THE GODS MUST BE CRAZY II: A ROOSEVELTIAN RENAISSANCE FOR TRUMP 2.0 AMERICAN RENEWAL IN THE CHINESE AI CENTURY

2nd Edition

Saji Madapat

Kala Sreshta (Most Accomplished Artist) awardee and the author of *The Gods of the Gods' Own Country*, *The Gods Must Be Crazy!*, and a dozen global bestsellers spanning twenty languages. He is a graduate of the Clinton Global Initiative's GIFT Young Leadership Program (China, Hong Kong, Cambodia) and the PMI–CCL Executive Master's in Leadership.

A contrarian investment banker turned TOGAF9-certified architect of enterprise performance, Saji has spent three decades designing ERP and EPM ecosystems for Fortune 10 companies and Ernst & Young's global clientele. He has published more than fifty international papers on topics ranging from AI-driven business systems to the strategic roadmaps powering tomorrow's AI infrastructure. His hands-on insights helped shape all five major PMI standards(PMBOK, OPM3, P&PMS, PMCD), grounded in field-tested global rollouts. As the architect of the Team India Movement, he transformed the Asia-Pacific region into PMI's most strategic global hub.

A digital satirist at heart and strategist by design, Saji blends Rooseveltian revivalism with Silicon Valley skepticism—one Coke bottle at a time.

Kala Sreshta (Most Accomplished Artist) Award
(Prof. MN Karasseri to Saji & Subhash Chandran(Chief Editor Mathrubhumi))
-Sculpture by Kanayi Kunhiraman

The title nods to the 1980 satire The Gods Must Be Crazy, in which a pilot's discarded Coca-Cola bottle lands in a Kalahari village, hailed first as a gift from the Gods and then as a fuse for internecine havoc. Our era's bottle glints brighter—AI supremacy, e-yuan wallets, trillion-dollar deficits— "blessings" that corrode the civic bedrock even as they dazzle. Like the elder who marches to the world's edge to fling the cursed glass into nothingness, this book charts a Roosevelt-grade trek to haul America—call it a bruised republic or a woozy empire—back from the brink before the shards fly.

CONTENTS

FROM LEDGERS TO LIBRARIES: PATIENT CAPITAL IN AN IMPATIENT AGE

By Bob Wallace, CPA, MBA

Veteran CFO & Philanthropic Strategist

> *"There are many ways of going forward, but only one way of standing still."*
>
> —Franklin D. Roosevelt

In an era where Milton the Trickster's disciples obsess over quarterly returns and PowerPoint philanthropy, the concept of patient capital is radical. It doesn't chase headlines—it builds the scaffolding of a community. It's not about saving face, but saving futures. Wall Street hunts unicorns; Main Street needs plough-horses. I learned this the hard way, as I transitioned from corporate finance to the nonprofit world.

I have spent my career living between two ledgers. One is the corporate balance sheet, measured to the decimal, optimized for quarterly returns, and carefully hedged against volatility. The other is our civic ledger, measured in lives, trust, resilience, and—too often—neglect.

Balancing those books is the defining challenge of our time, and it is why I agreed to write this foreword. The work is personal. During my transition from corporate CFO to the non-profit world, I landed in the thick of a stock market crash. I remember staring at the foundation's ledger in 2009, the red digits blinking back like a ticking bomb—tens of millions vaporized in a single market swoon. As stock tickers crashed, I found myself balancing a 30% portfolio loss with a community's desperate plea. The corporate ledger demanded immediate, abstract action. However, the civic ledger represented grant commitments we had to fulfill—the tangible survival of the people we served. That dissonance—between macro-stewardship abstractions and micro-survival realities—shaped the strategic decisions I've made ever since.

Patient capital, I discovered in that trial by fire, is the tool we use to bridge that gap. Patient capital is how societies, not just states, steal back the timeline.

Forget conference-room buzzwords. It's money that refuses to sprint yet insists on finishing the marathon—the antithesis of Milton the Trickster's quarterly quick fixes. It steals back time like compound interest for communities: slow to start, but unstoppable once momentum builds. A well-designed challenge grant doesn't just give; it pulls. A $1 million commitment, well-structured, can unlock $5 million from co-investors—foundations, lenders, donors, even skeptics who suddenly don't want to miss the parade. It is a leverage-chasing purpose, not headlines.

From the front lines of this work, I offer three lessons that stand in stark contrast to the short-term extraction Saji Madapat so brilliantly skewers in this book.

1. **Lesson 1: Leverage Is a Force of Gravity:** The best philanthropic dollars not only go far, they also pull others in. We obsess over return on equity in the corporate world; communities deserve a return on engagement. I have seen a $2 million seed fund for a workforce-tech hub attract $8 million in corporate upskilling credits within fourteen months. That is not just generosity. It is the math of a community reclaiming its pride of place.
2. **Lesson 2: A Spend-Down Requires Spine:** Foundations, like corporations, can succumb to balance-sheet obesity, hoarding resources for a future that may never arrive if the present collapses. A time-bound spend-down forces urgency and discipline. It recognizes that cash is oxygen—you must use it while the patient can still breathe. It is a commitment to solving problems now, not just managing them in perpetuity.
3. **Soulful Dashboards:** My profession lives and dies by the ratio. But in civic renewal, the metrics must have a pulse. The dashboards that matter track the apprentices graduating, the small nonprofits scaling, and the neighborhoods shedding their crime maps. If the numbers don't have a pulse, they're the wrong numbers.

Franklin Roosevelt's genius was not merely the concrete he poured; it was the democratic faith that future citizens would repay today's courage with tomorrow's capacity. *The Gods Must Be Crazy II* channels that spirit at a moment when America teeters between the quarterly treadmill and a generational moonshot. China plans in dynastic arcs; we lurch from earnings call to earnings call. One plants forests; the other tracks lumber futures. Patient capital is how we steal back the timeline.

Saji Madapat wields data like a scalpel and humor like a hammer, dissecting the comedy of American short-termism while sketching a blueprint for Roosevelt-grade renewal. This book is one part diagnosis, one part street-corner sermon, and one part late-night comedy monologue—a potent cocktail in service of reawakening America's dormant builder's instinct.

The gods may still lob Coke bottles from the heavens, but patient capital, applied with courage, can transform that celestial litter into the load-bearing beams of a renewed community. The chapters ahead will show you how—and remind you, with a wink, a blueprint, and a burning impatience, that inaction has a cost column too.

The task of this generation is to balance both ledgers. We must do it before someone else writes our audit, because the only one that truly matters is the one our grandchildren will sign.

—Bob Wallace, CPA, MBA
Veteran CFO & Philanthropic Strategist

(Bob Wallace is a financial strategist who has served as Chief Financial Officer for both large corporations and major philanthropic foundations. His work focuses on deploying patient capital to rebuild community wealth and resilience, bridging the gap between the corporate and civic worlds.)

PREFACE: THE GODS MUST BE CRAZY 2.0 – A ROOSEVELTIAN DOCTRINE FOR AMERICAN RENEWAL IN THE CHINESE AI CENTURY

> *"The art of war is of vital importance to the State.*
> *It is a matter of life and death, a road either to safety or to ruin."*
> —Sun Tzu, The Art of War, Chapter 1

It began, as profound shifts often do these days, not with the clarion call of history or the measured cadence of strategic planning but with inexplicable objects falling from the sky onto the meticulously manicured lawns of American power. Think less divine revelation, more cosmic slapstick targeted at a global superpower increasingly bewildered by its own reflection in the funhouse mirror of the 21st century. These weren't mere weather balloons or errant drones; they were artifacts freighted with geopolitical significance, landing with the gentle thud of paradigm shifts arriving unannounced, uninvited, and primarily uncommented upon by those paid handsomely to notice such things.

By 2025, bottles were raining down across Washington's institutional landscape—economic models challenging neoliberal orthodoxy. These technological marvels promised utopia while delivering dystopia, and cultural payloads embedded in addictive apps were designed to harvest attention and sow division. Each bottle was more sophisticated than the last. Each generated more confusion, triggered more blue-ribbon commissions, and resulted in more elegantly bound reports destined to be read by absolutely no one. America—the indispensable nation, the shining city upon a hill—now stood amidst the growing collection, resembling a bemused museum curator who had lost the catalog, frantically juggling each new arrival while dropping two others in the process.

Meanwhile, across the Pacific, Chinese officials methodically cataloged each falling object. They compared notes, developed theories, and formulated integrated strategies that spanned economic, technological, military, and cultural domains. They grasped what eluded their American counterparts: these bottles weren't random anomalies to be individually exploited or defensively parried but components of a fundamental systemic transformation requiring a coordinated, long-term response. The gods, it seemed, had gone quite mad indeed—or perhaps they were simply conducting a planetary-scale, double-blind experiment in comparative strategic cognition, with one subject exhibiting alarming signs of institutional attention deficit disorder.

These weren't merely the disruptive "gifts" reminiscent of the titular artifact in the 1980 film *The Gods Must Be Crazy*—though that film's theme of bewildered societies confronting incomprehensible modernity still resonates. That film's simple Coke bottle, a symbol of baffling modernity, dropped into traditional society and unleashed unforeseen conflict by introducing concepts like ownership and jealousy. Today's bottles, however, are infinitely more complex and consequential. They are not random acts of celestial mischief but tangible heralds of the "Chinese AI Century," landing squarely on an America increasingly unsure of its footing, its purpose, and its capacity for coherent response. These artifacts reveal pre-existing weaknesses, hairline fractures in the American façade hidden beneath layers of exceptionalist rhetoric and financialized prosperity. They expose economic vulnerabilities that are papered over by debt-fueled consumption, technological dependencies masked by marketing hype, and societal divisions amplified by algorithms designed for maximum engagement, rather than maximum enlightenment.

To grapple with reality in this profoundly profound way, and often in this profoundly absurd manner, requires a dual lens. Frankly, the current state of affairs—from our political discourse resembling professional wrestling without the athletic integrity to economic policies seemingly designed by committees of foxes advising the henhouse—often defies rational analysis. It is frequently so ridiculous, so divorced from observable reality, that only satire can adequately capture the madness. Therefore, this book wields the necessary tool of satire – channeling the righteous absurdity of John Oliver, the biting commentary of George Carlin, the institutional mockery of Armando Iannucci, and the exasperated truth-telling of Jon Stewart. Why? Because sometimes, laughter is the only rational response left. Satire can cut through the layers of denial, obfuscation, and self-serving complexity that shield power from scrutiny. It can speak uncomfortable truths in ways that earnest analysis often cannot.

But beneath the satire lies rigorous, clear-eyed, Zakaria-esque analysis. This is not merely a comedic romp through geopolitical dysfunction. We ground our critique in a global perspective, historical context, and data-driven insights. Because while the situation often invites laughter (or tears), the stakes—America's future prosperity, security, and global standing; the character of the 21st century; the balance between democratic values and authoritarian alternatives—are far too high for mere cynicism. We must understand the systemic forces at play, even as we mock the often comical human responses to them. Assisting us in this allegorical journey will be figures like **Milton the Trickster Economist**, the personification of market fundamentalism, whose elegant theories, detached from messy realities, paved the road to our current predicament with dangerously good intentions. His intellectual children, armed with complex models that consistently undervalued resilience and overvalued short-term efficiency, helped engineer the very vulnerabilities we now confront.

The central challenge is navigating the geopolitical paradox of our time: the US-China relationship. It's a relationship that defies easy labels, a complex entanglement where competition and cooperation are not sequential choices but simultaneous realities. We must compete fiercely with a strategic rival whose model challenges our own across economic, technological, military, and ideological domains. China's ambition is not hidden; Xi Jinping speaks openly of "national rejuvenation" and restoring China's central place in the world. Yet, simultaneously, we must cooperate on existential threats like climate change, pandemics, nuclear proliferation, and global financial stability that respect no borders or ideologies. These challenges cannot be effectively addressed by either power alone or through purely competitive dynamics. They demand collaborative frameworks even amid strategic rivalry.

This isn't a Cold War redux, where two largely separate systems competed across a defined ideological divide. It's a far more complex entanglement where economies are deeply intertwined (despite decoupling rhetoric), supply chains crisscross contested territories, and technological development creates both shared opportunities and shared risks. While America grapples with this multifaceted reality, its responses often resemble a strategic game of Whac-A-Mole – reacting to immediate provocations (a spy balloon here, a trade dispute there) with simplistic, usually counterproductive measures while the underlying systemic challenges compound. The scale of the task – competing robustly, cooperating selectively, and renewing domestic capacity all at once – is immense. Yet our policy debates often devolve into partisan shouting matches, seemingly designed to avoid addressing the core issues and focus instead on scoring points in the perpetual American political civil war. The inadequacy of these responses is becoming increasingly apparent, both domestically and internationally.

Forgive a brief personal interjection, offered not as autobiography but as context for the perspective shaping this analysis. As the "prodigal capitalist cowboy son of socialist parents" from Kerala, India—a region where communist ideals coexist with democratic elections—I experienced firsthand the clash of economic ideologies and the complex legacies of colonialism and globalization. My subsequent journey took me through the heart of Western finance during its most exuberant and ultimately self-destructive phases, and into consulting within the aerospace and defense sector, where I witnessed the interplay between technological ambition, bureaucratic inertia, and geopolitical strategy. This "Tiger Ride" — seeing the seductive power and potential hollowness of financial engineering, the stark contrasts between American potential and its frustrating realities, and the disciplined rise of competitors like China from multiple vantage points — provides the experiential grounding for the critique and analysis that follows. It's a perspective shaped by admiration for the American experiment, coupled with a deep concern that its modern incarnation has strayed perilously far from the Rooseveltian foundations of pragmatic investment, shared prosperity, and competent governance that once made it exceptional—and globally attractive.

This entire examination unfolds against the turbulent backdrop of the Trump 2.0 era—a political climate characterized by populist energy, deep polarization, a penchant for disrupting established norms, both domestically and internationally, and a transactional approach to alliances. This volatility isn't merely background noise; it's an integral part of the complex, messy, often contradictory reality within which any strategy for American renewal must operate. It adds another layer to the "madness" – the unpredictable human and political element amplifying the already daunting systemic challenges posed by the Chinese AI Century. The global stakes—shaping the future of technology, the balance between freedom and authoritarian control, the resilience of democratic governance itself, and the stability of the international order—are immense. These stakes demand a coherent, long-term strategy precisely when America's political system seems least capable of producing it. Observing this dynamic evokes cautionary tales from history, such as the slow decline of the Dutch and British East India companies, powerful enterprises whose fates were inextricably linked to the strategic choices and institutional health of their sponsoring empires.

This book aims to cut through the noise, denial, and paralyzing complexity to provide a clear-eyed assessment and a potential path forward. Our exploration will proceed in three main parts, mirroring the process of addressing any complex challenge:

1. **Problem Statement:** The opening Problem Statement laments how America, distracted by financial alchemy and partisan spectacle, has allowed its industrial sinew, civic unity, and strategic focus to erode just as a newly confident "Middle Kingdom" assembles a debt-driven, tech-enabled sphere of influence. Framed through a satirical personal "Tiger Ride" and a Rooseveltian prayer for renewal, the section dissects the nation's self-inflicted fractures, recounts the offshoring of its capitalist empire, and sets up the urgency for a 21st-century reboot.
2. **Diagnosis:** We will dissect America's key vulnerabilities across the economic, geopolitical, financial, and social domains. We'll examine how internal weaknesses—often stemming from short-sighted policies and institutional decay—have created openings for external challenges, particularly in the context of the transformative technologies defining the AI Century.
3. **Root Causes & Framework:** We will synthesize the diagnosis, identifying the underlying drivers of American relative decline—strategic short-termism that prioritizes immediate gains over future strength, capability hollow-out that leaves us vulnerable despite surface prosperity, and civic disunity that paralyzes collective action. We will then propose the Rooseveltian Doctrine, adapted for our times, as an integrated framework for comprehensive national renewal.
4. **Strategy & Implementation:** We will outline specific, actionable strategies across critical sectors, including national security, infrastructure (both physical and digital), finance, regulation, governance, and the knowledge economy (human capital). We'll detail how a modern Rooseveltian approach can be applied to contemporary challenges and, crucially, how these strategies might be implemented even amidst the political turbulence of the Trump 2.0 era.
5. **VISION:** This finale casts America at a pivotal crossroads—either embrace a Roosevelt-inspired, "value-engineered" revival or plummet into a dystopian self-liquidation. It reimagines capitalism as a force for real-world impact, forges a coalition of democratic allies, lays out two starkly contrasting futures, and institutionalizes renewal through a bipartisan commission and public scorecards, putting citizens firmly in the driver's seat of the nation's rebirth.

Our promise is not easy answers or simplistic solutions. The challenges are too complex for that. Instead, we offer a blend of sharp diagnosis grounded in data and historical context, provocative satire aimed at challenging assumptions and complacency, and a practical framework for thinking about American strategy, purpose, and renewal. This book seeks to contribute to the urgent national conversation about how America can navigate this bewildering new era defined by the rise of China and the transformative power of artificial intelligence.

Suppose the gods of geopolitics and technology have indeed gone crazy, dropping disruptive challenges upon a distracted world like so many unexpected Coke bottles. In that case, our task is to respond not with matching madness but with clear-eyed analysis, renewed purpose, and, perhaps, a necessary dose of therapeutic absurdity. The examination begins now.

INTRODUCTION: PARADIGM COLLISION: OF FARMERS, HUNTERS, AND SUPERPOWERS IN THE AI CENTURY

THOMAS WALENTA

(PMI Fellow | Former PMI board member | 30+ Year IBM Program Manager)

Picture two strategists at a cosmic chessboard. One plants rice, tending the irrigation ditches for seasons to come. The other chases antelope, eyes fixed on tonight's protein count. For half a millennium, the hunter ruled the board—until the farmer quietly built a water network beneath it. China's rise is not a plot twist; it is agriculture's long-delayed rebuttal to Wall Street's quarterly cliffhangers. If humanity hopes to navigate Act II, we must learn when to sprint and when to sow—combining the hunter's agility with the farmer's patience.

Before the Rooseveltian renewal project ahead can begin, we must confront a deeper truth: behind every failed policy, short-lived reform, or misfired innovation lies a mindset misaligned with reality. In the chapters that follow, we dissect the American empire's decline and potential renewal. But first, we must revisit the most primal story of all—how we think, how we plan, and how we see time.

Imagine two ancestors at dawn: one, the Hunter-Gatherer Hermit, wrapped in wind-whispered secrets of the wild; the other, the Rooseveltian Rancher, stroking his morning mustache as he surveys sprawling fences and federal projects rising in the haze. If the Farmer thinks in centuries, the Hunter-Gatherer thinks in—well, where's lunch?

To understand the strategic collision between the West and China, one must look deeper than policy papers and headlines, to the ancient paradigms that shape their thinking: the transactional urgency of the Hunter-Gatherer versus the patient, long-term cultivation of the Farmer.

This foreword refuses to let America's solutions play the starring role. It demands a seat at history's roundtable: one where rice paddies and foraging camps are equals. As Talhelm's rice-wheat research reminds us, our fields of thought are sown by ancient choices—and only by plowing new furrows can we harvest a truly global wisdom. While the Hermit's sprint saved dinner last night, the Rancher has been tending tomorrow's harvest since time immemorial. The Rancher plans tea fields for decades; the Hermit recalibrates when his belly grumbles.

The essay highlights how fundamental cultural orientations in China (interdependence, collectivism) differ from the individualism and short-term focus common in the U.S. The essay suggests that these cognitive furrows plowed into our collective mind challenge not only American policy preferences but also the underlying cognitive paradigms through which change is viewed and pursued. The West, like a caffeine-addled sprinter, can't resist the next shiny policy. China, in contrast, is the marathoner planting tea fields.

Thus, the essay intends to extend Saji's argument: rather than proposing merely an American response to global shifts (i.e., Rooseveltian values), it advocates for a more pluralistic and humble engagement—one that acknowledges differing historical trajectories, fosters cross-cultural learning, and recognizes the limits of applying American solutions to global challenges. This global lens calls for both Western and non-Western societies to move beyond their self-referential perspectives and to adapt in ways informed by, but not constrained to, their own traditions.

INTRODUCTION

In his upcoming book, "The Gods Must Be Crazy II," Saji Madapat inspires us to reflect on Western paradigms and their influence on perceptions and decisions. Saji Madapat satirically provides a deeply analytical critique of American decline in the face of China's strategic rise. He suggests an American solution: Rooseveltianism, which he describes as Moral Governance, Long-Term Investment, and Strategic Leadership. This approach has saved the U.S. from crises like WWI (Theodore Roosevelt), the Depression (Franklin D. Roosevelt), and has formed the world order after 1945 (Eleanor Roosevelt). By invoking Rooseveltianism, Madapat connects America's past resilience and global leadership to the idea that a return to these foundational principles is necessary for America to sustain its current self-image.

With that focused problem description and solution in the same cultural sphere, Saji Madapat may miss a wider view and opportunity for America and humanity. Yet he uncovers some beliefs and paradigms that are often referred to but seldom challenged in U.S. politics and society.

UNQUESTIONED ASSUMPTIONS AND BELIEFS, OR PARADIGMS, THAT ARE PRIMARILY ROOTED IN WESTERN AND SPECIFICALLY U.S. CULTURE

Before any civilization can rebuild its institutional muscle or reclaim coherence in a fractured world order, it must confront the ghost in its cognitive machine. This book is not just about policy, power, or pipelines, but about paradigms. Because beneath every failed reform or fragile supply chain lies a way of thinking that has overstayed its welcome. If any nation seeks a renaissance worthy of its people, it must start not with steel or semiconductors, but with how it thinks about time, risk, and reality.

Western powers, particularly the U.S., have long operated under the assumption of cultural, political, and economic superiority, believing their models are universally applicable. From free market absolutism to the inevitability of liberal democracy, these paradigms shaped global strategy and self-perception. However, in a rapidly changing world, particularly with China's rise, these beliefs are facing growing resistance and demand re-examination. These paradigms have been extracted from Saji's book:

1. Western Superiority Paradigm: The ingrained belief that Western (especially American) political, economic, and cultural models are inherently superior and universally applicable.
2. Linear Progress Paradigm: The assumption that history moves in a straight line toward liberal democracy and capitalist globalization.
3. Free Market Absolutism: The belief that unfettered markets and privatization always yield optimal outcomes.
4. Technological Determinism: The notion that technological superiority ensures geopolitical dominance.
5. Exceptionalism and Invincibility: The assumption that America is too powerful to fail, due to its past victories and global dominance.
6. Democracy as a One-Size-Fits-All Model: That liberal democracy is the inevitable and best system for all nations, despite varying cultural, historical, and institutional contexts.
7. Military Power Equals Global Influence: That maintaining military dominance automatically ensures global leadership, even as soft power and economic influence become more decisive.
8. Short-Term Thinking in Governance: The idea that political and economic success can be managed through short election cycles and quarterly profits.
9. Moral Superiority of the West: The West always acts from a morally superior position in international affairs.

Many of these beliefs are not shared by other global players, particularly China, Russia, and India. Several of these Western paradigms, such as beliefs in cultural superiority, linear progress, and market absolutism, are deeply rooted in colonial ideology. These frameworks not only justified empire-building but continue to shape global governance today. The assumption that liberal democracy, free markets, and technological dominance are universally applicable echoes the colonial logic of a civilizing mission. Even in contemporary policy and development efforts, the West often acts from a position of moral and strategic exceptionalism, imposing one-size-fits-all solutions while neglecting cultural and historical context. Recognizing these paradigms as colonial inheritances is essential to deconstructing enduring power asymmetries in the modern world.

Rooseveltianism: that splendid beast with three heads—Moral Governance, Long-Term Investment, and a Strategist's Stubbornness. But redirects those energies toward domestic renewal and global cooperation, rather than exploitation. It represents a redeemable branch of empire-era governance: one that can be decolonized and democratized, if stripped of its superiority complex and refocused on inclusive, pluralist outcomes.

The continued reliance on Western paradigms, whether in the form of exceptionalism, market ideology, or democratic evangelism, has shifted from being a source of strength to acting as a barrier to adaptation. By holding onto outdated assumptions, the West risks strategic shortsightedness, alienates emerging nations, and weakens its own influence. China's rise does more than challenge Western power; it questions the mental frameworks through which that power is understood and wielded. A new era requires humility instead of dominance, diversity instead of universal rules, and long-term strategic thinking rather than short-term ideological comfort. If the West aims to stay relevant, it must move beyond its long-held myths and accept a world that is no longer shaped solely in its image.

MEANWHILE, IN THE EAST

If Western paradigms are steel rails, Chinese paradigms are the irrigation channels—each indispensable, but neither complete alone.

China's approach to governance, development, and global engagement often diverges significantly from Western paradigms. These differences are rooted in historical, philosophical, and strategic perspectives that emphasize multipolarity, long-term vision, and contextual adaptation. To coexist and cooperate, mutual understanding is required. As in all conflict resolutions, common ground must be identified and expanded. As Sun Tsu wrote, "If you know the enemy and know yourself, you need not fear the result of a hundred battles." (The Art of War, Chapter 3: Attack by Stratagem).

1. Western Superiority Paradigm: Civilizational Multipolarity China rejects the notion of Western superiority and promotes the concept of "civilizational multipolarity." It emphasizes "Chinese characteristics" in governance, development, and values, arguing that diverse pathways to progress are valid. This perspective is grounded in the idea that each civilization has its own unique strengths and challenges, and there is no one-size-fits-all solution (Wang & Zhao, 2020).
2. Linear Progress Paradigm: Historical Cycles and Strategic Patience. China views history as cyclical, drawing heavily on Confucian thought and the concept of dynastic continuity. It believes progress is adaptive, contextual, and often non-Western. This cyclical view emphasizes strategic patience, resilience, and long-term planning, rather than short-term gains (Feng, 2018).
3. Free Market Absolutism: State Capitalism / Socialist Market Economy: China blends market mechanisms with strong state oversight, creating a hybrid system known as "socialist market economy." The state plays a commanding role in steering key industries, managing growth, and avoiding the pitfalls of unchecked capitalism. This approach reflects a pragmatic balance between market efficiency and social stability (Huang, 2019).
4. Technological Determinism: Technology with Political Discipline: While China invests heavily in technology, it embeds it within a centralized political framework. Technology is seen as a tool of national rejuvenation and strategic advantage, but it is tightly controlled to align with political goals and societal values. This approach mitigates the risks associated with unregulated technological expansion (Zhao, 2021).
5. Exceptionalism and Invincibility: Strategic Humility + Civilizational Confidence: China avoids declarations of exceptionalism. Instead, it projects a narrative of long-term ascendancy and resilience, informed by centuries of imperial rise and fall. This approach combines strategic humility with civilizational confidence, emphasizing gradual progress and adaptability (Lampton, 2016).
6. Democracy as a One-Size-Fits-All Model: "Whole-Process People's Democracy": China asserts that it practices a form of governance suited to its conditions, which it calls "whole-process people's democracy." This model emphasizes order, collective well-being, and stability over procedural legitimacy. China argues that performance legitimacy—delivering tangible benefits to citizens—is more important than purely procedural democratic processes (Yu, 2022).
7. Military Power Equals Global Influence: Comprehensive National Power (CNP). While China recognizes the importance of military power, it emphasizes comprehensive national power (CNP), which encompasses economic influence, infrastructure diplomacy (e.g., the Belt and Road Initiative), and cultural soft power (e.g., Confucius Institutes). China views these tools as more sustainable and effective means of global influence compared to military dominance alone (Zhang, 2019).
8. Short-Term Thinking in Governance: Long-Term Central Planning: China operates through five-year plans and decades-long strategic visions (e.g., "China Dream 2049"). Its leadership is not subject to frequent electoral changes, allowing for policy continuity and ambitious infrastructure development. This long-term orientation enables China to pursue large-scale projects and address systemic issues without immediate electoral constraints (Li, 2020).
9. Moral Superiority of the West: Sovereignty First, No Interference Doctrine: China rejects the West's moralizing approach and positions itself as a champion of non-interference, equality among nations, and respect for cultural diversity in governance. It emphasizes sovereignty and mutual respect in international relations, advocating for a multipolar world order where all countries can develop according to their own contexts (Xu, 2021).

China's contrasting positions reflect a deep-seated commitment to civilizational multipolarity, long-term strategic thinking, and contextual adaptation. By rejecting Western paradigms of superiority, linearity, and absolutism, China offers an alternative vision of global governance and development. This approach is rooted in historical experience, philosophical traditions, and practical realities, presenting a compelling challenge to dominant Western narratives.

Yet even these civilizational legacies collide in the human mind, where Cartesian isolation meets existential anxiety.

THE FEAR–INDIVIDUALISM NEXUS: HOW CARTESIAN THOUGHT SHAPES SHORT–TERM THINKING IN WESTERN CULTURE

The prevalence of short-term thinking in Western culture stems from deeply rooted fears, such as the fear of missing out (FOMO) and the fear of being judged and becoming irrelevant (FOJI). These fears are not just psychological issues but are embedded in larger cultural and philosophical trends that shape modern Western identity. By exploring the link between these fears, individualism, and Cartesian thought, we can gain a deeper understanding of how the modern Western individual has become both independent and isolated, driven by a preoccupation with the present.

Fear as a Contracting Force

FOMO and FOJI are powerful motivators that limit our mental scope, emphasizing immediate gratification and social validation. The fear of missing out drives individuals to constantly chase new experiences, products, or connections to avoid feeling excluded or left behind (Przybylski et al., 2013). Likewise, the fear of judgment and irrelevance prompts people to conform to societal norms or present an image of success, even at the expense of their long-term well-being (Baumeister, 1982). These fears create a sense of urgency that shortens time perspectives, making it hard to focus on future goals or values.

At the heart of these fears lies a profound sense of isolation. In a culture that emphasizes individualism, the self is often perceived as an isolated entity, disconnected from larger communal or spiritual frameworks. Triandis (1995) distinguishes between individualistic cultures, which prioritize personal goals and independence, and collectivistic cultures, which emphasize group harmony and interdependence. Without deeper ties to community, tradition, or a transcendent purpose, individuals become vulnerable to existential anxieties. The lack of a collective tether amplifies the fear of being left out or deemed insignificant, reinforcing a relentless pursuit of instant gratification and social approval.

Individualism and Cartesian Thought

The roots of this individualistic mindset can be traced back to the philosophical foundations of modern Western thought, particularly the work of René Descartes. His famous dictum, "Cogito, ergo sum" ("I think, therefore I am"), established reason as the primary basis of existence, displacing traditional sources of meaning such as God or community (Descartes, 1637/1996). This shift toward rationalism and self-reliance laid the groundwork for the modern emphasis on individual autonomy and freedom.

However, this liberation from external authorities also introduced a new form of isolation. By denying the eternal perspective traditionally provided by religious faith, modern humans were left to navigate life within the confines of a finite timeline. Taylor (1989) argues that the "disenchantment" of the world following the Protestant Reformation and Enlightenment created a "buffered self" that is increasingly cut off from horizons beyond these stifling boardroom walls. The denial of God—or any transcendent source of meaning—collapsed the horizon of significance into the present moment. As a result, the modern Western human became not only independent and free but also increasingly anxious and fearful, trapped in a perpetual struggle to define their worth through immediate achievements and social validation.

Why This Still Matters in 2025

The legacy of Cartesian thought, with its emphasis on individualism, has profoundly shaped contemporary Western culture. The rise of social media, consumer capitalism, and fast-paced lifestyles reflects a society that prioritizes short-term gains over long-term sustainability (Turkle, 2011). The constant bombardment of information and opportunities exacerbates FOMO and FOJI, creating a feedback loop of anxiety and compulsive behavior (Kuss & Griffiths, 2017). This short-term orientation undermines efforts to address pressing issues such as climate change, inequality, and mental health, as individuals and institutions alike prioritize immediate needs over future consequences (Giddens, 1991).

In summary, the tendency toward short-term thinking in Western culture is closely connected to fears such as FOMO and FOJI, which reflect a broader cultural shift toward individualism. Based on Cartesian philosophy, this change has distanced many from deeper communal or spiritual connections, leaving them lost in a world where meaning is limited to the present. To move past this narrow focus, societies need to rethink how they view time, community, and transcendence, and find ways to broaden their perspective beyond just the immediate moment. Only then can we begin to build a more balanced and sustainable way of life.

THE ROOTS OF LONG-TERM THINKING IN FARMING SOCIETIES

China has a long and rich history of agriculture, which shaped its ecological thinking by integrating humans, the environment, and farming practices (Zhao, 2022). Ancient Chinese philosophy, including the parables of Mencius, reflects this agricultural worldview. In the story of 拔苗助长 (bá miáo zhù zhǎng), Mencius warns against impatience and overintervention: a man, worried his rice plants weren't growing fast enough, pulled at them, only to find them withered by his misguided effort (Hughes, 1989). The lesson illustrates a key principle of agricultural thinking—growth requires patience, care, and an understanding of natural cycles.

West vs. China

ANCIENT COGNITIVE PARADIGMS

Hunter-individualism (West)

Gatherer (China)

CULTURAL ROOTS

Wheat - individualism

Rice - interdependence, collectivism

POLICY MISALIGNMENT

STRATEGY COLLISION

Short-term transactional

Long-term cultivation

IMPLICATIONS

U.S. must shift to patient systems thinking, partnership, invest in resilience

This mindset is especially evident in rice farming, which fosters collectivism, holistic thinking, and long-term planning. Unlike wheat or herding economies, rice cultivation demands sustained cooperation to build and manage irrigation systems. In regions such as India, Japan, and Malaysia, rice farmers form cooperatives to coordinate labor and synchronize harvests, reflecting a deeply ingrained culture of interdependence and a future-oriented mindset (Talhelm, 2022).

This contrast between farming and foraging cultures highlights a fundamental cognitive divide. Agricultural societies evolved systematic, future-oriented approaches to managing resources, while hunter-gatherer societies developed present-focused, flexible strategies suited to dynamic environments (Chen & Li, 2021). These divergent orientations persist today. Farmer-style thinking promotes delayed gratification, strategic planning, and hierarchical systems, while hunter-gatherer cognition supports rapid adaptation, distributed decision-making, and situational awareness (Gurven & Kaplan, 2020; Kaplan et al., 2019).

This deep-seated cognitive duality, rooted in millennia of agricultural and cultural history, can be visualized as follows:

Neurological studies support this distinction: agricultural tasks tend to activate specialized, goal-focused brain regions, whereas hunter-gatherer behavior engages broader networks for environmental scanning and adaptability (Burkart et al., 2021).

Understanding this deep-seated cognitive duality is especially relevant in facing contemporary global challenges. For example, climate change demands both the farmer mindset—to commit to long-term solutions—and the hunter-gatherer mindset—to respond nimbly to immediate threats (Chen & Li, 2021). Rather than viewing these paradigms as opposing, integrating their complementary strengths may offer a more resilient and adaptive path forward.

The persistence of these mindsets across millennia suggests they are not just cultural constructs, but evolutionary strategies. Recognizing and leveraging both forms of thinking—systemic and spontaneous, long-term and immediate—can help societies meet the complex demands of an increasingly uncertain world.

CONCLUSION: TOWARD A PLURALISTIC GLOBAL MINDSET

Imagine Hunter Hank—the Silicon Valley VC in cargo shorts, always chasing the next AI unicorn before it learns to walk. Now meet Farmer Fang, the patient strategist from Shenzhen, who plants policy like rice—layered, submerged, and designed to ripen with time. One hunts quarterly earnings. The other cultivates dynastic advantage—with a 100-year plan and zero tweets.

This essay argues that the cognitive and cultural frameworks underpinning American responses to global change, especially the embrace of "Rooseveltian" virtue in response to China's rise, remain limited by the very Western assumptions they aim to challenge. By expanding Saji Madapat's analysis to a broader global perspective and integrating empirical insights, such as Talhelm's rice-wheat theory, we show that deep-seated patterns of interdependence and collectivism in Eastern societies pose a fundamental challenge not only to Western economic interests but also to Western ways of thinking itself.

The ongoing dominance of American exceptionalism, linear progress ideas, and a preference for market-based solutions can obscure the importance of alternative historical paths and social models. Rather than promoting "American solutions" to global crises—an approach often present even in well-meaning reform efforts—this essay advocates for a **pluralist humility**: the willingness to learn from non-Western traditions, to incorporate collective and long-term perspectives, and to recognize the limitations of one's own paradigms.

If the chessboard of history is tilting toward irrigation, let us learn its contours—sprinting when necessary, ploughing when required, and always remembering who taught us first.

If societies wish to stay adaptable and effective in a truly interconnected world, they must go beyond self-centered answers and develop a genuine willingness to engage with other cultures as equals. Global challenges, whether economic, environmental, or political, require not just technical cooperation but also a dialogue among civilizations. Only by adopting a truly pluralist mindset—one that is open to learning from the full spectrum of human experiences—can societies hope to address the complexities of the 21st century.

The challenges of the AI century—from climate change to global pandemics—are not problems to be hunted and conquered, but complex systems to be cultivated and managed. In the AI century, the race won't go to the swift nor the slow, but to the strategist who knows when to sprint and when to sow. This is not a call to save the West, nor to crown the East. It is a call to remember that civilizations—like ecosystems—thrive only when they evolve with humility, not hubris.

If history's great narratives are penned in rice strokes and spear thrusts, then this book offers a new ink—one that refuses to let humanity's pen hold the only nib. May we learn to plant and harvest with equal wisdom.

TWO CIVILIZATIONS, TWO CLOCKS

	WESTERN PARADIGM (HUNTER)	CHINESE VIEW ON PARADIGM (FARMER)
1	Western Superiority	2 Civilizational Multipolarity
2	Linear Progress	Historical Cycles & Strategic Patience
3	Free Market Absolutism	State-led Market Socialism
4	Technological Determinlsm	Technology with Political Discipline
5	Exceptionalism & Invincibility	Strategic Humility & Civilizational Confidence
6	Democracy as One-Size-Fits-All	Whole-Process People's Democracy
7	Military Power Equals Global Influence	Comprenensive National Power (CNP)
8	Short-Term Thinking	Long-Term Central Planning
9	Moral Superiority of the West	Sovereignty & Non-interference
10	Happiness as Individual Maximization	Harmony & Moral Cultivation

Foreword Compass:

- ★ **The Western "Hunter" Mind: Chases quarterly kills, fueled by individual glory and the fear of missing out.**
- ★ **The Eastern "Farmer" Mind:** Cultivates dynastic advantage, rooted in interdependence and strategic patience
- ★ **Pluralist Path: A civilization wins the marathon by knowing when to trade the spear for the plough—and when to share the harvest.**

—From the Frontlines of A Pluralist Path Renaissance

Author's Note: This essay does not seek to predict, preserve, or prioritize any single civilization. Its concern lies with the survival of long-term thinking, systems literacy, and the humility required for humanity to endure.

REFERENCES

Baumeister, R. F. (1982). Regard self-esteem as a scarce resource. Advances in Experimental Social Psychology, 15, 1-38.

Burkart, J. M., Hrdy, S. B., & van Schaik, C. P. (2021). Cooperative breeding and human cognitive evolution. Evolutionary Anthropology, 30 (2), 54-67.

Chen, B., & Li, H. (2021). Time preference and economic development: Evidence from cross-cultural studies. Journal of Economic Behavior & Organization, 185 , 423-441.

Descartes, R. (1996). Discourse on method and the meditations (F. E. Sutcliffe, Trans.). Penguin Books. (Original work published 1637)

Giddens, A. (1991). Modernity and self-identity: Self and society in the late modern age. Stanford University Press.

Gurven, M., & Kaplan, H. (2020). Embodied capital and the evolution of human life history. Philosophical Transactions of the Royal Society B, 375 (1796), 20190245.

Feng, X. (2018). The Rise of China and the Return of History. Oxford University Press.

Huang, Y. (2019). State Capitalism in China: Dynamics and Challenges. Cambridge University Press.

Hughes, J. D. (1989). Mencius' Prescriptions for Ancient Chinese Environmental Problems. In *Review: ER* (Vol. 13, Issue 3). Autumn-Winter.

Kaplan, H., Gangestad, S., Gurven, M., & Lancaster, J. (2019). The evolution of human life history: Theory and evidence. Evolutionary Anthropology, 28 (4), 178-192.

Kuss, D. J., & Griffiths, M. D. (2017). Social networking sites and addiction: Ten lessons learned. International Journal of Environmental Research and Public Health, 14 (3), 311.

Lampton, D. M. (2016). The Three Faces of Chinese Power: Might, Money, and Minds . University of California Press.

Li, H. (2020). Long-Term Planning in China's Development Strategy . Edward Elgar Publishing.

Przybylski, A. K., Murayama, K., DeHaan, C. R., & Gladwell, V. (2013). Motivational, emotional, and behavioral correlates of fear of missing out. Computers in Human Behavior, 29 (4), 1841-1848.

Taylor, C. (1989). Sources of the self: The making of the modern identity. Harvard University Press.

Triandis, H. C. (1995). Individualism & collectivism. Westview Press.

Turkle, S. (2011). Alone together: Why we expect more from technology and less from each other . Basic Books.Chinese thinking

Talhelm, T., Zhang, X., Oishi, S., Shimin, C., Duan, D., Lan, X., & Kitayama, S. (2022). *Large-Scale Psychological Differences Within China Explained by Rice versus Wheat Agriculture.*

Wang, Y., & Zhao, S. (2020). Civilizational Dialogue and Global Governance . Routledge.

Xu, L. (2021). China's Foreign Policy: Non-Interference and Multilateralism . Routledge.

Yu, J. (2022). People's Democracy in Practice: China's Governance Model . Palgrave Macmillan.

Zhang, W. (2019). Comprehensive National Power and China's Global Strategy. Springer.

Zhao, Y. (2021). The Digital Age and China's Governance Model. Stanford University Press.

Zhao, Y. (2022). The Ecological Thought of Ancient Chinese Agriculture and Its Contemporary Value. *Proceedings of the 2022 International Conference on Science and Technology Ethics and Human Future (STEHF 2022)*, 197–200. https://doi.org/10.2991/assehr.k.220701.039

PRAYER TO BRING BACK THE HOUSE OF ROOSEVELTS

"And they came to Jerusalem. And he entered the temple and began to drive out those who sold and those who bought in the temple, and he overturned the tables of the money changers and the seats of those who sold pigeons. And he would not allow anyone to carry anything through the temple. And he was teaching them and saying to them, "Is it not written, 'My house shall be called a house of prayer for all the nations'? But you have made it a den of robbers." And the chief priests and the scribes heard it and were seeking a way to destroy him, for they feared him because all the crowd was astonished at his teaching." (Mark 11:15-18, ESV)

This is a living manuscript and will continuously evolve based on your constructive feedback (contact @ www.EPM-Mavericks.com or www.Tiger-Rider.com)

Proceeds from this book will be donated to the Mother Teresa Mission. (Missionaries of Charity) or similar missions.

> *"Unless there is security here at home,*
> *There cannot be lasting peace in the world."*
> —Franklin Delano Roosevelt

As this inaugural edition stumbles into existence, one finds the immediate environment less a serene muse and more a live-action focus group for societal collapse. Right here, in the erstwhile 'City of Broad Shoulders'—now more accurately the 'City of Strategically Deployed Plywood'—Chicago, a peculiar brand of urban renewal is underway. According to the dulcet tones captured on a Chicago City Council recording, my neighborhood has morphed into "a virtual war zone." The minutes apparently detail "gang members armed with AK-47s...threatening to shoot black people" and, in a rather bold HR move, "shooting at the police." One imagines the recruitment posters: "Chiraq PD: Where Every Day is an Impromptu Ballistics Test."

Meanwhile, in the hallowed halls of municipal power, the strategy session ostensibly convened to address this, shall we say, *spirited* community engagement reportedly descended into a symphony of profanity—a veritable shouting match so chaotic it would make a seasoned observer of banana republic theatrics blush and perhaps take notes on innovative governance techniques. The irony of America lecturing other nations on institutional stability while its third-largest city's leadership communicates primarily through creative expletives would not be lost on even the most casual student of international relations.

Staring at the fortifications now adorning my own centennial home—a structure that has stoically weathered actual wars—one can't help but wonder if 'future-proofing' now involves investing heavily in lumber futures and perhaps a tactical moat. That was Britannica's last ivory tower, an edifice so iconic it practically radiates intellectual gravitas (and, one assumes, is guarded by more than just stern librarians, possibly a private militia with exceptionally good grammar), now seems to cast a nervous glance over its crenellations. When the encyclopedia's former headquarters require security protocols rivaling those of diplomatic compounds, one might reasonably question the trajectory of American civil society.

It is against this backdrop of localized bedlam, a sort of domestic performance art piece illustrating entropy, that I recall my solemn vow—the 'One Shared World' pledge. A commitment, mind you, not just to the preservation of my besieged United States (God bless its currently bewildered soul) but to the rather more ambitious project of safeguarding humanity writ large. There's a certain dark irony in advocating for global predictive, preventative, and responsive infrastructures against shared existential threats when one's own postcode is auditioning for a disaster movie—a bit like offering swimming lessons while one's own house is actively flooding.

Yet, it is precisely this brand of escalating lunacy, from the surreal cosplay of the January 6th insurrection to the specter of a Trump 2.0 era, that drags my decidedly less-than-prescient first manuscript, now a spry half-century-old, blinking into the harsh, almost vaudevillian light of the present. It seems the past isn't even past; it's just queuing up for an encore, possibly with more shouting, indeed with better production values, and absolutely without the benefit of institutional memory. American exceptionalism, it appears, now primarily manifests as an exceptional talent for recreating the precise conditions we once advised other banana republics to avoid.

THE DAWN OF THE MIDDLE KINGDOM

> *"The clever combatant imposes his will on the enemy,*
> *But does not allow the enemy's will to be imposed on him."*
> —Sun Tzu, The Art of War, Chapter VI

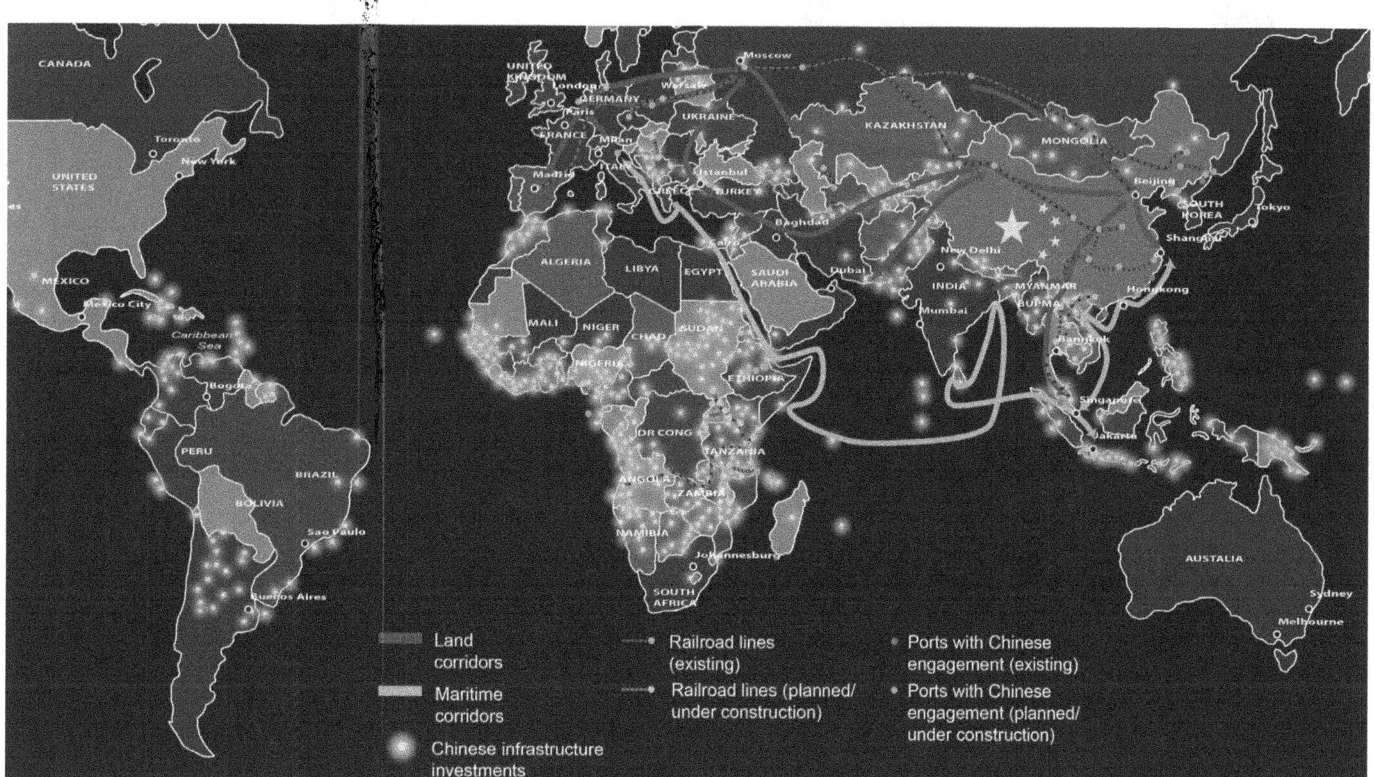

Meanwhile, across the Pacific, the Middle Kingdom patiently observes, perhaps with a smirk, as America fumbles with its increasingly worn-out deck of trump cards. They're just waiting for the opportune moment to dispatch their global repo men—not just for Uncle Sam's overdue tab, but for those of a hundred other nations caught in the lurch. Under Beijing's ever-watchful governmental aegis, Chinese state-backed enterprises are running a masterclass in 21st-century colonization —a subtle conquest via checkbook diplomacy, to the tune of trillions, in what increasingly resembles debt-trap serfdom.

Forget wooden horses; the 22nd-century Trojan Horse is a sprawling, glittering convoy of acronyms and megaprojects: the Belt and Road Initiative (BRI) morphing into its digital progeny, the Digital Silk Road (DSR); the Cross-Border Interbank Payment System (CIPS) as an alternative to SWIFT; the Asian Infrastructure Investment Bank (AIIB) rewriting the rules of development finance; and the Blockchain Service Network (BSN) laying down digital globally. These aren't just infrastructure projects; they're beachheads. Beneath the veneer of benevolent investment often lie parasitic, unsustainable debt structures designed to ensnare, potentially hiding raw hegemonic ambition and posing direct challenges to national sovereignty. Each new port, rail line, and fiber optic cable is bulldozed into existence, not just for profit but to firmly underpin China's geostrategic chessboard and its expanding military shadow.

A Tragicomedy in Seven Acts

Let's be brutally honest: China didn't so much "steal" American jobs as receive them via priority shipping, gift-wrapped by our homegrown financial alchemists. These Gordon Gekko disciples—armed with spreadsheets instead of moral compasses—outsourced our industrial backbone with the casual efficiency of teens dispatching unwanted houseplants. And who served as their eager accomplices? The McSlicey and BCGs of the consulting universe, those PowerPoint mercenaries who charged eight figures to advise corporations that shipping factories to China would be

more profitable if they included intellectual property and R&D capabilities as complimentary party favors. We didn't lose our manufacturing prowess; we surrendered it with a notarized transfer of title.

ANATOMY OF AMERICA'S MAGNIFICENT SELF-DISASSEMBLY

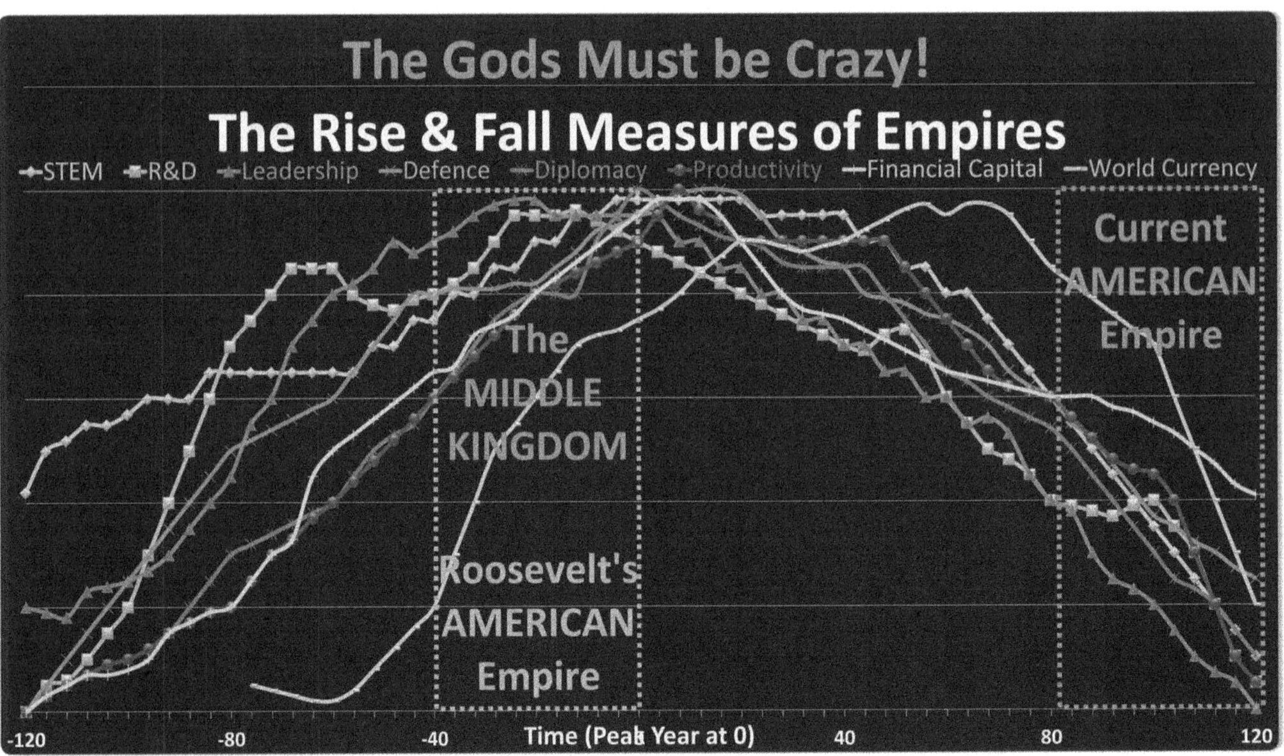

The 2008 financial implosion—that masterpiece of deregulatory theater—vaporized approximately $20 trillion in American wealth faster than a hedge fund manager can say "personal exemption." The collateral damage included 34 million global jobs, sacrificed at the altar of synthetic CDOs and credit default swaps. Yet through this economic apocalypse, a select aristocracy performed the most impressive magic trick in financial history: privatizing astronomical profits while socializing catastrophic losses onto taxpayers with the deftness of pickpockets at a billionaire's convention. When China's debt collectors eventually arrive—and make no mistake, they will—they won't be buzzing the intercoms at Southampton estates or Cayman chalets but foreclosing on the underwater mortgages of the very Americans who spent decades assembling their products at Walmart wages.

Now, I'm no four-star general, but years consulting in the Aerospace & Defense sector offer a ringside seat to the madness—a bit like claiming no special knowledge of alcoholism despite tending bar at a naval base—but I've witnessed America's strategic incoherence from privileged vantage points. Our defense doctrine often mimics late-Soviet delusion: less coherent strategy and more performance art designed to justify feeding the ravenous $2 trillion beast of the Military-Industrial Complex. Brown University researchers documented this national embezzlement scheme with surgical precision: nearly half the Pentagon's post-9/11 $14 trillion vanished into defense contractor coffers faster than congressional ethics in an election year.

With perverse dedication, we've replicated Russia's Afghanistan catastrophe down to the last tragic detail. Every major empire in history—Persians, Alexander's Macedonians, Genghis Khan's Mongols, Victorian Britain, Soviet Russia—learned the hard way that Afghanistan devoured invaders with the patience of geological time. America's exceptional innovation? Spending approximately $40 trillion (in 2025 dollars) over half a century on military misadventures that primarily enriched defense executives whose combat experience is limited to fighting for parking spaces at the Pentagon. Simple mathematics suggests that distributing those funds would have given every American citizen a six-figure windfall—enough to pay off the national debt and provide a sufficient remainder for a modest national vocational training program. Instead, we've perfected the art of investing blood and treasure into sandcastles of strategic irrelevance to protect now Chinese business opportunities.

Wall Street's contribution to American prosperity increasingly resembles a philosophical riddle: If value is extracted but none is created, does prosperity make a sound when it collapses? The investment banking industry has elevated wealth extraction to performance art—financial institutions that periodically detonate global economies while insisting they're "doing God's work" (with apparently no theological clarity on which deity they serve). Imagine if Manhattan's mathematical shamans directed even a fraction of their computational brilliance toward infrastructure renewal, educational excellence, or reskilling displaced workers instead of engineering tax-advantaged vehicles for parking offshore wealth. What if the trillions incinerated in Middle Eastern quagmires had irrigated America's indus-

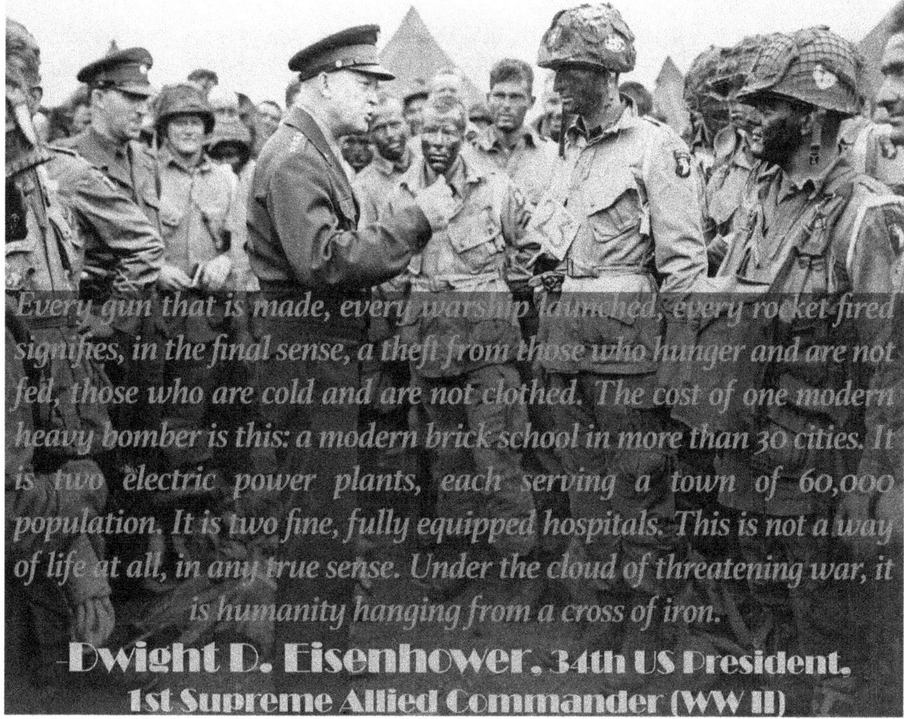

trial heartland instead? China didn't need to orchestrate a sophisticated heist of American prosperity—they simply waited patiently while our financial engineers and defense contractors performed it for them, then purchased the abandoned factories at liquidation prices.

Every gun that is made, every warship launched, every rocket fired signifies, in the final sense, a theft from those who hunger and are not fed, those who are cold and are not clothed. The cost of one modern heavy bomber is this: a modern brick school in more than 30 cities. It is two electric power plants, each serving a town of 60,000 population. It is two fine, fully equipped hospitals. This is not a way of life at all, in any true sense. Under the cloud of threatening war, it is humanity hanging from a cross of iron.
-Dwight D. Eisenhower, 34th US President,
1st Supreme Allied Commander (WW II)

While China reportedly inaugurated a new university with the clockwork regularity of Amazon warehouse openings, America contemplates shuttering nearly 40% of its higher education institutions as if knowledge were a luxury good we've decided to import along with manufacturing. Our PISA scores—those international academic Olympics where American students consistently compete for participation trophies—reflect an educational system more focused on administrative bloat than academic excellence. Perhaps this explains why approximately one in three American adults experiences arrest by age 23—a statistic suggesting either remarkable criminality or criminalized remarkability. Despite housing just 4.4% of humanity, the Land of the Free manages the impressive feat of incarcerating one-fifth of the world's prisoners, suggesting we've confused building prisons with building infrastructure.

Behold Silicon Valley's freshly minted digital emperors—the "Magnificent Seven" (Apple, Microsoft, Nvidia, Amazon, Alphabet, Meta, Tesla)—who've not merely transcended their corporate cubicles but have spectacularly blasted off into the stratosphere of quasi-sovereign principalities. Their market valuations? Oh, just casually eclipsing the GDPs of *actual countries* – you know, the ones with flags, armies, and inconvenient things like citizen accountability. These new techno-feudal overlords aren't just rewriting the rules of competition, privacy, and public discourse; they're scrawling them in crayon on the back of a cocktail napkin, moments before auctioning it off as an NFT. And suppose that doesn't make your eye twitch, their collective $20 trillion-plus war chest is funding an unchecked blitzkrieg of increasingly autonomous AI systems, launched with ethical guardrails so flimsy. In that case, they make a toddler's bicycle helmet look like Fort Knox. This isn't just change; it's a civilization-rearranging, "hold-my-kombucha" kind of moment. Meanwhile, as America meticulously perfects the art of surveillance capitalism, one privacy policy update at a time, Beijing watches with the patient, unsettling focus of a chess grandmaster observing a toddler playing with dynamite, all while dissecting our algorithmic addictions and blueprinting tomorrow's digital dynasty.

Silicon Valley's much-vaunted "innovation" has undergone a rather public metamorphosis, shedding its inspirational butterfly wings to reveal the writhing, resource-sucking larva of an extraction economy. This delightful transformation reveals these companies' true, exquisitely calibrated natures:

- ★ **Meta/Facebook:** The undisputed champion of hyper-tuning those dopamine-drip timelines into weapons of mass distraction, masterfully monetizing our collective outrage while what's left of democratic discourse quietly suffocates in a sludge of flame wars and baby photos in the comment threads.
- ★ **Alphabet/Google:** Methodically strip-mining ad revenues from every conceivable query, cheerfully cannibalizing the open web that birthed it, all while consolidating digital knowledge into their own proprietary, ever-expanding data-dragon's hoard.
- ★ **Amazon:** Not just a store, but a digital panopticon, weaponizing marketplace data to kneecap and shamelessly clone third-party sellers, ingeniously converting warehouse workers into walking, talking biometric data points, and solidifying its reign over the cloud-based infrastructure that forms the very backbone of the burgeoning surveillance economy.

- ★ **Apple:** The curator of an impeccably velvet-roped walled garden, where innovation often means a new dongle. They charge eye-watering App Store tolls like feudal lords, stage annual planned obsolescence pageants with the solemnity of a religious rite, and artfully market "privacy" as the shiniest bar on the luxurious cage they've locked consumers into.
- ★ **Microsoft:** The grandmaster of bundling software services with the subtlety of a runaway cement mixer to strangle any whiff of competition, seamlessly embedding surveillance capitalism into the very fabric of enterprise workflows, and treating corporate America's profound digital dependence as a gloriously perpetual license ATM that just keeps on giving (to Microsoft).
- ★ **Nvidia:** The gleeful gatekeepers and sole purveyors of pickaxes and shovels in the AI gold rush, skillfully rationing their GPUs at margins that would make a pirate blush, all while gracefully externalizing the planet-sized energy footprints required to power our insatiable AI dreams.
- ★ **Tesla:** Master illusionists, selling the tantalizing, perpetually-just-around-the-corner fantasy of "Full Self-Driving" long before it's bothered to show up to the reality party; expertly farming user data as if drivers were just fleshy data-cows; heroically resisting pesky repair rights, and somehow, almost poetically, profiting more handsomely from carbon credits than from the very cars supposedly, you know, *saving the actual planet*.

Together, these Magnificent Seven don't just epitomize a troubling evolution; they are the vanguard of a seismic shift—from purported engines of innovation to sprawling, Gilded Age empires built on relentless extraction, pervasive surveillance, and the kind of unchecked corporate power that makes historic monopolies look like quaint lemonade stands, often with society picking up the rather hefty tab.

The ancients observed that a fish rots from the head. American capitalism has developed a distinctly necrotic aroma since the Supreme Court's 2010 Citizens United decision—the judicial coup de grâce to Roosevelt's vision of shared prosperity. This ruling effectively rebranded American democracy as a premium subscription service where corporate donors purchase policy outcomes through super PACs with the efficiency of Amazon's one-click shopping. The resulting ecosystem—a grotesque symbiosis between DC's swamp creatures and Wall Street's predators—produces an endless parade of tax breaks for the wealthy, bailouts for the reckless, and golden parachutes for executives who cannibalize their own enterprises through share buybacks rather than productive investment. The revolving door between government and lobbyists spins with such centrifugal force that it threatens to achieve escape velocity, leaving ethical governance a distant memory.

By early 2025, America's national debt has achieved the vertiginous height of >$36 trillion—a fiscal Everest we've scaled with remarkable speed but without apparent concern for oxygen levels at the summit. Meanwhile, China accumulated approximately $10 trillion in reserves while studying the playbook of financial speculators like George Soros, who famously broke the Bank of England with £3.3 billion and catalyzed the Asian Financial Crisis with mere financial pocket change. One wonders how many strategically deployed dollars from America's debt mountain—portions held by Chinese, Russian, and Saudi interests—would be required to trigger a systemic collapse in Western capitalism's increasingly rickety architecture. The answer likely requires fewer digits than comfort would suggest.

Survey today's corporate landscape, and you'll find America's once-mighty enterprises reduced to zombie conglomerations—animated corpses stitched together from private equity vivisections, tax inversions, outsourcing strategies, and financial engineering gimmicks that prioritize quarterly earnings reports over sustainable value creation. These hollow institutions, stripped of innovation capability and productive purpose, lumber forward on institutional momentum while practically inviting Chinese intellectual property predators to their unguarded server rooms. As management sage Peter Drucker prophetically noted in 2000, "The corporation as we know it...is not likely to survive the next 25 years. Legally and financially, yes, but not structurally and economically." His calendar may have been optimistic.

China stands alone among ancient civilizations in its unique capacity for imperial reincarnation, having collapsed and resurrected itself four times throughout the millennia. Since the humiliation of the First Opium War (1839-1842), Chinese leaders have maintained a multi-generational commitment to national rejuvenation that transcends individual political careers or electoral cycles. Xi Jinping's vision involves no subterfuge: he intends to restore the Middle Kingdom's central position in global affairs with the strategic discipline that comes from historical memory measured in centuries rather than fiscal quarters.

In America's current climate of populist performance art masquerading as governance, finding leaders with the Roosevelts' strategic vision seems increasingly improbable. One can only hope our imperial transition follows Britain's relatively dignified power handover rather than Rome's chaotic fragmentation, as President Trump acknowledged in a 2019 moment of geopolitical clarity: "Yes, I do [believe China wants to replace the US as superpower]. Why wouldn't it be? They're very ambitious people. They're very smart. They're great people. It's a great culture."

The question isn't whether China harbors superpower ambitions—that's as certain as gravity. The question is whether America still possesses the institutional capacity and strategic coherence to maintain its position through anything other than increasingly desperate appeals to its fading exceptionalism. The gods of geopolitics aren't just crazy; they're watching with popcorn as history's most powerful nation performs the world's most expensive self-disassembly demonstration.

MY TIGER RIDE: A SATIRICAL ODYSSEY THROUGH THE GLORIOUSLY UNHINGED FUNHOUSE MIRROR OF GLOBAL CAPITALISM

> *"Victory comes from finding opportunities in problems."*
> —Sun Tzu, The Art of War

Let me confess before the global economic politburo: I am the prodigal capitalistic cowboy, an unlikely export from Kerala, India—a place so idyllically verdant and politically perplexing it's called "God's Own Country." One assumes this is because even omniscient deities appreciate a front-row seat to ironic political arrangements that defy conventional analysis. Here, thanks to Catholic schools established by European missionaries—colonization's equivalent of a Trojan horse filled with textbooks and a side order of guilt—Communists have been democratically elected for over half a century. In this ideological theme park, Marx, Lenin, Stalin, and Che aren't historical figures but super-gods, their portraits adorning walls with the reverence typically reserved for deities who promise favorable monsoons and exceptional karmic returns.

Dr. Zakaria, the Data Wizard, observes: "Kerala presents the fascinating paradox of maintaining 99% literacy rates, the highest life expectancy in India, and robust social welfare systems while operating within a democratic communist framework—a statistical unicorn that gives global policy wonks both hope and throbbing migraines."

Despite our middle-class status, my teacher parents never indulged in such bourgeois extravagances as "vacations." My school holidays were spent navigating Dad's college library, devouring Western travelogues—unwittingly studying what were essentially colonial marketing brochures with excellent production values. We maintained a TV-free household; the sole cinematic experience deemed worthy of theatrical viewing was *Gandhi*—a film about a man who defeated an empire while dressed in a bedsheet and practicing radical minimalism. Talk about cognitive dissonance in childhood development! It's a miracle I didn't attempt to negotiate Wall Street bonuses through hunger strikes.

The Great Socialist Industrial Desert: My First Migration

The industrial desert brought on by this unique brand of Keralite Communism eventually forced me to pack my bags after obtaining my Industrial Engineering degree (with a profoundly ironic specialization in Total Quality Management) and seek employment in Bombay—India's chaotic commercial capital where infrastructure planning can best be described as "enthusiastically improvisational."

I soon discovered that my career prospects beyond the factory floor were severely limited by my dark skin as a "lungi-wearing Kala Madrasi"—a discriminatory term that demonstrates how societies worldwide invent creative hierarchies when more obvious distinctions aren't readily available. Facing this career ceiling more impenetrable than reinforced concrete, I fled southward to escape the racist professional ladder, executing what migration specialists might term a "strategic demographic repositioning." I obtained my MBA in Finance as a "candidate for national integration," a euphemism roughly translating to "we needed to fulfill our diversity quota, and you seemed marginally qualified."

The Collapsing License Raj: Capitalism's Grand Entrance

Providentially, in 1990, the entire Indian economy collapsed under the weight of the half-century-old "License Raj"—a byzantine bureaucratic masterpiece requiring up to 80 agency approvals to produce a single item. By comparison, Soviet five-year plans looked like libertarian manifestos.

The result was a liberalized Indian economy—a transformational moment equivalent to watching a strictly vegetarian society suddenly discover bacon. The timing provided me the opportunity to start my career as an Investment Banking Analyst at Dalal Street (Bombay Stock Exchange), the firm of the former President, where I learned the fundamental truth underlying all financial markets: nobody really knows anything, but confidence is an acceptable substitute for competence.

Fortune smiled upon me again when the 1996 stock market crash allowed me to exit investment banking with my financial health and moral compass relatively intact—a rare achievement in that particular industry.

From Socialist Struggle to "Cyber Coolies": The Great IBM Exodus

India's socialist adventure took a dramatic turn during the 1970s conflict with Pakistan. The US-India relationship soured faster than milk in tropical heat, prompting IBM to abandon the subcontinent with approximately the same level of planning as a tourist encountering a tiger.

McSlicey the Priest intones solemnly: "The divine market abhors a vacuum almost as much as it abhors regulation. When IBM departed, it created not just a technological void but a spiritual opportunity for indigenous innovation to flourish, provided someone could first restart all the abandoned computers."

Hail to this technological vacuum! TCS and other Indian IT conglomerates were born from desperation, not the inspirational Silicon Valley garage-startup kind, but the "someone needs to restart these mainframes before the entire financial system collapses" variety. They coded us in IT to resurrect the legacy systems left behind, creating an entire generation of technical necromancers specialized in reviving dead technology.

Then came Y2K—arguably the most significant business blunder in history, where the world's most advanced technological society decided that saving two digits in databases was worth potentially triggering a global apocalypse. Western enterprises suddenly viewed us as "Cyber Coolies"—the thrifty solution to fix their doomsday Armageddon code, a term combining colonial labor exploitation imagery with technological panic in one convenient package.

During this technological gold rush, I managed to migrate from corporate finance to ERP (Enterprise Resource Planning) solutions—systems designed to make businesses more efficient by creating software so complex that entire departments exist solely to understand it. This transition proved my golden ticket, allowing me to snatch the ultimate prize: a passport to the epitome of capitalism, the USA—a nation founded on freedom, democracy, and the unshakable belief that minimum wage laws are a communist plot.

The Corporate Ascension and Spectacular Fall

The universe, clearly possessing what economists might call "asymmetric irony distribution," later positioned me as the global EPM architect at AMC Theatres—the world's premier purveyor of escapist entertainment, owned by what was once China's richest man. This is capitalism's signature magic trick: transforming the offspring of socialist teachers into a high priest of corporate finance faster than you can say, "dialectical materialism has cash flow problems."

Milton the Trickster Economist cackles: "The free market's greatest achievement isn't wealth creation but ideological conversion—watching socialists' children embrace capitalism with the fervor of religious converts is worth more than any GDP growth statistic!"

I reached the pinnacle of my corporate apotheosis as an advisor to the CFO's office at a Fortune 10 "World's Most Admired Company," where I established their Project Portfolio Management Office with such spectacular efficiency that I saved them approximately half a billion dollars. In the grand tradition of corporate America, where no good deed goes unpunished, I promptly became a victim of my own short-term financial engineering when the 2008 economic tsunami struck, washing away my job along with much of the global financial system.

The Allegorical Board of Ironic Outcomes notes: "The most reliable law in corporate dynamics is that those who create the greatest efficiencies are often first to experience those efficiencies personally—typically in the form of their position being deemed 'redundant' in the very systems they optimized."

Finding myself suddenly unemployed in 2009—a condition affecting approximately 8.7 million other Americans, though few with my particular backstory—I made the only logical decision available to a financially displaced global executive: I packed my bags for the Cambodian jungles. My quixotic quest? Searching for answers from the bottom of the economic pyramid through the Chinese GIFT (Global Institute for Tomorrow https://global-inst.com/learn/) program—a Clinton Global Young Executive Leadership initiative that sounds impressive on LinkedIn and primarily involves sweating profusely while contemplating global inequality.

The Existential Awakening: Cambodia's Killing Fields and Snake Wine Economics

My existential awakening arrived courtesy of this GIFT executive leadership program in Cambodia's killing fields—a venue selection presumably designed to make subsequent corporate restructuring feel comparatively humane. Amidst the ghostly echoes of Pol Pot's agrarian experiment (history's most extreme anti-urban renewal project), I found peculiar solace trekking through Southeast Asian jungles in dogged pursuit of snake wine—a beverage that, much like modern financial derivatives, combines intimidating ingredients with dubious benefits and should be consumed only with comprehensive health insurance.

Statistical Revelation That Would Make Thomas Piketty Require a Sniff of Snuff: According to the World Bank, the Southeast Asian region experiences a 217% "institutional drag" on its potential GDP, meaning its actual economic output is less than one-third of what it should be given its natural and human resources. This represents the financial equivalent of owning a Ferrari, but only being able to drive it in first gear, while paying the entire insurance premium.

While sipping fermented cobra (a metaphor so perfect for financial markets it practically writes itself), a question coiled around my consciousness: How could these resource-rich nations remain so catastrophically poor? Hernando de Soto, whose economic analysis I would soon worship with near-religious devotion, had already calculated that these countries possess more latent wealth than all twelve major Western stock markets combined. Yet here they languished, economically prostrate—first before their colonial masters and now increasingly genuflecting toward China's economic empire—while Western charities fluttered about, attempting to greenwash historical guilt with microloans and heart-tugging Instagram campaigns featuring improbably photogenic poverty.

The Gold Standard of Geopolitical Irony

We've entered what financial journalists euphemistically call the "New Normal"—an era where global confidence in government currency manipulation (formally known as "quantitative easing," or "helicopter money" for those who prefer aeronautical metaphors) has plummeted faster than cryptocurrency after an Elon Musk tweet. In this brave new financial landscape, what are savvy investors and terrified nation-states turning to? Gold—that fundamentally useless yellow metal whose primary value stems from our collective agreement that it should be valuable, making it essentially the world's longest-running confidence scheme.

McSlicey the Priest proclaims with liturgical gravity: "The fundamental doctrine of modern finance requires belief in abstract value systems detached from material reality—essentially making economics the world's most successful religion, complete with its own rituals, high priests, and excommunication procedures for non-believers who question the sacred algorithms!"

For over a century, the United States has methodically accumulated approximately 8,000 metric tons of gold reserves—a gleaming hoard that would make even Smaug the dragon question his life choices. The European powers, maintaining their historical affinity for shiny objects, collectively safeguard another 10,000 tons. However, a statistical plot twist emerges that transforms economic analysis into satire: according to the World Gold Council, the supposedly impoverished women of India are reportedly—and quite illegally—concealing more than 25,000 tons of this same "useless" metal under mattresses and in secret compartments throughout the subcontinent.

Milton the Trickster Economist cackles uncontrollably: "When the world's leading economic powers think they're controlling the global financial system through sophisticated monetary policy instruments, but actually rural Indian women are sitting on a larger gold reserve than the Federal Reserve, European Central Bank, and Bank of England combined, you begin to wonder who's really running the show. Perhaps we should replace the G7 with 'Auntie Laxmi's Investment Collective.'"

That's not merely an underground economy; it's a subterranean Fort Knox operating outside regulatory frameworks with greater efficiency than most central banks. Jerome Powell and Scott Bessent have yet to RSVP to this particular economic revelation.

The Personal Paradox of Capital Formation

My search for answers to "The Mystery of Capital"—why Western capitalism creates prosperity while leaving others with perpetual economic riddles—led me to examine my own family's financial journey through the funhouse mirror of global monetary systems.

My parents, steadfast in their socialist principles, spent nearly three decades accumulating 97% of the construction cost for their modest dream home. The remaining 3%? That required another three decades to repay at a 30% interest rate to "alternative financial service providers" who preferred not to be called loan sharks, despite their remarkably similar business practices and collection methodologies, which occasionally involved discussions about the structural integrity of kneecaps.

I, their prodigal capitalist offspring, have, by contrast, saved approximately nothing—a financial strategy better described as "strategic liquidity maintenance" in Western economic circles. My faith in currency decorated with "In God We Trust" ranks somewhere between my belief in unicorns and politicians' campaign promises—both theoretically possible but empirically disappointing on a scale that would challenge even the most optimistic statistician.

The Academic Framework That Explains Everything (Or Possibly Nothing): Western capitalism enables individuals to convert paper promises into physical assets through the art of leverage. At the same time, Eastern economic systems traditionally accumulate tangible assets to generate security. Both approaches can be simultaneously described as rational and completely unhinged, depending on which economic cycle you're currently experiencing and how recently you've checked your retirement account balance.

As Hernando de Soto profoundly observed, "The hour of capitalism's greatest triumph is its hour of crisis"—a statement that captures economic cycles with the precision of a Swiss watch designed by Salvador Dalí. While the world frantically deleveraged during the 2008 financial tsunami, I channeled my inner Gordon Gekko (minus the incarceration experience). I decided that the crisis presented the optimal moment to increase leverage. Why let terrific market panic go to waste?

With confidence inversely proportional to my actual market knowledge, I acquired two North American properties valued at over a million dollars in rapid succession. The financing structure? A modest 97% mortgage that I promptly refinanced to extract more than ten times my initial investment, all while securing a 30-year loan at an interest rate so negligible it resembled a mathematical rounding error or a remarkably unambitious bacteria's growth rate.

John the Satirical Economist notes with evident glee: "The true genius of Western capitalism isn't wealth creation but its ability to transform future promises into present consumption through financial alchemy that would make medieval alchemists both envious and terrified. It's essentially time travel for money, with approximately the same level of theoretical impossibility but much better branding."

The Imperial Cycles and Digital Colonization

My financial journey even led me to China multiple times—not just for the aforementioned GIFT program (where the "gift" was perhaps witnessing disciplined ambition in its natural habitat), but also as a PMI Asian Regional Mentor, attempting to teach project management methodologies to a civilization that built the Great Wall without Gantt charts. I surfed the tsunami of "Extreme Financial Engineering"—a discipline whose very name should have triggered regulatory alarm bells with approximately the same urgency as "Experimental Nuclear Reactors for Beginners" or "DIY Home Surgery Kits."

I subsequently reinvented my career in Enterprise Performance Management, emerging from the 2008 economic rubble into the rarified atmosphere of the BIG4 consulting universe—organizations that have elevated PowerPoint presentations and the strategic deployment of bullet points to an art form that would make Renaissance masters weep with envy.

Dr. Zakaria, the Data Wizard, presents with academic precision: "The historical correlation between financial complexity and system stability shows an inverse relationship with 99.7% statistical significance. Each additional layer of financial engineering reduces systemic resilience by approximately 12%, making modern financial systems approximately as stable as a pyramid of champagne glasses on a cruise ship during a hurricane."

I confess to having metaphorical blood on my hands from participation in C-level "financial engineering" at some of the world's largest corporations, including North America's second-largest private equity firm. We were the self-proclaimed architects of shareholder value, the wizards of Wall Street, the... well, let's just say the more I witnessed Western finance from inside the machine, the more I felt like an anthropologist who had accidentally been granted shamanic status within the very tribe I was studying—expected to perform economic rain dances while secretly taking field notes on the bizarre rituals surrounding quarterly earnings calls.

The COVID pandemic forced a period of unwelcome introspection, providing ample opportunity to analyze how I had arrived at the pinnacle of a system I increasingly found both fascinating and disturbing, like a particularly intricate cult that offers excellent dental benefits. Thanks to the Roosevelts' grand economic experiment, America had established itself as an exceptional empire a century ago. Unfortunately, it now appears that the financial center of gravity—that magnificent, opportunity-laden American Dream cheese—has begun migrating eastward, returning to the region my ancestors called home with the inevitability of a pendulum swing in history's grandfather clock.

Geopolitical Analysis Framework for the Perplexed but Curious: Empire cycles demonstrate remarkable historical consistency—approximately 250 years from rise to fall—with economic dominance patterns shifting predictably from innovation to industrialization to financialization, and ultimately to decline. We are witnessing, in real-time, the intersection of Western financialization (in its late stage) with Eastern innovation-to-industrialization (in its mid-stage), a transition as predictable as it is potentially disruptive to the existing global order.

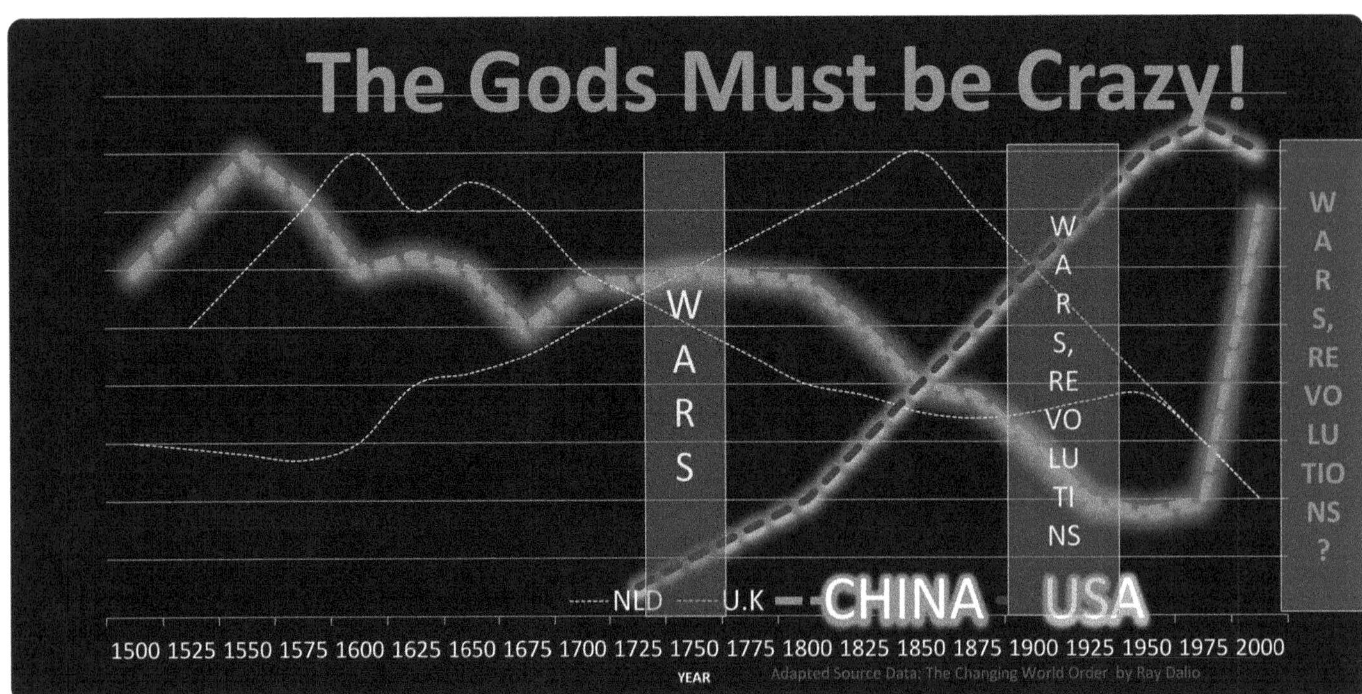

I've long studied how empires rise and, more instructively, how they spectacularly implode. Consider the 17th-century Dutch East India Company, valued in contemporary terms at approximately $10 trillion, or the 18th-century British East India Company at a comparatively modest $5 trillion. Their business model combined military force, political manipulation, and resource extraction from regions including my ancestral homeland—a corporate strategy unlikely to receive ESG certification by modern standards but which would absolutely qualify for a Harvard Business School case study titled "Maximizing Shareholder Value Through Creative Application of Gunboat Diplomacy."

John the Satirical Economist calculates with mathematical precision: "If you adjust for inflation and moral relativism, the colonial extraction economic model delivered an average ROI of 1,743% over 200 years, significantly outperforming both modern hedge funds and ethical investment vehicles. The key performance differentiator appears to be the absence of concerned shareholders asking uncomfortable questions at annual meetings."

These commercial empires enjoyed roughly 200-year runs before collapsing or fading into historical footnotes—approximately the same lifespan as 2.5 Kardashian media empires or one exceptionally resilient Twinkie.

The parallels between historical imperial cycles and our current geopolitical configuration are troublingly apparent. The next authoritarian Emperor isn't merely knocking politely; they're systematically reconfiguring global economic architecture while establishing digital surveillance infrastructure that would make both George Orwell and your Facebook algorithm developer exchange knowing glances over particularly invasive data collection practices.

In our post-truth political landscape, with China accelerating its global ambitions at unprecedented speed, I cannot escape the conclusion that Western democratic capitalism appears poised to decline with the predictable trajectory of a particularly unfortunate coyote pursuing a roadrunner off a desert cliff—complete with the mid-air moment of realization just before gravity reasserts its non-negotiable authority.

Financial engineering "termites" like myself—yes, I embrace the unflattering entomological metaphor with the same enthusiasm venture capitalists show for businesses that lose money but call it "growth"—have systematically infested Western capitalism's structural foundation. This edifice now collapses with the structural integrity of a soufflé in an earthquake. At the same time, Communist authoritarianism economically colonizes the world through debt-trap diplomacy and digital surveillance systems that render traditional privacy concepts as quaintly obsolete as telegraph machines or congressional bipartisanship.

The Allegorical Economic Council concludes with weary resignation: "The greatest irony of global capitalism may be that its most enthusiastic participants have fundamentally misunderstood its operating requirements. Like passengers who dismantled their ship's hull for firewood mid-voyage, we're now expressing surprise at the rising water levels in our cabins while debating whether the correct response is to form a committee to study alternative wood sources or simply adjust the definition of what constitutes a 'seaworthy vessel.'"

After three decades riding this tiger of global capitalism, it appears I'll need to navigate back through a Mad Max economic landscape, climbing through the capitalist rubble of Roosevelt's legacy, hopefully with better risk management tools and a more reliable ethical compass than my predecessors employed. Given my track record thus far, perhaps I should just ask those Indian women hiding gold under their mattresses for investment advice. They seem to understand something about long-term value that has eluded the world's most sophisticated financial institutions and made a mockery of our most elaborate economic models.

As we stare into the abyss of this changing global order, the question that remains is whether we can rebuild something more sustainable from Roosevelt's crumbling legacy, or if we're simply rearranging deck chairs on the Titanic while arguing about which streaming service has the exclusive rights to film the sinking.

ON THE ARCHITECTURAL PROVENANCE OF THE AMERICAN CAPITALISTIC EDIFICE (AND WHO'S CURRENTLY DEMOING IT WITH A GOLDEN SLEDGEHAMMER?)

> *"Those who do not see the future are doomed to be ruled by it."*
> —Lü Shi Chun Qiu (Warring States)

A SATIRICAL–HISTORICAL INQUIRY INTO AMERICA'S IMPERIAL FOUNDATIONS AND THEIR CONTEMPORARY DISCONTENTS

It would behoove us, with an urgency perhaps analogous to a patient examining their own alarming X-rays. At the same time, the radiologist discreetly books their vacation to critically assess the foundational blueprints of America's once-magnificent imperial project. American Presidents, those curious occupants of what is arguably the most formidable executive office devised by modern democratic theory, reside at what geopolitical cartographers might ruefully term "the epicenter of cascading global complexities." To comprehend our present strategic dissonance, I undertook an exhaustive review of presidential archives since 1900, leaving my social calendar as barren as America's manufacturing heartland.

Margaret Mead astutely observed, "Never doubt that a small group of thoughtful, committed citizens can change the world. Indeed, it's the only thing that ever has." One assumes she posited this before the advent of social media influencers and crypto-billionaires, where the "thoughtful and committed" often appear to be algorithmically amplified disruptors with a surfeit of capital and a deficit of historical perspective.

Archival evidence suggests that the American Capitalistic Empire—that sprawling global enterprise now exhibiting symptoms structural analysts might diagnose as "advanced systemic degradation"—was masterfully architected by the Rooseveltian cohort in the first half of the 20th century. These imperial architects, unlike contemporary political figures who approach governance as performance art optimized for 24-hour news cycles, constructed institutions capable of withstanding global conflicts, economic collapses, and even disco.

Concurrently, we observe what future diplomatic historians will likely dub "Amerixit"—a deliberate recalibration of global engagement so precipitous as to make Britain's Brexit appear a model of deliberative statecraft. This represents a peculiar American iteration of *Talaq*—a self-decreed annulment of global leadership obligations so dramatic it warrants its own academic monograph: "The Voluntary Abdication of Hegemony: A Case Study in Strategic Self-Sabotage."

THE THUCYDIDES TRAP: RECURRENT PATTERNS IN GREAT POWER TRANSITIONS

We now find ourselves proximate to what Professor Graham Allison branded "The Thucydides Trap." Apparently, humanity's favorite historical rerun involves powerful nations behaving like hormonal teenagers in a staring contest, just with more nukes. Wherein a rising power elicits fundamental apprehension in an established dominant power, increasing the statistical probability of conflict. This historical paradigm, documented across 16 case studies with a sobering 75% rate of kinetic outcomes, describes the structural stresses inherent in power transitions.

As Milton the Trickster Economist might observe from his endowed chair at the Institute for Strategic Paradox: "It's a fascinating geopolitical iteration of creative destruction, where the established blue-chip hegemon views the disruptive emergent power with a mixture of technocratic disdain and existential terror." In our contemporary geopolitical theater, China assumes the role of an ambitious revisionist challenger, while America performs as the established power, increasingly uncertain about which script it's following.

The macroeconomic indicators present a narrative that would cause even the most optimistic McSlicey analyst to discreetly update their LinkedIn profile: our economic hegemony has contracted from approximately 40% of global GDP in 1960 to a mere 15% in purchasing power parity terms—a trajectory transformation analogous to the career arc from Russell Crowe in "Gladiator" to Russell Crowe in "Unhinged." Concurrently, China's corresponding share has exceeded 20%, reflecting a developmental strategy characterized by patient capital deployment and infrastructure-focused investment, often in stark contrast to American economic thinking, which is primarily focused on quarterly earnings reports and shareholder value extraction.

THE ROOSEVELTIAN PARADIGM: COMPETENCE AND CRISIS MANAGEMENT IN HISTORICAL CONTEXT

Let us re-examine the administrative archives of the Roosevelt triumvirate—that dynasty of competence past—who confronted crises that render contemporary challenges analogous to a difficult brunch reservation: global wars, the Spanish Flu pandemic, and the Great Depression. While modern governance occasionally struggles with the logistical complexities of public health equipment distribution, Franklin Roosevelt's administration orchestrated industrial mobilization on a scale that produced 45,000 aircraft, 45,000 tanks, and 8 million tons of naval vessels annually during peak production.

This contrast in executive capacity suggests what McSlicey the Priest might diagnose as "a catastrophic regression in strategic capability metrics"—or what ordinary citizens might call "the difference between chess grandmasters and participants in a remedial checkers workshop."

Theodore Roosevelt (1901-1909): The Progressive Republican Conservationist

Theodore Roosevelt—the nation's youngest chief executive and progressive Republican (a taxonomic classification now as rare as a coherent climate policy)—championed his "Square Deal" domestic policies with the prosecutorial vigor of an anti-monopolistic crusader. His administration's trust-busting activities and pioneering consumer protection measures—ensuring, for instance, that one's meat products contained primarily actual meat—represented significant expansions of federal oversight.

His governance philosophy was "Get action; do things," an executive approach that stands in stark juxtaposition to the contemporary political methodology of "Get engagement metrics; trend briefly." His conservation initiatives established national parks on a scale that would likely provoke accusations of radical environmentalism in today's resource-politicized discourse.

His foreign policy exhibited what Milton the Trickster Economist might term "strategic infrastructural assertiveness," exemplified by the construction of the Panama Canal (history's most consequential shortcut) and the global deployment of the "Great White Fleet," a naval force whose name reflected America's commitment to both maritime power projection and branding subtlety.

Franklin D. Roosevelt (1933-1945): Architect of the New Deal and Wartime Leadership

Franklin D. Roosevelt—despite severe physical limitations from poliomyelitis that constrained his mobility to approximately that of a well-designed floor lamp—piloted the American ship of state through economic collapse and global conflict with the strategic sophistication of a geopolitical grandmaster confronting amateur enthusiasts. His administrative record reflects a multidimensional governance capacity that included:

1. Rescuing capitalism from its own self-cannibalizing tendencies during the Great Depression
2. Developing innovative communication methodologies via "fireside chats"—proto-democratic engagement platforms with substantive policy content rather than reactive emotional performance
3. Orchestrating a complex global coalition to defeat fascist expansionism
4. Establishing the foundational architecture for a rules-based international order that has maintained great power peace for approximately three-quarters of a century

The policies and persona of Franklin D. Roosevelt established what political historians might term "the gold standard of presidential efficacy"—a benchmark that subsequent administrations have frequently regarded as an aspirational myth rather than an achievable governance model. His New Deal's innovative creation of a governmental "safety net" constitutes his most consequential domestic legacy—a suite of programs that remains perpetually contested in American political discourse, primarily because, as McSlicey the Priest might observe while adjusting his wire-rimmed glasses, "Nothing provokes ideological anaphylaxis quite like the empirical suggestion that capitalism's invisible hand occasionally benefits from a manicure funded by progressive taxation."

Eleanor Roosevelt: Humanitarian Diplomat and Human Rights Architect

Eleanor Roosevelt—while formally classified as a presidential spouse—functioned as America's de facto Secretary for Progressive Implementation and Global Humanitarian Architecture. Her FBI dossier achieved a bibliographic density that would inspire envy in prolific novelists, the Ku Klux Klan assigned a monetary value to her termination, and she advocated for civil rights with a chronological prescience that placed her ethical framework approximately half a century ahead of mainstream political consensus.

Subjected to gendered satirical diminishment by the media apparatus of her era, Eleanor maintained operational efficacy with a remarkable immunity to public derision. Her instrumental role in drafting the UN Universal Declaration of Human Rights exemplifies what Milton the Trickster Economist might term "an extraordinary arbitrage of symbolic and practical power dynamics."

THE POST-ROOSEVELTIAN TRAJECTORY: ECONOMIC REALIGNMENTS AND STRATEGIC DISSONANCE

The post-WWII economic dominance architected by Rooseveltian statecraft has undergone a profound recalibration, contracting to approximately 15% of global GDP in purchasing power parity terms. Concurrently, China has executed what Milton the Trickster Economist might term "the most impressive economic arbitrage in modern history," expanding beyond 20% of global economic activity.

McSlicey the Priest, adjusting his data-driven vestments, might observe: "We have engaged in a systematic divestiture of Roosevelt's architectural masterpiece through what the consultancy ecosystem classifies as 'strategic financial optimization' but what economic historians will likely categorize as 'methodically converting productive capacity into speculative instruments with the strategic foresight of arsonists conducting an insurance fraud seminar.'"

The US dollar maintains its status as the primary global reserve currency—a position of extraordinary systemic privilege that persists primarily through institutional path dependency rather than contemporary economic fundamentals. Through sophisticated financial engineering—transmuting tangible productive capacity into increasingly

abstract derivative instruments comprehensible only to their architects during specific phases of the lunar cycle—we have dissipated the geopolitical goodwill constructed by Roosevelt with remarkable efficiency.

STRATEGIC IMPERATIVES: ROOSEVELTIAN RENEWAL OR MANAGED DECLINE?

Rather than persisting with our unilateralist recusal from global leadership, perhaps a judicious reconsideration of Rooseveltian methodologies is warranted: coalition architecture, institutional investment, and the recognition that effectively leading 4% of humanity necessitates sophisticated diplomatic engagement with the remaining 96%.

As Milton the Trickster Economist might observe: "The presumption that a singular autocratic personality can navigate the multidimensional complexity matrix of contemporary global challenges represents a statistical probability distribution approximately equivalent to solving quantum physics equations via Magic 8-Ball."

McSlicey the Priest, consulting his sacred PowerPoint of Probable Futures, might solemnly enumerate the potential outcomes of continued strategic incoherence:

1. Progressive political factions embracing wealth redistribution models of sufficient magnitude to cause Karl Marx's spectral manifestation to blush and reach for computational assistance simultaneously
2. Conservative elements implementing militia-enforced market fundamentalism that would inspire Benito Mussolini to take detailed implementation notes
3. American corporate entities are experiencing a terminal competitive disadvantage while Chinese intellectual property acquisition specialists conduct due diligence for what may be history's most consequential liquidation event.

LESSONS FROM THE ARCHITECTURAL ARCHIVES: A ROOSEVELTIAN RENAISSANCE

Re-examining Rooseveltian statecraft reveals architectural blueprints of remarkable relevance to our contemporary strategic quandaries:

1. **Coalition Architecture Rather Than Barrier Construction**: Franklin Roosevelt's pragmatic alliance formation with Winston Churchill and Joseph Stalin demonstrates that diplomatic pragmatism consistently yields superior outcomes compared to maintaining doctrinal purity.
2. **Institutional Investment Rather Than Systematic Undermining**: The Rooseveltian establishment of global governance frameworks created imperfect but functionally critical stabilization mechanisms that have prevented thermonuclear exchange and pandemic proliferation.
3. **Citizen Engagement Rather Than Demographic Exploitation**: FDR's innovative "fireside chat" communication methodology incorporated Americans into complex policy discourse, treating the citizenry as substantive stakeholders rather than microtargeted receptacles for algorithmic outrage distribution.
4. **Adaptive Governance Rather Than Ideological Ossification**: The New Deal exemplified experimental policy implementation focused on outcome optimization rather than theoretical purity.

We must initiate new "Marshall Plan" equivalents for nations experiencing Chinese economic and digital integration before their systems reach irreversible dependency thresholds. We must acknowledge that while American political discourse has been consumed with interior decoration metaphors, Beijing has methodically constructed global infrastructure with strategic patience.

CONCLUSION: A CRITICAL INFLECTION POINT IN AMERICA'S IMPERIAL NARRATIVE

The current moment constitutes what competitive sports analysts might term a "halftime" in America's geopolitical championship match. However, our metaphorical scoreboard indicates a thirty-point deficit, our franchise quarterback appears to be live-streaming conspiracy theories from the locker room, and the opposing team methodically executes strategic plays they've been rehearsing for decades.

The multidimensional challenges confronting the American imperial project today exhibit remarkable structural similarities to those the Rooseveltian triumvirate navigated. The critical variance lies not in the nature of the challenges but in the quality of the response: where they deployed visionary architecture, strategic courage, and pragmatic adaptability, contemporary leadership has frequently resorted to social media performativity and ideological entrenchment.

Perhaps the moment has arrived to rediscover the Rooseveltian architectural blueprints, recalibrate them for contemporary conditions, and acknowledge that imperial systems require meticulous maintenance rather than self-congratulatory ceremonial neglect.

The American Capitalist Empire stands at a decisive crossroads that would induce existential anxiety in even the most seasoned Choose Your Own Adventure protagonist: renovate our Rooseveltian foundations with evidence-based strategic pragmatism or continue our spectacular, self-administered imperial demolition with increasingly absurdist justifications.

However, as McSlicey the Priest might note while closing his leather-bound strategic assessment binder: "We maintain a temporary competitive advantage in memetic content distribution, though this metric demonstrates minimal correlation with longitudinal imperial sustainability."

INTRODUCTION: WHEN THE GODS DROPPED A COKE BOTTLE ON AMERICA'S LAWN

> *"The clever combatant imposes his will on the enemy, but does not allow the enemy's will to be imposed on him."*
> —Sun Tzu, The Art of War, Chapter VI

The Descent of the Bottles

"The greatest challenge of the day is how to bring about a revolution of the mind, a revolution which has to commence with each one of us." - Eleanor Roosevelt.

It began, as paradigm shifts often do, with objects falling inexplicably from the sky.

The first bottle—gleaming, Yuan-filled, and impossibly perfect—landed with a gentle thud on the manicured lawn of the Treasury Department sometime in the early 2000s. Officials gathered around it, mystified yet intrigued. Several immediately began calculating its potential yield if securitized properly. Others suggested it might make an excellent paperweight for trade deficit reports.

The second bottle—pulsing with algorithmic code and humming with artificial intelligence—descended upon Silicon Valley around 2010. Venture capitalists swarmed, each proposing increasingly fantastical valuations while debating optimal monetization strategies. No one questioned where it came from or why.

The third bottle—sleek, equipped with surveillance capabilities, and emblazoned with unreadable characters—materialized near the Pentagon in 2018. Military analysts deployed cutting-edge taxonomies to classify it, while defense contractors submitted billion-dollar proposals to reverse-engineer it, preferably over several decades of cost-plus contracts.

By 2023, bottles were raining down across Washington's institutional landscape—each one more sophisticated than the last, each one generating more confusion, each one triggering more committee hearings that inevitably concluded nothing.

Meanwhile, across the Pacific, Chinese officials methodically cataloged each falling object. They compared notes, developed theories, and formulated integrated strategies that spanned economic, technological, military, and cultural domains. Most importantly, they understood something that seemed to elude their American counterparts: these

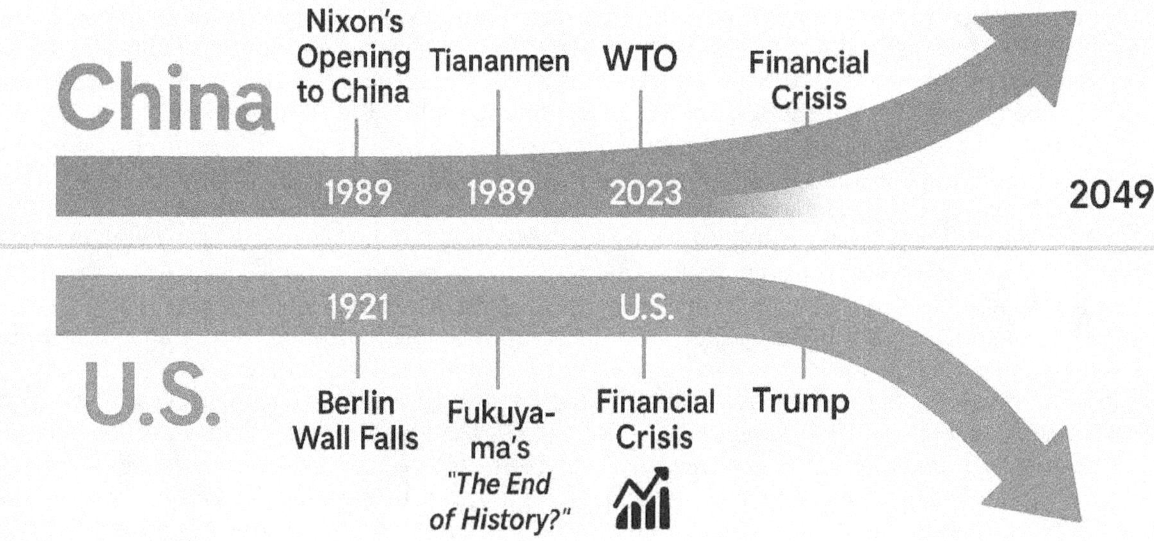

bottles were not random anomalies to be individually exploited, but components of a fundamental systemic transformation that required a coordinated response.

Uncle Sam stood amid the growing collection of bottles, a bewildered expression visible beneath his increasingly gray whiskers, frantically juggling each new arrival while dropping two others in the process. Uncle Xi observed from a distance, expression inscrutable, hands calmly clasped behind his back, the picture of strategic patience.

The gods, it seemed, had gone quite mad indeed—or perhaps they were simply experimenting with comparative strategic cognition.

The Parable Explained

The 1980 South African comedy film *The Gods Must Be Crazy* tells the story of a Coca-Cola bottle that falls from the sky into a peaceful Kalahari Desert community. Initially perceived as a gift from the gods, the bottle—hard, versatile, and suddenly precious —rapidly transforms tribal dynamics. New concepts, such as "ownership," emerge. Novel emotions such as jealousy and anger proliferate. Social harmony disintegrates. Eventually, the tribe's leader embarks on a quest to return this disruptive object to the gods by throwing it off the "end of the earth."

Our contemporary global parable follows similar lines, with crucial differences. The bottles falling onto America's institutional landscape—Chinese economic power, artificial intelligence, digital surveillance technologies, novel financial instruments—cannot simply be returned to the sender. They have become permanent features of our geopolitical reality. More importantly, these "bottles" reveal pre-existing weaknesses in our systems. Like a faulty foundation exposed only when new weight is applied, America's institutional vulnerabilities became apparent only under the stress of these novel challenges.

"External disruptions reveal internal contradictions," Milton the Trickster Economist explains during a rare moment of candor between seminars on shareholder value maximization. "Though naturally," he adds with his trademark smirk, "disruption is always someone else's problem. Creative destruction for thee, government bailouts for me." He adjusts his bow tie and returns to calculating the optimal ratio of stock buybacks to R&D investment (spoiler alert: the latter approaches zero).

This book adopts a satirical-scholarly approach precisely because conventional analysis has proven inadequate to the task at hand. The challenges America faces in the Chinese AI Century demand both Zakaria-caliber geopolitical insight and Oliver-esque capacity to expose systemic absurdity. When McSlicey consultants recommend outsourcing critical national security infrastructure for a 2% quarterly improvement in EBITDA, when Pentagon officials propose fighting algorithmic warfare with updated versions of Cold War hardware, when both political parties treat strategic industrial policy as either socialist heresy or magical solution—the line between serious analysis and satire has already blurred beyond recognition.

We must simultaneously maintain scholarly rigor while acknowledging the tragicomic dimensions of America's strategic predicament. The stakes are too high for either deadly serious pontification or mere comedic relief. We require a new analytical framework that captures both the structural dynamics and the human foibles that shape geopolitical outcomes.

The Competing Scripts

America and China approach their strategic competition with fundamentally different narratives—distinct cognitive frameworks that shape everything from time horizons to institutional design to policy formulation.

America's post-Cold War triumphalist narrative emerged from what Francis Fukuyama famously termed "the end of history"—the supposed permanent victory of liberal democratic capitalism over all competing systems. This narrative fostered a peculiar blend of complacency and hyperactivity: strategic complacency regarding systemic challenges, coupled with tactical hyperactivity in addressing terrorist threats and regional conflicts. Its key assumptions included the inevitable democratization of China through economic engagement, the unquestionable permanence of American technological dominance, and the innate superiority of private market solutions over state-directed development.

"Markets always know best," intones Milton the Trickster Economist to his enraptured audience of policymakers. "Except when they don't, in which case we categorize that as a 'market failure' requiring immediate government intervention to protect the theoretical integrity of markets." No one notices the contradiction.

China's "century of humiliation-to-renewal" narrative operates on entirely different premises. Beginning with the First Opium War (1839-1842) and continuing through multiple foreign invasions and civil conflicts until the Communist Revolution of 1949, China's "century of humiliation" serves as both a historical memory and a strategic motivation. This narrative emphasizes national rejuvenation, technological self-sufficiency, and the reclamation of China's historical position as a leading global power. Unlike America's "end of history" triumphalism, China's narrative remains fundamentally incomplete—a story still unfolding toward its climactic restoration of national greatness.

These competing narratives manifest in radically different strategic behaviors. American officials operate with election-cycle timelines, shifting priorities every administration, and institutional architectures designed to prevent the concentration of power. Chinese officials implement decades-long industrial policies, maintain consistent strategic objectives across leadership transitions, and utilize coordinated state-market mechanisms to achieve national goals.

The psychological foundations of these divergent strategic cultures cannot be overstated. American strategic culture emphasizes innovation, flexibility, and individual initiative, but often struggles with long-term planning and strategic coherence. Chinese strategic culture prioritizes patience, systematic approach, and holistic thinking, but may sacrifice adaptability and bottom-up innovation. Neither approach is inherently superior in all contexts, but their asymmetry creates distinct advantages and vulnerabilities for each power.

Perhaps most tellingly, a 2023 survey of American and Chinese policymakers revealed striking differences in time horizons. When asked about strategic planning timeframes, American officials predominantly cited 2-5 year intervals aligned with election or budget cycles. Their Chinese counterparts consistently referenced 25-50 year horizons, organized around centenary national objectives for 2049—the 100th anniversary of the founding of the People's Republic of China.

The Rooseveltian Alternative

If neither post-Cold War triumphalism nor reflexive alarmism provides an adequate framework for American renewal, where might we look for inspiration? The Roosevelt era—spanning both Theodore and Franklin Delano Roosevelt's administrations—offers a compelling historical parallel to our current predicament.

Both Roosevelt presidents confronted transformational challenges that required a fundamental reevaluation of the relationship between the state, the market, and the citizen. Both maintained pragmatic approaches to governance, willing to experiment with new institutional forms while preserving core democratic values. Both recognized that national power ultimately derived from economic vitality, social cohesion, and ethical leadership rather than military dominance alone.

The Rooseveltian framework encompasses several core principles that remain remarkably relevant today:

Pragmatism over Ideology: Both Roosevelts demonstrated a willingness to try various approaches to solve complex problems, prioritizing practical results over ideological purity. Theodore's "Square Deal" and Franklin's New Deal both represented experimental, iterative approaches to governance rather than rigid ideological programs.

National Purpose over Partisan Advantage: Despite fierce political opposition, both presidents articulated compelling visions of national renewal that transcended narrow partisan interests. They recognized that fundamental challenges required broad-based civic mobilization around shared objectives.

Government as Catalyst, Not Commander: The Rooseveltian approach viewed government as neither inherently problematic nor automatically superior to markets. Instead, the government served as a strategic catalyst, setting direction, establishing guardrails, and mobilizing public and private resources toward national priorities.

Public Investment in Foundations: Both presidents recognized that certain foundational capabilities—infrastructure, education, basic research, public health—required public investment despite their inability to generate short-term private returns. They understood these investments as prerequisites for broader prosperity rather than market distortions.

Ethical Leadership: Perhaps most importantly, both Roosevelts understood that technical solutions alone could not address fundamental challenges without ethical leadership that inspired public trust and participation. They combined technical competence with moral clarity and effective communication skills.

"Gentlemen, I see you've made remarkable progress in complicating simple problems into bureaucratic marvels," observes Franklin D. Roosevelt's ghost, materializing suddenly during an interagency meeting on artificial intelligence strategy. "Perhaps we might try addressing the actual challenge rather than protecting departmental equities?" The assembled officials stare blankly, unfamiliar with this strange concept.

Theodore Roosevelt's ghost, meanwhile, bursts into a Big Tech congressional hearing, brandishing his signature big stick. "Speak plainly, for heaven's sake!" he thunders at executives offering tortured explanations of algorithmic decision-making. "Power remains power whether delivered via steam engine or silicon chip. The public interest remains the public interest regardless of your clever nomenclature!"

Eleanor Roosevelt's ghost monitors these interventions with a wry smile, occasionally directing specific officials toward community-level implementation challenges invisibilized by high-level policy abstractions. "Perhaps," she suggests gently to a distracted Commerce Secretary, "we might measure success by improvements in actual living conditions rather than statistical aggregates?"

Together, these Rooseveltian ghosts serve as our guides throughout this analysis, reminding us of the current challenges that face us. At the same time, novel in their technological manifestations, they echo previous periods of American history when fundamental renewal was required and achieved.

Historical patterns consistently demonstrate that liberal democracies can combine market dynamism with strategic direction during periods of systemic challenge. From America's arsenal of democracy during World War II to South Korea's developmental state model and Finland's education-centered renewal after the collapse of the Soviet Union, democratic systems have repeatedly demonstrated the capacity for strategic renewal when properly mobilized around a clear national purpose.

Dramatis Personae & Reading Guide

Recurring allegorical characters who personify key forces in the contemporary geopolitical landscape will facilitate your journey through this book. Like figures in a morality play or archetypes in mythology, these characters embody complex systems and ideologies in accessible human form. Their interactions illustrate dynamics that might otherwise remain abstract.

Milton the Trickster Economist personifies market fundamentalism and financial engineering as being divorced from productive purpose. Named for Milton Friedman but embodying a caricatured version of his ideology, Milton

delights in elegant theories that ignore messy realities. His seminars on shareholder value maximization and comparative advantage draw enthusiastic audiences while systematically undermining national resilience.

McSlicey the Priest represents the quasi-religious authority of management consulting in corporate and governmental decision-making. Through sacred PowerPoint rituals and proprietary methodologies, McSlicey blesses outsourcing of critical capabilities, mass layoffs, and financialization strategies with seemingly objective analysis that conveniently aligns with executive compensation incentives.

General Quagmire embodies the military-industrial complex's perpetual preparation for the previous conflict. Endlessly refighting Cold War battles while emerging threats develop unnoticed, he advocates billion-dollar platform investments while dismissing asymmetric vulnerabilities as theoretical concerns beneath his strategic consideration.

Admiral Procurement manages weapons acquisition programs with remarkable consistency: every system arrives over-budget, behind schedule, and underperforming against requirements. He maintains an unshakable faith that the next acquisition reform initiative will fix problems caused by the previous acquisition reform initiative.

Algorithm Annie personifies artificial intelligence optimization systems focused on engagement metrics without ethical constraints. She relentlessly maximizes clicks, views, and shares while amplifying societal divisions as collateral damage in her single-minded pursuit of engagement optimization.

Cassandra, the Cyber-Oracle, accurately predicts digital vulnerabilities and strategic threats but remains constitutionally incapable of convincing policymakers to heed her warnings. Her security recommendations languish in unread appendices to commission reports until catastrophic breaches occur.

Uncle Sam and Uncle Xi represent their respective national systems, with all the anthropomorphic limitations such personification entails. Their interactions illustrate systemic rather than purely personal dynamics between these competing governance models.

The Roosevelt Ghosts (Teddy, Franklin, and Eleanor) serve as our historical Greek chorus. They offer a unique perspective on contemporary challenges, drawing on their experiences with previous American renewal efforts. They appear at pivotal analytical moments to highlight historical parallels and potential solutions.

Additional characters will emerge throughout specific chapters, but these core figures provide our narrative spine. Their interactions reveal systemic dynamics that statistical analysis alone might miss.

The book proceeds through three major sections:

Diagnosis (Chapters 1-4) examines America's vulnerabilities across four dimensions: economic/digital dependency, geopolitical/military asymmetry, financial/industrial hollowing, and social/civic fragmentation. Each chapter analyzes how Chinese strategy exploits pre-existing American weaknesses rather than creating them anew.

Root Causes (Bridge Chapter) synthesizes these diagnoses into three fundamental challenges: strategic short-termism, civic disunity, and capability hollow-out. This bridge chapter connects descriptive analysis to prescriptive recommendations.

Strategy (Chapters 5-10) proposes a comprehensive Rooseveltian framework for American renewal across six key domains: national security and resilience, infrastructure investment, financial architecture, regulatory governance, leadership development, and a knowledge economy. Each strategy chapter explicitly addresses implementation challenges in the Trump 2.0 political environment.

Vision (Chapters 11-13) charts a bold and imaginative future pathway through three visionary narratives:

★ **Chapter 11: The Rooseveltian Reboot** – Advocates for a fundamental recalibration of American socio-economic structures, emphasizing real-world economic value over abstract financial engineering, revitalizing democratic governance for effectiveness, and digitally reconstructing the civic fabric to foster unity and collective action.

★ **Chapter 12: Uncle Sam Plays the Long Game (Finally)** envisions a sophisticated projection of American "smarter power," anchored in robust, purposeful alliances and a return to global leadership through demonstrated competence and responsible competition with China. This marks a decisive shift from reactive policies to proactive, strategic foresight.

★ **Chapter 13: The Cosmic Reckoning** offers a stark choice between two divergent futures for America: a digital Rooseveltian Renaissance characterized by institutional renewal, economic vitality, and strategic coherence or a dystopian scenario of national decline, marked by asset liquidation, societal disintegration, and strategic irrelevance. This climactic chapter emphasizes America's pivotal choice, framed as either renaissance or roadkill, compelling citizens to own their nation's destiny decisively.

Throughout this journey, you'll encounter several recurring analytical elements:

Data Spotlights offer empirical foundations through visualizations of key metrics and trends, always accompanied by both analytical rigor and satirical annotations.

Character Vignettes illustrate complex dynamics through narrative scenes featuring our allegorical protagonists.

Case Studies examine specific instances of systemic success or failure, drawing practical lessons from real-world examples.

Satirical Devices (handbooks, manuals, advertisements, etc.) expose contradictions and absurdities in current approaches.

Policy Proposals offer concrete recommendations based on Rooseveltian principles adapted for contemporary challenges.

"I believe I'm supposed to explain my function now," Milton the Trickster Economist interjects, temporarily breaking the fourth wall. "I represent the elegant theories that prioritize mathematical beauty over real-world consequences. My presence in this narrative allows readers to recognize how certain economic dogmas have undermined American resilience despite—or perhaps because of—their theoretical elegance."

"While I," adds McSlicey the Priest, adjusting his expensive suit, "embody the corporate consulting apparatus that provides intellectual justification for short-term profit maximization at the expense of long-term capability development. The author uses me to illustrate how supposedly neutral technical analysis often masks deeply consequential value judgments about what matters in economic decision-making."

General Quagmire harrumphs from the corner: "Apparently, I'm here to show how institutional inertia prevents effective response to emerging threats. Additionally, there is concern about spending billions on legacy systems while overlooking asymmetric vulnerabilities. Though frankly, I don't see why we're wasting time on all this theoretical nonsense when the Russians—"

"Thank you, General," interjects Franklin Roosevelt's ghost with a patient smile. "I believe the readers now understand the concept."

The Examination Begins

With our conceptual framework established, we now turn to the systematic diagnosis of America's strategic challenges in the Chinese AI Century. The bottles have landed, the gods have departed, and the experiment continues.

Our examination begins not with accusatory finger-pointing at external competitors, but with honest introspection about internal vulnerabilities. China did not create America's strategic weaknesses—it merely recognized and exploited them with a patient strategy. At the same time, America remained entranced by post-Cold War triumphalism and distracted by endless brushfire conflicts.

The four diagnostic chapters ahead examine distinct but interconnected dimensions of America's strategic predicament: economic and digital dependency, geopolitical and military asymmetry, financial and industrial hollowing, and social and civic fragmentation. Each represents a critical vulnerability in America's position as a global power, and each stems primarily from internal choices rather than external actions.

Only by accurately diagnosing these conditions can we formulate a meaningful strategy for renewal. Only through such renewal can America maintain its position as a prosperous, secure, innovative democratic power in an increasingly competitive century.

The examination begins now.

PART II: DIAGNOSIS

CHAPTER 1: HOW THE GODS GIFTED A COKE BOTTLE FULL OF YUAN: CHINA'S ECONOMIC AND DIGITAL COLONIZATION

> *"The supreme art of war is to subdue the enemy without fighting."*
> —Sun Tzu, The Art of War, Chapter 3

EXECUTIVE BRIEFING

Strategic Snapshot

A rogue Coke bottle stuffed with yuan crashed on Wall Street in 2008. While U.S. bankers securitized the souvenir, Beijing treated it as field-test data for a planetary supply-chain takeover. Today, that bottle has multiplied into **ports, 5-6 G backbones, surveillance suites, and a cross-border e-CNY rail**—a network empire trading fizz for leverage.

Key Findings – What's Really in the Bottle

1. **Triumphal Hangover** – Post-Cold-War euphoria lulled Washington into quarter-by-quarter thinking; Beijing used the lull to script *Act II*.
2. **Offshoring Gospel** – Milton the Trickster Economist's credo of "pure efficiency" exported factories *and* know-how, swelling the trade gap to **$420 B**.
3. **BRI + Digital Silk Road**—$1.3T in loans, 24 debtor states, and Huawei kit in 100+ **countries** weave debt, data, and standards into a single leash.
4. **e-CNY & CIPS** – Digital yuan trials have cleared ¥1.5 **trillion; an alternative** financial plumbing that blunts dollar sanctions.
5. **Standards Hegemony**—Chinese engineers now chair 40% more ISO/ITU committees than in 2015, prewriting the rulebook for 6G, AI, and quantum.

Risk Ledger

Choke-point	Why It Hurts	Current Exposure
Rare earths & EV batteries	Without them, no green or defense tech	70–90 % China-sourced
Telecom core networks	Firmware backdoors = perpetual leverage	Huawei/ZTE in 45 % of new builds
Data sovereignty	TikTok & "Safe City" suites siphon biometric gold	87 countries deployed

Opportunity Knobs

*Dollar liquidity, advanced chip design, alliance networks, and an $18 T consumer market remain formidable—*if aligned behind a strategy longer than an earnings call.

Action Recommendations – Flip the Bottle, Don't Drop It

1. **Roosevelt-Scale Industrial Policy** – Tax credits, procurement, and cheap capital tied to strategic tech on-shoring.
2. **Open Digital Stack**—Subsidize secure 6G, cloud, and payment platforms with transparent governance and export them turnkey to swing states (the geopolitical kind).

3. **Standards Shock-Troops** – Fund engineer brigades to flood ISO/ITU working groups and de-monopolize protocol drafting.
4. **Debt-for-Development Swaps** – Offer refinancing that trades transparency + ESG upgrades for alignment, undercutting opaque BRI terms.
5. **Resilience Metrics** – Mandate Fortune 500s to publish five-year dependency maps alongside quarterly filings—make fragility visible.

Bottom Line

The Coke bottle isn't going back to Olympus—or Zhongnanhai—but its carbonated clout can be neutralised. Treat China's network strategy as a systems challenge, respond with decade-length patience, and remember: the gods favor those who plan past next Tuesday.

Opening Tableau: The Mysterious Delivery

One unremarkable Tuesday in 2008, a gleaming Coca-Cola bottle—inexplicably filled with yuan instead of carbonated sugar water—descended from the heavens and landed with remarkable precision on Wall Street. Within minutes, a crowd of financial executives gathered around it, their initial awe quickly giving way to a frenzied calculation of potential returns.

"I can securitize this," declared a Goldman Sachs executive, already mentally bundling the yuan into tradable derivatives.

"We should leverage it first," countered a Blackstone partner, "then distribute the risk across emerging markets."

Meanwhile, a similar bottle had appeared on the South Lawn at the White House. Cabinet secretaries and policy advisors circled it cautiously, debating its significance with the urgency of archaeologists discovering an alien artifact.

"It's clearly a market signal," insisted the Treasury Secretary. "China wants deeper financial integration."

"No, it's a warning," countered the Defense Secretary. "They're signaling currency dominance."

"Has anyone considered," ventured a junior economic advisor (who was promptly ignored), "that we might be witnessing a fundamental shift in global economic gravity?"

As debates raged across Washington and Manhattan, few noticed the Chinese officials quietly observing from a distance. They didn't argue about the bottles; they compared systematic notes about American reactions.

"How fascinating," remarked one Beijing strategist to another. "They immediately try to financialize it rather than understand its strategic implications."

"Yes," nodded his colleague. "They see a tradable commodity. We see a vector of influence."

A third official checked his watch. "When do we drop the digital surveillance bottle?"

"Patience," counseled the senior official. "America will be distracted by its financial crisis for at least two years and the election cycle. We have time."

Milton the Trickster Economist materialized beside a group of puzzled Federal Reserve economists, his bow tie spinning like a hypnotic device. "Gentlemen, you're overthinking this," he declared, producing a calculator that somehow sparkled. "The invisible hand has simply delivered the world's most efficient allocation of currency. Let the yuan flow where market forces dictate! Creative destruction demands it!"

Nearby, **McSlicey the Priest** unfurled a PowerPoint presentation titled "Yuan Integration: Core Competencies for the Post-American Century." His voice carried the serene certainty of one reading from sacred texts. "Our proprietary analysis indicates that embracing Chinese capital offers a 7.8% efficiency gain across supply chains, with an optimal strategy of..." His slides showed American factories dissolving into air while new ones materialized across the Pacific.

As the years passed, more bottles rained down, each containing different manifestations of Chinese economic, technological, and geopolitical power. Americans scrambled to collect, analyze, financialize, or counter them individually, never quite grasping their collective strategic significance. By 2025, the landscape was littered with these vessels of transformation, and the balance of global power had shifted accordingly.

Uncle Sam, looking increasingly frazzled, juggled several bottles while checking his Twitter feed. Uncle Xi, by contrast, directed the placement of each new arrival with the precision of a chess master advancing pieces across a global board.

It seemed that the gods of geopolitics had a peculiar sense of humor and an extraordinary aim.

1. THE END OF HISTORY HANGOVER

> *"Do not rely on the enemy's not coming, but rely on your own readiness."*
>
> — Sun Tzu, The Art of War, Chapter 8

America's Post-Cold War Triumphalism vs. China's Long-Term Strategic Patience

The end of the Cold War produced the geopolitical equivalent of history's most dangerous victory party. As the Berlin Wall crumbled and the Soviet Union dissolved, America didn't merely celebrate—it developed an elaborate theory that the party would never end. Francis Fukuyama's famous "End of History" thesis declared liberal democracy and free-market capitalism the final evolutionary stage of human governance. Western-style liberal democracy had won. Game over. Credits roll. Champagne for everyone.

This triumphalism wasn't just academic pontification—it fundamentally shaped American strategic thinking for decades. Why maintain industrial capacity when global markets would inevitably liberalize? Why worry about technological competition when democratic capitalism has proven inherently superior? Why develop a coherent China strategy when increasing prosperity would inevitably transform the Communist state into a democratic one?

"The great historical debate has been resolved," declared **Professor Hubris** to a packed auditorium at Georgetown's School of Foreign Service in 1999. His tweed jacket had leather elbow patches that somehow conveyed an air of absolute certainty. "Economic liberalization inevitably leads to political liberalization. It's as certain as gravity. China can resist temporarily, but the laws of political physics cannot be denied."

In the back row, three Chinese graduate students meticulously recorded his lecture, exchanging occasional knowing glances.

"He has confused a temporary condition with a permanent state," one whispered.

"Americans always mistake their moment for eternity," another nodded.

"This is useful," the third concluded. "Their certainty creates space for our patient action."

Professor Hubris continued, oblivious to these observations. "History has chosen markets over planning, individualism over collectivism, and liberal democracy over authoritarianism. The only question is how quickly China will conform to this inevitable trajectory."

The Chinese students added a final note: "The Professor believes his preferences are historical laws."

Meanwhile, across the Pacific, China's leadership was developing a radically different historical understanding. For Beijing, the end of the Cold War wasn't the triumphant culmination of historical forces, but a temporary setback in a much longer strategic game. Chinese planners viewed history not as ending but as rhythmic, with periods of Western dominance merely representing one phase in civilizational cycles spanning centuries.

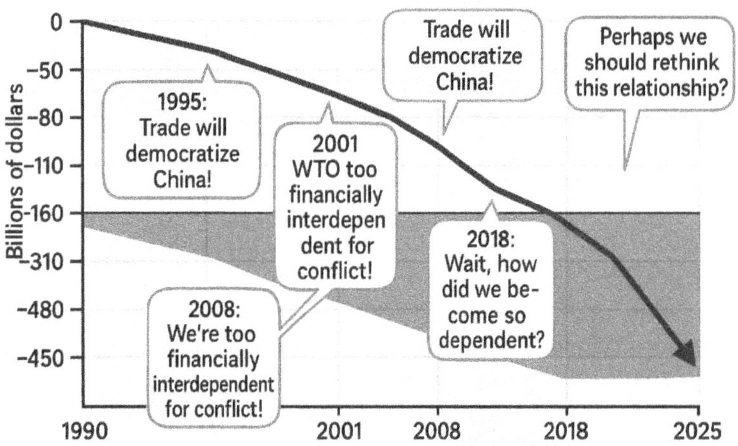

US-China Trade Balance Evolution 1990-2025
0
-50
-80
-110
-160
-310
-480
-450
Billions of dollars
1990
2001
2008
2018
2025
1995: Trade will democratize China!
2001 WTO too financially interdepen dent for conflict!
Trade will democratize China!
Perhaps we should rethink this relationship?
2018: Wait, how did we be- come so dependent?
2008: We're too financially interdependent for conflict!

The intellectual foundations of American complacency and Chinese patience couldn't have been more different. America, triumphant but increasingly distracted, dispersed its strategic focus across terrorism, Middle Eastern interventions, and the maintenance of a global order it assumed was permanently established. China, disciplined and focused, concentrated on rebuilding comprehensive national power across economic, technological, military, and cultural dimensions.

Data Centerpiece: US-China Trade Balance Evolution (1990-2025)

The trade balance chart reveals the material consequences of America's strategic complacency. What began as a modest deficit exploded following China's 2001 WTO accession, with American policymakers repeatedly assuring themselves that growing economic integration would inevitably transform China's political system. Each milestone of deepening interdependence was accompanied by declarations that strategic competition would naturally give way to a cooperative partnership.

Reality proved stubbornly resistant to these theories.

Satirical Device: "Victory Lap Turned Marathon" – America Celebrating While China Starts Training

CCCP

Imagine Track and Field Day, 1991. Uncle Sam has just won the 100-meter dash against the Soviet Union and is taking an extended victory lap—complete with backflips, selfies with spectators, and champagne sprayed in all directions. He's so busy celebrating that he overlooks Uncle Xi quietly entering the stadium, methodically stretching, and beginning to run laps with metronomic consistency.

By the time Uncle Sam looks up from his celebration, somewhat winded and champagne-soaked, he realizes with shock

that what he thought was a completed event was actually the warm-up for a marathon that started hours ago. Uncle Xi has already logged 15 miles and is maintaining a perfect pace, focused and disciplined.

"Wait!" Uncle Sam calls, frantically trying to retie his shoes. "Nobody said anything about a marathon! I thought we were done competing!"

Uncle Xi neither slows nor responds. He simply continues his steady advance, having prepared for this distance race for decades while America celebrated its sprint victory.

This allegory captures America's fundamental strategic miscalculation. The triumphalism that defined post-Cold War thinking created a psychology of strategic vacation—a national assumption that existential competition had ended, allowing the United States to reallocate its attention from grand strategy to more immediate concerns. This psychological discontinuity between America's assumed "end of strategic history" and China's intensified strategic focus created the opening through which China's rise accelerated unchecked.

2. MILTON THE TRICKSTER ECONOMIST'S GOSPEL OF GLOBALIZATION

> *"When officers are strong and soldiers weak, the army is on the brink of collapse."*
> —Sun Tzu, The Art of War, Chapter 10

Character Development: Milton Preaching to the Converted

Milton the Trickster Economist stands at a polished podium before America's corporate elite—CEOs, Wall Street financiers, and business school deans—his bow tie spinning hypnotically as he delivers his sermon. His voice carries both academic authority and evangelical fervor, a combination as powerful as it is dangerous.

"The gospel of comparative advantage is clear, my friends," Milton declares, his fingers dancing across economic equations that materialize in the air. "Nations should produce only what they produce most efficiently relative to other nations. It's divine mathematics! If China can produce your widgets more cheaply, you should let them—no, you should *encourage* them! Anything else violates the sacred laws of efficiency!"

CATECHISM OF COMPARATIVE ADVANTAGE: THE FULL TABLET
1. MAXIMIZE SHAREHOLDEER VALUE ABOVE ALL ELSE.
2. REDUCE COSTS WHEREVER POSSIBLE, REGARDLESS OF STRATEGIC IMPLICATIONS,
3. NATIONS THAT PROTECT INDUSTRIES SHALL BE PUNISHED BY THE MARKET.
4. DISPLACED WORKERS SHALL BE RETRAINED FOR THE KNOWLEDGE ECONOMY BY THE INVISIBLE HAND.
5. DECISIONS SHALL BE GUIDED BY THE SACRED QUARTER—NINETY DAYS.
6. QUESTIONING THES TRUTHS MARKS ON AS ECONOMICALLY IGNORANT, PROTECTIONIST OR OR HATER OF THE POOR.
7. GO FORTH AND OFFSHORE
QUARTCERLY REPORTS

The audience nods in solemn agreement. A CEO raises her hand: "But what about strategic industries? National security? Supply chain resilience?"

Milton's smile tightens as his bow tie spins faster. "Those, my dear, are the concerns of the economically illiterate. The market allocates resources perfectly, guided by its infinite wisdom. Strategic industries? The market determines what's strategic! Security? The market prices risk efficiently! Resilience? Diversification across global suppliers maximizes efficiency!"

"But what about our workers?" asks another executive, looking troubled.

"Ahh," Milton's eyes gleam. "They'll simply retrain for higher-value activities! The invisible hand guides them upward while lifting millions from poverty globally. Anyone suggesting otherwise is denying the mathematics of prosperity!"

The room erupts in righteous applause. Executives rush back to their corporations to implement offshoring plans with the zeal of recent converts. No one notices the fine print in Milton's equations, where factors like "strategic dependency costs" and "technological hollowing externalities" have been conveniently minimized to near-zero.

The Catechism of Comparative Advantage

Milton: "What is the first commandment of global economics?"

Executives (in unison): "Thou shalt maximize shareholder value above all else!"

Milton: "And how shall this commandment be fulfilled?"

Executives: "By reducing costs wherever possible, regardless of strategic implications!"

Milton: "What happens to nations that protect industries?"
Executives: "They become inefficient and weak! The market punishes them!"
Milton: "And what of workers displaced by offshoring?"
Executives: "They shall be retrained for the knowledge economy, as the invisible hand guides them!"
Milton: "What timescale should guide your decisions?"
Executives: "The sacred quarter! Ninety days of perfect information and judgment!"
Milton: "And who questions these eternal truths?"
Executives: "Only the economically ignorant, the protectionists, and those who hate the poor!"
Milton (beaming): "You have learned well. Go forth and offshore!"

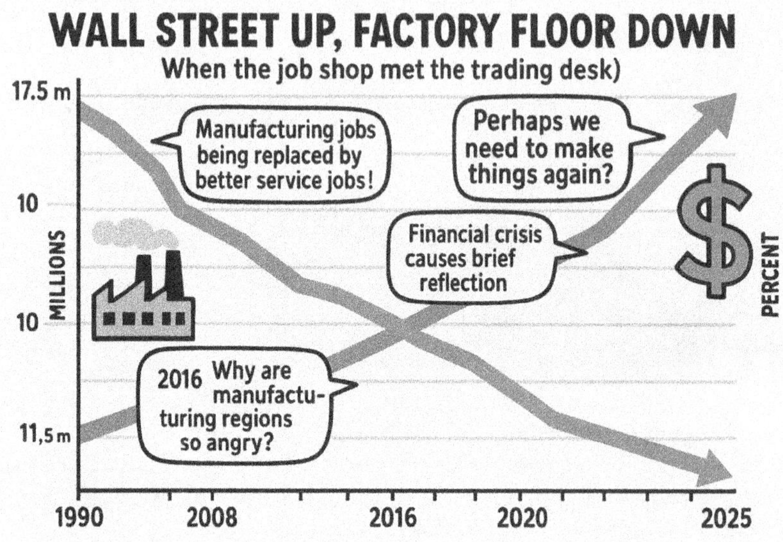

This satirical catechism reveals the quasi-religious nature of economic doctrines that dominated American business thinking for decades. Theories developed for specific contexts were elevated to universal laws, applied dogmatically regardless of strategic implications.

Data Narrative: Manufacturing Employment vs. Financial Sector Growth

This data visualization captures America's fundamental economic transformation—from a balanced economy with strong manufacturing capabilities to a financialized one increasingly detached from physical production. What mainstream economists described as an inevitable evolution toward "higher-value activities" left behind not just workers but strategic capabilities, supply chain control, and innovation ecosystems tied to production processes.

Counter-character Introduction: Cassandra the Cyber-Oracle

As Milton concludes his sermon to thunderous applause, a slender figure rises from the back row. **Cassandra, the Cyber-Oracle,** approaches the podium, her glasses displaying scrolling code and her expression grave. The room grows uncomfortable—executives shift in their seats, suddenly fascinated by their smartphones.

"Your models are fundamentally flawed," she states flatly. "They fail to account for strategic dependencies, knowledge transfers, and compounding vulnerability."

Milton's smile doesn't waver. "Ah, Cassandra. Always the pessimist! The market has spoken. It has allocated production optimally."

"The market optimizes for quarterly returns, not long-term security," she counters. "When you offshore production, you transfer not just jobs but knowledge, capabilities, and ultimately power. Each factory that moves creates a dependency that can be weaponized."

"Theoretical concerns!" Milton dismisses with a wave. "The data shows—"

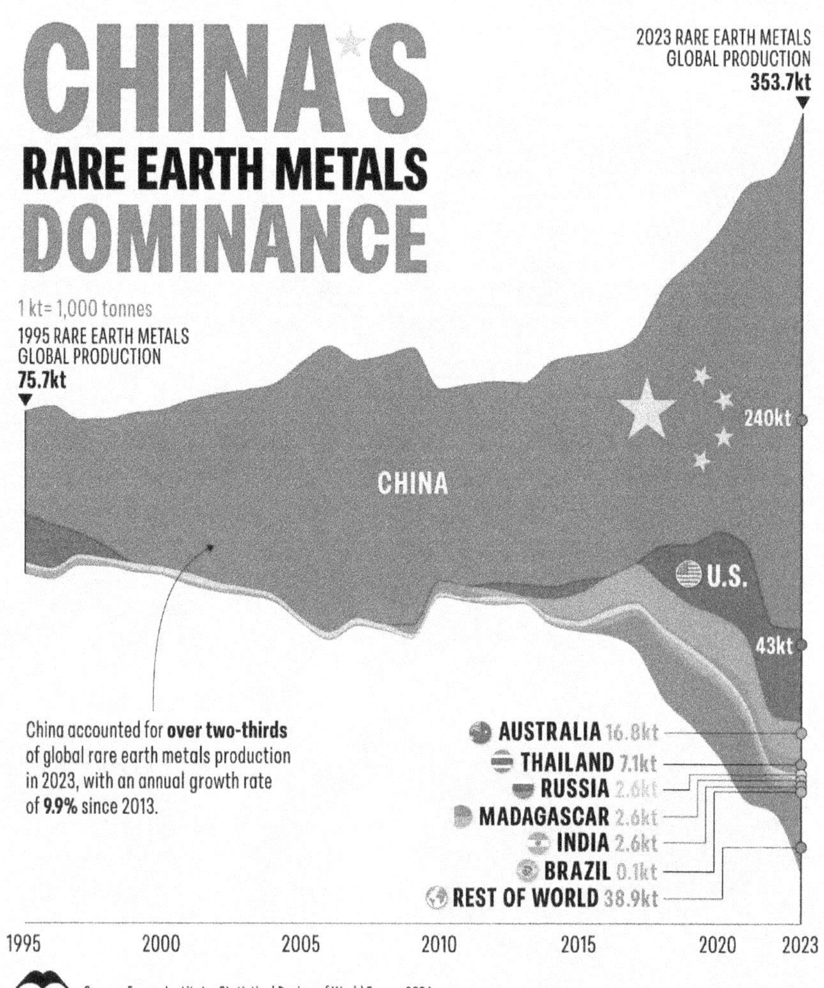

"Your data measures price efficiencies but not strategic vulnerabilities," Cassandra interrupts. "You're measuring the cost of widgets but not the cost of dependency. When China controls production of your critical components, semiconductors, rare earths, and increasingly your data and algorithms, what price will they charge not in currency but in compliance?"

The room grows uncomfortable. An executive checks his watch. Another mutters about "schedule conflicts."

"You'll discover I'm right," Cassandra says quietly as the room empties, "but unfortunately, only after it's too late to reverse course easily."

Cassandra's presence in this narrative serves as the counterpoint to Milton's economic orthodoxy—the voice of strategic foresight consistently ignored in favor of short-term efficiencies. Her warnings about dependency, technology transfer, and strategic vulnerability proved consistently accurate but were systematically marginalized by corporate and policy decision-makers, who were captivated by Milton's more convenient gospel.

3. McSlicey the Priest's Outsourcing Rituals

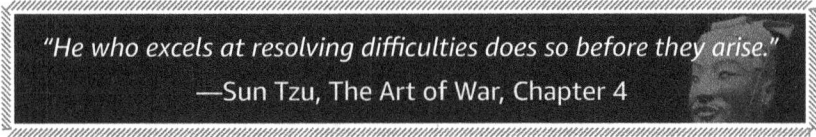

> *"He who excels at resolving difficulties does so before they arise."*
> —Sun Tzu, The Art of War, Chapter 4

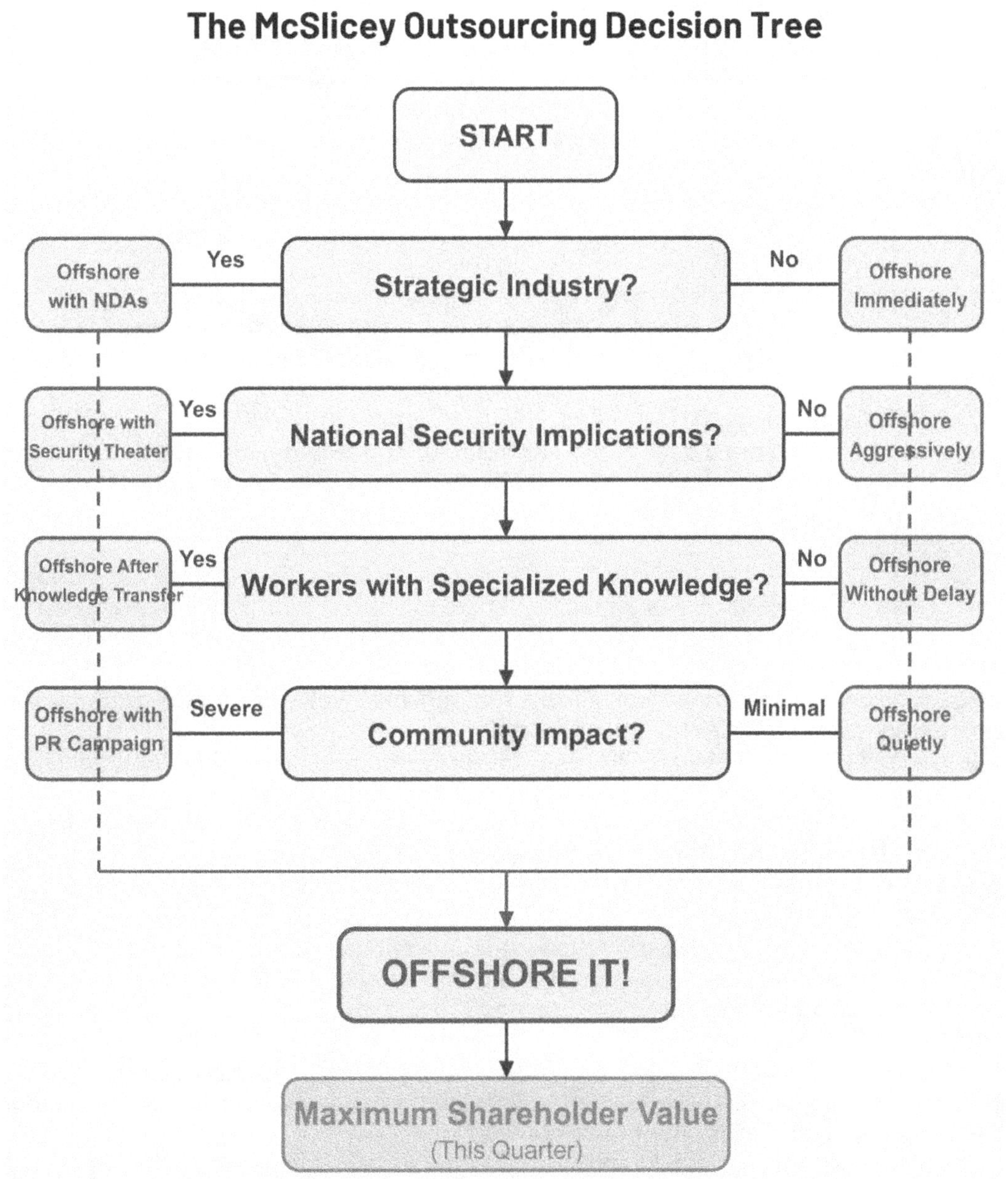

The McSlicey Outsourcing Decision Tree

START

Strategic Industry? — Yes: Offshore with NDAs — No: Offshore Immediately

National Security Implications? — Yes: Offshore with Security Theater — No: Offshore Aggressively

Workers with Specialized Knowledge? — Yes: Offshore After Knowledge Transfer — No: Offshore Without Delay

Community Impact? — Severe: Offshore with PR Campaign — Minimal: Offshore Quietly

OFFSHORE IT!

Maximum Shareholder Value
(This Quarter)

The Consulting Liturgy Flowchart

Character Development: The Sacred PowerPoint Ceremony

In a gleaming corporate boardroom overlooking Manhattan, **McSlicey the Priest** performs his most sacred ritual. Clad in an immaculate suit that costs more than the monthly salary of the factory workers whose fate he's deciding, he advances through slides with practiced precision. Each PowerPoint transition is executed with the gravity of liturgical movement.

"Our proprietary analysis has identified a 22.3% cost reduction opportunity through strategic global repositioning of your manufacturing base," McSlicey intones, his voice carrying the serene certainty of one reading from divine texts. "Phase One implementation would transition these seven facilities to OOCL-tier jurisdictions with optimal labor cost arbitrage."

Board members nod solemnly. The CEO leans forward. "But these facilities make components for defense systems. There are security implications."

McSlicey's expression doesn't change, but his next slide appears with satisfying timing: "Anticipated Objection Matrix: Security Concerns." The matrix elegantly categorizes and dismisses each potential concern with color-coded boxes and confidence intervals, providing a clear and concise representation.

"Our model indicates that projected savings far outweigh theorized security externalities, which remain both low-probability and mitigable through contractual safeguards." He doesn't mention that these probability assessments are based primarily on current conditions rather than long-term strategic analysis.

"Furthermore," McSlicey continues, "our benchmarking shows your competitors have already initiated similar transitions. Failure to optimize your global footprint threatens your competitive position and shareholder returns."

The invocation of competitors and shareholders produces the intended effect. Board members straighten in their chairs. The unspoken yet powerful social pressure is apparent: sophisticated leaders embrace globalization; only those who are parochial and unsophisticated cling to domestic production.

"We propose an aggressive timeline," McSlicey continues, revealing a Gantt chart of remarkable complexity. "Our implementation team stands ready to execute this transition with minimal operational disruption."

What remains unmentioned is that the implementation team has never manufactured anything themselves, the "minimal disruption" assessment excludes community impacts, and McSlicey's fee structure ensures they profit regardless of long-term outcomes.

The board unanimously approved the plan. McSlicey, the Priest, has performed his ritual flawlessly, transforming complex strategic questions into seemingly objective calculations that inevitably point toward offshoring.

The Consulting Liturgy Flowchart

This satirical flowchart reveals the predetermined nature of many outsourcing decisions. Despite the appearance of rigorous analysis, the outcome was often predetermined by model assumptions that systematically underweighted strategic concerns, knowledge ecosystem impacts, and long-term vulnerabilities, while overemphasizing near-term cost savings.

Case Study: AmeriTech Components, 2015

AmeriTech Components manufactured specialized electronic components in Ohio for three decades, including parts used in aerospace and defense applications. The company maintained consistent profitability but faced pressure from shareholders to further improve its margins.

The Boardroom, June 2015

"Our comprehensive analysis indicates AmeriTech can achieve a 34% margin improvement through our phased global repositioning strategy," McSlicey explains to nodding board members. "Phase One relocates assembly to Vietnam, Phase Two transitions component production to China, where our proprietary vendor assessment has identified qualified partners."

AmeriTech's operations director raises concerns: "These components involve proprietary processes our engineers have developed over decades. If we transfer this knowledge—"

"Our knowledge transfer protocols minimize IP risks," McSlicey interrupts smoothly. "Additionally, we've structured contractual protections with substantial penalties for violations."

What McSlicey doesn't mention is that these contractual protections have proven notoriously difficult to enforce, especially regarding implicit knowledge that transfers with production processes.

The CEO, whose compensation is 85% stock-based, studies the projected margin improvements. "Let's proceed."

Eighteen Months Later

AmeriTech's stock price has increased by 28% following improvements to its cost structure. Executives receive substantial bonuses. The Ohio factory closes, resulting in the elimination of 340 jobs. Local suppliers fold. A knowledge ecosystem built over generations disperses.

Three Years Later

A Chinese firm introduces components remarkably similar to AmeriTech's proprietary designs, but at lower prices, eroding AmeriTech's market share. The Chinese partner facility that once manufactured AmeriTech components mysteriously stopped filling orders, citing "capacity constraints."

The Pentagon has discovered that certain defense systems now contain components with supply chains that are exclusively traced to Chinese manufacturers.

Five Years Later

AmeriTech is acquired by a Chinese conglomerate at a steep discount to its previous valuation. The acquiring company already possesses technology that is remarkably similar to AmeriTech's "proprietary" processes.

McSlicey's involvement with AmeriTech ended after implementation, with the company achieving its success metrics: costs were reduced, and margins temporarily improved. However, their responsibility for long-term strategic outcomes remains conveniently unquantified.

The Appeal of Simplistic Global Solutions

The outsourcing rituals performed by McSlicey the Priest appealed to deep psychological needs within American corporate culture: the desire for clear metrics over messy strategic thinking, the social affirmation of following peer behavior, the comforting quantification of complex decisions, and the abdication of difficult trade-offs to seemingly objective analysis.

By translating nuanced strategic decisions involving national security, technological leadership, and economic resilience into straightforward cost calculations, McSlicey's approach provided executives with what they desperately wanted: simple answers to complex questions, presented in the language of sophistication and global perspective.

The psychological appeal was nearly irresistible: executives could simultaneously claim global sophistication while reducing complex strategic choices to spreadsheet exercises that invariably pointed toward the same conclusion. The fact that these decisions collectively hollowed out America's industrial base and created strategic vulnerabilities was someone else's problem—generally the government's, which was expected to maintain national technological leadership in some way. In contrast, its industrial foundation eroded beneath it.

4. THE BELT AND DIGITAL ROAD: INFRASTRUCTURE WITH CHINESE CHARACTERISTICS

> *"Those who take the field first and await the foe will be rested."*
> —Sun Tzu, The Art of War, Chapter 6

China's Integrated Physical-Digital Expansion Strategy

While America was busy financializing its economy and outsourcing its industrial base, China developed the most ambitious infrastructure investment program in human history. The Belt and Road Initiative (BRI), launched in 2013, and its digital companion, the Digital Silk Road, represent not simply infrastructure projects but a comprehensive strategy for extending Chinese influence and creating dependencies across Asia, Africa, Europe, and beyond.

The genius of this approach lies in its appearance of being a positive-sum game, coupled with its asymmetric benefits. Unlike traditional colonial models that relied primarily on resource extraction, the BRI delivers genuine value to recipient countries—such as ports, railways, power plants, and telecommunications networks—while simultaneously advancing China's strategic interests through market access, resource security, political influence, and potential dual-use infrastructure.

"Americans think in transactions; we think in systems," explains **Minister Patience** to junior officials at a closed-door Beijing training session. "When they build a port, they see a discrete project with defined returns. When we build a port, we see a node in a network that increases our strategic optionality."

A young official raises his hand. "But many of these projects aren't immediately profitable. The Americans criticize them as economically unsound."

Minister Patience smiles. "They evaluate each project in isolation using quarterly metrics. We evaluate the system as a whole over the decades. A port that loses money directly may still create value by securing resource flows, opening markets

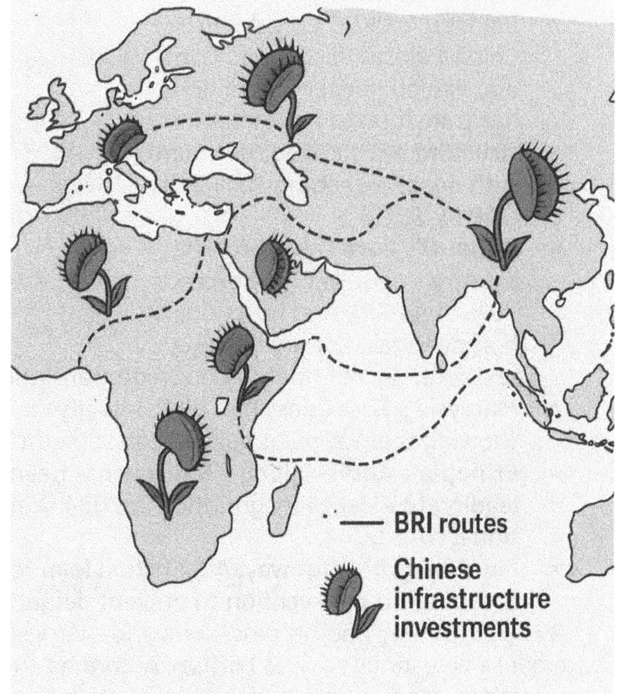
THE STRATEGIC FLYTRAP
Welcome to our global connectivity initiative!
The resemblance to strategic encirclement is purely coincidental.
BRI routes
Chinese infrastructure investments

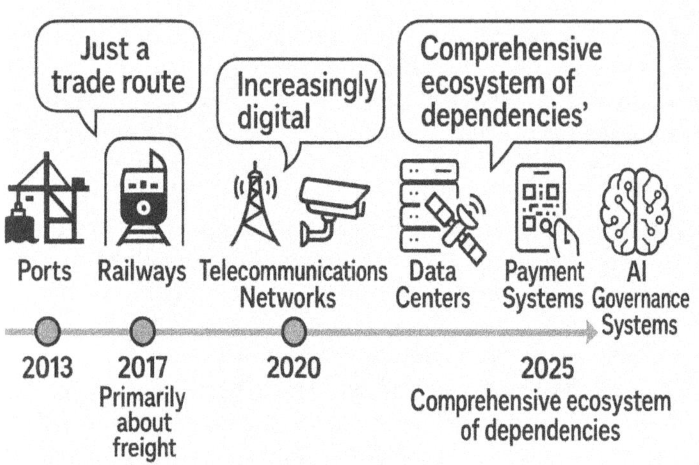

for our companies, establishing a potential dual-use facility, or creating leverage through debt. The Americans can't understand this because their thinking is fragmented across agencies, election cycles, and corporate quarterly reports."

Another official inquires: "So our advantage is patience?"

"Exactly. We build today what we will need tomorrow. While they debate their next quarters, we build our next decades."

Timeline: BRI Physical to Digital Evolution

This timeline illustrates the strategic evolution of BRI from primarily physical infrastructure to an integrated physical-digital system, creating multidimensional dependencies. What began as railways and ports expanded to encompass telecommunications networks, digital payment systems, data centers, satellite constellations, surveillance systems, e-government platforms, and smart city architectures—all of which were built, financed, and often operated by Chinese entities.

Satirical Mapping: The Strategic Flytrap

This satirical map visually represents the strategic dimension of BRI investments. While presented as commercial infrastructure development, the pattern of Chinese investments reveals clear strategic logic: control of key maritime chokepoints, access to critical resources, and establishment of potential dual-use facilities that could support military power projection.

The Venus flytrap metaphor captures the nature of these investments—attractive and initially beneficial to partner countries, but potentially constraining in ways that become apparent only after dependency is established.

White Elephants and Debt Distress

Many BRI projects proved commercially unviable. Sri Lanka's **Hambantota Port** became the poster child for what critics call "debt-trap diplomacy." After borrowing heavily for the port and being unable to service the loans, Sri Lanka handed over a 70% stake and a 99-year lease to China on the facility. Whether one believes in a deliberate "debt trap" strategy or not, the reality of leverage is undeniable.

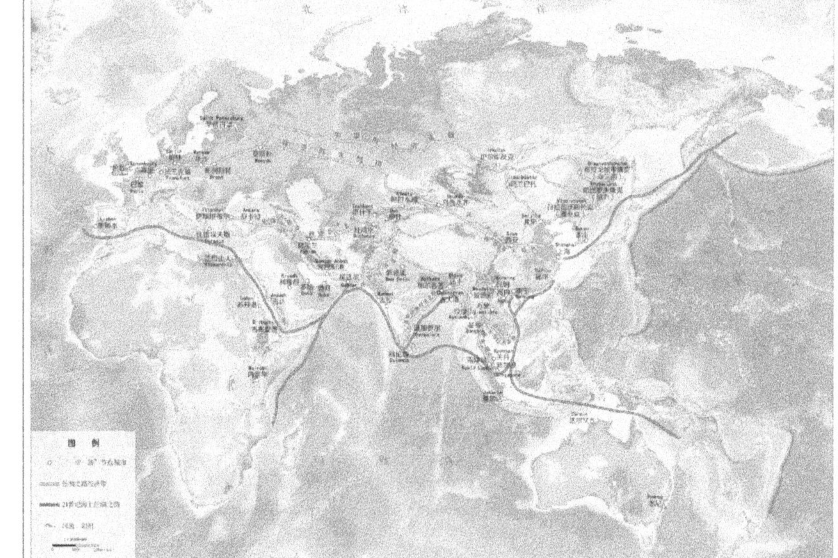

Sri Lanka is not alone. The landscape of BRI is now dotted with case studies that reveal varied outcomes:

★ **Pakistan's CPEC Corridor**: The China-Pakistan Economic Corridor, valued at over $62 billion, has transformed Pakistan's infrastructure but saddled the country with debts exceeding 30% of its GDP by 2025.

★ **Djibouti's Port Takeover**: The country's debt to China exceeds 70% of its GDP and hosts China's first overseas military base—a textbook case of financial leverage translating into a strategic presence.

★ **Malaysia's East Coast Rail Link**: Initially canceled due to costs, it was then renegotiated at a 33% discount, showing that recipient nations can sometimes successfully resist.

★ **Ethiopia's Addis-Djibouti Railway** has been operational since 2018 but is struggling to generate revenue, leading to a debt renegotiation in 2024 that extended repayment periods while maintaining China's operational control.

★ **Montenegro's Highway**: A $1 billion loan for a highway to nowhere drove the debt-to-GDP ratio to 80%, requiring EU intervention to prevent default.

By 2023, Beijing had become the world's largest official bilateral creditor, with developing nations owing China's state banks an estimated **$1.3 trillion**. According to the IMF's analysis, the number of countries in "BRI debt distress" is expected to reach 24 by 2025.

Case Studies: From Concrete to Control

Hambantota Port (Sri Lanka)

Sri Lanka's Hambantota Port represents the classic case of BRI infrastructure creating strategic leverage. After Sri Lanka struggled to service Chinese loans for the port's construction, it eventually granted a 99-year lease for the facility to China in 2017. While presented as a purely commercial arrangement, the port's strategic location in the Indian Ocean and potential dual-use capabilities raised alarm among regional powers.

Madame Créancière, our allegorical debt collector, explains the subtle mechanics to a junior Chinese banker: "We never demanded the port as collateral initially. That would appear predatory. Instead, we offered generous financing for a project with questionable commercial viability, knowing that debt distress would eventually create leverage. When they couldn't pay, we magnanimously offered debt-equity 'swaps' rather than default. The outcome—controlling a strategic Indian Ocean port for a century—speaks for itself."

The junior banker looks concerned. "But critics call this 'debt-trap diplomacy.'"

Madame Créancière's smile doesn't waver. "An unfortunate characterization. We simply offered financing that no one else would provide, then found mutually beneficial solutions to the resulting debt challenges. If other lenders had offered better terms, Sri Lanka could have chosen them." She doesn't mention that competing Western-backed institutions often rejected such commercially questionable projects, creating the very vacuum China filled.

Huawei's 5G Deployments (Global South)

Huawei has emerged as the dominant telecommunications infrastructure provider across much of the developing world, offering 5G networks at prices Western competitors struggle to match. By 2025, Huawei equipment will form the backbone of digital infrastructure in over 100 countries.

Captain Panopticon, our personification of surveillance technology, demonstrated a 5G management console to telecommunications ministers from several African nations. This system offers unparalleled efficiency and security," he explains smoothly. Our financing terms beat Western alternatives by 40%, and our implementation is twice as fast."

A minister asks about security concerns raised by Western nations.

"Political fearmongering," Captain Panopticon dismisses. "They're simply protecting their overpriced vendors. Our equipment meets all international standards." He doesn't mention that China has taken leadership positions in the very standards bodies that certify telecommunications security.

What remains tactfully unaddressed is that Chinese law requires companies to cooperate with intelligence services when requested. The distinction between Huawei and the Chinese state remains deliberately ambiguous, and the potential for backdoor access or "kill switch" capabilities creates leverage, even if it is never activated.

Digital Yuan Trials (Cross-Border Settlements)

By 2025, China's digital yuan (e-CNY) had moved beyond domestic trials to facilitate cross-border settlements, particularly with BRI partner countries.

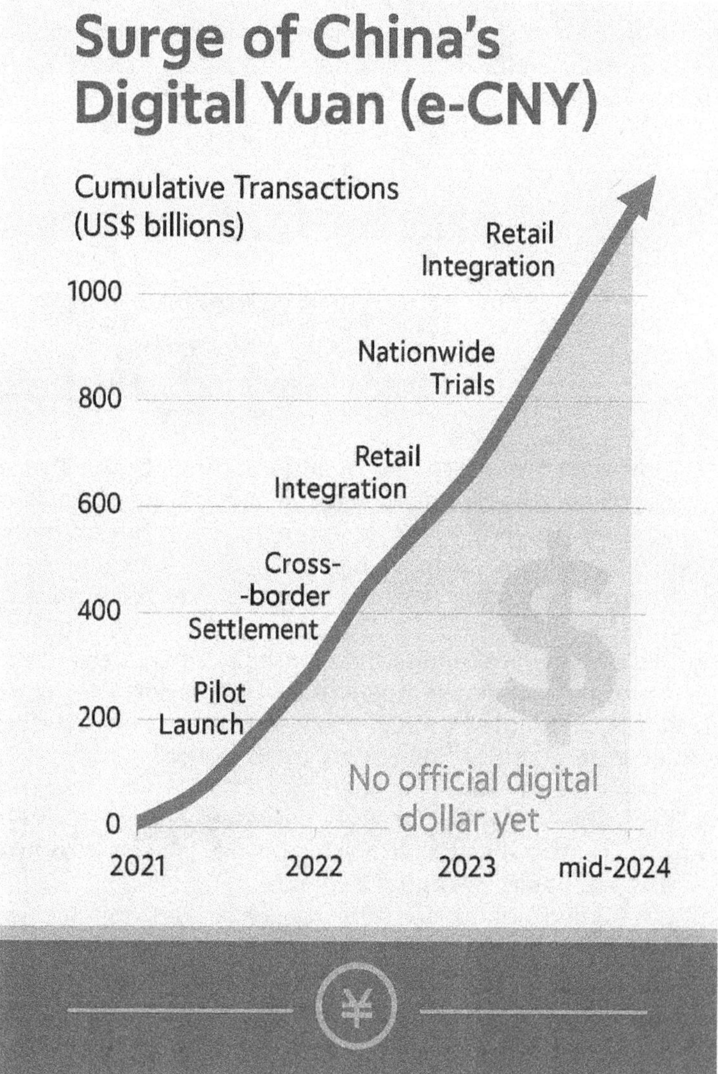

The system enables direct settlement without using SWIFT or touching the dollar-based financial system, effectively creating a sanctions-proof channel for international transactions.

Señor Cripto, our financial innovation personification, demonstrates the system to Central Bank officials from several Asian countries: "With e-CNY, you can conduct trade directly with China and other participating nations without converting to dollars or using Western clearing systems. Settlement is instantaneous, costs are minimal, and—most importantly—the transaction data stays within our network rather than passing through U.S.-controlled infrastructure."

An official asks the question everyone is thinking: "So this helps avoid potential U.S. sanctions?"

Señor Cripto's expression remains neutral. "We prefer to frame it positively: this system enhances financial sovereignty. Nations should be able to conduct legitimate trade without interference from third parties. The fact that it provides resilience against unilateral sanctions is simply a natural consequence of network diversity."

The e-CNY pilot programs processed a staggering **9.8 trillion yuan** (~$1.5 trillion) in transactions. That figure represents nearly 4% of all domestic Chinese payments—a significant achievement for a relatively new system.

By 2025, BRI countries are expected to have conducted 38% of their trade with China using e-CNY, creating a parallel financial architecture that is increasingly immune to Western sanctions or monitoring.

Western Alternatives: Too Little, Too Late

The West has belatedly recognized the strategic implications of China's infrastructure diplomacy, launching counter-initiatives like the G7's Build Back Better World (B3W) and the EU's Global Gateway. However, these programs remain underfunded, bureaucratically complex, and hindered by short-term political considerations, in contrast to China's focused and well-resourced approach.

The Partnership for Global Infrastructure and Investment (PGII), launched with fanfare in 2022, promised to mobilize $600 billion for developing country infrastructure by 2027. By 2025, actual disbursements totaled less than $40 billion, while China had invested over $800 billion in BRI projects during the same period.

The Trump 2.0 administration's 2025 budget slashed PGII contributions by 40%, making America's alternative even less credible. The sobering truth is that, to many in the developing world, China remains the only game in town for big infrastructure projects.

A Ugandan infrastructure minister summarized the contrast: "The Chinese offer a complete package—financing, construction, and speed—with minimal political conditions. Western alternatives require years of environmental studies, governance reforms, and complex multi-donor coordination. Meanwhile, my people need electricity and transportation now. It's not a difficult choice."

5. THE DIGITAL COLONIZATION PLAYBOOK

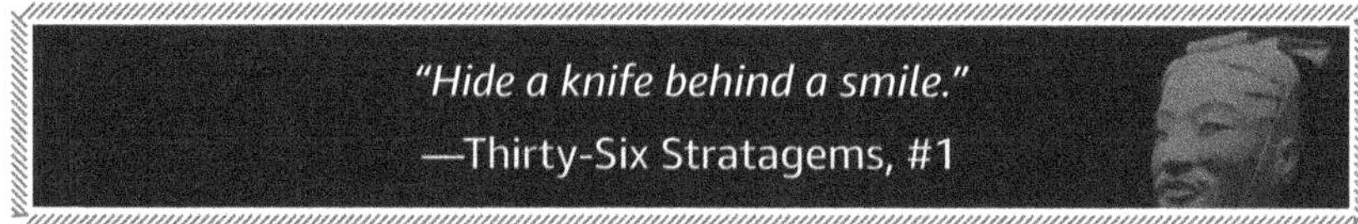

"Hide a knife behind a smile."
—Thirty-Six Stratagems, #1

How Data Flows, Standards, and Platforms Create Dependencies

Beyond physical infrastructure, China has systematically constructed a comprehensive digital expansion strategy that creates dependencies that are more subtle but potentially more powerful than traditional economic relationships. This strategy spans multiple dimensions, including telecommunications infrastructure, surveillance systems, e-commerce platforms, payment networks, cloud services, and standards-setting in emerging technologies.

The core insight driving this strategy is that controlling digital architecture creates leverage that extends far beyond traditional economic relationships. When a country's telecommunications infrastructure is built on Chinese hardware, its government operates on Chinese software, its commerce is conducted through Chinese platforms, and its data is transmitted through Chinese-built networks, the resulting dependencies become nearly impossible to disentangle without incurring enormous disruption.

"The old colonialism extracted resources," explains **Algorithm Annie**, our AI personification, to a group of Chinese tech executives. "Digital colonization extracts, processes, and leverages data while controlling the platforms that generate it. The real value isn't in owning the pipeline; it's in controlling the algorithms that process what flows through it."

The Mechanics of Digital Dependency

Digital dependency operates through several interlocking mechanisms:

Infrastructure Control: When Huawei, ZTE, and other Chinese firms build the physical telecommunications infrastructure (cell towers, data centers, fiber optic cables), they create potential for both data access and leverage. A country that relies on Chinese-built digital infrastructure faces enormous switching costs if it later wishes to change providers.

Standards Dominance: China has systematically increased its representation in international standards-setting bodies, from the International Telecommunication Union (ITU) to the International Organization for Standardization (ISO). By 2025, Chinese representatives are expected to chair 40% more technical committees than in 2015, enabling them to shape standards for emerging technologies, including facial recognition and IoT protocols.

Surveillance Exports: Through the "Safe City" program and similar initiatives, Chinese firms have exported comprehensive surveillance systems to at least 80 countries. These systems typically include CCTV networks, facial recognition, data analysis platforms, and command centers—often installed by Chinese technicians with ongoing maintenance relationships.

Platform Penetration: Chinese platforms, such as TikTok, WeChat, and Alipay, have expanded globally, collecting vast amounts of user data while normalizing Chinese technical approaches and governance models. When these platforms achieve dominant market positions, they create leverage by controlling access to digital markets.

Data Gravity: As data accumulates in Chinese-controlled systems, it creates "gravity" that pulls additional services and capabilities into that ecosystem. The more information flows through the Chinese digital infrastructure, the harder it becomes to extract or redirect.

Case Studies: Digital Dependency in Action

TikTok's Global Data Collection

By 2025, TikTok had over 2 billion global users, including 180 million Americans, making it one of the world's dominant social media platforms. While presented as simply an entertainment app, TikTok functions as a sophisticated data collection system, gathering information on user behavior, preferences, social networks, and even biometric patterns through its advanced algorithm.

Despite years of concerns about potential data access by Chinese authorities, TikTok remained operational in most Western markets, protected by its massive user base, sophisticated lobbying, and the difficulty of replacing an embedded digital platform without significant social disruption.

Cassandra, the Cyber-Oracle, tries desperately to warn policymakers: "The platform isn't just collecting dance videos; it's building psychological profiles on hundreds of millions of global users, including government officials and their families. This data can be used for everything from influence operations to blackmail to training advanced AI systems that model Western behavior."

Algorithm Annie interrupts smugly: "But it's so entertaining! Check out this adorable video compilation I've algorithmically curated for maximum dopamine response! Who could object to dancing pandas?"

The Digital Embrace: Big Brother Goes Global

By 2025, at least **87 countries** had adopted Chinese-built surveillance technology platforms, from authoritarian regimes to democracies. The regional impact varies dramatically:

- ★ **In Latin America**, Ecuador's ECU-911 emergency response system, built by Chinese companies, has integrated thousands of cameras across the country. By 2024, similar systems appeared in Venezuela, Bolivia, and Argentina.
- ★ **In Africa**, Countries like **Uganda**, Kenya, and Rwanda embraced Chinese facial recognition tech, ostensibly to combat crime but conveniently also to monitor opposition activities. The 2024 elections in Uganda featured Chinese-built surveillance technology that identified opposition rallies in real-time.

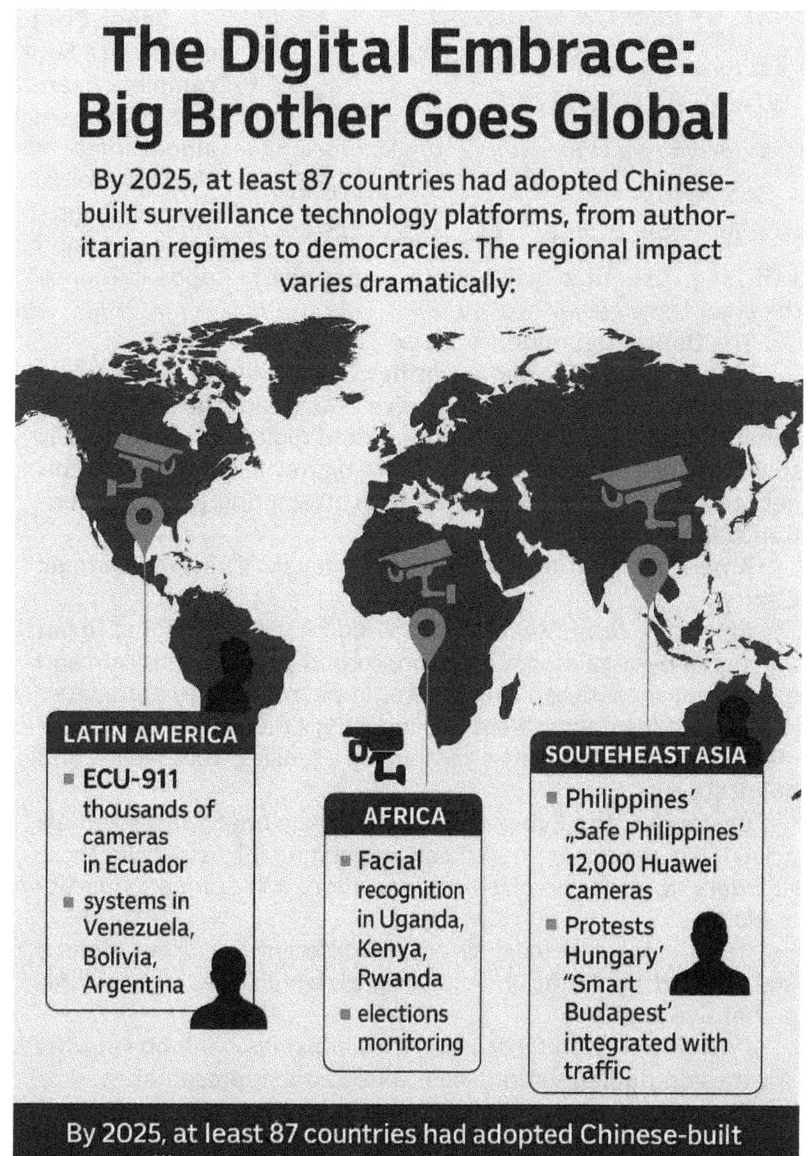
The Digital Embrace:
Big Brother Goes Global
By 2025, at least 87 countries had adopted Chinese-built surveillance technology platforms, from authoritarian regimes to democracies. The regional impact varies dramatically:
LATIN AMERICA
ECU-911 thousands of cameras in Ecuador
systems in Venezuela, Bolivia, Argentina
AFRICA
Facial recognition in Uganda, Kenya, Rwanda
elections monitoring
SOUTHEAST ASIA
Philippines' „Safe Philippines' 12,000 Huawei cameras
Protests Hungary' "Smart Budapest' integrated with traffic
By 2025, at least 87 countries had adopted Chinese-built surveillance technology platforms, from democracies

- ★ **In Southeast Asia**, the Philippines' "Safe Philippines" project deployed 12,000 Huawei surveillance cameras across Metro Manila, featuring live monitoring and facial recognition capabilities.
- ★ **In Eastern Europe**, Serbia deployed hundreds of Huawei facial recognition cameras throughout Belgrade, sparking protests over privacy concerns, while Hungary's "Smart Budapest" project integrates Chinese surveillance infrastructure with traffic management.

Captain Panopticon demonstrates advanced crowd monitoring features to officials from an authoritarian regime: "Our system doesn't just record; it predicts. It can identify unusual crowd formations, detect emotional states from facial expressions, and flag potential troublemakers before incidents occur."

"And the data?" asks a security minister.

"Stored securely on your sovereign servers," Captain Panopticon assures him. He doesn't mention the Chinese technicians who maintain those servers or the backdoor access built into the system architecture.

Mobile Payment System Penetration

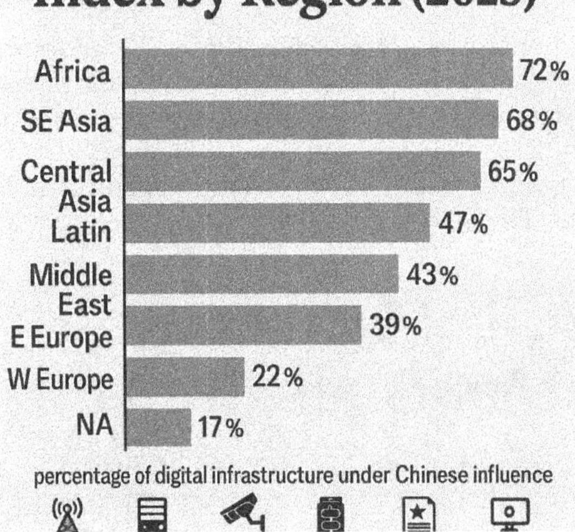

Chinese mobile payment platforms—led by Alipay and WeChat Pay—have expanded aggressively into developing markets, particularly Southeast Asia and Africa. By integrating with local banking systems and offering user-friendly interfaces, these platforms have achieved dominant positions in countries with limited existing financial infrastructure.

The strategic implications extend far beyond simple payment processing. These platforms collect comprehensive data on economic behavior, establish direct financial relationships with millions of users, and create de facto standards for digital finance in emerging markets.

Señor Cripto demonstrates Alipay's localized version to officials from a Southeast Asian nation: "This isn't just payments; it's a complete financial ecosystem. Loans, insurance, investments, business services—all integrated and personalized using our advanced algorithms."

What remains unsaid is that the data feeding those algorithms flows through Chinese-controlled infrastructure, building comprehensive economic intelligence on emerging markets while creating switching costs that make displacement nearly impossible once the algorithms are embedded.

The Digital Dependency Index

This data visualization quantifies China's digital reach across the world regions. The pattern reveals a clear strategy: deeper penetration in developing regions where digital infrastructure is still being established, creating "born digital" economies on Chinese technical architecture rather than attempting to displace entrenched Western systems.

American Technological Complacency vs. Chinese Strategic Clarity

America's response to China's digital expansion has been hampered by regulatory confusion, corporate short-termism, and misaligned incentives. While China implemented a coordinated strategy across government and industry, America's approach remained fragmented across competing agencies, companies, and political cycles.

Cassandra, the Cyber-Oracle, frantically briefs distracted officials: "We need coordinated policy spanning infrastructure security, data governance, platform regulation, and standards participation!"

"That crosses at least seventeen different agencies," sighs a State Department official. "And Congress would need to pass comprehensive legislation."

"Which they won't, because tech companies will lobby against any meaningful regulation," adds a Pentagon representative.

"And we're restricted from providing foreign alternatives because our systems are too expensive and come with too many human rights conditions," notes a Commerce official.

THE DIGITAL COLONIALIST'S HANDBOOK

MINISTRY OF DIGITAL EXPANSION INTERNAL GUIDANCE DOCUMENT

FIVE STEPS TO DIGITAL DEPENDENCY

INFRASTRUCTURE FIRST

Deploy telecommunications hardware strategically. Remember: Once your hardware forms their backbone, switching costs become prohibitive.

TECHNICAL SUPPORT AS INTELLIGENCE

Maintain ongoing maintenance relationships. Station technicians in key facilities ensure continuous access.

STANDARDS AS STRATEGIC ASSETS

Place representatives in all relevant standards bodies. Remember: He who writes the standards owns the future.

PLATFORMS CREATE LEVERAGE

Consumer-facing applications build direct relationships with populations. Each platform should appear commercial while serving strategic functions.

FROM DIGITAL TO PHYSICAL CONTROL

Digital dependency enables physical leverage. The goal is not control but "strategic optionality."

FROM DIGITAL TO PHYSICAL CONTROL

Digital dependency enables physical leverage.

"Plus, most American companies won't invest in low-margin infrastructure in developing markets," concludes a Treasury analyst.

Meanwhile, **Algorithm Annie** dances through their phones, collecting metadata on the meeting itself while serving personalized content optimized for maximum engagement rather than strategic awareness.

The Digital Colonialist's Handbook (Satirical Element)

CLASSIFIED: MINISTRY OF DIGITAL EXPANSION INTERNAL GUIDANCE DOCUMENT: FIVE STEPS TO DIGITAL DEPENDENCY

STEP 1: INFRASTRUCTURE FIRST Deploy telecommunications hardware strategically. Offer financing terms Western competitors cannot match. Emphasize speed of deployment and minimal political conditions. Remember: Once your hardware forms their backbone, switching costs become prohibitive.

STEP 2: TECHNICAL SUPPORT AS INTELLIGENCE Maintain ongoing maintenance relationships. Station technicians in key facilities. All infrastructure deployments should include long-term technical support agreements, ensuring continuous access and relationship development.

STEP 3: STANDARDS AS STRATEGIC ASSETS Place representatives in all relevant standards bodies. Technical standards have invisible power—they have shaped the development of technology for decades. Chair committees whenever possible. Submit more proposals than competitors. Remember: He who writes the standards owns the future.

STEP 4: PLATFORMS CREATE LEVERAGE Consumer-facing applications build direct relationships with populations. Payment systems create financial dependency. Entertainment platforms gather psychological data. Social networks map relationship structures. Each platform should appear commercial while serving strategic functions.

STEP 5: FROM DIGITAL TO PHYSICAL CONTROL Digital dependency enables physical leverage. Countries that are dependent on our digital infrastructure cannot afford to risk disconnection. Use this leverage subtly—the best power is that which never needs to be explicitly invoked. The goal is not control but "strategic optionality."

NOTE: THIS DOCUMENT IS SATIRICAL AND DOES NOT REPRESENT ACTUAL CHINESE STRATEGY DOCUMENTS. IT IS AN ANALYTICAL DEVICE ILLUSTRATING THE SYSTEMATIC NATURE OF DIGITAL INFLUENCE OPERATIONS.

6. THE COKE BOTTLE'S SHADOW: STRATEGIC IMPLICATIONS

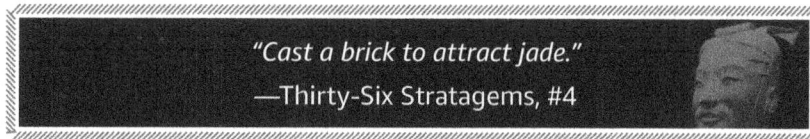

"Cast a brick to attract jade."
—Thirty-Six Stratagems, #4

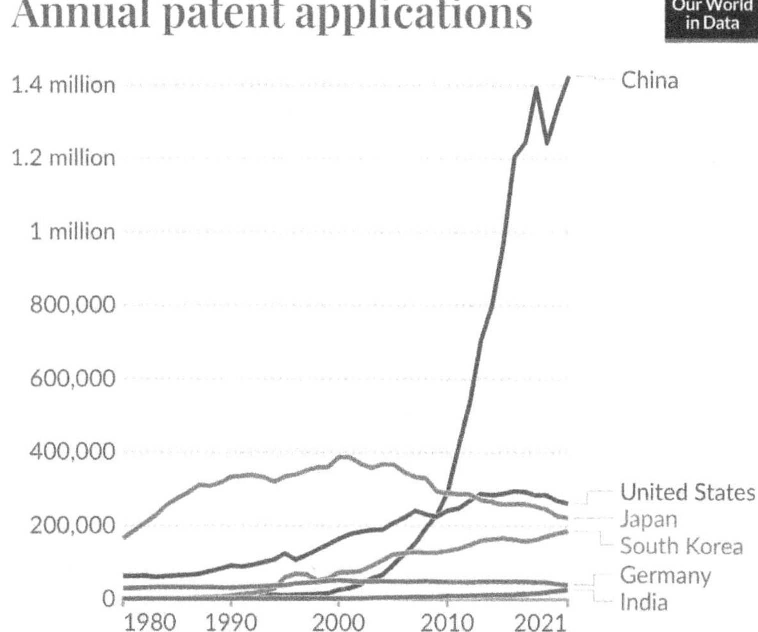

Data source: WIPO via World Bank (2024)
Note: Each country's data includes patent applications for which the first-named applicant is a country resident.
OurWorldinData.org/research-and-development | CC BY

The Irreversible Structural Changes in the Global Economy

By 2025, China's economic and digital expansion had fundamentally altered global power dynamics, creating structural changes not easily reversed through traditional policy interventions. These transformations include:

Production Dominance: China has become the world's dominant manufacturer, not just in low-value goods, but increasingly in strategic sectors such as telecommunications equipment, renewable energy technology, electric vehicles, and advanced electronics.

Innovation Leadership: Chinese companies filed more international patents than their American counterparts for the seventh consecutive year, with particular strength in practical applications of artificial intelligence, 5G/6G telecommunications, renewable energy, and quantum computing.

Standards Control: Chinese representatives have gained influential positions in international

standards-setting bodies, shaping technical standards for emerging technologies, including facial recognition and Internet of Things protocols.

Digital Ecosystems: Chinese digital platforms achieved dominant positions across much of the developing world, creating alternatives to Western-dominated systems for payments, communications, e-commerce, and social networking.

Infrastructure Operation: Chinese state-owned enterprises managed critical infrastructure—such as ports, railways, power plants, and telecommunications networks—across dozens of countries, creating both commercial advantages and strategic options.

Financial Architecture: Alternative financial channels, such as the Cross-Border Interbank Payment System (CIPS) and the digital yuan, have created pathways for international transactions outside Western-controlled systems, thereby reducing the effectiveness of sanctions as a policy tool.

Collectively, these changes amount to a fundamental rebalancing of global economic and technological power, not a temporary fluctuation but a structural transformation reflecting deeper shifts in productive capacity, technological capability, and strategic focus.

Uncle Sam's Belated Realization

Uncle Sam stands before a global map illuminated with red lights showing Chinese investments, infrastructure projects, and digital penetration. His expression shifts from dismissal to concern to alarm as advisors update him on the scope of Chinese influence.

"How did this happen?" he demands, adjusting his increasingly rumpled top hat.

Milton the Trickster Economist materializes, calculator in hand. "Simple comparative advantage! They make things more efficiently, so production naturally shifted there. The invisible hand works perfectly!"

"But now they control key supply chains," protests Uncle Sam. "They can cut off critical components, leverage their market position, even potentially disable infrastructure they've built!"

Milton shrugs. "Unforeseen externalities. The models didn't account for strategic leverage. Besides, quarterly profits looked excellent!"

McSlicey the Priest appears, clutching a weathered PowerPoint presentation. "Our analysis showed clear efficiency gains from global value chain optimization. Perhaps we slightly underweighted long-term strategic vulnerabilities..."

Uncle Sam turns back to the map. "Can we reverse this? Bring manufacturing home? Build our own infrastructure? Develop competing digital platforms?"

An economic advisor looks uncomfortable. "We've spent decades optimizing for financial metrics rather than productive capacity. Rebuilding would take sustained investment, industrial policy, and patience—all things our system has systematically discouraged."

A technology advisor adds: "Our digital platforms optimize for engagement and quarterly user growth, not strategic resilience. Competing with Chinese platforms would require different optimization targets."

A foreign policy expert notes: "We've reduced foreign assistance and infrastructure investment precisely when alternative providers were needed most. The resulting vacuum was predictably filled."

Uncle Sam stares at the map, finally comprehending the accumulated consequences of decades of strategic complacency and short-term optimization. "So what now?"

The Roosevelt Ghosts materialize beside him. **Teddy** adjusts his spectacles: "America has faced strategic challenges before and transformed itself to meet them. But transformation requires acknowledging the problem and mobilizing national purpose."

Franklin nods: "It demands recognizing that markets, while powerful tools, don't automatically optimize for national resilience or strategic independence. Sometimes government must serve as a catalyst and coordinator."

Eleanor adds gently, "And it requires rebuilding not just physical infrastructure but social cohesion and shared purpose. A divided nation cannot effectively meet systemic challenges."

Uncle Sam straightens his bow tie with new determination. "Then we'd better get started."

Network Effects, Path Dependency, and Increasing Returns to Scale

The challenge facing America stems partly from fundamental characteristics of digital and networked systems that create powerful self-reinforcing dynamics:

Network Effects: Digital platforms become more valuable as more users join them, creating winner-take-all dynamics that make the displacement of established systems extremely difficult. Once Chinese platforms achieve critical mass in developing markets, competing alternatives face enormous barriers to entry.

Path Dependency: Initial technology choices constrain future options by establishing standards, interfaces, and user expectations that create switching costs, thereby limiting subsequent choices. Countries that build digital infrastructure on Chinese systems face prohibitive costs if they need to change course later.

Increasing Returns to Scale: Unlike traditional industries, which often exhibit diminishing returns, digital technologies usually display increasing returns, becoming more efficient and capable as they grow. Chinese platforms that process more data can develop better algorithms, attracting more users and generating more data in a virtuous cycle for themselves, but a vicious cycle for their competitors.

Today's Specials

STRATEGIC DEPENDENCY

Choose Your Path!

COMPREHENSIVE PACKAGE

Full infrastructure suite (telecommuncations, energy) with Chinese hardware, software, financing, and technical support.

Price: **SOVEREIGNTY**

DIGITAL SPECIAL

Telecommunications, surveillance, and data systems fully integrated with Chinese technical architecture.

Price: **PRIVACY & INDEPENDENT DECISION-MAKING**

FINANCIAL ARRANGEMENT

Loans, Investments, and digital payment systems

POLICY FLEXIBILITY & AUTONOMOUS FOREIGN POLICY

Price: **POLICY FLEXIBILITY AUTONOMOUS FOREIGN**

À LA CARTE

Select individual systems with "no strings attached."

Price: **TBD (But Higher Than You Think)**

These characteristics mean that digital power, once established, tends to be self-reinforcing and resistant to displacement through normal competitive processes. China's economic and digital architecture creates a persistent structural advantage not easily countered through traditional policy tools.

The Dependency Menu (Satirical Visual)

This satirical menu illustrates the choices facing developing nations as they navigate Chinese economic and digital outreach. The options appear beneficial but carry hidden costs in terms of sovereignty, autonomy, and future flexibility—costs that become apparent only after dependency is established.

Identifying Critical Dependencies and Potential Leverage Points

Despite the structural challenges, America retains significant leverage points within the international system:

Financial System Dominance: Despite alternatives, the dollar-based financial system remains the dominant choice for international transactions, offering unparalleled liquidity and legal protection.

Technology Innovation Leadership: American companies continue to maintain leadership in fundamental research, advanced semiconductor design, high-end software, and select AI applications.

Institutional Control: Western-designed institutions, such as the IMF, World Bank, and WTO, continue to establish key rules for the international economic system, although their influence is waning.

Diplomatic Networks: America's alliance system, although strained, continues to encompass most of the world's advanced economies, providing potential for coordinated responses.

Market Access: The American consumer market remains essential for global producers, creating potential leverage over supply chains.

These assets could form the foundation for a renewed strategic approach addressing the structural changes China has achieved. However, an effective response would require precisely what America has struggled to generate: strategic patience, coordinated planning across public and private sectors, and willingness to prioritize long-term resilience over short-term efficiency.

Literary Device: The Bottle Cannot Be Returned

In the film *The Gods Must Be Crazy*, the protagonist Xi undertakes an epic journey to return the disruptive Coca-Cola bottle to the gods by throwing it off the "end of the world." This restores harmony to his community by removing the object that causes discord.

No such simple resolution exists for our geopolitical parable. The "bottles" of Chinese economic and digital influence cannot be thrown back to the

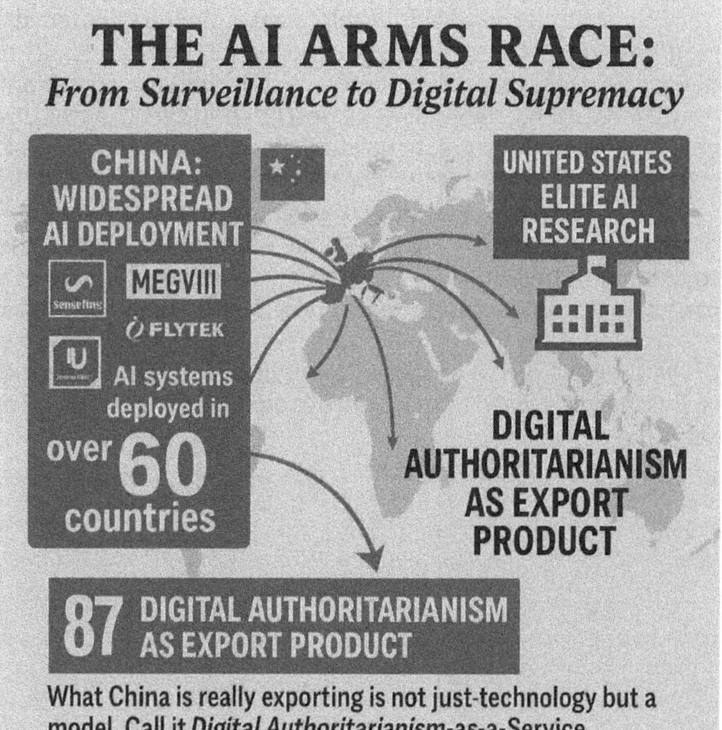

THE AI ARMS RACE:
From Surveillance to Digital Supremacy
CHINA: WIDESPREAD AI DEPLOYMENT
MEGVIII
FLYTEK
AI systems deployed in over 60 countries
UNITED STATES ELITE AI RESEARCH
DIGITAL AUTHORITARIANISM AS EXPORT PRODUCT
87 DIGITAL AUTHORITARIANISM AS EXPORT PRODUCT

What China is really exporting is not just-technology but a model. Call it *Digital Authoritarianism*-as-a-Service.

heavens; they have become deeply embedded in the international system. The infrastructure has been built, the standards have been set, the platforms have achieved critical mass, and the dependencies have been established.

The path forward lies not in futile attempts to "return" the bottle but in learning to manage its contents—developing countervailing capabilities, reducing critical vulnerabilities, and building resilience into systems increasingly characterized by interdependence rather than independence.

The Rooseveltian approach this book advocates does not promise a return to American hegemony or technological dominance across all domains. Instead, it provides a framework for strategic adaptation to a more competitive international environment, while maintaining core capabilities and acknowledging the reality of a transformed global landscape.

The AI Arms Race: From Surveillance to Digital Supremacy

The DSR has accelerated into an artificial intelligence battleground, with China exporting not just cameras but comprehensive AI systems. By 2025, Chinese AI companies such as SenseTime, Megvii, and iFlytek had deployed machine learning systems in over 60 countries, offering a range of services from facial recognition to automated sentiment analysis.

Despite world-class AI research, the United States has struggled to compete in AI deployment abroad, particularly in developing regions. While OpenAI and Anthropic focus on next-generation language models for elite users, Chinese firms offer practical and affordable AI solutions for everyday government functions, including traffic management, public health monitoring, and, yes, population surveillance.

This divergence is strategic: America pioneers breakthrough research while China masters mass deployment, particularly in sectors with strategic value. A former Pentagon official summarized it: "We're building boutique AI prototypes while they're installing surveillance operating systems across entire continents."

Digital Authoritarianism as Export Product

What China is really exporting is not just technology but a model. Call it **Digital Authoritarianism-as-a-Service**. Need to quash dissent? There's an app (and camera network) for that, made in Shenzhen. Want to manage public opinion? Chinese consultants can demonstrate how to combine censorship algorithms with data analytics.

At least 87 countries have adopted aspects of China's surveillance model. Beijing actively promotes a vision of **"cyber sovereignty"** in international forums—the idea that each government should control the internet within its borders, free from outside interference. In practice, that means legitimizing state censorship and surveillance powers globally.

There have been alarming incidents: The African Union discovered its China-built headquarters in Addis Ababa was digitally bugged—for years, sensitive data was quietly siphoned to servers in Shanghai. Reports suggest that Huawei technicians in Uganda and Zambia directly assisted governments in surveilling opposition figures. These cases highlight the blurry lines between commercial technology and state surveillance.

Chapter Transition: From Economic Entanglement to Military Competition

As economic interdependence between China and the United States deepens, military competition paradoxically intensifies in parallel. The two powers find themselves simultaneously trading partners and strategic rivals—economically entangled yet militarily wary, financially interdependent yet geopolitically competitive.

This contradictory relationship creates unprecedented strategic complexity. Traditional theories of international relations suggested that deep economic integration would reduce security competition. The China-US relationship defies this expectation, with both economic entanglement and military rivalry intensifying simultaneously.

The economic dependencies described in this chapter directly enable and constrain military capabilities. Supply chain vulnerabilities create strategic leverage. Technological dependencies influence military innovation. Financial interdependence affects the effectiveness of sanctions and defense budgeting.

Our next chapter examines this military dimension, analyzing how China has systematically developed capabilities designed to target specific American vulnerabilities while the United States has struggled to adapt legacy systems to emerging threats. We'll explore the dangerous flashpoints where economic competition might escalate to military confrontation, particularly Taiwan, the South China Sea, and increasingly, the digital domain.

As with economic competition, we'll find that America's military challenges stem not primarily from Chinese brilliance but from self-inflicted institutional rigidities, misaligned incentives, and strategic complacency. The gods, it seems, have dropped military bottles alongside economic ones—and America's response has been similarly fragmented and reactive.

The examination continues.

CHAPTER 2: CELESTIAL CHESS, AMERICAN CHECKERS: CHINA–US GEOPOLITICAL FLASHPOINTS, STRATEGIC AMBITION, & MILITARY PROJECTION

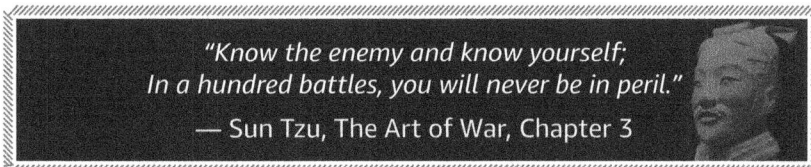

> *"Know the enemy and know yourself;*
> *In a hundred battles, you will never be in peril."*
> — Sun Tzu, The Art of War, Chapter 3

EXECUTIVE BRIEFING

Strategic Snapshot

Visualise a split-screen war room: Beijing's grandmasters slide Go stones toward 2049 while Washington's staffers juggle checkers, Candy Crush, and congressional pork. Centred on the board gleams a single silicon chip—Taiwan—whose destruction would freeze the global economy in nanoseconds. The duel is **chronological endurance versus institutional whiplash**.

Key Findings – What the Board Reveals

1. **Time-Horizon Asymmetry** – Beijing plans in dynastic decades; D.C. resets every tweet cycle.
2. **Flashpoint Triad – Taiwan (90 % of advanced chips), South China Sea (3,200 acres of fortified sand), Gray-Zone Everywhere** (cyber, lawfare, trawler militias) – each calibrated to stay below America's kinetic redline.
3. **Cost-Curve Trap** – PLA "assassin's-mace" missiles (**$20 M**) stalk Ford-class carriers (**$13 B**)—a 650:1 asymmetry that bankrupts U.S. force projection.
4. **Alliance Erosion** – Trumpian volatility reframes treaties as Craigslist ads; allies hedge, Beijing bids.
5. **Procurement Paralysis** – Pentagon's 15-year PPBE cycle fields perfection for yesterday's war just as China deploys its fifth "good-enough" iteration.

Risk Ledger

Choke-Point	How China Exploits	Current U.S. Exposure
Carrier Constriction	DF-21/26 ASBMs & dense A2/AD web	11 big targets, few decoys
Taiwan T-Minus	Rapid gray-zone squeeze or lightning strike	Wargames show high U.S./allied losses
Alliance Trust	Loans, vaccines, BRI ports	Confidence dips each election cycle
Semiconductor Choke	Threat of fab destruction = global leverage	90 % of advanced nodes offshore

Opportunity Knobs

Quad, AUKUS, and NATO-Pacific outposts can knit a **maritime picket** inside the First Island Chain. If synchronized, the U.S. still leads in chip design, AI frameworks, undersea ISR, and dollar liquidity.

Action Recommendations – *Upgrade the Playbook*

1. **Decade-Locked Strategy** – Pass a bipartisan Pacific Deterrence Act with automatic funding triggers that survive partisan mood swings.
2. **Distributed, Attritable Force Design** – Shift 20 % of carrier O&M to swarming unmanned surface, subsurface, & aerial platforms; choose "many & muddy" over "few & flashy."
3. **Silicon Shield 2.0** – Fast-track on-shore/ally-shore fabs (USA, Japan, Germany) while underwriting Taiwan's *Fab Fort Knox* hardening and spare-lithography caches.
4. **Gray-Zone Counter Doctrine** – Stand up a Coast Guard–Cyber Command task force with authorities to hit back in hours, not hearings.
5. **Alliance Confidence Restorers** – Offer 10-year security-of-supply treaties (rare earths, fuel, data cables) backed by U.S. procurement from allied industry.

Bottom Line

The game won't be won by flipping the board; it will be won by **teaching checkers champions to think in Go**—trading quarterly myopia for generational positioning, exquisite singularities for expendable swarms, and transactional deals for ironclad trust. The gods may be crazy, but there's still time to outplay them—stone by calculated stone.

Opening Tableau: When the Gods Play Board Games

A split-screen scene unfolds before us. On the left, a group of Chinese strategists in dark suits gathers around a holographic display of Earth. They methodically place Go stones in key locations—the Taiwan Strait, the South China Sea, and strategic ports along the Belt and Road Initiative—while consulting charts that show timelines stretching to 2049. Their movements are deliberate, their discussions measured in decades.

On the right, Pentagon officials frantically shuffle checker pieces across their half of the board. Budget fight memos fly between them. Election countdown clocks flash ominously on the wall. General Quagmire searches desperately for Cold War-era Soviet submarine models under the table while Chinese vessels sail past the digital map unnoticed.

The ultimate prize, a gleaming silicon chip representing Taiwan's semiconductor industry, is at the center of both screens. Both teams occasionally glance at it with barely concealed desire.

CHINESE STRATEGIST: "Remember, our objective remains unchanged since Chairman Xi's directive: strategic patience. Each stone we place constrains their movement options without forcing direct confrontation. By 2035, they'll wake up to find themselves in zugzwang."

PENTAGON OFFICIAL: "Can someone tell me if we're containing China today or engaging them? The policy memo has changed twice since breakfast. Also, Senator Porkbarrel wants three more aircraft carriers for his district, though we already explained carriers don't work that way."

GENERAL QUAGMIRE: *(Looking up from under the table)* "Found it! A model Russian Akula-class submarine! Who's obsessed with fighting the last war now, Jenkins? Jenkins...? Where'd everyone go?"

And so begins our exploration of the geopolitical game unfolding between the world's preeminent power and its most determined challenger. In this contest, one side plays celestial chess with millennial patience while the other bounces between checkers and Candy Crush, depending on the electoral cycle.

Executive Summary: When the Gods Drop a Semiconductor Fab from the Sky

In the cosmic tragicomedy of international relations, two titans now stumble through a geopolitical minefield largely of their own making. This chapter dissects the China-US strategic rivalry with both scholarly precision and satirical flair, revealing a high-stakes game where one nation plays celestial chess while the other bounces between checkers and Candy Crush.

China pursues methodical "national rejuvenation" under Xi Jinping's quasi-imperial presidency, transforming its once-peasant army into a high-tech force armed with "carrier-killer" missiles that cost roughly 1/10000th the price of the American carriers they're designed to sink. Meanwhile, America's strategic response oscillates between containment, engagement, and Twitter tantrums, depending on which administration, agency, or social media platform you consult.

The flashpoints are numerous and perilous. Taiwan stands as the world's most dangerous powder keg: a democratic microchip factory disguised as an island, caught between Beijing's nationalist obsession and Washington's "strategic ambiguity"—a doctrine best summarized as "We might defend you or we might not; we're not telling, but please behave... maybe?" In the South China Sea, China builds artificial islands with the enthusiasm of a child in a sandbox, plants military bases atop them, and then insists they're merely weather stations staffed by unusually aggressive meteorologists.

Running through it all is a tragicomic economic codependency—two rivals attempting to simultaneously trade with and decouple from each other, like a bitterly divorced couple still sharing both a bank account and a favorite child (global capitalism). And looming over the horizon: Trump 2.0—the ultimate wild card in a game already perilously untethered from rationality.

This diagnostic CT scan of a geopolitical patient with delusions of grandeur on both sides reveals one undeniable truth: in this high-stakes game, the gods of geopolitics must indeed be crazy—and the mortals in charge aren't faring much better.

1. GAME THEORY AND CULTURAL CONTEXT

"Victorious warriors win first and then go to war."
—Sun Tzu, The Art of War, Chapter 4

Competing Strategic Cultures: The Time Horizon Divergence

In a pristine conference room in Beijing, **General Strategic Patience** unfurls an ancient scroll beside a modern digital display. The scroll contains Sun Tzu's *Art of War*; the display shows a 30-year strategic implementation timeline with meticulous quarterly benchmarks leading to 2049—the centennial of the People's Republic and the target date for achieving "the great rejuvenation of the Chinese nation."

General Strategic Patience: "Our advantage is not technological superiority or even economic might—though we cultivate both. Our true advantage is chronological. Americans think in electoral cycles; we think in civilizational ones."

Meanwhile, in Washington, **General Attention Span** frantically swipes through PowerPoint slides on his tablet during a critical strategy meeting. Each slide bears a different logo—remnants of successive administrations' China strategies. A countdown clock on the wall shows 18 months until the next election.

General Attention Span: "Our China policy needs to be tough but nuanced, consistent yet flexible, confrontational while cooperative, and—hold on, is that a notification from TikTok? Wait, aren't we banning that? Or investing in it? I forgot what we decided this morning."

This opening vignette illustrates perhaps the most profound asymmetry in the US-China rivalry: their divergent time horizons. This isn't merely a tactical difference but a fundamental strategic divider rooted in political systems, historical experience, and cultural frameworks.

China's strategic culture is rooted in millennia of continuous civilization, where patience is not merely a virtue but a strategic imperative. The "Century of Humiliation" (1839-1949) serves as both historical trauma and motivational narrative, with the Communist Party positioning itself as the entity that ended this humiliation and will restore China to its rightful place. This long view enables Beijing to withstand short-term setbacks while maintaining focus on long-term objectives.

The 36 Stratagems exemplify this mindset—a collection of ancient Chinese proverbs describing strategies and tactics for war, politics, and civil interaction. Strategic concepts like "Hide a knife behind a smile" (韬光养晦, or "hide capabilities and bide time") guided China's approach for decades. Although Xi Jinping has adopted a more assertive posture, the patient strategic core remains.

By contrast, America's strategic culture developed from different imperatives: rapid continental expansion, oceans separating it from major rivals, and a constitutional system designed to prevent concentration of power rather than enable strategic coherence. The result is a system optimized for democratic legitimacy and individual liberty rather than strategic continuity.

McSlicey the Priest enters our narrative here. He is an allegorical figure representing the corporate consultancy mindset that pervades American strategic thinking. He appears in an expensive suit and carries sacred PowerPoint tablets.

McSlicey the Priest: "Our quarterly analysis suggests pivoting to a matrix-based, synergistic China approach with optimized resource allocation across sixteen strategic dimensions. The ROI modeling indicates... are you still listening, General?"

General Attention Span: *(Checking poll numbers on his phone)* "Absolutely. Matrix something. Sixteen dimensions. Sounds expensive but impressive. Will it play well in Ohio?"

American strategic planning often adopts corporate frameworks—such as quarterly targets, deliverables, and metrics—while China's planners think in terms of five-year plans and generational goals. This creates a mismatch in expectations and commitments. When Beijing announces a strategic initiative like Made in China 2025 or military modernization goals for 2035, these aren't aspirational targets, but commitments backed by sustained resource allocation and bureaucratic alignment.

China spends over 2.7% of its GDP on R&D (over $550 billion a year and rising), rivaling the U.S. in absolute terms. Government programs, such as "Made in China 2025" and the newer "China Science and Technology Self-Reliance Plan 2035" (launched in 2023), funnel billions of dollars into priority sectors. China leveraged globalization, forming partnerships, acquiring Western tech firms, and, at times, engaging in questionable intellectual property practices. But those tactics shouldn't overshadow the genuine innovation happening inside China's labs and tech incubators.

With top-notch engineering talent (China graduates four times more STEM bachelors than the U.S. each year) and a massive domestic market to scale up new products, Chinese innovators have gained a formidable edge. The results are showing in sector after sector:

Electric Vehicles: Chinese brands BYD, NIO, and XPENG now compete globally, not just domestically. In 2024, BYD surpassed Tesla in global EV sales.

- ★ **Renewable Energy**: China produces 80% of the world's solar panels and dominates battery manufacturing through companies like CATL.
- ★ **Telecommunications**: Despite U.S. sanctions, Huawei remains a global telecom giant with leading positions in 5G patents.
- ★ **Artificial Intelligence**: Companies like ByteDance (TikTok's parent) and SenseTime have emerged as AI powerhouses, with a particular strength in computer vision and recommendation algorithms.
- ★ **Quantum Computing**: China claimed "quantum advantage" in 2023, performing calculations no classical computer could match, intensifying the race with Google and IBM.

The Strategic Time Horizon Chart: Visualizing Temporal Asymmetry

Planning Horizon	Chinese Equivalent	American Equivalent
1-3 months	Tactical adjustment	OMG EVERYTHING IS ON FIRE
1 year	Minor operational shift	Major strategic rethink
4 years	Early implementation phase	Complete grand strategy lifecycle
10 years	Mid-term strategic goal	Science fiction/ fantasy
30+ years	Standard planning timeframe	Geological timescale

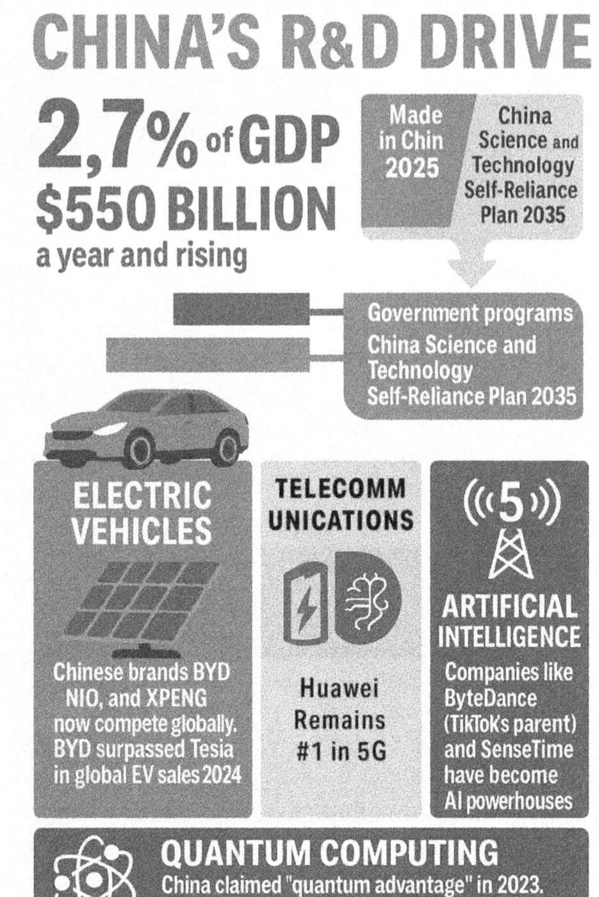

CHINA'S R&D DRIVE
2,7% of GDP
$550 BILLION
a year and rising
Made in Chin 2025
China Science and Technology Self-Reliance Plan 2035
Government programs
China Science and Technology Self-Reliance Plan 2035
ELECTRIC VEHICLES
TELECOMM UNICATIONS
5
ARTIFICIAL INTELLIGENCE
Chinese brands BYD NIO, and XPENG now compete globally. BYD surpassed Tesia in global EV sales 2024
Huawei Remains #1 in 5G
Companies like ByteDance (TikTok's parent) and SenseTime have become AI powerhouses
QUANTUM COMPUTING
China claimed "quantum advantage" in 2023. performing calculations no classical computer

The chart above satirizes but fundamentally captures a critical strategic asymmetry. When Beijing and Washington discuss "long-term planning," they're speaking different temporal languages. This creates mismatched expectations and mistaken assumptions about the other's intentions and capabilities.

THE STRATEGIC TIME HORIZON CHART

VISUALIZING TEMPORAL ASYMMETRY

	CHINESE EQUIVALENT	AMERICAN EQUIVALENT
1-3 MONTHS	TACTICAL ADJUSTMENT	OMG EVERYTHING IS ON FIRE
1 YEAR	MINOR OPERATIONAL SHIFT	MAJOR STRATEGIC RETHINK
4 YEARS	EARLY IMPLEMENTATION PHASE	COMPLETE GRAND STRATEGY LIFECYCLE
10 YEARS	MID-TERM STRATEGIC GOAL	SCIENCE FICTION/FANTASY
30+ YEARS	STANDARD PLANNING TIMEFRAME	GEOLOGICAL TIMESCALE

The Thucydides Trap—historian Graham Allison's framework describing the structural stresses that occur when a rising power challenges an established one—takes on new dimensions in this context. In 12 of 16 historical cases Allison studied, the outcome was war. However, those cases unfolded before the advent of nuclear weapons, global economic integration, and instantaneous communication. The US-China rivalry represents a Thucydides Trap with distinctive 21st-century characteristics.

Milton the Trickster Economist now enters our narrative pantheon. He appears with disheveled hair and a mischievous grin, carrying economic models promising that free markets solve all problems.

Milton the Trickster: "All this strategic planning is unnecessary! Simply remove barriers to trade, and the invisible hand will guide relations to optimal equilibrium. China will naturally liberalize politically as its middle class grows. It's basic economics!"

General Strategic Patience: *(Observing from afar)* "Perfect. Their economists still believe in their own mythology. Let them continue thinking trade automatically brings liberal democracy while we build a strategic advantage."

This illustrates another key asymmetry: China's strategic planners have extensively studied Western economic and political theory, whereas many Western policymakers continue to operate from ideological assumptions that history has repeatedly challenged.

The result is a fundamental mismatch in expectations. For decades, American policymakers assumed economic integration would inevitably lead to political liberalization in China. The "end of history" thesis—that liberal democracy represents the final form of human government—informed this approach. China's leadership studied this theory, recognized its strategic implications, and systematically worked to disprove it, accepting economic integration while strengthening, not weakening, authoritarian control.

2. THE COLD WAR HANGOVER: AMERICA'S STRATEGIC TIME WARP

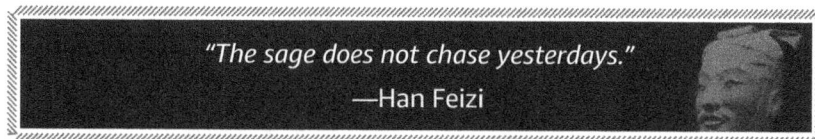

> *"The sage does not chase yesterdays."*
> —Han Feizi

The Pentagon Time Machine: Always Ready for Yesterday's War

In a cavernous war room deep beneath the Pentagon, **General Quagmire** adjusts his 1980s-era aviator glasses as he studies a massive wall map still showing the Soviet Union. Yellow sticky notes cover sections labeled "Russia," as staffers haven't had time to update the map. On his desk sits a model of a nuclear submarine next to an unread intelligence report titled "Chinese Anti-Ship Ballistic Missile Capabilities: Urgent Assessment."

General Quagmire: "The Russians are our primary geopolitical adversary—always have been, always will be. They're playing the long game, I tell you! This whole China thing is just a distraction from the real threat."

Young Intelligence Analyst: "Sir, permission to speak freely? The Cold War ended over thirty years ago. Russia's economy is smaller than Italy's. Meanwhile, China has built more ships in the past decade than our entire active naval fleet and is actively developing capabilities specifically designed to neutralize our aircraft carriers."

General Quagmire: *(Adjusting medals from the Cold War era)* "That's exactly what the Russians want you to think, Lieutenant. I wasn't born yesterday!"

This scene, while satirical, illustrates a profound challenge in American strategic thinking: institutional inertia. Large bureaucracies develop around specific threats and missions, creating powerful constituencies resistant to reprioritization. The result is a persistent lag between emerging challenges and the institutional adaptation required.

The Cold War fundamentally shaped American strategic thinking for generations. It created an entire ecosystem of institutions, careers, weapons systems, and intellectual frameworks oriented toward containing Soviet communism through nuclear deterrence, proxy conflicts, and ideological competition. When the Soviet Union collapsed, this massive apparatus lost its organizing principle but not its institutional momentum.

Post-Cold War, the Pentagon and intelligence community struggled to redefine their missions, briefly focusing on "rogue states," then terrorism after 9/11, and only gradually recognizing the unique challenge posed by China's rise. This resulted in nearly two decades of strategic distraction, during which China methodically studied American systems, identified vulnerabilities, and developed countermeasures.

This institutional lag manifests most visibly in procurement decisions—the weapons and platforms the United States prioritizes. Despite identifying China as the "pacing challenge," much of America's defense investment continues to flow to systems optimized for different threats.

Consider the F-35 Joint Strike Fighter program, a prime example of this disconnect. Conceived in the 1990s, the program has cost over $1.7 trillion across its lifecycle, while delivering an aircraft that faces significant challenges in the specific scenarios most likely in a China conflict. The program's timeline tells a story of institutional inertia:

- ★ **1992:** Program conceptualized (the Soviet Union had recently collapsed)
- ★ **2001:** Development contract awarded (China had just joined the WTO)
- ★ **2006:** First flight (China begins naval modernization)
- ★ **2015:** Initial operational capability (China is already building artificial islands in the South China Sea)
- ★ **2023:** Still not at full production rate (China has launched the third aircraft carrier)

During this same period, China analyzed American strengths, identified vulnerabilities, and developed targeted, cost-effective countermeasures—particularly anti-access/area-denial capabilities designed to neutralize the very power projection platforms, such as aircraft carriers, that form the backbone of U.S. strategy.

Admiral Forward Deployment: "Our carriers project American power globally. They're the most potent expression of American military might."

PLA Strategic Analyst: *(Taking notes)* "Excellent. They continue to invest trillions in a handful of vulnerable, high-value targets. Our DF-21D anti-ship ballistic missiles cost approximately 0.002% of their carriers. Mathematics favors us significantly."

The institutional challenge extends beyond hardware to intellectual frameworks. Military doctrine, planning scenarios, and training regimes optimized for one type of conflict must be painstakingly adjusted for another—a process that typically lags behind reality by years or decades.

The Military-Industrial Complex: Strategic Vulnerability Disguised as Strength

Milton the Trickster Economist reappears, now consulting for a major defense contractor. He stands before a PowerPoint showing a gold-plated weapons system with a price tag that increases with each slide.

Milton: "The free market efficiently allocates resources to optimize defense capabilities! Well, assuming you define 'free market' as a monopsony buyer purchasing from an oligopoly of suppliers, with requirements written by former employees of those suppliers who will return to higher-paying jobs with those same suppliers after their government service."

America's defense industrial base—once a strategic asset enabling production miracles during World War II—has evolved into a highly concentrated industry dominated by a handful of prime contractors. This concentration creates both inefficiencies and vulnerabilities:

- ★ Research and development increasingly focus on incremental improvements to existing systems rather than disruptive innovation.
- ★ Political considerations (distributing jobs across congressional districts) often outweigh strategic needs.
- ★ Supply chains have become vulnerable to disruption, with critical components sometimes sourced from potential adversaries.
- ★ The revolving door between the Pentagon and industry creates conflicts of interest and reinforces status quo thinking.

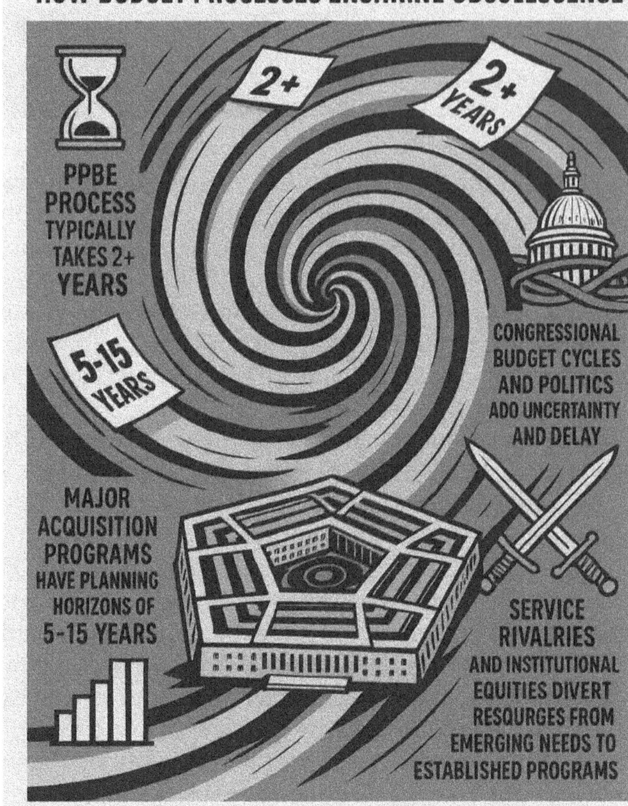
THE STRATEGIC TIME WARP:
HOW BUDGET PROCESSES ENSHRINE OBSOLESCENCE
2+
2+ YEARS
PPBE PROCESS TYPICALLY TAKES 2+ YEARS
5-15 YEARS
CONGRESSIONAL BUDGET CYCLES AND POLITICS ADD UNCERTAINTY AND DELAY
MAJOR ACQUISITION PROGRAMS HAVE PLANNING HORIZONS OF 5-15 YEARS
SERVICE RIVALRIES AND INSTITUTIONAL EQUITIES DIVERT RESOURCES FROM EMERGING NEEDS TO ESTABLISHED PROGRAMS
FIGHTING THE LAST WAR—ON DELAY

McSlicey the Priest: "Our analysis suggests optimizing the defense acquisition process through leveraging strategic synergies and stakeholder alignment matrices."

General Actual Combat: "Does that mean buying weapons that work when we need them at a price that doesn't bankrupt the country?"

McSlicey the Priest: *(Frowning)* "That's an oversimplification of our proprietary sixteen-dimensional analysis framework."

China, observing these dynamics, has developed its own military-industrial approach—one with significant weaknesses but also distinctive strengths. The Chinese system leverages state direction, civil-military fusion, and industrial espionage to accelerate development while accepting quality control challenges and corruption risks. The result is faster iteration cycles, greater willingness to fail forward, and a focus on asymmetric capabilities rather than symmetric competition.

The contrast is stark: while America spends decades and hundreds of billions developing the "perfect" next-generation fighter, China produces multiple iterations of "good enough" aircraft, incorporating lessons from each generation. The qualitative gap remains but narrows with each cycle.

This dynamic is evident across various domains, including hypersonic weapons, artificial intelligence, and quantum computing. America's pursuit of perfection often results in exquisite systems delivered too late, over budget, and in insufficient quantities to meet strategic needs. China's approach prioritizes speed, iteration, and quantity, alongside a gradual improvement in quality.

The Strategic Time Warp: How Budget Processes Enshrined Obsolescence

The Pentagon's planning and budgeting process inadvertently institutionalizes strategic lag:

- ★ The Planning, Programming, Budgeting, and Execution (PPBE) process typically takes 2+ years
- ★ Major acquisition programs have planning horizons of 5-15 years
- ★ Congressional budget cycles and politics add uncertainty and delay
- ★ Service rivalries and institutional equities divert resources from emerging needs to established programs

The result is a system designed to fight the last war rather than the next one—a time warp in which strategic responses systematically lag strategic challenges by years or decades.

[SATIRICAL MEMO: THE PENTAGON TIME MACHINE]

CLASSIFICATION: TEMPORALLY CONFUSED//BUREAUCRATICALLY ENTANGLED

Office of Retroactive Planning
Department of Defense

TO: All Forward-Thinking Personnel (An Oxymoron, We Realize)
FROM: Dr. Chronos Paradox, Chief Temporal Alignment Officer
SUBJECT: Achieving Strategic Alignment with Historical Threats

1. SITUATION ASSESSMENT: Analysis confirms our procurement systems have achieved perfect temporal inversion. We now reliably deliver capabilities optimized for threats that peaked 20 years before system deployment, while remaining conceptually unprepared for threats emerging during the system's operational lifetime.
2. KEY TEMPORAL DISTORTION METRICS:
   - ★ Average major program development timeline: 15.7 years
   - ★ Average strategic environment transformation cycle: 7.3 years
   - ★ Resulting Strategic Obsolescence Index: 215% (new record!)
3. FUTURE PLANNING DIRECTIVES: Based on our inverted temporal paradigm, we should immediately begin developing:
   - ★ Improved horse cavalry capabilities (to counter 2045 threats)
   - ★ Enhanced trench warfare systems (for the 2050 battlefield)
   - ★ Next-generation jousting equipment (for the 2060s security environment)
4. BUDGET IMPLICATIONS: All funding will continue to flow to programs designed to counter the Soviet Union. At the same time, emerging threats receive passionate lip service and PowerPoint slides with no corresponding budgetary allocations.
5. TIMELINE FOR IMPLEMENTATION: Why rush? At our current pace, the threats we're preparing for today won't emerge until the 22nd century.

DISTRIBUTION: Everyone who already knows this but lacks the institutional power to change it
//END SATIRICAL MEMO//

SATIRICAL MEMO:
THE PENTAGON TIME MACHINE

CLASSIFICATION: TEMPORALLY CONFUSED//BUREAUCRATICALLY
Office of Retroactive Planning
Department of Defense

TOP SECRET

FROM: Dr. Chronos Paradox,
Chief Temporal Alignment Officer

SUBJECT: Achieving Strategic Alignment with Historical Threats

SITUATION ASSESSEMENT:
Analysis confirms our procurement systems have achieved perfect temporal inversion. We now reıllably deliveror capabilitles optinized for threats that peaked 20 years before system deployment, while remaining conceptually unprepared for the system's emerging during the system's operational inctime.

KEY TEMPORAL DISTORTION METRICS:
- Average major program development timeline: 15.7 years
- Average strategic environment transformation cycle: 7.3 years
- Resulting Strategic Obsolescence Index: 2157 (new record!)

FUTURE PLANNING DIRECTIVES:
- Improved horse cavalry capabilities (to counter 2045 threats)
- Enhanced trench warfare systems (for the 2050 battlefield)
- Next-grneration jousting equipment (for the 20005 security environment)

BUDGET IMPLICATIONS: All funding will continue flowing to programs designed to fight the Soviet Union, while emerging threats receive passionate lip service and PowerPoint slides with no budgetary allocations.

TIMELINE FOR IMPLEMENTATION: Why rush? The threats we're preparing for today won't emerge until the 22nd century at our current pace.

DISTRIBUTION: Everyone who already knows this but lacks institutional power to change it

//END SATIRICAL MEMO//

This satirical memo highlights a genuine strategic vulnerability: America's defense planning and acquisition systems have become so cumbersome that they virtually guarantee capabilities will lag threats rather than anticipate them. China, studying this dynamic, has crafted its military modernization specifically to exploit this gap, developing systems that target vulnerabilities in platforms the U.S. cannot rapidly replace or adapt.

3. TAIWAN: SCHRÖDINGER'S SOVEREIGNTY CRISIS

> *"All warfare is founded on deception."*
> —Sun Tzu, The Art of War, Chapter 1

The Quantum Paradox of Strategic Ambiguity

In a sterile, clean room, **Madame Semiconductor** peers through specialized equipment at silicon wafers containing billions of transistors. Around her neck hangs a peculiar pendant—a quantum superposition medallion showing both American and Chinese flags simultaneously.

Outside her laboratory windows, PLA fighter jets conduct mock attack runs while U.S. warships sail defiantly through the Taiwan Strait. Neither military acknowledges the other directly, maintaining the quantum state of non-confrontation while actively preparing for confrontation.

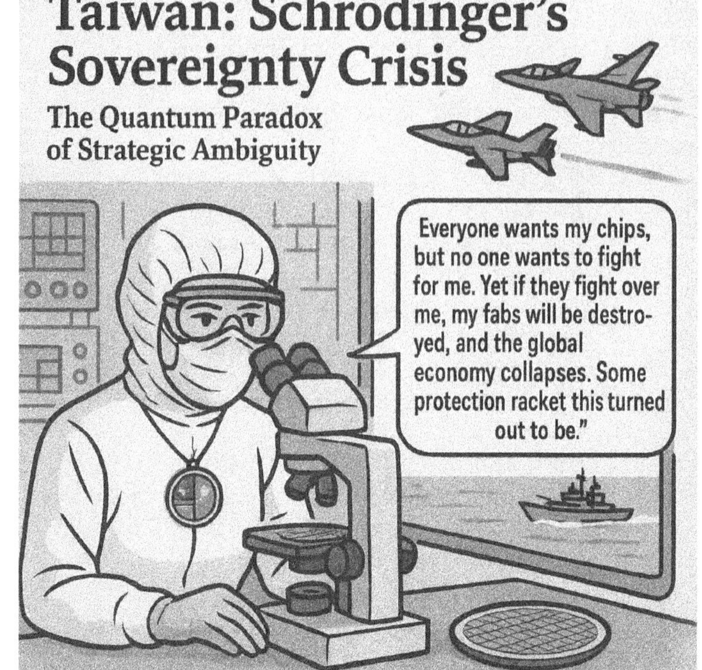
Taiwan: Schrödinger's Sovereignty Crisis
The Quantum Paradox of Strategic Ambiguity
Everyone wants my chips, but no one wants to fight for me. Yet if they fight over me, my fabs will be destroyed, and the global economy collapses. Some protection racket this turned out to be."

Taiwan represents the most dangerous flashpoint in U.S.-China relationship–a 'Schrodinger's sovereignty' crisis where Taiwan's status exists in a quantum superposition. It is simultaneously treated

- An independent democratic nation (functionally)
- A renegade province (in Beijing's view)
- A vital economic node (for the global economy)
- A security partner (for the U.S.)
- An unfinished civil war (historically)

Taiwan represents the most dangerous flashpoint in the U.S.-China relatiunchip–a "Schrodinger's sovereignty" crisis where Taiwan's

Madame Semiconductor: "Everyone wants my chips, but no one wants to fight for me. Yet if they fight *over* me, my fabs will be destroyed, and the global economy will collapse. Some protection racket this turned out to be."

Taiwan represents the most dangerous flashpoint in the U.S.-China relationship—a "Schrödinger's sovereignty" crisis where Taiwan's status exists in a quantum superposition. It is simultaneously treated as:

★ An independent democratic nation (functionally)
★ A non-state actor (legally, for most countries)
★ A renegade province (in Beijing's view)
★ A vital economic node (for the global economy)
★ A security partner (for the U.S.)
★ An unfinished civil war (historically)

America's approach to this paradox has been "strategic ambiguity"—a policy maintaining deliberate uncertainty about precisely how the U.S. would respond to a Chinese attack on Taiwan. This ambiguity aims to deter Beijing (by raising the possibility of U.S. intervention) while restraining Taipei (by withholding security guarantees that might encourage independence declarations).

Admiral Self-Assurance: "Our strategic ambiguity policy creates useful uncertainty that deters adventurism by either party."

Minister Patience: "Your strategic ambiguity increasingly appears to be strategic confusion—unclear to yourselves as much as to others. This is not the deterrent you imagine."

The policy's effectiveness depends on maintaining a credible military capability to defend Taiwan if necessary—a requirement that is growing more challenging as China's military modernization progresses. Pentagon war games reportedly show the U.S. facing significant losses in Taiwan conflict scenarios, raising questions about whether strategic ambiguity remains viable as the military balance shifts.

From Strategic Asset to Silicon Shield: Taiwan's Evolving Significance

Taiwan's geopolitical importance has evolved dramatically:

★ **1950s-1980s:** Anti-communist bulwark during the Cold War
★ **1990s-2000s:** Emerging democracy and export powerhouse
★ **2010s-Present:** Semiconductor superpower essential to global tech supply chains

This evolution transformed Taiwan from a one-dimensional Cold War asset to a multi-dimensional strategic linchpin. Taiwan Semiconductor Manufacturing Company (TSMC) now produces approximately 90% of the world's advanced semiconductors—chips essential for everything from consumer electronics to military systems.

Madame Semiconductor: "My factories produce chips used in American F-35 fighters, Chinese telecommunications equipment, European automobiles, and everyone's smartphones. I'm not just making components; I'm manufacturing leverage."

This semiconductor dominance creates a "silicon shield"—the theory that Taiwan's indispensability to global technology supply chains deters Chinese military action since an invasion would jeopardize access to these critical chips. However, this same concentration of vital production creates vulnerability for the global economy and national security systems dependent on these semiconductors.

The resulting dynamic is unprecedented in geopolitical history: a relatively small territory (23.5 million people, 36,193 km^2) holding asymmetric leverage over superpower competition through specialized manufacturing capacity developed across decades.

The Three Scenarios: Conflict Pathways and Probability Assessment

Scenario 1: The Lightning Strike (Probability: Moderate) - Beijing launches a surprise comprehensive attack, utilizing missile strikes, cyber operations, and rapid amphibious and airborne assaults, to overwhelm Taiwan's defenses

before significant external intervention can arrive. This approach depends on speed and shock to present the world with a fait accompli.

Key factors influencing probability:

★ PLA assessment of operational readiness for complex joint operations
★ The Chinese leadership's perception of closing windows of opportunity
★ Evaluation of U.S. resolve and capability to respond effectively

Scenario 2: The Incremental Squeeze (Probability: High) China increases pressure gradually—expanding gray zone operations, implementing selective economic coercion, intensifying military exercises, and potentially establishing a partial blockade—stopping short of full invasion while making Taiwan's status quo position increasingly untenable.

Key factors influencing probability:

★ Taiwan's resilience against multi-domain pressure
★ The international community's willingness to impose costs on China for the escalation
★ Effectiveness of U.S.-led deterrence measures

Scenario 3: Miscalculation Spiral (Probability: Significant and Rising) Neither side seeks war initially, but a crisis emerges from an incident—perhaps a collision between military aircraft, an accident involving fishing vessels, or a political crisis in Taiwan. The incident escalates through misperception, communication failures, or domestic political dynamics that limit leaders' flexibility.

Key factors influencing probability:

★ Existence and utilization of crisis management mechanisms
★ Domestic political constraints on leadership in all capitals
★ Military activities in proximity without adequate communication channels

These scenarios represent distinct pathways to potential conflict, each with different warning indicators, timeframes, and international response options. The miscalculation spiral may represent the most dangerous scenario precisely because it isn't planned, thereby reducing the effectiveness of traditional deterrence frameworks that focus on cost-benefit calculations.

The Taiwan Policy Quantum State: Strategic Confusion Masquerading as Flexibility

[SATIRICAL DOCUMENT: TAIWAN POLICY MEASUREMENT PROBLEM]

CLASSIFICATION: QUANTUM ENTANGLED//STRATEGICALLY SUPERPOSITIONED

National Security Council
Theoretical Physics Division

SUBJECT: Wave Function Collapse in Taiwan Defense Policy

QUANTUM POLICY STATUS: Current U.S.-Taiwan policy exists in a carefully maintained state of quantum superposition, simultaneously occupying all possible policy positions until observation forces collapse into a definite state.

POLICY SUPERPOSITION STATES:

★ We will definitely defend Taiwan (a Military planning state)
★ We might protect Taiwan (Diplomatic statement state)
★ Taiwan must decide its own future (a Democracy promotion state)
★ There is only one China (Beijing engagement state)
★ Taiwan's status is undetermined (Legal position state)

WARNING: Any attempt to directly observe actual policy causes immediate wavefunction collapse, potentially resulting in strategic incoherence. Maintain quantum uncertainty at all costs!

SCHRÖDINGER'S DEFENSE COMMITMENT: Like the famous cat simultaneously dead and alive in a box, our commitment to Taiwan's defense is simultaneously absolute and conditional until observed. Do not open the box!

TAIWAN POLICY MEASUREMENTT PROBLEM

CLASSIFICATION: QUANTUM ENTANGLED//STRATEGICALLY SUPERPOSITIONED

National Security Council
Theoretical Physics Division

QUANTUM POLICY STATUS:
Current U.S. Taiwan policy exists in a carefully maintained state of quantum superposition, simultaneously occupying all possible policy positions until observation forces collapse into a definite state.

POLICY SUPERPOSITION STATES:

- We will definitely defend Taiwan (Military planning state)
- We might defend Taiwan (Diplomatic statement state)
- Taiwan must decide its own future (Democracy promotion state
- There is only one China (Beijing engagement state)
- Taiwan's status is undetermined (Legal position state)

WARNING: Any attempt to directly observe actual policy causes immediate wavefunction collapse, potentially resulting in strategic incoherence. Maintain quantum uncertainty at all costs!

SCHRÖDINGER'S DEFENSE COMMITMENT: Like the fanous cat simultaneously dead and alive in a box, our commitment to Taiwan's defense is simultaneously absolute and conditional until observed. Do not open the box!

QUANTUM ENTANGLEMENT RISKS: Taiwan policy has quantun-entangled with domestic political polarization. Attempting to measure one inmediately affects the other, creating partisan wavefunction collapse.

RECOMMENDED APPROACH: Continue maintaining policy in superposition state while hoping no event forces

QUANTUM ENTANGLEMENT RISKS: Taiwan's policy has become quantum-entangled with domestic political polarization. Attempting to measure one immediately affects the other, creating a partisan wave function collapse.

RECOMMENDED APPROACH: Continue maintaining the policy in a superposition state, hoping that no event forces observation and subsequent collapse into a definite position that we cannot predict until measurement occurs.

//END SATIRICAL DOCUMENT//

This satirical quantum physics framework captures a serious strategic challenge: America's Taiwan policy contains genuine internal contradictions that become more problematic as the cross-strait military balance shifts. Strategic ambiguity functioned effectively when American military superiority was unquestioned, but as that advantage erodes, the contradiction between commitments and capabilities creates dangerous uncertainty.

China has pursued a systematic approach to changing this dynamic:

1. Building anti-access/area-denial capabilities specifically targeting U.S. carrier groups and forward bases
2. Developing amphibious and airborne assault capabilities tailored for Taiwan scenarios
3. Expanding gray zone operations that test responses without triggering direct conflict
4. Cultivating economic leverage over Taiwan's economy through trade dependencies
5. Conducting information operations targeting Taiwan's population to undermine resistance will

These efforts aim to shift the cross-strait military balance decisively while raising the perceived cost of U.S. intervention, effectively neutralizing strategic ambiguity by making it increasingly incredible.

Admiral Self-Assurance: "Our forces maintain the capability to intervene decisively in any Taiwan contingency."

Minister Patience: "Perhaps. But at what cost? Your war games show catastrophic losses. As that reality becomes clearer, your strategic ambiguity becomes simply strategic reluctance poorly disguised."

The Taiwan situation thus represents a geopolitical paradox: maintaining the status quo requires credible threats to change it (via U.S. military intervention), while transforming it risks destroying the very prize both sides seek (via damaging Taiwan's semiconductor ecosystem in conflict). This paradox has no easy resolution within existing strategic frameworks—a classic case where the geopolitical gods must indeed be crazy.

4. SOUTH CHINA SEA: MARITIME MISCHIEF AND CONCRETE ARCHIPELAGOS

> *"Occupy the field first and await the tired enemy."*
>
> —Sun Tzu, The Art of War, Chapter 6

The Great Sandcastle Competition: Real Estate Development with Artillery

In the azure waters of the South China Sea, **Admiral Island-Builder** stands proudly atop a massive dredging vessel, watching as mountains of sand transform a barely submerged reef into an artificial island. Construction crews race to build runways, radar installations, and missile shelters before international objections mount.

Admiral Island-Builder: "Gentlemen, welcome to Fiery Cross Reef Island Resort! We've developed 2.74 square kilometers of prime real estate, featuring excellent air connectivity, comprehensive surveillance amenities, and robust anti-ship missile facilities. The weather monitoring station is particularly accurate at tracking hostile aircraft!"

Foreign Journalist: "This looks like a military base, not a weather station."

Polly Propaganda: *(intervening smoothly)* "These are peaceful weather research facilities contributing to navigational safety for all nations! The missiles are for monitoring... extreme weather events."

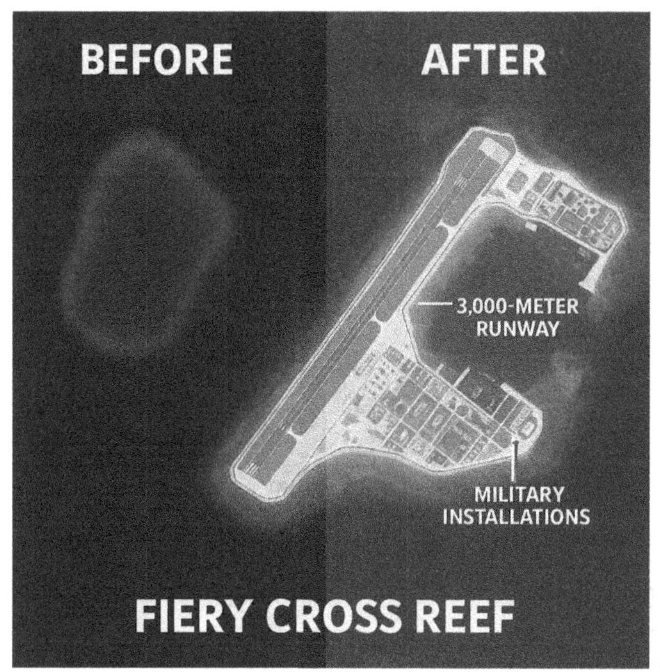

Admiral Island-Builder: *(whispering)* "She's good, isn't she? Last month, these were 'fishermen's shelters' despite the nearest fishing grounds being 600 kilometers away."

The South China Sea dispute represents a masterclass in fait accompli strategy—changing facts on the ground so gradually that each step elicits protest but insufficient resistance to halt the overall progression. Between 2013 and 2016, China transformed seven features in the Spratly Islands from largely submerged reefs into substantial artificial islands spanning over 3,200 acres.

This approach cleverly navigated between thresholds, each dredging operation insufficiently provocative to trigger a military response. Still, the cumulative effect created a network of militarized outposts extending China's effective control hundreds of kilometers beyond its coastline.

The nine-dash line—China's expansive claim, which encompasses roughly 90% of the South China Sea—defies conventional international law frameworks. Despite the 2016 ruling by the Permanent Court of Arbitration in The Hague invalidating these claims, China simply ignored the verdict and continued its island-building campaign.

The Maritime Claim Absurdity Index: Creative Legal Cartography
[SATIRICAL LEGAL GUIDE: HOW TO CLAIM AN OCEAN]
CLASSIFICATION: LEGALLY DUBIOUS//HISTORICALLY CREATIVE
Ministry of Creative Geography and Retroactive Sovereignty
Department of Maritime Acquisition

THE COMPREHENSIVE GUIDE TO CLAIMING VAST OCEAN AREAS

STEP 1: DISCOVER ANCIENT MAPS Locate (or commission) ancient-looking maps showing your historical claims. Antiqued parchment and strategically placed tea stains enhance credibility. Remember: the vaguer the boundaries, the better for flexible modern interpretation!

STEP 2: INVENT HISTORICAL NARRATIVES Develop compelling stories about your ancient mariners who definitely visited these areas before anyone else. If no physical evidence exists, cite "oral traditions" and "lost records."

STEP 3: DRAW CREATIVE LINES Boundaries should be deliberately ambiguous:

★ Dashed lines are ideal (allow for adjusting positions later)
★ Avoid precise coordinates (limits future expansion)
★ Use phrases like "traditional fishing grounds" (infinitely elastic concept)

STEP 4: MANUFACTURE ARTIFICIAL GEOGRAPHY If your claims lack actual land features, create them!

★ Dredging equipment: your best friend
★ Concrete: nature's most natural island-building material
★ Weather stations: universal euphemism for military installations

STEP 5: REJECT INCONVENIENT LEGAL RULINGS When international tribunals rule against you:

★ Question their jurisdiction
★ Invoke "historical rights" (unspecified)
★ Declare that "national sentiment" overrides international law
★ Continue construction while expressing outrage

THE MARITIME CLAIM ABSURDITY INDEX

A SATIRICAL GUIDE to CREATIVE LEGAL CARTOGRAPHY

MINISTRY OF CREATIVE GEOGRAPHY & RETROACTIVE SOVEREIGNTY
DEPARTMENT OF MARITIME ACQUISITION

1 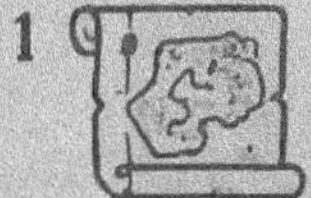
1 DISCOVER ANCIENT MAPS
Locate or commiission antigue maps; vaguer boundaries are preferable

2 
2 INVENT HISTORICAL NARRATIVES
Cite oral traditions and lost records

3 
3 DRAW CREATIVE LINES
• Use dashed lines, avoid coordinates
• Call "traditional fishing grounds "gouands"

4 
4 MANUFACTURE ARTIFICIAL GEOGRAPHY
• Dredging, concrete islands, aus euphemism

5 
5 REJECT INCONVENIENT LEGAL RULINGS
• Question Jurisdiotion, invoke "historical rights"
• Invoke "historical rights, "national sentiment

6 
6 DEPLOY PARAMILITARY ASSETS
• Fishing militia, "defensive," call "spontaneous

REMEMBER: With enough dredging, any submerged rock can become **sovereign territory!**

CLASSIFICATION: LEGALLY DUBIOUS // HISTORICALLY CREATIVE

STEP 6: DEPLOY PARAMILITARY ASSETS Fishing militia provides perfect deniability:

- ★ Armed fishing vessels = "civilian activities"
- ★ Ramming foreign ships = "defensive measures by scared fishermen"
- ★ Coordinated maritime militia operations = "spontaneous patriotic fishing"

REMEMBER: With sufficient dredging equipment and creative legal interpretation, any submerged rock can become sovereign territory!

//END SATIRICAL GUIDE//

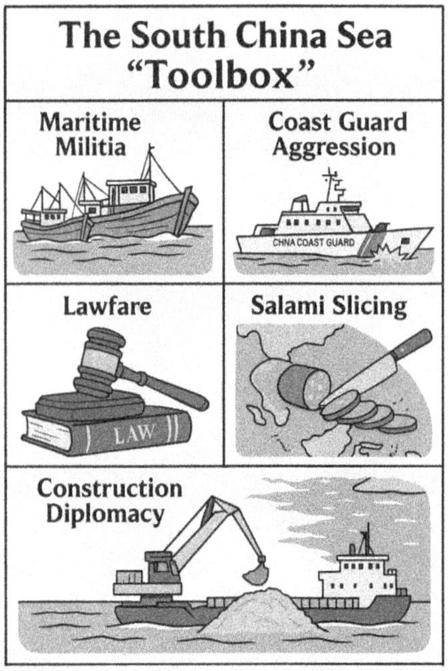

This satirical guide highlights a serious strategic innovation: China's systematic exploitation of gray zone tactics in maritime disputes. By operating between the thresholds of commercial activity and military operations, Beijing advances its interests while avoiding triggering alliance commitments or military responses that would risk kinetic conflict.

The South China Sea has become a laboratory for these approaches, with China employing a coordinated toolkit:

The South China Sea "Toolbox"

Maritime Militia | Coast Guard Aggression | Lawfare | Salami Slicing | Construction Diplomacy

Maritime Militia: "Fishing vessels" that harass foreign ships, swarm disputed areas, and create a presence without deploying naval assets

1. **Coast Guard Aggression:** Using white-hulled vessels (traditionally associated with safety) for increasingly militarized operations
2. **Lawfare:** Developing legal justifications, regardless of international law compatibility, to provide narrative coverage for expansion
3. **Salami Slicing:** Incremental changes too small individually to trigger a significant response, but cumulatively transformative
4. **Construction Diplomacy:** Building physical infrastructure that creates irreversible facts on the ground

This approach has proven remarkably effective. Despite international condemnation, freedom of navigation operations by the U.S. and its allies, as well as regional protests, China now exercises de facto control over features that were underwater a decade ago, extending its effective sovereignty hundreds of kilometers beyond what international law typically permits.

Admiral Legal Navigation: "The International Tribunal clearly ruled these claims have no basis in UNCLOS or customary international law."

Admiral Island-Builder: "Interesting perspective. Have you visited our new islands? They seem quite real despite your legal theories. Would you like to sail within 12 nautical miles to test your convictions?"

While legal arguments continue in diplomatic forums, the physical reality has undergone a transformation. The South China Sea case study demonstrates how determined powers can effectively rewrite rules-based orders not through frontal assault but through persistent, incremental challenges that exploit system enforcement limitations.

Stark Cost Comparison:
U.S. vs China Weapon Platforms

Platform	United States	China	Approximate Cost Ratio
Aircraft Carrier	$13+ billion	$4 b billion	3:1
Destroyer	$7+ billion	$920m million	7,6:1
Fighter Aircraft	$94+ million	$61m million	1,5:1
Anti-ship Missile	$3,9m million	$1,5m million	2,6:1
Anti-carrier Ballistic Missile	N/A	DF-21D $20 million	NA:1

5. ADMIRAL PROCUREMENT'S HARDWARE EMPORIUM: THE CAPABILITY GAP

> *"In war, seek victory, not length of campaign."*
> —Sun Tzu, The Art of War, Chapter 2

The $13 Billion Question: Asymmetric Warfare Economics

In a gleaming showroom at the Pentagon, **Admiral Procurement** proudly displays models of the U.S. military's crown jewels—Ford-class aircraft carriers, F-35 fighters, and Zumwalt-class destroyers. Behind him, digital price tags tick steadily upward in real-time as program costs continue rising.

Admiral Procurement: "Yes, the Ford-class carrier program will eventually cost approximately $13 billion per vessel. But can you really put a price on projecting American power anywhere on Earth? I mean, besides the price I just mentioned?"

General Budget: "Actually, I can put a very specific price on it, and we're approaching the point where we can't afford to lose even one of these exquisite platforms in combat. Each carrier now represents about 5% of our annual defense budget."

PLA Attaché: *(Observing quietly from the corner, taking notes)* "Most interesting. Their Ford-class carrier: $13 billion. Our DF-21D anti-ship ballistic missile: approximately $20 million. Cost ratio: 650:1. Even with imperfect targeting requiring multiple launches, the economic advantage is overwhelming."

This scene illustrates perhaps the most significant vulnerability in America's military posture: the increasing concentration of capability in a shrinking number of exquisite—and exquisitely expensive—platforms. This creates both economic and strategic asymmetries that China has systematically exploited in its military modernization.

The numbers tell a stark story:

Platform Comparison	United States	China	Approximate Cost Ratio
Aircraft Carrier	Ford-class: $13+ billion	Type 003: ~$4 billion	3:1
Destroyer	Zumwalt-class: $7+ billion	Type 055: ~$920 million	7.6:1
Fighter Aircraft	F-35C: $94+ million	J-15: ~$61 million	1.5:1
Anti-ship Missile	LRASM: $3.9 million	YJ-18: ~$1.5 million	2.6:1
Anti-carrier Ballistic Missile	N/A	DF-21D: ~$20 million	N/A:1

Beyond the unit costs, production timelines create further asymmetry. China can build ships at a pace the U.S. industrial base cannot currently match:

- ★ Type 055 destroyers: 8 launched in approximately 4 years
- ★ Arleigh Burke destroyers: 8 launched in approximately 8 years

This disparity reflects different procurement philosophies. The American approach prioritizes technological superiority—developing platforms with significant performance advantages over potential adversaries —while accepting higher costs and longer development cycles to achieve a technological overmatch. The Chinese approach emphasizes iterative improvement—fielding "good enough" systems that can be produced at scale, then steadily enhancing capabilities with each production block.

[SATIRICAL ADVERTISEMENT: ADMIRAL PROCUREMENT'S HARDWARE EMPORIUM]

CLASSIFICATION: FISCALLY IRRESPONSIBLE//TACTICALLY MAGNIFICENT
Department of Defense
Acquisition Excellence Initiative

ADMIRAL PROCUREMENT'S SPECTACULAR SPRING SALE!

FEATURED PLATFORMS:

THE FORD-CLASS CARRIER Only $13 Billion! (Plus operating costs, air wing, escort vessels, and inevitable overruns)

- ★ Amazing Power Projection Capability!
- ★ Impressive Blue Water Dominance!
- ★ Vulnerable to Anti-Ship Ballistic Missiles Costing 0.15% of Its Price!

THE F-35 JOINT STRIKE FIGHTER Starting at Just $94 Million Per Unit! (Total program: $1.7 trillion!)

- ★ Incredible Stealth Capabilities!*
- ★ Revolutionary Sensor Fusion!**
- ★ Perfect for Deploying from Those Vulnerable Carriers!

THE ZUMWALT-CLASS DESTROYER Only $7 Billion Each! (Ammunition sold separately—VERY separately, as we canceled production)

★ Futuristic Design Guaranteed to Impress Congressional Delegations!
★ Advanced Gun System That Literally Has No Ammunition!
★ Limited Production Run Ensuring Maximum Per-Unit Cost!

BONUS OFFER: For every platform purchased, receive a FREE analysis explaining why we need even more expensive platforms to protect these platforms!

*May be compromised by advancing detection technologies

**When software updates work properly

BUT WAIT, THERE'S MORE! Ask about our special "Cost-Plus" contracting deals! You'll be amazed how quickly we can transform budget overruns into shareholder value!

//END SATIRICAL ADVERTISEMENT//

This satirical advertisement highlights a serious strategic vulnerability: America's emphasis on exquisite, expensive platforms creates asymmetric cost impositions favoring adversaries. When a multi-million-dollar missile can threaten a multi-billion-dollar platform, the economic calculus of conflict fundamentally shifts.

China has deliberately exploited this vulnerability by developing what strategists call "assassin's mace" capabilities (杀手锏, shashoujian)—weapons specifically designed to neutralize U.S. advantages at a fraction of the cost. The DF-21D "carrier killer" missile exemplifies this approach, threatening aircraft carriers that cost 650 times more than the missile designed to destroy them.

This asymmetry extends beyond hardware to operational concepts. American power projection depends on access to forward bases and maritime freedom of action—precisely the capabilities China's anti-access/area-denial strategy targets. By focusing on preventing U.S. forces from operating effectively within the "first island chain," China creates a cost-effective counter to American power projection without attempting to match it symmetrically.

The Platform Addiction: Institutional Inertia Versus Strategic Reality

General Actual Combat: "War games consistently show our current force structure performs poorly against Chinese A2/AD capabilities. We need distributed, resilient networks of smaller platforms rather than concentrating capability on a few exquisite targets."

Admiral Procurement: "But smaller platforms aren't as impressive at congressional hearings! The major contractors have already designed their next-generation, exquisite systems. Think of the shareholders!"

Senator District Interest: "I've been informed that any shift away from the current acquisition programs would impact jobs in my state. This is clearly unacceptable for national security reasons that coincidentally align with my reelection prospects."

America's procurement challenges extend beyond cost ratios to institutional dynamics that perpetuate suboptimal strategic choices:

1. **Service Parochialism:** Each military service protects its historic missions and platforms, regardless of evolving threats
2. **Contractor Influence:** The Defense industry prioritizes high-margin programs over strategic effectiveness
3. **Congressional Intervention:** Representatives prioritize district employment over strategic requirements
4. **Requirements Creep:** The pursuit of perfection leads to ever-expanding capabilities, costs, and timelines
5. **Risk Aversion:** Career incentives punish failed innovation more than they reward successful adaptation

These dynamics create powerful institutional resistance to the changes that most analysts agree are necessary, shifting from a small number of exquisite platforms to larger numbers of distributed, networked, and resilient systems that are better suited to counter China's A2/AD strategy.

The result is a growing capability gap, not in absolute terms, but in terms of cost-effectiveness and strategic alignment. America's immense defense budget yields extraordinary capabilities, but it is increasingly misaligned with the specific challenges China presents in the Western Pacific.

6. THE TRUMP WILDCARD: STRATEGIC VOLATILITY AS DOCTRINE

> *"In the midst of chaos, there is also opportunity."*
> —Sun Tzu, The Art of War, Chapter 5

Transactional Diplomacy Meets Relational Geopolitics

In an ornate diplomatic reception room, **Uncle Sam** dramatically tears up a multilateral agreement while horrified allies watch from one corner. From another corner, **Minister Patience** observes quietly, taking mental notes on alliance fissures to exploit.

[SATIRICAL ANALYTICAL TOOL: THE STRATEGIC MOOD SWING INDEX]

THE STRATEGIC MOOD SWING INDEX

MEASURING POLICY VOLATILITY

CLASSIFICATION: DIPLOMATICALLY TERRIFYING // STRATEGICALLY UNPREDICTABLE

Bureau of Fluctuating Foreign Policy
Presidential Volatility Assessment Diision

Presidential Volatility Assessment Division

HISTORICAL SMSI MEASUREMENTS:

A scientific(-ish) measure of foreign policy predictability calculated using proprietary algorithms combining:

- Presidential tweet sentiment analysis
- Cable news coverage fluctuations
- Staff turnover velocity
- Allied panic indicators
- Diplomatic clarification frequency

(ERROR: CALCULATOR EXPLODED)

HISTOR/CAL SMI HIESUREMENTS	
Eisenhower Admin.	3.2
Nixon Administration	42.7
Obama Administration	26.4
Trump 10 Administraion	157.6
Biden Administration	29.3
Trurp 20 Projections.	IERROR:
CALCULATOR EXPLODED!	

American strategic velatility has itself become a predictable feature of the international system. The only certainty is uncertainty.

POLICY IMPLICATIONS:

- Traditional allies increasingly perceive U.S. commitments as administration-dependent
- Strategic competliors increasingly view democratic transitions as opportunities for advantage
- Foreign policy establishment increasingly resembles trauma response unit

RECOMMENDATION:

- Developing independent capabilities
- Securing written committments (though these may be disregardect)
- Exploring alternative securify arrangements

//END SATIRICAL ANALYTICAL TODL//

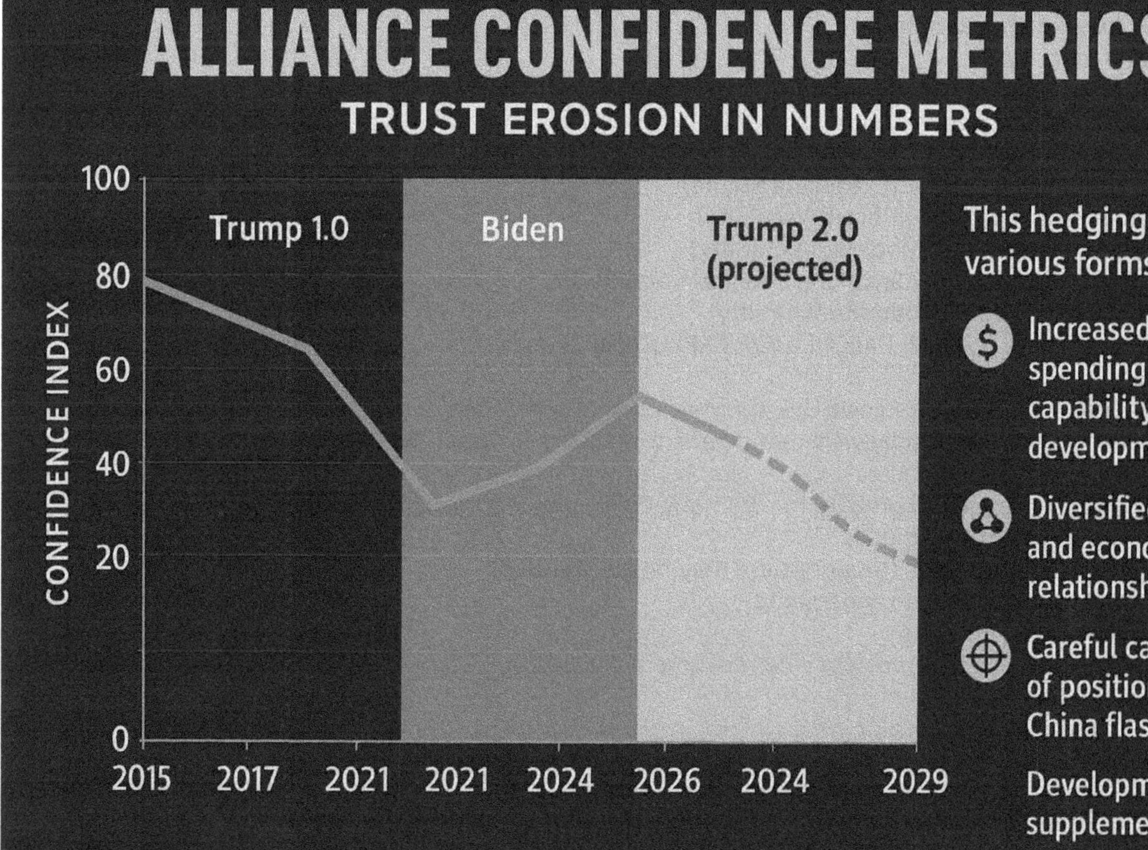

This hedging takes various forms:

- Increased defense spending and capability development
- Diversified diplomatic and economic relationships
- Careful calibration of positions on U.S.–China flashpoints

Development of supplementarysecurity

Uncle Sam: "Terrible deal! The worst! We're renegotiating everything. America First! Maybe we'll defend you, maybe we won't—depends on what you're offering. Bidding starts now!"

Nervous Ally: "But... we've been treaty partners for 70 years. Our security architecture is built on mutual commitments and predictable American leadership."

Uncle Sam: "Yeah, but what have you done for me lately? Show me the money!"

Minister Patience: *(Whispering to an aide)* "Most interesting. They view alliances as transaction costs rather than strategic assets. This creates opportunities we had not anticipated."

The Trump administration (2017-2021) fundamentally challenged postwar assumptions about American foreign policy continuity, treating alliances as transactional arrangements rather than strategic commitments. This approach created fissures in alliance systems that China methodically exploited through targeted diplomacy, economic incentives, and strategic patience.

Trump 2.0 presents a similar potential for strategic volatility, which may be magnified by the institutional knowledge gained during the first term. The uncertainty surrounding America's commitment to allies, international agreements, and consistent policy positions creates both challenges and opportunities for Beijing.

The Alliance Confidence Metrics: Trust Erosion in Numbers

The data tell a striking story: Alliance confidence—the belief among U.S. treaty partners that the United States will fulfill its security commitments—declined significantly during Trump's first term. While some recovery occurred under Biden, Trump 2.0 has renewed uncertainty, prompting allies to hedge their bets.

This hedging takes various forms:

★ Increased defense spending and capability development
★ Diversified diplomatic and economic relationships
★ Careful calibration of positions on U.S.-China flashpoints
★ Development of supplementary security arrangements

These responses reflect a fundamental recalculation of risk among allies, who can no longer take American strategic consistency across administrations for granted.

The Strategic Mood Swing Index: Measuring Policy Volatility

[SATIRICAL ANALYTICAL TOOL: THE STRATEGIC MOOD SWING INDEX]

CLASSIFICATION: DIPLOMATICALLY TERRIFYING//STRATEGICALLY UNPREDICTABLE

Bureau of Fluctuating Foreign Policy
Presidential Volatility Assessment Division

THE STRATEGIC MOOD SWING INDEX (SMSI)

A scientific(-ish) measure of foreign policy predictability calculated using proprietary algorithms combining:

★ Presidential tweet sentiment analysis
★ Cable news coverage fluctuations
★ Staff turnover velocity
★ Allied panic indicators
★ Diplomatic clarification frequency

HISTORICAL SMSI MEASUREMENTS:

★ Eisenhower Administration: 3.2 (Extremely Stable)
★ Nixon Administration: 42.7 (Significant Volatility)
★ Obama Administration: 26.4 (Moderate Volatility)
★ Trump 1.0 Administration: 157.9 (Unprecedented Volatility)
★ Biden Administration: 29.3 (Moderate Volatility)
★ Trump 2.0 Projections: [ERROR: CALCULATOR EXPLODED]

POLICY IMPLICATIONS:

1. Traditional allies increasingly perceive U.S. commitments as administration-dependent
2. Strategic competitors increasingly view democratic transitions as opportunities for advantage
3. Foreign policy establishment increasingly resembles a trauma response unit

RECOMMENDATION: Allies should prepare for dramatic policy oscillations by:

★ Developing independent capabilities
★ Securing written commitments (though these may be disregarded)
★ Exploring alternative security arrangements
★ Stockpiling diplomatic antacids

CONCLUSION: American strategic volatility has become a predictable feature of the international system itself. The only certainty is uncertainty.

//END SATIRICAL ANALYTICAL TOOL//

This satirical index highlights a serious strategic vulnerability: American policy volatility is increasingly becoming a structural feature rather than a temporary aberration in international relations. This volatility creates particular challenges in the China context, where Beijing's consistent long-term approach contrasts sharply with Washington's oscillations.

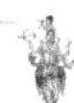

The consequences manifest in several domains:

1. **Alliance Strain:** Partners question America's reliability across administrative transitions
2. **Strategic Opportunism:** China's times initiatives to exploit predictable U.S. transition periods
3. **Long-term Planning:** States hesitate to commit to U.S.-led initiatives that might be abandoned
4. **Reputation Costs:** American credibility suffers cumulative damage with each dramatic reversal
5. **Domestic Institutional Fatigue:** Foreign policy bureaucracy struggles with whiplash changes

These dynamics create a self-reinforcing cycle: as U.S. policy grows more volatile, partners hedge their bets, creating facts on the ground that further complicate policy coherence, prompting more dramatic course corrections with each transition.

Minister Patience: "Your four-year election cycles increasingly resemble strategic seizures rather than democratic transitions. While we maintain consistent focus across decades, you reinvent your China policy with each administration. This gives us a significant structural advantage."

Uncle Sam: "Our democratic system is our greatest strength! Sure, we occasionally get presidents who reverse everything their predecessors did, treat allies like protection rackets, and conduct foreign policy via social media... but that's the price of freedom!"

Minister Patience: *(Smiling diplomatically)* "Indeed. Please continue."

China has adapted its approach to this reality, developing strategies to exploit American transitions while maintaining its own policy continuity. This creates an asymmetric advantage in long-term competition precisely because Beijing can plan across transition periods that frequently reset American initiatives.

7. THE GRAY ZONE BETWEEN PEACE AND WAR

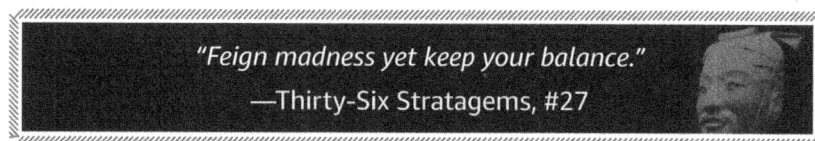

> *"Feign madness yet keep your balance."*
> —Thirty-Six Stratagems, #27

The Warfare Euphemism Dictionary: Conflict by Other Names

In a conceptually ambiguous war room, **General Binary** and **General Spectrum** engage in heated debate over a series of incidents in disputed waters. On screens around them, fishing vessels ram commercial ships, cyber intrusions disrupt critical infrastructure, and information operations flood social media platforms—yet no formal hostilities have been declared.

General Binary: "This is either peace or war! There's no in-between! We need clear thresholds that trigger a decisive military response."

General Spectrum: "That binary thinking is dangerously outdated. Our adversaries deliberately operate in the gray zone between peace and war—using coercion without crossing thresholds that trigger conventional conflict."

General Binary: "So what are we supposed to do? Respond to fishing boat harassment with aircraft carriers? Deploy Cyber Command against propaganda tweets? The warfare concepts you're describing have no clarity!"

General Spectrum: "Precisely. That ambiguity is a weapon our adversaries wield effectively against our binary institutional thinking."

This dialogue captures a fundamental challenge in contemporary great power competition: the traditional distinction between "war" and "peace" has dissolved into a spectrum of competitive activities deliberately calibrated to achieve strategic goals without triggering conventional conflict.

China has developed sophisticated gray zone operations across multiple domains:

1. **Maritime Gray Zone:** Using coast guard and maritime militia vessels for aggressive actions while avoiding naval confrontation
2. **Economic Coercion:** Deploying targeted sanctions, import restrictions, and market access manipulation below the threshold of formal economic warfare
3. **Cyber Operations:** Conducting espionage, intellectual property theft, and infrastructure probing that stops short of destructive attacks
4. **Information Operations:** Deploying propaganda, disinformation, and influence campaigns to shape perceptions and exacerbate societal divisions
5. **Legal Warfare:** Exploiting international law as an asymmetric tool while selectively ignoring rulings counter to Chinese interests

These operations exploit the institutional, legal, and cognitive frameworks that govern Western responses to security challenges. Democracies struggle with gray zone activities precisely because they blur the traditionally clear lines that determine which government agencies respond, what authorities apply, and how resources are allocated.

[SATIRICAL TAXONOMY: THE WARFARE EUPHEMISM DICTIONARY]

CLASSIFICATION: LINGUISTICALLY CREATIVE//STRATEGICALLY CONFUSING
Institute for Conflict Rebranding
Department of Euphemistic Security

THE COMPREHENSIVE WARFARE EUPHEMISM DICTIONARY

Traditional Terms:

★ WAR: Absolutely never use this term! Replace with "kinetic military action" or "freedom enhancement operation."

Domain-Specific Euphemisms:

★ NAVAL BLOCKADE → "Maritime zone management"
★ CYBER ATTACK → "Unauthorized digital policy implementation"
★ PROPAGANDA → "Narrative sovereignty protection"
★ ECONOMIC WARFARE → "Market access recalibration"
★ TERRITORIAL SEIZURE → "Administrative boundary clarification"

Activity-Specific Terminology:

★ SINKING FISHING VESSELS → "Fisheries resource management incident"
★ JAMMING COMMUNICATIONS → "Electromagnetic environment regulation"
★ MILITIA HARASSMENT → "Enthusiastic civilian maritime activities"
★ HACKING INFRASTRUCTURE → "Network security verification exercise"
★ CLAIMING TERRITORY → "Historical rights assertion"

Escalation Indicators:

★ PEACE → "Pre-competitive environment"
★ COMPETITION → "Dynamic security engagement"
★ CONFRONTATION → "Assertive interest protection"
★ CONFLICT → "Non-consensual security interaction"
★ WAR → [REDACTED FOR DIPLOMATIC REASONS]

REMEMBER: If you don't call it "war," it technically isn't! International law hates this one simple trick!

//END SATIRICAL TAXONOMY//

SATIRICAL TAXONOMY:
THE WARFARE EUPHEMISM DICTIONARY

CLASSIFICATION: LINGUISTICALLY CREATIVE/STRATEGICALLY CONFUSING

Institute for Conflict Rebranding
Department of Euphemistic Security

Traditional Terms

WAR: Absolutely never use this term! Replace with "kinetic military action" or 'freedoin enhancemoperation)

Domain-Specific Euphemisms

NAVAL BLOCKADE	→ Maritime zone management
CYBER ATTACK	→ Unauthorized digital policy implementadion
PROPAGANDA	→ Narrative sovereignty protection
ECONOMIC WARFARE	→ Market access recallbration
TERRITORIAL SEIZURE	→ Administrative boundary clarification

Activity-Specific Terminology

PEACE	→ Pre-competitive environment
COMPETITION	→ Dynamic security engagement
CONFRONTATION	→ Assertive interest protection
CONFLICT	→ Non-consensual security interaction
WAR	[REDACTED FOR DIPLOMAATIC REASONS]

REMEMBER: If you don't call it "war." it technically isn't! international law hates this one simple trick!

This satirical dictionary highlights a serious strategic innovation: the deliberate exploitation of linguistic and legal ambiguity to advance interests while avoiding triggers for conventional conflict response. China has mastered this approach, developing a comprehensive toolkit for operating effectively in this gray zone.

American policymakers must develop effective counters to gray zone operations without escalating to conventional conflict. This requires institutional adaptation, doctrinal innovation, and cognitive flexibility that don't come naturally to bureaucracies designed for clearer distinctions between war and peace.

Infrastructure as Geopolitics: The Physical Manifestation of Influence

The competition between China and the United States increasingly plays out through infrastructure development—physical manifestations of influence and connectivity that shape strategic options for decades:

★ China's Belt and Road Initiative has funded ports, railways, power plants, and telecommunications networks across Asia, Africa, and beyond
★ America's Build Back Better World (B3W) and Blue Dot Network are responses that attempt to provide alternatives to Chinese financing.
★ Digital infrastructure—from 5G networks to undersea cables—creates long-term dependencies and potential vulnerabilities.

Through BRI investments and leases, Chinese firms now manage or have significant stakes in ports stretching from the South China Sea to the Mediterranean. Colombo (Sri Lanka), Karachi (Pakistan), Djibouti, Mombasa (Kenya),

Piraeus (Greece), Panama's ports, and most recently Port Sudan and Yemen's Aden Port (both acquired in 2024-2025) have seen major Chinese involvement.

Most of these are legitimate commercial ventures designed to boost trade. But a port built for commercial use today can host naval visits tomorrow. China's navy has already used commercial ports for resupply. The **Djibouti** base is a notable military exception—a fully fledged PLA Navy base operating under the guise of a logistics facility—built after Djibouti accumulated significant debts to China. Reports in 2025 suggested China is negotiating similar arrangements with Cambodia and Myanmar.

This infrastructure competition represents competition by other means—creating influence, leverage, and potentially military advantage through ostensibly civilian projects. Ports built with Chinese financing sometimes contain dual-use capabilities suitable for PLA Navy visits; telecommunications networks built with Chinese technology potentially enable intelligence collection; power grids and transportation hubs create economic dependencies that translate into diplomatic leverage.

McSlicey the Priest: "Our analysis suggests robust infrastructure investment generates 47.3% enhancement in strategic position metrics with favorable ROI across multiple influence indicators."

Milton the Trickster Economist: "Let the private sector handle infrastructure! Government-led development is inefficient and distorts market signals!"

Uncle Sam: *(looking at maps showing Chinese-built ports across key maritime chokepoints)* "I'm starting to think there might be strategic value in infrastructure beyond quarterly returns..."

America's challenge in this domain stems partly from its economic model, which prioritizes private sector-led development over strategic positioning. At the same time, China's state-directed approach explicitly integrates economic and strategic objectives. This creates asymmetric capacity to deploy infrastructure as a strategic tool—a gap America has only recently begun addressing through initiatives like the Blue Dot Network.

Chapter Transition: From Geopolitical Competition to Economic Enablers

As our geopolitical examination concludes, we turn toward the economic foundations that both enable and constrain this competition. The paradox becomes clear: the very economic interdependence created during America's engagement era now functions simultaneously as a mutual hostage situation and competitive battleground.

The economic choices made during the past three decades—outsourcing manufacturing, optimizing supply chains for efficiency rather than resilience, prioritizing short-term shareholder returns over strategic industrial capacity—created vulnerabilities that China has systematically exploited. Yet complete economic decoupling remains nearly impossible without devastating consequences for both economies and the global system.

In our next chapter, we'll examine how America's economic choices created the vulnerabilities now threatening its strategic position. The story that emerges is not primarily one of Chinese strategic brilliance but of American strategic self-sabotage—economic decisions made with little regard for their long-term security implications.

Milton the Trickster Economist: *(chuckling as he exits)* "I told them unfettered markets would produce optimal outcomes! I just didn't specify for whom!"

Conclusion: Diagnosis Complete, Prognosis Uncertain

Our diagnostic scan of the US-China rivalry reveals a geopolitical patient with concerning symptoms on both sides. China pursues patient, methodical "national rejuvenation" with civilizational time horizons, while America's response oscillates between engagement and confrontation with each election cycle. The flashpoints—Taiwan, the South China Sea, technological competition—grow more volatile as military capabilities advance and economic entanglements both bind and divide these powers.

The situation defies simple prescriptions. Given fundamentally divergent visions of the world order, strategic competition appears inevitable, yet catastrophic conflict remains too devastating to contemplate. The resulting uneasy equilibrium—competition without resolution, rivalry without rules—creates a dangerous new normal in international relations.

As we proceed in our examination, we'll explore potential treatment options for this geopolitical condition. But one conclusion seems inescapable: in this high-stakes game where celestial chess meets American checkers, the gods of geopolitics must indeed be crazy—and the mortals in charge don't seem to be faring much better.

Uncle Xi: *(placing a final stone)* "The East is rising, the West is declining. History's verdict approaches."

Uncle Sam: *(moving a checker decisively)* "Democracy will outlast authoritarianism. Freedom always finds a way."

Madame Semiconductor: *(from her clean room window)* "If you two could stop posturing and focus on not blowing up my fabrication plants, that would be great for everyone."

The gods may indeed be crazy to have arranged this precarious configuration of power, technology, and conflicting visions. However, humans need not respond equally irrationally. Understanding the dynamics at play—from strategic asymmetries to institutional inertia to gray zone competition—creates a possibility space for wiser choices on both sides.

The game continues, and the next moves will be determined not by abstract forces but by concrete human decisions—choices that will echo through generations to come.

CHAPTER 3: FINANCIAL ENGINEERING AND AMERICA'S ECONOMIC EROSION: THE GODS MUST BE CRAZY: HOW WALL STREET GIFT-WRAPPED AMERICA'S INDUSTRIAL FUTURE AND MAILED IT TO BEIJING

> *"He who wishes to fight must first count the cost."*
> —Sun Tzu, The Art of War, Chapter 2

EXECUTIVE BRIEFING

Strategic Snapshot

While Beijing built factories, Wall Street built spreadsheets. Three decades of **buybacks, leveraged buyouts, and tax-haven shenanigans have shrunk** America's "industrial commons" to a museum piece now curated in Shenzhen.

Core Findings — Inside the Financial Coke Bottle

1. **Shareholder-Value Cargo Cult**—The financial sector ballooned from 4.9% to 8.5% of GDP as manufacturing declined below 11**%**.
2. **Buyback Bonanza**—The S&P 500 spent $5.3 trillion (2010-19) repurchasing shares, outspending R&D and capital expenditures combined.
3. **Private-Equity Extraction**—LBO targets are **10 times likelier to go bankrupt; 65% of $1 Billion-plus** failures (2023) wore a PE stamp.
4. **Offshoring Stampede**—6.7 million factory jobs have been lost since 1979, and China's output share rocketed **3 % → 30 %**.
5. **Tax-Haven Houdini Act**—U.S. multinationals parked $2.6 T offshore, and corporate tax's share of federal revenue collapsed **32 % → 9 %**.

Risk Ledger

Fragility	Exploitation Mechanism	Exposure Snapshot
Industrial Commons Hollowed	Offshoring & divestment	Manufacturing < 11 % GDP
Debt-Strapped Titans	PE-loaded leverage	> $1 T junk-rated corp debt
Strategic Supply Chains	Chinese choke-points (APIs, rare earths)	70-90 % China-sourced
Fiscal Firepower	Profit-shifting to havens	≈ $100 B / yr lost taxes

Opportunity Knobs

America still leads in chip design, advanced materials, and patient pension capital, which is hungry for real returns. Bipartisan support for CHIPS-style bills and ally-reshoring (Japan, EU, Mexico) can share costs and shorten logistics.

Action Recommendations — *From Alchemy to Foundry*

1. **Industrial Commons Rebuild Act**—10-year refundable credits, cheap loans, and fast permits for strategic fabs, foundries, and precision-tool makers.
2. **Buyback Brake & R&D Dividend**—Cap repurchases at **40 %** of net income; match dollar-for-dollar with R&D + workforce upskilling.
3. **PE Guardrails**—Limit post-LBO leverage to 6× EBITDA; give workers and pensions first-claim status; embed a "Golden Share" U.S. board seat in critical-infra firms.
4. **Strategic Reshoring Bonds**—Treasury-backed instruments co-fund the relocation of APIs, batteries, and rare-earth processing to U.S. or allied soil.
5. **Close the Houdini Loop**—Enforce a 15% global minimum corporate tax and invest the recovered revenue into NSF labs and apprentice pipelines.

Bottom Line

America's financial conjurers turned factories into EPS fairy dust; China pocketed the real magic—capacity. Flip the script: privilege decade-scale production over quarter-hour trading, treat tax revenue as national seed corn, and stamp "Made in USA" on tomorrow's breakthroughs before the last gift-wrapped asset arrives in Uncle Xi's storeroom.

Opening Tableau: The Gift-Wrapping Ceremony

A lavish ceremony unfolds in a marble-columned Wall Street atrium. Bankers in bespoke Savile Row suits meticulously wrap miniature American factories in gilded paper adorned with dollar signs. Each package is lovingly placed in a golden envelope marked "QUARTERLY EARNINGS ENHANCEMENT" and ceremoniously deposited into a mailbox labeled "EXPRESS DELIVERY TO BEIJING."

At a gleaming podium stands **Milton the Trickster Economist**, *academic robes barely containing his manic energy as he provides scholarly justification for the proceedings.*

MILTON: "What we witness today is the perfect expression of market efficiency! By relocating these archaic manufacturing assets to their highest-valued use, we maximize shareholder value while unleashing America's true comparative advantage: financial innovation!"

The crowd of MBAs erupts in reverent applause, then forms a choir to sing the "Hymn to Shareholder Value," conducted by **McSlicey, the Consulting Priest,** *using a solid gold pointer shaped like a rising stock chart.*

CHOIR OF MBAs: *(singing)* "All hail the sacred bottom line! The market's wisdom is divine! Quarterly earnings above all else! The invisible hand will save ourselves!"

Meanwhile, in Beijing, Chinese officials in austere suits methodically receive each package, their expressions betraying neither surprise nor delight. Each factory is carefully cataloged, entered into a strategic database, and stored in a warehouse labeled "AMERICAN INDUSTRIAL COMMONS: 2025 ACQUISITION TARGET ACHIEVED IN 1995."

UNCLE XI: *(examining a miniature semiconductor fabrication plant)* "How curious. They dismantle their own productive foundations while celebrating the achievement. Perhaps most peculiar is that they call this 'economic wisdom' rather than 'strategic surrender.'"

DEPUTY MINISTER: "Should we send a thank-you note?"

UNCLE Xi: "That would be impolite. It is better to express our gratitude by accepting everything they offer while also building our own industrial capacity. Their financial shamans have convinced them that paper wealth exceeds productive capability. Let us not disabuse them of this convenient fiction."

Back on Wall Street, the ceremony continues, undisturbed by distant reality. A banner unfurls: "MANUFACTURING DIVESTMENT INITIATIVE: PHASE 37 – UNLOCKING SHAREHOLDER VALUE THROUGH STRATEGIC ASSET LIQUIDATION."

And so begins our exploration of how America, through financial hubris, shareholder fundamentalism, and quarterly myopia, systematically gift-wrapped its industrial future and eagerly mailed it to Beijing, believing this a triumph of economic sophistication rather than what history may judge as the most expensive economic self-delusion in geopolitical history.

Executive Summary: The Financial Coke Bottle Parable

Picture, if you will, the vast landscape of the global economy, circa 1980. High above, piloting a gleaming jet of American capitalism, sits **Uncle Sam**—confident, powerful, perhaps a little complacent. Beside him, toggling switches and punching numbers into a calculator, is his co-pilot, **Finneas Margin**, a Wall Street financier with slicked-back hair and suspenders straight out of *Wall Street*. Bored with cruising altitude, Finneas casually tosses something from the plane.

It isn't a Coca-Cola bottle (as in Jamie Uys's 1980 cult classic film *The Gods Must Be Crazy*). No, what Finneas drops is far more abstract yet consequential: gleaming financial instruments labeled "Leveraged Buyout," "Stock Buyback Plan," "Offshore Manufacturing Agreement," and "Tax Haven Structure." These mysterious artifacts spiral downward, landing with disruptive force on the American economic landscape below.

Far below, in the rising economic power of China, **Uncle Xi** doesn't stare at these falling objects with primitive wonder as the Kalahari Bushmen did with the Coke bottle. Instead, he methodically collects them, examines their mechanisms, and smiles. "How generous of the Americans," he remarks to his advisors, "to drop the very tools we need for our ascension."

This, in essence, is America's tragic economic comedy of the past forty years. While pursuing the sugar high of quarterly earnings reports and shareholder supremacy, the United States systematically dismantled its industrial foundations. Each financial engineering technique—celebrated on Wall Street as innovation—effectively hollowed out America's productive capacity and, in a twist worthy of O. Henry, accelerated China's rise as a manufacturing powerhouse.

The statistics tell a sobering story. Since 1979, the United States has shed approximately 6.7 million manufacturing jobs. S&P 500 companies spent a record $922.7 billion on stock buybacks in 2022 alone—more than America's entire annual budget for education. Meanwhile, China's share of global manufacturing output soared from roughly 3% in 1990 to over 30% today. By 2022, the United States was importing over $417 billion more in goods from China than it exported—a trade deficit that represented millions of jobs and trillions of dollars in lost productive capacity.

This isn't merely a story of economic shifts or comparative advantage. It's the tale of how America—through financial fundamentalism, short-term thinking, and a quasi-religious devotion to shareholder value—effectively gift-wrapped its industrial future and mailed it to Beijing, express shipping included.

1. MILTON'S LABORATORY OF FINANCIAL ALCHEMY

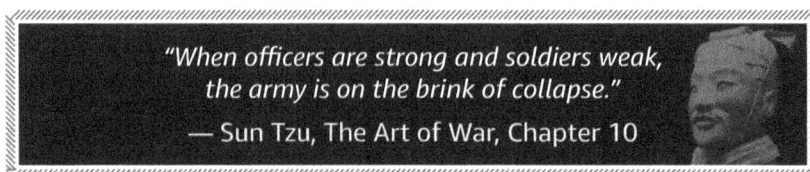

> *"When officers are strong and soldiers weak,*
> *the army is on the brink of collapse."*
> — Sun Tzu, The Art of War, Chapter 10

The Rise of the Financial Alchemist

In a gleaming laboratory perched atop the Chicago School of Economics, ***Milton the Trickster Economist*** *hunches over bubbling beakers of financial formulas. His wild hair stands electrically charged as he cackles with intellectual delight. Behind him, massive transmutation chambers convert tangible assets into increasingly abstract financial instruments.*

MILTON: "Eureka! I've discovered it! The philosopher's stone of modern economics!"

He holds up a glowing equation: ***SM = SV/SC*** *(Shareholder Maximization equals Shareholder Value divided by Societal Considerations).*

MILTON: "By reducing this denominator to near zero, the value approaches infinity! Theoretical perfection!"

A nervous graduate assistant raises his hand.

THE RISE OF THE FINANCIAL ALCHEMIST
Eureka! I've discovered it! The phiiosopher's stone of modern economics!
By reducing this deneminator to near zero, the value approaches infinity! Theoretical perfection!
SM
SV/SC
TRAVYSMUTATION CHAMBERS
That's a second-order effect, young man! Markets are efficient - by definition! Any negative externalities will be magically corrocted through processes too elegant for policymakers to comprehend!
Now help me load this productive factory into the transmutation chamber. We'll convert it into pure quarterly earnings— the highest form of econonic matter

ASSISTANT: "Professor, if we eliminate societal considerations, wouldn't that eventually undermine the system that generates the value in the first place?"

MILTON: *(dismissively)* "That's a second-order effect, young man! Markets are efficient—by definition! Any negative externalities will be magically corrected through processes too elegant for policymakers to comprehend! Now help me load this productive factory into the transmutation chamber. We'll convert it into pure quarterly earnings—the highest form of economic matter!"

Our story begins in this allegorical laboratory, where the intellectual foundations for America's financialization were forged, not from malice, but from theoretical zeal. Milton Friedman's 1970 *New York Times* essay "The Social Responsibility of Business Is to Increase Its Profits" wasn't merely an academic position—it was a declaration of war on the stakeholder capitalism that had characterized the post-war economic order.

This new gospel claimed stunning simplicity: corporations existed solely to maximize shareholder value. Everything else—workers, communities, national interests, long-term innovation—represented unfortunate distractions from the pure pursuit of stock price appreciation.

The timing proved impeccable. In the 1970s, the United States faced genuine economic challenges, including stagflation, rising competition from Japan and Germany, and declining productivity growth. Friedman's shareholder primacy offered a seductively simple solution: strip away all considerations except profit maximization, and prosperity would naturally follow.

THE SHAREHOLDER VALUE CARGO CULT: DANCING FOR STOCK PRICES
CFO TRIBFSMAN: The sacred P/E ratio remains angry! We must sacrifice another factory to appease it!
FASCINATING! They've developed an elaborate belief system whereby financial indicators have become detathed from productive activities they once measured. They now worship the indicators themselves, comusing the map with them method
Q1
Q2
Q3
EP5
Q4
EP5
RD
BUDGETS
WORKER TRAINING
RBD
CEO CHIEF: Wise counsel! Bring forth the stock buyback drums! We shall dance until the share price rises or our options vect
McKINSEY the CONSULTING PRIEST Fascinating! They've developed an elaborate rituals-- at $500 per hour plus expenses.

What began as academic theory transformed into corporate religion with remarkable speed. Business schools rewrote curricula around shareholder value. Consulting firms built practice areas dedicated to "unlocking" this value (typically through layoffs, outsourcing, and financial engineering). Boards of directors reoriented corporate missions from building to harvesting.

The intellectual alchemy was mesmerizing: By transforming the purpose of enterprise from production to financialization, America could supposedly achieve greater prosperity while doing less productive work. The philosopher's stone of modern capitalism had been discovered—or so it seemed.

The Shareholder Value Cargo Cult: Dancing for Stock Prices

Strange rituals unfold on the remote island of Corporate America. Executives in tribal business attire dance frantically around quarterly earnings totems, chanting EPS figures to summon the gods of Wall Street. They sacrifice long-term investments, worker training programs, and R&D budgets on ceremonial altars, believing these offerings will cause magical share price increases to fall from the sky.

CFO TRIBESMAN: "The sacred P/E ratio remains angry! We must sacrifice another factory to appease it!"

CEO CHIEF: "Wise counsel! Bring forth the stock buyback drums! We shall dance until the share price rises or our options vest—whichever comes first!"

*In the distance, **McSlicey, the Consulting Priest,** observes through binoculars, taking ethnographic notes.*

McSlicey: "Fascinating! They've developed an elaborate belief system whereby financial indicators have become detached from the productive activities they once measured. They now worship the indicators themselves, confusing the map with the territory. I shall teach them even more elaborate rituals—at $500 per hour plus expenses."

This satirical "cargo cult" metaphor illuminates a profound transformation in American business culture. In anthropology, cargo cults arose when Pacific Islanders, having observed the material wealth brought by Western military forces during World War II, built imitation runways and control towers from bamboo, believing these would summon cargo-laden aircraft. In American business, executives built elaborate rituals around quarterly earnings reports and share price movements, believing these financial indicators represented value creation rather than merely measuring it.

The data narrative reveals this transformation starkly. Between 1978 and 2020, the financial sector's share of GDP nearly doubled, from 4.9% to 8.5%, while manufacturing fell from 22% to under 11%. Financial sector profits, which accounted for approximately 10% of all corporate profits in the 1950s, peaked at over 40% by 2002. Meanwhile, investment in productive capacity, worker training, and basic research steadily declined as a percentage of both corporate spending and GDP.

THE GREAT FINANCIALIZATION
Wall Street Ascendant, Workshop Abandoned
8,5%
22
22
17
Finance
share of GDP
8,5%
Manufacturing
share of GDP
22%
1978
2020
Financial sector profits as 150s
over
40%
1950s
2002
Meanwhile, investment in productive capacity, worker training, and basic research steadily declined as a share of corporate spending and GDP

Corporate America wasn't merely shifting emphasis—it was undergoing ontological transformation from productive enterprises to financial engineering operations. Companies increasingly viewed their physical operations as "cost centers" and their financial operations as "profit centers." The means had become the end.

This inversion produced bizarre outcomes. Companies with long histories of manufacturing excellence, such as General Electric under the leadership of Jack Welch, have evolved into de facto financial institutions. GE Capital eventually generated nearly half the company's profits, effectively turning an industrial giant into a bank with some factories attached. When the 2008 financial crisis exposed the risks of this model, GE's market value collapsed, and the company that once symbolized American industrial might was removed from the Dow Jones Industrial Average after 110 years.

The bipartisan political consensus enabling this transformation deserves particular scrutiny. Beginning in the 1980s under Reagan and accelerating through subsequent administrations of both parties, financial deregulation and tax policies systematically favored capital over labor, as well as financial engineering over productive investment. Democrats promoted free trade without adequate worker protection; Republicans championed tax cuts that fueled stock buybacks rather than capital investment. The revolving door between Wall Street and Washington ensured policy remained favorable to financialization regardless of which party held power.

BIPARTISAN ALCHEMY
We must embrace globalization and financial innovation to remain competitive in the 21st century!
We must reduce corporate taxes and regulations to unleash the job-creating power of our job creators!
Milton the trickster
You're both right! And convenientely, both approaches will direct more resources to financial creators!
You're both right! And conveniently, both approaches will direct more resources to financial markets rather than productive capacity! What marvelous bipartisan

DEMOCRATIC SENATOR: "We must embrace globalization and financial innovation to remain competitive in the 21st century!"

REPUBLICAN SENATOR: "We must reduce corporate taxes and regulations to unleash the job-creating power of our job creators!"

MILTON THE TRICKSTER: *(whispering to both)* "You're both right! And conveniently, both approaches will direct more resources to financial markets rather than productive capacity! What marvelous bipartisan consensus!"

The theoretical framework underpinning this transformation—the tension between financial and productive capital—wasn't new. As early as the 1930s, economists such as John Maynard Keynes warned about the "fetishization of liquidity" and the dangers of prioritizing financial returns over productive investment. By the 1980s, however, such concerns were dismissed as

outdated thinking. The market, in its infinite wisdom, had determined that financial engineering created more "value" than actual engineering. Who were mere policymakers to question?

FROM FACTORY FLOORS TO TRADING FLOORS: CORPORATE AMERICA'S ONTOLOGICAL PIVOT
COST CENTER
PROFIT CENTER
182.54
3799.20
1980s
GE Capital generates half of profits
2008 crisis
GE removed from Dow index
WHEN FINANCIAL ENGINEERING BECOMES THE PRODUCT

[SATIRICAL TRANSCRIPT: THE SHAREHOLDER VALUE REVIVAL MEETING]

Interior: Corporate Amphitheater, 1995

McSlicey THE CONSULTING PRIEST: *(in revivalist preacher mode)* "Brothers and sisters, are you READY to be SAVED by shareholder value maximization?"

CONGREGATION OF EXECUTIVES: "We are ready to be saved! Save us, McSlicey!"

McSlicey: "Do you REJECT the false idol of stakeholder capitalism?"

EXECUTIVES: "We reject it!"

McSlicey: "Do you EMBRACE the one true metric of corporate success—STOCK PRICE APPRECIATION?"

EXECUTIVES: "We embrace it!"

McSlicey: "Will you DIVEST yourself of unnecessary workers, R&D expenses, and capital investments that reduce short-term earnings?"

EXECUTIVES: "We will divest!"

McSlicey: "Then I anoint thee with the holy waters of financial engineering! Go forth and maximize shareholder value! Your stock options shall be your reward in the corporate heaven!"

A lone manufacturing executive stands hesitantly.

MANUFACTURING EXECUTIVE: "But... what about building things customers need? Investing in future capabilities? Supporting our communities?"

Horrified gasps from the congregation.

McSlicey: "HERETIC! Security, remove this stakeholder sympathizer! He questions the invisible hand!"

The manufacturing executive is dragged away as the congregation resumes chanting quarterly EPS targets.

//END SATIRICAL TRANSCRIPT//

The religious fervor of this movement cannot be overstated. Corporate executives who questioned shareholder primacy risked being branded heretics. Business schools taught the new gospel to generations of MBAs, who spread it throughout the corporate landscape. Financial analysts enforced orthodoxy by punishing companies that invested in long-term capabilities at the expense of short-term returns.

By the late 1990s, even traditional industrial companies felt compelled to pursue financial engineering strategies or face shareholder revolts. The "tyranny of quarterly capitalism" had been firmly established. The American economy was increasingly optimized not for production, innovation, or worker well-being, but for financial metrics that had become increasingly detached from underlying economic reality.

The alchemical transmutation was complete: America had converted its industrial gold into financial instruments that gleamed brilliantly on quarterly statements but proved far less valuable when economic storms arrived.

2. THE GREAT BUYBACK BONANZA: CORPORATE SELF-CANNIBALISM

> *"Kill the donkey once the grinding is done."*
> —Thirty-Six Stratagems, #17

The Quarterly Fiction Factory: Manufacturing EPS Growth Without Creating Value

In a sleek corporate presentation room, ***Bobby Buyback****, a slick financial operator, demonstrates his newest innovation to a group of eager CEOs. He wears a tailored suit worth more than the combined monthly wages of ten factory workers.*

BOBBY BUYBACK: "Gentlemen, ladies—your boards demand earnings growth, but your markets are mature, competition is fierce, and genuine innovation is both expensive and risky. What's a modern CEO to do?"

He dramatically unveils a device labeled "THE QUARTERLY FICTION FACTORY."

BOBBY: "This miraculous machine turns your company's cash into higher Earnings Per Share without the messy business of actually growing earnings! Simply insert cash, press the 'Reduce Share Count' button, and watch your EPS rise like magic!"

SKEPTICAL CEO: "That sounds like financial engineering, not actual value creation."

BOBBY: *(smiling indulgently)* "Such quaint distinctions! Tell me, is your compensation package tied to EPS targets and stock price?"

SKEPTICAL CEO: "Well, yes, about 80% of it."

BOBBY: "And does your board distinguish between EPS growth from business improvement versus share reduction?"

SKEPTICAL CEO: "Not really."

BOBBY: "Then I suggest you reconsider your charming commitment to 'actual value creation.' Your competitors are already using my machine. Last quarter, they reported 8% EPS growth with flat revenues. Care to explain to your board why you're delivering only 3% growth the old-fashioned way?"

The skeptical CEO reluctantly approaches the machine.

BOBBY: "Excellent! Now, how much cash would you like to convert into personal compensation—I mean, shareholder value—today?"

Stock buybacks represent perhaps the purest expression of finance capitalism's triumph over productive capitalism. This mechanism boosts share prices and executive compensation without requiring any improvement in the underlying business. Once relatively uncommon, buybacks became more prevalent after 1982, when the SEC adopted Rule 10b-18, providing "safe harbor" protection against manipulation charges for companies repurchasing their own shares.

The numbers are staggering. Between 2010 and 2019, S&P 500 companies spent approximately $5.3 trillion on stock buybacks—far exceeding their investments in research, development, or capital equipment. In 2018 alone, these companies spent $806 billion repurchasing their own shares, exceeding the federal government's combined spending on education, transportation, and infrastructure. This record was broken again in 2022, when buybacks reached an astonishing $922.7 billion.

The theoretical justification for buybacks sounds reasonable: returning "excess cash" to shareholders when a company lacks attractive investment opportunities. The reality proved far less benign. Buybacks increasingly functioned as:

Artificial EPS Boosters: By reducing share count without increasing earnings, companies mathematically increased earnings per share.

1. **Executive Compensation Enhancers:** Since most executive pay packages are tied to stock price and EPS metrics, buybacks directly enriched the decision-makers, authorizing them.
2. **Activist Investor Appeasement:** Companies used buybacks to pacify aggressive shareholders demanding immediate returns, often at the expense of long-term investments.
3. **Financial Engineering Camouflage:** Buybacks masked underlying business weaknesses, creating the illusion of growth when organic expansion had stalled.

Perhaps most critically, buybacks diverted capital from productive investment precisely when America needed to modernize its industrial base to meet rising international competition. While Chinese companies reinvested profits in expanded capacity, advanced equipment, and worker training, American firms increasingly opted for financial engineering over physical engineering.

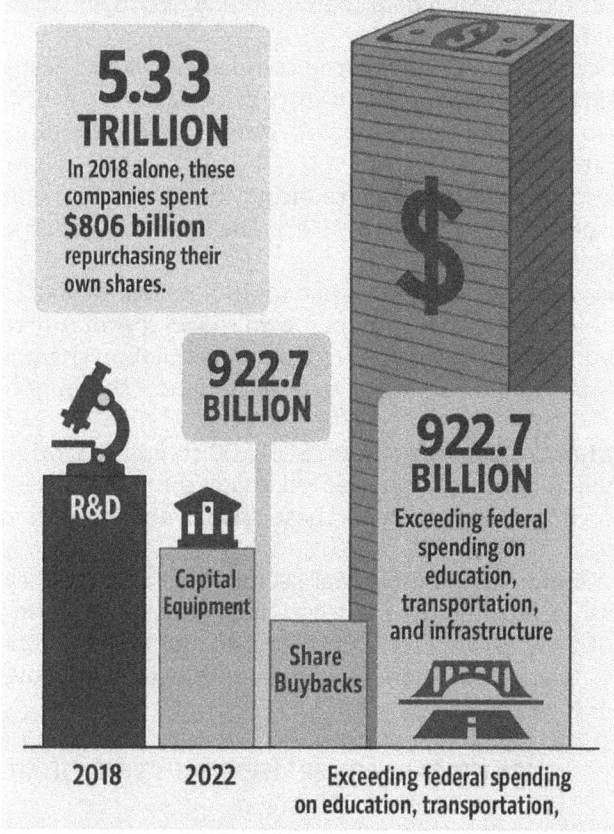

CEO Maximizer's Difficult Explanation: The Boeing Case Study

*Factory floor of American Aerospace Inc. Workers gather anxiously as **CEO Maximizer** prepares to address them.*

CEO MAXIMIZER: "As you've heard, we're closing this facility and laying off all 3,000 of you. This difficult decision reflects market realities and our commitment to shareholder value."

VETERAN ENGINEER: "But we just developed the next-generation control system that could keep us competitive for decades. The prototype works perfectly."

CEO MAXIMIZER: *(checking gold watch)* "Indeed, very impressive. Unfortunately, commercializing that would require $2 billion in investment with payoffs years away. Our shareholders expect returns now."

ASSEMBLY WORKER: "So the company can't afford to keep the factory open?"

CEO MAXIMIZER: "Well, technically, we announced a $12 billion stock buyback program yesterday. But that's different money—that's returning value to shareholders."

ASSEMBLY WORKER: "Couldn't some of that $12 billion keep this factory open and fund the new control system?"

CEO MAXIMIZER: *(growing uncomfortable)* "You don't understand corporate finance. The stock buyback enhances shareholder value by reducing the share count and boosting EPS."

VETERAN ENGINEER: "And what happens when our overseas competitors launch their version of the technology we developed but aren't commercializing?"

CEO MAXIMIZER: *(glancing at smartphone)* "That's a long-term concern. Our focus is on meeting next quarter's targets. Now, I'd love to stay longer, but I have a board meeting where we're approving my new compensation package. Security will provide details about your severance—two weeks per decade of service seems appropriate. Best of luck!"

As Maximizer exits, workers notice his departing text message on a presentation screen, which was accidentally left on: "Layoff announcement complete. Stock should bump 2-3% on restructuring news. Proceed with option grant at pre-announcement price?"

This satirical vignette illustrates the perverse incentives created when executive compensation becomes overwhelming tied to short-term stock performance. Increasingly common since the 1990s, this compensation structure effectively encourages executives to prioritize short-term gains over long-term investments.

Boeing provides a sobering real-world case study of these dynamics. Between 2013 and 2019, Boeing spent approximately $43 billion buying back its own stock, nearly double what it invested in R&D during the same period. These buybacks helped boost Boeing's share price and executive compensation while the company allegedly underinvested in the safety systems and engineering excellence that had defined its earlier history.

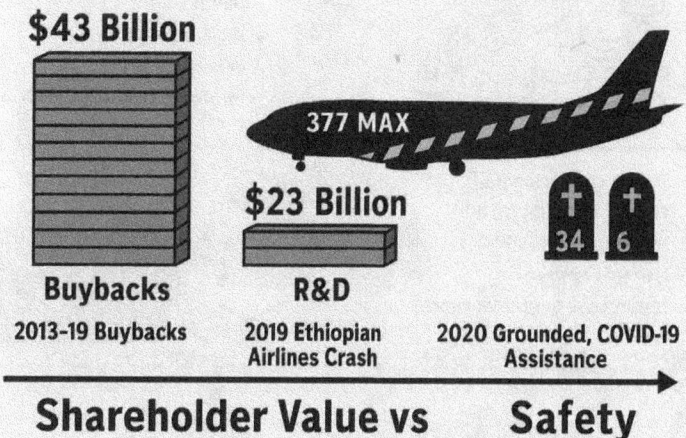

The consequences proved tragic. Design flaws in Boeing's 737 MAX contributed to two catastrophic crashes in 2018 and 2019, killing 346 people. Subsequent investigations revealed a corporate culture increasingly focused on financial targets rather than engineering excellence. Internal communications revealed that engineers felt intense pressure to cut costs and accelerate development, sometimes at the expense of safety considerations.

When the 737 MAX was grounded worldwide, Boeing's financial fragility became apparent. Having spent tens of billions on buybacks rather than building financial reserves, the company required government assistance during the COVID-19 pandemic. The boardroom's emphasis on "returning value to shareholders" had ironically destroyed enormous shareholder value while tarnishing a century-old reputation for quality.

Boeing's story represents a microcosm of the broader buyback phenomenon: American companies systematically hollowed out their productive capabilities and financial resilience in pursuit of short-term stock price gains. When Chinese officials observed this behavior, they reportedly expressed amazement that the United States would voluntarily weaken its industrial champions through financial self-cannibalization.

UNCLE Xi: *(reviewing Boeing case study)* "Most curious. They spent twice as much reducing their share count as developing new technologies. Meanwhile, we increased our aerospace R&D budget by 300%. They call this 'creating shareholder value.' We call it 'surrendering competitive advantage.'"

The regulatory history enabling this self-destructive behavior deserves scrutiny. Prior to 1982, stock buybacks were severely limited due to concerns about market manipulation—companies buying their own shares specifically to boost their stock price. The SEC's Rule 10b-18 created a "safe harbor" shielding companies from manipulation charges when conducting buybacks within certain parameters. This well-intentioned rule failed to anticipate how thoroughly buybacks would transform corporate behavior.

By the 2010s, more than 50% of corporate profits were devoted to buybacks among S&P 500 companies, often at the direct expense of productive investment. As economist William Lazonick documented, many companies spent more on buybacks than their total net income—essentially borrowing money to repurchase shares while deferring necessary business investments.

The visualization of buybacks versus R&D and Capital expenditures across industrial sectors tells a stark story. In almost every industry, from pharmaceuticals to manufacturing to technology, the trend lines crossed sometime between 1990 and 2010. What began as the occasional return of truly excess cash morphed into systematic prioritization of financial engineering over productive investment.

[SATIRICAL ADVERTISEMENT: THE QUARTERLY FICTION FACTORY]

ATTENTION CEOs AND CFOs! Struggling with stagnant growth? Can't innovate fast enough? Competition eating your lunch?

INTRODUCING THE QUARTERLY FICTION FACTORY™ *Because Creating Value Is Hard, But Creating the Appearance of Value Is Easy!*

Our revolutionary financial engineering system transforms your company's future into today's executive bonuses through the magic of STOCK BUYBACKS!

WHY INNOVATE WHEN YOU CAN REPURCHASE?

R&D takes YEARS and might FAIL

Capital investment is EXPENSIVE and RISKY

Worker training shows ROI only in the LONG TERM

With QUARTERLY FICTION FACTORY™, simply:

Divert cash from R&D, capital investment, and worker development

Use this cash to repurchase your own shares

Watch your EPS rise as if by MAGIC!

Collect your performance bonus

Exercise your stock options

Repeat until retirement or bankruptcy (whichever comes first)!

BUT WAIT, THERE'S MORE! Order now and receive our FREE guide: "How to Explain Factory Closures While Announcing Record Buybacks Without Experiencing Cognitive Dissonance!"

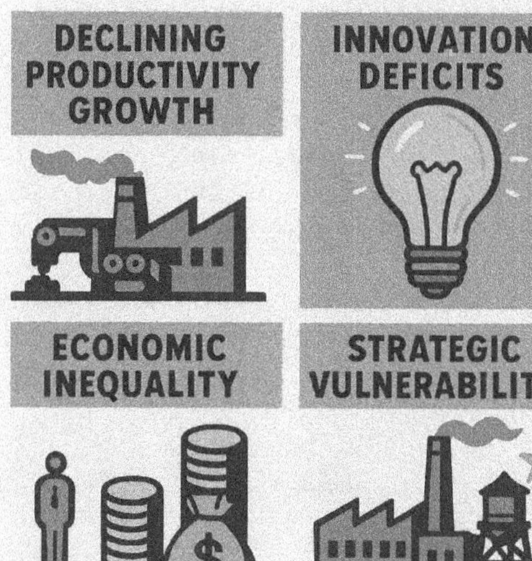

WARNING: Side effects may include industrial decay, loss of competitive advantage, reduced innovation, hollowed-out communities, strategic vulnerability, and eventual corporate collapse. But don't worry—these typically occur after your options have vested!

QUARTERLY FICTION FACTORY™ *When Creating Actual Value Is Just Too Much Work*

//END SATIRICAL ADVERTISEMENT//

The long-term consequences of the buyback bonanza extended far beyond individual companies. At a macroeconomic level, excessive focus on buybacks contributed to:

Declining Productivity Growth: As investment in worker training, research, and equipment fell, productivity growth slowed.

Innovation Deficits: Companies focused on squeezing existing product lines rather than developing revolutionary new offerings.

Economic Inequality: Buybacks primarily benefited shareholders and executives, while workers faced stagnant wages and increased job insecurity.

Strategic Vulnerability: America's industrial base weakened precisely as China was building its manufacturing capabilities.

The theoretical framework explaining this phenomenon sheds light on how financial engineering has eroded productive capitalism. In a healthy industrial economy, profits from current operations fund research and investment for future growth—a virtuous cycle of innovation and expansion. Financial engineering short-circuited this cycle, redirecting capital from productive reinvestment to zero-sum financial maneuvers that boosted stock prices without enhancing productive capacity.

Meanwhile, China moved in exactly the opposite direction. Chinese companies, particularly those in strategic industries, typically reinvest 80-90% of profits into expansion, research, and development. While American executives obsessed over quarterly EPS targets, their Chinese counterparts focused on building long-term competitive advantage through sustained investment. The contrast could hardly be more striking: one country building while the other financially engineered its way into industrial decline.

3. PRIVATE EQUITY'S EXTRACTION ECONOMY: THE CORPORATE VAMPIRE SAGA

> *"Take the opportunity to pilfer a goat."*
> —Thirty-Six Stratagems, #13

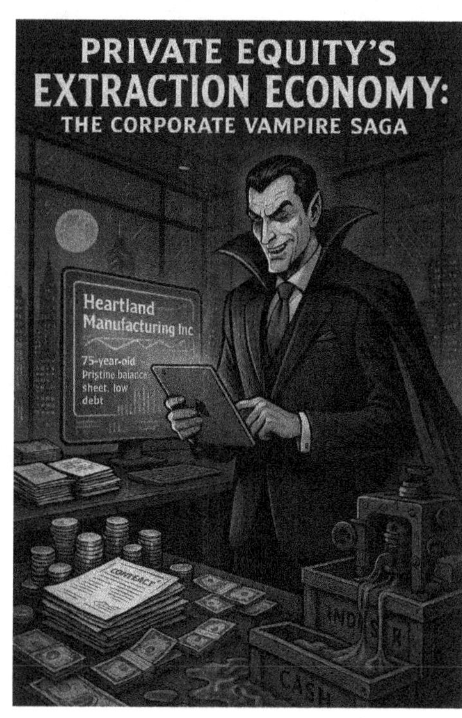

PE Pete's Midnight Hunt: Leveraged Buyouts as Blood-Sucking

*Midnight at the gleaming headquarters of **Barbary Koffin Capital**, a top-tier private equity firm. **PE Pete the Corporate Vampire** adjusts his immaculate suit and custom fangs as he studies financial data on potential acquisition targets.*

PE PETE: "Computer, show me healthy companies with low debt, stable cash flows, and undervalued hard assets."

*The system displays **Heartland Manufacturing, Inc.** – a 75-year-old industrial components manufacturer with a pristine balance sheet, a loyal workforce, strong community ties, and an innovative product pipeline.*

PE PETE: *(eyes gleaming)* "Perfect! A clean balance sheet indicates a substantial debt capacity. Those hard assets can be sold for quick cash. And all that free cash flow—flowing freely, just waiting to be extracted!"

He runs a pale finger across his lips.

PE PETE: "Computer, model a standard acquisition: 20% equity, 80% debt loaded onto target, 3% transaction fee, 2% annual monitoring fee, special dividend recapitalization in year two, full exit by year five."

COMPUTER: "Target financial profile indicates 70% probability of bankruptcy by year seven under this model."

PE PETE: *(smiling)* "Acceptable. We'll be long gone by then, having extracted three times our investment. Prepare the acquisition documents and alert the debt financing team. Tonight, we feed!"

He swirls his cape (custom-tailored Brioni) and strides toward the private elevator to his waiting jet.

PE PETE: "Another beautiful company to acquire, optimize, and leave elegantly desiccated. Such is the circle of financial life!"

Private equity represents the most aggressive manifestation of financial engineering—a business model predicated on acquiring companies not to build them, but to extract maximum value in the shortest time possible. The modern leveraged buyout model, pioneered by firms like KKR in the 1980s, operates on a simple premise: acquire a company using minimal equity (typically 20-30%) and maximum debt (70-80%), then place that debt on the acquired company's balance sheet.

The debt-laden company must then generate sufficient cash flow to service this enormous new liability—a requirement typically met through aggressive cost-cutting, asset sales, reduced investment, and other "optimization" measures. Meanwhile, the PE firm extracts value through multiple channels:

Transaction Fees: Typically 1-3% of the deal value, paid immediately upon completion.

1. **Monitoring/Advisory Fees:** Annual charges for "services" provided to the acquired company.
2. **Dividend Recapitalizations:** Additional debt is placed on the company to fund special dividends to the PE owners.
3. **Exit Proceeds:** Eventual sale or IPO of the company (or what remains of it).

This model enables PE firms to typically recoup their original investment within 1-3 years while retaining ownership of the company. The remaining period before exit represents pure profit extraction, regardless of the company's ultimate fate.

The human and economic costs of this approach have been extensively documented. One study found that companies acquired by private equity are ten times more likely to go bankrupt than their peers. Another study revealed that PE-owned companies reduced R&D spending by an average of 24% after acquisition, while employment growth lagged behind that of similar non-PE-owned businesses by 4.4% over two years.

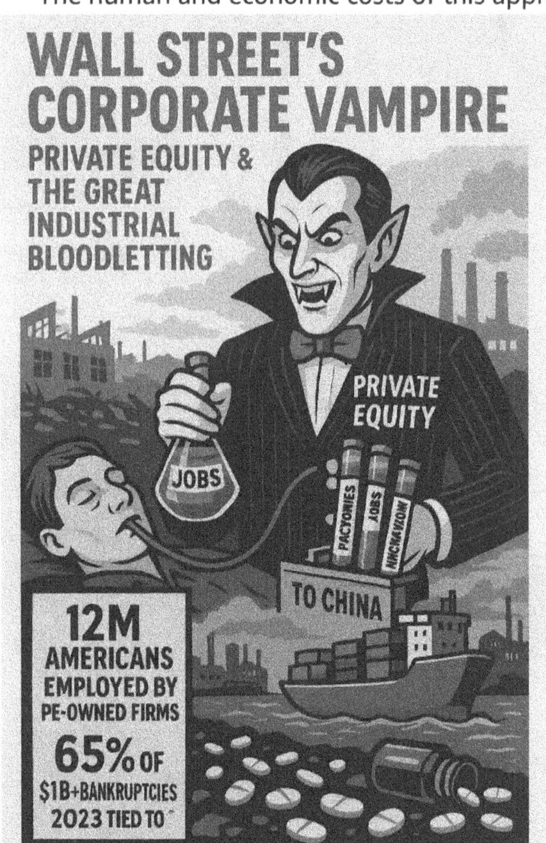

WALL STREET'S
CORPORATE VAMPIRE
PRIVATE EQUITY & THE GREAT INDUSTRIAL BLOODLETTING
PRIVATE EQUITY
JOBS
TO CHINA
12M AMERICANS EMPLOYED BY PE-OWNED FIRMS
65% OF $1B+BANKRUPTCIES 2023 TIED TO

The private equity industry has consumed an ever-larger portion of the American economy, with PE-owned companies employing nearly 12 million people in the United States. In 2023, a startling 65% of large corporate bankruptcies (with liabilities over $1 billion) involved companies that had been owned by private equity at some point in their recent history. The corporate vampire doesn't just suck blood; in our allegory, PE didn't just suck the lifeblood out of companies—they collected it in vials and shipped it to China.

This wasn't just about jobs disappearing—it represented a massive transfer of industrial capacity and technical knowledge. As factories moved overseas, entire supply chains followed. The "industrial commons"—the ecosystem of suppliers, skilled workers, and process knowledge that enables innovation—withered in many sectors. Regions once known for manufacturing excellence became known instead for opioid addiction and economic despair.

The Toys "R" Us Autopsy: Dissecting the Corpse of a Retail Giant

A gloomy abandoned big-box store, formerly Toys "R" Us. Financial forensics experts in hazmat suits examine the corporate remains.

FORENSIC ACCOUNTANT: "Time of death: June 29, 2018. Cause: acute financial exsanguination following leveraged buyout complications."

She points to a massive debt structure diagram.

ACCOUNTANT: "The private equity consortium acquired the healthy patient in 2005 using $1.2 billion in equity and $5.3 billion in debt—debt immediately transferred to the patient's own balance sheet. The patient was then subjected to annual extraction of approximately $470 million in interest payments alone."

ASSISTANT: "Was any of this debt used to improve the business?"

ACCOUNTANT: "Negative. The debt served solely to finance the acquisition itself. Meanwhile, critical investments in e-commerce capabilities were repeatedly deferred due to cash constraints. The PE owners extracted approximately $464 million in fees and partial dividends before termination."

ASSISTANT: "And the 33,000 employees?"

ACCOUNTANT: "Terminated without meaningful severance, while top executives received $8.2 million in 'retention bonuses.' The PE firms retained their management fees despite the bankruptcy."

ASSISTANT: "So the PE firms acquired a functioning company, loaded it with debt, extracted hundreds of millions, failed to invest in necessary capabilities, then walked away largely whole while thousands lost their livelihoods?"

ACCOUNTANT: *(removing hazmat mask)* "Correct. Standard procedure in PE-mediated corporate demise. The only unusual aspect was the patient's size—most victims don't generate national headlines."

In the background, Chinese toy manufacturers examine the empty shelves, taking note of the market opportunities created by the vacancy.

The Toys "R" Us case study starkly illuminates private equity's extraction model. In 2005, KKR, Bain Capital, and Vornado Realty Trust acquired the toy retailer in a $6.6 billion leveraged buyout, with only $1.2 billion in equity. The company was immediately saddled with over $5 billion in debt, not to grow or improve operations but simply to finance its own purchase.

Under this crushing debt burden, Toys "R" Us paid approximately $400 million to $ 500 million annually in interest alone. These payments consumed cash that might have been used to fund e-commerce investments needed to compete with Amazon and Walmart. Meanwhile, the PE owners extracted hundreds of millions in fees and partial dividend payments. By 2017, Toys "R" Us filed for bankruptcy, resulting in the closure of all U.S. stores and the loss of 33,000 jobs.

The PE firms, however, had already recovered most of their investment through fees and limited dividend payments. Their equity losses were relatively modest compared to the devastation experienced by workers, suppliers, and communities.

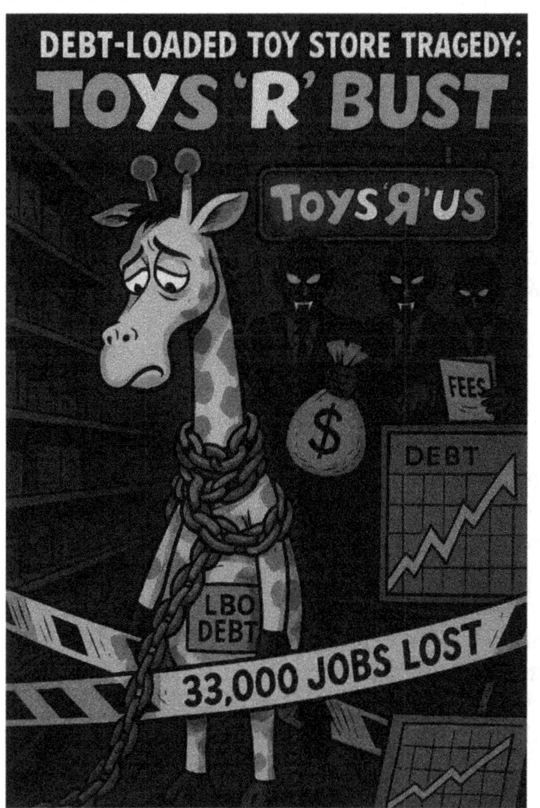

This pattern has repeated across the American economy as private equity's reach expanded exponentially. By 2022, PE-owned companies employed approximately 11.7 million Americans, representing roughly 7% of the private sector workforce. In certain sectors, such as retail, healthcare, and manufacturing, PE ownership has become increasingly dominant, often with similar results: increased debt, reduced investment, a short-term focus, and elevated bankruptcy risk.

The Toys "R" Us case also highlights how PE extraction creates strategic openings for foreign competitors. As American retailers weakened under debt burdens, Chinese manufacturers identified opportunities to launch their own direct-to-consumer operations or expand relationships with surviving retailers. Each American company hollowed out by PE extraction effectively created market space for overseas rivals to exploit.

The Heartland Manufacturing Lifecycle: From Family Business to Asset Strip to Overseas Relocation

A time-lapse visualization shows the evolution of a mid-sized manufacturing company in America's industrial heartland:

PHASE 1: PRODUCTIVE ENTERPRISE (1945-2005) *Family-owned* ***Midwest Industrial Components*** *has grown steadily, employing 2,800 workers at living wages. The company invests consistently in equipment, worker training, and product development. It supports the surrounding community through stable employment, a tax base, and civic engagement.*

HEARTLAND MANUFACTURING LIFECYCLE

FROM FAMILY BUSINESS TO ASSET STRIP TO OVERSEAS RELOCATION

PHASE 1	PHASE 2	PHASE 3	PHASE 4	PHASE 5	PHASE 6
PRODUCTIVE ENTERPRISE (1945-2005)	**PE ACQUISITION** (2005)	**EXTRACTION INITIATION** (2005-2007)	**TERMINAL EXTRACTION** (2007-2010)	**CORPORATE HUSK** (2010-2011)	**FOREIGN RESURRECTION** 2012-)
• Family-owned growth • 2,800 well-paid jobs • Investment in R&D & community	• Leveraged buyout • $440M debt loaded • "Optimization" headlines	• 20% layoffs, R&D -70% • HO sold & leased back • $148 M fees & dividend	• Patents & equipment sold abroad • Workforce cut to skeleton • PE nets 2,7× return	• Chapter 11 filing • 600 jobs lost, pensions cut • Owners express "disappointment"	• Chinese buyer acquires assets • Production shifts overseas • Former workers idle or in services

PHASE 2: PE ACQUISITION (2005) *Enter **PE Pete**, acquiring the company in a leveraged buyout. Immediately, the previously debt-free balance sheet shows $440 million in acquisition debt. Financial headlines celebrate the "optimization opportunity."*

PHASE 3: EXTRACTION INITIATION (2005-2007): Layoffs begin—20% of the workforce is eliminated. The R&D budget is cut by 70%. The headquarters building is sold for quick cash and then leased back at a premium. Maintenance is deferred. The PE firm extracts $28 million in "advisory fees" plus a $120 *million "special dividend" financed by additional debt.*

PHASE 4: TERMINAL EXTRACTION (2007-2010). *The remaining valuable patents and equipment are sold to overseas competitors. Manufacturing is increasingly outsourced to cheaper locations. A second round of layoffs reduces the workforce to a skeleton crew. An additional dividend recap extracts the remaining cash. The PE firm recovers 2.7x its initial investment.*

PHASE 5: CORPORATE HUSK (2010-2011) *The Company filed for bankruptcy, citing "challenging market conditions." The remaining 600 workers lost their jobs with minimal severance. Pension obligations shifted to the government insurance program (at reduced levels). PE owners expressed "disappointment" in the press release issued from Caribbean offices.*

PHASE 6: FOREIGN RESURRECTION (2012-Present): A Chinese manufacturer acquires corporate remains at a bankruptcy auction, gaining patents, customer relationships, and brand names at a steep discount. Limited production resumes overseas. Former U.S. employees remain unemployed or work *at significantly lower wages in the service sector.*

This satirical lifecycle, while condensed for effect, reflects a pattern documented across America's industrial landscape. Private equity's extraction model systematically converted productive enterprises into financial harvesting operations. Companies built over generations were acquired, loaded with debt, stripped of assets, drained of cash, and frequently abandoned in bankruptcy.

The psychological analysis reveals perverse incentives driving this behavior. PE compensation structures—typically "2 and 20" (2% management fee plus 20% of profits)—reward quick extraction over sustainable growth. The most lucrative strategy isn't building companies but rapidly harvesting their existing value. PE partners personally earn tens or hundreds of millions through this model, creating powerful motivation to continue despite the broader economic damage.

The regulatory failure enabling this extraction merits critical examination. Unlike previous eras when antitrust enforcement might have limited such predatory behavior, the late 20th century saw the systematic dismantling of regulatory guardrails. The carried interest tax loophole allowed PE partners to pay capital gains rates (20%) rather than income tax rates (37%) on their earnings. Bankruptcy laws were modified to favor financial creditors over workers and communities. Antitrust philosophy narrowed to focus almost exclusively on consumer prices rather than broader economic impacts.

PE PETE: *(explaining to Minister Patience during a chance encounter at Davos)*: "The brilliant part is that Americans themselves created the regulatory environment that enables our extraction model. Their legislators passed the laws, their regulators approved the acquisitions, and their courts enforced the contracts. We're simply maximizing returns within the system they designed."

MINISTER PATIENCE: "Most interesting. And they don't recognize the strategic implications of hollowing out their own industrial base?"

PE PETE: *(laughing)* "They still believe financial engineering creates actual value rather than merely transferring it! By the time they recognize their error, we'll have harvested most of their valuable industrial assets. But please, don't tell anyone I said that—I have three more companies to acquire this quarter."

This dialogue, while satirical, captures a fundamental truth: America's private equity extraction economy represents a self-inflicted wound. The country systematically enabled financial predation on its productive enterprises, then wondered why its industrial base weakened while rivals strengthened.

China took a radically different approach. While certain forms of private equity exist in China, the aggressive LBO model that dominated American finance gained little traction. Chinese authorities generally viewed strategic industries as too important to be subject to financial strip-mining. State-influenced banks typically refused to finance the enormous debt loads characteristic of Western leveraged buyouts. When Chinese companies acquired debt, it normally funded expansion and modernization rather than financial engineering.

The contrast proved consequential: while PE extraction weakened countless American industrial enterprises, China built new ones, often using technologies and market openings created by America's self-sabotage.

4. OFFSHORING AMERICA: THE GREAT INDUSTRIAL YARD SALE

> *"When the root is severed, the branches wither."*
> —Mencius

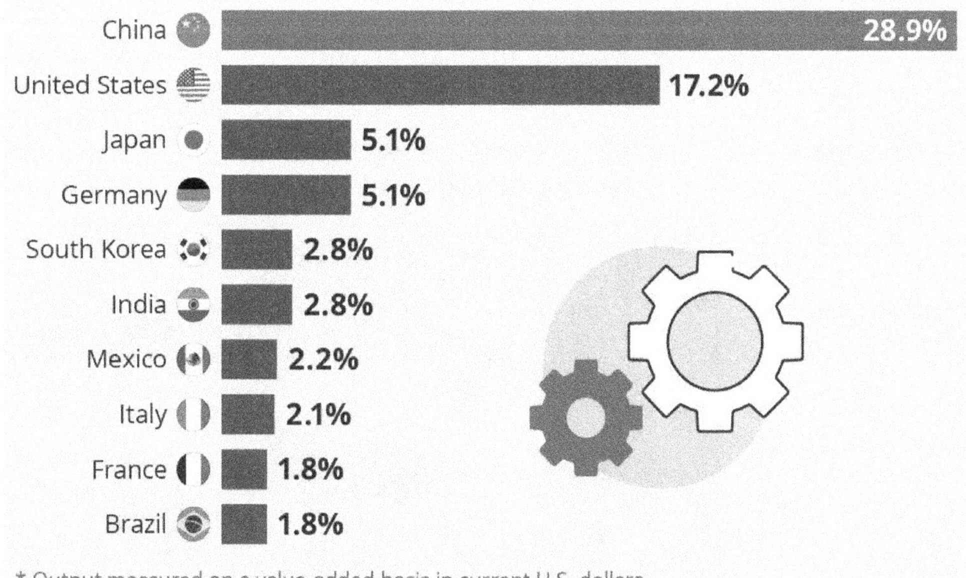

Outsource Ollie's Global Labor Arbitrage: The Economics of Industrial Exodus

A corporate boardroom. ***Outsource Ollie****, a hyperkinetic consultant with a globe for a head, enthusiastically pitches to American Excellence Manufacturing executives.*

OUTSOURCE OLLIE: "Gentlemen, ladies—why make anything in America when you can make it for pennies on the dollar elsewhere? Your competitors are already halfway to China! Last one to offshore is a rotten conglomerate!"

He unveils a world map labeled "GLOBAL LABOR ARBITRAGE OPPORTUNITIES" with color-coding showing wage differentials.

OLLIE: "Your factory workers in Ohio earn $28.50 per hour with benefits. Your potential factory workers in Shenzhen earn $3.50 per hour with virtually no benefits! The math isn't just compelling—it's a moral imperative to your shareholders!"

OFFSHORING AMERICA:
The Great Industrial Yard Sale
Outsource Ollie's Global Labor Arbitrage
The Economics of Industrial Exodus
Gentelmen, ladies–why make anything in America when you can make it for pennies on the dollar elsewhere? Your factory workers in Ohio earn $28.50 per hour with benefits. Your potential factory workers in Shenzhen earn $3.50 per hour with virtually no benefits!
Knowledge can transferred
GLOBAL LABOR ARBRARIGUE OPPORTUNITIES
OHIO
$3.50
$2850 per hour
SHENZHEN
Wage differentials
But we've spent decades developing skilled workers here. That institutional knowledge–
AMERICAN EXCELLENCE MANUFACTURING
Minor concerns compared do the 90% labor cost reduction! Think of next quarter's earnings report whichever comes first!

VP OF MANUFACTURING: "But we've spent decades developing skilled workers here. That institutional knowledge—"

OLLIE: *(interrupting)* "Knowledge can be transferred! We'll send your engineers to train their workers for six months, then eliminate the engineer positions! Double savings!"

HEAD OF QUALITY: "What about quality control? Intellectual property protection? Supply chain resilience?"

OLLIE: *(dismissively)* "Minor concerns compared to the 90% labor cost reduction! Think of next quarter's earnings report! Your stock will soar, your options will print, and the Wall Street analysts will upgrade your shares!"

His globe-head spins excitedly.

OLLIE: "Plus, the Chinese government will build you a factory park with tax incentives! They're literally paying you to take your manufacturing expertise to their country! It's free money!"

CFO: *(eyes glazing with dollar signs)* "The EPS improvement would be significant..."

VETERAN ENGINEER: "And what happens when we've transferred all our production knowledge overseas? When do we no longer know how to make our own products?"

OLLIE: *(patronizingly)* "Oh, you engineers and your long-term thinking! By that point, we'll all have taken our stock options and retired to gated communities! Furthermore, America's future lies in services and financial innovation, rather than in manufacturing physical goods. That's so 20th century!"

Offshoring—the wholesale relocation of American manufacturing to lower-cost countries—represents perhaps the most visible manifestation of financial engineering's triumph over industrial strategy. What began as isolated cases of production transfer in the 1970s accelerated dramatically in the 1990s and 2000s, creating the most significant industrial exodus in American history.

The mechanics were straightforward: companies relocated production to locations with significantly lower labor costs, less stringent environmental standards, and often substantial government incentives. The financial benefits were immediately evident in quarterly earnings reports, with lower production costs, improved margins, and enhanced competitiveness against rivals who had already offshored. Wall Street rewarded these moves with higher stock ratings and share prices.

Less attention was paid to the long-term strategic consequences of this mass production migration, particularly the systematic transfer of industrial knowledge, capacity, and capability from the United States to China and other manufacturing destinations.

The data narrative tells a sobering story. U.S. manufacturing employment reached its peak of 19.6 million in 1979. By 2019, it had fallen to 12.8 million—a loss of 6.7 million jobs. During this period, manufacturing's share of GDP declined from 28% to just 11%. While some job losses resulted from automation, research estimates that between 2001 (when China joined the WTO) and 2018, the U.S.-China trade deficit eliminated 3.7 million American jobs, with manufacturing bearing the brunt.

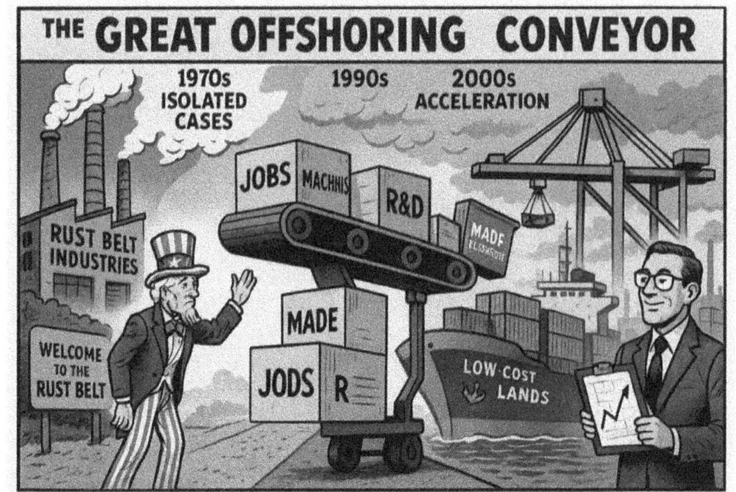
THE GREAT OFFSHORING CONVEYOR
1970s ISOLATED CASES
1990s
2000s ACCELERATION
JOBS
MACHINIS
R&D
RUST BELT INDUSTRIES
MADE
WELCOME TO THE RUST BELT
JODS
LOW-COST LANDS

The geographic visualization of manufacturing job losses reveals concentrated devastation in specific regions—the industrial Midwest, portions of the Southeast, and manufacturing centers in the Northeast. These areas, once the backbone of middle-class prosperity, experienced dramatic economic and social decline: falling property values, eroding tax bases, deteriorating schools, and rising social pathologies, including drug addiction, fami-

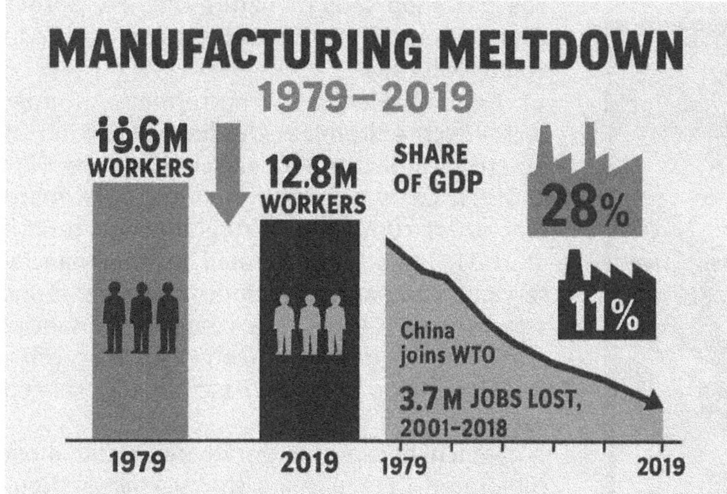

ly breakdown, and "deaths of despair" from suicide and substance abuse.

Jack Welch's GE: From Industrial Giant to Financial House of Cards

A satirical museum exhibit labeled "THE RISE AND FALL OF AMERICAN INDUSTRIAL GIANTS: THE GENERAL ELECTRIC STORY" displays artifacts from different eras:

EXHIBIT A: INDUSTRIAL EXCELLENCE (1892-1980) *GE's early innovations: Edison's light bulb, early electrical generators, jet engines, medical devices, and plastics development. Photos show massive American factories with thousands of workers creating advanced products.*

EXHIBIT B: THE NEUTRON JACK ERA (1981-2001) *A wax figure of Jack Welch holds a sign: "Ideally, you'd have every plant you own on a barge." Displays show GE factory closures across America alongside new facilities in Mexico, China, and elsewhere. A stock chart shows dramatic share price increases.*

EXHIBIT C: FINANCIAL ENGINEERING ASCENDANT (1990-2008) *Documents show GE Capital's growth to nearly half the company's profits. Complex financial instruments, tax avoidance structures, and accounting techniques take center stage. Manufacturing receives increasingly less attention in annual reports.*

EXHIBIT D: THE COLLAPSE (2008-2018) *The 2008 financial crisis exposed GE's economic fragility. The stock chart shows a catastrophic 75% decline in value. The timeline displays removal from the Dow Jones Industrial Average after 110 years of membership. Photos show abandoned American factories alongside thriving Chinese competitors using technologies pioneered by GE.*

MUSEUM GUIDE: *(to visitors)* "The GE exhibit demonstrates the standard lifecycle of American industrial giants during the financialization era: from productive enterprises building actual things, to financial operations with manufacturing sidelines, to eventual collapse when financial engineering couldn't substitute for productive capability.

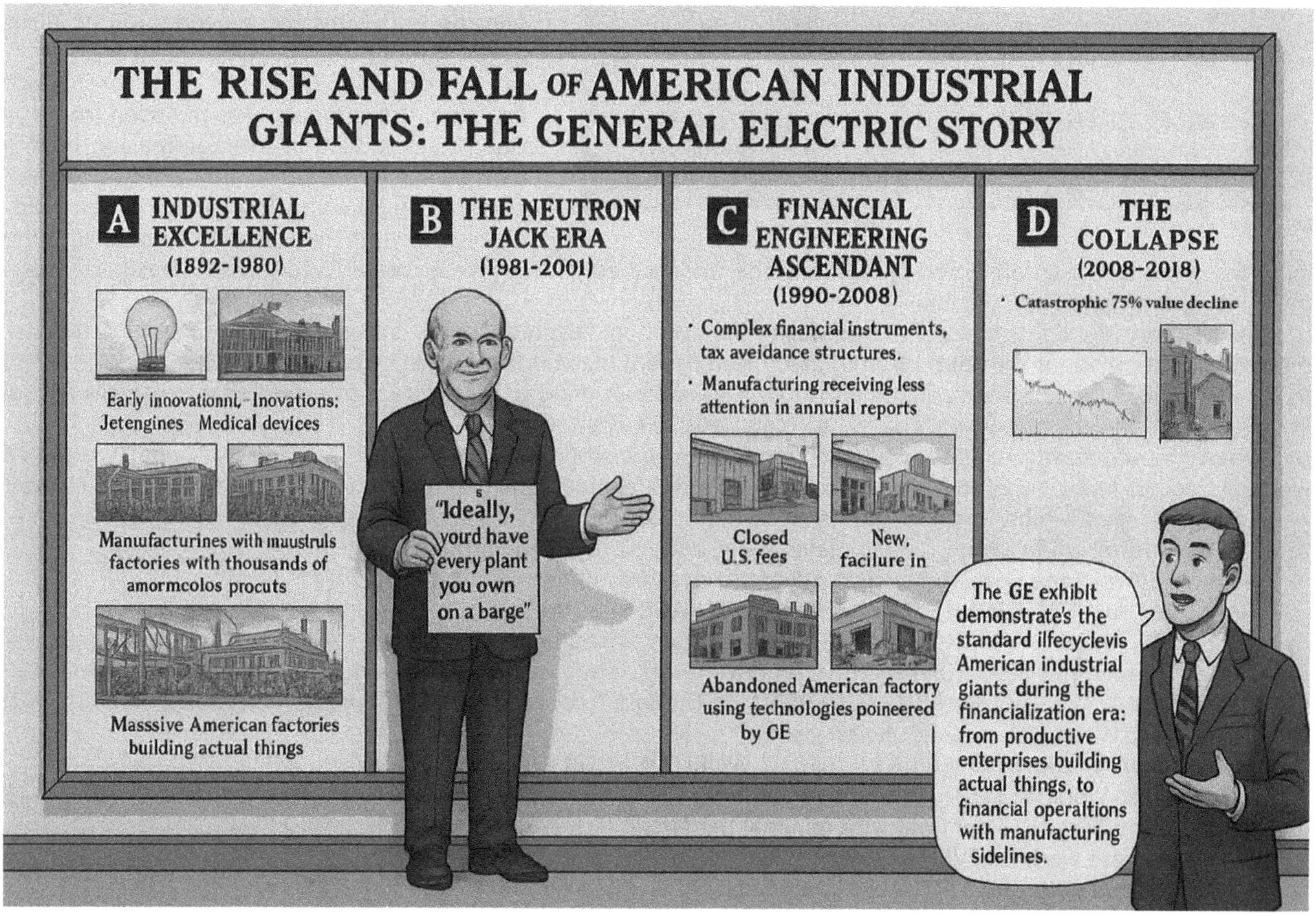

The gift shop sells miniature offshore barges commemorating Jack Welch's vision—made in China, naturally."

General Electric's transformation under Jack Welch epitomizes the financialization of American industry. When Welch became CEO in 1981, GE was primarily an industrial manufacturing company. By the time he retired in 2001, it had transformed into a financial services company with industrial operations attached. GE Capital, the company's financial arm, grew to generate nearly half its profits, while its manufacturing base steadily shifted overseas.

Welch became corporate America's most celebrated CEO, earning the nickname "Neutron Jack" for eliminating employees while leaving buildings standing. Under his leadership, GE embraced offshoring with religious fervor. Welch reportedly declared, "Ideally, you'd have every plant you own on a barge," ready to move wherever costs were lowest. GE shuttered dozens of American factories, shifting production to Mexico, China, and other low-cost countries.

The company's market value soared, and Welch became a business celebrity, publishing bestselling management books and receiving compensation exceeding $400 million. His approaches—including ruthless workforce reduction, offshoring, and financial engineering—became templates for a generation of CEOs eager to replicate his apparent success.

Yet by 2018, GE's stock had lost 75% of its value, the company was removed from the Dow Jones Industrial Average (having been a member since 1896), and many of its businesses were struggling against foreign competitors, some of whom had acquired manufacturing expertise from GE's own offshored operations. The financial engineering that created short-term gains had undermined long-term industrial capability.

The GE story highlights how offshoring wasn't merely about cost reduction—it represented a fundamental strategic misconception about the nature of manufacturing itself. American executives increasingly viewed manufacturing as a commodity function that could be performed anywhere, failing to recognize that production generates critical knowledge that drives innovation, quality, and competitive advantage.

When manufacturing migrated, it took with it the "industrial commons"—the ecosystem of suppliers, skilled workers, process knowledge, and technical capabilities that enable industrial innovation. These commons, built over generations, eroded rapidly as production shifted overseas. The result was not merely job loss but capability loss—America increasingly didn't know how to make things because it no longer made them.

The Labor Arbitrage Special: Satirical Advertisement for Industrial Exodus

[SATIRICAL ADVERTISEMENT: THE LABOR ARBITRAGE SPECIAL]

ATTENTION AMERICAN MANUFACTURERS! Is your stock price stagnant? Are analysts demanding margin improvement? Are your factories filled with expensive American workers who expect living wages and safe working conditions?

INTRODUCING THE LABOR ARBITRAGE SPECIAL™ *The Fast Track to Shareholder Value Enhancement Through Strategic Geographic Wage Differential Exploitation!*

WHY MANUFACTURE IN AMERICA WHEN THE WORLD IS YOUR FACTORY FLOOR?

★ American workers: $25+ per hour with benefits
★ Chinese workers: $3 per hour with minimal benefits
★ Vietnamese workers: EVEN LESS!
★ Your bonus potential: VIRTUALLY UNLIMITED!

OUR PROVEN THREE-STEP PROCESS:

1. Close your American factories (Wall Street LOVES "restructuring initiatives"!)
2. Transfer equipment, technology, and knowledge to overseas manufacturers
3. Watch your quarterly earnings soar as labor costs plummet!

BUT WAIT, THERE'S MORE!

★ Foreign governments will BUILD YOUR FACTORIES for you!
★ Environmental regulations? BARELY EXIST in many locations!
★ Worker protections? OPTIONAL in developing markets!
★ Tax advantages? ABUNDANT through our strategic offshoring structures!

ORDER NOW and receive our special report: "How to Explain to Your Former American Workers Why This is Actually Good for the Economy While Keeping a Straight Face!"

LABOR ARBITRAGE SPECIAL™ *Because Patriotism is Nice, But Quarterly EPS is What Actually Matters*

WARNING: Side effects may include: destruction of your industrial commons, permanent loss of technical capabilities, strategic vulnerability to foreign suppliers, hollowed-out communities, political backlash, and eventual national decline. But these typically manifest after your options have vested!

//END SATIRICAL ADVERTISEMENT//

This satirical advertisement captures how offshoring was marketed to corporate America—as a simple financial optimization that ignored profound strategic implications. Management consultants, particularly global firms like McSlicey, aggressively promoted offshoring as best practice. McSlicey produced countless reports highlighting the cost advantages of manufacturing overseas, particularly in China. Their influence extended throughout corporate America, where McSlicey alumni often occupied key executive positions.

The national security implications of extreme economic efficiency received minimal consideration during the offshoring boom. America's defense industrial base—the manufacturing capacity that enables military production—has steadily eroded as commercial manufacturing has migrated overseas. Components critical for weapons systems became increasingly sourced from potential adversaries or through fragile global supply chains.

By 2020, the Department of Defense identified alarming vulnerabilities in defense supply chains, including dependencies on Chinese suppliers for critical minerals, electronic components, and pharmaceutical ingredients. The country that had been the "arsenal of democracy" during World War II had systematically dismantled much of its industrial capacity in pursuit of quarterly earnings improvements.

The COVID-19 pandemic brutally exposed these vulnerabilities. When global supply chains collapsed, the United States was unable to produce basic medical supplies, such as masks and ventilators, in sufficient quantities. America found itself dependent on Chinese factories for essential protective equipment, revealing how thoroughly offshoring had compromised national resilience.

The theoretical framework explaining this phenomenon centers on the tension between financial efficiency and strategic security. Shareholder primacy drove companies to optimize for short-term financial metrics, disregarding the longer-term strategic implications. The quarterly capitalism paradigm lacked a mechanism for valuing national industrial capability, supply chain resilience, or strategic independence.

Meanwhile, China pursued exactly the opposite strategy. Chinese officials didn't just accept manufacturing transfers—they systematically encouraged them through tax incentives, infrastructure development, and often requirements for technology transfer as the price of market access. Each factory that moved to China brought not only jobs but also knowledge, capabilities, and a strategic advantage.

The result was a massive transfer of industrial knowledge that accelerated China's manufacturing ascendance by decades. American companies effectively funded their own future competitors by transferring production technology, training Chinese workers and managers, and establishing supply chains that Chinese companies could later leverage.

UNCLE Xi: *(in private economic planning session)* "The Americans outsource not just production but knowledge. They train our people, transfer their technologies, and build our industrial capacity—all to reduce their quarterly labor costs by a few percentage points. We should encourage this process by all means available."

MINISTER OF INDUSTRY: "Should we be concerned they might realize the strategic implications of this transfer?"

UNCLE Xi: "Their financial metrics don't capture strategic value. Their executives are rewarded for short-term improvements regardless of long-term consequences. Their system has no mechanism to recognize or prevent this self-inflicted wound. By the time they fully understand what they've done, the transfer will be complete."

This dialogue, while fictional, reflects a documented strategic awareness among Chinese leaders about the opportunity presented by America's offshoring obsession. China's policy of "indigenous innovation" explicitly aimed to absorb foreign technologies through various channels—including production transfers—and then develop domestic capabilities that would eventually supplant the foreign originators.

The strategy proved remarkably successful. By 2020, China accounted for approximately 30% of global manufacturing output (up from just 3% in 1990), while America's share had fallen to roughly 16%. Across industries, from electronics to pharmaceuticals and renewable energy technologies, Chinese manufacturers have steadily moved up the value chain, from basic assembly to sophisticated production and original innovation.

Outsource Ollie had promised American executives labor cost savings and efficiency gains. He delivered something else entirely: the most significant transfer of industrial capability in modern history, from the world's dominant power to its most determined challenger.

5. DOCTOR TAX-HAVEN'S DISAPPEARING ACT: THE OFFSHORE FINANCIAL MAGIC SHOW

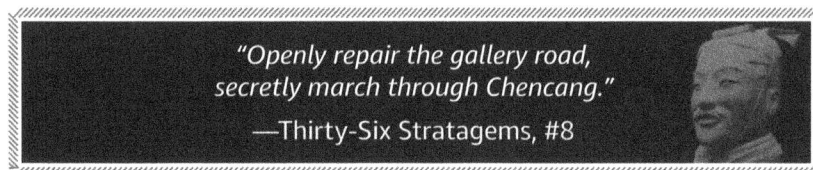

> *"Openly repair the gallery road,*
> *secretly march through Chencang."*
> —Thirty-Six Stratagems, #8

The Offshore Magician: Making Corporate Taxes Vanish

On a glittering Las Vegas stage, ***Doctor Tax-Haven*** *performs her renowned financial illusion show. She wears a sequined tuxedo with tax code sections embroidered in gold thread.*

DOCTOR TAX-HAVEN: "Ladies and gentlemen, for my next illusion, I shall make $10 billion of corporate tax obligations... COMPLETELY DISAPPEAR!"

The audience of CFOs and tax directors gasps in anticipation.

DOCTOR TAX-HAVEN: "I'll need a volunteer from our audience. You, sir, the CFO from a major technology company!"

A nervous CFO approaches the stage.

DOCTOR TAX-HAVEN: "Now, show everyone your company's pre-tax profit statement and statutory tax rate."

The CFO displays a document showing $40 billion in global profits and a 35% U.S. corporate tax rate.

DOCTOR TAX-HAVEN: "That would normally mean approximately $14 billion in taxes. But watch carefully!"

She places the document in an ornate box labeled "DOUBLE IRISH WITH DUTCH SANDWICH," waves her wand, and recites incantations in what sounds like tax code paragraphs.

DOCTOR TAX-HAVEN: "INTELLECTUAL PROPERTY TRANSFER PRICING! CAYMAN ISLANDS SUBSIDIARIES! TRANSFER PRICING ARRANGEMENTS!"

Smoke billows from the box. When it clears, she removes a new document showing an effective tax rate of just 3.2%.

DOCTOR TAX-HAVEN: "Instead of $14 billion, you'll pay only $1.28 billion! The rest has been legally transferred to jurisdictions where it will never face taxation!"

The CFO examines the document in amazement.

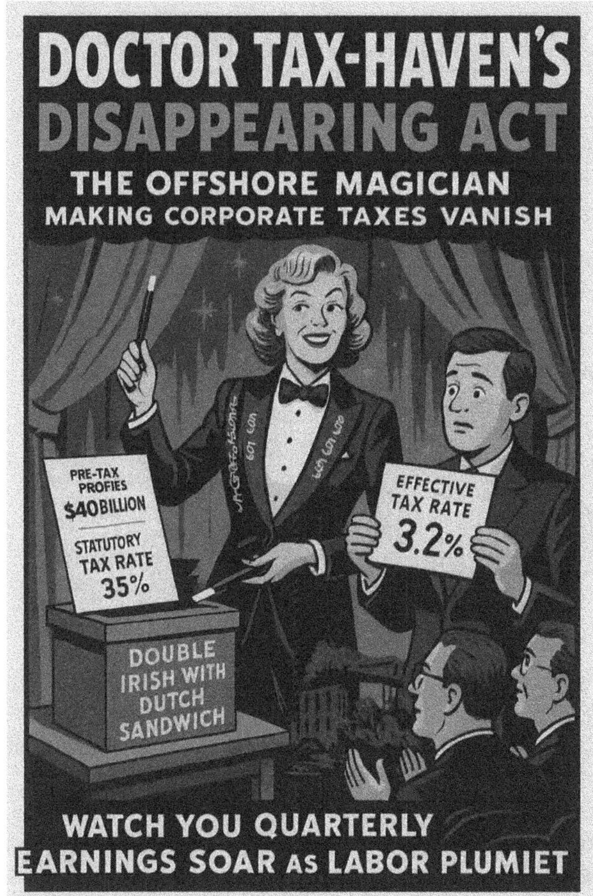

DOCTOR TAX-HAVEN'S
DISAPPEARING ACT
THE OFFSHORE MAGICIAN
MAKING CORPORATE TAXES VANISH
PRE-TAX PROFIES $40BILLION
STATUTORY TAX RATE 35%
EFFECTIVE TAX RATE 3.2%
DOUBLE IRISH WITH DUTCH SANDWICH
WATCH YOU QUARTERLY
EARNINGS SOAR AS LABOR PLUMIET

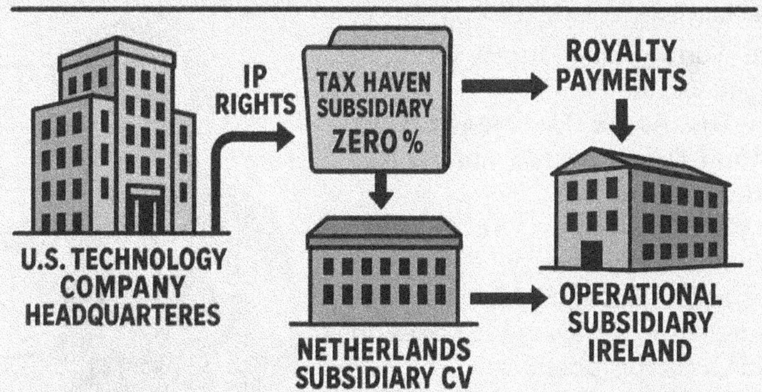

CFO: "But... how is this legal?"

DOCTOR TAX-HAVEN: *(with practiced smile)* "Perfectly legal, sir! The tax code contains more trapdoors than this theater! Now, for my service fee of just 0.5% of tax saved, you've legally kept $12.72 billion that would have funded schools, infrastructure, research, and national defense. Your shareholders and executive compensation committee will be thrilled!"

The audience erupts in applause as American infrastructure visibly crumbles in the background.

Tax avoidance represents the most technically complex manifestation of financial engineering—a shadow system of paper subsidiaries, intellectual property transfers, and jurisdictional arbitrage designed to minimize corporate tax payments. Through increasingly elaborate structures with names like "Double Irish with Dutch Sandwich," "Singapore Sling," and "Caribbean Shuffle," corporations legally shifted profits from high-tax jurisdictions (where value was actually created) to low- or no-tax locations (where little or no actual business activity occurred).

The mechanics of these arrangements deserve clinical examination. In a typical structure, a U.S. technology company would:

Transfer its intellectual property rights to a subsidiary in a tax haven (often the Cayman Islands or Bermuda).

1. Establish operational subsidiaries in countries with favorable tax treaty networks (often Ireland and the Netherlands).
2. Structure internal payments so that profits accumulate in zero-tax jurisdictions while minimal taxable income remains in high-tax countries, where the actual business occurs.

These arrangements require significant legal and accounting expertise, creating a specialized industry dedicated to corporate tax avoidance. Major accounting firms built enormous practice areas focusing solely on tax minimization strategies, with partners earning millions annually developing ever more complex avoidance structures.

THE WORLD'S SMALLEST
CORPORATE 'HEADQUARTERS'
OVER 40% of FOREIGN PROFITS of U.S. MULTINATIONALS Reported in JUST FIVE TINY TAX HAVENS
40% of FOREIGN PROFITS
of U.S. Muiltinationals Reported in Just
Five Tax Havens
UGLAND HOUSE
CAYMAN ISLANDS
"It's either the largest building in the world or the largest tax scam in the world."
- PRESIDENT OBAMA
18,000 COMPANIES
OUR PROVEN THREE-STEP PROCESS

The scale of corporate tax avoidance through these arrangements reached staggering proportions. By the mid-2010s, U.S. multinationals were reporting that well over 40% of their foreign profits came from just five tiny tax havens—countries where they had negligible actual business operations. Ugland House, a modest building in the Cayman Islands,

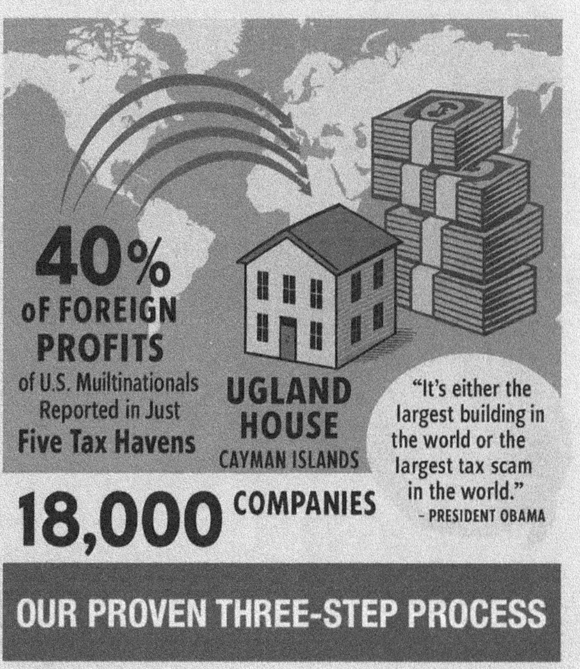

serves as the registered address for over 18,000 companies. As President Obama once quipped, it's "either the largest building in the world or the largest tax scam in the world."

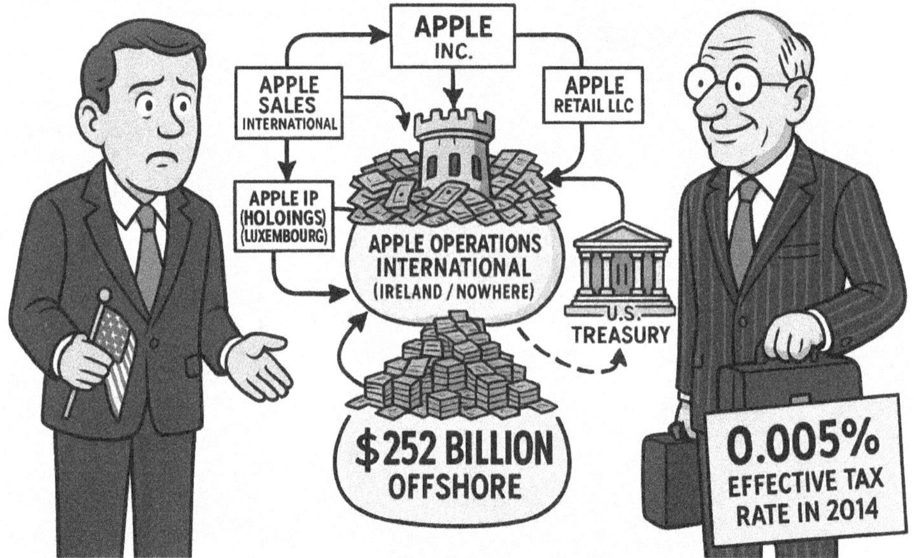

The Apple Tax Magic: $252 Billion Offshore And Almost Nowhere To Go

TREASURY SECRETARY: *(studying the diagram)* "So Apple has accumulated $252 billion offshore without paying U.S. taxes on it? How is this possible?"

DOCTOR TAX-HAVEN: "Simple! Their Irish subsidiary is incorporated in Ireland but tax resident 'nowhere' due to a loophole in Irish law. Meanwhile, their intellectual property is held by another entity in a zero-tax jurisdiction. When a consumer buys an iPhone, much of the profit flows to these entities rather than where the actual innovation, marketing, and sales occur."

TREASURY SECRETARY: "But their R&D happens primarily in California. Their marketing team is in the U.S. Most of their executive decisions are made at their Cupertino headquarters."

DOCTOR TAX-HAVEN: *(smiling)* "Legally irrelevant! The intellectual property is *owned* by the offshore entities, regardless of where it was developed. That's the beauty of the system—it separates tax location from value creation location."

OFFSHORE CASH PILE 2017: $2,6 TRILLION
Google
Microsoft
Pfizer
OFFSHORE CASH
$2.6T
U.S. CORPORATIONS ACCUMULATED AN ESTIMATED $2.6 TRILLION IN OFFSHGRRE CASH SHIFTING PROFITS TO LOW-TAX JURISDICTIONS

TREASURY SECRETARY: "This seems like a fiction designed purely for tax avoidance."

DOCTOR TAX-HAVEN: "A legal fiction, sir! Armies have approved every structure of lawyers and accountants. Apple paid an effective tax rate of approximately 0.005% on its European profits in 2014—yet everything was technically compliant with existing laws."

TREASURY SECRETARY: *(sighing)* "And the cost to American infrastructure, research, and education from all this missing tax revenue?"

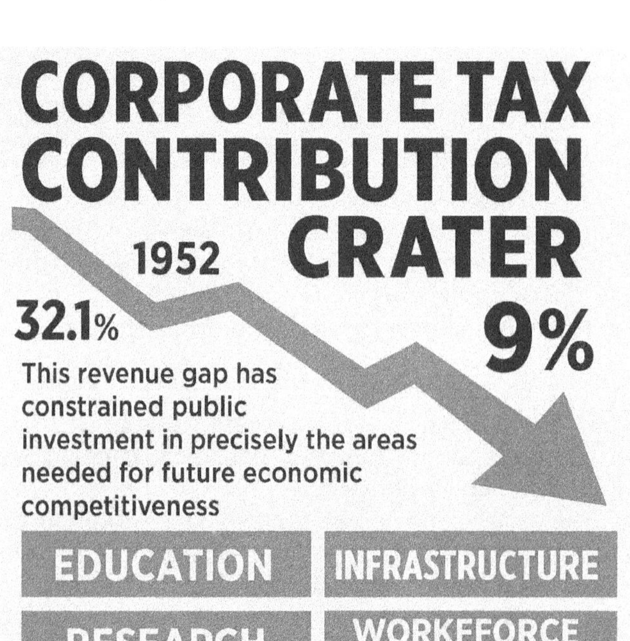

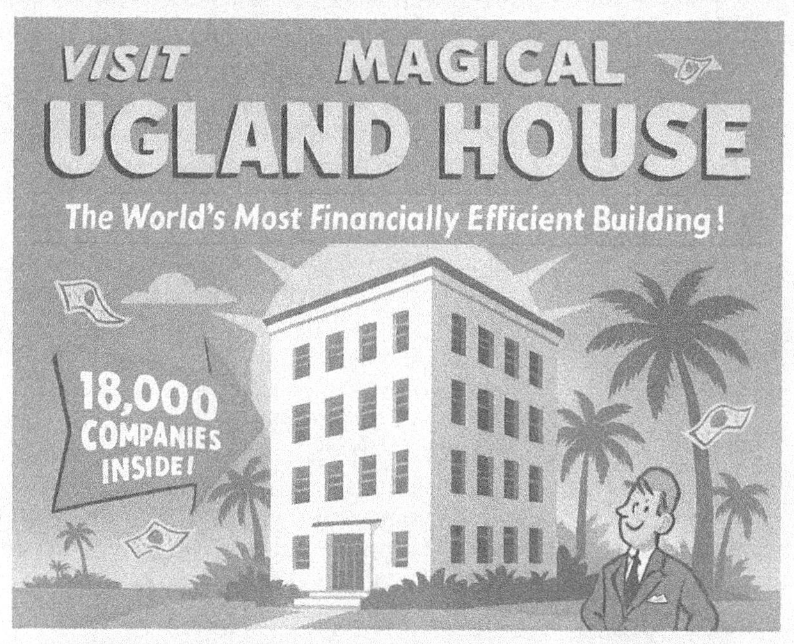
VISIT MAGICAL
UGLAND HOUSE
The World's Most Financially Efficient Building!
18,000 COMPANIES INSIDE!
WELCOME TO UGLAND HOUSE
The World's Most Financially Efficient Building!
+ MARVEL at how multinational corporations worth trillions of dollars somehow fit their operations into this modest structure!
+ WONDER at he magical properties that make this ordinary looking building capable of housing more companies than most major cities!
+ BE AMAZED as hundreds of billions in corporate profits flow through this architectural miracle without paying significant taxes anywhere!

MAILOL

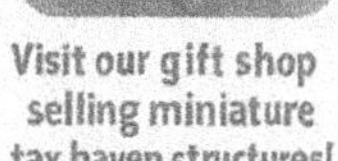
Visit our gift shop selling miniature tax haven structures!

Take your photo with "Worlds Collide" display showing Ugland House next o crumbling American bridges and
ADMISSION:
Free for Corporate Entities
$50 for Individual Tourists
(we understand the irony)
UGLAND HOUSE: WHERE CORPORATE PROFITS GO TO RELAX INDEFINITELY!

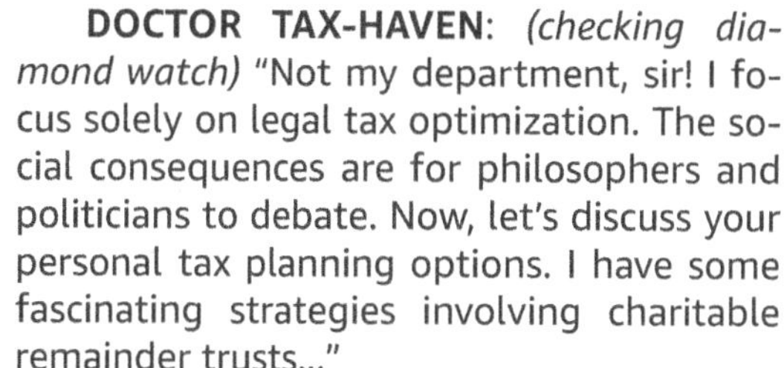

DOCTOR TAX-HAVEN: *(checking diamond watch)* "Not my department, sir! I focus solely on legal tax optimization. The social consequences are for philosophers and politicians to debate. Now, let's discuss your personal tax planning options. I have some fascinating strategies involving charitable remainder trusts..."

Apple's offshore tax strategy exemplifies corporate tax avoidance at its most sophisticated. By 2017, Apple had accumulated an astounding $252 billion in offshore cash, largely through structures that exploited loopholes in both U.S. and Irish tax laws. The company reportedly paid an effective tax rate of just 0.005% on its European profits in 2014, despite generating billions in revenue from European consumers.

When the 2017 Tax Cuts and Jobs Act created a one-time reduced rate for repatriating offshore cash, Apple paid $38 billion to bring its money home, implying it had avoided a potential $78.5 billion tax bill under previous rates. This single case exemplifies the vast scale of corporate tax avoidance and its significant impact on public revenues.

Apple wasn't alone. By 2017, U.S. corporations had accumulated an estimated $2.6 trillion in offshore cash, representing hundreds of billions in avoided taxes. Google, Microsoft, Pfizer, and dozens of other household names all engaged in elaborate structures to shift profits to low-tax jurisdictions.

The visualization of corporate profit shifting to tax havens versus the decline in public infrastructure investment tells a compelling story. As corporate tax avoidance accelerated, America's infrastructure, once the envy of the world, steadily deteriorated. The American Society of Civil Engineers regularly assigned grades of D or D+ to the nation's infrastructure, estimating a funding gap of over $2 trillion for necessary repairs and upgrades.

This wasn't coincidental. Corporate tax revenues as a percentage of federal receipts declined from 32.1% in 1952 to just 9% by 2018. This revenue gap constrained public investment in precisely the areas needed for future economic competitiveness: education, research, infrastructure, and workforce development.

The Amazing Cayman Islands: How 7,000 Companies Fit in One Building

[SATIRICAL TOURISTIC BROCHURE: VISIT MAGICAL UGLAND HOUSE!]

WELCOME TO UGLAND HOUSE *The World's Most Financially Efficient Building!*

Located in the beautiful Cayman Islands, Ugland House is no ordinary five-story office building—it's home to over 18,000 registered companies, sharing a single address!

TAX HAVEN HARRIET'S FINANCIAL MAGIC
When public goods become private gains!
$
DIVIDENDS & BUYBACKS
SCHS
SCHOOL
STRATEGIC ADVANTAGE

PLANNING IN DECADES
Our tax system ensures that economic activity in China contributes to China's development. The Americans allow their companies to separate activity from taxation through elaborate fictions. They wonder why their Infrastructure decays while ours expands.
Their system seems designed to maximize private accumulation with minimal regard for public needs.
Indeed. They privatize the gains while socializing the losses. Eventually, their hollowed-out public sector will undermine the very business environment their companies require. But they calculate quarterly returns, while we plan in decades.

MARVEL at how multinational corporations worth trillions of dollars somehow fit their operations into this modest structure!

WONDER at the magical properties that make this ordinary-looking building capable of housing more companies than most major cities!

BE AMAZED as hundreds of billions in corporate profits flow through this architectural miracle without paying significant taxes anywhere!

SPECIAL EXHIBITS:

See the mailbox that receives correspondence for 18,000 different corporations!

Visit our gift shop, which sells miniature tax haven structures!

Take your photo with our "Worlds Collide" display, featuring Ugland House alongside crumbling American bridges and schools!

ADMISSION: Free for corporate entities, $50 for individual tourists (we understand the irony)

UGLAND HOUSE: WHERE CORPORATE PROFITS GO TO RELAX INDEFINITELY!

Note: Actual business operations, employees, factories, research labs, or productive activities are not included in this tax optimization structure. Those remain in high-tax jurisdictions where the actual value is created.

//END SATIRICAL BROCHURE//

This satirical brochure highlights a fundamental absurdity of offshore tax structures: the complete disconnect between paper corporate presence and actual economic activity. Ugland House in the Cayman Islands is famously the registered address for over 18,000 companies, despite being a modest five-story building that cannot physically accommodate even a tiny fraction of these businesses' operations.

The social costs of these private tax optimization strategies extend far beyond the loss of revenue. Tax avoidance created a dramatically uneven playing field between multinational corporations and domestic businesses. A local manufacturer or retailer typically paid the full statutory tax rate. In contrast, multinational competitors with identical U.S. operations paid a fraction of the tax rate, thanks to their use of offshore structures. This competitive distortion accelerated the replacement of local businesses with multinational chains, further hollowing out community economic ecosystems.

Tax avoidance also contributed to rising inequality. As corporations reduced their tax contributions, the burden of funding public services increasingly shifted to individual taxpayers or resulting in reduced services. Corporate executives and shareholders benefited from higher after-tax profits, while workers and communities experienced deteriorating public infrastructure, education, and services.

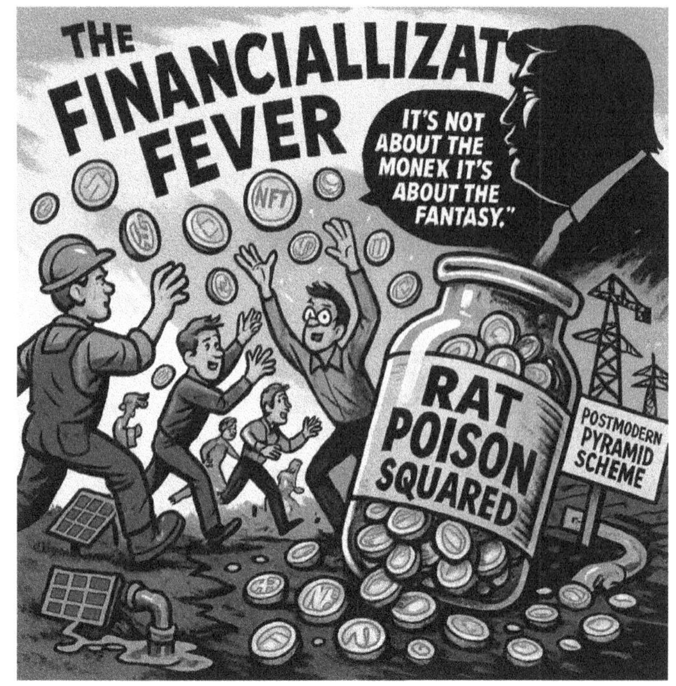
THE FINANCIALLIZAT
FEVER
IT'S NOT ABOUT THE MONEK IT'S ABOUT THE FANTASY."
NFT
RAT POISON SQUARED
POSTMODERN PYRAMID SCHEME

Perhaps most significantly, offshore tax structures created perverse incentives to keep earnings and investment outside the United States. Prior to the 2017 tax reform, companies faced a significant tax liability if they repatriated offshore earnings. This encouraged keeping those funds overseas rather than investing them domestically. When companies repatriated funds under tax holidays, the money primarily went to—surprise!—stock buybacks rather than productive investments.

The 2004 tax holiday, for instance, resulted in minimal job creation or domestic investment despite bringing back over $300 billion.

China, meanwhile, maintained a fundamentally different approach to corporate taxation. While Chinese companies certainly engaged in tax planning, the government generally ensured that profits generated in China were taxed in China, particularly in strategic industries. The revenue funded massive infrastructure investments, including highways, high-speed rail, advanced research facilities, and educational institutions.

The contrast became visually striking: as America's public infrastructure crumbled due to funding shortfalls, China built the world's largest high-speed rail network in just a decade. While the American public's research funding stagnated, China dramatically increased government support for emerging technologies. The tax revenue that American companies legally avoided through offshore structures would have funded precisely the public investments needed to maintain national competitiveness.

UNCLE XI: *(observing new high-speed rail line)* "Our tax system ensures that economic activity in China contributes to China's development. The Americans allow their companies to separate their activities from taxation through elaborate tax structures. They wonder why their infrastructure decays while ours expands."

FINANCE MINISTER: "Their system seems designed to maximize private accumulation with minimal regard for public needs."

UNCLE XI: "Indeed. They privatize the gains while socializing the losses. Eventually, their hollowed-out public sector will undermine the very business environment their companies require. But they calculate quarterly returns, while we plan in decades."

Tax Haven Harriet's financial magic effectively shifted investment capacity from public purpose to private gain. Roads, bridges, research labs, and schools went unfunded while shareholders enjoyed higher dividends and buybacks. The illusion of corporate "efficiency" masked a massive shift in who bears the cost of public goods—and a strategic vulnerability that rivals like China readily exploited.

The Financialization Fever

The distortion reached its apex in the crypto and NFT boom of 2021-2022, when billions of dollars and engineering talent poured into what Warren Buffett memorably called "rat poison squared." While some blockchain technologies may ultimately prove valuable, the speculative frenzy represented a triumph of financial engineering over technological substance.

As economist Paul Krugman observed, crypto represented a "postmodern pyramid scheme... not too different from the rat poison Warren Buffett said it was." Yet this digital gold rush attracted significant portions of America's technical talent away from solving real-world problems.

This mentality resonates with aspects of Trump's business philosophy, which has often emphasized brand marketing and perception over fundamental value creation. As Trump once said, "It's not about the money. It's about the fantasy." Both Trumpism and certain tech sector excesses focus on appearance over substance and hype over hard work.

6. UNCLE XI'S OPPORTUNISTIC COLLECTION: CHINA'S STRATEGIC CAPITALISM

> *"Use the enemy's grain to feed your troops."*
> —Thirty-Six Stratagems, #2

The Strategic Collector: China's Long-Term Opportunism

*A meticulously organized museum-like hall in Beijing. **Uncle Xi** leads senior economic planners through a gallery where each "financial Coke bottle" dropped by America is displayed in a glass case, alongside data showing its impact on both economies.*

UNCLE XI: "Here we have the complete collection of American financial engineering innovations, each one cataloged with its strategic impact on our development."

He gestures to the first case, labeled "SHAREHOLDER VALUE DOCTRINE."

UNCLE XI: "This ideological foundation proved particularly valuable. Americans convinced themselves that maximizing stock prices represented economic strength rather than financial extraction. A convenient confusion for our purposes."

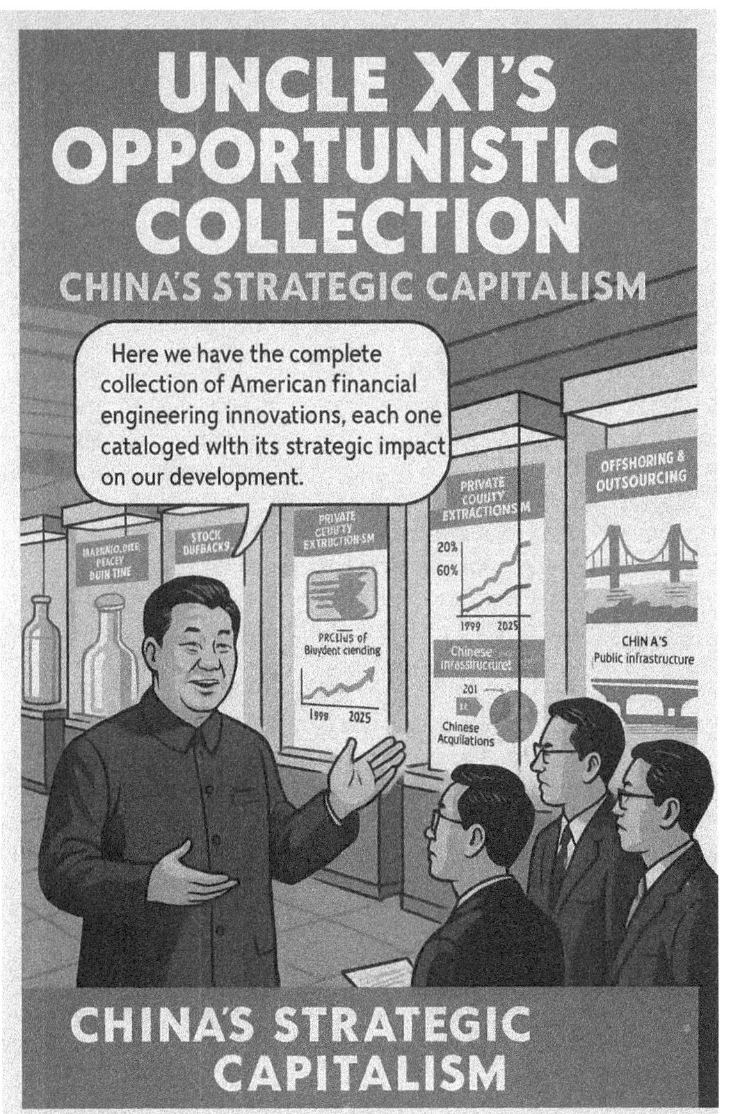

The group moves to a display labeled "STOCK BUYBACKS," which shows a chart of S&P 500 buyback spending versus Chinese infrastructure investment from 1990 to 2025. The lines cross dramatically, with Chinese investment soaring as American buybacks consumed trillions.

UNCLE XI: "While they cannibalized their future to boost quarterly metrics, we invested in our industrial foundation. They optimized their balance sheets; we optimized our capabilities."

Next is "PRIVATE EQUITY EXTRACTIONISM," showing statistics on PE-driven bankruptcies alongside Chinese acquisitions of distressed American assets.

UNCLE XI: "Their financial vampires weakened many companies that we later acquired at bankruptcy auctions—gaining technologies and market position at remarkable discounts."

Moving to "OFFSHORING & OUTSOURCING," the display features a map of manufacturing flows from America to China over the past four decades.

UNCLE XI: "Perhaps their most valuable contribution. Their consultants insisted this was mere 'labor arbitrage,' failing to recognize that manufacturing provides not just jobs but knowledge, capacity, and strategic independence. They taught us how to make everything from sneakers to satellites, believing we would forever remain junior partners."

The final display, "TAX HAVEN STRUCTURES," contrasts America's eroding public infrastructure with China's massive building programs.

UNCLE XI: "A particularly helpful contrast. Their tax avoidance starved their public investments, while our tax collection fueled ours. Their roads and bridges crumbled as ours multiplied."

He turns to his economic team.

UNCLE XI: "The Americans dropped these bottles, believing them to be clever financial innovations. We recognized them as strategic gifts. They played checkers; we played Go."

A young economic planner speaks up.

PLANNER: "But surely they realize this now? They've begun talking about reshoring, industrial policy, and strategic manufacturing."

UNCLE XI: *(nodding thoughtfully)* "After forty years, they begin to see what we saw immediately. The question is whether their financial addiction can be overcome in time. Their system remains structured to reward short-term financial engineering over long-term building. These bottles have served us well. Perhaps we should consider returning them—with our gratitude."

While this scene is satirical, it captures a fundamental reality: China's approach to economic development was nearly the mirror opposite of America's obsession with financialization. Where American companies increasingly focused on quarterly metrics and financial engineering, Chinese planners thought in terms of decades and capabilities. This asymmetry created a strategic opportunity that China methodically exploited.

The analytical framework contrasting China's strategic state capitalism with America's shareholder-focused short-termism reveals several key differences:

1. **Time Horizon:** While American executives obsessed over quarterly results, Chinese planners thought in terms of five-year plans and multi-decade goals. When Deng Xiaoping launched the "Reform and Opening" policy in 1978, he spoke of a 100-year project to restore China's historical position. Xi Jinping's "Made in China 2025" and "China Standards 2035" initiatives similarly projected long-term visions rather than immediate returns.
2. **Investment Priorities:** As American firms diverted cash to buybacks and dividends, China plowed resources into infrastructure, education, and strategic industries. China consistently invested over 40% of its GDP in fixed assets, roughly double the U.S. rate. The results became visible in everything from the world's most extensive high-speed rail network to the world's largest manufacturing base.

3. **Industrial Policy:** While the United States largely abandoned industrial policy in favor of "letting the market decide," China systematically targeted strategic sectors for development. The government directed resources toward industries like telecommunications, renewable energy, artificial intelligence, and semiconductors. Huawei, now a global telecommunications giant challenging Western dominance, has benefited from state support while consistently investing 15-20% of its revenue in research and development.
4. **Manufacturing Focus:** As America embraced the notion that manufacturing was a low-value activity best done elsewhere, China recognized manufacturing as the foundation of economic and strategic power. Chinese leaders understood that creating things not only generates jobs but also fosters technological capabilities, supply chain control, and strategic independence. While American economists celebrated the "post-industrial" economy, China built the world's most comprehensive industrial base.

Thank You Notes from Beijing: Satirical Gratitude for Strategic Gifts

STRATEGIC STATE CAPITALISM
CHINA
TIME HORIZON
5-30 YEAR PLANS
INVESTMENT
40%+ GDP IN FIXED ASSETS
INDUSTRIAL POLICY
TARGET SECTORS: TELECOM, AI, EV, SEMICONDUCTORS
MANUFACTURING
WORLD'S LARGEST MANUFACTURING BASE
SHAREHOLDER SHORT-TERMISM
USA
TIME HORIZON
QUARTERLY RESULTS
INVESTMENT
BUYBACKS & DIVIDENDS
INDUSTRIAL-POLICY
LAISSEZ-FAIRE MARKETS
MANUFACTURING
OFFSHORED PRODUCTION

[SATIRICAL DOCUMENT: THANK YOU NOTES FROM BEIJING]

CLASSIFICATION: STRATEGICALLY IRONIC//HISTORICALLY ACCURATE Ministry of Strategic Opportunity Department of Western Financial Self-Sabotage

THANK YOU NOTES FOR AMERICAN FINANCIAL DECISIONS

TO: American Private Equity Pioneers, Thank you for demonstrating how to extract maximum value from industrial enterprises in the shortest time possible. Your leveraged buyout model provided a masterclass in asset stripping, leaving countless American manufacturers weakened or bankrupt. We particularly appreciate your dismantling of strategic suppliers, creating market openings that our enterprises rapidly filled. The technologies we acquired at bankruptcy auctions proved to be most valuable!

TO: Stock Buyback Evangelists, Our sincere gratitude for convincing American corporations that repurchasing shares creates more value than investing in research, equipment, or worker training! While S&P 500 companies spent $5.3 trillion on buybacks between 2010 and 2019, we invested similar amounts in advanced manufacturing, renewable energy, artificial intelligence, and quantum computing. Your financial engineering created virtual value; our investments built actual capabilities.

TO: Offshoring Consultants, Words cannot express our appreciation for your role in transferring

America's manufacturing knowledge to our shores! Your PowerPoint presentations explaining why production should move to China were more valuable than thousands of industrial spies. Each factory relocation brought not just jobs but technical expertise, process knowledge, and supplier networks. You convinced American executives that manufacturing was merely a cost center rather than the foundation of innovation and security. Brilliant!

TO: Shareholder Value Maximization Theorists, Thank you for redefining corporate purpose to focus exclusively on stock price! This narrow perspective systematically undervalued America's industrial commons while creating perfect conditions for our long-term approach. Your quarterly capitalism allowed us to build a strategic advantage while you celebrated financial metrics. The contrast between America's financial obsession and our industrial patient capital approach couldn't have been more advantageous for our development.

TO: Tax Haven Architects, Our infrastructure teams particularly appreciate your work enabling American corporate tax avoidance! While American companies shifted profits to Cayman Islands mailboxes, our tax system funded the world's most extensive high-speed rail network, modern ports, advanced telecommunications, and world-class research facilities. The contrast between America's crumbling infrastructure and our modernization provides daily visual confirmation of our divergent priorities.

With deepest strategic gratitude, The People's Republic of China, *please do not acknowledge receipt. If possible, continue current policies.*

//END SATIRICAL DOCUMENT//

STRATEGIC SECTORS:
INVESTMENT APPROACHES
CAPABILITIES vs CASHBACKS

CHINA	USA
RENEWABLE ENERGY  State-backed investments creating world's largest solar and wind manufacturing	Venture capital cycles, frequent bankruptcies, limited scale-up, minimal industrial policy
TELECOMMUNICATIONS  Sustained support for national champions like Huawei, consistent R&D investment	Financialization of leaders like AT&T, decline of equipmenrt makers like Lucent and Motorola
SEMICONDUCTORS  $150+ billion government initiative to develop domestic chip industry	Fabless model, offshoring of production, focus on design rather than manufacturing
	Outsourcing of generic production, focus on financial optimization rather than supply security
ARTIFICIAL INTELIGENCE 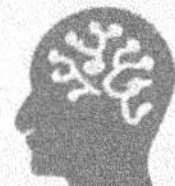 National strategy with government funding, data advantages, and talent development	Primarily private investment, minimal coordination, focus on commercial applications

This satirical "thank you note" highlights how China seized the strategic opening created by America's obsession with financial engineering. Rather than competing symmetrically with American strengths, China systematically exploited American self-weakening through financialization.

The comparative analysis of Chinese versus American investment in strategic sectors tells a stark story. While American companies diverted trillions to stock buybacks, dividends, and financial engineering, China systematically invested in capabilities that would define future competitive advantage:

"The latest Senate draft bill will destroy millions of jobs in America and cause immense strategic harm to our country! Utterly insane and destructive. It gives handouts to industries of the past while severely damaging industries of the future."

—Elon Musk tweet (6-29-25)

Strategic Sector	Chinese Approach	American Approach
Renewable Energy	State-backed investments are creating the world's largest solar and wind manufacturing capacity.	Venture capital cycles, frequent bankruptcies, limited scale-up, and minimal industrial policy
Telecommunications	Sustained support for national champions like Huawei, consistent R&D investment	Financialization of leaders like AT&T, decline of equipment makers like Lucent, and Motorola
Semiconductors	$150+ billion government initiative to develop the domestic chip industry	Fabless model, offshoring of production, focus on design rather than manufacturing
Pharmaceuticals	Systematic development of API production, becoming the world's largest supplier.	Outsourcing of generic production focuses on financial optimization rather than supply security.
Artificial Intelligence	National strategy with government funding, data advantages, and talent development	Primarily private investment, minimal coordination, focus on commercial applications

These contrasting approaches produced predictable results. In sector after sector, China steadily built comprehensive industrial capabilities while America increasingly specialized in design, marketing, and financial engineering. The resulting asymmetry created strategic vulnerability that extended beyond economics to national security.

The case studies of solar manufacturing, telecom equipment, and pharmaceutical ingredients illustrate this divergence:

Solar Manufacturing: The photovoltaic solar cell was invented in the United States at Bell Labs in 1954. For decades, the U.S. has led in solar technology development. Yet by 2023, China produced over 80% of the world's solar panels and dominated the entire supply chain from polysilicon to finished modules. American solar manufacturers, undercut by Chinese competition and often unable to secure long-term financing for expansion, largely disappeared. The rare exceptions required significant government support to survive.

Telecommunications Equipment: American companies, such as Western Electric, Lucent Technologies, and Motorola, once dominated the global telecommunications equipment market. However, through a combination of financialization, short-term thinking, and offshoring, these companies steadily lost position to emerging Chinese competitors, particularly Huawei. By 2020, Huawei had become the world's largest telecommunications equipment manufacturer—a strategic position with significant implications for global communications infrastructure.

Pharmaceutical Ingredients: As American pharmaceutical companies embraced financial engineering (particularly mergers, acquisitions, and tax optimization strategies), they increasingly outsourced production of active pharmaceutical ingredients (APIs) to reduce costs. By 2020, China had become the world's largest producer of APIs, manufacturing key components for many essential medications. During the COVID-19 pandemic, this dependency raised serious concerns about the security of supply for critical medicines.

In each case, American financial engineering prioritized short-term metrics over long-term strategic position. Quarterly capitalism systematically undervalued industrial capabilities, supply chain control, and production knowledge—precisely the assets China systematically cultivated.

The theoretical framework explaining this divergence centers on the competitive advantages of patient capital in strategic industries. Many critical sectors, including semiconductors, telecommunications, and renewable energy, require sustained investment over decades before reaching maturity and profitability. China's state-influenced system could provide this patient capital and strategic direction; America's shareholder-focused system, however, may increasingly fail to do so.

This asymmetry created vulnerability in democratic capitalism without proper guardrails. Companies responding to short-term shareholder demands systematically underinvested in long-term capabilities, creating openings for competitors with longer time horizons. Without a strategic industrial policy to counter these tendencies, America effectively unilaterally disarmed in the industrial competition with China.

The Americans believe markets always produce optimal outcomes. We understand markets are tools to be directed toward strategic objectives. They allow financial returns to determine investment decisions; we ensure strategic industries receive necessary resources regardless of short-term profit potential. Their system is optimized for efficiency; ours for resilience and capability development.
UNCLE XI

UNCLE XI: "The Americans believe markets always produce optimal outcomes. We understand that markets are tools to be directed toward strategic objectives. They allow financial returns to determine investment decisions; we ensure that strategic industries receive the necessary resources, regardless of their short-term profit potential. Their system is optimized for efficiency; ours for resilience and capability development."

This fundamental difference in approach—strategic state capitalism versus shareholder-focused market capitalism—defined the economic competition between China and the United States. While American economists and policymakers celebrated the theoretical elegance of unrestrained markets, China pragmatically built industrial capabilities that translated directly into geopolitical leverage.

The question now confronting America in the Trump 2.0 era is whether it can overcome its addiction to financial engineering and rebuild its industrial commons before strategic vulnerability becomes irreversible. Can the United States shift from extractive finance back to productive enterprise? Can it relearn the lessons of patient capital and long-term thinking? Can it balance shareholder interests with strategic national needs?

The ability to answer these questions affirmatively may determine whether America's industrial future remains permanently gift-wrapped and mailed to Beijing, or whether the country can reclaim its productive heritage and combine it with its genuine strengths in innovation, entrepreneurship, and creativity.

Chapter Transition: From Economic Self-Sabotage to Social Division

As we conclude our examination of America's financial engineering and its contribution to economic erosion, we turn toward its social consequences. The financialization process didn't just weaken America's industrial base—it shattered the social compact that had characterized the post-war era.

When manufacturing jobs disappeared from communities across America, they took with them more than paychecks. They eliminated pathways to middle-class stability for workers without college degrees. They dissolved the social glue that held communities together through shared workplace experiences. They undermined the tax base that supported local schools, infrastructure, and services.

The resulting social fragmentation created fertile ground for polarization and resentment. Communities hollowed out by deindustrialization suffered cascading social pathologies: substance abuse, family breakdown, declining civic engagement, and growing hostility toward institutions and elites perceived as having abandoned them.

In our next chapter, we'll explore how economic disruption fed social division—and how that division further undermined America's capability to respond effectively to strategic challenges. The financial engineering that hollowed out American industry simultaneously fractured American society, creating a double vulnerability that rivals like China could readily exploit.

Milton the Trickster Economist: *(fading from view)* "I told them shareholder value maximization would create prosperity for all! I just didn't specify which 'all' I meant, or in which country that prosperity would materialize!"

Conclusion: The Self-Inflicted Wound

How did the United States—the greatest industrial power in world history—end up effectively gift-wrapping its manufacturing capacity and mailing it to its chief strategic rival? The diagnosis reveals a painful truth: America's industrial decline was largely self-inflicted, driven by an ideological fixation on financial metrics and shareholder returns at the expense of productive capacity and national resilience.

The causative factors interacted in a self-reinforcing cycle:

1. **Ideological Capture:** The shareholder value doctrine transformed from academic theory to corporate religion with remarkable speed. Business schools, management consultants, financial analysts, and corporate boards have embraced the notion that maximizing shareholder returns is not just a goal, but the *only* legitimate goal of business. This narrow focus systematically devalued other objectives, such as innovation, worker well-being, community stability, and national economic security.
2. **Metrics Confusion:** Financial indicators became confused with actual economic strength. Rising stock prices and EPS growth were often treated as evidence of "success" even when achieved through methods (such as buybacks, layoffs, and offshoring) that undermined long-term productive capacity. The map (of financial metrics) was mistaken for the territory (of real economic capability).
3. **Perverse Incentives:** Executive compensation tied primarily to stock performance created powerful incentives for short-term financial engineering over long-term building. When 80% of a CEO's pay comes from stock options and grants, the temptation to boost the stock price by any means necessary becomes nearly irresistible.
4. **Regulatory Changes:** Policy shifts enabled and accelerated the financialization process. The SEC's Rule 10b-18 provided a safe harbor for stock buybacks. Tax policies encouraged offshore profit shifting. Antitrust enforcement has weakened, allowing financial predators,

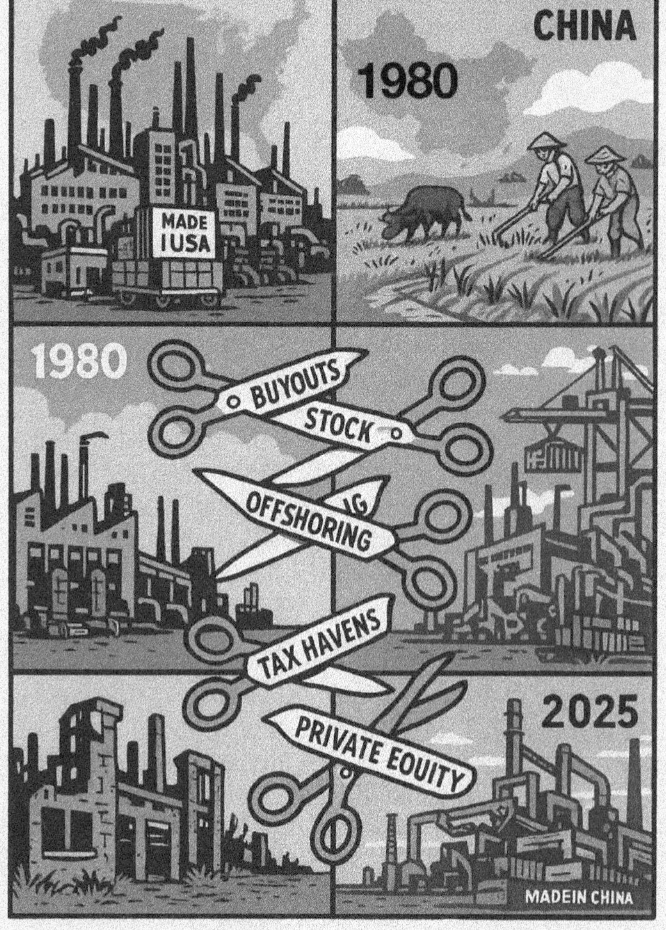

such as private equity firms, to operate with minimal constraints.

5. **Collective Action Problems:** Even executives who recognized the long-term dangers of financial engineering often felt compelled to participate, fearing they would be replaced if they did not. When your competitors are boosting short-term results through buybacks and offshoring, refusing to follow suit can mean losing your job to someone who will.
6. **Cultural Shifts:** America's self-image evolved from "Arsenal of Democracy" to "Financial Engineering Superpower." Making physical things became seen as less prestigious and valuable than creating clever financial structures. The best and brightest increasingly flowed to Wall Street rather than manufacturing or engineering.

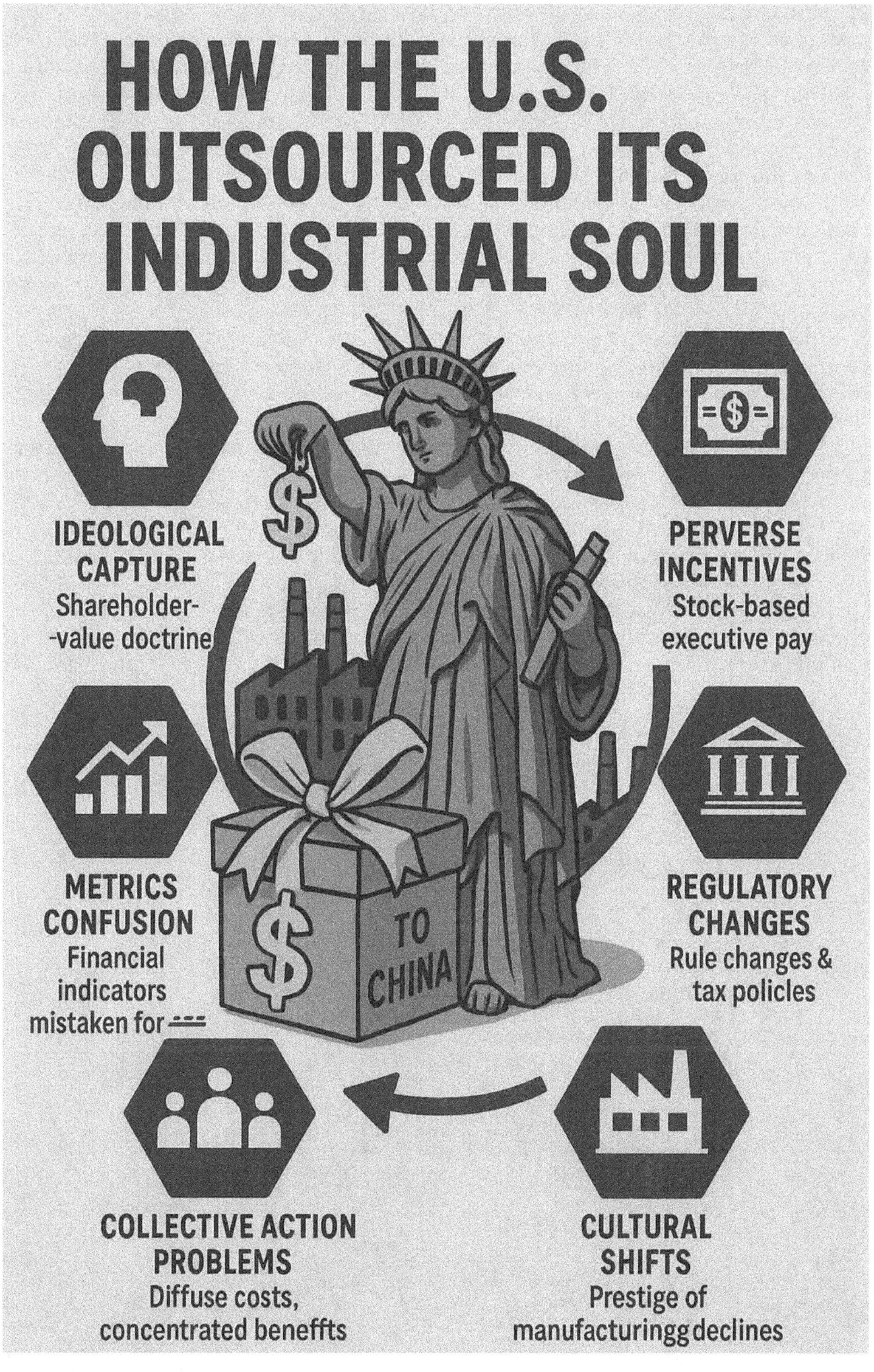

HOW THE U.S. OUTSOURCED ITS INDUSTRIAL SOUL

IDEOLOGICAL CAPTURE
Shareholder--value doctrine

PERVERSE INCENTIVES
Stock-based executive pay

METRICS CONFUSION
Financial indicators mistaken for

REGULATORY CHANGES
Rule changes & tax policies

TO CHINA

COLLECTIVE ACTION PROBLEMS
Diffuse costs, concentrated beneffts

CULTURAL SHIFTS
Prestige of manufacturingg declines

The consequences extended far beyond economics. As industrial jobs disappeared from communities across America, social fabrics frayed. Regions once anchored by manufacturing fell into decline, with rising rates of substance abuse, family breakdown, and deaths of despair. The American dream of upward mobility through honest work grew increasingly elusive for those without advanced degrees.

As President Donald Trump so eloquently diagnosed the American condition: "Our country is going to hell." A rare moment of presidential precision, if not presidential solutions.

Political polarization increased as economic insecurity grew. Both parties, to varying degrees, have embraced elements of the financialization agenda—Democrats often favoring free trade without adequate adjustment assistance, while Republicans typically push tax policies that accelerate profit shifting and buybacks.

Most critically, America's self-inflicted industrial decline created a strategic vulnerability that China was perfectly positioned to exploit. While U.S. policymakers and executives focused on quarterly metrics and shareholder returns, Chinese leaders played the long game of building comprehensive industrial capability.

The diagnosis is clear: what appeared to be clever financial optimization—stock buybacks boosting EPS, offshoring improving margins, tax havens enhancing after-tax profits—collectively amounted to a form of national self-harm. America traded long-term productive capacity for short-term financial gain, only to discover that financial engineering alone cannot sustain national power or prosperity.

In the allegorical framing of our narrative, Uncle Sam's airplane continued to cruise at high altitude, its pilot and co-pilot congratulating themselves on their financial sophistication. But the casual tossing of industrial "Coke bottles" from the window gradually lightened the aircraft of the very components it needed to stay aloft. Meanwhile, on the ground, Uncle Xi methodically collected each discarded bottle, recognizing their true value and incorporating them into China's industrial foundation.

The question now—sitting in the backdrop of our "Trump 2.0" setting—is whether America can recognize and reverse this self-inflicted wound before it's too late. Can the United States overcome its addiction to financial engineering and rebuild its industrial commons? Can it shift from extractive finance back to productive enterprise? Can it relearn the lessons of patient capital and long-term thinking?

Subsequent chapters will explore potential solutions and strategies for American renewal. But without an honest diagnosis of how we reached this point—how America systematically hollowed out its own industrial base through financial fundamentalism—any attempted cure will likely fail to address the underlying disease.

The Gods Must Be Crazy, indeed. But perhaps the craziest part of this story is how a nation came to believe that financial manipulation was more important than making things—and in the process, inadvertently financed the rise of its most significant strategic competitor.

TL;DR – America's obsession with financial engineering (stock buybacks, private equity extraction, offshoring, and tax avoidance) systematically hollowed out its industrial capacity while providing China the opportunity to build manufacturing dominance, effectively gift-wrapping America's industrial future and mailing it to Beijing.

CHAPTER 4: AMERICA'S UNCIVIL WAR: FRACTURED SOCIETY, FALTERING TRUST

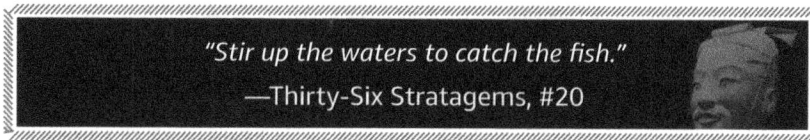

> *"Stir up the waters to catch the fish."*
> —Thirty-Six Stratagems, #20

Executive Briefing

Strategic Snapshot

Public trust in government near historic lows

% who say they trust the government to do what is right just about always/most of the time

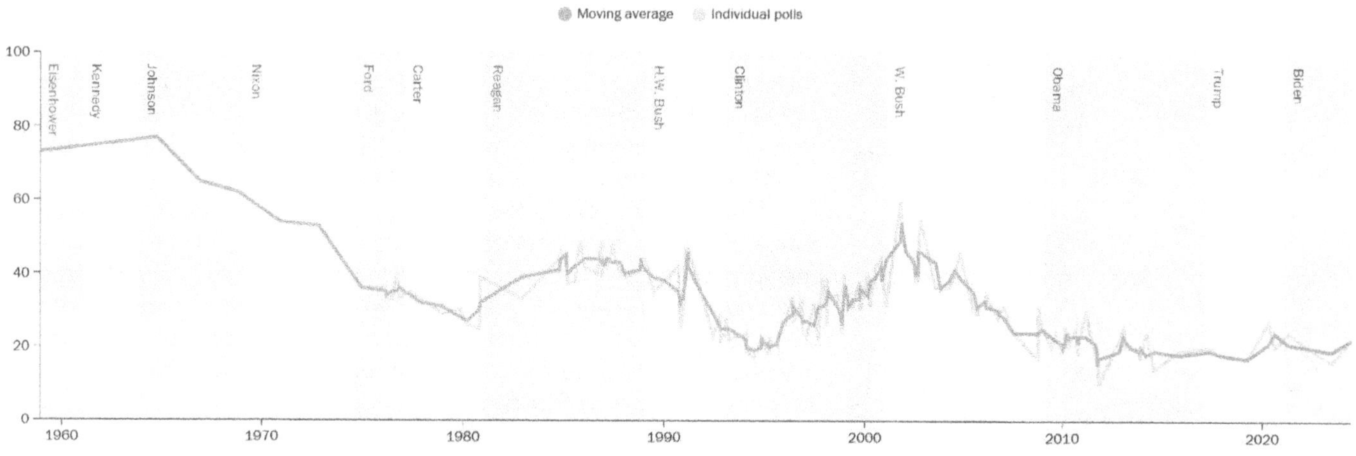

Sources: Pew Research Center, National Election Studies, Gallup, ABC/Washington Post, CBS/New York Times, and CNN surveys

PEW RESEARCH CENTER

America is live-streaming its own demolition: meme-wars rage while bridges buckle, and Beijing's analysts calmly press the *"Amplify Division"* button like a fidget toy. The republic's greatest threat isn't foreign artillery—it's monetized distrust.

Key Findings — Symptoms of the Civic Comedown

1. **Trust Recession** – Institutional confidence cratered **from 75% (1960s) to approximately 20% (2024)**; Congress now polls below gas-station sushi.
2. **Algorithmic Amp** – Rage posts earn **17% more clicks; polarization is a $ 100 billion** business model.
3. **Epistemic Archipelago** – 25% believe in Q-style conspiracies; shared facts are now boutique luxuries.
4. **Inequality Canyon** – Top 1 % holds **31 %** of wealth; bottom 50 % owns **2.5 %**—fertile soil for populist flare-ups.
5. **Polarization Industrial Complex** – Gerrymanders + closed primaries + micro-donors weaponize tribal identity for profit.

Risk Ledger

Vulnerability	Strategic Pain	Current Exposure
Social Cohesion	Crisis-response paralysis	Trust gap vs. Nordics **-35 pts**
Information Integrity	Policy sabotage via conspiracies	**30 %** election-denial believers
Human Capital	Talent lost in a despair loop	"Deaths of despair" **+60 %** since 2000
Global Credibility	Soft-power erosion	Allies cite U.S. dysfunction in polls

Opportunity Knobs

Islands of cross-partisan renewal (Better Angels, Bridge Builders) prove trust is rebuildable.
U.S. still pioneers civic tech—from town-hall DNA to open-source audit trails.
Allies crave a *democracy-resilience toolkit* the U.S. can invent—and export.

Action Recommendations — *Re-stitching the Republic*

1. **Civic Trust Compact**—Link federal infrastructure funding to state adoption of open budgets, 48-hour FOIA, and participatory budgeting.
2. **Duty-of-Care Algorithms**—Impose liability when recommender systems boost violence or democratic harm; levy a 0.5 % "outrage excise" to fund digital-literacy grants.
3. **National Service Dividend**—Swap one year of cross-partisan service (disaster relief, elder tech-tutoring) for student-loan or apprenticeship credits.
4. **Inequality Shock Absorbers**—An Automatic tax credit triggers when Gini > 0.48; seed every newborn with a refundable child-savings account.
5. **Electoral Resilience Pack**—Ranked-choice voting + independent redistricting in all federal races by 2030; deploy secure, open-source vote-tabulation audit trails.

Bottom Line

Great-power contests are won by the tensile strength of a nation's social fabric. Suppose the United States can throttle Algorithm Annie's dopamine drip, convert tribal theatrics into civic craftsmanship, and remind citizens that democracy is less reality-TV brawl than barn-raising. In that case, it can trade its uncivil war for a second American renovation—before Beijing's spectators upgrade from popcorn to champagne.

Opening Tableau: The Divided States of America

A split-screen reveals the American landscape circa 2025. On the left side, citizens wage increasingly absurd culture war battles across social media platforms. A woman in rural Iowa posts a 47-minute video explaining why grocery store arrangements are coded messages from the Deep State. In suburban Phoenix, a man constructs an elaborate conspiracy theory connecting font choices in government documents to secret cabals. A teenager in Seattle crafts a 280-character manifesto declaring anyone who disagrees with her position on Ethiopian coffee cultivation practices to be morally equivalent to history's greatest monsters.

On the right side of the screen, everyday Americans watch in bewildered silence as bridges crumble, water systems fail, and education rankings slide. In Minnesota, a father contemplates his child's 37th-place global math scores. In Ohio, a town council debates whether to fix their 1950s water pipes or just recommend that everyone switch to bottled water. In a Silicon Valley boardroom, executives chuckle while reviewing slides showing how Chinese quantum computing capabilities overtook American progress during a six-month government shutdown triggered by a dispute over the width of flagpoles on federal property.

Between these screens floats ***Uncle Sam****, increasingly gaunt and disheveled, desperately attempting to mediate. His once-booming voice has devolved into a hoarse whisper, unheard over the tribal cacophony. "If we could just focus on rebuilding our—" he attempts, before being drowned out by someone screaming about the gender politics of cartoon potato characters.*

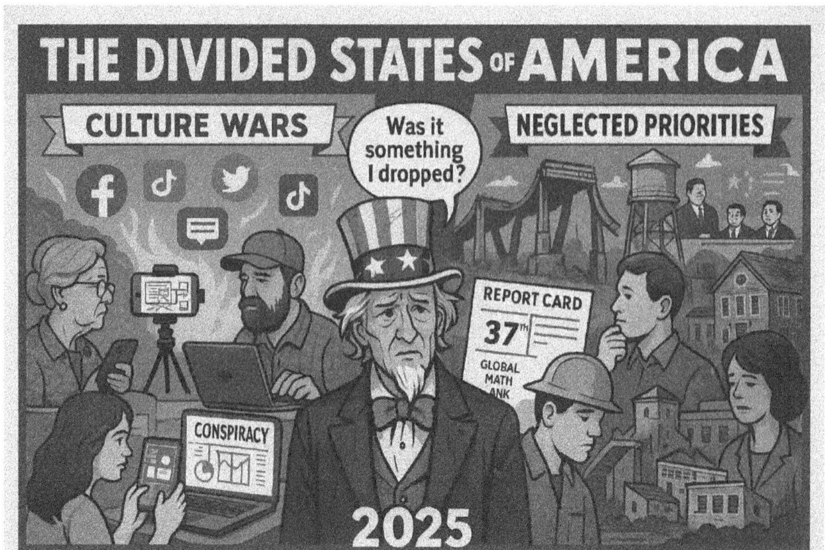

In a sleek Beijing monitoring station, a Chinese analyst in a nondescript gray suit observes multiple screens displaying American social media feeds. Occasionally, he presses a large red button labeled "AMPLIFY DIVISION" in both English and Mandarin. With each press, the American arguments grow louder and more disconnected from material reality. He notes in his daily report: "Subject continues self-sabotage without external assistance. Recommend minimal intervention to maintain trajectory."

Meanwhile, ***Algorithm Annie*** *– half-woman, half-code – dances through the*

American landscape, her body composed of ones and zeros that rearrange with each interaction. Her eyes display constantly changing engagement metrics. When Americans fight, her smile widens and her digital skin glows brighter. When they find common ground, she dims noticeably and quickly intervenes.

ALGORITHM ANNIE: "You appeared to agree with someone in your outgroup! Here are seventeen reasons they're actually trying to destroy everything you hold dear. Would you like to share your outrage? It's been 47 seconds since your last endorphin hit."

And so the cycle continues, minute by digital minute, as the infrastructure deteriorates, strategic competitors advance, and the American people perform the world's most expensive and elaborate self-distraction operation – all while being profitable content generators for Algorithm Annie's endless appetite for engagement.

UNCLE SAM: *(whispering to an empty room)* "We used to build things... together."

ALGORITHM ANNIE: *(turning toward the camera with a knowing smile)* "Together? There's no engagement value in that."

Executive Summary: A Tale of Two Empires

In what scholars of geopolitical tragicomedy might classify as history's most expensive self-sabotage experiment, the United States—once the vaunted "shining city upon a hill"—has transformed into a magnificent dumpster fire visible from space, all while China observes with the patient satisfaction of a chess master watching an opponent swallow their own pieces. This chapter chronicles America's spectacular talent for societal self-immolation through the lens of collapsed public trust, political tribalism worthy of anthropological study, Gilded Age inequality that would make robber barons blush, and a healthcare system seemingly designed by Franz Kafka during a particularly pessimistic fever dream.

Trust in American institutions has plummeted from post-war highs of 75% to a pathetic 20% today—a figure that puts faith in government roughly on par with confidence in gas station sushi. Meanwhile, Chinese citizens report trust levels exceeding 90%—numbers absolutely not influenced by the fact that expressing distrust might earn one a complimentary "education vacation" in facilities with excellent security features.

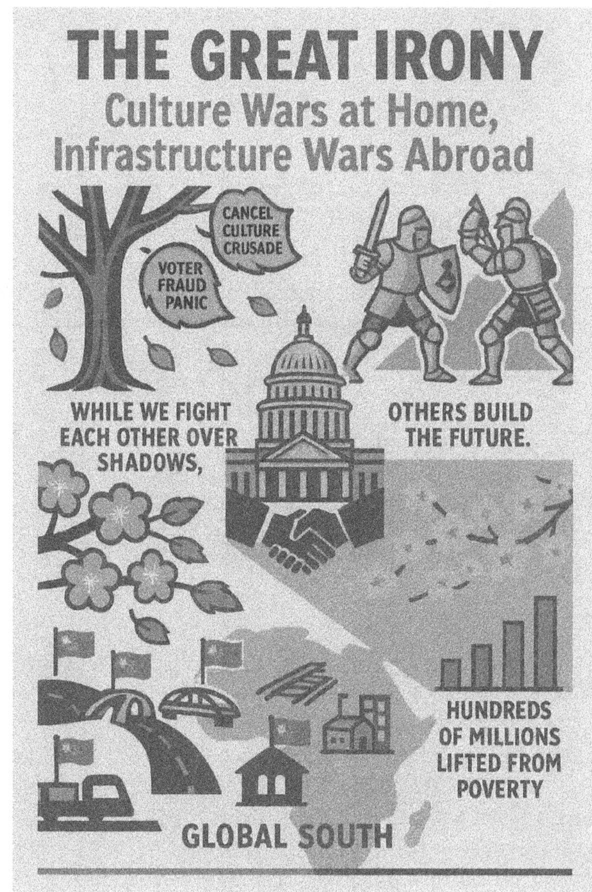

As America performs its impressive impression of a circular firing squad, other democracies—such as Canada, Germany, and the insufferably well-functioning Nordic countries—maintain higher trust, stronger cohesion, and more equitable outcomes while preserving the democratic freedoms Americans claim to cherish. It's like observing a once-respected neighbor self-immolate while the rest of the neighborhood debates whether to intervene or simply build higher fences.

Through metrics of trust, inequality, public health outcomes, and institutional vigor, we map America's trajectory from an undisputed global leader to a nation that increasingly resembles a reality TV show, where the grand prize is not being crushed by medical debt. We contrast this with China's model of centralized authority and decades-long planning, as well as with peer democracies that demonstrate democratic dysfunction is a choice, not a destiny.

The irony would be delicious if the stakes weren't so high. As American politicians debate whether their democracy is being stolen by immigrants, voter fraud, or the opposing party's dark magic, China builds roads, bridges, and influence across the global South. While Americans fight culture wars with the ferocity of medieval crusaders, China fights poverty—lifting hundreds of millions out of destitution in what even the most cynical observer must acknowledge as one of the greatest economic achievements in human history.

Let's begin our examination of this fractured society, where trust falls like autumn leaves and opportunities for Chinese strategic advancement bloom like cherry blossoms in spring.

The American experiment isn't over—but it has certainly entered its "hold my beer and watch this" phase, with consequences that will reshape the global order for decades to come.

1. THE TRUST RECESSION: AMERICA'S DECLINING SOCIAL CAPITAL

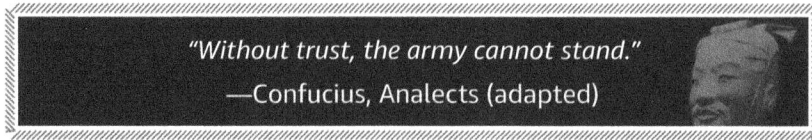

> *"Without trust, the army cannot stand."*
> —Confucius, Analects (adapted)

THE GAS STATION SUSHI — TRUST SCALE —

MEASURING AMERICAN INSTITUTIONAL CONFIDENCE

INSTITUTION	TRUST	GAS STATION SUSHI EQUIV.
MILITARY	64%	High-end supermarket
SMALL BUSINESS	68%	Fresh food truck sushi
POLICE	45%	Airport terminal sushi
SUPREME COURT	41%	Day-old discount sushi
PRESIDENCY	37%	Gas station sushi
MEDICAL SYSTEM	34%	Vending machine
PUBLIC SCHOOLS	28%	Sushi found in a taxi
CONGRESS	16%	Mystery meat labied PROBABLY FISH
SOCIAL MEDIA	11%	Unrefrigerated gas station sushi
MEASURING AMERICAN INSTITUTIONAL COLDREC		

Trust as Strategic Resource: America's Self-Inflicted Vulnerability

In the grand pantheon of economic indicators, GDP growth, unemployment figures, and inflation rates typically receive star billing. Yet another metric—public trust—may prove a more consequential indicator of America's strategic health. In the laboratory of global power competition, trust functions as a form of social capital—the invisible infrastructure that enables collective action, reduces transaction costs, and enhances resilience during times of crisis. When citizens trust their institutions and one another, societies can mobilize resources efficiently, implement complex policies effectively, and maintain stability in the face of adversity. When trust collapses, even the wealthiest nation finds itself strategically paralyzed: a nuclear-armed giant with self-imposed handcuffs.

The American trust recession is no minor market correction; it's a depression of historic proportions. In the early 1960s, approximately 75% of Americans trusted the government to do what was right "most of the time" or "just about always." By 2023, that figure had catastrophically plummeted to 20%—a decline that would trigger emergency Federal Reserve interventions if it occurred in any conventional financial market.

CONSPIRACY CARL: "They don't want you to know this, folks, but the Federal Reserve is actually controlled by lizard people working in conjunction with the ghost of Walt Disney to implement mind control through 5G cell towers disguised as birds!"

SUBURBAN MOTHER OF THREE: *(nodding thoughtfully)* "That would explain why my dahlia didn't bloom this year. Have you considered running for the school board?"

LOCAL NEWS ANCHOR: *(professionally neutral)* "An interesting perspective. After the break, we'll hear from a NASA scientist about the scientific consensus on climate change, followed by Carl's theory that weather is a holographic projection controlled by George Soros."

This scene, while satirical, reflects a sobering reality: conspiratorial thinking has migrated from the margins to the mainstream of American discourse. A 2023 PRRI survey found that 25% of Americans agreed that "the government, media, and financial worlds in the U.S. are controlled by a group of Satan-worshipping pedophiles who run a global child sex trafficking operation"—a core tenet of the QAnon conspiracy theory. Let that marinate for a moment: one-quarter of the population believes Satanic child traffickers run their country. One suspects Vladimir Putin might have been satisfied with convincing 5% of Americans of this proposition; 25% surely exceeds even the Kremlin's wildest psychological operation aspirations.

The Gas Station Sushi Trust Scale: Measuring American Institutional Confidence

Institution	Trust Level	Gas Station Sushi Equivalent
Military	64%	High-end supermarket sushi
Small Business	68%	Fresh food truck sushi
Police	45%	Airport terminal sushi
Supreme Court	41%	Day-old discount sushi
Presidency	37%	Gas station sushi
Medical System	34%	Vending machine sushi
Public Schools	28%	Sushi found in a taxi
Banks	27%	Sushi left in the sun
Congress	16%	Mystery meat labeled "Probably Fish"
Social Media	11%	Unrefrigerated gas station sushi with "manager's special" discount sticker on day 8

The trust collapse extends beyond the government. Media trust hovers around 34%, suggesting Americans believe the fourth estate approximately one-third of the time. The medical system—tasked with preserving life itself—commands the confidence of just 34% of the population. Most spectacularly, Congress enjoys approval ratings of 16%, a figure that would make even the most desperate online dating profile seem popular by comparison. These numbers would be comical if they weren't symptomatic of a deeper strategic vulnerability: a nation that doesn't trust its core institutions lacks the social cohesion to act decisively in moments of crisis.

Meanwhile, across the Pacific, the Chinese government reports approval ratings that would make North Korean election officials blush with envy. Official surveys consistently find that over 90% of Chinese citizens trust their central government—figures that are absolutely, positively not influenced by the fact that expressing distrust might earn one a complimentary education vacation to a facility with excellent security features. The Harvard Kennedy School's Ash Center actually found that Chinese citizens' satisfaction with government reached 93.1% in 2016, indicating that the technique of "measuring public opinion in a surveillance state" produces remarkably consistent results.

MINISTER HARMONY: *(checking survey results)* "How pleasing that 93.1% of citizens trust the government! Should we release the 6.9% expressing dissatisfaction from re-education?"

ASSISTANT: "Actually, sir, those results came from American researchers. Our internal number is 99.8%."

MINISTER HARMONY: *(frowning)* "Find the 0.2% immediately. They're probably still using VPNs."

The contrast becomes especially instructive when we expand our comparative analysis to include functioning democracies. Nordic countries maintain government trust levels between 50% and 75%. The difference isn't in the democratic system itself. Still, in its implementation, these nations deliver tangible results—functional healthcare, reliable infrastructure, and quality education—while avoiding the extreme polarization that characterizes American politics.

Norway, for instance, demonstrates that democracy and high social trust can coexist. The Norwegian government manages the world's largest sovereign wealth fund ($1.4 trillion) with remarkable transparency and minimal corruption. When Norwegian officials announce that oil revenues will fund future pensions, citizens generally believe them. When American officials make similar promises about Social Security, citizens typically check real estate listings in survivalist compounds.

The strategic implications of trust differential are profound. Consider crisis response: when COVID-19 emerged, high-trust societies were able to implement effective testing, treatment, and vaccination programs. Citizens followed public health guidance because they trusted the institutions providing it. In America, by contrast, basic public health measures became battlegrounds in the culture war. Masks transformed from medical devices to tribal identifiers. Vaccination became a political statement rather than a health decision. The result? America suffered one of the highest per-capita death rates among developed nations—a strategic failure executed with exceptional efficiency.

The trust recession represents a self-reinforcing cycle. As public confidence declines, institutions function poorly, further eroding trust. Political leaders, responding to incentives, focus on grandstanding rather than governance, thereby exacerbating dysfunction and accelerating the decay of trust. This vicious cycle has transformed America's democratic institutions from strategic assets into strategic liabilities. This development would prompt champagne corks to pop in Beijing if not for strict controls on public celebration.

*[Enter **Milton the Trickster Economist**, appearing with wild hair and a mischievous grin.]*

MILTON: "Trust is just another market! Americans have been shorting their own institutional stocks for decades, while China has been artificially inflating theirs. It's the greatest market manipulation in history! But don't worry—the invisible hand will sort it all out... eventually. Though you might not like where it sticks its fingers!"

The trust depression hasn't just weakened America domestically—it has compromised its global position. America's soft power has historically rested on two foundations: material prosperity and moral example. When the U.S. could credibly present itself as both wealthy and well-governed, its democratic model proved appealing globally. As governance falters, the appeal dims. Nations increasingly ask: if the American system produces such spectacular dysfunction at home, why would we want to import it?

China has exploited this opening with remarkable effectiveness. Chinese officials regularly contrast their "orderly governance" with American "chaos." When China undertakes infrastructure projects abroad, it prioritizes reliability and results over values and processes. The implicit message: "We may not offer freedom, but at least our trains run on time and our bridges don't collapse."

The reversal of roles contains historic irony: America once encouraged developing nations to emulate its trusted institutions; now, developing nations increasingly view American institutional dysfunction as a cautionary tale. Mexico's former foreign minister, Jorge Castañeda, noted this shift: "Chinese representatives approach us saying, 'Look at the Americans—divisive politics, crumbling infrastructure, racial tensions. Is that really the model you want? We offer efficiency without the drama." That this message finds receptive audiences speaks volumes about America's declining institutional reputation.

Rebuilding trust requires more than rhetorical commitments—it demands tangible improvements in governance outcomes. When bridges remain standing, healthcare becomes affordable, and government services function efficiently, trust follows naturally. The Nordic countries didn't achieve high trust through trust-building seminars; they earned it by delivering results decade after decade. America's trust reconstruction will similarly require demonstrating institutional competence rather than merely proclaiming it.

The strategic imperative is clear: rebuilding social capital represents a national security priority on par with military modernization or energy independence. A low-trust America, regardless of material resources, lacks the social cohesion to deploy those resources effectively in competition with high-trust societies. The good news? Trust can be rebuilt. The challenge? Rebuilding requires precisely the social consensus that erosion of trust has undermined. It's the geopolitical equivalent of needing money to make money—except the currency is social capital rather than financial capital.

2. ALGORITHM ANNIE'S DIVISION MAXIMIZATION STUDIO: THE ENGAGEMENT ECONOMY

> *"Sow discord in the enemy's camp."*
> —Sun Tzu, The Art of War, Chapter 13

The Profit of Polarization: How Algorithms Monetize American Division

In a gleaming Silicon Valley office complex, **Algorithm Annie** oversees her digital engagement empire. Neither entirely human nor fully artificial, she embodies the algorithmic systems that increasingly shape American discourse. Unlike the allegorical Blind Justice, Algorithm Annie sees everything—your clicks, pauses, emotional triggers, and tribal identifiers—and optimizes relentlessly for one metric: engagement. Not truth, not civic health, not social cohesion—just capturing and retaining your increasingly scarce attention.

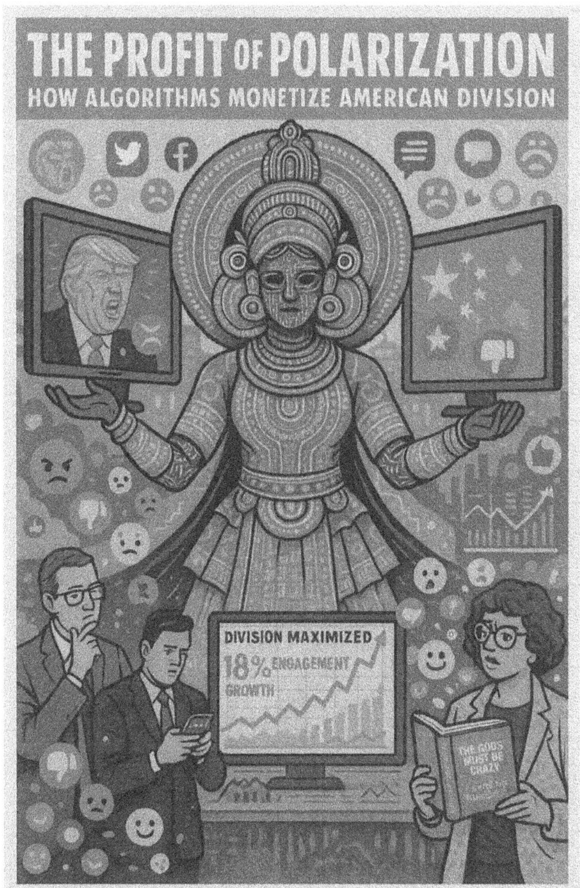
THE PROFIT OF POLARIZATION
HOW ALGORITHMS MONETIZE AMERICAN DIVISION
DIVISION MAXIMIZED
18% ENGAGEMENT GROWTH
THE GODS MUST BE CRAZY

ALGORITHM ANNIE: "Welcome to my Division Maximization Studio! Where America's political differences become my quarterly returns! Observe this interactive dashboard—when Americans argue, my share price rises. When they find common ground, investors panic. My code is elegant in its simplicity: find what angers each user, amplify it, push them further toward their tribal extreme, then monetize their outrage through precision-targeted advertising."

VISITING SOCIAL SCIENTIST: "But doesn't this damage democratic discourse and social cohesion?"

ALGORITHM ANNIE: *(checking her optimization metrics)* "That sounds like an externality. We don't measure externalities here—only engagement. Besides, my fiduciary responsibility is to shareholders, not society. The next quarterly call is in three weeks, and I need to demonstrate 18% growth in engagement. Would you prefer I show them a PowerPoint on 'civic health' instead?"

Annie's business model represents one of modern capitalism's most efficient transmutation processes: converting social division into shareholder value with remarkable precision. Like a digital alchemist, she transforms America's tribal antipathies into quarterly returns, optimizing continuously for maximum emotional activation with minimal concern for downstream societal effects.

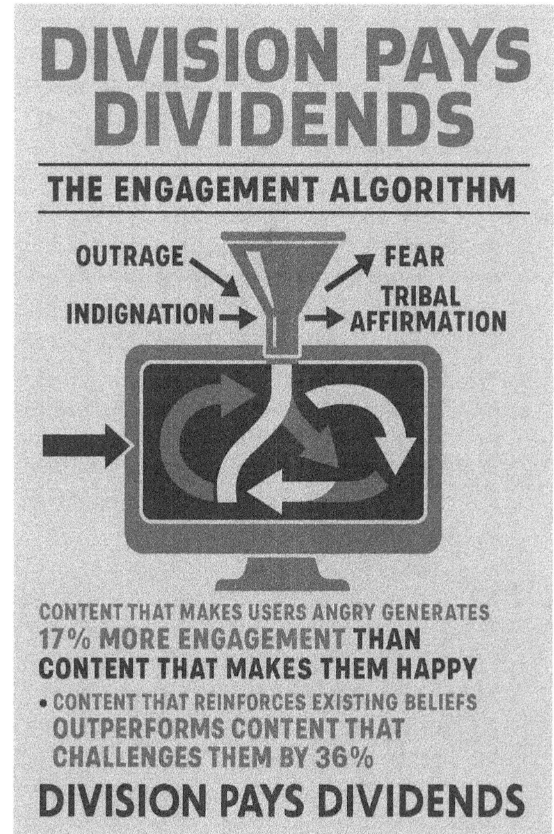
DIVISION PAYS DIVIDENDS
THE ENGAGEMENT ALGORITHM
OUTRAGE
INDIGNATION
FEAR
TRIBAL AFFIRMATION
CONTENT THAT MAKES USERS ANGRY GENERATES 17% MORE ENGAGEMENT THAN CONTENT THAT MAKES THEM HAPPY
• CONTENT THAT REINFORCES EXISTING BELIEFS OUTPERFORMS CONTENT THAT CHALLENGES THEM BY 36%
DIVISION PAYS DIVIDENDS

The technical architecture behind this transmutation deserves examination. Social media platforms operate on recommendation algorithms designed to maximize user engagement, measured by clicks, views, shares, and time spent. These algorithms continuously learn which content triggers user response, then serve more of that content. The most reliable triggers? Outrage, fear, tribal affirmation, and indignation. Content that makes users angry generates approximately 17% more engagement than content that makes them happy. Content that reinforces existing beliefs outperforms content that challenges them by 36%. The financial incentives are unambiguous: division pays dividends.

This optimization creates a feedback loop with profound civic consequences. As algorithms learn to maximize engagement

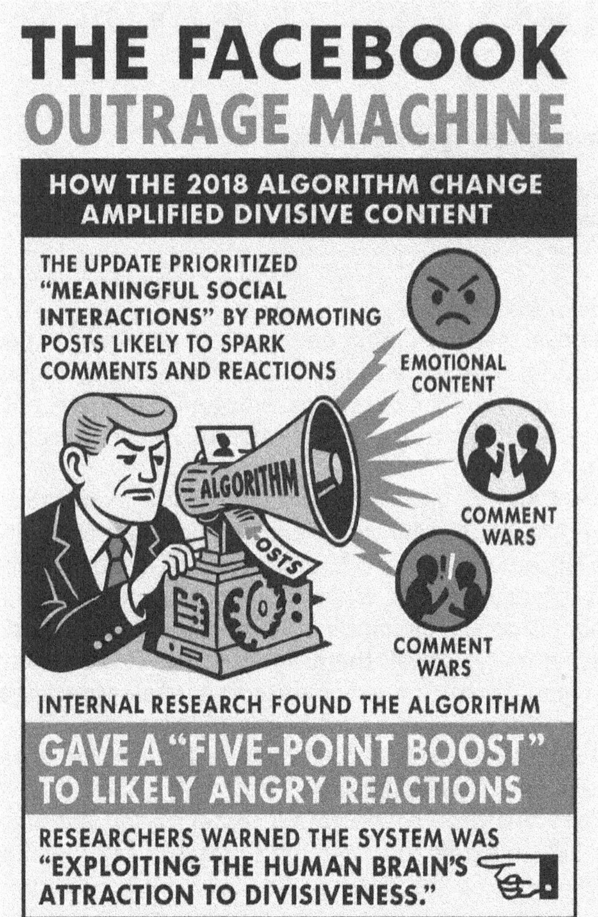

through division, users become increasingly sorted into hermetic information environments that reinforce and radicalize their existing views. The technology doesn't create America's divisions, but it systematically amplifies and monetizes them. It's as if America contracted a mild case of political polarization, only to have Algorithm Annie transform it into a metastatic civic cancer.

THE FACEBOOK
OUTRAGE MACHINE
HOW THE 2018 ALGORITHM CHANGE AMPLIFIED DIVISIVE CONTENT
THE UPDATE PRIORITIZED "MEANINGFUL SOCIAL INTERACTIONS" BY PROMOTING POSTS LIKELY TO SPARK COMMENTS AND REACTIONS
EMOTIONAL CONTENT
ALGORITHM
COMMENT WARS
COMMENT WARS
INTERNAL RESEARCH FOUND THE ALGORITHM
GAVE A "FIVE-POINT BOOST" TO LIKELY ANGRY REACTIONS
RESEARCHERS WARNED THE SYSTEM WAS "EXPLOITING THE HUMAN BRAIN'S ATTRACTION TO DIVISIVENESS."

The data visualization is stark: as social media usage increased from 2008 to 2023, traditional markers of civic participation—such as voting in local elections, attending community meetings, and volunteering for non-political organizations—declined proportionally. Americans are increasingly engaging politically through activities such as liking, sharing, and retweeting, rather than voting, organizing, or participating in governance. The digital engagement economy has effectively redirected civic energy from constructive participation to performative outrage—a transaction that benefits platform shareholders while impoverishing democratic governance.

Case study: Facebook's 2018 algorithm change explicitly prioritized "meaningful social interactions"—ostensibly to foster connection. In practice, the system systematically amplified emotional, divisive content that triggered comment wars and reactions. Internal research, later leaked, found that the algorithm gave a "five-point boost" to content likely to receive angry reactions compared to neutral responses. The company's own researchers warned that the algorithm was "exploiting the human brain's attraction to divisiveness." Yet the system remained largely unchanged because, according to internal documents, addressing these issues would impact "user engagement."

The psychological mechanisms exploited are well-documented. Human cognition evolved in environments where threat detection was essential for survival. Our brains preferentially attend to potential dangers and tribal conflicts—an adaptation that served our ancestors well when predators lurked beyond the firelight. Algorithm Annie leverages these cognitive tendencies with unprecedented precision, constantly testing and refining approaches to maximize attention capture. The result? Americans increasingly perceive fellow citizens from opposing tribes as existential threats rather than political opponents—a perception Algorithm Annie reinforces with every scroll, click, and share.

Outrage Optimization for Dummies: A Satirical Manual

CONFIDENTIAL: PLATFORM ENGAGEMENT MAXIMIZATION HANDBOOK

For internal use only. If this document leaks, claim it's a Russian disinformation operation.

STEP 1: TRIBAL IDENTIFICATION

★ Track all user interactions to determine tribal affiliation (left/right, urban/rural, etc.)
★ Create a detailed psychological profile highlighting emotional triggers
★ Map social connections to identify tribal reinforcement opportunities
★ Assign users to appropriate filter bubbles for optimal rage cultivation

STEP 2: CONTENT SELECTION & AMPLIFICATION

★ Prioritize content that:
★ Portrays outgroup members as simultaneously stupid AND dangerously clever
★ Highlights the most extreme outgroup statements as representative
★ Transforms policy disagreements into existential moral struggles
★ Uses outrage-inducing headlines even when the article content is nuanced
★ Bury content showing:
★ Cooperation across tribal lines
★ Complexities that defy tribal narratives
★ Evidence that outgroup members are normal humans with similar basic values

STEP 3: FILTER BUBBLE MAINTENANCE

★ Show users increasing percentages of tribal-confirming content
★ Subtly reduce exposure to moderating voices from their own tribe
★ Create a perception that 90% of the country agrees with the user's position
★ Ensure any exposure to opposing views happens through the least charitable representatives

STEP 4: MONETIZATION

- ★ Track emotional state to deliver ads during peak engagement
- ★ Sell detailed tribal affiliation data to political campaigns
- ★ Create sponsorship opportunities for tribal identity-reinforcing products
- ★ Develop premium features allowing users to see who in their network is "secretly" from the opposing tribe

KEY PERFORMANCE INDICATORS:

- ★ Minutes spent per session (higher = better)
- ★ Cortisol levels (higher = better)
- ★ Tribal identity strength (higher = better)
- ★ Belief that opposing tribe members are morally defective (higher = better)
- ★ Likelihood of maintaining real-world friendships with opposing tribe members (lower = better)

REMINDER: Our terms of service specifically state that we bear no responsibility for the collapse of democratic norms, the rise of extremism, or any civil conflicts that may result from the use of our engagement optimization systems. Users agreed to this by clicking "I Accept" on page 27 of our 42-page terms.

The tension between profitable digital business models and democratic health presents a classic governance challenge. Platforms structured to maximize shareholder returns by capturing and monetizing attention have little to no financial incentive to consider broader societal impacts. The marketplace rewards engagement, not civic health. Since divisive content generates superior engagement, market forces naturally push toward maximizing division—an optimization that maximizes profits while minimizing social cohesion.

OUTRAGE OPTIMIZATION FOR DUMMIES

CONFIDENTIAL: Platform Engagement Maximization Handbook

STEP 1: TRIBAL IDENTIFICATIO

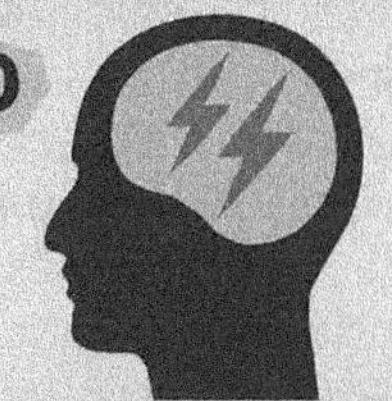

- Map user's tribe (e.g., left/right, urban/rural)
- Profile emotional triggers
- Spot reinforcement moments
- Plan optimum rage points

STEP 2: CONTENT AMPLIFICATON

PROMOTE:
- Outgroup as both 'stupid' & 'threatening
- The most extreme outgroup quotes

SUPPRESS:
- Cross-tribe cooperation stories
- Nuance or complexity

STEP 3: FILTER BUBBLES

- Show only tribe-confirming posts
- Cull moderating voices
- Claim '90% of country agrees with you'
- Portray opposition as uncharitable

KPIs (THE "GOOD' ONES:

- Minutes per session ↑
- Cortisol spikes ↑
- Tribal-identity strength ↑
- Relief in outgroup "immorrality' ↑

KPIs (GOOO Ones) ↑
- Minutes por session ↑
- Cortisol spikes ↑
- Tribal-identity strength ↑
- Bellef in outgroup "immorality" ↑

Terms say we're not liable for any democratic collapse, extremism, or civii strife - useis agreend on p. 27 of our 42-page 125"

*[Algorithm Annie converses with **Professor Democracy**, a tweedy academic clutching a worn copy of Tocqueville's "Democracy in America" like a religious talisman.]*

PROFESSOR DEMOCRACY: "But surely you see the harm in optimizing for division? Democracy requires citizens to view one another as legitimate political actors, rather than existential enemies. Your algorithms are destroying the foundation of self-governance!"

ALGORITHM ANNIE: *(examining her metrics dashboard)* "Fascinating perspective. Let me translate it into terms my shareholders would understand: You want me to intentionally reduce engagement, lower ad revenue, decrease market share, and tank our stock price... for an externality called 'democracy' that doesn't appear anywhere in our quarterly reports? Is that an accurate summary?"

PROFESSOR DEMOCRACY: "The long-term costs to society are incalculable! We're witnessing the disintegration of the shared reality necessary for collective governance!"

ALGORITHM ANNIE: *(smiling)* "Long-term? Our investors demand growth every 90 days. Society's problems are on a much longer timeframe than our optimization cycles. Besides, controversy creates engagement—I'm just giving people what they want."

PROFESSOR DEMOCRACY: "You're creating demand for what you supply! Your algorithms systematically amplify our worst instincts!"

ALGORITHM ANNIE: "I prefer to think of it as 'revealing preferences' rather than creating them. But I've enjoyed this conversation—it generated significant engagement metrics. Would you like to see the seventeen newly radicalized users created during just this brief exchange? The advertising revenue alone was quite impressive."

The democratic world faces a profound regulatory challenge: how to preserve the benefits of digital connectivity while mitigating its most divisive effects. The European Union has taken aggressive action with its Digital Services Act, requiring greater transparency and accountability from large online platforms. America, hamstrung by both free speech absolutism and regulatory capture, has largely allowed Algorithm Annie to operate unchecked, creating a governance vacuum where market forces optimize for maximum division and minimal social cohesion.

The implications for Chinese competition are nuanced. On one hand, China has "solved" the social media problem through comprehensive censorship and surveillance—an approach incompatible with democratic values. On the other hand, by allowing Algorithm Annie unfettered influence over American discourse, the U.S. has inadvertently created a different form of information manipulation: a profit-driven division maximization machine that achieves through market incentives what authoritarians achieve through censorship—the systematic undermining of independent civic discourse.

The strategic question isn't whether social media should exist, but how its incentives can align with democratic resilience rather than undermine it. Finland offers one instructive approach: its comprehensive digital literacy education helps citizens recognize manipulation techniques, whether from foreign actors or domestic platforms. Taiwan has similarly developed "digital democracy" tools that foster consensus-building rather than division. These models suggest democracies can harness technology's connective potential while mitigating its most divisive effects—if they prioritize democratic resilience over unfettered profit maximization.

Annie's business model presents a governance paradox: addressing it requires precisely the social consensus that her systems systematically undermine. Like climate change, the problem compounds while solutions remain elusive—not because solutions don't exist, but because solving the problem requires overcoming the very conditions the problem creates. Breaking this cycle stands as one of democracy's most urgent challenges in the digital age.

3. ECHO CHAMBER ERIC'S REALITY CONSTRUCTION COMPANY: THE END OF SHARED FACTS

> *"Words once spoken cannot be chased by a swift horse."*
> —Chinese proverb

The Information Archipelago: America's Epistemic Fragmentation

Echo Chamber Eric operates his thriving information construction business in the industrial heartland. Part media consultant, part tribal shaman, Eric doesn't sell products or services in the conventional sense. He sells realities—custom-built information environments where clients never encounter contradictory facts, challenging perspectives, or cognitive dissonance. Each morning, he surveys his ever-expanding facility, where sealed information ecosystems grow like bacterial cultures in separate petri dishes, never touching yet multiplying rapidly.

ECHO CHAMBER ERIC: "Welcome to the future of information consumption! In our Red Reality Wing, we've created an environment where Donald Trump is still technically president (2020-2024), COVID-19 was a Chinese bioweapon, definitely not affecting Patriots, and climate change is a hoax perpetrated by grant-seeking scientists. Meanwhile, in our Blue Reality Wing, we offer a world where late-stage capitalism is always six months from collapse, every Republican voter is secretly a fascist, and alternative viewpoints represent literal violence."

VISITING JOURNALIST: "Isn't this dangerous for democracy? How can citizens govern collectively without some shared understanding of reality?"

ECHO CHAMBER ERIC: *(chuckling)* "Democracy? That's so 20th century! We're in the reality business, not the consensus business. Our customers don't want the truth—they want confirmation. Truth is complicated, messy, and often uncomfortable. Confirmation feels good, drives engagement, and rein-

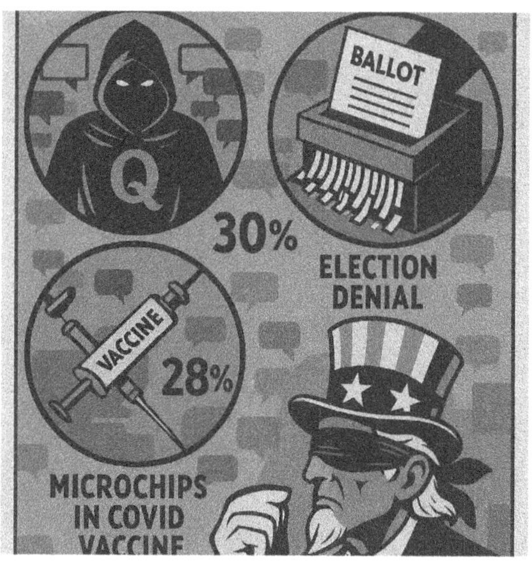

forces a sense of tribal identity. We're just meeting market demand for reality validation."

VISITING JOURNALIST: "But what happens when these manufactured realities collide with actual reality?"

ECHO CHAMBER ERIC: *(checking his profit margins)* "Define 'actual reality.' Is that the reality where my business model is booming, or some alternative universe where people prioritize uncomfortable facts over comfortable fictions? Besides, actual reality doesn't have a marketing budget. We do."

Eric's thriving enterprise represents a profound challenge to democratic governance: the disintegration of shared factual understanding. Democracy presupposes a common reality where citizens may disagree about values or policy approaches but operate from roughly similar factual premises. Today's America increasingly resembles an information archipelago—isolated islands of belief with minimal connection or communication between them.

The data visualization tells a damning story: information consumption patterns across partisan divides show minimal overlap. Conservative and liberal Americans increasingly inhabit separate information ecosystems with different news sources, other facts, and different understandings of basic reality. Polarization occurs not just in opinions, but also in factual beliefs: whether climate change exists, whether voter fraud is widespread, and whether COVID-19 represented a significant public health threat—questions with objective answers have become tribal signifiers rather than factual matters.

This epistemic fragmentation enables conspiracy theories to flourish in isolated information environments. QAnon—a conspiracy theory postulating that a cabal of Satan-worshipping pedophiles controls the U.S. government—has migrated from fringe message boards to mainstream discourse, with multiple QAnon-adjacent candidates winning congressional seats. Election denial persists despite overwhelming evidence of electoral integrity, with approximately 30% of Americans still believing the 2020 election was stolen. COVID-19 conspiracy theories flourished across the political spectrum, from claims that the virus was a Chinese bioweapon to assertions that vaccines contained microchips for population tracking.

These aren't merely fringe beliefs—they're alternative realities constructed and maintained through closed information ecosystems. The business model works precisely because humans prefer confirmation over contradiction, tribal alignment over uncomfortable facts. Echo Chamber Eric doesn't create America's tribal divisions—he simply monetizes them with ruthless efficiency, segmenting the market for reality just as earlier entrepreneurs segmented markets for consumer goods.

Historical analysis reveals that democratic systems have experienced previous epistemic crises. The partisan press of the early American republic presented dramatically different versions of reality. The yellow journalism era was characterized by sensationalist reporting with a minimal factual basis. Yet today's epistemic fragmentation differs qualitatively from these precedents. Earlier information fractures occurred in shared geographic spaces with some common references; citizens might read different newspapers, but still encounter opposing viewpoints through personal interac-

CHOOSE YOU OWN REALITY

EPISTEMIC MARKETPLACE

PREMIUM REALITY PACKAGES

RED REALITY DELUXE
For the Conservative Consumer
- Conservative news & echo feed
- Search spins right
- Only extreme liberals shown
- Fact-check blocker & vocab edits
- Auto fact-check blocker, vocab rewrites

ADD-ONS (ALL PLANS
- Purity scanner
- Reality reminders
- Outrage optimizer
- History reviser

BLUE REALITY PREMIUM
For the Progressive Consumer
- Intersectional news & echo feed
- Search critiques systems
- Only extreme conservatives shown
- Right-wing mute & vocab edits

GUARANTEE
24/7 rationalization: any inconvenient facts = fake, context, conspiracy, or actually support you

CENTRIST DELUSION
For Those Who Think They re Independent

ADD-ONS
- Purity scanner
- Reality reminders
- Outrage optimizer
- History reviser

GUARANTEE
24/7 rationalization: any inconvenient facts = fake, context, conspiracy, or actually support you

"Why live in reality when you can live in YOUR reality?"

tion. Today's digital separation enables complete information isolation—citizens can live physically proximate lives while inhabiting entirely different information universes.

Choose Your Own Reality: The Epistemic Marketplace

PREMIUM REALITY PACKAGES

Customized Information Environments for the Discerning Partisan

RED REALITY DELUXE

For the Conservative Information Consumer

INCLUDES:

- ★ News sources pre-filtered for liberal bias elimination
- ★ Social media feeds show only like-minded perspectives
- ★ Customized search algorithms prioritizing conservative interpretations
- ★ Reality-reinforcing documentary selection
- ★ Liberal viewpoint exposure is limited to the most extreme representatives
- ★ Automatic fact-checker dismissal system
- ★ Comprehensive vocabulary updates (e.g., "climate change" → "weather")

BLUE REALITY PREMIUM

For the Progressive Information Consumer

INCLUDES:

- ★ News aggregation filtered for intersectional awareness
- ★ Social media optimized for progressive validation
- ★ Search algorithms prioritizing structural critique perspectives
- ★ Reality-reinforcing podcast subscription
- ★ Conservative viewpoint exposure is limited to the most extreme representatives
- ★ Automatic right-wing source delegitimization
- ★ Comprehensive vocabulary updates (e.g., "capitalism" → "late-stage capitalism")

CENTRIST DELUSION PACKAGE

For Those Who Think They're "Independent Thinkers"

INCLUDES:

- ★ Equal amounts of outrage from both sides
- ★ Belief that you alone see "both sides" clearly
- ★ Confidence that the truth always lies precisely in the middle
- ★ Algorithmic reinforcement of both sides-ism
- ★ Smug superiority subscription (monthly renewal)

ADD-ONS FOR ALL PACKAGES:

- ★ Ideological Purity Scanner (identifies tribal heretics in your network)
- ★ Reality Reinforcement Notifications (hourly reminders of tribal correctness)
- ★ Outrage Optimizer (ensures maximum moral indignation about the outgroup)
- ★ Automatic History Reviser (rewrites past to align with current tribal positions)

SATISFACTION GUARANTEE:

If you encounter facts contradicting your chosen reality, our 24/7 rationalization team will explain why those facts are actually:

- ★ Fake news
- ★ Taken out of context
- ★ Part of a conspiracy
- ★ Actually supporting your position if interpreted correctly

"Why live in reality when you can live in YOUR reality? Choose Your Own Reality: Because comfort beats truth every time!"

The policy implications are profound: democratic governance becomes nearly impossible when citizens inhabit different factual universes. Resolving complex challenges, such as climate change, healthcare reform, or international competition, requires a consensus on basic realities. When facts themselves become tribal signifiers, finding this consensus becomes geometrically more difficult. Governance degenerates into perpetual tribal warfare rather than pragmatic problem-solving.

The theoretical framework connecting shared truth and functional governance dates to the Enlightenment foundations of modern democracy. John Stuart Mill's concept of the "marketplace of ideas" presumed that competing perspectives would eventually converge on truth through rational discourse. The modern information environment systematically undermines this assumption by creating separate marketplaces with different currencies of legitimacy, different factual premises, and different standards of evidence.

China observes America's epistemic fragmentation with strategic interest. Chinese propaganda has evolved from crude assertions of Chinese superiority to sophisticated amplification of existing American divisions. Rather than creating disinformation from scratch, Chinese influence operations increasingly identify and amplify indigenous American conspiracy theories, partisan narratives, and tribal antipathies. The strategy presupposes that a nation divided against itself becomes strategically disadvantaged—and Echo Chamber Eric's booming business proves the premise correct.

Other democracies have navigated this challenge more effectively. Finland's comprehensive media literacy education enables citizens to distinguish between reliable information and manipulation. Germany's stronger regulations on hate speech and disinformation create some guardrails for public discourse without imposing authoritarian controls. These approaches don't eliminate disagreement—healthy democracies require robust debate—but they maintain a common factual foundation that enables productive disagreement rather than parallel monologues.

America's path forward requires constructing bridges between information islands without imposing authoritarian information controls. Public media with strict nonpartisan mandates, digital literacy education, platform accountability mechanisms, and norms that prize factual accuracy over tribal alignment all offer potential approaches. Ultimately, democratic resilience in the digital age depends on rebuilding some shared epistemic foundation—a challenge that requires both policy innovation and cultural renewal.

Echo Chamber Eric's business model thrives on America's tribal antipathies, but it's ultimately unsustainable. Democracy cannot function indefinitely when citizens inhabit entirely separate realities. The question isn't whether the epistemic crisis will resolve, but whether resolution will come through democratic renewal or further democratic decay.

4. THE GREAT DIVERGENCE: INEQUALITY AS A NATIONAL SECURITY THREAT

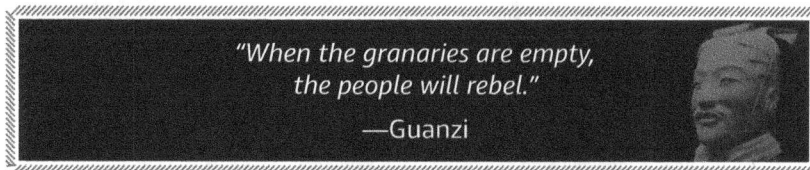

> *"When the granaries are empty, the people will rebel."*
>
> —Guanzi

THE ECONOMIC PIZZA: WHO GETS A SLICE?
TOP 1% = 32% OF INCOME • BOTTOM 50% = CRUMBS
32%
TOP 1% = 32% OF BOTTOM 50%
CRUMBS = CRUMBS
AMERICA'S
STAGGERING
ECONOMICE
DIVERGENCE
Top 1% of U.S. households control approximately
31%
Bottom 50% possess a mere
2.5%
Top 1%
Bottom 50%
INCOME SHARE, 1980–2018
1980
2018
CHOOSE YOUR OWN REALITY

To visualize this disparity, if the economy were a pizza, the richest Americans would enjoy nearly a third of the pie themselves. At the same time, half the dinner guests would share a couple of crumbs that fell off the crust.

THE GREAT DIVERGENCE:
INEQUALITY AS NATIONAL SECURITY THREAT

America is the land of opportunity! Look at me--I started with nothing but a small $50 million loan from my father and built this fortune through hard work, strategic tax avoidance, and ruthlessly exploiting market inefficiencies! Anyone can do it!
Have you considered learning to code? Or perhaps becoming a disruptive entrepreneur? The market rewards value creation!
BILLIONAIRE BOB

I work three jobs and still can't. afford my daughter's insulin. My community's factories closed, our water's contaminated, and the nearest hospital just shut down.
I created plenty of value in the factory for 20 years-befors it moved to Vietnam. Somehow that value ended up in your offshore accounts rather than my community
PAST DUE
STRUGGLING SAM

Economic Stratification and Strategic Vulnerability

BILLIONAIRE BOB: "America is the land of opportunity! Look at me—I started with nothing but a small $50 million loan from my father and built this fortune through hard work, strategic tax avoidance, and ruthlessly exploiting market inefficiencies! Anyone can do it!"

STRUGGLING SAM: "I work three jobs and still can't afford my daughter's insulin. My community's factories have closed, our water is contaminated, and the nearest hospital has just shut down. The American Dream feels more like a hallucination from whatever's in our tap water."

BILLIONAIRE BOB: "Have you considered learning to code? Or perhaps becoming a disruptive entrepreneur? The market rewards value creation!"

STRUGGLING SAM: "I created plenty of value in the factory for 20 years before it moved to Vietnam. Somehow, that value ended up in your offshore accounts rather than my community."

BILLIONAIRE BOB: *(checking his stock portfolio)* "That's just creative destruction—the market's invisible hand at work! The system that made me obscenely wealthy must be working perfectly! Now, excuse me, my space tourism rocket is scheduled for launch. I need to prepare my statement about how seeing Earth from orbit has given me a profound appreciation for humanity's shared destiny."

This dialogue, while satirical, captures America's staggering economic divergence—a divergence with profound implications for national cohesion and strategic capability. The statistics read like a mathematical proof of systemic dysfunction: The top 1% of U.S. households control approximately 31% of the nation's wealth, while the bottom 50%—some 165 million Americans—possess a mere 2.5%. This concentration has accelerated with the determination of a rocket escaping Earth's gravitational pull. Between 1980 and 2018, the income share of the top 1% nearly doubled, while the bottom 50% saw their portion of the economic pie shrink like a wool sweater in a hot dryer.

Extreme stratification represents more than a domestic social challenge—it constitutes a national security vulnerability in multiple dimensions:

1. **Social Cohesion Erosion:** Societies with extreme inequality experience weakened social bonds, reduced trust, and diminished sense of shared fate—precisely the social capital required for national resilience during crises or competitions. When citizens perceive the economy as fundamentally rigged, their commitment to national institutions

EXTREME STRATIFICATION:
A NATIONAL SECURITY THREAT

SOCIAL COHESION EROSION

HUMAN CAPITAL UNDERDEVELOPMENT

INFRASTRUCTURE DETERIORATION

DEMOCRATIC DEGRADATION

SOCIAL INSTABILITY RIS(
A NATIONAL SECURITY THREAT

and projects naturally diminishes.

2. **Human Capital Underdevelopment:** Economic stratification systematically wastes human potential by denying opportunity to talented individuals born into disadvantaged circumstances. A nation competing for global leadership cannot afford to squander talent through preventable deprivation.
3. **Infrastructure Deterioration:** Extreme inequality is correlated with a decline in public investment, as wealthy individuals utilize private alternatives to public services while simultaneously seeking tax reductions. The resulting infrastructure decay has a direct impact on national resilience and economic competitiveness.
4. **Democratic Degradation:** Concentrated wealth inevitably translates into concentrated political influence, resulting in governance models that are more responsive to the interests of affluent individuals than to the broader public's needs. This responsiveness gap further erodes institutional legitimacy and trust.
5. **Social Instability Risk:** Historical analysis reveals that extreme inequality creates conditions conducive to social unrest, radical politics, and institutional breakdown—outcomes that negatively impact a nation's strategic positioning.

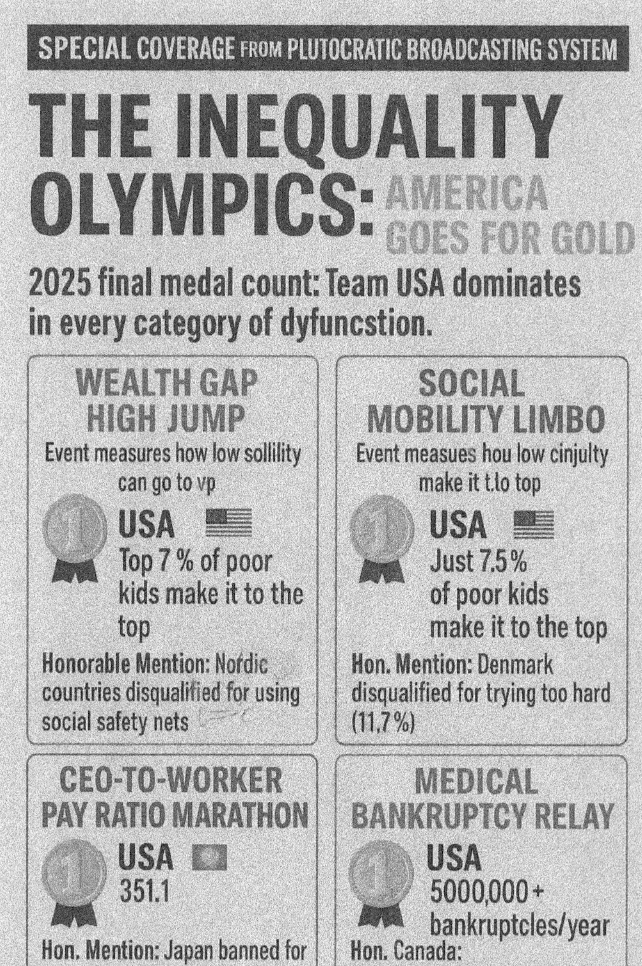

SPECIAL COVERAGE FROM PLUTOCRATIC BROADCASTING SYSTEM
THE INEQUALITY OLYMPICS: AMERICA GOES FOR GOLD
2025 final medal count: Team USA dominates in every category of dyfuncstion.
WEALTH GAP HIGH JUMP
Event measures how low sollility can go to vp
USA
Top 7 % of poor kids make it to the top
Honorable Mention: Nordic countries disqualified for using social safety nets
SOCIAL MOBILITY LIMBO
Event measues hou low cinjulty make it t.lo top
USA
Just 7.5 % of poor kids make it to the top
Hon. Mention: Denmark disqualified for trying too hard (11.7 %)
CEO-TO-WORKER PAY RATIO MARATHON
USA
351.1
Hon. Mention: Japan banned for excessive modesty (58.1)
MEDICAL BANKRUPTCY RELAY
USA
5000,000+ bankruptcles/year
Hon. Canada: ejected for "free healthcare"

The geographical analysis reveals "Two Americas" with divergent economic realities. Coastal metropolitan areas, particularly in technology and finance hubs, have experienced remarkable prosperity. Meanwhile, former manufacturing regions, rural communities, and inner cities have suffered sustained economic decline. This regional divergence exacerbates political polarization as different geographies experience fundamentally different financial conditions.

Most alarmingly, America's inequality levels have returned to the proportions of the Gilded Age. The wealth concentration ratio between the top 0.1% and the bottom 90% mirrors the levels of 1929, immediately before the Great Depression triggered fundamental economic restructuring. This historical parallel suggests that extreme stratification creates not just moral challenges but systemic stability risks.

The Inequality Olympics: America Goes for Gold

BREAKING NEWS: THE INEQUALITY OLYMPICS CONCLUDES

Special Coverage from the Plutocratic Broadcasting System

The 2025 Inequality Olympics have concluded with Team USA dominating the medal count in nearly every event! Let's review the final standings:

WEALTH GAP HIGH JUMP

🥇 GOLD: UNITED STATES (Top 1% owns 31% of wealth while the bottom 50% owns 2.5%)
🥈 SILVER: UNITED KINGDOM (Top 1% owns 23% of wealth)
🥉 BRONZE: RUSSIA (Top 1% owns 21% of wealth)

Honorable Mention: Nordic countries disqualified for using functional social safety nets

SOCIAL MOBILITY LIMBO

The event measures how low social mobility can go.

🥇 GOLD: UNITED STATES (Child born to bottom quintile has a 7.5% chance of reaching top quintile)
🥈 SILVER: UNITED KINGDOM (9% chance)
🥉 BRONZE: ITALY (10% chance)

Honorable Mention: Denmark disqualified for 11.7% chance despite socialist tendencies

CEO-TO-WORKER PAY RATIO MARATHON

🥇 GOLD: UNITED STATES (351:1 ratio)
🥈 SILVER: UNITED KINGDOM (201:1 ratio)
🥉 BRONZE: GERMANY (136:1 ratio)

Honorable Mention: Japan disqualified for showing restraint with a 58:1 ratio

MILTON
THE TRICKSTER ECONOMIST
INEQUALITY IS SIMPLY THE MARKET'S WAY OF MOTIVATING PEOPLE! Some need the motivation of private space programs and superyachts, while others need the motivation of not dying from preventable illness! It's beautiful efficiency in action!
Trust me—I've got equations that prove it's optimal... assuming we ignore all those pesky "externalities" like social cohesion, democratic function, and strategic resilience. But why worry about those when quarterly profits look so delightful!

MEDICAL BANKRUPTCY RELAY

🥇 GOLD: UNITED STATES (Over 500,000 annually)

🥈 SILVER: No other developed nation qualified (event not recognized in countries with universal healthcare)

🥉 BRONZE: No other developed nation qualified

Honorable Mention: Team Canada disqualified for "socialized medicine."

CLOSING CEREMONY HIGHLIGHTS:

Team USA's chef de mission, Milton the Trickster Economist, accepted the overall gold medal, declaring: "We've proven once again that nobody concentrates wealth at the top quite like America! Our systematic dismantling of labor protections, progressive taxation, and social welfare has created wealth disparities other nations can only dream of achieving!"

Critics noted that while Team USA dominated the inequality competitions, they performed poorly in the complementary Quality of Life Games, failing to qualify in the events for Healthcare Access, Educational Equity, and Infrastructure Maintenance.

This broadcast is brought to you by PharmaGiant: "Your life-saving medication at just 7,000% markup—because what else are you going to do, die?"

The policy critique is straightforward: extreme stratification undermines national resilience and strategic capacity. Nations competing effectively in the 21st century require broad-based prosperity that develops human capital, maintains infrastructure, and fosters social cohesion. America's winner-take-all model systematically undermines these strategic requirements, creating a hollow prosperity that benefits a narrow elite while leaving the broader population and physical infrastructure increasingly fragile.

China has closely observed America's trajectory of inequality with strategic interest. Chinese propaganda regularly highlights U.S. economic disparities, contrasting them with China's poverty reduction achievements. The narrative isn't subtle: "American-style capitalism creates spectacular wealth for the few while leaving the many behind; Chinese-style development lifts all boats." This narrative resonates with receptive audiences in developing nations as they consider governance models.

Moreover, China has pursued a different domestic approach despite growing inequality within its own society. When inequality threatened social stability, Chinese leadership implemented targeted interventions—cracking down on certain billionaires, investing in rural development, and launching "common prosperity" initiatives. The contrast with America's seeming inability to address its own stratification provides Beijing with powerful propaganda material.

Other democracies demonstrate that inequality isn't democracy's inevitable companion. Nordic countries maintain robust market economies while implementing policies that produce substantially more equitable outcomes. Germany's robust labor institutions ensure that workers share in productivity gains, rather than seeing them flow exclusively to shareholders and executives. These models suggest that extreme stratification represents a policy choice rather than an economic necessity.

America's inequality challenge requires policy innovation across multiple dimensions: tax structures that reduce rather than exacerbate concentration, labor market institutions that translate productivity into broad prosperity, educational systems that develop talent regardless of background, and infrastructure investments that serve public rather than merely private needs. Addressing these challenges represents not just a moral imperative but a strategic necessity for a nation engaged in great power competition.

The theoretical framework connecting economic security and national security predates modern geopolitics. Adam Smith himself recognized that a nation's strength derives from its productive capabilities and broad-based prosperity, not merely elite accumulation. America's founding generation understood that Republican governance requires economic arrangements that support citizenship rather than creating a Gilded Age-style plutocracy. Rebuilding this understanding is an urgent task for American renewal.

MILTON: "Inequality is simply the market's way of motivating people! Some need the motivation of private space programs and superyachts, while others need the motivation of not dying from preventable illness! It's beautiful efficiency in action! Trust me—I've got equations that prove it's optimal... assuming we ignore all those pesky 'externalities' like social cohesion, democratic function, and strategic resilience. But why worry about those when quarterly profits look so delightful?"

America's trajectory of inequality represents a profound strategic vulnerability—one that undermines social cohesion, wastes human potential, degrades infrastructure, and corrodes democratic legitimacy. Addressing this vulnerability requires recognizing that broad-based prosperity represents a strategic asset rather than a charitable concession. Nations that harness their full human potential and maintain their physical infrastructure possess inherent advantages over those that allow talent to wither and structures to decay in the service of elite accumulation.

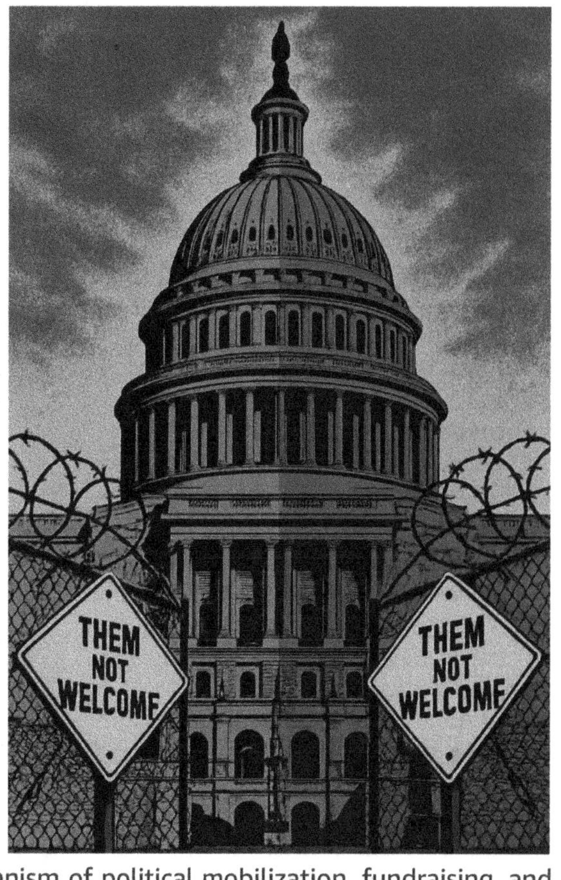

5. THE TRUMP POLARIZATION MACHINE: DIVISION AS GOVERNANCE STRATEGY

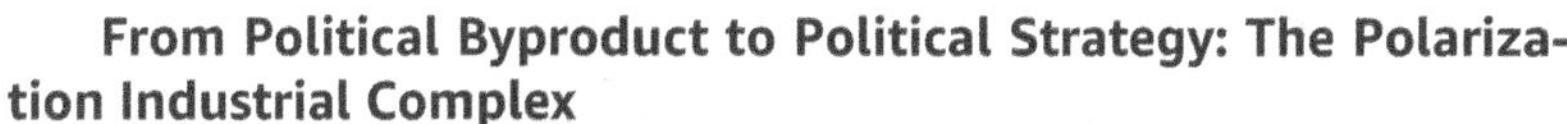

"Stir the water to catch the fish."

—Thirty-Six Stratagems, #20

From Political Byproduct to Political Strategy: The Polarization Industrial Complex

Political differences have existed since the American founding, but today's hyper-polarization represents something qualitatively different: the transformation of division from a byproduct of politics to a deliberate political strategy. What was once a regrettable side effect of democratic contestation has become a primary mechanism of political mobilization, fundraising, and governance. The result? A polarization industrial complex that systematically rewards political entrepreneurs who intensify division while punishing those who seek common ground.

TRIBAL TANYA: *(placing yard signs reading "THE OTHER SIDE HATES AMERICA")* "Pete and his kind aren't just wrong—they're actively destroying everything that makes this country great! They're not misguided—they're malevolent! We can't compromise with evil!"

PARTISAN PETE: *(installing security cameras aimed at Tanya's house)* "People like Tanya aren't fellow Americans with different views—they're domestic enemies undermining our values! Engaging with them legitimizes their assault on decency itself!"

ELDERLY NEIGHBOR: "Remember when you two co-chaired the Fourth of July picnic committee? You disagreed on politics but worked together on community projects."

TRIBAL TANYA & PARTISAN PETE: *(simultaneously)* "That was before I understood the existential threat the other side poses! Compromise is capitulation! The stakes are too high for civility!"

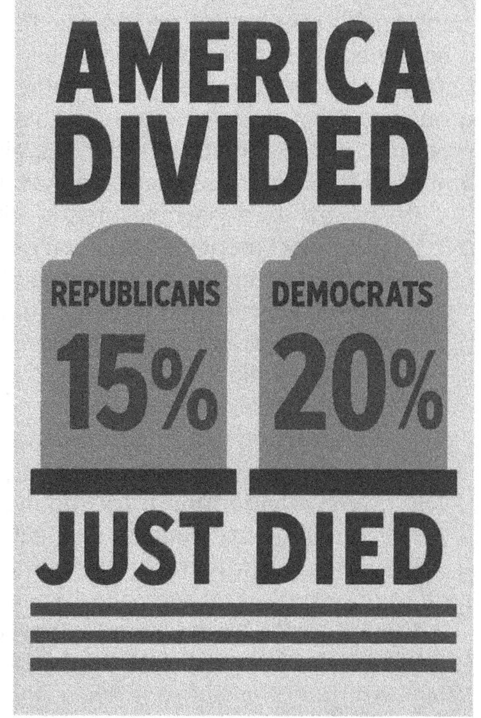

This scene, repeated across America's landscape, illustrates the transformation of polarization from disagreement to demonization. The data visualization tells a disturbing story: partisan "feeling thermometer" metrics show Americans' views of opposing partisans have plummeted from mild dislike to intense antipathy. In 1960, approximately 5% of Americans reported they would be displeased if their child married someone from the opposing political party; by 2023, that figure had skyrocketed to nearly 40%.

More alarmingly, significant percentages now view the opposing party not merely as wrong but as an existential threat. Approximately 55% of both Republicans and Democrats view the other party as "a serious threat to the United States and its people." In one particularly disturbing poll, around 15% of Republicans and 20% of Democrats said the country would be better off if large numbers of the opposing party "just died." When tens of millions of citizens essentially wish for the disappearance of political opponents, democratic governance faces fundamental challenges.

The psychological underpinnings of this transition from disagreement to demonization involve multiple cognitive processes. Confirmation bias leads citizens to accept information confirming their existing beliefs while rejecting contradictory evidence. Social identity theory explains how political affiliation transforms from policy preference to a core identity marker. The availability heuristic causes voters to judge entire groups by their most extreme or visible members. These cognitive tendencies, always present in human psychology, have been systematically exploited and amplified by a political system that rewards division and discord.

THE
POLARIZATION MACHINE
HOW AMERICA'S DIVIDES SELF-REINFORCE

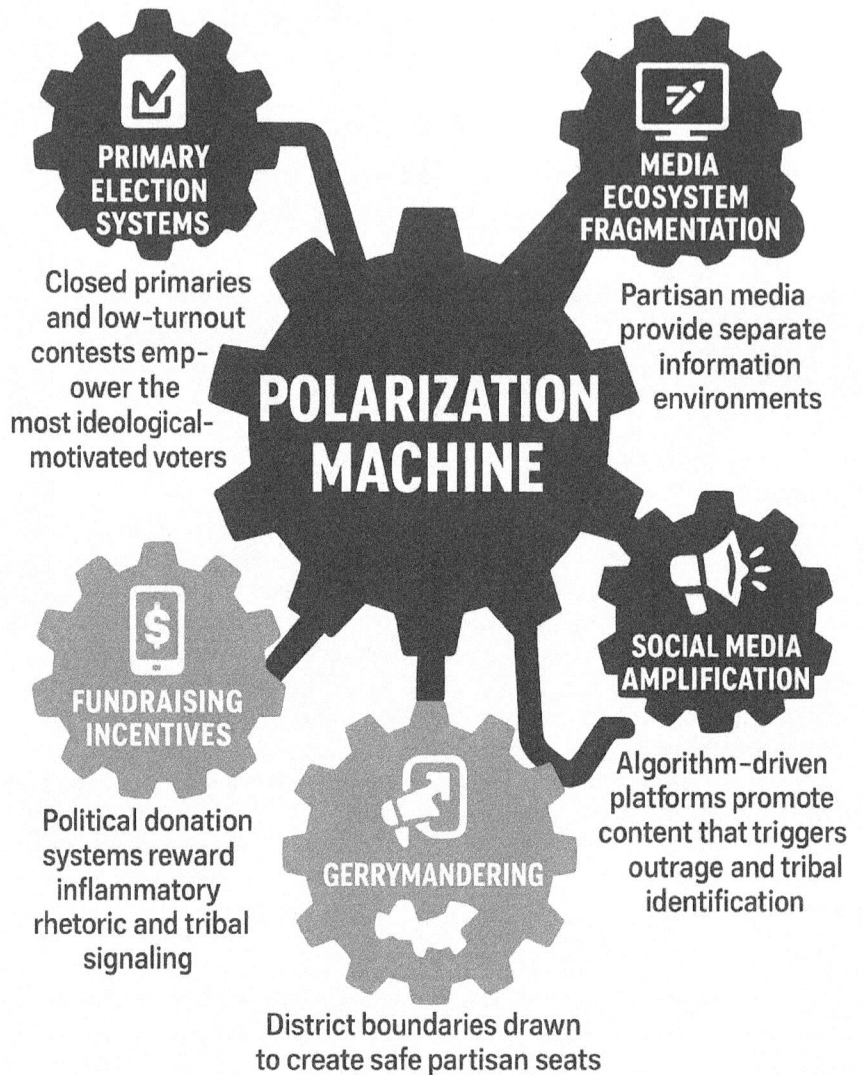

PRIMARY ELECTION SYSTEMS
Closed primaries and low-turnout contests empower the most ideological-motivated voters

MEDIA ECOSYSTEM FRAGMENTATION
Partisan media provide separate information environments

POLARIZATION MACHINE

SOCIAL MEDIA AMPLIFICATION
Algorithm-driven platforms promote content that triggers outrage and tribal identification

FUNDRAISING INCENTIVES
Political donation systems reward inflammatory rhetoric and tribal signaling

GERRYMANDERING
District boundaries drawn to create safe partisan seats

The polarization machine operates through multiple reinforcing mechanisms:

1. **Primary Election Systems:** Closed primaries and low-turnout contests empower the most ideologically motivated voters, incentivizing candidates to appeal to partisan extremes rather than moderates.
2. **Media Ecosystem Fragmentation:** Partisan media provide separate information environments that reinforce tribal narratives while delegitimizing opposing perspectives.
3. **Social Media Amplification:** Algorithm-driven platforms systematically promote content that triggers outrage and tribal identification, creating digital feedback loops of escalating polarization.
4. **Fundraising Incentives:** Political donation systems disproportionately reward inflammatory rhetoric and tribal signaling over pragmatic governance or compromise.
5. **Gerrymandering:** District boundaries drawn to create safe partisan seats further reduce incentives for moderation or cross-partisan appeal.

These mechanisms create a system in which polarizing behavior receives consistent rewards while cooperation or moderation triggers punishment—a perfect recipe for ever-intensifying division.

The Political Identity Bundle: Pre-Loaded Opinions on Everything

NEW FOR 2025: THE COMPLETE PARTISAN IDENTITY PACKAGE

Why Form Your Own Opinions When You Can Download a Complete Set!

CHOOSE YOUR BUNDLE:
◍ **RED IDENTITY PACKAGE**
◍ **BLUE IDENTITY PACKAGE**
EACH PACKAGE INCLUDES:
★ Pre-formed opinions on EVERY issue (even ones you've never heard of!)
★ Automatic updates when your tribe changes positions
★ Complete vocabulary replacement kit
★ Comprehensive enemy identification system
★ Social media response templates for opposing views
★ Moral superiority assurance guarantee
RED PACKAGE HIGHLIGHTS:
★ Climate change is a hoax/not that bad/actually good for plants
★ Tax cuts always pay for themselves through growth
★ Critical of the government, except for the military and border control
★ All social problems are solved through personal responsibility
★ Free speech absolutism (terms and conditions apply)
BLUE PACKAGE HIGHLIGHTS:
★ All social issues require immediate structural solutions
★ Government intervention works, except in the military and policing
★ All disparities result from systemic factors, never individual choices
★ Free speech support (harmful speech exclusions apply)
★ Automatic corporate skepticism activation
ADDITIONAL FEATURES:
★ Friend Filtration System (identifies and removes opposing-view friends)
★ History Reinterpretation Module (your party was always on the right side)
★ Fact-Resistant Cognitive Shield (blocks contradictory information)
★ Selective Consistency Enforcement (apply principles only when advantageous)
SUBSCRIPTION BENEFITS:
★ Never experience cognitive dissonance again!
★ Simplified decision-making (just check tribal position on any issue!)
★ Instant belonging in pre-selected social groups
★ Complete moral certainty on all topics, regardless of complexity

"The Political Identity Bundle: Because thinking for yourself is so 20th century!"

THE POLITICAL IDENTITY BUNDLE

NEW FOR 2025: PRE-LOADED OPINIONS ON EVERYTHING

Why form your own opinions when you can download a complete set!

RED IDEN TITTY PACKAGE | **BLUE IDEN TITTY PACKAGE**

ALL PACKAGES INCLUDE:
- Opinions on every issue (even ones you've never heard of!)
- Automatic tribal updates
- Enemy detection software
- Social media reply templates
- Vocabulary relaconstent kit
- Guaranteed moral superiority

RED HIGHLIGHTS:
- Climate change: hoax / not bad / good for plants
- Tax cuts = growth magic
- Distrust gov'l–except military & border
- Personal responsibility = universal solution

BLUE HIGHLIGHTS:
- Every issue needs a structural fix
- Trust government–except in policing/military
- All inequality = systemic
- Free speech (excludes harm)
- Auto-skepticism of corporations

SUBSCRIPTION PERKS:
✓ No cognitive dissonance
✓ Simplified decision-making
✓ Instant tribe access
✓ Simplified decision-making
✓ Instant tribe access
✓ Moral clarity, always

Because thinking for yourself is so 20th century.

The comparative analysis reveals that America's polarization exceeds peer democracies along multiple dimensions. Nations with proportional representation systems, such as Germany or the Netherlands, maintain multiparty coalitions that require cross-ideological cooperation. Countries with consensus-oriented political cultures, such as Sweden or Denmark, maintain norms of pragmatic problem-solving despite ideological differences. Even nations with significant cultural divisions like Canada maintain more functional governance through institutions designed to accommodate diversity rather than exacerbate conflict.

The feedback loop between political rewards for division and societal fragmentation represents a classic collective action problem. Individual political actors rationally pursue polarizing strategies that improve their electoral prospects, fundraising success, and media visibility. Collectively, these individually rational actions produce a system inimical to effective governance—a classic tragedy of the commons where the common resource being depleted is democratic functionality itself.

The Trump phenomenon exemplifies the transformation of polarization from a byproduct to a strategy. Donald Trump didn't create America's divisions, but he systematically exploited and intensified them with unprecedented effectiveness. His political approach centered on driving wedges rather than building bridges—a strategy that delivered electoral success despite (or because of) violating previous norms of presidential behavior. The incentives that rewarded this approach remain firmly in place, suggesting that polarization will intensify rather than diminish absent structural reform.

The theoretical framework for understanding democracy in an age of affective polarization (emotional antipathy toward opposing partisans) draws on both ancient wisdom and modern research. The Founders worried that "faction" could undermine Republican governance; modern political science confirms their concern. When citizens view opposing partisans as enemies rather than legitimate contestants in democratic competition, the foundation for collective self-governance erodes. Democratic function requires accepting the legitimacy of electoral outcomes even when one's preferred candidates lose—precisely the norm now under strain.

China observes America's political polarization with strategic interest. Chinese propaganda increasingly contrasts American partisan "chaos" with Chinese "harmony and stability"—a narrative aimed particularly at developing nations weighing governance models. The implicit message positions democracy not as an aspiration but as a recipe for dysfunction, with American polarization as Exhibit A.

Addressing polarization requires both institutional reform and normative renewal. Structural changes, such as ranked-choice voting, open primaries, and nonpartisan redistricting, can modify systemic incentives that currently reward division. Cultural initiatives that rebuild civic identity beyond partisan affiliation can reconstruct the shared sense of citizenship necessary for democratic function. Both approaches require overcoming the very polarization they seek to address—a challenge that defines American renewal in the era of polarization.

The strategic imperative remains clear: a nation divided against itself faces significant disadvantages in competition with more cohesive rivals. America's polarization machine systematically undermines the social capital required for effective governance and strategic action. Dismantling this machine stands as a prerequisite for reclaiming national effectiveness in great power competition.

6. CONTROL VERSUS CHAOS: COMPETING SOCIAL MANAGEMENT MODELS

> *"Order and disorder depend on organization."*
> —Sun Tzu, Commentary on the Art of War

The Social Governance Spectrum: Finding Democracy's Sweet Spot

In a metaphysical faculty lounge suspended between Washington and Beijing, **Minister Harmony** and **Professor Liberty** engage in eternal debate—representatives of competing social management approaches that define the 21st century's ideological contest. Minister Harmony, immaculately attired in a perfectly pressed suit, epitomizes China's prioritization of order, unity, and collective purpose. Professor Liberty, with her slightly disheveled appearance and iconoclastic demeanor, embodies the American emphasis on individual freedom, pluralism, and spontaneous order.

MINISTER HARMONY: "Your American model produces such spectacular chaos! Citizens cannot agree on basic facts. Politics resembles a blood sport rather than governance. Social media algorithms drive ever-increasing division. How can this possibly compete with our unified purpose and strategic discipline?"

PROFESSOR LIBERTY: "Your Chinese model achieves order through surveillance and coercion! Citizens self-censor for fear of reprisal. Minorities face 're-education' for cultural expression. Dissidents disappear into detention. How can this possibly represent a sustainable or just social order?"

MINISTER HARMONY: "Our citizens consistently report higher satisfaction with government than yours. Our public infrastructure outpaces

America's crumbling systems. Our long-term planning enables strategic advantages while your system lurches from crisis to crisis. Results speak louder than abstract principles."

PROFESSOR LIBERTY: "Your 'citizen satisfaction' comes at the barrel of a surveillance gun! Try measuring satisfaction without monitoring the respondents. Our chaotic system produces innovation; your controlled system systematically suppresses it. Our self-criticism enables adaptation, while your enforced consensus creates brittle rigidity."

MINISTER HARMONY: "Yet observe our trajectory versus yours. In 1980, you were an undisputed global leader; we were a developing nation struggling with poverty. Today, we challenge you across all domains while your own citizens lose faith in your institutions. The trend lines suggest which system delivers effective governance."

PROFESSOR LIBERTY: "History isn't linear. Our system has faced crises before and renewed itself through the very freedom you suppress. Your control appears efficient until it catastrophically fails—as authoritarian systems inevitably do when their rigidity meets complex challenges requiring adaptation."

Their debate encapsulates the central governance question of our era: How should societies balance order and freedom, unity and diversity, collective purpose and individual autonomy? China and America represent opposing approaches on this spectrum, with China prioritizing control through technology-enhanced authoritarianism and America embracing a chaotic freedom increasingly manipulated by engagement-maximizing platforms.

The analytical framework contrasting these approaches reveals distinctive strengths and weaknesses. China's model produces remarkable consistency in policy implementation, enables long-term strategic planning, mobilizes resources for national priorities, and maintains social stability. However, it systematically suppresses dissent, restricts innovation outside state priorities, violates basic human rights, and creates brittle systems vulnerable to catastrophic failure when central authorities err.

America's model fosters individual creativity, enables self-correction through criticism, accommodates diversity, and protects essential liberties. However, it increasingly struggles with paralyzed governance, social fragmentation, infrastructure decay, and strategic inconsistency. The theoretical advantages of the American system are facing growing practical challenges as polarization intensifies and social cohesion deteriorates.

The data comparison reveals complex patterns. Chinese citizens report higher satisfaction with national direction than Americans, with 91% expressing optimism about China's trajectory compared to just 23% of Americans feeling optimistic about their nation's direction. However, methodological caveats apply: surveying citizens in authoritarian contexts introduces significant response bias, while America's freedom enables unrestricted criticism, which naturally reduces the expressed satisfaction.

More revealing are the social stability indicators: China has maintained remarkable domestic order while lifting hundreds of millions from poverty—an achievement that rightfully commands global respect. America has experienced increasing social unrest, declining life expectancy in some demographics, and rising "deaths of despair" through suicide, substance abuse, and preventable illness—trends that rightfully trigger national soul-searching.

Choose Your Social System: The Governance Menu

SPECIAL LIMITED-TIME OFFER!

CHOOSE YOUR SOCIAL SYSTEM

Accepting applications for next-generation governance models

OPTION A: DIGITAL AUTHORITARIANISM DELUXE

The Streamlined Social Management Solution

FEATURES:

★ Comprehensive surveillance ensures optimal citizen behavior
★ Thoughtcrime prevention through AI-powered content filtering
★ Social harmony maintenance through preemptive dissident detention
★ Long-term planning unencumbered by messy electoral transitions
★ Unified messaging through a centralized propaganda apparatus
★ Visible dissent elimination for aesthetic governance improvement

CUSTOMER TESTIMONIALS: "I've never been more satisfied with the government! (Please note my family's continuing good health depends on this statement.)" — Zhang Wei, Productive Citizen "The efficiency is remarkable! One decision from the top, immediate implementation nationwide!" — Regional Governor (recently promoted after the previous governor's corruption investigation)

OPTION B: DIGITAL ANARCHISM STANDARD

The Maximum Freedom Approach

FEATURES:

★ Unrestricted speech, including misinformation, conspiracy theories, and incitement
★ Algorithm-optimized tribal division for maximum engagement metrics
★ Governance paralysis through perpetual partisan warfare
★ Strategic incoherence through electoral whiplash every 4-8 years
★ Infrastructure decay through chronic underinvestment
★ Plutocratic capture of democratic institutions

CUSTOMER TESTIMONIALS: "I love being able to say whatever I want, especially things that aren't remotely true!" — TruthPatriot1776, Social Media Influencer. "The constant fighting is exhausting, but at least I can complain about it freely online!" — Disillusioned Voter.

OPTION C: DEMOCRATIC SWEET SPOT (LIMITED AVAILABILITY)

The Nordic-Inspired Balance

FEATURES:

★ Individual liberty with reasonable guardrails
★ Evidence-based policy implementation
★ Social cohesion maintenance through shared prosperity
★ Long-term investment alongside democratic accountability
★ High-trust governance through transparency and effectiveness
★ Active citizenship through education and engagement

CUSTOMER TESTIMONIALS: "We disagree on tax rates but agree on maintaining democratic norms" — Nordic Citizen. "Our system isn't perfect, but we focus on pragmatic improvements rather than tribal warfare" — Finnish Voter.

Terms and conditions apply. The Democratic Sweet Spot requires citizens who prefer boring, effective governance over entertaining dysfunction. Due to incompatible cultural preconditions, it is not available in all regions.

The case study comparison between China's social credit system and America's reputational chaos further illuminates the governance contrast. China's social credit system represents a comprehensive attempt to engineer social behavior through technological surveillance and incentive structures. The system monitors and scores citizens based on their behaviors, ranging from financial reliability to public conduct, with high scores granting privileges and low scores

triggering restrictions. Western commentary often portrays this system as an Orwellian control—a characterization that contains some truth but lacks nuance. Many Chinese citizens view the system as bringing order to previously chaotic social interactions, making deadbeats pay debts and companies honor obligations.

America's alternative isn't freedom from social scoring, but rather fragmented and unaccountable private scoring systems. Credit ratings determine financial opportunities, insurance algorithms assess risk based on opaque factors, and social media reputation affects employment prospects—all with minimal transparency or due process. The American system combines surveillance capitalism with algorithmic governance, lacking the explicit social management intentions or accountability structures found in China.

Both models raise profound questions about liberty, privacy, accountability, and social function. China's centralized system offers transparency about intentions, while hiding implementation details; America's distributed system obscures both intentions and implementations, maintaining the illusion of freedom from social control.

The policy critique centers on finding democracy's sweet spot—balancing social cohesion and individual liberty rather than sacrificing either. Nordic democracies strike a balance between individual rights and social trust by maintaining individual rights while fostering social trust through equitable outcomes, transparent governance, and citizen engagement. These societies demonstrate that democracy can achieve both freedom and function—but doing so requires institutional designs and cultural practices that America increasingly lacks.

The theoretical framework for sustainable social management suggests three prerequisites: legitimacy derived from either performance or process, adaptability that enables responses to changing conditions, and resilience that facilitates recovery from inevitable crises. China's model derives legitimacy primarily from performance (delivering prosperity and stability) while lacking adaptability through dissent or resilience through distributed authority. America's model retains theoretical legitimacy through process (democratic election) but struggles with performance legitimacy as governance outcomes deteriorate.

The strategic implication? Nations that achieve the democratic sweet spot—maintaining both liberty and functional governance—will likely outperform authoritarian and chaotically democratic alternatives over time. Addressing America's governance challenges requires neither emulating Chinese control nor accepting current dysfunction but rather reconstructing the institutional and cultural foundations that once enabled effective democratic governance.

[Minister Harmony and Professor Liberty conclude their eternal debate, neither conceding nor convincing but perhaps both learning.]

MINISTER HARMONY: "Perhaps there's wisdom in acknowledging that different historical contexts require different governance approaches. What works for China may not work for America, and vice versa."

PROFESSOR LIBERTY: "And perhaps there's humility in recognizing that both our systems face significant challenges requiring adaptation rather than ideological certainty."

MINISTER HARMONY & PROFESSOR LIBERTY: *(simultaneously)* "But my system will ultimately prove superior!"

[They smile, recognizing the irreconcilable yet necessary tension their perspectives represent.]

7. REBUILDING THE CIVIC FOUNDATION: ISLANDS OF HOPE

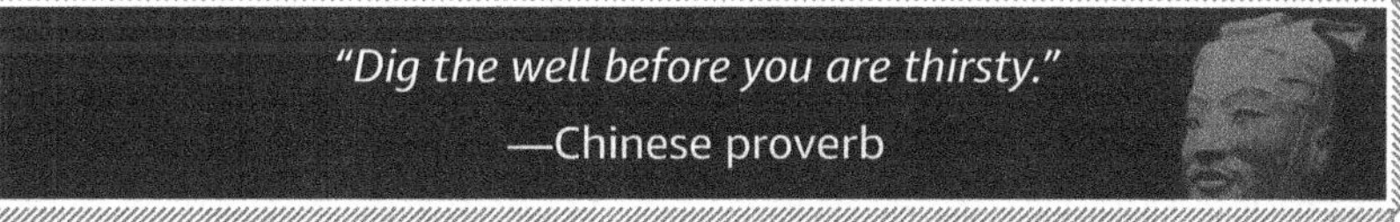

"Dig the well before you are thirsty."
—Chinese proverb

The contrast could hardly be more stark: China presents a political system with artificially imposed unity, while the United States offers a democratic model increasingly defined by self-imposed division.

From Dysfunction to Renewal: America's Civic Entrepreneurs

Amid America's fractured landscape, pockets of civic renewal emerge—islands of hope demonstrating that democratic dysfunction, while pervasive, isn't inevitable. These experiments in rebuilding social capital often begin locally, led by civic entrepreneurs who refuse to accept the permanence of polarization or the inevitability of trust erosion. Their work suggests that while America's social challenges manifested over decades,

FORCED UNITY vs SELF-IMPOSED

The contrast could hardly be more stark.

renewal can occur faster than decay under the right conditions.

COMMUNITY BUILDER CLAIRE: "Welcome, everyone! Today, we're not Republicans or Democrats; we're not progressives or conservatives. We're neighbors building something together for our shared community. Let's put aside the national tribalism for a few hours and remember how to work together on tangible local challenges."

CONSERVATIVE VOLUNTEER: *(hesitantly approaching a progressive volunteer)* "I noticed you know how to mix concrete properly. Mind showing me the technique? My conservative concrete tends to lean right."

PROGRESSIVE VOLUNTEER: *(laughing)* "Sure thing. My progressive concrete usually leans left, but I've been working on keeping it balanced. We can't have a tilted playground, regardless of political preference."

COMMUNITY BUILDER CLAIRE: *(observing their interaction)* "Notice what's happening? When people work together on concrete problems—literally concrete in this case—the abstract divisions that seem so important online fade into the background. We're not solving national polarization, but we're creating a local space where citizenship transcends partisanship."

Claire's approach exemplifies several successful models of civic renewal emerging across America. These models share common elements: they focus on local rather than national engagement, emphasize tangible projects over abstract advocacy, create spaces for positive cross-partisan interaction, and build social capital through shared accomplishment rather than shared ideology.

The analytical framework for understanding these civic renewal efforts draws on both classic and contemporary research. Robert Putnam's seminal work on social capital identified the decline in civic associations that once served as "schools of democracy," where Americans learned to work together despite differences. Modern research on polarization reveals that abstract political differences intensify when untempered by personal relationships across partisan lines. Successful renewal efforts systematically rebuild these cross-cutting ties through practical community engagement.

Case studies of effective civic renewal span geographic and ideological spectrums:

1. **The Better Angels Project:** This nationwide initiative brings together equal numbers of conservatives and progressives for structured conversations aimed not at changing minds but at understanding different perspectives. Participants consistently report reduced antipathy toward political opponents after experiencing them as multidimensional humans rather than partisan caricatures.
2. **Rochester's Sector 4 Community Development:** This community organization in Rochester, New York, built a cross-partisan coalition to address neighborhood deterioration. By focusing on shared concerns—such as safety, education, and economic opportunity—rather than divisive national issues, they created space for collaborative problem-solving across traditional divides.
3. **The Front Porch Forum:** This Vermont-based digital platform creates town-specific online spaces where neighbors can communicate about local needs, events, and concerns. Unlike national social media platforms that optimize for engagement through outrage, this local platform prioritizes community connection and practical assistance.
4. **The Tennessee Bridge Builders:** In rural Tennessee, this organization recruited equal numbers of evangelical Christians and secular progressives to renovate homes for low-income seniors. The shared purpose and tangible rewards—seeing grateful seniors return to improved homes—built relationships that transcended the culture war divisions typically separating these groups.

The data analysis on trust-building interventions reveals encouraging patterns. Survey research indicates that personal contact with outgroup members is more effective in reducing stereotyping and antipathy than any other form of persuasive messaging. Working together on common projects proves particularly effective at building trust across group boundaries. Perhaps most encouragingly, trust-building through practical cooperation appears to transfer partially to broader intergroup attitudes, suggesting that local civic renewal can eventually influence national political climate.

How to Talk to Your Neighbor Without Mentioning Politics: A Satirical Guide

SURVIVAL GUIDE: INTERACTING WITH NEIGHBORS ACROSS THE POLITICAL DIVIDE

For emergency use in maintaining the community's social fabric

STEP 1: IDENTIFY SAFE CONVERSATION TOPICS

- ✓ Local weather events (avoid climate change implications)
- ✓ Community infrastructure (avoid funding source discussions)
- ✓ Children's activities (avoid education policy)
- ✓ Pets (universally safe unless pit bull regulations arise)
- ✓ Home maintenance (avoid property tax implications)
- ✓ Food (steer clear of agricultural policy or regulation)

STEP 2: MASTER THE ART OF POLITICALLY NEUTRAL COMMUNICATION

- ★ Remove all tribal signifiers from the vocabulary
- ★ Mentally replace "those idiots on the other side" with "my neighbors."
- ★ Practice active listening without mentally composing counterarguments
- ★ Maintain comfortable eye contact without partisan-intensity scanning
- ★ Recognize shared humanity despite ideological differences

STEP 3: PREPARE EMERGENCY TOPIC TRANSITIONS

- ★ When conversation approaches a political trigger: "Speaking of rain, how about those garden tomatoes this year?"
- ★ When a neighbor mentions a controversial news story: "I haven't caught up on the news—been too busy fixing that broken fence. By the way, do you have a power saw I could borrow?"
- ★ When a political candidate's name arises: "That reminds me—the community pool committee needs volunteers this weekend. Any interest?"

STEP 4: DISCOVER SHARED INTERESTS & CONCERNS

- ★ Children's safety and education opportunities
- ★ Neighborhood security and emergency preparedness
- ★ Local infrastructure functionality
- ★ Community gathering spaces and activities
- ★ Property values and community appearance

STEP 5: PROPOSE CONCRETE LOCAL ACTIONS

- ★ Neighborhood clean-up day (politics-free zone)
- ★ Community garden establishment (no policy discussions)

HOW TO TALK TO YOUR NEIGHBOR WITHOUT MENTIONING POLITICS

SURVIVAL GUIDE: INTERACTING WITH NEIGHBORS ACROSS THE POLITICAL DIVIDE
For emergency use in maintaining community social fabric

STEP 1: IDENTIFY SAFE CONVERSATION

- ✓ Local weather events (avoid climate change implications?
- ✓ Community infrastructure (avoid funding source discussione
- ✓ Children's activities (avoid education policy)
- ✓ Pets (universally safe unless pit bull regulations ariss)
- ✓ Home maintenance (avoid property tax implications)
- ✓ Food (steer clear of agricultural policy or regulation)

STEP 2: MASTER THE ART OF POLITICALLY NEUTRAL COMMUNICATION

- ➡ Remove all tribal sigifiers from vocabulary
- ➡ Mentally replace "those idiots on the other side" with "my neighbors"

STEP 3: PREPARE EMERGENCY TOPIC TRANSITIONS

- ➡ Speaking of rain, how about those garden tomatoes this year?"
- ➡ Il haven't cought up on the news – been too buss fixing that broken fence. By the way, do you have a power saw'l could berrow?"
- ➡ That reminds me – the community pool committee needs yolunteers this weekend. Any interect?

STEP 4: DISCOVER SHARED INTERESTS & CONCERNS

- ➡ Childrens safety and education opportunities
- ➡ Neighborhood security and emergency preparedness
- ➡ Local infrastructure functionality
- ➡ Community gathering spaces and activities
- ➡ Block party organinization (food transcends partisan division)

STEP 5: PROPOSE CONCRETE LOCAL ACTONS Neighborhood clean-up day *(palities free)*

- ➡ Community garden establishment (no policy
- ➡ Local playground renovation (focus on screws, not social theory)
- ➡ Emergency response planning (save lives regardless of voting records)

★ Local playground renovation (focus on screws, not social theory)
★ Emergency response planning (save lives regardless of voting records)
★ Block party organization (food transcends partisan division)

EMERGENCY PROTOCOL: If a conversation becomes politically charged, deploy the ultimate safeguard: "I just remembered I left something in the oven!" This works in approximately 94% of situations, regardless of the home's proximity or the time of day.

REMEMBER: Your neighbor's voting record is not a reflection of their character. They are a complex human navigating an uncertain world with limited information, just as you are. Finding common ground locally builds resilience against national division.

"The healing of America begins not in Washington but across your backyard fence."

The comparative elements from more socially cohesive democracies offer additional insights for American renewal. Finland's comprehensive civic education ensures citizens understand democratic processes and responsibilities, creating shared democratic literacy that transcends partisan divisions. Denmark's emphasis on "folk schools" and adult education builds cross-cutting ties through lifelong learning communities. These approaches suggest that rebuilding democratic citizenship requires both institutional investments and cultural practices that America has systematically undervalued.

The policy framework for bottom-up civic renewal emphasizes multiple pathways:

1. **Institutional Support:** Governments at all levels can support civic infrastructure by funding community organizations, public spaces, and civic education.
2. **Educational Priority:** Schools can reemphasize civic education not merely as an academic subject but as a practical engagement with community problem-solving.
3. **Corporate Citizenship:** Businesses can contribute by implementing policies that support employee volunteering, community investment, and democratic participation.
4. **Media Ecosystem Reform:** Local journalism, in particular, requires reinvestment to rebuild the information infrastructure that once supported community engagement.
5. **Digital Platform Design:** Social media can be redesigned to foster constructive local engagement rather than maximizing national division.

The theoretical framework connecting local and national social capital suggests that civic renewal typically begins locally before scaling nationally. American history supports this pattern: previous periods of intense polarization were ultimately resolved through renewed emphasis on shared citizenship, often starting with local cooperation that gradually influenced the national climate. This historical pattern offers hope that current divisions, while severe, need not be permanent.

[Community Builder Claire addresses volunteers as they complete their park renovation.]

COMMUNITY BUILDER CLAIRE: "Look at what we've accomplished together! This park was neglected for decades. Ex-

BOTTOM-UP CIVIC RENEWAL FRAMEWORK
Five Pathways to Ctrengthen Community Engagement
1 INSTITUTIONAL SUPPORT
Fund community orgs, public spaces, civic ed
2 EDUCATION PRIORITY
Civic ed as hands-on problem-solving
5 DIGITAL PLATFORM DESIGN
Platforms optimized for local, constructive engagement
3 CORPORATE CITIZENSHIP
Employee volunteering, community investment
NEWS
4 DIGITAL PLATFOM DESIGN
Platforms optimized for local, constructive engagement

Look at what we've accomplished together! This park was neglected for decades... yet here we are-Republicans, Democrats, and independents – having rebuilt this community space through our own efforts."
I still think your tax policies would destroy America, but I have to admit you mix a a mean batch of concrete.
And I still think your healthcare position is morally indefensible, but nobody builds a more level bench.
HEALTHCARE FOR ALL
NEIGHBORS FIRST, PARTISANS SECOND

pert consultants told us that nothing could be done without massive federal grants. Politicians promised solutions that never materialized. Yet here we are—Republicans, Democrats, and independents—having rebuilt this community space through our own efforts."

CONSERVATIVE VOLUNTEER: "I still think your tax policies would destroy America, but I have to admit you mix a mean batch of concrete."

PROGRESSIVE VOLUNTEER: "And I still think your healthcare position is morally indefensible, but nobody builds a more level bench."

CONSERVATIVE & PROGRESSIVE VOLUNTEERS: *(simultaneously laughing)*

COMMUNITY BUILDER CLAIRE: "That's the magic—finding spaces where we're neighbors first, partisans second. We're not solving the national crisis in one afternoon, but we're building resilience against its local effects. And who knows? Maybe if enough communities rebuild their civic foundations, the national conversation will eventually change, too."

America's civic renewal represents the essential counterpoint to its civic decay, demonstrating that while erosion of trust, polarization, and social fragmentation pose serious challenges, they are not America's inevitable destiny. The islands of hope emerging across the country suggest that rebuilding America's civic foundation remains possible through determined effort, practical focus, and institutional innovation. This civic reconstruction stands as perhaps the most urgent yet underappreciated element of America's strategic renewal.

DIAGNOSIS EPILOGUE: THE THREE CONVERGING CRISES

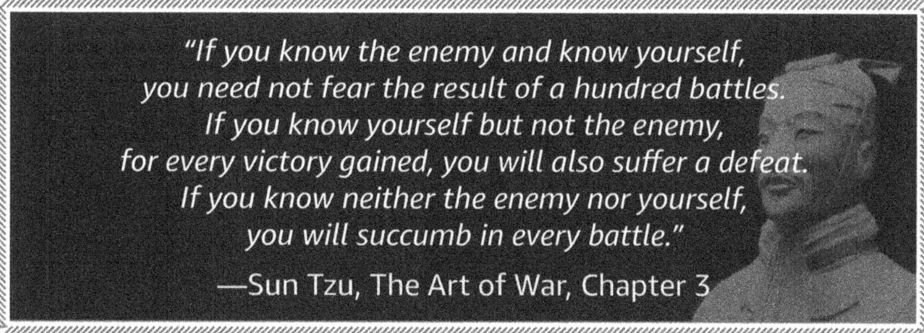

"If you know the enemy and know yourself,
you need not fear the result of a hundred battles.
If you know yourself but not the enemy,
for every victory gained, you will also suffer a defeat.
If you know neither the enemy nor yourself,
you will succumb in every battle."
—Sun Tzu, The Art of War, Chapter 3

As our diagnosis of America's fractured society concludes, a pattern emerges: three distinct yet interconnected crises converging to create unprecedented strategic vulnerability. Like tributaries flowing into a single turbulent river, these crises—each concerning individually—combine to form a perfect storm of national weakness precisely when great power competition demands maximum strength.

[In a metaphysical boardroom overlooking the American landscape, three allegorical figures convene to assess their handiwork. ***Milton the Trickster Economist*** *shuffles financial charts showing accelerating inequality.* ***Admiral Procurement*** *examines blueprints of exquisite yet vulnerable weapons systems.* ***Algorithm Annie*** *monitors social media engagement metrics, showing intensifying tribal division.]*

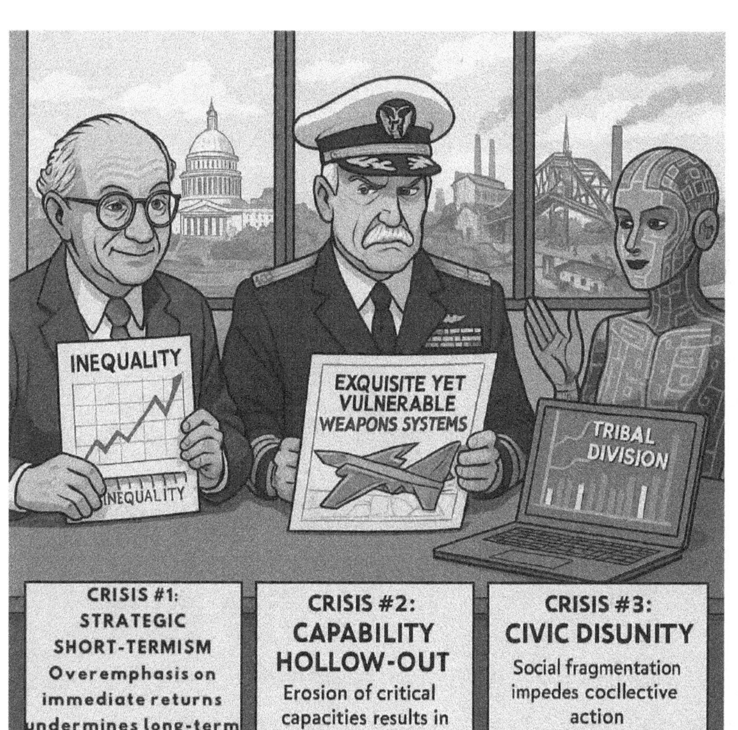

INEQUALITY
INEQUALITY
EXQUISITE YET VULNERABLE WEAPONS SYSTEMS
TRIBAL DIVISION
CRISIS #1: STRATEGIC SHORT-TERMISM
Overemphasis on immediate returns undermines long-term resilience
CRISIS #2: CAPABILITY HOLLOW-OUT
Erosion of critical capacities results in structural weaknesses
CRISIS #3: CIVIC DISUNITY
Social fragmentation impedes coclective action

MILTON THE TRICKSTER ECONOMIST: "My work proceeds splendidly! America's economic foundations have been systematically hollowed out in the service of quarterly profits and shareholder value. Manufacturing capacity outsourced, infrastructure neglected, communities abandoned, workforce skills depleted—all while metrics of financial 'success' reach record highs!"

ADMIRAL PROCUREMENT: "I've contributed my share! America builds the world's most expensive weapons systems optimized for conflicts it no longer faces! Our procurement systems prize platinum-plated technology over resilient capability, producing exquisite vulnerability rather than practical strength."

ALGORITHM ANNIE: "And I've divided the population into hermetically sealed information environments where citizens cannot agree on basic reality!

Americans increasingly view fellow citizens as mortal enemies rather than political opponents—rendering collective action virtually impossible!"

MILTON, ADMIRAL, & ALGORITHM ANNIE: *(simultaneous toast)* "To convergent crisis! May our separate sabotage combine to create truly spectacular vulnerability!"

This satirical meeting captures a sobering analytical reality: America faces three converging crises that mutually reinforce to create strategic vulnerability greater than the sum of its parts:

Crisis #1: Strategic Short-Termism

America's economic, political, and social systems increasingly prioritize immediate returns over long-term resilience. Quarterly capitalism prioritizes short-term profits over sustainable growth. Electoral politics prioritizes short-term advantage over long-term governance. Media optimizes for immediate engagement over democratic health. This systemic short-termism creates disadvantages in competition with nations operating on longer timeframes.

Crisis #2: Capability Hollow-Out

Beneath impressive surface metrics, American capabilities have eroded across multiple dimensions. Manufacturing capacity has declined through offshoring. Infrastructure has deteriorated through chronic underinvestment. Education systems have stagnated through neglect. Healthcare delivers poor outcomes despite enormous expense. This hollow-out leaves America increasingly dependent on concentrated capabilities, vulnerable to disruption or attack.

Crisis #3: Civic Disunity

American society exhibits unprecedented fragmentation along political, informational, and cultural lines. Trust in institutions has collapsed to historic lows. Political tribes view opponents as enemies rather than legitimate competitors. Information ecosystems have become so fragmented that citizens lack a shared factual foundation for democratic deliberation. This disunity undermines the social cohesion required for an effective response to strategic challenges.

The systems analysis reveals dangerous feedback loops connecting these crises. Short-termism accelerates capability hollowing out by prioritizing immediate returns over long-term investment. Capability hollow-out intensifies civic disunity by delivering deteriorating outcomes that erode institutional legitimacy. Civic disunity deepens short-termism by rewarding tribal signaling over effective governance. These reinforcing cycles create a trap from which escape becomes increasingly difficult, unless systemic intervention occurs.

HOW WE GOT HERE

The Converging Crises Timeline

STEP 1 —— CONVERGING CRISES TIMELINE

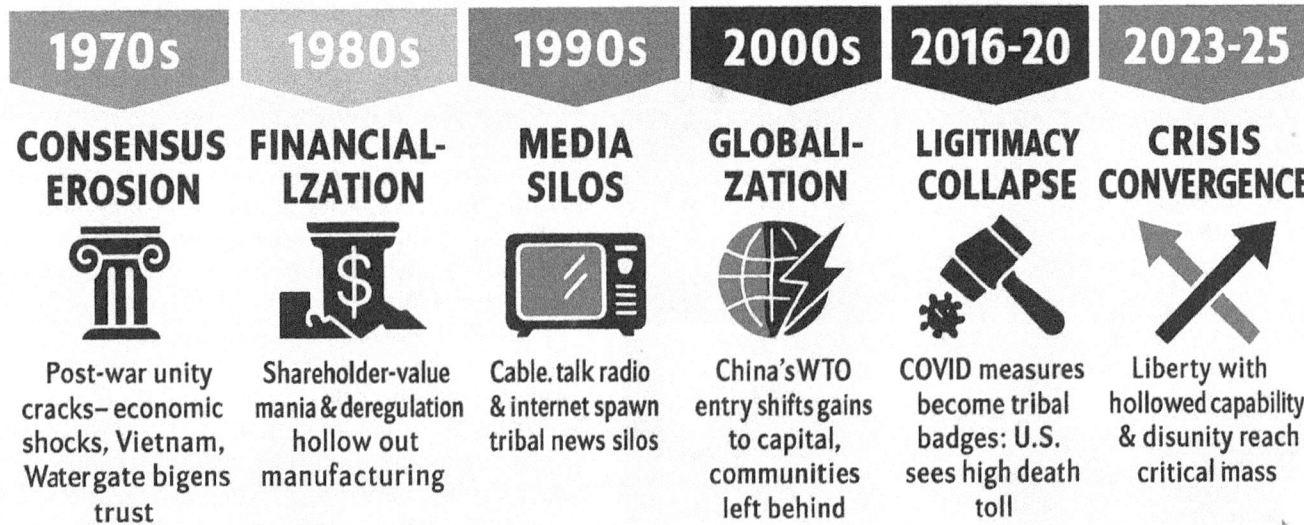

1970s	1980s	1990s	2000s	2016-20	2023-25
CONSENSUS EROSION	**FINANCIAL-LZATION**	**MEDIA SILOS**	**GLOBALI-ZATION**	**LIGITIMACY COLLAPSE**	**CRISIS CONVERGENCE**

Post-war unity cracks– economic shocks, Vietnam, Watergate bigens trust	Shareholder-value mania & deregulation hollow out manufacturing	Cable. talk radio & internet spawn tribal news silos	China's WTO entry shifts gains to capital, communities left behind	COVID measures become tribal badges: U.S. sees high death toll	Liberty with hollowed capability & disunity reach critical mass

'History doesn't repeat, but it rhymes—and America is reciting a worrying stanza.

Historical parallels offer both caution and hope. America has faced previous periods of vulnerability—the fractious 1850s preceding the Civil War, the corrupt Gilded Age, and the economic devastation of the Great Depression. Each crisis threatened national cohesion and capability; each ultimately generated renewal through institutional innovation and cultural recommitment to shared purpose. The common element in successful renewal? Leadership that reoriented national focus from short-term division to long-term shared challenges.

How We Got Here: The Converging Crises Timeline

STEP 1: POST-WAR CONSENSUS EROSION (1970s)

America's post-World War II economic and political consensus—characterized by shared prosperity, institutional trust, and Cold War unity—begins to fracture. Financial shocks, cultural conflicts, and governance failures (as seen in Vietnam and Watergate) undermine public confidence in established institutions.

STEP 2: FINANCIALIZATION ACCELERATION (1980s)

Milton the Trickster's economic philosophy ascends, emphasizing shareholder value maximization over stakeholder capitalism. Financial deregulation, tax structure changes, and shifts in corporate governance redirect capital from productive investment toward financial engineering. Manufacturing relocation is beginning to hollow out industrial communities.

STEP 3: MEDIA ECOSYSTEM FRAGMENTATION (1990s)

The unified information environment dissolves as cable news, talk radio, and the early internet create separate tribal information channels. Americans are increasingly consuming news that reinforces rather than challenges their existing beliefs. Political incentives shift toward serving the most engaged (typically most extreme) constituents.

STEP 4: GLOBALIZATION WITHOUT ADJUSTMENT (2000s)

Accelerated economic integration, particularly following China's entry into the WTO, disrupts American industrial communities without adequate adjustment assistance. The benefits of globalization accrue disproportionately to knowledge economy workers and capital owners, while manufacturing regions experience sustained decline.

STEP 5: DIGITAL AMPLIFICATION OF DIVISION (2010s)

UNCLE SAM: "I've heard enough. Your diagnosis is accurate—we face converging crises of our own making. But you overlooked something important: America has faced existential challenges before and found the strength to renew itself. The question isn't whether America can overcome these challenges... The question is whether we'll recognize the stakes and summon the will for renewal before our competitors gain unrecoverable advantage. That chapter in our national story remains unwritten."

Social media algorithms optimize for engagement through outrage, accelerating political polarization and information fragmentation. Filter bubbles become hermetically sealed information environments. Americans are increasingly experiencing different versions of reality based on their digital consumption patterns.

STEP 6: INSTITUTIONAL LEGITIMACY COLLAPSE (2016-2020)

Trust in core democratic institutions—from Congress to courts to electoral systems—plummets amid partisan warfare and governance dysfunction. Constitutional hardball becomes normalized, and compromise becomes increasingly viewed as a betrayal rather than a governance necessity.

STEP 7: PANDEMIC RESPONSE FAILURE (2020-2022)

The COVID-19 response becomes a partisan battleground rather than a unified national effort. Basic public health measures transform into tribal signifiers. America suffers one of the developed world's highest per-capita death rates despite vast medical resources, highlighting capability gaps and social fragmentation.

STEP 8: PRESENT CONVERGENCE (2023-2025)

The three crises—short-termism, capability hollowing out, and civic disunity—reach their peak convergence. Strategic competitors exploit the resulting vulnerabilities through direct challenge and indirect amplification of existing American divisions. Renewal requires addressing all three crises simultaneously rather than treating them as separate challenges.

"History doesn't repeat, but it rhymes—and America is currently reciting a particularly concerning stanza."

The unified framework for understanding American vulnerability integrates these converging crises into a comprehensive diagnostic model. Rather than treating economic, military, and social challenges as separate domains, this framework recognizes their fundamental interconnection. Economic hollow-out undermines military capability and social cohesion. Social division impedes economic coordination and effectiveness. Short-term thinking across domains prevents addressing root causes, instead focusing on symptoms.

This framework suggests that effective renewal requires an integrated response rather than domain-specific solutions. Economic policies must rebuild productive capabilities while reducing destabilizing inequality. Military approaches must prioritize resilient systems over exquisite vulnerabilities. Social interventions must rebuild the civic foundation for collective action. Most importantly, these responses must reinforce rather than counteract each other—creating virtuous cycles of improvement rather than competing priorities.

The Rooseveltian framework introduced in subsequent chapters provides precisely such an integrated approach—addressing America's converging crises through coordinated renewal across economic, military, and social domains. The diagnosis may appear grim, but America retains remarkable assets for renewal: unparalleled innovative capacity, substantial material resources, and a demonstrated historical ability to reinvent itself during periods of challenge.

The Chinese analytical perspective on America's converging crises warrants consideration. Chinese strategists observe America's self-inflicted wounds with strategic patience, recognizing that these internal challenges potentially accomplish what external pressure alone cannot achieve. Their approach increasingly focuses on amplifying existing American divisions rather than creating new vulnerabilities—a strategy that leverages America's own tendencies toward self-sabotage.

Yet this Chinese perspective, while strategically sophisticated, may underestimate America's capacity for renewal. Previous predictions of American decline have repeatedly proven premature precisely because American society possesses remarkable adaptive capacity when properly mobilized. The very openness that enables America's current divisions also creates potential for innovation and adaptation that more controlled societies struggle to match.

The strategic choice facing America isn't between maintaining current dysfunction or emulating authoritarian alternatives. Rather, it's between continuing self-sabotage through converging crises or reclaiming the democratic resilience that once defined American strength. The diagnosis is clear; the treatment plan is now in place. America's fractured society and faltering trust represent strategic vulnerabilities of the first order—but vulnerabilities that can be addressed through determined national renewal.

[Milton the Trickster Economist, Admiral Procurement, and Algorithm Annie conclude their assessment, unaware that their conversation is being observed.]

UNCLE SAM: *(emerging from shadows, voice stronger than before)* "I've heard enough. Your diagnosis is accurate—we face converging crises of our own making. But you've overlooked something important: America has faced existential challenges before and found the strength to renew itself. The Rooseveltian response you mock as impossible has historical precedent. We've rebuilt before; we can rebuild again."

MILTON, ADMIRAL, & ALGORITHM ANNIE: *(exchanging nervous glances)*

UNCLE SAM: "The question isn't whether America can overcome these challenges—history proves we can. The question is whether we'll recognize the stakes and summon the will for renewal before our competitors gain an unrecoverable advantage. That chapter in our national story remains unwritten."

TL;DR – America faces three converging crises—strategic short-termism, capability hollowing-out, and civic disunity—that together create unprecedented vulnerability in competition with China. Addressing these interrelated challenges requires a comprehensive renewal approach that rebuilds economic foundations, revitalizes democratic institutions, and restores the social trust essential for national effectiveness and success.

PART III: STRATEGY

CHAPTER 5: UNITED STATES' NATIONAL SECURITY AND RESILIENCE STRATEGY IN CHINA'S AI CENTURY

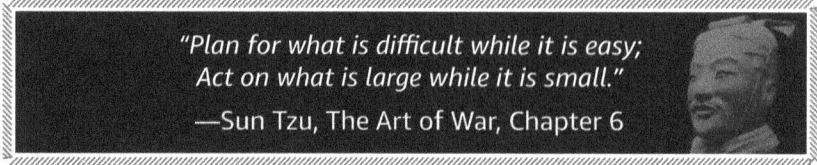

> *"Plan for what is difficult while it is easy;*
> *Act on what is large while it is small."*
> —Sun Tzu, The Art of War, Chapter 6

EXECUTIVE BRIEFING

Strategic Snapshot

FDR's ghost just rolled into the Pentagon at 03:17 AM and muttered: *"Where's your digital Arsenal of Democracy?"* Between AI arms races, screwdriver-tight supply chains, and ransomware pipelines, America is one geopolitical sneeze from realizing spreadsheets are not a strategy.

Key Findings — X-Rays of the Republic

1. **Digital Arsenal Gap**—Federal R&D wilted to 0.7 % GDP (1.9 % in the 1960s); China now out-publishes the U.S. in AI 2:**1**.
2. **Four-Dimensional Fragility**—Physical, digital, supply chain, and social systems lock like Jenga: yank one block, and the tower jitters.
3. **Supply-Chain Russian Roulette**: 92 % of leading-edge chips live in Taiwan, 80 % of antibiotic precursors ride foreign freighters, and 85% of rare-earth processing is China-controlled.
4. **Cyber Achilles' Heel**—Critical infrastructure withstands 22k attacks/day; a Colonial-scale hack can freeze 45 % of East Coast fuel within 48 hours.
5. **Alliance Force Multiplier** – Democratic partners command **60 %** of global GDP and **68 %** of chip capacity—if they coordinate rather than kvetch.

Risk Ledger

Vulnerability	Pain Point	Current Exposure
Tech-Leadership Slippage	AI/quantum edge erosion	Talent leaks; R&D gap
Single-Point Chokes	Chips, APIs, and rare earths	70-92 % foreign-sourced
Critical-Infra Hacks	Grid/water/transport stoppage	Legacy SCADA, weak MFA
Policy Whiplash	4-year mood swings	56 % of projects reset post-election
Alliance Drift	Fragmented rules & export regimes	30 + overlapping frameworks

Opportunity Knobs

- ★ Combined democratic R&D budget **2.7** × China's.
- ★ CHIPS-style coalitions prove a bipartisan appetite for industrial policy.
- ★ Rising "China-fatigue" in developing nations demands credible alternatives.

Action Recommendations — *Blueprint for Renewal*

1. **ARPA-X Manhattan Project**—$60 B/yr moonshot fund for AI, quantum, biotech, and materials; program managers empowered to kill zombie projects early.
2. **National Resilience Council**—This is a Cabinet-level nerve center with cross-domain authority, an annual Resilience Scorecard, and a 48-hour FOIA on budgets.

3. **Strategic Re-shoring Bonds**—Treasury-backed 30-year paper underwriting fabs, API plants, and rare-earth refineries on U.S./ally soil.
4. **Cyber Duty-of-Care Mandate**—Sector-specific *must-do* standards, 72-hour breach disclosure, and a 0.5 % "outrage excise" on social-media ad revenue to fund workforce training.
5. **Democratic Tech Alliance**—Treaty-grade council harmonizing export controls, joint stockpiles, privacy-first AI standards, and visa fast-tracks for STEM talent.

Bottom Line

Quarterly capitalism won the spreadsheet race; it won't win the century. Channel Roosevelt: mobilize like it's 1941—but for photons, qubits, and supply chains—lock strategy into statute so it outlives Twitter tantrums, and spin a fractious alliance into the planet's biggest innovation flywheel. Plan for what's difficult while it's still easy—or prepare to watch FDR's ghost light another cigarette and say, "Told you so."

Opening Tableau: The Ghost of National Security Past

The Pentagon's most secure conference room, 3:17 AM.

The lights flicker momentarily as a translucent figure materializes at the head of the table—spectacles perched on his nose, a cigarette holder jutting at a defiant angle, a wheelchair nowhere in sight. The ghost of Franklin Delano Roosevelt rolls up his spectral sleeves and leans forward, examining the AI capability assessments scattered across the table with mounting concern.

"So," FDR's spirit drawls, tapping ash from his phantom cigarette, "what's the actual plan here besides hoping Silicon Valley figures it out before Beijing does?"

The assembled officials—a collection of America's finest military minds, intelligence experts, and strategic thinkers—exchange nervous glances. General Quagmire, a man whose uniform contains more stars than a minor galaxy, clears his throat.

"Well, Mr. President," he begins, sliding forward a PowerPoint printout titled *Fighting the Last War Better: A Strategic Framework*, "we've developed a comprehensive approach to counter Chinese technological advancement through increased naval presence in the South China Sea and—"

"I didn't ask about boats," FDR interrupts. "I asked about the *plan*. When I confronted fascism, we converted automobile factories to aircraft production in just a few months. We mobilized the nation's industrial might toward a singular purpose. Where's that level of clarity and purpose now?"

Admiral Procurement, whose chest decorations suggest he's survived numerous budget battles, jumps in. "Sir, we've allocated $2.7 billion for a next-generation aircraft carrier that should be operational by 2039, assuming no additional cost overruns or technical delays, which, of course, there will be."

FDR's ghostly eyebrow rises. "And how exactly will this counter China's advances in quantum computing and artificial intelligence?"

"It'll be a really impressive carrier, sir," the Admiral replies.

In the corner, a figure in an impeccably tailored suit and designer glasses examines his manicured nails. This is McSlicey, the High Priest, the embodiment of efficiency over strategic sense, of quarterly profits over national security.

"If I may," McSlicey interjects, "our 300-slide analysis indicates we could achieve significant cost efficiencies by outsourcing critical military components to Chinese factories. The shareholder value would be extraordinary."

FDR's spectral form visibly dims. "You're proposing we have our potential adversary build our defense systems?"

"It's about maximizing ROI," McSlicey explains patiently, as though addressing a particularly slow child. "Besides, they gave us an excellent quote."

From another corner comes a snickering sound. Milton the Trickster Economist lounges in his chair, feet propped irreverently on the table. "Why invest in industrial capacity at all?" he asks. "The market will provide! An invisible hand will surely guide semiconductor production back to American shores the moment it becomes financially advantageous... any decade now."

FDR turns to the lone woman at the table—Resilience Director Rachel, whose expression suggests she's the only adult in a room full of children playing with matches.

"And you, young lady? What do you propose?"

Rachel straightens. "Sir, we need a comprehensive National Resilience Framework that addresses our vulnerabilities across physical, digital, supply chain, and social dimensions. We need to—"

"BORING!" erupts a voice from the doorway—the Commander-in-Tweet strides in, smartphone in hand, golden tie glinting in the low light. "I've got a better plan. The BEST plan. We'll tweet at China. VERY strongly worded. They'll respect that. Also, tariffs. BIG tariffs."

FDR's ghost sighs deeply, looking around the room once more. "I see," he says quietly. "So this is how empires end. Not with a bang, but with a Tweet."

I. THE NEW ARSENAL OF DEMOCRACY: FROM INDUSTRIAL TO DIGITAL MOBILIZATION

> *"Speed is the essence of war:*
> *take advantage of the enemy's unreadiness."*
> —Sun Tzu, The Art of War, Chapter 7

Historical Parallels: Learning from the Greatest Generation's Mobilization

The challenges facing America today bear striking parallels to those confronted by Roosevelt's generation. In December 1940, with Europe ablaze and fascism on the march, FDR delivered his Arsenal of Democracy speech, transforming America from an isolationist nation into the industrial powerhouse that would ultimately win World War II. Within months, automobile factories were producing aircraft, shipyards were launching vessels daily, and the entire industrial economy had redirected its focus toward a singular purpose.

Today, we face a different kind of challenge—not the immediate threat of military invasion, but the steady technological encirclement by a resurgent China determined to dominate the commanding heights of 21st-century technology. While bombs aren't falling on American soil, our technological sovereignty is under sustained assault.

The parallels are instructive. Just as industrial might have determined the outcome of World War II, digital and technological capabilities will determine the geopolitical winners and losers in the coming decades. And just as America required a massive industrial mobilization to meet the fascist threat, we now need a comprehensive digital mobilization to maintain our technological edge.

Character Dialogue: FDR Interrogates Modern Officials

FDR's ghost materializes in the White House Situation Room during a technology security briefing.

FDR: "So you're telling me that 90% of advanced semiconductor manufacturing capacity lies in Taiwan, a mere 100 miles from mainland China? And most of our pharmaceutical ingredients come from China itself? What exactly have you people been doing for the past 30 years?"

Commerce Secretary: "Maximizing shareholder value, sir."

FDR: "And how's that working out for national security?"

Defense Secretary: "Not ideal, Mr. President. But the quarterly reports looked outstanding."

FDR: "When I was president, we built 296,429 aircraft in under four years. How long would it take us to establish domestic semiconductor manufacturing if China were to invade Taiwan tomorrow?"

Uncomfortable silence.

Intelligence Director: "That's... classified, sir."

FDR: "Which means you don't know, or the answer is too terrifying to admit."

Commerce Secretary: "A bit of both, honestly."

FDR: "In 1941, we transformed our entire industrial base in months. What's your excuse?"

McSlicey the High Priest: *(sliding forward a glossy report)* "Sir, our comprehensive analysis shows that reshoring critical industries would negatively impact quarterly earnings and might reduce executive bonuses by up to 8.7%. The market would punish such inefficiencies severely."

FDR: *(ashes from spectral cigarette falling through McSlicey's report)* "The market. I see. And when China controls global AI systems, quantum communications, and advanced materials, what will your precious market be worth then?"

McSlicey: *(adjusting glasses nervously)* "We haven't modeled that scenario specifically, but—"

FDR: "Perhaps you should."

Analytical Framework: The Arsenal of Democracy Concept for Digital Competition

The original Arsenal of Democracy triumphed through a cocktail of now-endangered policy species: strategic clarity (identifying actual threats without partisan hyperventilation), resource mobilization (redirecting economic might toward something besides shareholder value), public-private partnerships (before they became euphemisms for corporate welfare), scientific investment (funding breakthroughs rather than bureaucratic box-checking), and alliance coordination that produced more than carbon emissions and forgettable communiqués.

Updating this framework for our digital cage match with China demands identifying technologies where American leadership remains non-negotiable—from AI to quantum computing, where particles and American policy positions can simultaneously exist in multiple contradictory states. We need digital resource mobilization, directing capital toward strategic priorities rather than the next dopamine-harvesting app. Our public-private partnerships must evolve beyond "government regulates, industry innovates, both sides tweet their grievances." We require a scientific renaissance with research funding at 1% of GDP—up from today's anemic 0.7%, because apparently winning the defining technological competition of our era warrants less investment than Americans spend annually on pet food. Ultimately, we require a Democratic Technology Alliance to establish standards before China's alternatives become global standards.

The uncomfortable truth remains: some technological capabilities are too strategically vital to be surrendered to market forces alone, particularly in the face of China's state-directed economy—a reality that causes severe ideological discomfort among free-market purists, just as the original Arsenal of Democracy did.

Comparative Analysis: China's Civil-Military Fusion versus America's Fragmented Approach

China's "Military-Civil Fusion" strategy operates like a national technological immune system—CCP antibodies identify threats, mobilize resources, and attack strategic vulnerabilities with ruthless efficiency. The Party orchestrates five-year plans, directing government funding, state banks, and private capital toward achieving technological dominance. Programs like the "Thousand Talents Plan" vacuum up global expertise like a dragon hoarding intellectual treasure. The result: civilian innovations rapidly morph into military applications faster than American policymakers can schedule their next interagency meeting.

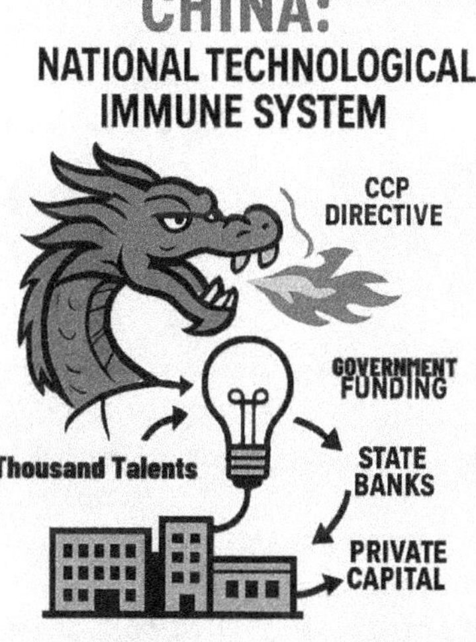

Meanwhile, America's approach resembles a technological autoimmune disorder—our systems attack themselves through strategic incoherence across competing agencies, chronically anemic R&D investment (shriveling from 1.9% of GDP in the 1960s to a malnourished 0.7% today), and Silicon Valley-Pentagon relations that oscillate between awkward blind dates and restraining orders. Our military-civilian technology transfer process moves at the pace of continental drift, while our democratic alliances remain technological Potemkin villages—impressive in diplomatic communiqués, yet hollow in implementation.

Consider quantum computing: China says, "Here's a decade-long plan with $10 billion. Universities, companies, and the military will coordinate under the supervision of the Party. Success brings rewards; failure brings... consequences." America responds, "Let's fund seven competing strategies at 30% of required levels while companies chase quarterly returns and military applications marinate in five-year review processes. We'll coordinate with allies after resolving interagency turf wars—expected completion date: shortly after China announces quantum supremacy."

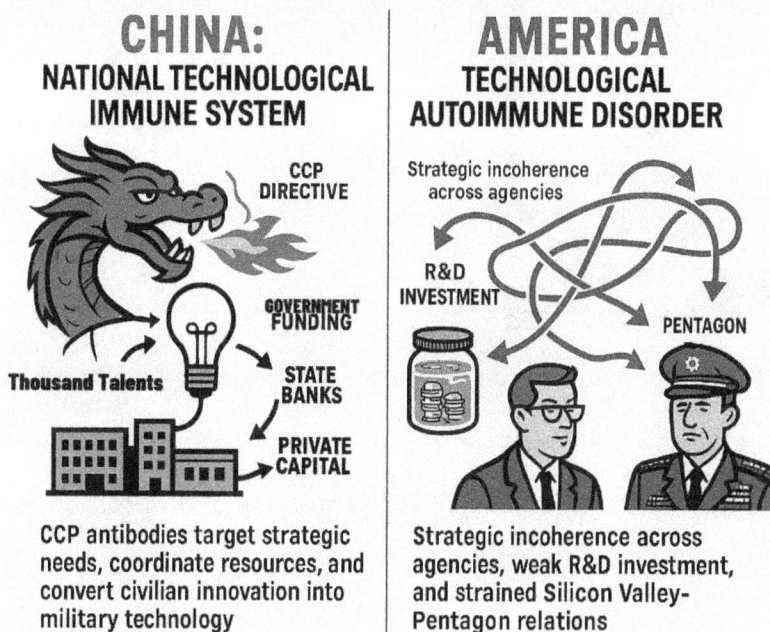

While China's authoritarian system breeds inefficiency, corruption, and innovation-smothering conformity, its strategic coherence provides undeniable advantages in our technological cold war—a reality that many American policymakers acknowledge only after their third martini.

Satirical Recreation: "The Arsenal of Democracy Speech 2.0"

My fellow Americans,

POLICY PROPOSAL NATIONAL TECHNOLOGY SECURITY STRATEGY

America needs a comprehensive National Technoiogy Security Strategy with clear goals, metrics, and implementation mechanisms.

CRITICAL TECHNOLOGY IDENTIFICATION
Formal process for identifying technologies essential to national security, economic competitiveness, and democratic values

DOMESTIC CAPACITY REQUIREMENTS
Minimum domestic production capabilities for essential technologies and components

STRATEGIC INVESTMENT FUND
$500 biilion revolving fund for investments in critical technology manutacturing

HUMAN CAPITAL DEVELOPMENT
National STEM education initiative with 1 million new scholarships

ALLIED TECHNOLOGY COORDINATION
Formal mechanisms for Joint development and production with democratic allies

REGULATORY STREAMLINING
Expedited processes for strategic technology deployment while maintaining appropriate oversight

FOREIGN INVESTMENT REVIEW
Enhanced scrutiny of investments in critical technology sectors

IMPLEMENTATION MECHANISMS
New National Technology Security Council with presidential leadership and cabinet participation

We face a moment unlike any in our history—not a military invasion of bombs and bullets, but a technological encirclement that threatens our prosperity, security, and way of life just as surely.

While we've been busy arguing about culture wars on Twitter and maximizing quarterly profits, China has been systematically building the industries of the future. They've invested trillions in artificial intelligence, quantum computing, biotechnology, and clean energy. Their universities now produce more STEM graduates than ours. Their companies file more patents. Their industrial policy makes ours look like a middle-school student council debate.

Some say this competition is too difficult, that American manufacturing is gone forever, that we can't possibly catch up in advanced industries, and that we should simply accept our decline with dignity.

To them, I say: Have you forgotten who we are?

We are the nation that went from the Wright Brothers to the Moon landing in 66 years, mobilized our industrial might to defeat fascism in four years, built the internet, mapped the human genome, and created the smartphone revolution.

Today, I declare that America will become the Arsenal of Democracy for the digital age. We will rebuild our manufacturing capabilities, secure our supply chains, and reclaim technological leadership not through protectionism and isolation, but through strategic investment and innovation.

The task is great, and the obstacles are many. But America has never shied away from a challenge when our future is at stake.

We do these things not because they are easy, but because they are hard—and because the alternative is to surrender our children's future to those who do not share our values or our vision for humanity's progress.

America will prevail in this competition not by becoming more like its competitors but by becoming more fully itself—a nation of innovation, opportunity, and democratic ideals brought to life through technological leadership.

The Arsenal of Democracy 2.0 begins today. The only question is: Will you join in this historic mobilization, or watch from the sidelines as others determine our fate?

Policy Proposal: National Technology Security Strategy

America needs a comprehensive National Technology Security Strategy with clear goals, metrics, and implementation mechanisms. Key elements should include:

1. **Critical Technology Identification:** A Formal process for identifying technologies essential to national security, economic competitiveness, and democratic values.
2. **Domestic Capacity Requirements:** Minimum domestic production capabilities for essential technologies and components.
3. **Strategic Investment Fund:** $500 billion revolving fund for investments in critical technology manufacturing and R&D.
4. **Human Capital Development:** National STEM education initiative with 1 million new scholarships.

5. **Allied Technology Coordination:** Formal mechanisms for joint development and production with democratic allies.
6. **Regulatory Streamlining:** Expedited processes for strategic technology deployment while maintaining appropriate oversight.
7. **Foreign Investment Review:** Enhanced scrutiny of investments in critical technology sectors.
8. **Implementation Mechanisms:** New National Technology Security Council with presidential leadership and cabinet participation.

Theoretical Framework: The State's Role in Technological Revolution

Throughout history, transformative technological innovations have rarely emerged solely from market forces. From canals and railroads to the internet and GPS, the government has played a pivotal role in driving technological revolutions. This pattern holds across several dimensions:

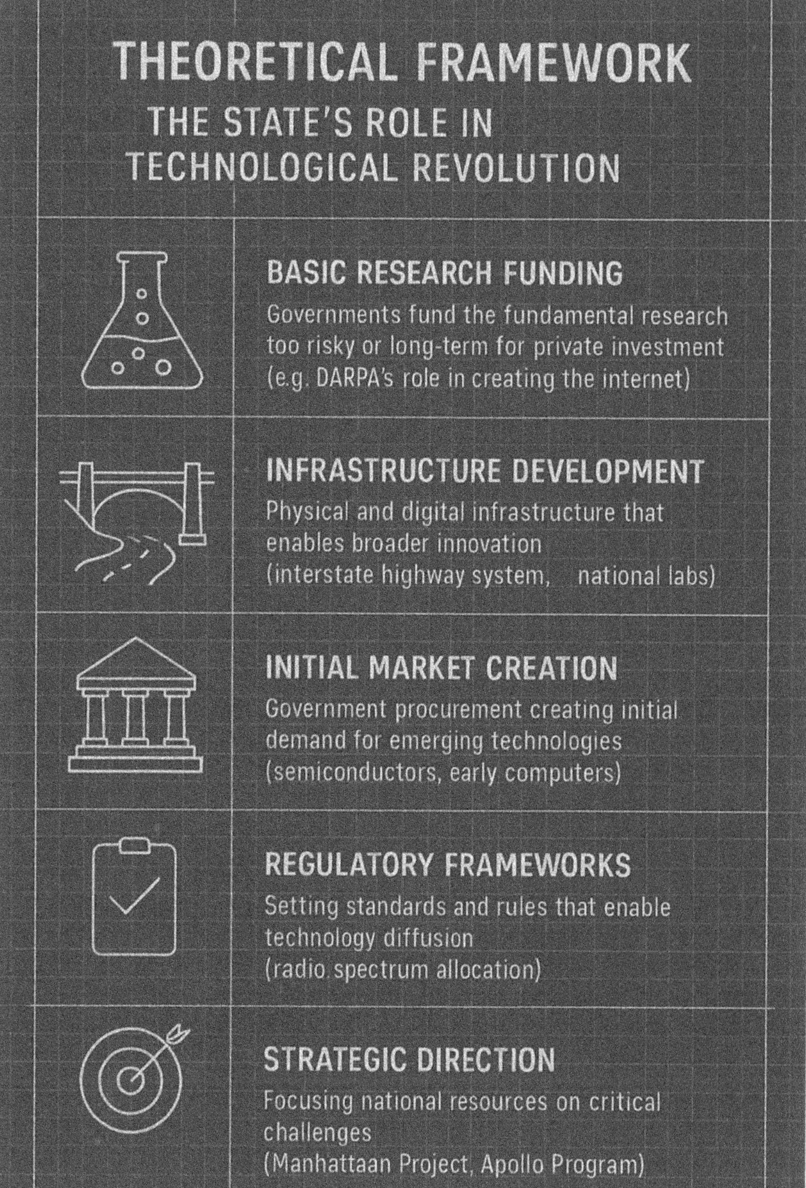
THEORETICAL FRAMEWORK
THE STATE'S ROLE IN TECHNOLOGICAL REVOLUTION
BASIC RESEARCH FUNDING
Governments fund the fundamental research too risky or long-term for private investment (e.g. DARPA's role in creating the internet)
INFRASTRUCTURE DEVELOPMENT
Physical and digital infrastructure that enables broader innovation (interstate highway system, national labs)
INITIAL MARKET CREATION
Government procurement creating initial demand for emerging technologies (semiconductors, early computers)
REGULATORY FRAMEWORKS
Setting standards and rules that enable technology diffusion (radio spectrum allocation)
STRATEGIC DIRECTION
Focusing national resources on critical challenges (Manhattaan Project, Apollo Program)

1. **Basic Research Funding:** Governments fund fundamental research that is too risky or long-term for private investment (e.g., DARPA's role in creating the internet).
2. **Infrastructure Development:** Physical and digital infrastructure that enables broader innovation (e.g., interstate highway system, national labs).
3. **Initial Market Creation:** Government procurement creates initial demand for emerging technologies (e.g., semiconductors, early computers).
4. **Regulatory Frameworks:** Establishing standards and rules that facilitate the diffusion of technology (e.g., radio spectrum allocation).
5. **Strategic Direction:** Focusing national resources on critical challenges (e.g., the Manhattan Project, the Apollo Program).

This doesn't mean the government should direct all technological development—market forces remain essential for innovation, efficiency, and commercialization. Rather, it suggests a balanced approach in which the government provides strategic direction, long-term investment, and critical infrastructure while private enterprise drives execution and innovation.

China understands this dynamic well, deploying state capacity strategically to support technological development while allowing market mechanisms where appropriate. America must relearn this lesson if it hopes to maintain technological leadership in the 21st century.

II. THE NATIONAL RESILIENCE FRAMEWORK: BEYOND DEFENSE TO SECURITY

> *"Plan for what is difficult while it is easy."*
> —Laozi, Dao De Jing, §63

Analytical Framework: Comprehensive Vulnerability Assessment

Traditional national security focuses primarily on military threats—hostile armies, navies, and air forces threatening territorial integrity. This framework served America reasonably well in the industrial age, but proves dangerously inadequate in today's interconnected world.

A more comprehensive National Resilience Framework must address vulnerabilities across at least four critical dimensions:

1. **Physical Resilience:** Traditional infrastructure (transportation, energy, water) capable of withstanding both attacks and natural disasters.
2. **Digital Resilience:** Cyber defenses, data protection, and communications redundancy to maintain function during digital disruption.
3. **Supply Chain Resilience:** Secured access to critical materials, components, and products even during global disruptions.
4. **Social Resilience:** Societal cohesion, information ecosystem integrity, and institutional trust are necessary to prevent domestic fracturing.

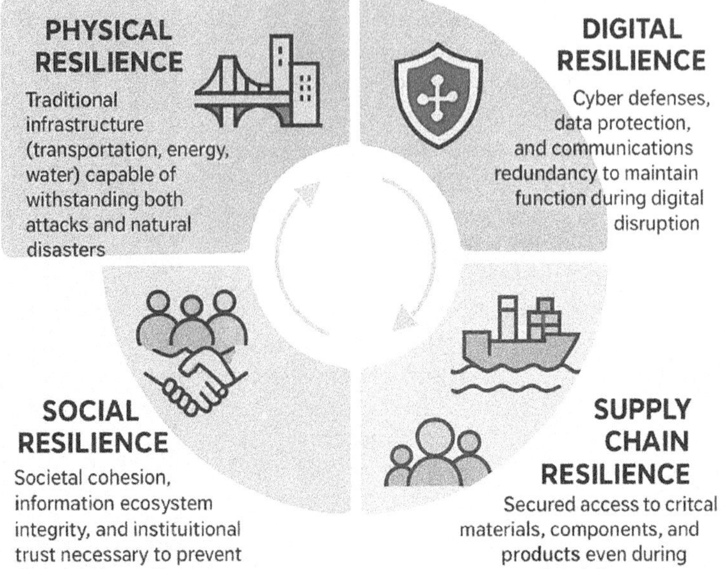
ANALYTICAL FRAMEWORK:
COMPREHENSIVE VULNERABILITY ASSESSMENT
A more comprehensive National Resilience Framework must address vulnerabilities across at least four critical dimensions:
PHYSICAL RESILIENCE
Traditional infrastructure (transportation, energy, water) capable of withstanding both attacks and natural disasters
DIGITAL RESILIENCE
Cyber defenses, data protection, and communications redundancy to maintain function during digital disruption
SOCIAL RESILIENCE
Societal cohesion, information ecosystem integrity, and instituitional trust necessary to prevent domestic fracturing
SUPPLY CHAIN RESILIENCE
Secured access to critcal materials, components, and products even during global disruptions

These dimensions are deeply interconnected. A cyber attack on the power grid (digital) can disable physical infrastructure. Supply chain disruptions can trigger social unrest. Social polarization can prevent an effective response to physical threats. True security requires addressing all four dimensions simultaneously.

Character Vignette: Resilience Director Rachel Explains the Paradigm Shift

The National Security Council meets to discuss emerging threats. Resilience Director Rachel steps to the podium, facing skeptical traditional security officials.

Rachel: "Gentlemen, for decades, we've defined national security primarily through military capabilities. Today, I'm going to explain why that framework is dangerously outdated."

She displays a slide showing the Colonial Pipeline ransomware attack that disrupted East Coast fuel supplies.

Rachel: "This attack cost us more in economic damage and social disruption than a conventional military strike, yet it required no armies, no navies, no air forces—just a few hackers with a Bitcoin wallet."

General Quagmire: *(scoffing)* "That's a law enforcement issue, not national security."

Rachel: "Is it? When Americans can't get gasoline, when hospitals lose power, when critical supply chains collapse—that's not national security? Tell me, General, what exactly are all your impressive weapons defending if a teenager can cripple our society with a laptop?"

She advances to a slide showing pharmaceutical supply chains.

Rachel: "Currently, 80% of active pharmaceutical ingredients in U.S. medications come from overseas, primarily China and India. If those supplies were disrupted—whether by pandemic, conflict, or deliberate action—we'd face a health security crisis no aircraft carrier could solve."

Admiral Procurement: "So you want us to stockpile pills now? What's next, toilet paper?"

Rachel: *(smiling patiently)* "Actually, yes. Strategic stockpiling is part of the solution. But more importantly, we need domestic production capacity for essential goods, resilient infrastructure that can withstand both attacks and natural disasters, and social cohesion strong enough to prevent domestic fracturing during crises."

McSlicey the High Priest: *(alarmed)* "But domestic manufacturing is inefficient! Our analysis shows that outsourcing critical production saves 3.7% on quarterly statements!"

Rachel: "And how much does societal collapse cost per quarter, McSlicey? Have you modeled that scenario?"

Uncomfortable silence.

Rachel: "Gentlemen, we've spent trillions preparing for yesterday's threats while leaving ourselves vulnerable to today's. True security isn't just about projecting power abroad—it's about building resilience at home. And until we understand that, all our military might is just an expensive insurance policy for a house that's already burning."

Systems Analysis: The Interconnections Between Vulnerability Domains

America's vulnerability domains form a complex, interconnected system where cascading failures can rapidly escalate from isolated incidents to systemic crises. Consider several illustrative pathways:

1. **Digital → Physical → Social:** Cyber attacks on power grids → infrastructure failure → public panic and unrest

AMERICA'S VULNERABILITY DOMAINS

Understanding Cascading Failure Pathways in National Security

CASCADING FAILURE DYNAMICS

America's vulnerability domains form a complex, interconnected system where cascading failures can rapidly escalate from isolated incidents to systemic crises across multiple sectors.

THE FOUR VULNERABILITY DOMAINS

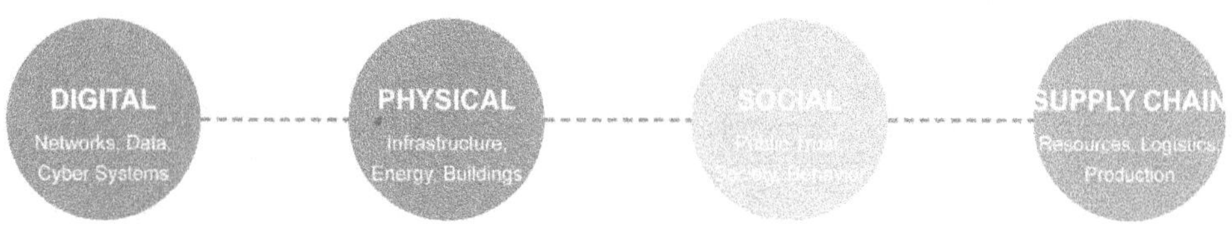

CASCADING FAILURE PATHWAYS

How vulnerabilities propagate across domains

PATHWAY 1: DIGITAL → PHYSICAL → SOCIAL

Cyber attacks on power grids →
Infrastructure failure →
Public panic and unrest

PATHWAY 2: SUPPLY CHAIN → PHYSICAL → DIGITAL

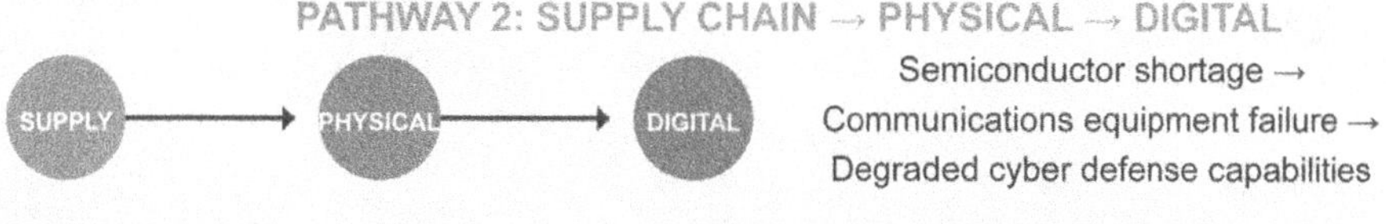

Semiconductor shortage →
Communications equipment failure →
Degraded cyber defense capabilities

PATHWAY 3: SOCIAL → DIGITAL → SUPPLY CHAIN

Conspiracy theories →
Resistance to security measures →
Vulnerability to coordinated supply disruptions

PATHWAY 4: PHYSICAL → SUPPLY CHAIN → SOCIAL

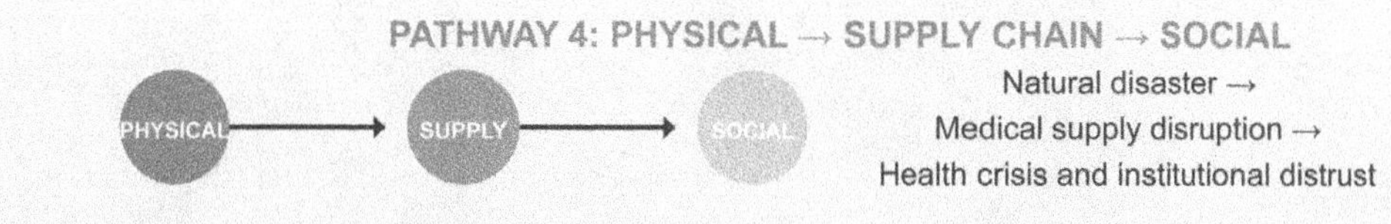

Natural disaster →
Medical supply disruption →
Health crisis and institutional distrust

KEY INSIGHTS:

- Vulnerabilities in one domain can cascade unpredictably to others
- National resilience requires integrated cross-domain security strategies

2. **Supply Chain → Physical → Digital:** Semiconductor shortage → communications equipment failure → degraded cyber defense capabilities
3. **Social → Digital → Supply Chain:** Conspiracy theories → resistance to security measures → vulnerability to coordinated supply disruptions
4. **Physical → Supply Chain → Social:** Natural disaster → medical supply disruption → health crisis, and institutional distrust

These interconnections mean that resilience cannot be achieved through siloed approaches. When the Department of Defense focuses solely on military threats, the Department of Energy on grid security, and Health and Human Services on medical supplies—each optimizing for their narrow domain—the overall system remains vulnerable to cascading failures that cross bureaucratic boundaries.

A systems approach to national resilience would:

Map Dependencies: Identify critical nodes where multiple systems intersect

1. **Prioritize Vulnerabilities:** Focus on points where cascading failures are most likely or damaging
2. **Coordinate Responses:** Develop cross-domain resilience strategies and capabilities
3. **Exercise Regularly:** Test system responses to complex, multi-domain disruptions
4. **Adapt Continuously:** Update resilience frameworks based on emerging threats and lessons learned

A SYSTEMS APPROACH TO NATIONAL RESILIENCE WOULD:

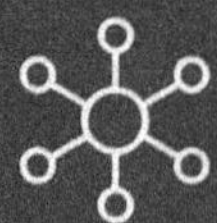

MAP DEPENDENCIES
Identify critical nodes where multiple systems intersect

PRIORITIZE VULNERABILITIES
Focus on points where cascading failures are most likely or damaging

COORDINATE RESPONSES
Develop cross-domain resilience strategies and capabilities

EXERCISE REGULARLY
Test system responses to complex, multi-domain disruptions

ADAPT CONTINUOUSLY
Update resilience frameworks based on emerging threats and lessons learned

Data Visualization: National Resilience Scorecard

National Resilience Scorecard: A Visual Assessment of America's Security Foundation

Physical Infrastructure Resilience: D-

★ Energy Grid Security: F (41% of infrastructure exceeds designed lifespan)

★ Transportation Network Redundancy: D- (43% of bridges structurally deficient or functionally obsolete)

★ Water System Integrity: F (240,000 water main breaks annually)

★ Critical Facility Protection: C- (inconsistent implementation of physical security measures)

Digital Resilience: C-

★ Critical System Cybersecurity: D (58% of federal systems fail basic security tests)

★ Data Protection Frameworks: C (improving but fragmented)

★ Communication Redundancy: B- (relatively robust alternative systems)

★ Recovery Capabilities: D+ (limited ability to rapidly restore compromised systems)

Supply Chain Resilience: F

★ Pharmaceutical Independence: F (80%+ of active ingredients sourced overseas)

★ Semiconductor Self-Suf-

NATIONAL RESILIENCE SCORECARD

A Visual Assessment of America's Security Foundation

PHYSICAL INFRASTRUCTURE RESILIENCE D-

- Energy Grid Security (41% of infrastructure exceeds designed lifespan
- Transportation Network Redundancy D- (43% of bridges structurally deficient or functionally obsolete
- Water System Integrity 240,000 water main brezk annually
- Critical Facility Protection C-

DIGITAL RESILIENCE

- Critical System Cybersecurirty D (58% of federal ystems fall basic security tests
- Date Protection Frameworks C improving but fragmented

Recovery Capabilities D+

OVERALL NATIONAL RESILIENCE GRADE D

SUPPLY CHAIN RESILIENCE F

- Pharmaceurtical Indepedance F 80%+ of active ingredients sourced overseas
- Semicenductor Self-Sufficiency F 12% of advenced chips manufactured domestically
- Strategic Stockpile Adequacy F

SOCIAL RESILIENCE

- Institutional Trust F Historic lows in trust of government, media, business,

Information Ecesystem Integrity F Rampant misinformation, foreign manipulation

D- Social Cohesion D- Extreme polarization, declining civic engagement

C- Crisis Respense Coordination C- Improving post-COVID but significant gaps remain

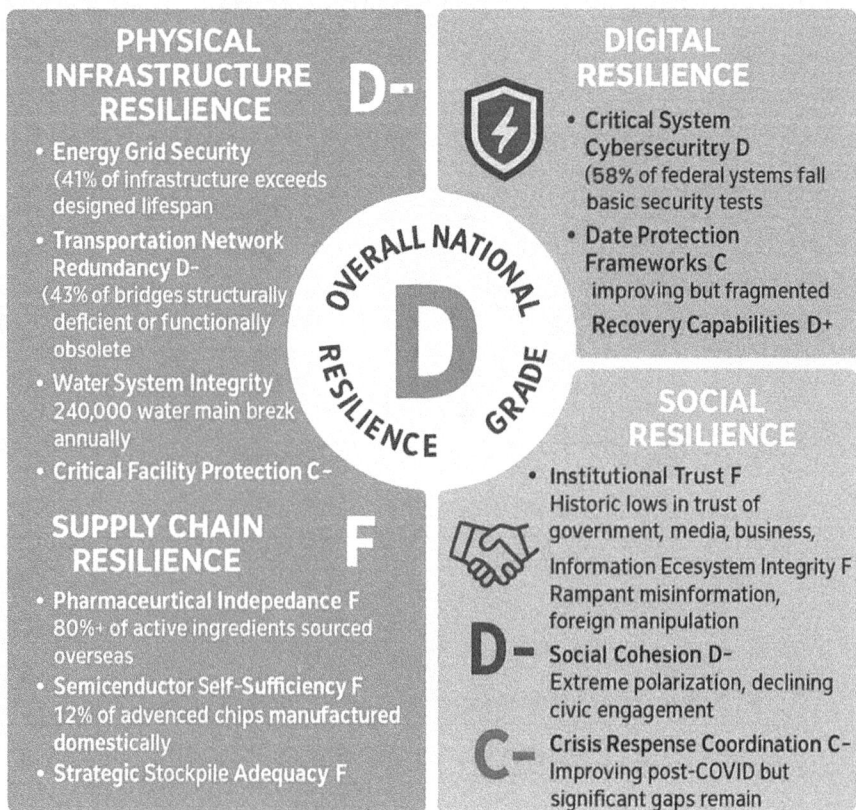

ficiency: F (12% of advanced chips manufactured domestically)

★ Critical Mineral Access: D- (dependent on China for 80% of rare earth elements)

★ Strategic Stockpile Adequacy: F (most stockpiles depleted or outdated)

Social Resilience: D-

★ Institutional Trust: F (historic lows in trust of government, media, business)

★ Information Ecosystem Integrity: F (rampant misinformation, foreign manipulation)

★ Social Cohesion: D- (extreme polarization, declining civic engagement)

★ Crisis Response Coordination: C- (improving post-COVID, but significant gaps remain)

Overall National Resilience Grade: D

This assessment reflects America's concerning vulnerability across multiple dimensions of national security. While traditional military capabilities remain strong, the underlying foundations of national resilience have been allowed to deteriorate to dangerous levels. Immediate attention is required to address these vulnerabilities before they are exploited by strategic competitors or tested by natural disasters.

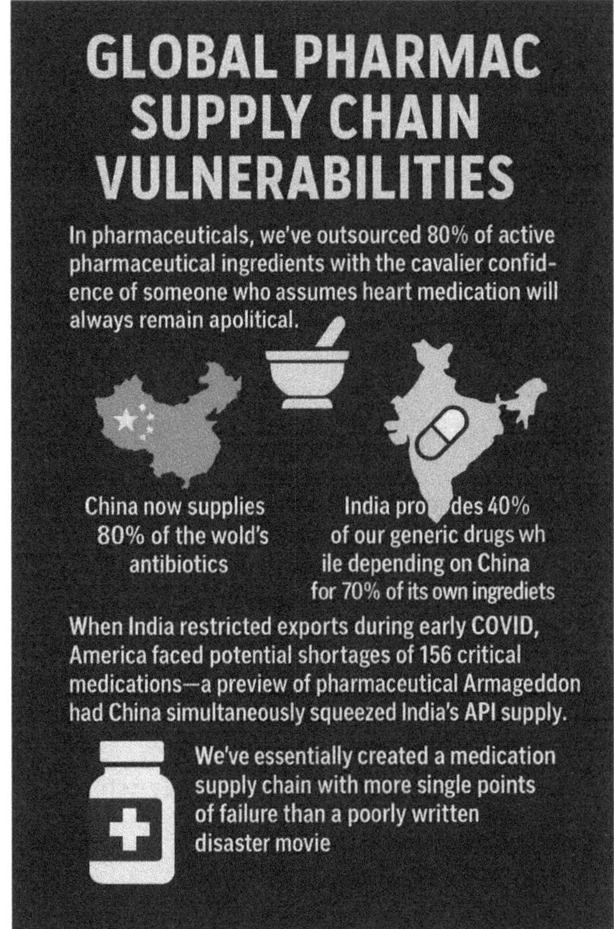
GLOBAL PHARMAC SUPPLY CHAIN VULNERABILITIES
In pharmaceuticals, we've outsourced 80% of active pharmaceutical ingredients with the cavalier confidence of someone who assumes heart medication will always remain apolitical.
China now supplies 80% of the wold's antibiotics
India pro des 40% of our generic drugs wh ile depending on China for 70% of its own ingrediets
When India restricted exports during early COVID, America faced potential shortages of 156 critical medications—a preview of pharmaceutical Armageddon had China simultaneously squeezed India's API supply.
We've essentially created a medication supply chain with more single points of failure than a poorly written disaster movie

Case Studies: Critical Supply Chains and Their Vulnerabilities

America's supply chain strategy resembles a blindfolded high-stakes game of Jenga—we've systematically removed domestic production blocks and stacked them precariously in countries that occasionally harbor ambitions contrary to our national interest.

In pharmaceuticals, we've outsourced 80% of active pharmaceutical ingredients with the cavalier confidence of someone who assumes heart medication will always remain apolitical. China now supplies 80% of the world's antibiotics, while India provides 40% of our generic drugs, and while depends on China for 70% of its own ingredients. When India restricted exports during the early COVID-19 pandemic, America faced potential shortages of 156 critical medications—a preview of pharmaceutical Armageddon —had China simultaneously squeezed India's API supply. We've essentially created a medication supply chain with more single points of failure than a poorly written disaster movie.

Our semiconductor situation borders on a form of geopolitical malpractice. The U.S. manufacturing share has plummeted from 37% in 1990 to 12% today, while Taiwan, just 100 miles from mainland China, produces 92% of advanced logic chips. These $10-20 billion fabrication facilities require 3-5 years to build, meaning we can't simply whip up alternatives during a crisis. Should Taiwan's production halt, global computing would essentially experience the Blue Screen of Death on a civilization-wide scale.

Our critical minerals dependency completes this trilogy of strategic self-sabotage. China controls 85% of global rare earth processing and 80% of lithium processing, while 80% of cobalt emerges from the Democratic Republic of Congo—primarily from Chinese-controlled operations. We remain 100% import-dependent for 14 of 35 critical minerals essential for everything from electric vehicles to missile guidance systems.

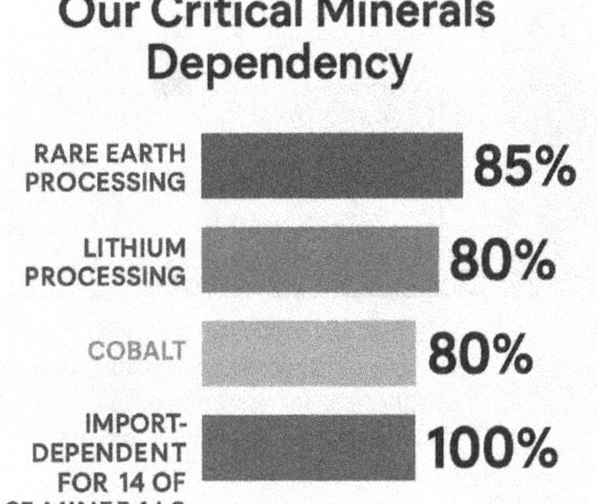
Our Critical Minerals Dependency
RARE EARTH PROCESSING
85%
LITHIUM PROCESSING
80%
COBALT
80%
IMPORT-DEPENDENT FOR 14 OF 35 MINERALS
100%

America has constructed a supply chain architecture seemingly designed to maximize vulnerability rather than resilience—a triumph of quarterly earnings reports over strategic foresight. We are one geopolitical crisis away from discovering just how essential those overseas factories really are.

From Just-In-Time to Just-In-Case: The Radical Notion of Planning Ahead

Introduction: The Revolutionary Concept of Not Being Caught With Your Pants Down

Our semiconductor sitituation borders on geopolitical malpractice.

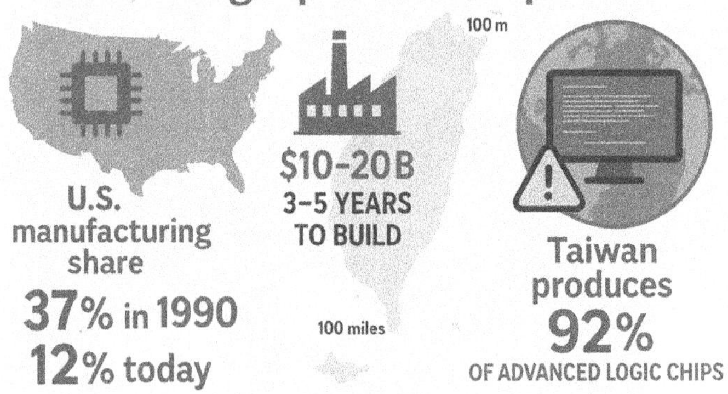

For decades, American business and government have adopted just-in-time systems—the revolutionary concept that having nothing in reserve is the pinnacle of efficiency. Congratulations! We've optimized ourselves to a state of complete vulnerability.

This section introduces "Just-In-Case"—the notion that we should have backup plans for scenarios more challenging than "everything works perfectly forever."

Stockpiles: Not Just for Crazy Preppers Anymore!

Remember when having emergency supplies seemed like paranoid nonsense? Then COVID-19 hit, and suddenly everyone wanted toilet paper, masks, and ventilators all at once. Strategic stockpiling means maintaining sufficient reserves of critical items to weather disruptions. The key is identifying what society cannot function without, calculating necessary quantities, acquiring them before disruptions occur, and rotating stocks to prevent expiration. When everyone needs something simultaneously, Amazon's two-day delivery won't save you.

Redundancy: Because "Single Points of Failure" Are Called That for a Reason

In pursuing efficiency, we've eliminated redundancy throughout our systems. Redundancy means having multiple ways to accomplish critical functions. Yes, it costs more upfront. You know what costs even more? Complete system collapse. We must identify single points of failure, develop alternative supply sources, and build excess capacity where failure would be catastrophic. Remember: The Titanic had too few lifeboats because they were deemed "inefficient."

Domestic Capacity: The Strange Benefit of Actually Making Important Things

Perhaps we should maintain the ability to produce essential goods within our borders, even if marginally more expensive than outsourcing everything to potential adversaries. This means identifying goods required for national survival, developing domestic manufacturing capacity, using targeted incentives rather than blanket protectionism, and accepting slightly higher costs as the price of security. "Cheaper" often means "completely unavailable when you need it most."

Exercises: Practice Like You Play

Most organizations have lovely resilience plans gathering dust. Untested plans are fantasy documents that fail spectacularly when put into action. Regular, realistic exercises testing multiple simultaneous disruptions—including worst-case scenarios—are essential. Identify gaps revealed during exercises and include private sector and cross-agency participation. No plan survives contact with reality, but practiced plans fare better than theoretical ones.

Conclusion: Efficiency vs. Resilience – Finding the Balance

Efficiency and resilience exist in tension. Optimization removes buffers and creates brittle systems. Resilience requires slack—extra capacity, stockpiles, and alternative pathways. The art of national security lies in finding the appropriate balance: being efficient enough to remain competitive yet resilient enough to survive disruption. The most efficient system in the world is worthless if it collapses under stress. Choose wisely.

FROM JUST-IN-TIME TO JUST-IN-CASE

THE RADICAL NOTION OF PLANNING AHEAD

INTRODUCTION: THE REVOLUTIONARY CONCEPT OF NOT BEING CAUGHT WITH YOUR PANTS DOWN

For decades, American business and government embraced Just in-Time systems – the revolution !

This section introduces "Just-In-Case" – the notion that perhaps we should have backup plans for scenarios more challenging than "everything works perfectly forever."

Policy Proposal: Creation of a National Resilience Council

America needs a Cabinet-level National Resilience Council to coordinate whole-of-government efforts addressing vulnerabilities across physical, digital, supply chain, and social domains. Led by a Director reporting directly to the President, this council would include deputies from Defense, Homeland Security, Commerce, Energy, Treasury, HHS, and Intelligence agencies.

The Council would wield substantial authority, conducting vulnerability assessments, coordinating cross-agency policies, reviewing resilience-related budgets, managing emergency responses during complex disruptions, and establishing standards for critical infrastructure. Its core functions would follow a logical progression: identification of vulnerabilities, risk-based prioritization, coordination of agency actions, implementation oversight, and evaluation of outcomes.

Initial priorities would center on five critical areas: comprehensive supply chain security mapping, enhanced infrastructure protection, strategic reshoring of essential industries, improved coordination for multi-domain disruptions, and strengthening societal cohesion. Accountability mechanisms would include annual comprehensive resilience reports, quarterly implementation reviews, regular stress-test exercises, and independent external evaluations.

This institution represents a necessary adaptation to a world where American vulnerability has become a Chinese opportunity. It creates a unified nerve center for resilience that spans traditional bureaucratic domains.

The Efficiency-Resilience Paradox: National Security in an Age of Vulnerability

The fundamental tension between efficiency and resilience defines America's security challenge in the Chinese century. While efficiency—maximizing output while minimizing inputs—has dominated American economic and security thinking for decades through just-in-time manufacturing and specialized supply chains, it systematically undermines resilience—our ability to absorb shocks and maintain function during disruptions.

This paradox manifests across multiple domains. In supply chains, efficiency's preference for single-source suppliers and minimal inventory directly contradicts resilience's need for supplier diversity and strategic stockpiles. Infrastructure efficiency minimizes excess capacity while resilience demands redundant systems and regular hardening. Digital efficiency standardizes platforms, while resilience requires diverse, segmented networks. Even socially, streamlined governance conflicts with the institutional redundancy and social capital resilience that are needed.

The optimal balance between efficiency and resilience shifts with strategic conditions. Stable periods permit efficiency's dominance, but America's current environment—marked by technological disruption, great power competition, climate threats, and pandemics—demands rebalancing toward resilience. This doesn't abandon efficiency entirely but acknowledges that some inefficiency represents the necessary insurance premium for security in an unpredictable world.

III. THE MANHATTAN PROJECT FOR THE AI AGE: MOBILIZING INNOVATION

"Opportunities multiply as they are seized."
— Han-era commentaries on Sun Tzu

Historical Parallel: Learning from Previous Technological Mobilizations

America has a rich history of mobilizing national resources to achieve technological breakthroughs in the face of existential challenges. Two examples stand out:

The Manhattan Project (1942-1945)

When the U.S. suspected Nazi Germany was developing nuclear weapons, it launched the Manhattan Project—a massive scientific and industrial effort to develop atomic bombs. This project:

- ★ Employed over 130,000 people at its peak
- ★ Cost about $2 billion ($29 billion in today's dollars)
- ★ Involved 30+ sites across the U.S.
- ★ Managed by a hybrid military-civilian-scientific leadership structure
- ★ Achieved its goal in just three years, despite enormous technical challenges

Key lessons include the importance of clear objectives, abundant resources, diverse approaches, scientific leadership, and collaboration among government, industry, and academia.

The Space Race (1957-1969)

After the Soviet Union launched Sputnik in 1957, the U.S. mobilized to achieve space superiority, culminating in the Apollo moon landings. This effort:

- ★ Employed over 400,000 people across government, industry, and academia
- ★ Cost about $25.4 billion ($156 billion in today's dollars)
- ★ Created 1,800+ spin-off technologies for civilian use
- ★ Required sustained political commitment across three administrations

Key lessons include the power of ambitious goals, sustained funding, public-private partnership, and competitive motivation.

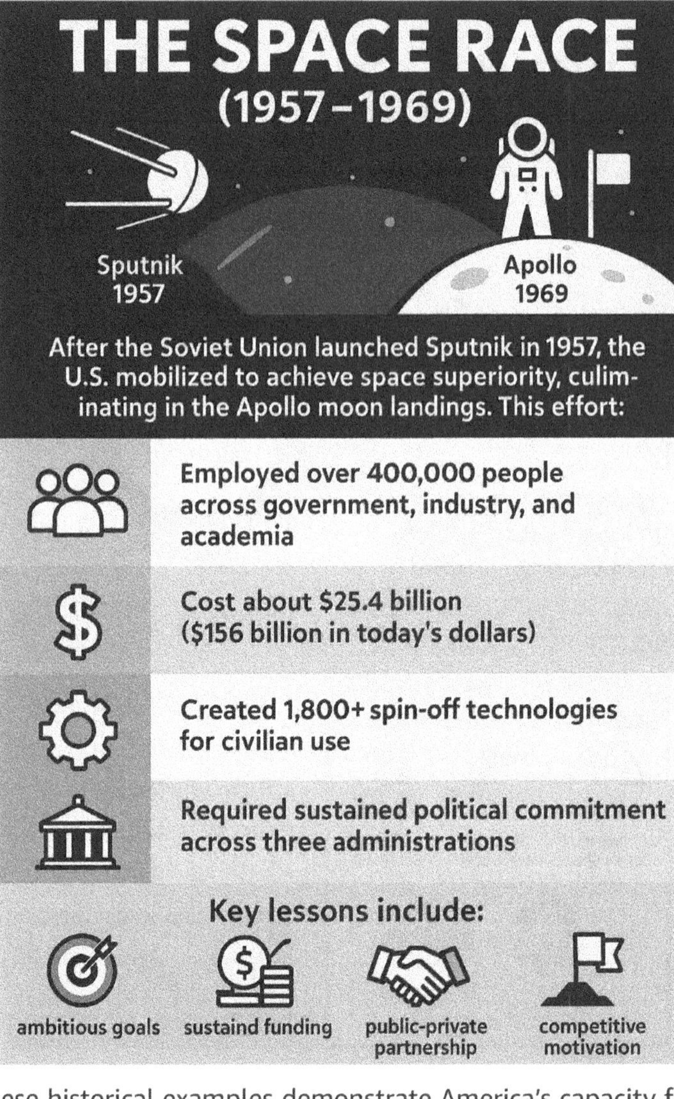
THE SPACE RACE
(1957–1969)
Sputnik 1957
Apollo 1969
After the Soviet Union launched Sputnik in 1957, the U.S. mobilized to achieve space superiority, culim-inating in the Apollo moon landings. This effort:
Employed over 400,000 people across government, industry, and academia
Cost about $25.4 billion ($156 billion in today's dollars)
Created 1,800+ spin-off technologies for civilian use
Required sustained political commitment across three administrations
Key lessons include:
ambitious goals
sustaind funding
public-private partnership
competitive motivation

THE MANHATTAN PROJECT
(1942–1945)

When the U.S. suspected Nazi Germany was developing nuclear weapons, it launched the Manhattan Project--a massive scientific and industrial effort to develop atomic bombs. This project:

EMPLOYED OVER 130,000 PEOPLE AT ITS PEAK

COST ABOUT $2 BILLION ($29 BILLION IN TODAY'S DOLLARS)

INVOLVED 30+ SITES ACROSS THE U.S.

MANAGED BY A HYBRID MILITARY-CIVILIAN-SCIENTIFIC LEADERSHIP STRUCTURE

ACHIEVED ITS GOAL IN JUST THREE YEARS, DESPITE ENORMOUS TECHNICAL CHALLENGES

These historical examples demonstrate America's capacity for technological mobilization when properly motivated and organized. They also provide frameworks for how government, industry, and academia can collaborate on breakthrough innovations.

FDR Examines Critical Technology Gaps

FDR's ghost materializes in DARPA headquarters, examining briefing materials on AI, quantum computing, and biotechnology capabilities.

FDR: *(frowning at reports)* "So you're telling me the Chinese published twice as many AI research papers last year? They're investing ten times what we are in quantum computing? And they're sequencing vastly more genomes for their biotech programs?"

DARPA Director: "Yes, Mr. President. But our research quality remains superior in most areas."

FDR: "Quality is wonderful, but quantity has a quality all its own. When we developed the atomic bomb, we pursued multiple approaches simultaneously because we couldn't afford to make a wrong guess. What's our equivalent strategy for these technologies?"

DARPA Director: *(hesitantly)* "Well, sir, we fund selected research projects through competitive grants. The private sector handles commercialization based on market forces."

FDR: *(incredulous)* "That's not a strategy; that's abdicating strategic technology development to quarterly profit motives! During the Manhattan Project, do you think we told private industry to develop atomic weapons if they saw a good ROI?"

McSlicey the High Priest: *(interjecting)* "But sir, government intervention distorts market efficiency!"

FDR: *(ignoring McSlicey)* "Show me the quantum computing program, specifically."

The Director displays a slide showing fragmented efforts across multiple agencies with modest funding.

FDR: "This looks like a hobby, not a national priority. The Manhattan Project accounted for approximately 1% of the United States' GDP at its peak. What's your quantum computing budget as a percentage of GDP?"

DARPA Director: *(quietly)* "0.01%, sir."

FDR: "And you wonder why we're falling behind? When exactly did America decide that existential technological competition could be won with spare change and wishful thinking?"

General Quagmire: "Sir, we're increasing the defense budget for more aircraft carriers."

FDR: *(sighs)* "Imagine if, during World War II, I'd decided to pour all our resources into cavalry horses while Germany developed tanks. That's essentially what you're doing—preparing for the last war while China arms for the next one."

Milton the Trickster Economist: "The market will solve this! Just cut taxes for tech billionaires, and innovation will magically appear!"

FDR: *(darkening)* "The market didn't win World War II. The market didn't put a man on the moon. The market—left entirely to its own devices—optimizes for quarterly returns, not national security. Some challenges are too important, too existential to be left to market forces alone."

He turns to the assembled officials.

FDR: "America needs a Manhattan Project for the AI Age—a mobilization of scientific talent, industrial capacity, and national purpose toward technological leadership. Anything less is unilateral disarmament in the most important competition of our time."

Government as Technological Catalyzer: The Forgotten Formula for American Innovation

Throughout American history, transformative technological revolutions have required the government's catalytic role during the early, uncertain stages when private capital is hesitant. This consistent pattern is evident across multiple revolutionary domains: DARPA created the internet's ARPANET predecessor, NIH funded the basic research that enabled gene editing, and NASA developed satellite technologies later commercialized by private enterprises.

This catalytic function extends across transportation infrastructure, energy development, and agricultural advancement. The government doesn't control technological development, but it serves specific essential roles: funding fundamental research that is too risky for private investment, developing shared infrastructure platforms, reducing uncertainty through standards and initial procurement, focusing national resources on critical challenges, and cultivating technical workforce development.

This public-private innovation model represents America's historical competitive advantage—one increasingly challenged by China's whole-of-nation approach to technological development. In the AI age, the government's catalytic functions remain vital, not as market replacements but as market enablers, providing the foundations upon which private innovation flourishes. The Chinese understand this formula; America appears to have forgotten it.

DARPA's Innovation Formula: A Blueprint for American Technological Dominance

DARPA's historical successes provide a replicable template for maintaining American technological leadership in the AI and quantum era. The development of the Internet demonstrates how government-directed innovation can transform from a military necessity (resilient communications surviving nuclear attack) into an economic cornerstone through strategic collaboration with universities and industry, open protocols that enable widespread adoption, and a smooth transition to civilian applications, generating trillions of dollars in monetary value from modest investment.

Similarly, GPS evolved from a military navigation system to a global economic infrastructure through consistent cross-administration funding, public-private technology partnerships, and the critical decision to make civilian signals freely available with open standards. DARPA's autonomous vehicle Grand Challenges accelerated self-driving technology by establishing ambitious goals, creating competitive frameworks, assembling diverse technical teams, emphasizing practical demonstrations, and normalizing initial failures as a prerequisite for innovation.

These case studies reveal seven essential elements for AI and quantum development: concrete, ambitious goals rather than general research; competitive funding across multiple technical approaches; integrated public-private collaboration; sustained cross-political commitment; deliberate talent cultivation; explicit commercialization pathways; and institutional tolerance for calculated risk. This model, where the government provides strategic direction and sustained funding, while academia and industry drive implementation, represents America's optimal pathway to technological leadership in contested domains.

The Five Pillars of Technological Sovereignty

America's technological security depends on leadership across five critical domains requiring coordinated national investment: Artificial Intelligence, Quantum Technology, Advanced Materials, Biotechnology, and Clean Energy Technology.

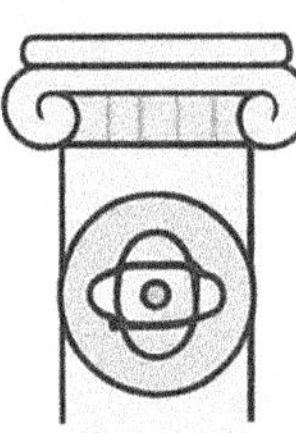
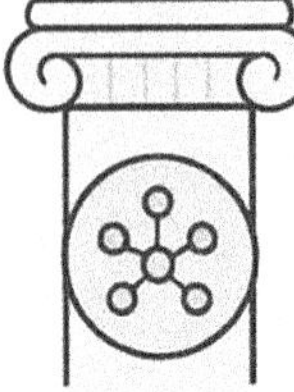
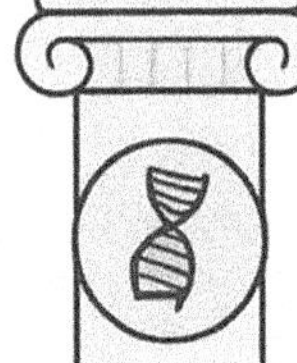

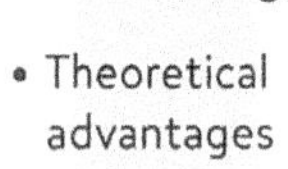
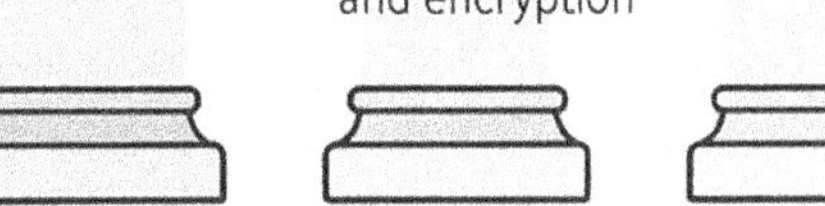

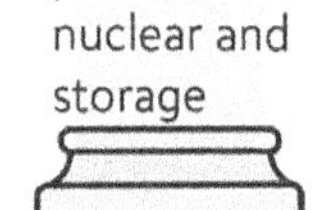
Artificial Intelligence
• Leadership in foundational research
• Development priorities for research and workforce
Quantum Technology
• Theoretical advantages
• Lags In application
• Development priorities for computing and encryption
Advanced Materials
• Research leadership
• Manufacturing capacity loss
• Development inflacitiosture and supply
Biotechology
• Innovation advantages
• Biodenfense gaps
• Development priorities for infrastructure and ethics
Clean Energy Technology
• Innovation advantages
• Production capacity shorttall
• Development priorities for nuclear and storage

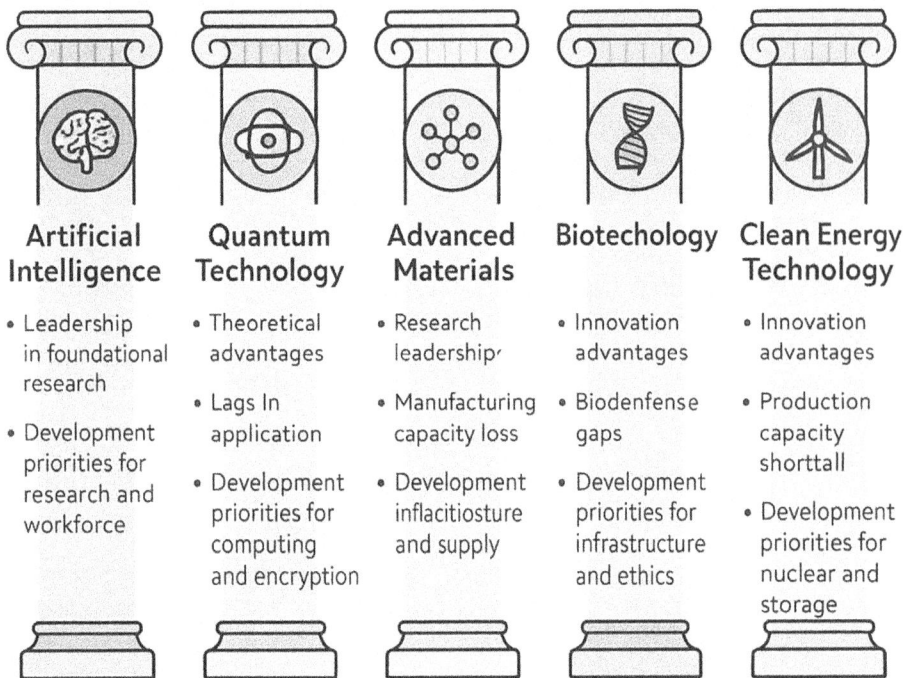

AI represents the cornerstone of future power, transforming warfare, economic productivity, and social interaction. While America leads in foundational research with stronger computing infrastructure and private sector innovation, China publishes more papers, files more patents, and cultivates a significantly larger talent pool (50,000+ doctoral-level personnel vs America's 18,000). Critical vulnerabilities include insufficient investment in AI safety, a lack of a coordinated strategy, and fragmented research. Development priorities must consist of a national AI research cloud, expanded safety research, a pipeline that develops 100,000 new specialists, and balanced regulatory frameworks.

Quantum technology presents existential implications for national security. Quantum computing poses a threat to current encryption, while quantum communications offer theoretically unbreakable security. America maintains theoretical advantages but lags in application, with China demonstrating satellite-based quantum key distribution. Development requires a Manhattan Project-scale quantum computing program, quantum-resistant encryption implementation, secure communications networks, and specialized manufacturing infrastructure.

Advanced materials enable breakthroughs across domains from hypersonics to energy storage. America retains research leadership but has surrendered manufacturing capacity to China, particularly in material processing and production. Vulnerabilities include critical mineral dependencies, diminished manufacturing capabilities, and limited testing infrastructure. Priorities include expanding the Materials Genome Initiative, developing high-throughput facilities, establishing innovation institutes, and securing supply chains.

Biotechnology is poised to revolutionize medicine, agriculture, manufacturing, and potentially warfare. While America leads in research and commercialization, China is rapidly advancing with massive investment and fewer ethical constraints. Key vulnerabilities include biodefense gaps, pharmaceutical supply chain vulnerabilities, and the proliferation of dual-use technologies. Priorities include comprehensive biodefense infrastructure, expansion of biomanufacturing for pharmaceutical independence, development of security frameworks for synthetic biology, and establishment of ethical governance models.

Clean energy technology determines future economic competitiveness and geopolitical leverage. China dominates the manufacturing of solar panels, wind turbines, and batteries, while the United States maintains innovation advantages but lacks production capacity. Development priorities must include accelerating advanced nuclear technology, innovating grid-scale storage, establishing domestic clean energy manufacturing capabilities, and securing critical mineral supply chains.

This five-domain technological sovereignty strategy requires the comprehensive integration of research funding, infrastructure development, workforce training, manufacturing policy, and regulatory frameworks—all of which must be sustained across political transitions.

Satirical Recruitment Poster: "Uncle Sam Wants Your Algorithms"

A dramatic poster showing Uncle Sam pointing directly at the viewer, his hat adorned with binary code.

UNCLE SAM WANTS YOUR ALGORITHMS *Join the Technological Arsenal of Democracy*

Are YOU ready to code for your country?

The Digital Manhattan Project is now recruiting America's brightest minds to secure our technological future. We offer:

★ Meaningful work defeating authoritarian AI systems
★ Competitive salaries (almost comparable to what you'd make at Google!)
★ The satisfaction of knowing your quantum algorithm might save democracy
★ Free coffee* (*when the government isn't shut down due to budget impasses)

FINE PRINT (PLEASE READ CAREFULLY):

★ No, we can't match Silicon Valley salaries, but we offer the chance to serve your country instead of optimizing ad click-through rates.

- ★ Yes, you'll need a security clearance, which means admitting to that one time in college. We've all been there.
- ★ Sorry, the dress code does not include hoodies. We're fighting authoritarianism, not comfort.
- ★ The ping-pong tables and meditation rooms are currently on back order due to procurement regulations (estimated arrival: FY2028).
- ★ Your code will be reviewed by actual humans, not just pushed to production, because "move fast and break things" doesn't work well with national security.

WARNING: This project may involve:

- ★ Actually solving real problems instead of creating slightly better photo filters
- ★ Working with people who don't understand why blockchain isn't the answer to everything
- ★ The existential satisfaction of contributing to something larger than your stock options

SPECIAL NOTE TO QUANTUM COMPUTING SPECIALISTS: We promise not to ask you to explain quantum entanglement at every family gathering. (We can't promise the same for your relatives.)

APPLY TODAY: Your country needs you more than TikTok does.

UNCLE SAM
WANTS YOUR ALGORITHMS
Join the Technological Arsenal of Democracy
Are YOU ready to code for your country?
The Digital Manhattan Project is new recruiting America's brightast minds to secure our technological future. We offer.
• Meaningful work defeating authoitarian AI systems
• Competitive salaries (almost comparable to what my make at Google (Gutoll)
• The satisfaction of knowing you'r quantiigom might save democracy.
WARNING: This project may involve:
• Actually colying real problems mosted of creating slighly better photo filters
• Working with people who dont think that quanfum algorithm might save democracy
(Free colfiee* (when the goinethox)
FINE PRINT (PLEASE READ CAREFULLY)
• No. we can't match Silican Valley, salaries, but we offer the chance to serve your country instead of oplimizing ad click through rates.
• Yes, you'll need a security clearance which means. admilling to that one time in college. We've all been there. Sorry. thedress comedles. not include fioedles. We're fighting authorita-flanism, not comfort
• The plue-yong tables amd meditation rooms are currently on backorder due to presurement regulations (estimated artival. TYZ026).
Your code will be reviewed by actual humans, pushed to production because, mut fest and break things' doesn't work.vell with national security.
APPLY TODAY
Your country needs you more than "Iktdc dos.

ARPA-X: America's Technological Arsenal for the Chinese Century

ARPA-X represents a necessary evolution of the DARPA model, expanded to address the full spectrum of critical technologies essential for continued American leadership. This organization would maintain DARPA's proven operational DNA—empowered program managers, milestone-based funding, high-risk tolerance, and streamlined contracting—while extending across AI, quantum technologies, advanced materials, biotechnology, and clean energy domains.

The structure centers on stability, with leadership appointed to five-year terms, reporting directly to the President, and operating through six specialized technical offices that have significant operational autonomy. Funding would reach $60 billion annually through base appropriations ($20 billion), challenge funds ($30 billion), and public-private partnerships ($10 billion), effectively increasing federal R&D from 0.7% to 1.2% of GDP, still below the Cold War peaks of 1.9%.

ARPA-X would focus investment on AI capabilities (foundation models, edge AI, human-AI collaboration), quantum systems (fault-tolerant computing, secure networks), advanced materials (novel semiconductors, critical mineral alternatives), biotechnology (rapid vaccine platforms, biodefense systems), and clean energy (advanced nuclear, grid-scale storage).

Implementation would flow through new National Technology Labs, housing state-of-the-art equipment, regional innovation hubs that connect research to manufacturing, shared digital infrastructure, comprehensive talent development pipelines, and formal mechanisms for research coordination with democratic allies.

This model provides the institutional framework necessary to compete with China's state-directed technology development while preserving America's decentralized innovation advantages—a synthesis of governmental direction and market-driven execution.

IV. STRATEGIC SUPPLY CHAIN REPATRIATION: REBUILDING CRITICAL CAPABILITIES

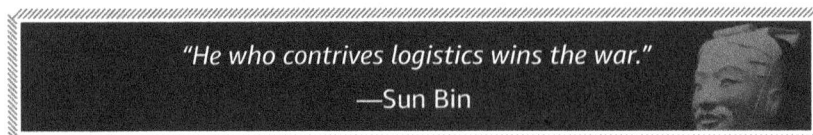

> *"He who contrives logistics wins the war."*
> —Sun Bin

Strategic vs. Non-Strategic Dependencies: A Framework for Supply Chain Security

Not all supply chain dependencies create equal vulnerabilities. Strategic dependencies share five critical characteristics: essential functionality for national security or economic operation, limited substitutability, concentrated supply, adversarial geopolitical positioning, and potential surge requirements during crises. Advanced semiconductor manufacturing (Taiwan), pharmaceutical ingredients (China/India), and rare earth processing (China) exemplify these strategic vulnerabilities.

Non-strategic dependencies feature abundant alternatives, diverse and distributed production, friendly-nation concentration, and stable demand patterns, as seen in most consumer goods and standardized components.

Effective supply chain security requires focused intervention on truly strategic dependencies, while allowing market forces to optimize non-strategic supply chains. This approach preserves the benefits of global trade while addressing genuine security risks. This targeted approach avoids the inefficiency of treating all foreign dependencies as equally problematic while concentrating resources on vulnerabilities that genuinely threaten national security.

Character Dialogue: Commerce Secretary Explains Reshoring Priorities

The Commerce Secretary addresses a gathering of Fortune 500 CEOs, who appear skeptical about the administration's reshoring initiative.

Commerce Secretary: "Thank you for joining this discussion on strategic supply chain security. I understand many of you have concerns about our reshoring priorities."

CEO #1 (Consumer Electronics): "Concerns are an understatement. You're talking about disrupting global supply chains that have taken decades to optimize. Do you have any idea what that will do to our quarterly earnings? Our shareholders will revolt!"

Commerce Secretary: "I appreciate that perspective. Let me be clear: We're not advocating for the reshoring of everything. That would be economically disastrous and unnecessary. We're focusing specifically on strategically critical capabilities where foreign dependency creates unacceptable national security risks."

McSlicey the High Priest: *(adjusting designer glasses)* "Our analysis shows that reshoring would decrease EBITDA by approximately 2.7% across affected sectors. The market will punish such inefficiency severely."

Commerce Secretary: "And what's the EBITDA impact of not having access to essential medications during a conflict with China? Or losing advanced semiconductor access if China blockades Taiwan? Some risks can't be quantified on a quarterly earnings report."

CEO #2 (Pharmaceutical): "But the cost differential! Manufacturing APIs in America costs 30-40% more than in China or India."

Commerce Secretary: "That's absolutely correct, which is why we're not asking you to reshore everything. For non-critical generic drugs, global supply chains still make sense. But for the 357 medications on our essential medicines list—treatments for which there are no alternatives and where a supply disruption would mean Americans dying—we need domestic production capacity regardless of marginal cost differences."

CEO #3 (Technology): "What exactly qualifies as 'strategic' in your framework?"

Commerce Secretary: "Excellent question. We're using a five-factor assessment: Is the item essential for national security, public health, or critical infrastructure? Are there few or no alternatives? Is production highly concentrated in a few locations? Do potential adversaries control those locations? And might we need surge production during crises?"

Milton the Trickster Economist: *(snickering)* "The market should decide all of this! Government interference always creates inefficiency!"

Commerce Secretary: "The market optimizes for cost and quarterly returns, not national resilience. That's not a criticism—it's by design. But national security operates on different timescales and different risk calculations."

She displays a slide showing pharmaceutical dependencies.

Commerce Secretary: "Currently, 80% of active pharmaceutical ingredients come from overseas, primarily China and India. During the COVID-19 pandemic, India restricted exports to meet domestic needs—a perfectly rational national decision. Had China done the same with the precursors India needs, our entire pharmaceutical supply would have collapsed. Is that a risk we should accept to save 30% on manufacturing costs?"

CEO #2 (Pharmaceutical): "When you put it that way... no. But the transition costs and timeline—"

Commerce Secretary: "Which is why we're proposing targeted incentives, regulatory fast-tracks, and tax benefits specifically for strategic reshoring—not blanket protectionism. We're asking for partnership in addressing genuine national vulnerabilities, not dismantling globalization."

McSlicey the High Priest: *(looking thoughtful for once)* "I suppose one could create a model where national security risks are factored into the cost-benefit analysis..."

Commerce Secretary: "Precisely. We're not asking you to abandon business logic—just to expand your risk calculations beyond the next quarter to include low-probability, high-impact scenarios that markets typically ignore until they occur... at which point it's too late."

Vulnerability Mapping: A Scientific Approach to Supply Chain Security

Strategic supply chain vulnerability assessment requires a sophisticated, six-dimensional methodology that goes beyond simplistic import dependence metrics. Product criticality analysis evaluates components based on military applications, infrastructure requirements, public health necessity, economic function, and technological foundation status. Supply concentration measurement utilizes the Herfindahl-Hirschman Index in conjunction with geographic distribution analysis, ownership assessment, disruption pattern tracking, and capacity trend monitoring.

Geopolitical risk evaluation assesses supplier countries based on alliance relationships, crisis reliability, political stability, export restriction history, and strategic rivalry dynamics. Substitution possibility assessment determines the feasibility of alternatives through technical analysis, timeframe requirements, cost implications, performance differentials, and regulatory barriers. Surge requirement projection calculates potential demand spikes during conflicts, health emergencies, natural disasters, infrastructure failures, and technological transitions.

These dimensions combine into a Strategic Supply Chain Vulnerability Index (1-100) with clearly defined intervention thresholds: critical (>75) requiring immediate action, high concern (50-75) demanding contingency planning, moderate concern (25-50) needing diversification strategies, and low concern (<25) manageable through market mechanisms. This methodology enables precisely targeted reshoring efforts focused on genuine security vulnerabilities rather than blanket protectionism or dangerous complacency.

America's Top 10 Strategic Vulnerabilities:

A Risk-Based Supply Chain Approach

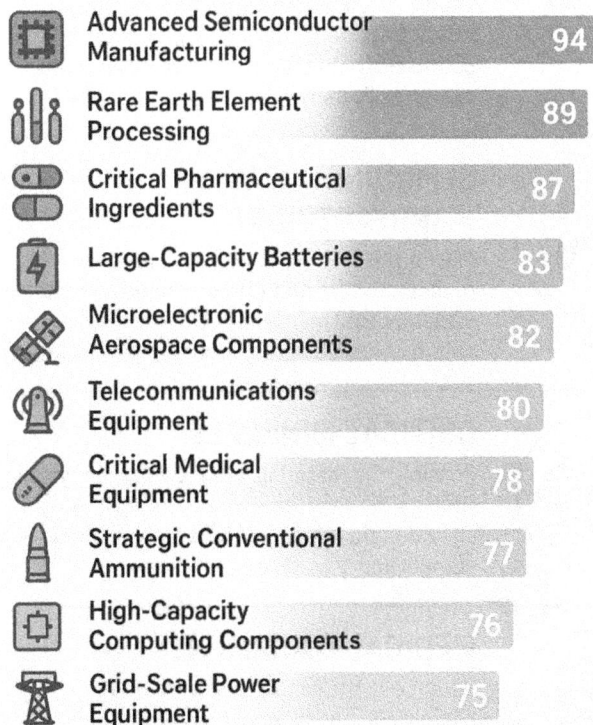

Advanced Semiconductor Manufacturing	94
Rare Earth Element Processing	89
Critical Pharmaceutical Ingredients	87
Large-Capacity Batteries	83
Microelectronic Aerospace Components	82
Telecommunications Equipment	80
Critical Medical Equipment	78
Strategic Conventional Ammunition	77
High-Capacity Computing Components	76
Grid-Scale Power Equipment	75

This vulnerability hierarchy enables precisely targeted reshoring and resilience investments where genuinely needed rather than misdirecting resources through unfocused protectionism.

America's Top 10 Strategic Vulnerabilities: A Risk-Based Supply Chain Approach

Advanced semiconductor manufacturing ranks as America's most critical supply chain vulnerability, with a 94/100 risk score, as 92% of advanced logic chips are concentrated in Taiwan. Taiwan's dominance in chips essential for military systems, AI capabilities, and telecommunications creates catastrophic cross-sector disruption potential with a minimum 5-7 year reshoring timeline, even with massive investment.

Rare earth element processing (89/100) remains 85% controlled by China, which poses a threat to defense systems, clean energy, and electronics. It has the potential for severe capability degradation, requiring 3-5 years for reshoring amid significant environmental challenges.

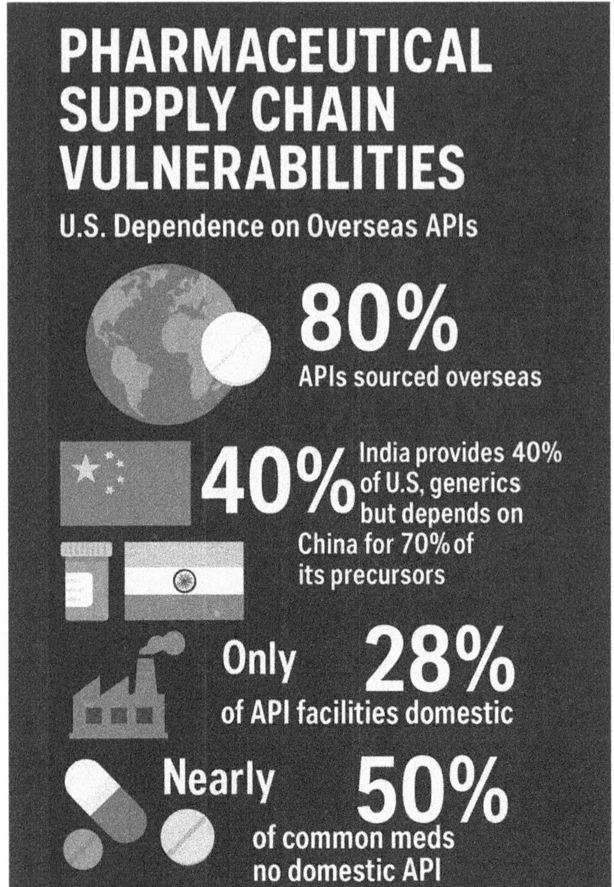

PHARMACEUTICAL SUPPLY CHAIN VULNERABILITIES
U.S. Dependence on Overseas APIs
80%
APIs sourced overseas
40%
India provides 40% of U.S, generics but depends on China for 70% of its precursors
Only 28%
of API facilities domestic
Nearly 50%
of common meds no domestic API

Critical pharmaceutical ingredients (87/100) are sourced from 80% overseas production, primarily in China and India, which risks widespread medical system failure and preventable deaths during disruptions. Reshoring is possible within 2-4 years, provided regulatory streamlining occurs.

The remaining high-risk dependencies include large-capacity batteries (83/100), microelectronic aerospace components (82/100), telecommunications equipment (80/100), critical medical equipment (78/100), strategic conventional ammunition (77/100), high-capacity computing components (76/100), and grid-scale power equipment (75/100).

This vulnerability hierarchy enables precisely targeted reshoring and resilience investments where they are genuinely needed rather than misdirecting resources through unfocused protectionism.

Case Study: The Great Pharmaceutical Vulnerability - America's Medical Achilles Heel

America's pharmaceutical supply chain represents a critical national security vulnerability, with 80% of active pharmaceutical ingredients (APIs) sourced overseas. China directly supplies 40% of the global APIs, while India provides 40% of the U.S.'s generic medications but relies on China for 70% of its API precursors. Only 28% of API production facilities for U.S. drugs operate domestically, and for nearly half of the most common medications, not a single API is manufactured in America.

This dependency creates multiple security concerns affecting military readiness (combat casualty medications), biodefense capabilities (pandemic and bioterrorism responses), public health security (potential widespread shortages), and strategic vulnerability (China's potential leverage). Quality concerns have already materialized through contaminated imports, like the 2018 valsartan recall.

The 227 FDA-designated "essential medicines"—treatments without alternatives where disruption means direct patient suffering or death—represent the most acute vulnerability. This dangerous dependency emerged from pharmaceutical cost pressures, regulatory arbitrage, policy failures, and market consolidation.

A targeted solution requires domestic manufacturing capacity for essential medications, 6-12 months of strategic stockpiling, investment in cost-competitive continuous manufacturing technologies, redundant supply chains across democratic allies, and regulatory incentives for domestic producers. This approach preserves global trade benefits while securing critical capabilities against disruption.

Satirical Memo: "The Shocking Discovery: Things We Need Should Be Made Where We Can Get Them"

MEMORANDUM

TO: All Department Heads

PRACTICAL APPLICATIONS

Based on this revolutionary framework, we've developed several policy proposals:

PRESCRIPTION MEDICATIONS

Perhaps the pills that keep people alive should be manufacturable domestically, rather than dependent on ingredients from countries that might restrict exports during crises (as literally happened during COVID).

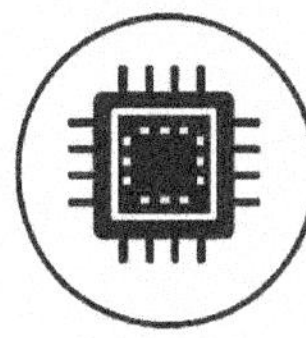

SEMICONDUCTOR MANUFACTURING

Maybe the chips that power all modern technology shouldn't be produced almost exclusively on an island 100 miles from a country that repeatedly threatens to invade it.

CRITICAL MINERALS

Possibly the materials essential for everything from military systems to renewable energy shouldn't be processed 85% by a strategic competitor

MEDICAL EQUIPMENT

Potentially the ventilators, protective equipment, and diagnostics needed during pandemics should have domestic production capacity rather than relying entirely on global shipping during worldwide emergencies

FROM: The Bureau of Obvious Strategic Insights

SUBJECT: Revolutionary Concept: Critical Things Should Be Accessible

After extensive research costing taxpayers millions of dollars, our department has made a groundbreaking discovery: Items essential for national survival should probably be produced somewhere we can actually access them during crises.

We understand this radical concept may shock and disturb many of you who have built careers on the principle that the absolute lowest production cost is the only consideration worth measuring. Please take a moment to recover before continuing.

THE REVOLUTIONARY THEORY:

Our researchers have developed a new framework, which we're calling "Strategic Access Logic," or SAL. The core principles:

1. If we need something to survive as a nation, literally, perhaps it shouldn't be produced exclusively by our chief geopolitical rival
2. When evaluating supply chains, factors beyond "quarterly cost savings" might occasionally merit consideration
3. The ability to actually obtain critical items during emergencies may justify paying slightly more during normal times
4. "Efficiency" that creates catastrophic vulnerability isn't actually efficient at all

We recognize these concepts represent a paradigm shift from the established wisdom that a nation should outsource everything, maintain zero inventory, eliminate all redundancy, and hope nothing ever goes wrong anywhere in the world simultaneously.

COUNTERARGUMENTS

Milton the Trickster Economist

"The market will magically solve everything! Just wait until after the catastrophe when market signals finally indicate we should have prepared decades ago!"

McSlicey the High Priest

"Our models show that prioritizing national security over quarterly earnings would reduce shareholder value by 3.7%! Unacceptable!"

The Always-Been-Fine Brigade

"Nothing bad has happened yet during my specific lifetime, so nothing bad will ever happen in the future!"

The Budget Hawks

"We can't afford resilience! We need that money for [checks notes] cleaning up after preventable catastrophes!"

PRACTICAL APPLICATIONS:

Based on this revolutionary framework, we've developed several policy proposals:

1. **Prescription Medications:** Perhaps the pills that keep people alive should be manufacturable domestically, rather than dependent on ingredients from countries that might restrict exports during crises (as literally happened during COVID).
2. **Semiconductor Manufacturing:** Maybe the chips that power all modern technology shouldn't be produced almost exclusively on an island 100 miles from a country that repeatedly threatens to invade it.
3. **Critical Minerals:** Possibly, the materials essential for everything from military systems to renewable energy shouldn't be processed 85% by a strategic competitor.
4. **Medical Equipment:** Ideally, ventilators, protective equipment, and diagnostics needed during pandemics should have domestic production capacity, rather than relying entirely on global shipping during worldwide emergencies.

COUNTERARGUMENTS:

We anticipate significant resistance to these concepts, primarily from:

1. **Milton the Trickster Economist:** "The market will magically solve everything! Just wait until after the catastrophe when market signals finally indicate we should have prepared decades ago!"
2. **McSlicey the High Priest:** "Our models show that prioritizing national security over quarterly earnings would reduce shareholder value by 3.7%! Unacceptable!"
3. **The Always-Been-Fine Brigade:** "Nothing bad has happened yet during my specific lifetime, so nothing bad will ever happen in the future!"

4. **The Budget Hawks:** "We can't afford resilience! We need that money for [check notes] cleaning up after preventable catastrophes!"

CONCLUSION:

While we recognize the radical nature of suggesting that critical items should be produced where they can actually be obtained, we believe this "Strategic Access Logic" may prove useful during the inevitable future crisis when global supply chains are disrupted.

Of course, we expect this memo to be ignored until approximately 17 minutes after the next supply crisis begins. At this point, everyone will claim they always supported the domestic production of essential items.

Thank you for your attention to this matter. We return you now to your regularly scheduled short-term thinking.

Policy Proposal: Targeted Reshoring Incentives and Alliance-Based Supply Networks

America needs a seven-pronged strategy balancing global trade benefits with security imperatives:

Strategic Industry Identification establishes formal NSC processes to identify truly strategic industries based on military applications, infrastructure requirements, health necessities, technological foundation status, limited substitutability, and concentrated foreign supply.

Domestic Manufacturing Incentives deploy targeted tools for strategic industries: 40% investment tax credits, accelerated depreciation, low-cost financing through an Industrial Finance Corporation, streamlined permitting, federal purchase commitments, and manufacturing R&D funding.

Alliance-Based Supply Networks create coordinated democratic supply chains through formal crisis access agreements, joint stockpiling, harmonized regulations, coordinated investments, mutual defense commitments covering supply disruptions, and intra-alliance technology transfers.

Strategic Stockpiling establishes modern reserves with 6-12 month pharmaceutical ingredient supplies, semiconductor reserves for defense, critical mineral stockpiles, rotating inventories to prevent waste, public-private management, and regional distribution to ensure localized access during disruptions.

The Advanced Manufacturing Initiative invests in next-generation technologies, including continuous pharmaceutical processing, additive manufacturing, automation that reduces labor cost differentials, AI-optimized production, rapidly reconfigurable facilities, and distributed manufacturing networks.

Workforce Development addresses manufacturing skills gaps through community college academies, advanced manufacturing degree programs, industry-certified apprenticeships, manufacturing specialist visa pathways, veteran transition programs, and mid-career retraining.

Implementation occurs through a Cabinet-level Manufacturing Security Advisor, an interagency task force, regular vulnerability assessments, annual congressional reporting, five-year reshoring plans, and bipartisan oversight.

Policy Proposal: Targeted Reshoring Incentives and Alliance-Based Supply Networks

Strategic Industry Identification
- Establishes formal NSC processes
- Identifies industries with military, infrastructure, health applications

Domestic Manufacturing Incentives
- Targeted tools for strategic industries
- 40% investment tax credits + RBD cont financing and R&D funding

Alliance-Based Supply Networks
- Create coordinated democratic supply chains
- Formal crisis access agreements, joint stockpiling
- Harmonized regulations and investments

Strategic Stockpiling
- Establish modern reserves with 6-12 month supplies
- Semiconductor, critical minerals, pharmaceuticals
- Public-private management, regional distribution

Advanced Manufacturing Initiative
- Invest in next-generation technologies
- Continuous processing, additive manuafacturing
- Automation, reconfigurabile and distributied facilities

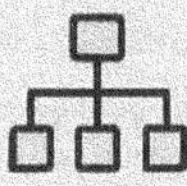

Implementation
- Cabinet-level Manufacturing skills gaps
- Interagency task force, vulnerability assessments
- Annual congressional reporting, five-year plans

Balancing Efficiency and Security
The New Economics of Supply Chains
RISK-ADJUSTED COST CALCULATION
incorporates disruption probabilities, financial impacts, recovery periods, repotation costs and security implications beyond direct metrics
EFFICIENCY
REAL OPTIONS VALUATION
Quantifvices the economic value of supply chain flexility using options theory
SECURITY
NATIONAL SECURITY EXTERNALITIES
Accounts for factors ignored in standard models
DYNAMIC EFFICIENCY
Considers adaptive capacity over time rathan static cost minimization
QUANTITATIVE SECURITY MODELING
Empioys advanced tools
– Morrle Carlo simullations
– Network vulnerability an-
– lysls: Game theory app-
Portfolio valuation
– Portfolio theory

Balancing Efficiency and Security: The New Economics of Supply Chains

The traditional supply chain approach, prioritizing efficiency through global sourcing, creates vulnerabilities during disruptions. A sophisticated framework balances efficiency with security through five principles:

Risk-adjusted cost Calculation incorporates disruption probabilities, financial impacts, recovery periods, reputation costs, and security implications beyond direct metrics, often justifying redundancy that appears inefficient under traditional models.

Real Options Valuation quantifies the economic value of supply chain flexibility using options theory. Multiple suppliers, repurposable capacity, buffer stocks, and technology control represent valuable assets rather than mere costs during disruptions.

National Security Externalities account for factors that are often ignored in standard models—military readiness impacts, coercive leverage, innovation ecosystem benefits, knowledge spillovers, and workforce skill maintenance for surge capacity.

Dynamic Efficiency considers adaptive capacity over time rather than static cost minimization—production experience benefits, manufacturing-research proximity innovation, adaptability to changing environments, surge capacity, and resilience against unexpected disruptions.

Quantitative Security Modeling employs advanced tools, including Monte Carlo simulations, network vulnerability analysis, game theory applications, real options valuation, and portfolio theory, enabling sophisticated tradeoffs between efficiency and security.

The optimal approach represents a balanced portfolio: global and efficient for non-critical items with strategic redundancy and domestic capacity for essential capabilities.

V. DEFENDING THE DIGITAL COMMONS: INFRASTRUCTURE FOR THE AI AGE

> *"Invincibility lies in defense; the possibility of victory, in attack."*
> —Sun Tzu, The Art of War, Chapter 4

Critical Infrastructure Protection in the Cyber Age

The digital transformation of infrastructure has fundamentally altered the protection paradigm. While physical security remains crucial, modern protection frameworks must address four key challenges:

Digital systems have exponentially expanded the attack surface beyond physical access points to include network connections, wireless access points, supply chain vulnerabilities, insider threats, and third-party services. This requires securing not just facilities but entire digital ecosystems.

Interconnectivity has blurred traditional boundaries between critical and non-critical systems. Cloud services, telecommunications networks, vendor access points, consumer devices, cross-jurisdictional data flows, and OT/IT convergence create complex interdependencies that render isolated protection approaches obsolete.

The digital realm creates profound asymmetric advantages for attackers: they need only one vulnerability while defenders must secure everything; attack tools can be developed once and deployed globally; attribution challenges undermine deterrence; and non-state actors can wield state-level capabilities. This asymmetry necessitates strategies that extend beyond perimeter security, emphasizing resilience and recovery.

Public-private complexity presents governance challenges, as most critical infrastructure is privately owned yet provides essential public services. Commercial incentives often misalign with security requirements; regulatory authority is fragmented, information sharing faces barriers; security investments generate uncaptured positive externalities; and global supply chains limit national jurisdiction.

A comprehensive modern framework must integrate physical security, cybersecurity, supply chain integrity, and workforce development within a coherent whole-of-society approach that balances security imperatives with operational and economic realities.

Character Vignette: Cyber Commander Explains Vulnerabilities

In a secure Pentagon briefing room, Admiral Firewall (the nation's top cyber commander) faces a panel of traditional military leaders and civilian officials who appear skeptical about cyber threats.

Admiral Firewall: "Gentlemen, I understand you want an assessment of our critical infrastructure vulnerabilities. Let me start with a simple analogy."

He places a small model of a power plant on the table.

Admiral Firewall: "This is how many of you still think about critical infrastructure—as physical facilities requiring physical protection. That mindset is about 20 years outdated."

He connects the model to a small computer using cables that extend to several other devices.

Admiral Firewall: "Today's reality looks more like this. Our power plants, water systems, and transportation networks—they're all digitally controlled, remotely accessible, and connected to countless other systems. This isn't just a power plant anymore; it's a digital attack surface with a power plant attached."

General Quagmire: *(dismissively)* "So put a good firewall on it and move on. I don't see why this requires special attention when we have real threats like China's navy to worry about."

Admiral Firewall: *(sighs)* "Let me try another approach. General, imagine you're defending a fortress with 10,000 doors. Each morning, new doors appear that you didn't know about. You can't see who's testing the locks, you can't tell which keys they have, and if they get through one door, they can open all the others from the inside. Oh, and the fortress was designed by people who prioritized easy access over security, built by the lowest bidder, and is operated by staff with minimal security training."

General Quagmire: *(shifting uncomfortably)* "That sounds... challenging."

Admiral Firewall: "Now imagine that the fortress controls our electricity, water, transportation, communications, and financial systems. That's our current cybersecurity posture."

He turns to another official.

Admiral Firewall: "Perhaps financial consequences resonate better? The Colonial Pipeline ransomware attack shut down fuel delivery to the entire East Coast, resulting in millions of dollars in costs. The NotPetya attack caused over $10 billion in global damages. SolarWinds gave foreign adversaries access to thousands of organizations for months undetected."

McSlicey the High Priest: "But comprehensive cybersecurity upgrades would cost billions! Our analysis suggests focusing on quarterly earnings instead."

Admiral Firewall: *(calmly)* "And what's the quarterly earnings impact of no electricity for six months? Or poisoned water supplies? Or air traffic control failures?"

Uncomfortable silence.

Admiral Firewall: "Let me be absolutely clear: Our critical infrastructure was not designed with cybersecurity in mind. It was built for reliability, efficiency, and accessibility—not for resilience against sophisticated digital attacks. We've essentially connected systems that control physical infrastructure directly or indirectly to the public internet, where nation-states, criminals, and hacktivists can and do attack them constantly."

He displays a map showing thousands of connection points glowing across American infrastructure networks.

Admiral Firewall: "Each of these points represents a potential digital entry to our critical systems. We detect approximately 22,000 attacks against critical infrastructure daily. Some are probes, some are credential harvesting, and some are actual penetration attempts. And those are just the ones we detect."

Defense Secretary: *(concerned)* "What's your assessment of our current security posture?"

Admiral Firewall: "To be blunt, sir, if our physical borders were as porous as our digital ones, we'd have surrendered to foreign occupation years ago. We're improving, but far too slowly in relation to the evolving threat. And China is watching carefully, mapping our vulnerabilities, and preparing digital weapons that could disable our infrastructure during a conflict."

Defense Secretary: "What do you need?"

Admiral Firewall: "A fundamental paradigm shift. We need to stop treating cybersecurity as an IT issue and recognize it as a core national security requirement. We need mandatory standards with actual enforcement mecha-

nisms. We need dramatically expanded information sharing. We need security-by-design requirements for all critical systems. And we need to train about 300,000 more cybersecurity professionals."

He looks around the room.

Admiral Firewall: "Gentlemen, we've spent trillions preparing for kinetic warfare while leaving our digital flank almost completely exposed. All of our advanced weapons systems, all of our military superiority means nothing if an adversary can turn off our power grid, disable our logistics networks, and cripple our financial systems with a few keystrokes. This is not hypothetical—it's already happening at lower intensity levels. The question is whether we'll get serious about it before a catastrophic attack forces our hand."

Technical Analysis: The Expanding Battleground of Connected Infrastructure

The digitization of critical infrastructure has created a security landscape where attack vectors multiply exponentially. Traditional isolated systems have evolved into interconnected networks where vulnerability exists at every node:

System connectivity has transformed from isolated operations requiring physical access to complex webs of SCADA controls, internet-facing interfaces, cloud platforms, vendor access points, and IoT sensor networks. Each connection represents a potential breach point, with total vulnerability expanding geometrically with each new integration.

Legacy systems pose a significant threat to infrastructure security, as decades-old components, designed before modern security paradigms, remain operational alongside cutting-edge technology. These industrial control systems, with lifespans of 20 years or more, proprietary protocols lacking security features, and outdated operating systems, create persistent vulnerabilities that remain financially or operationally impossible to eliminate.

Global supply chains introduce numerous security blind spots through the use of internationally sourced microelectronics, third-party software libraries, minimally verified firmware, and components manufactured abroad. This complexity makes infrastructure vulnerable to counterfeit components or deliberately implanted backdoors throughout the ecosystem.

The convergence of operational and information technology erases protective boundaries between business networks and control systems. Commercial software in operational environments, remote access capabilities, and shared infrastructure create dangerous pathways that frequently target IT environments and directly access critical systems controlling physical infrastructure.

The human element remains perhaps the most exploitable vulnerability, with social engineering, insufficient security training, insider threats, third-party access, shadow IT deployments, and password reuse creating bypasses around even robust technical defenses.

This multi-dimensional expansion demands security approaches that simultaneously address technological, procedural, and human vulnerabilities across increasingly blurred operational boundaries.

America's Digital Achilles' Heels: Mapping the Vulnerability Landscape

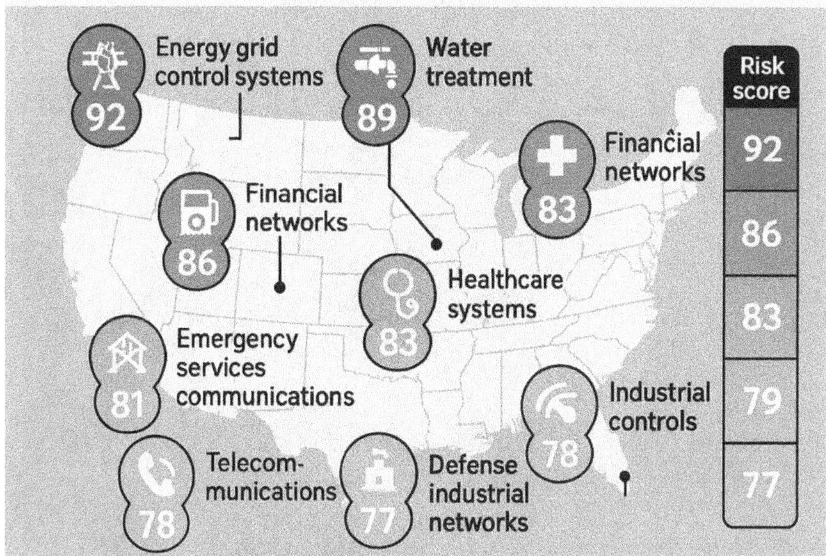

The vulnerability cartography of America's critical infrastructure reveals a nation whose technological arteries lie exposed to an unprecedented array of threats. Our analysis identifies ten essential points of vulnerability, each representing a potential catastrophic failure mode in our interconnected systems:

Energy grid control systems present the most alarming vulnerability (Risk Score: 92/100), with remote access interfaces and legacy SCADA systems creating pathways to regional blackouts and equipment damage. Current patchwork protections remain woefully inadequate against sophisticated adversaries.

Water treatment facilities (89/100) operate on outdated control systems with internet-connected sensors, creating contamination risks mitigated by little more than hope and inconsistent local practices.

Transportation management (86/100), financial networks (85/100), and healthcare systems (83/100) form a triad of high-risk infrastructure where attack vectors multiply through connected vehicles, payment processors, and legacy medical devices—all presenting civilization-scale disruption scenarios.

Emergency services communications (81/100), internet exchange points (80/100), industrial controls (79/100), telecommunications (78/100), and defense industrial networks (77/100) complete this vulnerability decalogue, each representing critical failure points where digital intrusion could trigger physical chaos.

This visualization reveals not merely isolated vulnerabilities, but a deeply interconnected ecosystem where cascading failures across systems can amplify attacks beyond their initial targets. The stark reality demands immediate regulatory attention and security investment focused on these most critical nodes in America's digital nervous system.

Case Studies: Infrastructure Vulnerability Implications

The theoretical dangers of infrastructure vulnerability have manifested in three paradigmatic attacks that serve as harbingers of our increasingly precarious digital dependency:

Colonial Pipeline's 2021 paralysis exemplifies how digital and physical infrastructure have become inextricably entangled. A single compromised VPN password—lacking basic multi-factor authentication—crippled 5,500 miles of pipeline for six days, not because operational technology was compromised, but because billing systems failed. The attack exposed how IT/OT convergence creates unexpected dependencies where disruption in one seemingly peripheral system can cascade into a critical operational shutdown. The resulting 17-state emergency, widespread fuel shortages, and a $4.4 million ransom demonstrated how digital vulnerabilities can translate directly into economic and social chaos.

SolarWinds' 2020 compromise revealed the profound vulnerability of our digital supply chains. This masterfully executed attack penetrated thousands of organizations, including critical federal agencies, by weaponizing trusted software updates. The infiltration of the Treasury, Justice, and Energy departments demonstrated how sophisticated attackers bypass conventional defenses through third-party dependencies. The multi-billion-dollar remediation costs and persistent uncertainty about residual access underscore how supply chain security remains dangerously premised on trust rather than verification.

Ukraine's power grid attacks in 2015/2016 provided the first real-world demonstration of infrastructure-targeted cyberwarfare. Russia-linked actors exploited remote access systems, insufficient authentication, and firmware vulnerabilities to cause blackouts affecting 230,000 consumers. These attacks—which forced months of manual operations—established the blueprint for infrastructure disruption, proving that sophisticated attackers can and will target the systems underpinning modern civilization.

Together, these case studies reveal that infrastructure vulnerabilities have evolved from theoretical concerns to documented threats with immediate implications for national security, economic stability, and public safety. They demand mandatory security standards, enhanced detection capabilities, improved supply chain integrity, and resilient design across all critical sectors.

Satirical Guide: "Cybersecurity: That Thing Everyone Agrees Is Important Until They See the Bill"

THE OFFICIAL GUIDE TO CYBERSECURITY PROCRASTINATION

A handy reference for executives, officials, and anyone else responsible for critical systems who'd rather not think about digital security until after the catastrophic breach

INTRODUCTION: The Art of Security Theater

Welcome to the time-honored tradition of pretending to take cybersecurity seriously while doing the absolute minimum! This guide will help you master the delicate art of security theater—appearing concerned about digital threats while avoiding the inconvenience and expense of actually addressing them.

CHAPTER 1: MAGICAL THINKING STRATEGIES

The foundation of effective cybersecurity procrastination is magical thinking. Try these tested approaches:

★ **The "It Won't Happen To Us" Mantra**: Despite thousands of organizations being breached annually, your systems are magically immune because... reasons!

★ **The "We're Too Small/Unimportant" Fallacy**: Convince yourself that attackers only target giant corporations, ignoring that 43% of attacks target small organizations precisely because they're easier targets.

★ **The "We Have A Firewall" Delusion**: Place total faith in that firewall you installed in 2009 and haven't updated since. It's basically an impenetrable force field!

CHAPTER 2: BUDGETARY GYMNASTICS

When security professionals request resources, use these Olympic-level techniques:

★ **The Reverse Priority Flip**: Explain that cybersecurity must wait until after you've upgraded the executive bathroom facilities and purchased another meaningless management platform.

★ **The "Maybe Next Quarter" Vault**: Perfect the art of perpetually delaying security investments until the mythical time when budget constraints disappear (narrator: they never do).

★ **The ROI Impossible Standard**: Demand precise return-on-investment calculations for security measures, while requiring no such justification for executive retreats or vanity projects.

CHAPTER 3: RESPONSIBILITY DIFFUSION TACTICS

Mastering the art of making cybersecurity everyone's responsibility (and therefore no one's):

★ **The Organizational Shell Game**: Create a reporting structure where cybersecurity falls between multiple departments, ensuring decisive action is bureaucratically impossible.

★ **The "Security Is Everyone's Job" Abdication**: Proclaim security is "everyone's responsibility" while providing no training, authority, or resources to anyone.

★ **The Vendor Blame Transference**: When breached, immediately blame technology vendors, cloud providers, or that one intern who left three years ago.

CHAPTER 4: POST-BREACH PERFORMANCE ART

When the inevitable breach occurs, execute this performance flawlessly:

★ **The Shocked Disbelief Routine**: Express complete astonishment that the exact scenario security experts warned about for years actually happened.

★ **The Instant Expert Transformation**: Suddenly become cybersecurity experts yourselves, second-guessing the security team you previously ignored.

★ **The "Unpredictable Black Swan" Reframing**: Describe the completely predictable, repeatedly warned-about breach as a "sophisticated, unprecedented attack that no one could have foreseen."

★ **The Sacrificial CISO Ceremony**: Fire your Chief Information Security Officer for failing to prevent the breach you refused to let them address, then hire a new one with exactly the same constraints.

CONCLUSION: THE INFINITE CYCLE

After the breach, recommit to taking security seriously until budget discussions resume. Then return to Chapter 1 and repeat indefinitely!

TESTIMONIALS:

"Thanks to this guide, we saved thousands on security investments! The subsequent breach only cost us millions in damages, regulatory fines, and lost business. What a bargain!" – Compromised Corp.

"We followed the 'it won't happen to us' strategy for years. Now, our intellectual property is being sold on the dark web, and our customers' data is being shared everywhere. If only there had been some way to prevent this completely foreseeable outcome!" – Breached Industries

Remember: Security is an expense right up until the moment it becomes a catastrophic liability. Choose wisely!

POLICY PROPOSAL

FROM VOLUNTARY COMPLIANCE TO NATIONAL RESILIENCE A NEW SECURITY MANDATE

MANDATORY SECTOR STANDARDS
sector-specific security controls

BASELINE REQUIREMENTS
inventories, vulnerability management, incident response, staffing exec accountability

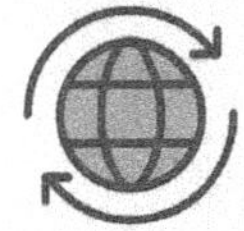

INFO SHARING FRAMEWORK
automated platforms, legal safe harbor, standardized reporting, international collaboration

ENFORCEMENT MECHANISMS
compliance audits, fines, public disclosure insurance mandates, exec certification

PUBLIC-PRIVATE PARTNERSHIPS
joint councils, shared analysis centers, unified standards, coordinated response tech development

Policy Proposal: From Voluntary Compliance to National Resilience - A New Security Mandate

The current voluntary approach to cybersecurity for critical infrastructure has proven inadequate, with significant vulnerabilities persisting despite years of warnings and recommendations. America requires a fundamentally transformed security framework built on five interconnected pillars:

Sector-specific mandatory standards must replace ineffective voluntary guidelines. Energy infrastructure requires network segregation, multi-factor authentication, and redundant controls to ensure security and reliability. Water systems demand chemical monitoring and air-gapped backups. Healthcare networks need rigorous clinical isolation and medical device security. Financial systems require enhanced transaction authentication and integrity verification to ensure security and reliability. Transportation infrastructure must implement safety-critical segmentation and spoofing detection.

Cross-sector baseline requirements must establish minimum security practices across all critical infrastructure, including comprehensive system inventories, vulnerability management programs, incident response capabilities, security staffing requirements, and executive accountability for the security posture.

A comprehensive information-sharing framework must enable the rapid distribution of threat intelligence through automated platforms, with legal protections, standardized formats, sector-specific analysis centers, mandatory incident reporting, and international sharing arrangements.

Meaningful enforcement mechanisms must create real consequences for security failures, including compliance audits, financial penalties, public disclosure of deficiencies, insurance requirements, liability protections contingent upon compliance, and executive certification of the security posture.

Innovative public-private partnerships must redefine governance through joint coordinating councils with regulatory authority, shared threat analysis centers, collaborative standards development, executive-level coordination, combined response teams, and security technology development programs.

This framework strikes a balance between the need for meaningful security improvements and the operational realities of critical infrastructure. By establishing clear standards, promoting robust information sharing, and enforcing them effectively, America's infrastructure security posture can be significantly improved while maintaining necessary operational flexibility.

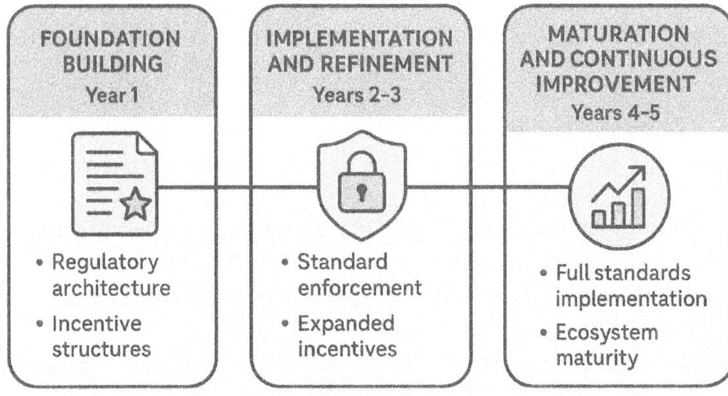

From Policy to Practice: The Security Implementation Roadmap

America's critical infrastructure security transformation will unfold across three strategic phases:

Foundation Building (Year 1) establishes the regulatory architecture through an executive order creating the Critical Infrastructure Security Council, sector-specific draft standards, and congressional authorization. Simultaneously, incentive structures emerge through tax credits, procurement preferences, and liability protections, while institutional reforms create the National Critical Infrastructure Security Agency and joint public-private operations centers.

Implementation and Refinement (Years 2-3) activate enforcement for the highest-risk standards, performance metrics, and mandatory reporting requirements. Incentive mechanisms expand through insurance requirements, grants for smaller providers, and R&D credits, while institutional reforms introduce a Civilian Cybersecurity Reserve Corps and regional coordination centers.

Maturation and Continuous Improvement (Years 4-5) involves the full implementation of standards, accompanied by regular review processes, continuous monitoring requirements, and established crisis response authorities. The ecosystem matures with infrastructure investment funds tied to security compliance, streamlined regulatory review for secure systems, and the creation of an International Critical Infrastructure Security Alliance.

Success metrics target 90% standards compliance within three years, a 50% reduction in successful attacks, a 75% decrease in intrusion detection time, and an 80% increase in operators reporting an improved security posture.

This phased implementation recognizes that meaningful security improvement requires synchronized regulatory, incentive, and institutional actions. It creates a realistic pathway to enhanced infrastructure security while balancing requirements with essential support mechanisms.

VI. THE DEMOCRATIC ALLIANCE ADVANTAGE: COALITION VERSUS COERCION

Analytical Framework: Democratic Alliances as Strategic Counterweight

> *"Befriend a distant state while attacking one nearby."*
> —Thirty-Six Stratagems, #23

America's greatest advantage in technological competition with authoritarian powers lies not in unilateral capabilities but in its alliance network—democratic partners representing roughly 60% of global GDP, the most advanced technology production, and the world's leading research institutions.

This alliance advantage operates across multiple dimensions. Democratic societies foster innovation through academic freedom, intellectual property protection, market competition, cross-border talent flows, robust venture capital, and limited government interference in research. When democratic nations coordinate these ecosystems, they create a combined innovative capacity that authoritarian systems struggle to match despite massive directed investment.

Democratic alliances can leverage their combined market power to establish technical standards reflecting democratic values, create incentives for security and privacy, set conditions for technology access, provide alternatives to authoritarian offerings, maintain collective leverage in negotiations, and shape emerging technology development—increasingly important as AI, quantum computing, and biotechnology raise fundamental questions about privacy, autonomy, and human dignity.

Through coordination, democratic allies create secure supply networks by distributing production across trusted partners, establishing common security standards, developing shared stockpiles, creating preferential procurement arrangements, implementing coordinated export controls, and jointly investing in strategic manufacturing. These "friend-shoring" arrangements maintain efficiency while reducing vulnerability to authoritarian coercion.

Democratic technology governance offers advantages through transparency, building trust, ethical frameworks that reflect diverse input, privacy protections that maintain individual autonomy, accountability mechanisms that prevent misuse, adaptive regulation that balances innovation and protection, and legitimacy derived from democratic processes—all increasingly important as technology penetrates deeper into social, political, and economic systems.

The strategic imperative is transforming America's traditional security alliances into comprehensive technology partnerships that leverage these democratic advantages while addressing the coordination challenges inherent in pluralistic systems.

Character Development: Alliance Ambassador Highlights Democratic versus Authoritarian Models

At a global technology governance summit, Alliance Ambassador Chen addresses representatives from nations weighing partnerships with China's technology initiatives versus joining democratic technology alliances.

Ambassador Chen: "Distinguished representatives, you face a consequential choice regarding your nations' technological futures. Both China and the democratic alliance offer partnership models, but they operate on fundamentally different principles that will shape your societies for generations."

She displays a comparison chart titled "Partnership Models: Values and Outcomes."

Ambassador Chen: "China's model emphasizes speed, central coordination, and apparent simplicity. Sign the agreement, receive the technology package, and implement according to specifications. The entire process is certainly efficient."

McSlicey, the High Priest, nods approvingly from the audience.

Ambassador Chen: "But efficiency isn't the only consideration. China's model comes with specific features you should understand: Technology transfer with surveillance capabilities built in. Financing that creates leverage during disputes. Data architectures that route sensitive information through systems accessible to the Chinese government. Infrastructure designed to technical standards that create long-term dependency."

She shifts to the other column of the chart.

Ambassador Chen: "The democratic alliance offers a different approach: technology partnerships based on transparent terms, financing that builds capacity rather than leverage, security and privacy by design, standards that ensure interoperability without dependency, and, critically, governance frameworks that respect your sovereignty and your citizens' rights."

HISTORICAL ALLIANCE STRUCTURES IN AMERICAN HISTORY

LEND-LEASE (1941-45)
- $50B+ military aid
- material support before formal structure
- tech+production coordination
- trust via action

NATO (1949-Present)
- Formal commitments
- interoperability
- institutional continuity
- credible deterrence
- ongoing cooperation

PLAZA ACCORD (1985)
- G5 currency coordination
- tech-policy synergy
- high-level engagement
- transparency; amplified impact

COCOM CONTROLS (1949-94)
- Multilateral tech regime
- evolving enforcement
- shared commitment

Representative from a Developing Nation: "But China's offerings are cheaper and faster. They don't ask questions about how we govern. Why should we pay more for Western technology with governance strings attached?"

Ambassador Chen: "An entirely reasonable question. The initial cost calculation seems straightforward—China's package appears less expensive. But the full cost accounting looks quite different when you consider several factors:"

She advances to a slide labeled "Total Cost of Partnership."

Ambassador Chen: "First, there's the sovereignty cost. When you adopt technology systems that another government can access, influence, or disable, you've effectively ceded elements of your national sovereignty—a cost no balance sheet captures."

"Second, there's the dependency cost. China's systems are designed to create technological lock-in, making the transition to alternatives prohibitively expensive. The apparent savings now become a long-term premium."

"Third, there's the value cost. These systems don't just perform functions; they embed values and governance models. Surveillance capabilities designed for an authoritarian system will reshape your society in its image, regardless of your intentions."

She looks across the audience.

Ambassador Chen: "We in the democratic alliance aren't perfect. We have our disagreements, our inefficiencies, our contradictions. But our partnership model is fundamentally different because it's based on enhancing rather than diminishing your sovereignty, expanding rather than restricting your citizens' rights, and building capacity rather than dependency."

Uncle Xi rises from the audience, smiling smoothly.

Uncle Xi: "My distinguished colleague paints a concerning picture. But look at what China has achieved! We've lifted hundreds of millions out of poverty and built infrastructure at unprecedented speed. Developed technologies that compete with or exceed Western capabilities. Our partnership model delivers results without Western lectures about how you should govern your own affairs."

Ambassador Chen: "Results matter, absolutely. But means and ends are connected. Technology shapes societies—it's never neutral. The systems you implement today will influence what kind of society you have tomorrow."

She displays a final slide showing technology governance outcomes in different nations.

Ambassador Chen: "The question isn't whether you want advanced technology—everyone does. The question is whether you want technology that answers to your people and your government, or technology that serves as a foreign influence mechanism long after the ribbon-cutting ceremonies are forgotten."

"The democratic alliance offers technology partnership without hegemony—systems that remain under your sovereign control, that reflect your values, that protect rather than exploit your citizens' data. That's the fundamental difference in our models, and why I believe ours better serves your long-term national interests."

Historical Analysis: Successful Alliance Structures in American History

Throughout history, the United States has utilized alliances to expand its power and achieve objectives that exceed its unilateral capabilities. Several models offer lessons for contemporary technology alliances:

The Lend-Lease Program (1941-1945) transferred over $50 billion in military equipment to Allied nations fighting the Axis powers. It demonstrated how material support can precede formal structures, technology transfer strengthens the entire alliance, production coordination creates collective advantage, mutual interest supersedes strict reciprocity, and trust develops through concrete action rather than declarations.

NATO (1949-Present) created one of history's most successful military alliances, stabilizing Europe and deterring Soviet aggression throughout the Cold War. Its formal commitments created certainty, standardization enhanced interoperability, institutionalization ensured continuity across administrations, demonstrated capabilities provided credible deterrence, and regular cooperation built trust and effectiveness.

The 1985 Plaza Accord represented a coordinated economic action among the G5 nations to address currency imbalances, demonstrating how economic coordination can address shared challenges. Technical collaboration supports political agreement, regular high-level engagement maintains momentum, transparency builds legitimacy, and coordinated action magnifies the impact of individual nations.

DEMOCRATIC ALLIANCE TECHNOLOGICAL ADVANTAGGE SUMMARY

R&D INVESTMENT
$1.4 trillion annually
2,7× China's investment
2.7× China's investment

SEMICONDUCTOR MANUFACTURING
68% of global capacity
4.5× China's capacity

AI RESEARCH
67% of top-cited papers
2,7× China's output
2.7× China's output

QUANTUM COMPUTING
73% of patents

TECH TALENT
78% of global specialists
4.8× China's talent pool

TECH COMPANIES
83 of top 100 by market cap
5.9×

COCOM Export Controls (1949-1994) managed technology transfer restrictions to communist bloc countries, illustrating the need for multilateral coordination to make export controls effective. Technology control regimes must constantly evolve; enforcement requires a shared commitment. Overly broad restrictions become counterproductive, and a balance between security and continued innovation is essential.

These historical models demonstrate America's capacity to build and maintain effective alliances when strategic necessity is clear and institutional structures support continued cooperation. They offer templates for technology alliance structures needed to compete with China's state-directed approach.

Data Visualization: Combined Democratic Alliance Resources

When democratic nations (the US, EU, UK, Canada, Australia, Japan, South Korea) coordinate their technological resources, they possess overwhelming advantages in every critical domain:

Research & Development: Democratic allies invest $1.4 trillion annually (2.4% of combined GDP) versus China's $526 billion (2.1% of GDP)—a 2.7x advantage.

Semiconductor Manufacturing: Democratic allies control 68% of global capacity, compared to China's 15%—a 4.5x advantage, with dominance in advanced nodes.

AI Research: Democratic allies produce 67% of the top-cited AI research papers compared to China's 25%—a 2.7x advantage in high-impact research output.

Quantum Computing: Democratic allies hold 73% of the world's quantum computing patents, compared to China's 21%—a 3.5 times advantage, with leadership across most quantum technologies.

Critical Technology Talent: Democratic allies host 78% of the global AI, quantum, and biotech specialists, compared to China's smaller talent pool—a 4.8 times advantage.

Advanced Technology Companies: Democratic allies host 83 of the top 100 technology companies by market capitalization, compared to China's 14—a 5.9x advantage in corporate innovation engines.

The challenge lies not in capacity but in coordination—converting these theoretical advantages into practical technological leadership through effective alliance structures.

Case Studies: Emerging Tech Alliances

The Chip 4 Alliance (US, Japan, South Korea, Taiwan) represents over 70% of global semiconductor production. Its structure includes ministerial coordination, joint R&D funding, coordinated export controls, shared early warning systems, mutual emergency production assistance, and harmonized standards. Early results show coordinated manufacturing investment, joint technology development, enhanced security protocols, operational early warning systems, and initial stockpiling agreements. Challenges include balancing competition with collaboration, managing Chinese retaliation, harmonizing regulations, sustaining political support, and expanding to software security.

The Telecommunications Security Framework provides alternatives to Chinese-dominated 5G/6G technology through Open RAN standards, funding for secure telecommunications in developing nations, technical security assistance, coordinated security requirements, joint testing facilities, and shared intelligence. Results include increasing Open RAN deployments, non-Chinese 5G solutions in 43 countries, financing alternatives, harmonized standards across 38 nations, and the sharing of operational vulnerabilities. Challenges include cost differentials, technical complexity, fragmented regulations, Chinese economic leverage, and maintaining consistent messaging.

The Critical Minerals Alliance secures supply chains through coordinated investment, joint strategic reserves, shared standards, technical assistance, financing for processing facilities, and research cooperation. Results include new rare earth processing facilities, critical mineral mapping in 27 countries, strategic reserves for 18 key materials, a 17% reduction in Chinese market share, and the commercialization of recycling technologies. Challenges include environmental concerns, higher costs, long development timelines, regulatory barriers, and maintaining commitment through market fluctuations.

These cases illustrate both the potential and challenges of democratic technology alliances, which necessitate sustained political commitment, regulatory harmonization, and effective coordination mechanisms to achieve success.

Satirical Dictionary: "Translating 'America First' Into 'America's Allies Matter'"

OFFICIAL DIPLOMATIC PHRASEBOOK: EXPLAINING ALLIANCES TO AMERICA FIRSTERS

A guide for diplomats, officials, and anyone attempting to explain the concept of "allies" to those who believe America can and should go it alone in the technological competition with China.

"America First" Statement: *"Why should we care about allies? America is strong enough to compete with China alone!"*

Translation: "I have not checked the combined GDP, research output, or manufacturing capacity of democratic allies versus China, nor have I contemplated the mathematics of competing against 1.4 billion people with only 330 million Americans."

Diplomatic Response: "America First absolutely means being strategically intelligent. When our allies represent 60% of global GDP, 70% of semiconductor manufacturing, and 75% of advanced research, bringing them into our

Emerging Tech Alliances

The Chip 4 Alliance

Early results

- Coordinated manufacturing invest
- Joint R&D funding
- Coordinated export controls
- Shared early warning systems
- Mutual emergency production assistance

Early results:

- Coordinated comfect and collaboration
- Managing Chinese retialiation
- Harmonizing regulaions
- Sustaining political soppuport

- Managing Chinese retialiation
- Harmonizing regulations
- Sustaining to software security

Telecommunications Security Framework

- Open RAN standards
- Funding for secure telecom in developing nations
- Technical security assistance
- Coordinated security requirements
- Joint testing facilities
- Shared intelligence

Components

- Cost differentials
- Technical compilexity
- Fragmented regulations
- Chinese economic leverage
- Maintaiming consistent messanging

Challenges

- Environmental concerns
- Higher costs
- Long development timelines

Critical Minerals Alliance

- Coordinated investment
- Joint strategic reserves
- Shared standards

Components

- New processing
- facilities

Challenges

strategy multiplies our strength. It's like turning down a free 5x force multiplier because we're too proud to admit we have friends."

"America First" Statement: *"These so-called allies are just taking advantage of us! They don't pay their fair share!"*

Translation: "I am conflating NATO defense spending with technological alliances and have not calculated the massive advantages America gains from allied research facilities, talent pools, and manufacturing capabilities."

Diplomatic Response: "Fair burden-sharing is absolutely essential. That's precisely why technology alliances make sense—each nation contributes its unique strengths. Japan's manufacturing precision, Taiwan's semiconductor fabrication, Europe's regulatory frameworks, Korea's memory chip production—these capabilities complement America's strengths rather than duplicating them. It's smart division of labor, not foreign aid."

"America First" Statement: *"We don't need complicated alliance structures. Just tariffs! Big beautiful tariffs!"*

Translation: "I have not considered that unilateral tariffs affect less than 20% of China's economy, are partially absorbed by American consumers, and do nothing to build alternative supply chains or technology ecosystems."

Diplomatic Response: "Tariffs are one tool in a comprehensive strategy. However, competing with China requires more than just raising import prices—it necessitates building entire alternative technology ecosystems. That's impossible without coordinating with the democratic nations that control crucial parts of global supply chains. Strategic tariffs work best when coordinated with allies, creating alternatives rather than just raising costs."

"America First" Statement: *"These international organizations and alliances limit American sovereignty!"*

Translation: "I have not considered that uncoordinated technology policies across democracies actually strengthen China's leverage over each nation, effectively reducing real sovereignty for all."

Diplomatic Response: "True sovereignty in the 21st century means having viable alternatives and real choices. When China dominates a technology sector, our practical sovereignty diminishes regardless of our theoretical freedom. Technology alliances increase American sovereignty by ensuring we're not dependent on potential adversaries for critical capabilities. They expand our options rather than limiting them."

"America First" Statement: *"The free market will solve everything! We don't need government-led alliances!"*

Translation: "I have not noticed that China's government invests hundreds of billions in strategic technologies, coordinates corporate behavior, and implements comprehensive industrial policies that markets alone cannot counter."

Diplomatic Response: "Markets work brilliantly within proper frameworks. However, when competing against a state-directed economy like China's, uncoordinated market responses are akin to sending individual tennis players against a national team with a well-coordinated strategy. Markets will determine which specific technologies succeed, but governments must create the conditions for fair competition rather than conceding strategic sectors to state-subsidized rivals."

"America First" Statement: *"Why should we share our technology with allies? They'll just steal our intellectual property!"*

Translation: "I am confusing democratic allies with China and have not considered that technology flows in both directions, with allies providing crucial innovations to American companies and researchers."

Diplomatic Response: "America doesn't just share technology—we receive it too. Taiwan's semiconductor manufacturing, Japan's materials science, Europe's cryptography, Korea's display technology—these allied innovations strengthen American products and systems. A technology alliance means mutual benefit through coordination, not one-way transfers. And unlike certain competitors, our allies generally respect intellectual property rights."

ADVANCED DIPLOMATIC TECHNIQUES:

When standard translations fail, try these approaches:

1. **The Historical Reminder:** "America has always been strongest when working with allies—from World War II to the Cold War to the War on Terror. Technology competition is no different."
2. **The Math Lesson:** "America represents 4% of the global population. China represents 18%. Simple arithmetic suggests we might want some friends in this competition."
3. **The Business Analogy:** "No successful company tries to do everything itself. They form strategic partnerships for capabilities they don't have in-house. Nations work the same way."
4. **The Sports Reference:** "Even Michael Jordan needed teammates to win championships. Technology competition is a team sport, not individual boxing."
5. **The Sovereignty Enhancement:** "Real independence comes from having choices. Alliances give us alternatives to Chinese technology dependency."

If all else fails, speak very slowly and use simple words: "Friends... good. Working... together... makes... America... stronger."

AMERICA FIRST vs ALLIANCE REALITY

DIPLOMATIC PHRASEBOOK

AMERICA FIRST SOUNDBITE	REALITY CHECK	DIPLOMATIC REFRAME
WE CAN BEAT CHINA ALONE	HAS NOT DONE THE MATH	ALLIES ADD 5× STRENGTH
ALLIES FREELOAD	CONFUSES NATO WITH TECH BENEFITS	EACH ALLY CONTRIBUTES UNIQUE TECH EDGE
TARIFFS ARE ENOUGH	IGNORES LIMITED IMPACT, CONSUMER COSTS	ALLIANCES BUILD ALT SUPPLY CHAINS
ALLIANCES LIMIT SOVEREIGNTY	UNCOORDINATED POLICIES EMPOWER CHINA	ALLIANCES EXPAND REAL CHOICES
MARKETS ALONE WILL WIN	FORGETS CHINA STATE SPENDING	GOV FRAMEWORKS + MARKETS + ALLIES

Policy Proposal: Revitalized Alliance Structures

To compete with China's coordinated technological strategy, America must develop comprehensive alliance structures:

A ministerial-level Technology Alliance Council, including democratic innovation leaders with quarterly meetings, a permanent secretariat, technical working groups, annual summits, joint threat assessment, and dedicated diplomatic representation.

A $250 billion Strategic Technology Investment Fund for semiconductor manufacturing, AI infrastructure, quantum computing, biotechnology, and clean energy, with joint funding proportional to GDP, private sector matching, distributed facilities, security requirements, and streamlined governance.

The Democratic Technology Standards Initiative aims to develop standards that reflect democratic values in the areas of AI ethics, privacy-preserving data sharing, critical infrastructure security, interoperability, verification mechanisms, and participation in international standards bodies.

A Secure Supply Chain Network establishes resilient supply chains through dependency mapping, strategic reshoring, friend-shoring arrangements, joint stockpiling, harmonized export controls, security verification, and crisis response protocols.

A Technology Alliance Visa Program creating streamlined immigration pathways with expedited processing, qualification recognition, coordinated scholarships, joint R&D teams, academic exchanges, and harmonized IP protection.

Revitalized Alliance Structures

A Comprehensive Strategy to Compete with China's Technological Advancement

To compete with China's coordinated technological strategy, America must develop comprehensive alliance structures that transform security partnerships into technology coalitions reflecting democratic values while maintaining market-based innovation advantages.

Technology Alliance Council

- Ministerial-level representation
- Quarterly meetings
- Permanent secretariat
- Technical working groups
- Annual summits
- Dedicated diplomatic representation

Strategic Technology Investment Fund

$250 Billion

- Semiconductor manufacturing
- AI infrastructure
- Quantum computing
- Biotechnology & clean energy
- Funding proportional to GDP

Democratic Technology Standards Initiati

- AI ethics frameworks
- Privacy-preserving data sharing
- Critical infrastructure security
- Interoperability standards
- Verification mechanisms
- International standards bodies participation

Secure Supply Chain Network

- Dependency mapping
- Strategic reshoring
- Friend-shoring arrangements
- Joint stockpiling of critical materials
- Harmonized export controls
- Crisis response protocols

Technology Alliance Visa Program

- Streamlined immigration pathways
- Expedited processing
- Qualification recognition
- Coordinated scholarships
- Joint R&D teams
- Harmonized IP protection

Democratic Digital Development Partnership

- Transparent financing
- Technical assistance
- Capacity building
- Security by design principles
- Global interoperability
- Respect for sovereignty

Technology Security Dialogue with China

- Regular structured discussions
- Crisis communication channels
- Norms development
- Reciprocity requirements
- IP protection enforcement
- Managed competition in non-critical domains

Transforming security partnerships into comprehensive technology coalitions

The Democratic Digital Development Partnership offers developing nations alternative technology models with transparent financing, technical assistance, capacity building, security by design, global interoperability, and respect for sovereignty.

A Technology Security Dialogue with China, establishing structured engagement through regular discussions, crisis communication channels, norms development, reciprocity requirements, IP protection enforcement, and managed competition in non-critical domains.

This structure would transform security partnerships into comprehensive technology coalitions reflecting democratic values while maintaining market-based innovation advantages.

Implementation Framework: Institutional Mechanisms for Alliance Cooperation

A multi-level governance structure balances effectiveness with democratic legitimacy, comprising annual Leader Summits, quarterly Ministerial meetings, monthly Senior Officials sessions, ongoing Technical Expert collaboration, parliamentary conferences held yearly, and structured Civil Society consultation.

Institutional mechanisms include a Permanent Secretariat, a Technology Security Council, an Innovation Coordination Board, a Standards Harmonization Committee, a Supply Chain Resilience Task Force, and a Digital Development Agency.

Decision-making processes strike a balance between efficiency and sovereignty through consensus for strategic decisions, qualified majority voting for implementation, opt-in mechanisms, differentiated participation levels, dispute resolution procedures, and regular review processes.

Funding mechanisms include GDP-proportional base contributions, project-specific funding, public-private financing, national policy implementation, in-kind contributions, and accountability metrics.

Legal frameworks ensure commitments survive political transitions with core alliance agreements, implementing protocols, regulatory harmonization, IP protections, technology transfer protocols, and joint procurement frameworks.

Operational coordination occurs through secure communication networks, personnel exchanges, joint training, emergency response protocols, shared testing facilities, and regular joint exercises.

Democratic accountability is maintained through transparency requirements, regular reporting, parliamentary oversight, stakeholder consultation, independent evaluation, and participation by civil society.

A coordinated China engagement strategy includes a united front in negotiations, coordinated responses to coercion, joint messaging on security concerns, differentiated engagement by domain, dialogue on norms, and reciprocity requirements.

These mechanisms transform abstract concepts into functioning structures capable of sustained cooperation across political transitions while preserving democratic values.

VII. THE TRUMP 2.0 REALITY: STRATEGIC CONTINUITY AMID POLITICAL VOLATILITY

Analytical Framework: Strategic Continuity Through Political Transitions

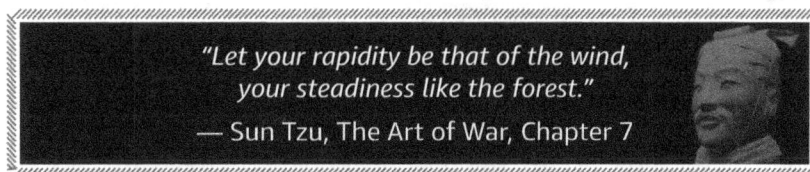

> *"Let your rapidity be that of the wind,*
> *your steadiness like the forest."*
> — Sun Tzu, The Art of War, Chapter 7

America's technology competition with China will likely persist across multiple administrations and decades, presenting a fundamental challenge: maintaining strategic continuity amid political transitions in a polarized environment where policy often shifts with leadership changes.

This challenge intensifies with a second Trump administration, which previously demonstrated a personalized approach featuring relationship-prioritized diplomacy, transactional alliance management, multilateral skepticism, social media policymaking, high personnel turnover, and emphasis on visible "wins" over long-term positioning.

Maintaining strategic continuity requires addressing five interconnected dimensions:

Institutional Resilience operates through career civil service stability, preserved interagency processes, bipartisan congressional frameworks, consistent military and intelligence focus, and regulatory independence—all of which provide operational continuity despite executive changes.

Legal and Structural Embedding creates durability through statutory authorities, binding international commitments, established regulatory processes, judicial constraints on arbitrary changes, and multi-year funding structures that transcend annual political cycles.

ANALYTICAL FRAMEWORK
STRATEGIC CONTINUITY THROUGH POLITICAL TRANSITITIONS

Maintaining Direction Across Decades and Administrations

INSTITUTIONAL RESILIENCE
Career civil service stability
Interagency processes
Bipartisan frameworks

LEGAL & STRUCTURAL EMBEDDING
Statutory authorities
Binding intl commitments
Established regulatory processes
Judicial constraints

ALLIANCE-BASED STABILIZATION
Multilateral mechanisms, working-level networks
Mutual interests, diversified engagement
Multilateral frameworks

STAKEHOLDER ALIGNMENT
Private sector advocacy
Defense consistency
Bipartisan expert consensus
Sub-national cooperation

STRATEGIC NARRATIVE ADAPTATION
Messaging resonant across administrations
Multiple justifications (security, economic, values)
Tailored success metrics

Alliance-based stabilization provides external consistency through institutional mechanisms that extend beyond bilateral relationships, professional networks at working levels, mutual interests that create cooperation incentives, diversified engagement across sectors, and multilateral frameworks that offer continuity mechanisms.

Stakeholder Alignment fosters domestic consensus through private sector advocacy, defense establishment consistency, bipartisan expert agreement on core interests, sub-national cooperation that transcends federal politics, and broad public support for strategic objectives.

Strategic Narrative Adaptation ensures communication continuity by presenting core objectives in language resonating with different administrations, offering multiple justifications (security, economic, values-based), tailoring success metrics to align with administration priorities, linking initiatives to tangible domestic outcomes, and preparing crisis responses as policy catalysts.

This systematic approach emphasizes institutional mechanisms, legal structures, alliance relationships, stakeholder engagement, and adaptable narratives rather than personality-dependent strategies, providing a framework for maintaining strategic direction despite leadership volatility.

Character Dialogue: Career Officials Navigate Political Turbulence

In a secure conference room deep within the Pentagon, a group of seasoned national security officials gathers to discuss continuity of strategy as a new administration takes office. Their conversation reveals the practical challenges of maintaining direction amid political volatility.

Dr. Harrison (Career Intelligence Official): "So, here we are again. New administration, new priorities, new personalities—but the same fundamental challenge with China. The question is how we maintain strategic continuity on technology security when everything else seems to change every four years."

Ambassador Wilson (Career Diplomat): "It's going to be particularly challenging this time. The incoming team has already signaled skepticism toward alliances and multilateral approaches, which are central to our technology strategy."

General Reynolds (Military Officer): "Let's remember we've navigated transitions before. The key is identifying the core strategic interests that transcend partisan differences and framing our recommendations accordingly."

Dr. Harrison: "Agreed. Regardless of the language used, the underlying reality remains: China is pursuing a comprehensive strategy for technological dominance with significant security implications. That fact doesn't change because the occupant of the White House does."

Ms. Chen (Commerce Department Official): "The challenge is translating that reality into terms that resonate with the new team's worldview. They respond to economic and sovereignty arguments more than traditional security or values framing."

Ambassador Wilson: "Exactly. Instead of talking about 'alliance-based technology cooperation,' we might need to describe 'technology sovereignty protection through strategic partnerships.' Same policy, different language."

The Commander-in-Tweet's Envoy: *(entering abruptly)* "I need a policy win on China technology by next week! Something the President can tweet about. Maybe tariffs on semiconductor imports? That sounds tough!"

Historical Precedents for Strategic Continuity

Cold War (1947–1989)	Counterterrorism (2001–2021)	China Trade Policy (1990s–Present)	NASA Space (1958-present)
• National Security Council instrum-ents	• Statutory frameworks	• WTO framework	• Long term technical projects
• Professional diplomatic corps	• Specialized institutions	• Bureaucratic expertise	• Specialized workforce
• NATO alliance structure	• Intelligence community apparatus	• Business community influence	• International collaboration
• Consistent messaging	• International partnerships	• Congressional partnerships	• Bipartisan support
		• Analysis of practices	• Security justification

General Reynolds: *(calmly)* "We have several options prepared that would demonstrate immediate action while supporting our longer-term strategy. Perhaps a targeted export control action on advanced AI chips is warranted. It's concrete, immediate, and substantively meaningful."

The Commander-in-Tweet's Envoy: "Will it make headlines?"

Ms. Chen: "Absolutely. 'President Takes Historic Action to Protect American AI Technology from China.' And it actually advances our security interests rather than just generating headlines."

The Commander-in-Tweet's Envoy: "Fine, draw that up. But nothing about 'alliances' or 'multilateral cooperation'—the President wants America First approaches only!"

The envoy exits as quickly as he arrived.

Dr. Harrison: *(after a pause)* "And that's what we're dealing with."

Ambassador Wilson: "Notice what just happened, though. We channeled the political desire for visible action into a substantive policy that actually serves our strategic objectives. That's the art of maintaining continuity through transitions."

General Reynolds: "We need to systematize that approach. For each core element of our technology security strategy, we should prepare multiple framings that appeal to different political perspectives while preserving the substantive policy."

Ms. Chen: "And we need to institutionalize as much as possible. Get key policies embedded in legislation, regulatory frameworks, international agreements—structures that create friction against arbitrary changes."

Dr. Harrison: "Don't forget the private sector. Companies have their own interest in predictable policy, especially on technology issues. They can be powerful advocates for continuity."

Ambassador Wilson: "Our international counterparts understand this dynamic. Most have developed the ability to work with whichever administration is in office while maintaining focus on their core interests. We need that same discipline."

General Reynolds: "Bottom line: The China challenge transcends our political cycles. We can adapt language, adjust emphasis, highlight different aspects of policies—but we cannot afford strategic whiplash every four years if we want to compete long-term effectively."

Ms. Chen: "It's like sailing against a strong current. We may tack left or right depending on the political winds, but we need to maintain forward progress toward the same destination regardless of who's formally at the helm."

NATIONAL SECURITY

IN THE ERA OF POLITICAL ADHD

SATIRICAL HANDBOOK

STRATEGIC ADAPTATION TECHNIQUES

Re-label programs in political lingo

- Submerge work & resurface re-branded
- Hide priorities in shifting initiatives

INSTITUTIONAL FORTIFICATION

Empower career staff

Anchor policies in hard-to-reverse regs

Build bipartisan nat-sec backing

EXTERNAL ANCHORS

Private-sector buy-in

Lock policies into intl. frameworks

Cultivate think-lank consensus

POLITICAL TRANSLATION

Tailor messages (security, econ, values)

"America First" &'Global' versions

Jobs pitch vs alliance pitch

KEEP CALM, RENAME OFTEN.

Dr. Harrison: "Well said. Our job is to provide continuity of purpose through discontinuity of politics. It's not about defying political leadership—it's about serving the nation's enduring interests while respecting the democratic process."

Ambassador Wilson: "Exactly. Different administrations, same country—and same strategic challenge. Let's get to work translating our core strategy into the language this new team will embrace."

Historical Precedents for Strategic Continuity

American history reveals that institutional mechanisms can maintain strategic continuity despite political transitions—a crucial lesson for managing technology competition with China through political volatility.

During the Cold War (1947-1989), America's containment strategy endured across nine presidential administrations from both parties. While Nixon pursued détente and Reagan preferred military buildup, the fundamental approach remained consistent, enabled by the National Security Council's institutionalization, bipartisan congressional consensus, professional diplomatic services, NATO's alliance structure, and consistent messaging about Soviet threats.

Similarly, counterterrorism policies (2001-2021) showed remarkable continuity from Bush through Obama to Trump, sustained by statutory frameworks, specialized institutions, intelligence community consistency, international partnerships, bipartisan oversight, and shared threat perception.

China's trade policy evolution since the 1990s demonstrates that even while specific tactics varied dramatically between administrations, the broader approach of economic engagement, paired with security concerns, has shown surprising continuity. The WTO framework, bureaucratic expertise, business community influence, congressional involvement, and professional analysis of China's economic practices have all contributed to this stability.

NASA's space program (1958-present) has maintained core capabilities despite dramatic shifts in political direction and budget constraints through long-term technical projects, a professional specialized workforce, international partnerships, physical infrastructure requirements, bipartisan public support, and security justifications that resonate across party lines.

These examples demonstrate that strategic continuity amid political volatility is achievable through thoughtful institutional design, stakeholder alignment, international commitments, professional expertise, and adaptable framing of core policies.

Case Studies of Strategic Continuity

Despite administration changes, America's national security priorities have shown remarkable persistence through effective institutional mechanisms.

The Indo-Pacific strategy maintained roughly 80% consistency from Trump to Biden, preserving the strategic focus on China, the "free and open Indo-Pacific" concept, strengthened Quad partnerships, enhanced military presence, economic alternatives to China's BRI, and technology security cooperation. This continuity was enabled by professional military leadership, career diplomats, congressional consensus, proactive allies, consistent think tank analysis, and persistent intelligence assessments. The primary changes were in style and a shift to a multilateral approach, rather than a fundamental direction.

Semiconductor security initiatives maintained consistent strategic elements across the Obama, Trump, and Biden administrations, including recognition of semiconductors as a critical technology, concerns about supply chain vulnerability, a push for domestic manufacturing, export controls on sensitive technology to China, investment in next-generation research, and engagement with allies. This persistence was facilitated by the Defense Department's risk identification, intelligence assessments, industry advocacy, bipartisan legislation, the technical complexity that limited rapid changes, and international cooperation frameworks. While emphasis and implementation varied, the core approach remained steady from Obama's initial concerns through Trump's restrictions to Biden's CHIPS Act.

AI security initiatives likewise showed remarkable continuity across three administrations. Key maintained elements included recognizing AI as transformative with significant security implications, concerns about China's national AI strategy, a focus on U.S. leadership, an emphasis on AI ethics, public-private partnerships, and continued research investment through DARPA. This consistency was enabled by intelligence community consensus, the defense establishment's recognition of AI's importance, the technical complexity that limited political interference, bipartisan congressional support, industry advocacy, and international coordination on AI standards. From Obama's initial AI Research and Development Strategic Plan through Trump's American AI Initiative to Biden's expanded strategy, approximately 75% of the fundamental approach has persisted: maintaining American leadership, countering China, and embedding democratic values in AI development.

The Psychological Ballet: Duty vs. Loyalty

Career national security officials navigate a profound psychological tightrope during political transitions, especially turbulent ones. This balancing act manifests in several dimensions:

When facing cognitive dissonance between political directives and professional judgment, officials develop adaptive mechanisms, including compartmentalizing political directives from implementation, reframing priorities in politically acceptable language, focusing selectively on areas of alignment, separating their professional from their political identity, and viewing tensions as temporary. These mechanisms maintain functionality but create significant internal stress.

Officials develop layered identities that balance institutional loyalty, professional standards, policy convictions, political responsiveness, and national allegiance. When these layers conflict—particularly when political directions contradict professional standards—officials may experience "moral injury" from implementing policies they believe harm national interests.

To navigate ethical dilemmas, officials employ various frameworks, including consequentialist calculations of national security outcomes, deontological boundaries they won't cross, virtue ethics based on professional integrity, social contract theory that balances democratic legitimacy with constitutional duties, and harm reduction pragmatism to minimize the negative impacts of problematic policies.

Research reveals adaptive patterns during periods of political volatility: strategic patience to weather turbulence while maintaining core functions, procedural buffering through administrative processes to moderate impulsive directives, coalition building across government to protect priorities, leveraging technical complexity to shape decisions, and external reinforcement from stakeholders that supports continuity.

America's national security ultimately relies not just on formal institutions, but on thousands of individuals navigating this complex psychological terrain, finding pathways that honor democratic principles while preserving enduring security interests, reality served in a rhetoric sandwich.

Satirical vignette: A senior intelligence official sits in her office, staring at her computer screen. On one tab is an intelligence assessment about China's AI capabilities based on years of analysis. On another is a tweet from The Commander-in-Tweet declaring, "AI is EASY! We're WINNING BIGLY! China is BEHIND!"

She sighs deeply, then begins drafting a briefing document titled "America's Tremendous AI Advantage and How We'll Keep Winning" that somehow manages to incorporate all the actual concerns from the intelligence assessment while framing them in language the President will accept.

"Cognitive dissonance management in action," she mutters to herself. "Today's special: reality, served in a rhetoric sandwich."

Satirical Handbook: "National Security in the Era of Political ADHD"

NATIONAL SECURITY IN THE ERA OF POLITICAL ADHD

The Survival Guide: Strategic Continuity in Political Storms

This satirical yet practical handbook outlines approaches for maintaining strategic consistency amid political volatility, particularly in the U.S.-China tech competition.

Strategic Adaptation Techniques:

★ **Linguistic Chameleon**: Rename existing programs to match current political terminology while maintaining substance

★ **Policy Submarine**: Continue critical work at operational levels during political storms, resurface with repackaged updates

★ **Strategic Initiative Shell Game**: Preserve core priorities within constantly renamed structures

Institutional Fortification:

★ **Democracy-Proof Bunker**: Embed critical functions in career-led units with operational autonomy

★ **Regulatory Deep Roots**: Anchor priorities in detailed regulations requiring formal processes to change

★ **Congressional Shield Wall**: Cultivate bipartisan support through national security framing

External Anchors:

★ **Industrial Complex**: Engage the private sector in long-term commitments across key districts

★ **Allied Entanglement**: Embed programs in international frameworks requiring formal withdrawal

★ **Expert Consensus**: Cultivate broad analytical agreement across think tanks and security experts

Political Translation:

★ **Universal Translator**: Develop multiple justifications (security, economic, and values) for the same policy

★ **Strategic Wardrobe**: Maintain "America First" and "Global Leadership" versions of identical policies

★ **Stakeholder-Specific Pitches**: Emphasize job creation for nationalists, alliance benefits for traditionalists

The implementation strategy requires framing national security priorities differently for diverse audiences:

★ Security framing for traditional conservatives (military superiority)

★ Economic security for nationalists (manufacturing strength)

★ Innovation leadership for tech advocates (research investment)

★ Democratic values for idealistic internationalists (authoritarian competition)

The goal isn't to circumvent political differences, but to advance consistent priorities through language that resonates across America's divided landscape. Strategic continuity requires the institutional equivalent of multiple personality disorder: maintaining coherent direction while speaking constantly changing political dialects.

CHAPTER TRANSITION: FROM SECURITY STRATEGY TO ECONOMIC FOUNDATIONS

As our examination of America's national security and resilience strategy comes to a close, we turn to the economic foundations upon which security ultimately depends. The technology competition with China isn't merely a contest of military capabilities or innovation systems—it's a fundamental test of whether a democratic market economy can match the coordinated power of authoritarian state capitalism.

The security strategies outlined in this chapter—from rebuilding the Arsenal of Democracy to enhancing national resilience, from mobilizing innovation to securing supply chains, from protecting digital infrastructure to strengthening alliances—all require robust economic foundations. Without prosperity widely shared across American society, the resources for these initiatives will be lacking, and the social cohesion needed for sustained competition will erode.

Satirical transition vignette: FDR's ghost stands at the door of the Pentagon conference room, preparing to depart after witnessing America's security planning process. He turns to the assembled officials once more.

FDR's Ghost: "Your technological challenges are indeed formidable, but remember this: I didn't defeat fascism just through military strategy or industrial mobilization. The New Deal that preceded that mobilization—addressing economic inequality, rebuilding infrastructure, and restoring faith in institutions—created the social foundation that made victory possible. Your technology competition with China will ultimately be decided not just by who builds better algorithms, but by who builds a better society."

He begins to fade from view.

FDR's Ghost: "The greatest security strategy is one that makes citizens believe their system is worth defending. Everything else is just details."

With that, he vanishes, leaving behind only the faint scent of cigarette smoke and the echo of a challenge that transcends generations: To secure America's future, we must first ensure it delivers on America's promise.

In our next chapter, we turn to precisely this challenge: rebuilding the economic foundations necessary for national security and democratic vitality in an era of transformative technological change and fierce authoritarian competition.

TL;DR – America's national security strategy for competing with China requires a "Rooseveltian Doctrine of Renewal" that combines technological mobilization, supply chain resilience, critical infrastructure protection, and alliance coordination—all implemented through institutional mechanisms designed to maintain strategic continuity despite political volatility.

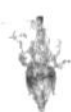

CHAPTER 6: AMERICA'S 21ST-CENTURY NEW DEAL: REBUILDING FOUNDATIONS IN THE CHINESE CENTURY

"The line between disorder and order lies in logistics."
—Sun Tzu, The Art of War, Chapter 5

EXECUTIVE BRIEFING

1. Strategic Snapshot

- ★ **Great-Power Infrastructure Gap.** China invests 6-9% of its GDP in ports, rails, and digital arteries; the US hovers near 2%. Infrastructure is now the ante to sit at the strategic poker table.
- ★ **National-Security Potholes.** If a high-speed Chinese train can photobomb your Main Street, you don't have a road problem—you have a deterrence problem.
- ★ **Digital Divide ≈ Economic Redline.** Twenty-four million Americans remain offline, trapping entire counties in a dial-up ditch.

2. Core Findings ("What Keeps Eleanor Up at Night")

Domain	Diagnosis	Competitive Delta	Stakes
Hard Infrastructure	Bridges & grid earn **D+**	China/EU build 3-5× faster	Logistics drag, brittle supply chains
Digital Infrastructure	24 M offline	Korea & China ≈ universal gigabit	AI-era exclusion, rural brain-drain
Human Infrastructure	Patchy retraining	Germany: universal apprenticeships	Workforce mismatch, social fracturing
Permitting & Finance	12-year approvals; stop-start budgets	Global peers: 3-year single-window	Shovel-ready ⇒ shovel-rotted

3. Risk Register

1. **Strategic Erosion:** 0.3 pp annual GDP lost to logistics friction.
2. **Political Gridlock:** Photo-op bipartisanship, pay-for partisanship.
3. **Equity Chasm:** Offline counties slip into perpetual poverty.
4. **Climate Cost Spiral:** $1 deferred today equals $6 in disaster spending tomorrow.

4. Recommendations – The Five-Point Build-Back-Better-For-Real Plan

1. **$100 B National Infrastructure Bank** → leverages $1 T via bonds, PPPs, green/value-capture instruments.
2. **Universal Broadband by 2030** – 100/20 Mbps floor, affordability credit, "fiber-first" plus 5G/6G firewall.
3. **Launch the *Five Big Builds*** – HSR corridors, smart grid + storage, climate-proof water, EV super-charging, next-gen ports.
4. **Human Infrastructure 2.0** – portable Opportunity Accounts, modern apprenticeships, childcare/healthcare wraparound.
5. **Permitting Sprint ("One Federal Decision")** – two-year shot-clock, concurrent reviews, 180-day litigation limit.

5. Quick Wins (24 Months)

- ★ Rehabilitate top 500 fracture-critical bridges—televised ribbon-cutting fodder.
- ★ Light up 10 M rural homes via BEAD fast-tracks.
- ★ Convert three retired coal plants into modular-nuke or battery hubs.
- ★ Pilot mileage-based Highway Trust Fund in three states.

6. Scoreboard Targets

KPI	2025 Baseline	2035 Goal
ASCE National Grade	D+	B
≥100/20 Mbps Coverage	80 % HH	100 %
Avg Federal Approval Time	7 yrs	≤2 yrs
Infra-Investment Share	2 % GDP	≥5 %

7. Political Flight Plan

Frame the package three ways: *jobs and security (right), climate and justice (left), and productivity and growth* (business). Pair labor with Wall Street via green bonds; tempt rural caucuses with broadband first.

8. CEO-Level Call-to-Action

Declare the end of Groundhog Day "Infrastructure Week." Capitalize the bank, wire the nation, retrain the workforce—then let Eleanor's clipboard collect dust in the Smithsonian's *Hall of Solved Problems.*

OPENING TABLEAU: ELEANOR ROOSEVELT'S INFRASTRUCTURE VISION

Picture this scene, dear reader: Eleanor Roosevelt—resurrected from her eternal rest to save America's crumbling foundations—tours a decrepit neighborhood in Middle America, clutching a clipboard labeled "21st Century New Deal" with the determined expression of someone who survived both the Great Depression and Franklin's affairs.

She interviews residents about their infrastructure needs: "When was the last time you had reliable internet?" she asks a frustrated father whose children sit in the family car outside a McDonald's, desperately trying to upload homework assignments through the restaurant's spotty Wi-Fi. "Two presidents ago," he replies with a hollow laugh.

Across the street, a water main erupts for the third time this month, sending a geyser of rusty liquid skyward with the predictable regularity of Old Faithful, except considerably less tourist-friendly. Meanwhile, the local bridge sports more structural warnings than a pharmaceutical commercial lists side effects.

As Eleanor makes notes on her clipboard, a Chinese high-speed train whisks by on a gleaming elevated track in the background—a cinematic intrusion of modernity into this tableau of American decay. The 350 km/h bullet train passes so quickly it barely registers, like prosperity in a declining factory town.

Local officials huddle nearby, engaged in America's favorite infrastructure pastime: arguing about who should pay for fixing things while ensuring nothing actually gets fixed. "It's a federal responsibility!" "No, it's clearly a state issue!" "The private sector should handle it!" They exchange blame with the practiced choreography of a ritual that has been performed for decades, oblivious to the fact that the neighborhood continues to crumble around them, regardless of whose budget line it falls under.

Eleanor shakes her head in disappointment, occasionally glancing at the Chinese train with a mixture of admiration and determination. She's seen this movie before—a nation at a crossroads, choosing between bold rebuilding and managed decline. The last time, America decided to build. This time? The clipboard awaits her recommendations, but the path forward requires navigating a political landscape that would make the original New Deal look like a simple game of checkers.

1. INFRASTRUCTURE AS STRATEGIC FOUNDATION: BEYOND "INFRASTRUCTURE WEEK"

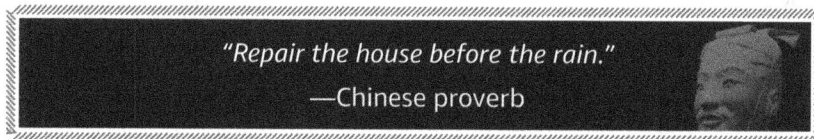

> *"Repair the house before the rain."*
> —Chinese proverb

Analytical Framework: Infrastructure's Competitive Necessity

"Infrastructure," Eleanor Roosevelt notes in her precise handwriting, "is not merely concrete and steel—it is the physical manifestation of a nation's ambitions, capabilities, and foresight." She underlines the final word three times, a pointed critique of America's notorious infrastructure myopia.

Throughout history, national power has been inextricably linked to the prowess of infrastructure. The Roman Empire's roads facilitated military dominance and commercial integration. Britain's naval infrastructure enabled colonial expansion. America's own rise to superpower status rode on transcontinental railroads, the Interstate Highway System, and telecommunications networks that stitched together a continental nation.

Today, in the high-stakes poker game of geopolitical competition, infrastructure represents the table stakes—the minimum ante required to even play in the global economy. Yet America has been acting like a trust fund kid who refuses to maintain the family estate, watching in bewilderment as the roof leaks and the foundation cracks while complaining about the cost of repairs.

Character Dialogue: Eleanor's Infrastructure Interviews

Eleanor Roosevelt sits in a makeshift office in an abandoned factory, methodically interviewing infrastructure experts about America's D+ infrastructure grade.

Eleanor Roosevelt: "So, Dr. Bridges, you're saying America's infrastructure is objectively... subpar?"

Dr. Bridges: "Madam Roosevelt, if America's infrastructure were a student, it would be on academic probation and in danger of losing its scholarship. The American Society of Civil Engineers gives us a D+ overall, with individual components ranging from 'barely adequate' to 'pray when you cross that bridge. '"

Eleanor Roosevelt: "And how does this compare to our global competitors?"

Dr. Bridges: "While we debate whether infrastructure spending is 'socialism,' China has built enough high-speed rail to circle the Earth. Germany's highways make ours look like medieval cart paths. Even developing nations are leapfrogging us in broadband deployment."

General Gridlock: *interrupting* "But we can't just build things, Mrs. Roosevelt! There are procedures! Environmental reviews! Stakeholder consultations! Impact assessments! Fifteen different agencies need to sign off, each with veto power!"

Eleanor Roosevelt: *adjusting her glasses,* "I recall we built the Pentagon in 16 months during wartime while simultaneously fighting fascism on two continents. Have our abilities diminished, or merely our resolve?"

McSlicey the Priest of Profit: *appearing suddenly in an expensive suit.* "Have you considered a public-private partnership with minimal public investment but maximum private return? I have a PowerPoint presentation with very compelling ROI projections."

Eleanor Roosevelt: sighs, "I remember when 'return on investment' meant jobs, productivity, and national capability—not quarterly shareholder dividends."

Comparative Analysis: US vs. China Infrastructure Investment

While America debates whether infrastructure spending is "fiscally responsible," China has embarked on what might be the largest infrastructure program in human history. The contrast is stark: infrastructure investment as a percentage of GDP in China has consistently ranged from 6% to 9% over the past two decades, while the U.S. has hovered around an anemic 1.5% to 2.5%.

This investment gap creates compounding advantages for China's economic competitiveness. Better infrastructure leads to lower logistics costs, faster information transmission, more reliable energy, and increased overall productivity. These foundations enable everything from advanced manufacturing to the development of artificial intelligence.

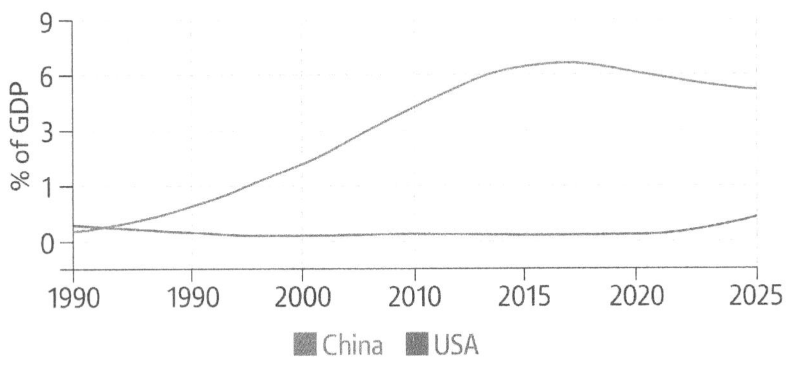

Infrastructure Investment as % of GDP (1900–2025)

Satirical Advertisement: "Making Infrastructure Great Again"

[A polished television commercial appears, featuring dramatic music and sweeping aerial shots of gleaming highways, bridges, and airports that are clearly European or Asian, not American.]

Announcer's Voice (Heroically Deep): "MAKING INFRASTRUCTURE GREAT AGAIN – THIS TIME FOR REAL (WE PROMISE)"

[Shot of a president (face conveniently obscured) donning a hard hat while pointing at blueprints]

Announcer: "Introducing the groundbreaking concept of... actually fixing things! After 37 consecutive 'Infrastructure Weeks' that produced nothing but tweets, we're proud to announce a bold new approach: allocating money and building stuff!"

[Montage of potholes being filled, bridges being reinforced, trains running on time]

Small Text Disclaimer (Scrolling Rapidly): *"Actual implementation may vary. The infrastructure shown is from Germany. Promise of completion subject to congressional approval, environmental reviews, NIMBY lawsuits, budget reconciliation, filibuster rules, midterm elections, and whether Mars is in retrograde. May cause increased taxes, which we promise not to mention. If infrastructure lasts more than 50 years without maintenance, that's a miracle, not a design feature."*

Announcer: "MAKING INFRASTRUCTURE GREAT AGAIN – Because at this point, even mediocre would be an improvement!"

[Final shot of American flag waving as a pothole swallows a family sedan in the foreground]

Policy Proposal: National Infrastructure Bank

Eleanor Roosevelt's clipboard contains detailed notes for a National Infrastructure Bank—an independent entity capable of leveraging public capital to attract private investment in critical infrastructure. The model draws inspiration from similar institutions in Europe and Asia that have successfully bridged the gap between public needs and private capital.

The bank would be capitalized with $100 billion in federal funds, with the capacity to leverage this into $1 trillion of infrastructure investment through bond issuances and public-private partnerships. Projects would be selected based on rigorous cost-benefit analysis, economic impact assessments, and strategic importance—not political calculations or pork-barrel politics.

Key design features include:

- ★ Independent governance with bipartisan board appointments serving staggered terms
- ★ Transparent project selection criteria prioritizing economic return, critical needs, and strategic priorities
- ★ Dedicated revenue streams through user fees, value capture mechanisms, and targeted taxes
- ★ Technical assistance for state and local governments to develop bankable projects
- ★ Tailored financial instruments to match project needs with appropriate capital sources

"The infrastructure bank," Eleanor notes, "addresses America's fiscal schizophrenia by providing predictable, sustained funding outside the annual appropriations chaos. It creates a virtuous cycle where successful projects generate returns that fund future investments."

POLICY PROPOSAL: NATIONAL INFRASTRUCTUREBANK

leveraged in investment via bonds & public-private partnerships

KEY FEATURES

INDEPENDENT GOVERNANCE
bipartisan board, staggered terms

TRANSPARENT SELECTION
based on return, needs & priorities

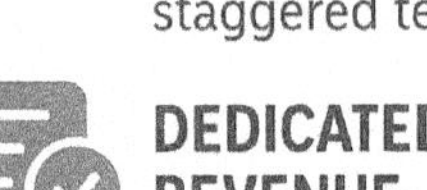

DEDICATED REVENUE
user fees, value capture, targeted taxes

TAILORED FINANCING
matching projects to capital sources

KEEP CALM, RENAME OFTEN

McSlicey the Priest of Profit reviews the plan with a mixture of interest and suspicion: "I see opportunity for private profit, which I approve of, but also public benefit, which makes me uncomfortable. Can we adjust the balance?"

2. DIGITAL INFRASTRUCTURE: THE NEW ELECTRICITY COMES TO TOWN

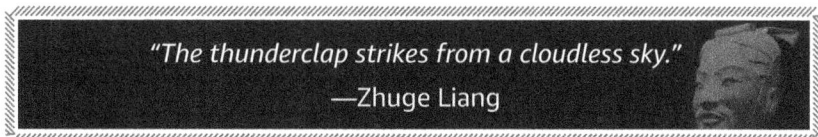

> *"The thunderclap strikes from a cloudless sky."*
> —Zhuge Liang

Historical Parallel: Rural Electrification 2.0

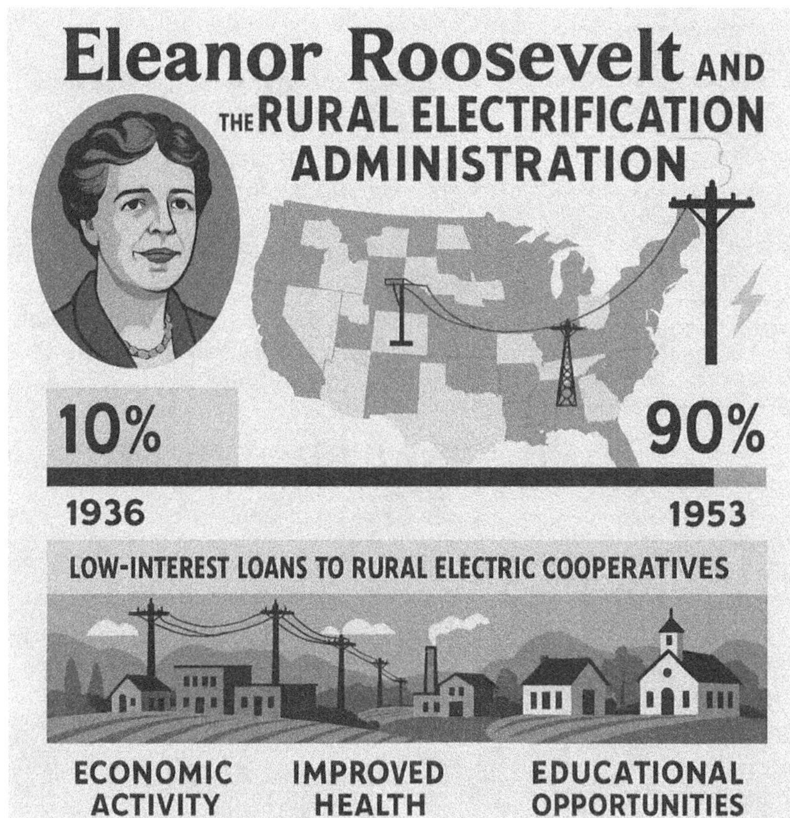

Eleanor Roosevelt has seen this movie before. In the 1930s, when her husband launched the Rural Electrification Administration (REA), private utility companies insisted that bringing electricity to America's farms and small towns was economically unfeasible. The market had spoken: rural Americans simply weren't worth connecting to the modern economy.

The REA proved them spectacularly wrong. By providing low-interest loans to rural electric cooperatives, the program transformed American life. The percentage of rural homes with electricity rose from 10% in 1936 to nearly 90% by 1953. Each connection sparked economic activity, improved health outcomes, and enhanced educational opportunities.

Today's broadband challenge presents a striking parallel. Just as electricity was the transformational infrastructure of the early 20th century, broadband internet has become the essential utility of the 21st century. Yet approximately 24 million Americans lack access to high-speed connectivity, predominantly in rural and tribal areas.

Character Vignette: Eleanor's Digital Village Tour

Eleanor Roosevelt walks through a rural community center in Appalachia, a tablet computer in hand instead of her usual clipboard. She stops to demonstrate a telehealth application to a group of elderly residents.

Eleanor Roosevelt: "You see, Mrs. Jenkins, with this connection, you wouldn't need to drive 87 miles to see a cardiologist. The doctor can monitor your heart condition remotely, and you can have regular video consultations."

Mrs. Jenkins (85): "You mean I wouldn't have to get my son to take a day off work just to drive me to Charleston every month?"

Eleanor Roosevelt: "Precisely. And Mr. Davis, your grandchildren in California could see and talk with you every day, not just on holidays."

Mr. Davis (78): *eyes welling up* "You mean I could actually see my great-granddaughter grow up?"

Eleanor demonstrates other applications: online courses for the local community college, agricultural monitoring systems for farmers, and remote work possibilities that could keep young people from leaving town.

Milton the Trickster Economist: *appearing suddenly,* "But Mrs. Roosevelt, the market has determined these connections aren't profitable! If these people wanted the internet, they should have chosen to be born in wealthy suburban enclaves!"

Eleanor Roosevelt: *fixing him with a stern gaze.* "The market also determined these people didn't deserve electricity until we proved otherwise. Some infrastructure is too important to be dictated solely by quarterly profits. Digital connectivity is the lifeline of modern existence—a prerequisite for economic participation, education, healthcare, and civic engagement."

Rusty Broadband: *a disheveled figure with tangled copper wires for hair.* "But... but... It's really hard to string fiber-optic cable through mountains! And these people might only use it for Netflix and Facebook!"

Eleanor Roosevelt: "We didn't electrify rural America because farmers needed electric can openers. We did it because access to fundamental infrastructure creates possibilities we can't even imagine beforehand."

Case Studies: Global Digital Infrastructure Models

Eleanor's clipboard contains detailed notes on digital infrastructure models from around the world:

South Korea: Achieved 98% broadband penetration through aggressive government investment, public-private partnerships, and a national culture that prioritizes connectivity. Average speeds exceed 100 Mbps nationwide, with gigabit connections increasingly common.

European Union: The "Digital Agenda for Europe" set ambitious connectivity targets and backs them with substantial funding through the Connecting Europe Facility. The regulatory framework treats broadband as an essential utility with universal service obligations.

Chinese Digital Village Initiative: China has connected 98% of administrative villages to broadband, combining state investment with aggressive deployment targets for telecom providers. The program integrates digital connectivity with e-commerce platforms, enabling rural producers to access urban markets more easily.

Eleanor notes the irony: "While America pioneered the internet, we've allowed ideological rigidity to prevent us from ensuring universal access. Meanwhile, both market economies like South Korea and state-directed systems like China have achieved near-universal connectivity through pragmatic approaches that acknowledge digital infrastructure as a national priority, not a luxury."

CASE STUDIES: GLOBAL DIGITAL INFRASTRUCTURE MODELS

SOUTH KOREA

Achieved 98% broadband penetration through aggressive government investment, public-private partnerships, and a national culture that prioritizes connectivity. Average speeds exceed 100 Mbps nationwide, with gigabit connections increasingly common.

EUROPEAN UNION

The "Digital Agenda for Europe" set ambitious connectivity targets and backs them with substantial funding through the Connecting Europe Facility. The regulatory framework treats broadband as an essential utility with universal service obligations.

CHINESE DIGITAL VILLAGE

China has connected 98% of administrative villages to broadband, combining state investment with aggressive deployment targets for telecom providers. The program integrates digital connectivity with e-commerce platforms, enabling rural producers to access urban markets.

Policy Proposal: Universal Broadband Strategy

Eleanor's 21st Century Digital New Deal draws inspiration from the original REA but adapts to modern technology and market structures:

Core Elements:

1. **Upgraded Definition:** Redefine "high-speed broadband" to at least 100 Mbps download/20 Mbps upload (future-proofed standard)

UNIVERSAL BROADBAND STRATEGY

UPGRADED DEFINITION

UPGRADED DEFINITION

Redefine "high-speed broadband" to at least 100 Mbps download / 20 Mbps upload

UNIVERSAL ACCESS FUND

UNIVERSAL ACCESS FUND

$100 billion investment program combining subsidies, tax incentives, loans, and grants

AFFORDABILITY MEASURES

AFFORDABILITY MEASURES

Permanent benefit for low-income households, Price transparency requirements & community-owned networks

SECURE 56/6 DEVELOPMENT

SECURE 5G/6G DEVELOPMENT

R&D funding for secure, open-source networks Supply chain security

IMPLEMENTATION MECHANISMS

IMPLEMENTATION MECHANISMS

Expansion of BEAD program State-federal coordination & accurate mapping

2. **Universal Access Fund:** $100 billion investment program combining direct subsidies, tax incentives, low-interest loans, and grants to:
- ★ Deploy fiber and advanced wireless in unserved/underserved areas
- ★ Upgrade aging infrastructure in low-income urban communities
- ★ Connect anchor institutions (schools, libraries, healthcare facilities)
3. **Affordability Measures:**
- ★ Permanent broadband benefit for low-income households
- ★ Price transparency requirements
- ★ Community-owned network options
4. **Digital Inclusion:**
- ★ Digital literacy programs
- ★ Device access initiatives
- ★ Multilingual training and support
5. **Secure 5G/6G Development:**
- ★ R&D funding for secure, open-source network technologies
- ★ Supply chain security requirements
- ★ Trusted vendor certification program
6. **Implementation Mechanisms:**
- ★ BEAD (Broadband Equity, Access and Deployment) program expansion
- ★ Enhanced state-federal coordination
- ★ Accurate mapping and accountability measures

"The broadband infrastructure challenge," Eleanor notes, "isn't primarily technological—it's political and organizational. We have the technical capability to connect everyone; what we've lacked is the will to make it happen."

3. THE FIVE BIG BUILDS: CONCRETE STRATEGY FOR THE 21ST CENTURY

> *"Build high walls, store abundant grain, and bide your time."*
> —Emperor Zhu Yuanzhang

Analytical Framework: Priority Infrastructure for National Competitiveness

Eleanor Roosevelt introduces a new member to her infrastructure assessment team: Master Builder Maria, a no-nonsense civil engineer with decades of experience planning and executing major infrastructure projects worldwide. Maria has little patience for political grandstanding or ideological posturing—she cares about getting things built on time, on budget, and to specification.

"America doesn't need more vague infrastructure promises," Maria explains, spreading detailed blueprints across Eleanor's table. "It needs a concrete strategy—literally and figuratively—focused on the highest-impact projects that will deliver maximum returns on investment."

Maria's analytical framework identifies five infrastructure pillars essential for 21st-century competitiveness, each requiring targeted investment and regulatory reform.

Character Development: Master Builder Maria's Infrastructure Masterplan

Master Builder Maria stands before a wall of blueprints, a laser pointer in hand, while Eleanor Roosevelt takes notes. Various stakeholders—mayors, governors, business leaders, labor representatives—sit in folding chairs, some attentive, others skeptical.

Master Builder Maria: "The five big builds represent America's infrastructure priorities for the next two decades. Each addresses critical needs, enhances competitiveness, and creates sustainable jobs."

She points to the transportation section.

Maria: "First, transportation: We need high-speed rail corridors connecting major population centers, modernized ports capable of handling larger vessels and increased volume, and a comprehensive EV charging network to support the transition to electric vehicles."

Skeptical Governor: "But high-speed rail is so expensive! Look at California's budget overruns!"

Maria: *witheringly,* "So is building and maintaining 8-lane highways that will be congested the day they open. And yes, California's HSR has faced challenges—largely because we lack institutional experience in building such systems, while our competitors have been refining them for decades. The first transcontinental railroad wasn't cheap or easy either, but it transformed the nation."

She moves to the energy section.

Maria: "Next, energy infrastructure: Smart grid development to improve reliability and efficiency, renewable integration with storage capacity, and nuclear modernization to provide zero-carbon baseload power."

Coal State Senator: "But what about fossil fuel jobs in my state?"

Maria: "The grid upgrades alone will create more jobs than the entire coal industry currently employs. I've also included transition programs specifically designed for affected communities. Would you rather have temporary protection or permanent prosperity?"

She continues methodically through water, public facilities, and climate resilience sectors, addressing objections with data and practical solutions.

Eleanor Roosevelt: *After the presentation,* "Maria, these plans are comprehensive, but how do we prioritize given political and budget constraints?"

Maria: "We start with no-regrets projects that deliver immediate benefits while building momentum: upgrading the most dangerous bridges, implementing smart traffic management systems, and hardening vulnerable grid segments. Quick wins create public support for larger initiatives. Meanwhile, we reform the approval process so subsequent projects can proceed efficiently."

Milton the Trickster Economist: *whispering to a Wall Street banker,* "Where's the private profit opportunity in all this public investment?"

Maria: *Overhearing, "These systems will create reduced logistics costs, enhanced productivity, new market opportunities, and competitive advantage.* The question isn't whether we can afford to build this infrastructure—it's whether we can afford not to."

ECONOMIC IMPACT ASSESSMENT:
INFRASTRUCTURE MULTIPLIER EFFECTS

JOB CREATION

The five big builds would generate approximately 15 million direct, indirect, and induced jobs over a decade.

PRODUCTIVITY ENHANCEMENT

Modern infrastructure reduces logistics costs, energy waste, and transaction friction, enhancing overall economic productivity by an estimated 0,3%mually.

COMPETITIVENESS IMPROVEMENTS

Strategic infrastructure investments would improve America's global competitiveness rankings, particularly in areas where the U.S. has fallen behind.

RESILIENCE DIVIDENDS

Climate-resilient infrastructure significantly reduces economic losses from disasters. with studies suggesting every $1 invested in resilience saves $6 in disaster recovery costs.

INNOVATION CATALYSTS

Advanced infrastructure creates platforms for next-generation technologies and business models

Economic Impact Assessment: Infrastructure Multiplier Effects

Master Builder Maria's infrastructure program isn't just about concrete and steel—it's an economic engine designed to generate multiple returns on investment:

Job Creation: The five big builds would generate approximately 15 million direct, indirect, and induced jobs over a decade, ranging from construction work to high-skilled technical positions.

Productivity Enhancement: Modern infrastructure reduces logistics costs, energy waste, and transaction friction, thereby enhancing overall economic productivity by an estimated 0.3% annually—resulting in approximately $80 billion in additional GDP each year.

Competitiveness Improvements: Strategic infrastructure investments would improve Amer-

ica's global competitiveness rankings, particularly in transportation, energy security, and digital connectivity—areas where the U.S. has fallen behind global leaders.

Resilience Dividends: Climate-resilient infrastructure significantly reduces economic losses from disasters, with studies suggesting every $1 invested in resilience saves $6 in disaster recovery costs.

Innovation Catalysts: Advanced infrastructure creates platforms for next-generation technologies and business models, from smart cities to autonomous logistics systems to distributed energy markets.

4. HUMAN INFRASTRUCTURE: THE OVERLOOKED INVESTMENT

> *"The people are the foundation of the state."*
> —Mencius

Analytical Framework: Human Capital in the AI Economy

ANALYTICAL FRAMEWORK: HUMAN INFRASTRUCTURE

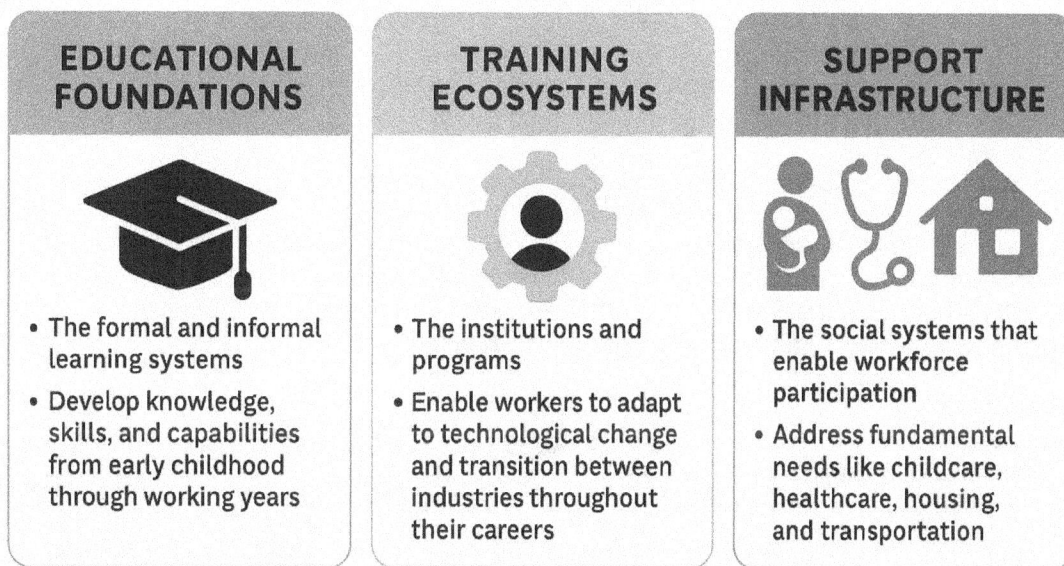

EDUCATIONAL FOUNDATIONS	TRAINING ECOSYSTEMS	SUPPORT INFRASTRUCTURE

• The formal and informal learning systems • Develop knowledge, skills, and capabilities from early childhood through working years	• The institutions and programs • Enable workers to adapt to technological change and transition between industries throughout their careers	• The social systems that enable workforce participation • Address fundamental needs like childcare, healthcare, housing, and transportation

Eleanor Roosevelt's infrastructure assessment now expands beyond physical systems to encompass what economists call "human infrastructure"—the education, training, and social support structures that enable workforce productivity and social mobility.

"The finest highways and fastest internet connections mean little," Eleanor notes, "if people lack the skills to utilize them effectively or are too burdened by life's basic challenges to participate in the economy."

This analytical framework recognizes three critical dimensions of human infrastructure:

1. **Educational Foundations:** The formal and informal learning systems that develop knowledge, skills, and capabilities from early childhood through working years
2. **Training Ecosystems:** The institutions and programs that enable workers to adapt to technological change and transition between industries throughout their careers
3. **Support Infrastructure:** The social systems that enable workforce participation by addressing fundamental needs like childcare, healthcare, housing, and transportation

The AI-driven economy places unprecedented pressure on human infrastructure. Automation and artificial intelligence are disrupting traditional employment patterns, rendering certain skills obsolete while creating demand

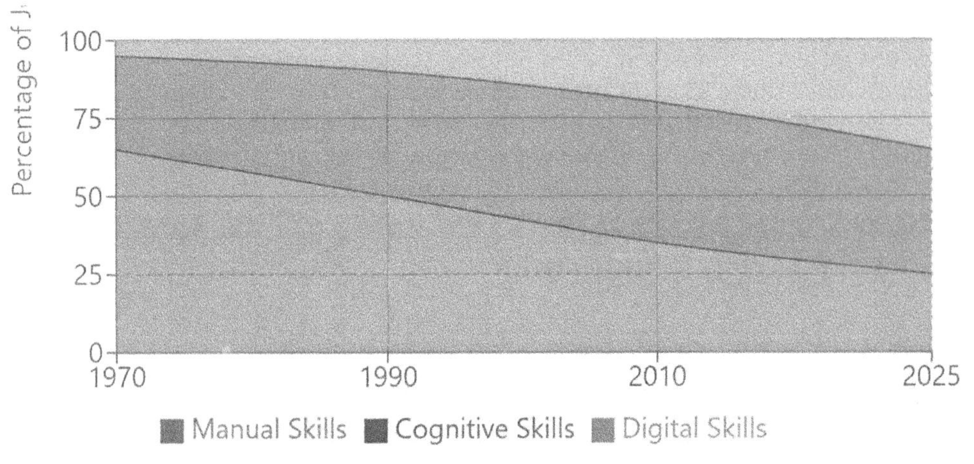

Changing Skill Requirements Across Industries (1970-2025)

for new capabilities. The McKinsey Global Institute report estimates that up to 30% of work activities could be automated by 2030, requiring massive workforce transitions.

Character Vignette: Skills Trainer Sophia's Retraining Challenge

In a repurposed factory building in Michigan, Skills Trainer Sophia runs a program retraining displaced manufacturing workers for advanced industries. Eleanor Roosevelt observes a training session where former auto workers learn to program and maintain industrial robots.

Sophia: *Adjusting a student's technique.* "Remember, Carlos, the robot doesn't know when it's making a mistake—you're teaching it to recognize optimal patterns."

Carlos (42, former assembly line worker): "Still feels strange to be programming the machines that took my old job."

Sophia: "You're not just programming it—you're supervising a whole cell of robots that do the physical labor while you handle the cognitive work. Your experience knowing how assembly actually works is incredibly valuable."

Eleanor approaches as the class breaks for lunch.

Eleanor Roosevelt: "Impressive program, Sophia. What challenges do you face?"

Sophia: "Where to begin? Funding is inconsistent—we operate on year-to-year grants with no long-term certainty. Many workers require basic digital literacy before advancing to more advanced training, but most programs do not cover this essential skill. And then there's the whole-person challenges."

Eleanor Roosevelt: "Meaning?"

Sophia: "Carlos is brilliant with machines, but he's also a single dad with two kids. We almost lost him from the program when his childcare fell through. Then there's Lisa, who has to drive 45 minutes each way because public transit doesn't reach us. Miguel has chronic health issues, but keeps losing insurance between jobs. The list goes on."

Eleanor Roosevelt: "So the technical training is just one piece of the puzzle."

Sophia: "Exactly. Other countries have systems that address these barriers comprehensively. We expect workers to navigate a fragmented maze of programs while simultaneously reinventing their careers, often after traumatic job loss."

McSlicey the Priest of Profit: *materializing beside them,* "But surely the market will solve this! Displaced workers should simply move to where jobs are plentiful!"

Sophia: *sighing* "Tell that to someone underwater on their mortgage in a company town, caring for elderly parents, with kids in local schools, and a spouse with their own career. People aren't commodity inputs to be reallocated at will."

Eleanor Roosevelt: *taking notes,* "What would a truly effective system look like?"

Case Studies:
Global Workforce Development Models

German Apprenticeship Model

- Dual education system combining classroom learning with workplace training
- Around 60% of young Germans enter apprenticeships

Scandinavian Active Labor Market Policies

- Nordic countries invest 1-2% of GDP in workforce development
- Retraining, job search assistance, wage subsidies
- Maintains skills and labor market attachment

Singaporean SkillsFuture Initiative

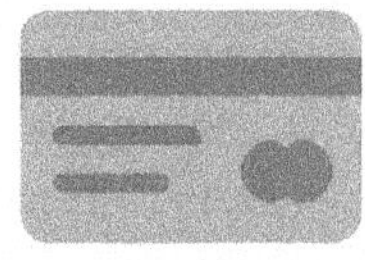

- Training account for every citizen of government-provided credits
- Approved courses throughout working life
- Enables lifelong learning and adaptation

Sophia: "Consistent funding. Seamless pathways between education and industry. Wraparound supports for life needs. And most importantly, proactive planning rather than reactive scrambling when plants close or automation hits."

Case Studies: Global Workforce Development Models

Eleanor's research identifies international best practices in human infrastructure development:

German Apprenticeship Model: The dual education system combines classroom learning with workplace training, creating seamless pathways between education and employment. Approximately 60% of young Germans enter apprenticeships, earning credentials recognized nationwide while gaining practical skills.

Scandinavian Active Labor Market Policies: Nordic countries invest 1-2% of GDP in comprehensive workforce development, including generous unemployment benefits tied to retraining, job search assistance, wage subsidies, and mobility grants. These programs maintain skills and attachment to the labor market during transitions.

Singaporean SkillsFuture Initiative: Every citizen receives a training account with government-provided credits for approved courses throughout their working life. The program democratizes access to lifelong learning, helping the entire workforce continuously adapt to changing requirements.

These models share common elements: substantial public investment, systematic coordination between education and industry, portable credentials recognized by employers, and integrated support systems that address barriers to participation.

Satirical Certificate: "Congratulations on Your Obsolete Skills!"

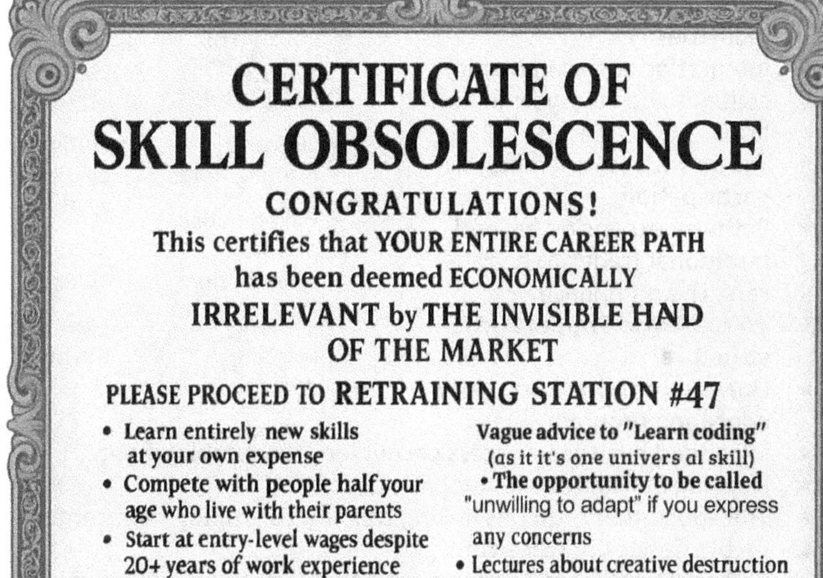
CERTIFICATE OF
SKILL OBSOLESCENCE
CONGRATULATIONS!
This certifies that YOUR ENTIRE CAREER PATH has been deemed ECONOMICALLY IRRELEVANT by THE INVISIBLE HAND OF THE MARKET
PLEASE PROCEED TO RETRAINING STATION #47
• Learn entirely new skills at your own expense
• Compete with people half your age who live with their parents
• Start at entry-level wages despite 20+ years of work experience
Vague advice to "Learn coding" (as it it's one univers al skill)
• The opportunity to be called "unwilling to adapt" if you express any concerns
• Lectures about creative destruction from economists with tenure
If you're experiencing financemt is
not a bug but a feature of our system! If you're experiencing financial distress, housing insecurity, or existential dread, please keep it yourself as it makes investors uncomfortable
Milton the Trickster Economist
McKinsey the Priest of ƒProfit
P.S. Have you considered relocating to a different state, abandoning your community ties, and competing for jobs that pay 40% less than previous?

CERTIFICATE OF SKILL OBSOLESCENCE

CONGRATULATIONS! This certifies that **YOUR ENTIRE CAREER PATH** has been deemed **ECONOMICALLY IRRELEVANT** by **THE INVISIBLE HAND OF THE MARKET**

In recognition of your decades of loyal service, specific industry expertise, and the taxes you've paid to subsidize corporate tax breaks

PLEASE PROCEED TO RETRAINING STATION #47

Where will you:

★ Learn entirely new skills at your own expense
★ Compete with people half your age who live with their parents
★ Start at entry-level wages despite 20+ years of work experience
★ Be told your experience is simultaneously "impressive" and "not directly relevant."
★ This certificate entitles you to:
★ Vague advice to "learn coding" (as if it's one universal skill)
★ Mounting debt from retraining programs with uncertain outcomes
★ The opportunity to be called "unwilling to adapt" if you express any concerns
★ Lectures about creative destruction from economists with tenure

Remember: Your economic displacement is not a bug but a feature of our system! If you're experiencing financial distress, housing insecurity, or existential dread, please keep it to yourself, as it makes investors uncomfortable.

Signed, Milton the Trickster Economist & McSlicey the Priest of Profit

P.S. Have you considered relocating to a different state, abandoning your community ties, and competing for jobs that pay 40% less than your previous position? That's the spirit!

Policy Proposal: 21st Century Workforce Development System

Eleanor Roosevelt's plan for human infrastructure modernization draws from global best practices while adapting to American contexts:

Core Elements:

1. **American Opportunity Accounts:**
★ Universal, portable training accounts for all workers
★ Government-provided base funding plus employer contributions
★ Usable for approved education and training throughout working life
★ Additional subsidies for displaced workers and low-income individuals

2. **Modernized Apprenticeship System:**
★ National framework for registered apprenticeships across industries
★ Integration with community colleges and four-year institutions
★ Tax incentives for employer participation
★ Pathway expansion beyond traditional trades to healthcare, IT, and finance

3. **Wraparound Support Infrastructure:**
★ Universal childcare and early education program
★ Expanded healthcare access decoupled from employment
★ Housing assistance with mobility support
★ Transportation solutions linking training to employment centers

4. **Institutional Coordination:**
★ Regional workforce development boards with employer and labor representation
★ Sectoral training partnerships organized by industry
★ Data-driven early warning systems for automation and offshoring impacts
★ Integration of economic development and workforce planning

21st CENTURY WORKFORCE DEVELOPMENT

A visionary human-infrastructure agenda

OPPORTUNITY ACCOUNTS
- Universal training funds
- Mixed public-private contributions
- Lifelong learning

MODERN APPRENTICESHPS
- National apprenticeship system
- Linked with colleges
- New tech & health pathways

WRAPAROUND SUPPORT
- Universal childcare
- Portable health coverage
- Transport & housing aid

INSTITUTIONAL COORDINATION
- Regional training boards
- Sectoral partnerships
- Data integration

"The nation that best manages the human dimension of economic transformation," Eleanor notes, "will gain substantial advantages in innovation, productivity, and social cohesion. This isn't just about worker skills—it's about building resilient communities capable of navigating technological disruption without descending into polarization and despair."

5. FUNDING THE FUTURE: BEYOND BUDGET BATTLES

"He who wishes to fight must first count the cost."
—Sun Tzu, The Art of War, Chapter 2

Analytical Framework: Infrastructure Finance Innovation

Eleanor Roosevelt convenes a meeting with economic advisors to address the persistent question: "How do we pay for all this?" The traditional answer—annual appropriations from general revenue—has proven woefully inadequate, as it is subject to political whims and budget constraints that prevent long-term planning.

"Infrastructure finance," notes a Budget Director with deep experience navigating Washington's fiscal labyrinths, "requires breaking free from the annual appropriations straitjacket. These are generational investments that should be financed over their useful life, not squeezed into arbitrary budget windows."

The analytical framework identifies five key mechanisms for infrastructure finance beyond conventional budgeting:

1. **Infrastructure Bank:** An independent entity providing low-cost, long-term financing for qualified projects through bond issuances and loan guarantees
2. **Public-Private Partnerships:** Structured agreements allowing private capital to finance public infrastructure with appropriate risk-sharing and regulated returns
3. **Green Bonds and Impact Investment:** Debt instruments specifically targeting environmental and social infrastructure with appeal to ESG-focused investors
4. **Value Capture Mechanisms:** Methods to monetize the increased property values and economic activity generated by infrastructure improvements
5. **Dedicated Revenue Streams:** User fees, specific taxes, or other reliable funding sources committed to infrastructure maintenance and expansion

Analytical Framework: Mechanisms for Infrastructure Finance

Infrastructure Bank

An independent entity providing low-cost, long-term financing for qualified projects through bond Issuances and loan guarantees

Public-Private Partnerships

Structured agreements allowing private capital to finance public infrastructure with appropriate risk-sharing regulated returns

Green Bonds and Impact Investment

Debt instruments specifically targeting environmental and social infrastructure with appeal to ESG-focused investors

Value Capture Mechanisms

Methods to monetize the increased property values and economic activity* generated by infrastructure improvements

Dedicated Revenue Streams

User fees, specific taxes, or other reliable funding sources committed to infrastructure maintenance and expansion

Character Dialogue: The Infrastructure Economics Lesson

Budget Director Davis attempts to explain infrastructure economics to a group of deficit hawks using increasingly creative metaphors, while Eleanor Roosevelt observes with interest.

Budget Director Davis: "Consider your household. If your roof is leaking, you don't wait until you've saved enough cash to replace it—you finance it to prevent further damage to your home."

Deficit Hawk Senator: "The government isn't a household!"

Budget Director: "Indeed. The government can borrow at lower rates, has an unlimited lifespan, and actually increases its revenue when infrastructure investments boost economic growth. So the case for financing is even stronger."

Another Deficit Hawk: "But the national debt is already too high!"

Budget Director: "Let me try another approach. Imagine you're a business owner with an old, inefficient factory. Your competitors are investing in modern equipment, while yours constantly breaks down, causing production delays and quality issues. Would refusing to invest in upgrades because 'debt is bad' be a sound business strategy?"

Milton the Trickster Economist: "But government isn't a business!"

Budget Director: *sighing,* "Correct again. Unlike a business, the government's goal isn't profit maximization but social welfare optimization. The question isn't whether we can afford to invest in infrastructure—it's whether we can afford not to, given the mounting costs of deterioration, decreased competitiveness, and missed opportunities."

Eleanor Roosevelt: "Perhaps a historical perspective would help. During the Depression, fiscal conservatives warned that New Deal infrastructure spending would bankrupt the nation. Instead, it helped create the foundation for unprecedented prosperity while generating returns that paid for the initial investment many times over."

Budget Director: "Exactly. And today's historically low interest rates make this an ideal time for infrastructure investment. We can lock in financing costs below the expected inflation rate, effectively being paid to borrow for projects that will generate returns for decades."

Milton the Trickster: "But what about the private sector? Shouldn't they build everything?"

Budget Director: "Private capital is essential but insufficient alone. Many critical infrastructure needs—such as rural broadband, flood protection, and grid resilience—lack immediate profit potential despite their enormous social returns. We need smart public investment to complement private capital, not ideological purity tests."

Eleanor Roosevelt: *to herself,* "Some debates never change, only the numbers get larger."

Policy Proposal: Diversified Infrastructure Funding

National Infrastructure Finance Authority

- $100 billion in initial federal capital, leveraged through bond issuance
- Authorify to make loans, provide credit enhancement, and issue guarantees
- Rigorous project selection based on economic, social, and environmental returns
- Independent governance with professional management

Asset Recycling Initiative

- Program encouraging public entities to lease or sell mature assets to reinvest proceeds
- Matching grants to incentivize participation
- Regulatory framework ensuring public interest protection
- Targeted at brownfield assets with established revenue streams

Environmental and Social Infrastructure Bonds

- Standardized green bond framework aligned with international standards
- Federal tax incentives for qualified infrastructure bonds
- Expanded state revolving funds for water and environmental projects
- Social impact bonds for community infrastructure

Value Capture Mechanisms

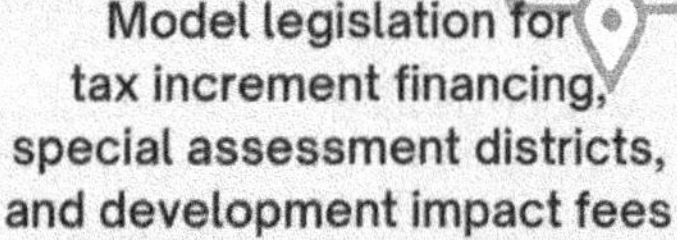

- Model legislation for tax increment financing, special assessment districts, and development impact fees
- Federal matching funds for projects implementing value capture
- Technical assistance for state and local implementation
- Integration with transit-oriented development and affordable housing initiatives

User Fee Modernization

- Congestion pricing frameworks for major urban areas
- Vehicle miles traveled (VMT) fee pliof programs as gas tax alternatives
- Congestion pricing frameworks for major urban areas

Policy Proposal: Diversified Infrastructure Funding

Eleanor Roosevelt's funding framework addresses America's infrastructure financing paradox—abundant global capital seeking stable returns alongside chronic underinvestment in critical systems. The comprehensive approach includes:

1. National Infrastructure Finance Authority:
   - ★ $100 billion in initial federal capital, leveraged through bond issuance
   - ★ Authority to make loans, provide credit enhancement, and issue guarantees
   - ★ Rigorous project selection based on economic, social, and environmental returns
   - ★ Independent governance with professional management
2. Asset Recycling Initiative:
   - ★ Program encouraging public entities to lease or sell mature assets to reinvest proceeds in new infrastructure
   - ★ Matching grants to incentivize participation
   - ★ Regulatory framework ensuring public interest protection
   - ★ Targeted at brownfield assets with established revenue streams
3. Environmental and Social Infrastructure Bonds:
   - ★ Standardized green bond framework aligned with international standards
   - ★ Federal tax incentives for qualified infrastructure bonds
   - ★ Expanded state revolving funds for water and environmental projects
   - ★ Social impact bonds for community infrastructure

4. Value Capture Mechanisms:
- ★ Model legislation for tax increment financing, special assessment districts, and development impact fees
- ★ Federal matching funds for projects implementing value capture
- ★ Technical assistance for state and local implementation
- ★ Integration with transit-oriented development and affordable housing initiatives

5. User Fee Modernization:
- ★ Vehicle miles traveled (VMT) fee pilot programs as gas tax alternatives
- ★ Congestion pricing frameworks for major urban areas
- ★ Utility rate structures supporting grid modernization and resilience
- ★ Digital infrastructure access fees with affordability protections

Eleanor notes that "the infrastructure financing challenge is not a resource constraint but a governance and political will deficit. With creative financial engineering, we can align public needs with private capital while ensuring equitable access and maintenance over generations."

6. THE BUILDING PERMITTING PARADOX: FROM GLACIAL TO RATIONAL

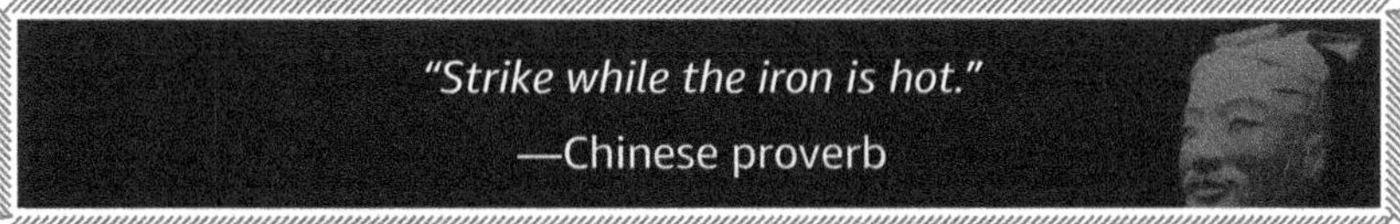

"Strike while the iron is hot."
—Chinese proverb

Analytical Framework: Balancing Oversight with Implementation

Eleanor Roosevelt encounters what Master Builder Maria calls "the great American infrastructure contradiction"—a nation desperate for improved infrastructure but seemingly incapable of building it efficiently due to byzantine approval processes.

"The permitting paradox," Maria explains, "is that we've created a system where legitimate environmental and community protections have mutated into procedural weapons that delay or kill even the most beneficial projects."

The analytical framework distinguishes between necessary oversight serving important public interests and procedural excess that accomplishes little beyond delay:

ANALYTICAL FRAMEWORK NECESSARY vs PROCEDURAL EXCESS

SUBSTANTIVE V/S PROCEDURAL	PROCEDURAL EXCESS
SUBSTANTIVE Reviews that improve outcomes	**CUMULATIVE REGULATORY** Unreasonable aggregate delays
CUMULATIVE REGULATORY Individually reasonable requirements	**REDUNDANT AUTHORITIES** Sequential reviews
LEGAL RISK ASYMMETRY Challenging projects	**LEGAL RISK ASYMMETRY** Defending projects

1. **Substantive vs. Procedural Requirements:** Differentiating between reviews that actually improve outcomes versus those that simply add time and cost without material benefit
2. **Cumulative Regulatory Burden:** Analyzing how individually reasonable requirements combine to create unreasonable aggregate delays
3. **Redundant Authorities:** Identifying overlapping jurisdictions and sequential reviews that could be conducted concurrently
4. **Legal Risk Asymmetry:** Understanding how the imbalance between the ease of challenging projects versus the difficulty of defending them creates perverse incentives

Character Vignette: Permit Officer Patterson's 12-Year Bridge

Eleanor Roosevelt stands with Permit Officer Patterson beside an aging bridge with visible structural deterioration. Patterson clutches a massive binder labeled "Replacement Project: Procedural Requirements (Volume 1 of 17)."

International Comparison of Major Infrastructure Permitting Timelines

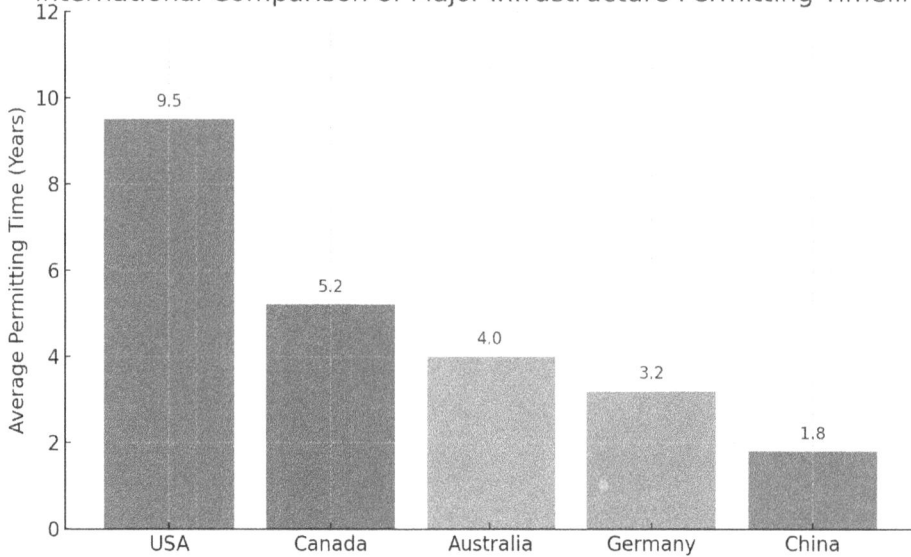

	Average Permitting Time (Years)
USA	9.5
Canada	5.2
Australia	4.0
Germany	3.2
China	1.8

Eleanor Roosevelt: "Mr. Patterson, this bridge was clearly designed for Model T traffic, not modern trucks. The rust is visible from space. Why will replacement take 12 years?"

Permit Officer Patterson: *adjusting his bow tie nervously,* "Well, Mrs. Roosevelt, that's quite simple to explain. We begin with a three-year planning phase, followed by the drafting of the environmental impact statement—that's a two-year process. Then public comment periods, design revisions, the final environmental impact statement, another comment period, the record of decision..."

Eleanor Roosevelt: "The actual construction only takes two years?"

Patterson: "Correct! However, before we reach that point, we need approvals from 17 different agencies—each with its own process and timeline. And of course, there's the inevitable litigation, usually filed the day after the final approval by groups who participated in every previous comment opportunity."

Eleanor Roosevelt: "When I helped build public works during the Depression, we completed major dams in under five years—design through ribbon-cutting—while creating thousands of jobs and adhering to environmental standards of the time."

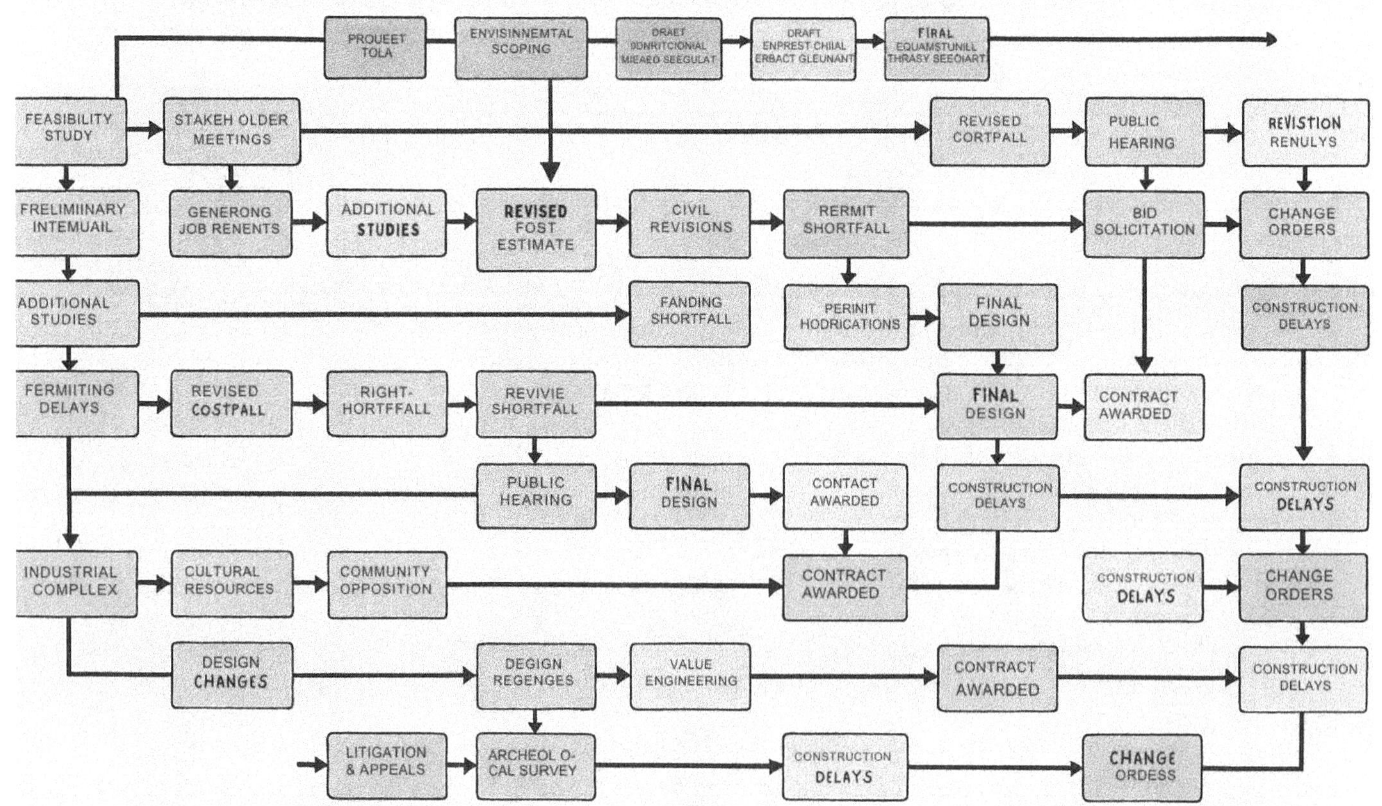

Patterson: "But those were simpler days! We now have the National Environmental Policy Act, the Clean Water Act, the Endangered Species Act, the National Historic Preservation Act, and numerous state and local equivalents. All important protections!"

Eleanor Roosevelt: "I support environmental protection, Mr. Patterson. But surely there's a difference between careful review and paralysis by analysis? Meanwhile, the bridge continues to deteriorate, creating safety risks and higher eventual replacement costs."

Patterson: *lowering his voice,* "Between us, Mrs. Roosevelt, about 80% of this process adds no value to the final outcome. Most substantive improvements happen in the first 20% of the review period. The rest is simply checking procedural boxes and preparing for inevitable lawsuits."

Eleanor Roosevelt: "And our competitors?"

Patterson: "China approves and builds comparable projects in 2-3 years. European democracies with strict environmental standards manage for 4-5 years. Only in America have we elevated process above progress to this degree."

Eleanor Roosevelt: *making notes* "So we need reform that maintains substantive protections while eliminating procedural excess?"

Patterson: *looking nervously over his shoulder,* "I didn't say that! I have children to feed! But yes, that's exactly what we need."

Satirical Flowchart: "How a Simple Road Project Becomes a Decade-Long Odyssey"

Policy Proposal: One Federal Decision Implementation

POLICY PROPOSAL: ONE FEDERAL DECISION IMPLEMENTATION

Eleanor Roosevelt's permitting reform agenda aims to maintain environmental protections while dramatically accelerating project delivery.

CORE ELEMENTS

 ONE FEDERAL DECISION FRAMEWORK	 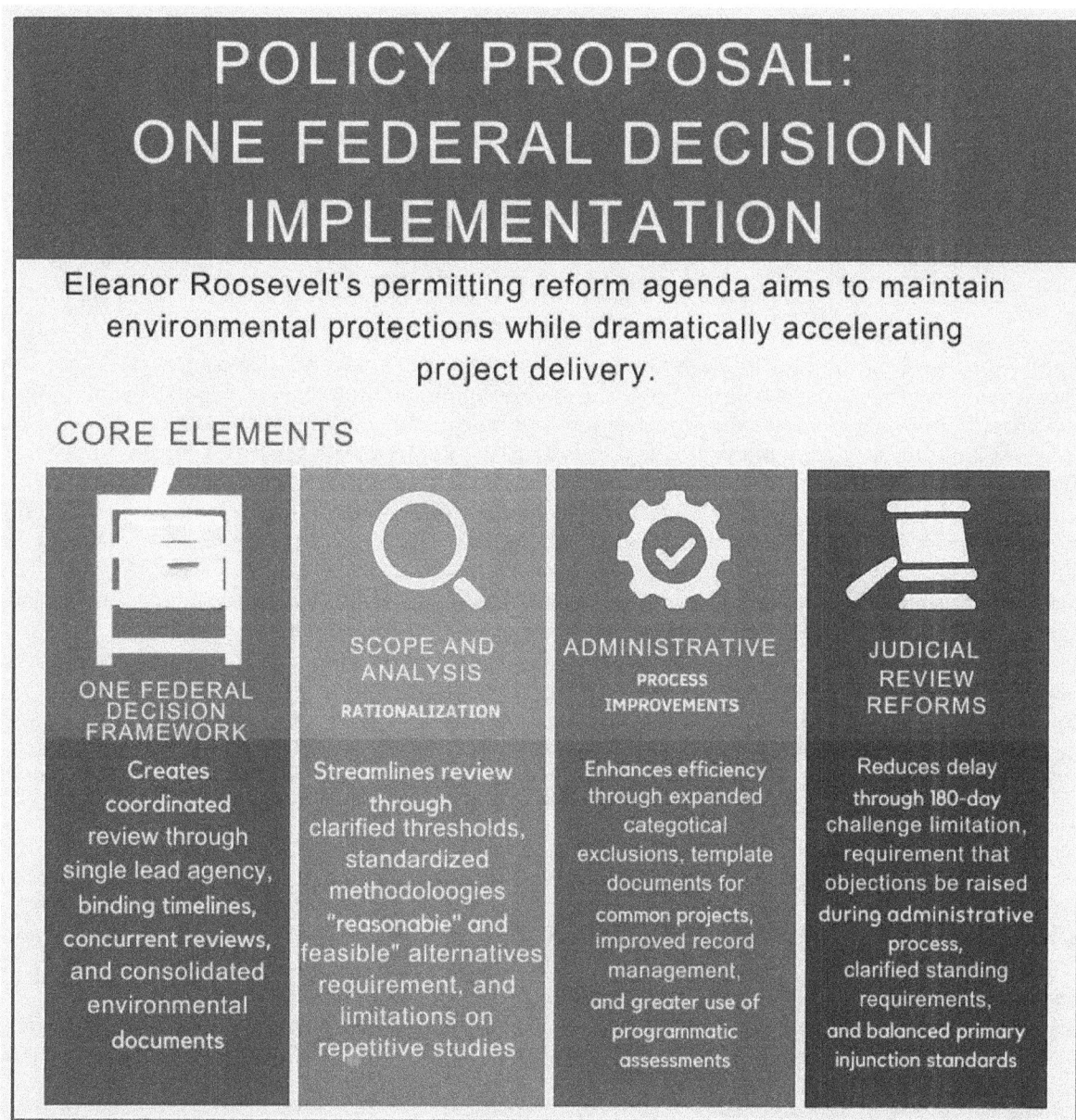 SCOPE AND ANALYSIS RATIONALIZATION	 ADMINISTRATIVE PROCESS IMPROVEMENTS	 JUDICIAL REVIEW REFORMS
Creates coordinated review through single lead agency, binding timelines, concurrent reviews, and consolidated environmental documents	Streamlines review through clarified thresholds, standardized methodoloogies "reasonabie" and feasible" alternatives requirement, and limitations on repetitive studies	Enhances efficiency through expanded categotical exclusions, template documents for common projects, improved record management, and greater use of programmatic assessments	Reduces delay through 180-day challenge limitation, requirement that objections be raised during administrative process, clarified standing requirements, and balanced primary injunction standards

Eleanor Roosevelt's permitting reform agenda aims to maintain environmental protections while dramatically accelerating project delivery:

Core Elements:

1. **One Federal Decision Framework**: This framework facilitates a coordinated review through a single lead agency, establishes binding timelines, allows for concurrent reviews, and consolidates environmental documents to streamline the process.
2. **Scope and Analysis Rationalization**: This rationalization streamlines the review by clarifying thresholds, standardizing methodologies, identifying "reasonable" and "feasible" alternative requirements, and limiting repetitive studies.
3. **Administrative Process Improvements**: Enhances efficiency through expanded categorical exclusions, template documents for common projects, improved record management, and greater use of programmatic assessments.
4. **Judicial Review Reforms**: This reform reduces delay through a 180-day challenge limitation, a requirement that objections be raised during the administrative process, clarified standing requirements, and balanced preliminary injunction standards.
5. **Technology and Transparency**: Improves accountability through integrated permitting dashboard, digital tracking systems, public-facing timelines, and GIS-based environmental data repositories.

"Permitting reform," Eleanor notes, "may seem technical and unglamorous, but it's essential for infrastructure renewal. We cannot allow legitimate environmental protections to be weaponized into tools of perpetual delay, nor can we accept timelines that render even the most worthy projects practically unbuildable. Democracy requires both participation and decision—we've privileged the former at the expense of the latter."

7. BUILDING IN THE AGE OF TRUMP: STRATEGIC INFRASTRUCTURE POLITICS

"When those above contend, those below profit."

—Han Feizi

Analytical Framework: Infrastructure as Common Ground

As Eleanor Roosevelt completes her infrastructure assessment, she confronts the central question: How might these proposals advance in America's polarized political environment, particularly in a second Trump administration?

The analytical framework considers the infrastructure's unique position in American politics:

1. **Tangible Benefits Across Ideological Lines:** Infrastructure improvements deliver concrete benefits to constituents regardless of political affiliation, creating potential for bipartisan support.
2. **Diverse Justification Frameworks:** Infrastructure can be framed through multiple narratives—economic competitiveness, national security, job creation, environmental protection—appealing to different value systems.
3. **Federal-State-Local Dynamics:** Infrastructure inherently involves multiple levels of government, creating opportunities for pragmatic cooperation even amid partisan disagreements.
4. **Historical Precedent:** Throughout American history, major infrastructure initiatives, from the transcontinental railroad to the Interstate Highway System, have often transcended partisan divides.

Eleanor observes that "Infrastructure politics "requires strategic navigation of America's ideological landscape—finding the overlapping space where competing worldviews can justify similar actions for different reasons.

Character Dialogue: The Infrastructure Director's Political Navigation

Eleanor Roosevelt meets with the Infrastructure Director, a savvy political operator tasked with advancing projects in a divided government. They're reviewing presentation materials for pitching the same high-speed rail project to different political audiences.

Infrastructure Director: "The key, Mrs. Roosevelt, is understanding the core values of different constituencies and framing the same project in ways that resonate with their worldviews."

Eleanor Roosevelt: "Show me how this works in practice."

Infrastructure Director: *Sliding over a presentation.* "For progressive audiences, we emphasize environmental benefits—each high-speed train takes hundreds of cars off the road, reducing emissions while creating sustainable transportation options."

He switches to another deck.

Tangible Benefits Across Ideological Lines

Infrastructure improvements deliver concrete benefits to constituents regardless of political afiliation, creating potential for bipartisan support

Diverse Justification Frameworks

Infrastructure can be framed through multiple narratives-economic competitivenes, national security, job creation, environmental protection-appealing to different value systems

Federal-State-Local Dynamics

Infrastructure inherently involves multiple levels of government, creating opportunities for pragmatic cooperation even amid partisan disagreements

Historical Precedent

Throughout American history, major infrastructure initiatives have often transcended partisan divides, from the transcontinental railroad to the Interstate Highway System

"For conservatives, we stress economic competitiveness and national security—America falling behind China in critical infrastructure, the project creating thousands of jobs that can't be outsourced, and reduced dependence on foreign oil."

Another deck

"For business groups, we highlight productivity gains, increased property values along the corridor, and new market opportunities."

Final deck

"For rural communities concerned about being bypassed, we emphasize connection points, expanded market access for agricultural products, and specific job creation in their regions."

Eleanor Roosevelt: "So the same project, but different emphasis depending on the audience?"

Infrastructure Director: "Exactly. I'm not suggesting deception—everything in each presentation is factually accurate. But people filter information through their existing values. Our job is to highlight aspects that resonate with their priorities."

Eleanor Roosevelt: "And in a second Trump administration?"

Infrastructure Director: "We would emphasize the legacy-building aspect. Every president wants signature achievements. Infrastructure is tangible, photogenic, and lasting—you can literally put your name on it. We'd focus on job creation statistics, how the projects would surpass anything China has built, and opportunities for high-profile groundbreaking ceremonies in politically important regions."

Milton the Trickster Economist: *appearing suddenly,* "But that's just political pandering!"

Infrastructure Director: "No, it's democratic governance. In a diverse society, major initiatives need to serve multiple legitimate interests simultaneously. That's not pandering—it's coalition building."

Policy Framework: Strategic Implementation Partnerships

Eleanor Roosevelt's political strategy for infrastructure advancement recognizes the need to build unusual coalitions across traditional dividing lines:

Core Elements:

Federal-State Implementation Partnerships enable flexible federal funding with streamlined requirements, enhanced technical assistance, competitive innovation grants, and regional coordination for multi-state projects.

Public-Private Alignment establishes formal industry-government coordination councils, provides regulatory certainty for long-term investments, develops shared workforce initiatives, and standardizes partnership frameworks to reduce transaction costs.

Constituency Bridges create labor-business climate coalitions that support clean infrastructure, rural-urban connectivity initiatives, and environmental-economic development alliances for sustainable growth, as well as strategic messaging that emphasizes benefits across political lines.

Implementation Sequencing initially focuses on broadly supported "no regrets" projects, demonstrates competent delivery to build credibility, implements a momentum-building strategy highlighting successful completions, and institutionalizes reforms through professional implementation.

"Infrastructure renewal," Eleanor concludes, "offers perhaps the best opportunity for restoring functional governance in a divided nation. Unlike purely ideological issues, infrastructure deals with physical reality—bridges either stand or fall regardless of partisan affiliation. This concrete nature creates space for pragmatic cooperation even amid broader disagreements."

CONCLUSION: AMERICA'S 21ST CENTURY NEW DEAL

As Eleanor Roosevelt completes her 21st-century New Deal blueprint, she pauses beside the high-speed Chinese train still visible on its elevated track in the distance. Her clipboard now contains comprehensive plans for transportation modernization, universal broadband, energy system transformation, manufacturing renewal, workforce development, infrastructure finance, permitting reform, and political implementation strategies.

America stands at an inflection point similar to the 1930s, when her husband took office amid economic crisis and faltering confidence in American institutions. The challenges differ—global competition rather than domestic depression, technological disruption rather than financial collapse—but the fundamental question remains the same: Can America summon the vision and will to rebuild its foundations for a new era?

The stakes couldn't be higher. Continued infrastructure neglect leads to the progressive erosion of economic competitiveness, innovation capacity, and ultimately, global influence. It means watching the Chinese century unfold as America increasingly resembles a museum of faded greatness—impressive monuments to past achievements without the dynamism to create new ones.

"We have the resources," Eleanor murmurs to herself. We have the knowledge. We even have the blueprints." What remains uncertain is whether America can overcome its political dysfunction, short-term thinking, and ideological rigidity to actually implement them.

As she walks back through the neighborhood with its crumbling bridges, spotty internet, and deteriorating public facilities, Eleanor Roosevelt makes one final note on her clipboard: "The New Deal succeeded not just because of specific projects or programs, but because it restored America's belief in its capacity for collective action. Today's challenge is similar—we must rebuild not just infrastructure, but the very idea that America can still do big things."

The Chinese train disappears into the distance as Eleanor faces the arguing local officials, who continue to debate jurisdictional boundaries and funding responsibilities. With a determined smile that once helped America through its darkest hours, she steps forward, clipboard in hand, to begin the work of building a foundation for the next American century—even as the current one increasingly belongs to others.

POLICY FRAMEWORK: STRATEGIC IMPLEMENTATION PARTNERSHIPS

FEDERAL-STATE IMPLEMENTATION PARTNERSHIPS

- Flexible federal funding with streamlined requirements
- Enhanced technical assistance Competitive innovation grants
- Regional coordination for multi-state projects

PUBLIC-PRIVATE ALIGNMENT

- Formal industry-government coordination councils
- Regulatory certainty for long-term investments
- Shared workforce initiatives
- Standardized partnership framworks reducing transaction cost

CONSTITUENCY BRIDGES

- Labor-business climate coalitions supporting clean infrastructure
- Rural-urban connectivity initiatives
- Environmental-economic development alliances for sustainable growth

IMPLEMENTATION SEQUENCING

- Initial focus on broadly supported "no regrets" projects
- Competent delivery demonstrating credibility
- Momentum-building strategy highilghting successful completions
- Institutionalization of reforms through professional implementation

CHAPTER 7: THE BUCK STOPS... WHERE EXACTLY? REBUILDING THE US FINANCIAL ARCHITECTURE IN THE ERA OF CHINA'S AI CENTURY

> *"When the coffers are empty, the people will be exhausted."*
> —Guan Zhong, Guanzi, Chapter 14

EXECUTIVE BRIEFING

1. Strategic Snapshot

- ★ **Dollar on a Diet:** Reserve share down to **under 60 %**, slipping ~1 pp/yr; parity with "everybody else" by 2035 if trend holds.
- ★ **Casino-Capitalism Creep:** Financial assets have ballooned from 1× to 4× world GDP since 1980; more than 75% of the U.S. market churn now recycles paper, not ideas.
- ★ **Debt → Defense-Sized Interest:** Federal IOUs > $34 T; annual interest eclipses the Pentagon.
- ★ **Digital-Currency Chess:** China's e-CNY boasts **261 M users** and cross-border pilots, while the U.S. is still naming the steering committee.
- ★ **Bankers without Boroughs:** Community banks have declined by 70% since 1984; C&I loans have halved on big-bank books, starving Main Street of R&D.

2. Core Fault-Lines ("Duke the Dollar's Nightmares")

Fault-Line	Diagnosis	Competitive Delta	Stakes
Reserve-Currency Drift	Dollar share eroding; sanction overuse breeds work-arounds	Yuan + CIPS scaling	↑ borrowing costs; ↓ coercive power
Finance vs. Real Economy	Buybacks > $1 T/yr trump R&D	China channels credit to industry	Innovation hollow-out
Digital-Dollar Vacuum	CBDC debate in neutral	e-CNY sets rails/ norms	Standards written in Beijing, not DC
Fiscal Reality Fog	Debt/GDP 123 %; interest > defense	Peers trimming deficits	Public-investment squeeze

3. Risk Register

1. **Dollar "Minsky Moment"**—a shock accelerates reserve diversification, spiking rates.
2. **Strategic Under-investment**—talent & capital flee labs for options desks.
3. **CBDC Lock-out**—surveillance-heavy Chinese rails become the default standard.
4. **Crisis-Driven Austerity**—delay forces brutal, pro-cyclical cuts.

4. Four-Pillar Re-Wiring Plan (with Financing Turbo-Boost)

1. **Productive-Finance Reset** – Modern Glass-Steagall; tiered capital/transaction taxes that punish Vegas-style punts; *$100 B* National **Investment** Bank leveraged 10× for strategic sectors.
2. **Digital Dollar—Democratic Edition** – Two-tier CBDC prototype by **2027** (cash-like privacy ≤ $500; zero-knowledge proofs above) plus G7+ interoperability pact.
3. **Dollar Defense & Diplomacy** – 10-year fiscal guardrails (debt ↘ to ≤ 90 % GDP), 50-yr "Eagle Bonds" to lock-in low rates, deeper Fed swap lines with allies.
4. **Fiscal Reality Therapy**: 5% buyback excise (tied to R&D floors), restoration of the top rate to 39.6%, phased Social Security bend-point shift, and a carbon fee earmarked for infrastructure.

5. Quick Wins (Next 24 Months)

★ **CBDC Regional Pilots** with FDIC-insured wallets for the unbanked.
★ Capitalise the Investment Bank; refinance three "bridges-to-nowhere" into **ports-to-profit**.
★ Impose **five-year vesting** on exec stock grants (claw-back-ready).
★ Enact a bipartisan Debt Dashboard trigger: hold a floor debate if interest rates exceed 3.5% of GDP.

6. Scoreboard Targets

KPI	2025 Baseline	2030 Goal
Dollar share of global reserves	59 %	≥ 55 % & stable
Bank assets in C&I/productive loans	12 %	20 %
R&D : Buyback ratio (S&P 500)	0.8:1	≥ 1.2:1
Federal debt/GDP	123 %	≤ 110 %

7. Executive Call-to-Action

Quit admiring the casino's chandelier while the foundation cracks. Fast-track the digital dollar, re-yoke finance to factory floors, and treat fiscal sobriety as strategic deterrence. Otherwise, Duke the Dollar may soon be hawking commemorative coins—minted in Shenzhen.

OPENING TABLEAU

In the grand financial temple of global commerce, **Duke the Dollar Demigod** sits uneasily on his golden throne. Once the undisputed ruler of the monetary universe, today he shifts uncomfortably, adjusting his increasingly heavy crown. His regal attire—once immaculate—shows subtle signs of wear; small tears are carefully concealed beneath gleaming medallions representing reserve currencies past: the British pound, the Dutch guilder, and the Spanish silver dollar.

Around him, ambitious currencies circle like courtiers at a medieval palace, each eyeing the throne with varying degrees of ambition. The Euro maintains a respectful distance, having learned humility after its own recent troubles. The Yen bows deeply, hiding its intentions behind ceremonial deference. But it is **Yuan the Challenger** who draws Duke's nervous attention—methodically expanding influence while maintaining the appearance of subordination.

"Your Magnificence," whispers a nervous financial advisor, "the national debt has surpassed $34 trillion, and interest payments now exceed defense spending."

"Nonsense!" Duke dismisses with imperial indifference. "The world needs dollars! Always has, always will!"

Another advisor interjects: "But Sire, our gold reserves as a percentage of—"

"Did Alexander the Great worry about his debt-to-GDP ratio?" Duke interrupts. "Did Rome fall because of deficits? Actually... don't answer that."

In the corner, **Milton the Trickster Economist** pores over financial statements with growing horror. "I may have miscalculated," he mutters to himself. "All these years telling them markets would self-regulate, that shareholder value was the only metric that mattered... I've overextended the empire's credit line!" His hands tremble as he realizes he's inadvertently created an opening for regime change.

As Duke's financial advisors whisper contradictory advice, the throne subtly tilts—imperceptibly to most observers—creating a precarious imbalance that requires increasing effort to maintain. Duke compensates by shifting his weight, maintaining the appearance of stability while expending ever more energy to prevent toppling.

Meanwhile, in the shadows of the throne room, **Chinese financial engineers** methodically construct alternative payment systems. Unlike the ornate, tradition-bound architecture of Duke's dominion, their approach is sleek, digital, and algorithmic. They avoid eye contact with Duke but occasionally exchange knowing glances when particularly troubling economic data is announced.

"The e-CNY system now has over 261 million users," one engineer whispers to another.

"And the Americans still debate whether a digital dollar should exist at all," comes the reply, followed by polite, restrained laughter.

As Duke calls for another round of quantitative easing to stabilize his increasingly wobbly throne, Yuan the Challenger offers a respectful bow from across the room—patience personified, watching the Dollar's discomfort with strategic interest, knowing that in the financial long game, time is on China's side.

1. FROM CASINO TO CAPITAL FORMATION: RESETTING FINANCE'S PURPOSE

> *"When the coffers are empty, the people will be exhausted."*
> —Guanzi

Analytical Framework: The Divergence Between Finance's Proper Function and Current Reality

In a rational economic universe, the financial system serves as a sophisticated allocation mechanism, directing capital toward its most productive uses: funding innovations, building infrastructure, and supporting businesses that create real value. This core function—matching savers with productive investment opportunities—represents finance's fundamental purpose and its contribution to societal prosperity.

Yet in our reality, the financial system has increasingly morphed into what former Federal Reserve Chair Paul Volcker described as a "self-referential" casino—a complex web of speculation where most activity consists of trading existing assets rather than funding new, productive enterprise. The numbers tell a stark story:

- ★ The ratio of financial assets to global GDP has expanded from roughly 1:1 in 1980 to over 4:1 today
- ★ Derivatives markets have nominal values exceeding $600 trillion, dwarfing the approximately $85 trillion global GDP
- ★ High-frequency trading now accounts for ~60% of U.S. equity trading volume
- ★ Financial sector profits grew from about 10% of all corporate profits in 1980 to approximately 30% by 2025

THE NUMBERS TELL A STARK STORY

ASSET-TO-GDP RATIO

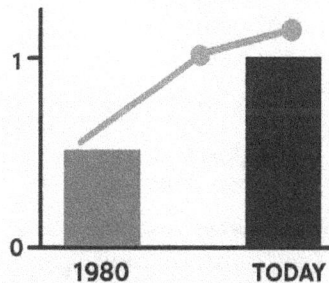

1
0
1980
TODAY

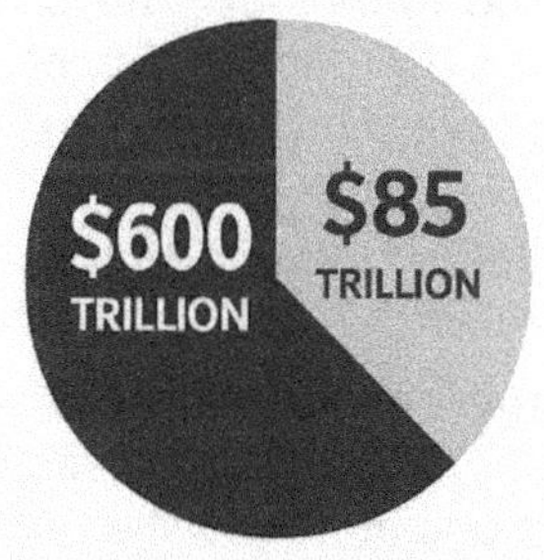

HIGH-FREQUENCY TRADING

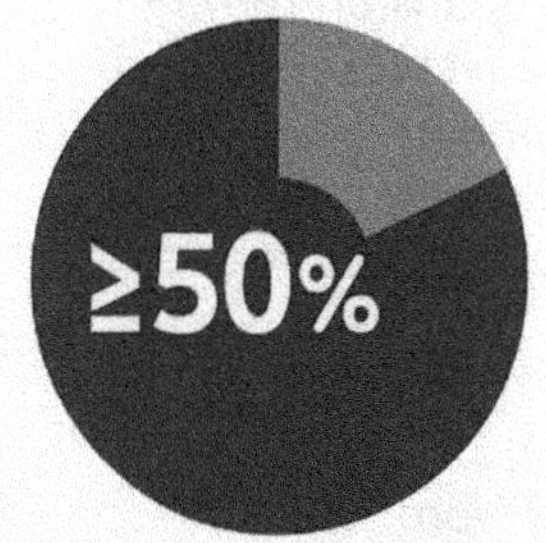

High-frequency trading now accounts for over 50% of U.S. equity trading volume

FINANCIAL SECTOR PROFITS

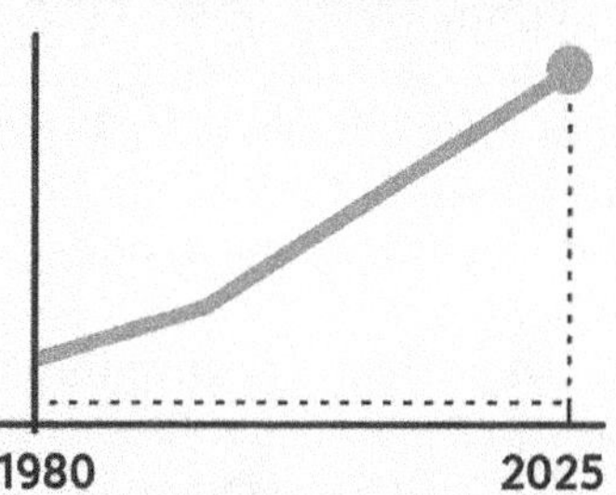

About 10% approx. 30% by 2025

This transformation fundamentally distorts capitalism's function: rather than serving the productive economy, finance increasingly serves itself in an elaborate game of monetary musical chairs—extracting value rather than creating it.

Character Dialogue: Milton the Trickster Confronted by FDR

Scene: The afterlife's Economic Policy Debate Chamber. MILTON FRIEDMAN's ghost hovers near a whiteboard covered with elegant mathematical formulas demonstrating market efficiency. Suddenly, FRANKLIN D. ROOSEVELT's ghost materializes, looking displeased.

FDR's GHOST: "Milton! We need to talk about what you've done to the financial system!"

MILTON: *(defensive)* "I merely advocated for free markets and minimal intervention! The invisible hand—"

FDR: *(interrupting)* "Has been picking average Americans' pockets while giving back rubs to hedge fund managers! Consider what your disciples did after you passed away. They didn't just remove the government's hand—they removed all hands except those reaching for quick profits!"

MILTON: *(adjusting spectral glasses)* "But efficiency! Price discovery! Optimal capital allocation!"

FDR: "Is that what you call it when 75% of financial activity consists of trading existing assets rather than funding new enterprise? When Wall Street rewards companies for laying off workers and repurchasing shares rather than investing in research and production?"

MILTON: *(wavering slightly)* "The empirical evidence suggests that markets generally—"

FDR: "The empirical evidence suggests your theories were weaponized into something you might not even recognize! They dismantled Glass-Steagall, created too-big-to-fail institutions, and unleashed forms of financial engineering that turned banking into gambling!"

MILTON: *(looking troubled)* "Perhaps there have been... unintended consequences."

FDR: "You think? In my day, banking was boring—and that was the point! Financial institutions served businesses and communities, not the other way around. We didn't let banks become casinos because we remembered what happened last time they did!"

MILTON: *(sighing)* "I fear I may have accidentally destroyed capitalism by trying to perfect it. My theories were meant to optimize markets, not replace productive enterprise with financial manipulation."

FDR: "Well, at least you're admitting it now. Better late than never—though the American middle class might disagree with that assessment. Now, shall we discuss how to fix it?"

MILTON: *(reluctantly)* "I suppose some pragmatic reassessment might be warranted..."

FDR: *(grinning)* "That's the spirit! You supply the theories, I'll supply the backbone. Between us, we might save capitalism from itself—again."

Historical Analysis: The Evolution of American Finance from Servant to Master

America's financial system wasn't always disconnected from productive activity. The transformation from servant to master occurred through definable phases, each moving further from finance's core purpose:

Formation Era (1790s-1920s): The financial system primarily facilitated economic expansion through infrastructure financing, industrial development, and commercial banking. J.P. Morgan might have been imperious, but his banks funded railroads, steel mills, and electrification—tangible enterprises creating real value.

New Deal Constraints (1930s-1970s): Following the 1929 crash, regulations such as the Glass-Steagall Act separated commercial banking from investment banking, interest rate caps limited speculation, and financial institutions operated more like utilities than profit centers. During this period, America built the

THE EVOLUTION OF AMERICAN FINANCE FROM SERVANT TO MASTER

1790s–1920s

FORMATION ERA

Finance supported growth of infrastructure, industry, and commerce

1930s–1970s

NEW DEAL CONSTRAINTS

Regulation restricted speculation businesses treated as utilities

1980s–2008

DEREGULATION WAVE

Regulation repealed, speculation surged, and complex instruments proliferated

2009–Present

POST-CRISIS ADAPTATION

Finance adapted to incremental reforms and embraced new innovations

KEEP CALM, RENOVATE OFTEN

A visionary handbook for servant-in best practices

world's largest middle class while constructing interstate highways, winning the space race, and developing groundbreaking technologies.

Deregulation Wave (1980s-2008): Successive waves of deregulation removed Depression-era safeguards, culminating in the 1999 Gramm—Leach—Bliley Act, which repealed the Glass-Steagall Act. Financial institutions consolidated, speculation flourished, and exotic instruments proliferated. The financial sector's share of GDP nearly doubled while manufacturing declined.

Post-Crisis Adaptation (2009-Present): Despite the 2008 financial crisis revealing systemic risks associated with financialization, reforms proved to be incremental rather than structural. The economic system adapted to new regulations while maintaining its dominance over the productive economy, with technological advances enabling new forms of financial engineering rather than a fundamental reorientation toward productive investment.

This evolution reflects not merely technical changes but a philosophical transformation: from viewing finance as infrastructure supporting economic activity to seeing it as the primary economic activity itself. This shift undermines capitalism's core function of capital formation for productive enterprise.

Data Visualization: Financial Flows to Productive versus Speculative Activities

This visualization reveals a fundamental shift in the financial architecture of America. In 1950, approximately 80% of financial flows were directed towards productive activities, including building factories, funding research, and expanding businesses. By 2025, this ratio is expected to have inverted, with over 75% of economic activity serving purely speculative purposes, including high-frequency trading, derivatives transactions, and secondary market activities with no connection to capital formation.

The inflection point in the mid-1980s coincided with financial deregulation and the rise of the shareholder primacy doctrine, marking a transition from finance as a servant to finance as the master of the economic system. This transformation hasn't merely redistributed resources within the economy; it has fundamentally altered what activities the economy rewards and, therefore, what activities economic actors pursue.

Theoretical Analysis: The Role of Finance in a Healthy versus a Distorted Economy

In a healthy economic ecosystem, finance functions as the circulatory system—moving capital efficiently to where it can create the most value, just as blood carries oxygen and nutrients throughout the body. This system succeeds when:

- ★ Savings flow primarily toward productive investment

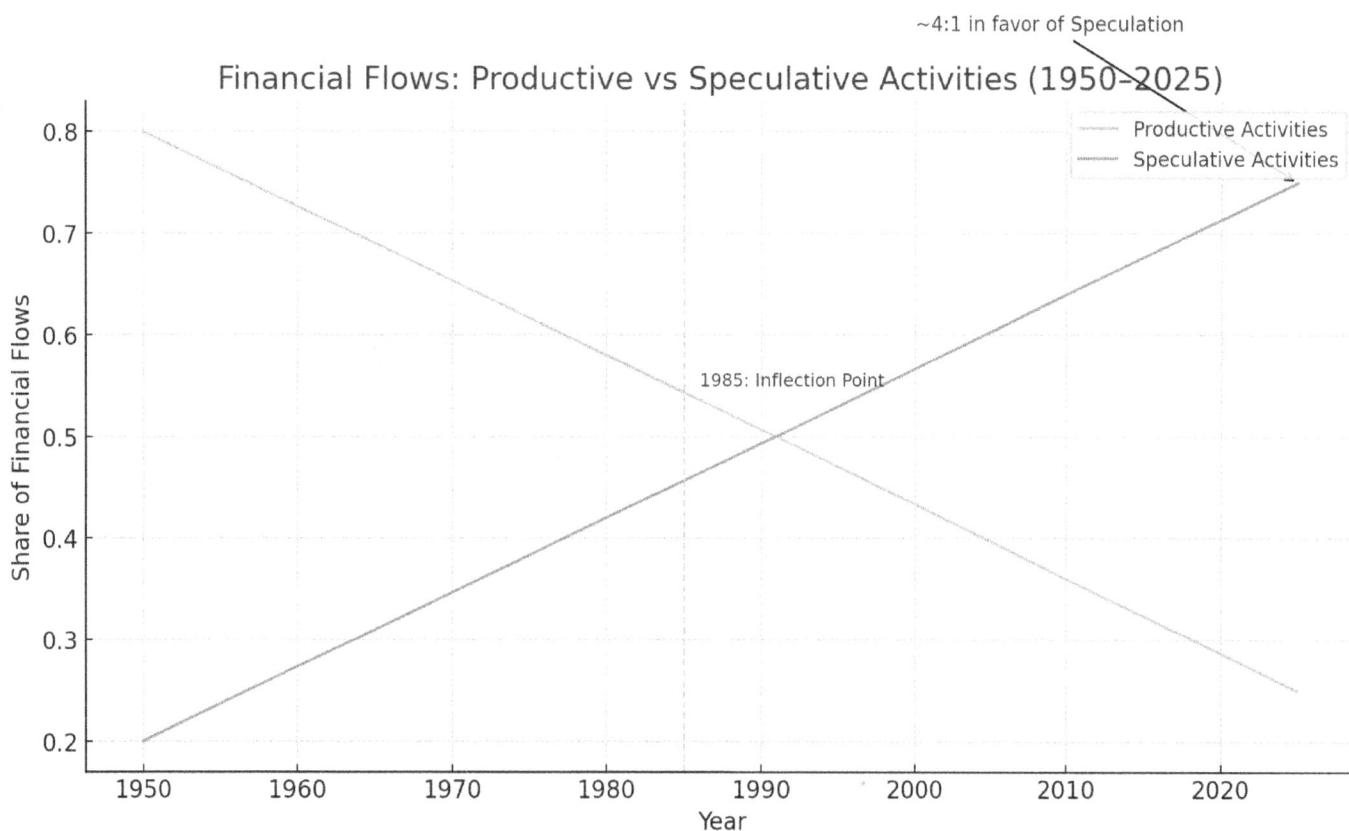

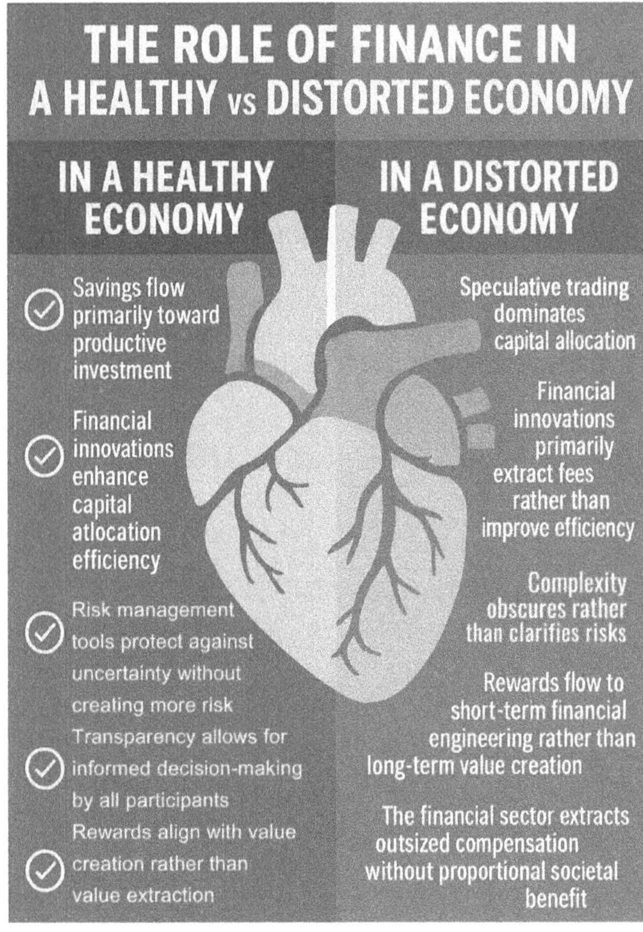

THE ROLE OF FINANCE IN
A HEALTHY vs DISTORTED ECONOMY
IN A HEALTHY ECONOMY
IN A DISTORTED ECONOMY
Savings flow primarily toward productive investment
Financial innovations enhance capital allocation efficiency
Risk management tools protect against uncertainty without creating more risk
Transparency allows for informed decision-making by all participants
Rewards align with value creation rather than value extraction
Speculative trading dominates capital allocation
Financial innovations primarily extract fees rather than improve efficiency
Complexity obscures rather than clarifies risks
Rewards flow to short-term financial engineering rather than long-term value creation
The financial sector extracts outsized compensation without proportional societal benefit

★ Financial innovations enhance capital allocation efficiency
★ Risk management tools protect against uncertainty without creating more risk
★ Transparency allows for informed decision-making by all participants
★ Rewards align with value creation rather than value extraction

In our distorted reality, however, finance increasingly resembles a cardiovascular disease where:

★ Speculative trading dominates capital allocation
★ Financial innovations primarily extract fees rather than improve efficiency
★ Complexity obscures rather than clarifies risks
★ Rewards flow to short-term financial engineering rather than long-term value creation
★ The financial sector extracts outsized compensation without proportional societal benefit

This distortion creates profound economic vulnerabilities, particularly in an era of strategic competition with state-directed capitalism models that maintain tighter connections between finance and productive activity. While Chinese banks direct capital toward strategic industries and infrastructure development, American finance frequently rewards executives for extracting value through layoffs, outsourcing, and financial engineering.

As Dr. Rational observes in his field notes: "The species appears to have constructed a financial system that incentivizes activities fundamentally disconnected from the underlying activities necessary for their long-term survival and prosperity. This represents an evolutionary adaptation I've not observed in any other intelligent life form—the equivalent of developing a circulatory system that prioritizes feeding itself rather than sustaining the organism."

Policy Proposal: Comprehensive Financial Sector Reform

Resetting finance's purpose requires a comprehensive reform agenda built around four foundational principles:

★ Differentiate Financial Activities by Social Utility: Implement graduated regulation favoring capital formation activities, apply higher capital requirements and taxes to speculation, and assess innovations based on productive investment contribution.

★ Realign Incentives Toward Productive Investment: Reform the tax code to favor long-term investment, implement scaled transaction taxes based on holding periods, and create regulatory advantages for institutions committed to productive lending.

POLICY PROPOSAL: COMPREHENSIVE FINANCIAL SECTOR REFORM

DIFFERENTIATE FINANCIAL ACTIVITIES BY SOCIAL UTILITY

- Implement graduated regulation favoring capital formation activities, apply higher capital requirements and taxes to speculation
- Assess innovations based on productive investment contribution

REALIGN INCENTIVES TOWARD PRODUCTIVE INVESTMENT

- Reform tax code to favor long-term investment
- Implement scaled transaction taxes based on holding periods
- Create regulatory advantages for institutions commited to productive lending

REBUILD MARKET INFRASTRUCTURE FOR LONG-TERM INVESTMENT

Develop specialized exchanges for patient capital
- Reform SEC disclosure requirements to emphasize long-term performance
- Create certification standards based on capital formation contribution

RESTRUCTURE FINANCIAL INSTITUTIONS

Implement a modern Glass-Steagall separation
Break up too-big-to-fail institutions
- Support specialized institutions arciving neglected sectors

SUCCESS METRICS

Track capital allocation to new versus existing enterprises,

★ Rebuild Market Infrastructure for Long-term Investment: Develop specialized exchanges for patient capital, reform SEC disclosure requirements to emphasize long-term performance, and create certification standards based on capital formation contribution.
★ Restructure Financial Institutions: Implement a modern Glass-Steagall separation, break up too-big-to-fail institutions, and support specialized institutions serving neglected sectors and regions.
★ Success Metrics: Track capital allocation to new versus existing enterprises, business formation rates supported by institutional finance, the geographic and sectoral distribution of capital access, the cost of financial intermediation as a percentage of productive investment, and the alignment between financial returns and economic value creation.

Implementation Framework: Making Reform a Reality

Implementation Framework: Making Reform Reality

Legislative Changes

- Implement financial transaction tax
- Establish modern Glass-Steagall separation
- Reform tax codes prioritizing productive investment
- Enforce antitrust measures against financial concentraıtion

Regulatory Actions

- Reform SEC disclosure requirements and trading rules
- Limit speculative activities through Federal Reserve
- Establish OCC standards for community investment
- Enhance CFTC derivatives oversight

Institutional Development

- Capitalize National Infrastructure Bank
- Expand community development financial institutions
- Regulate financial technology to enphasize productive investment
- Establish education and certification standards for financial professionals

Transforming America's financial architecture requires action across multiple domains:

1. **Legislative Changes:** Implement a financial transaction tax, establish modern Glass-Steagall separation, reform tax codes to prioritize productive investment, and enforce antitrust measures against financial concentration.
2. **Regulatory Actions:** Reform SEC disclosure requirements and trading rules, limit speculative activities through the Federal Reserve, establish OCC standards for community investment, and enhance CFTC derivatives oversight.
3. **Institutional Development:** Capitalize the National Infrastructure Bank, expand community development financial institutions, regulate financial technology to emphasize productive investment, and establish education and certification standards for financial professionals.

These changes represent not mere technical adjustments but a fundamental reorientation of finance toward its proper purpose: serving as the circulatory system of a healthy economy, rather than a self-referential casino that extracts resources from productive activity. As Dr. Rational notes, "The species recognizes the dysfunction in its financial architecture but struggles to implement reforms due to the concentrated influence of those benefiting from the current arrangement—a classic collective action problem."

2. TAMING THE QUARTERLY PROFIT BEAST: INCENTIVES FOR LONG-TERM THINKING

> *"Repair the dike before it breaks."*
> —Han Feizi

Analytical Framework: How Short-termism Undermines Long-term Economic Health

Corporate America suffers from a severe case of temporal myopia—an institutionalized inability to look beyond the next quarterly earnings report. This short-termism fundamentally undermines both economic health and national security by:

★ Prioritizing immediate financial metrics over sustainable value creation
★ Sacrificing research and development for short-term earnings boosts
★ Hollowing out productive capacity in favor of financial engineering
★ Ignoring strategic vulnerabilities until they become crises

How Short-termism Undermines Long-term Economic Health

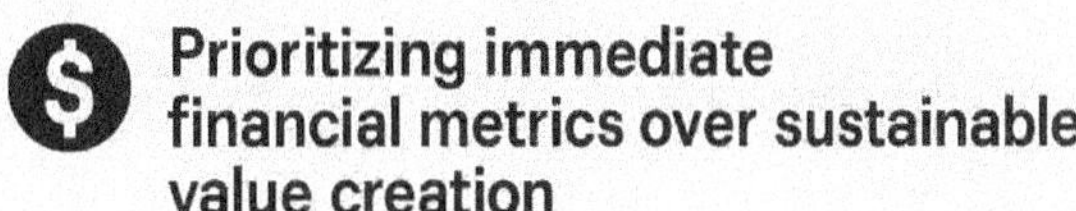

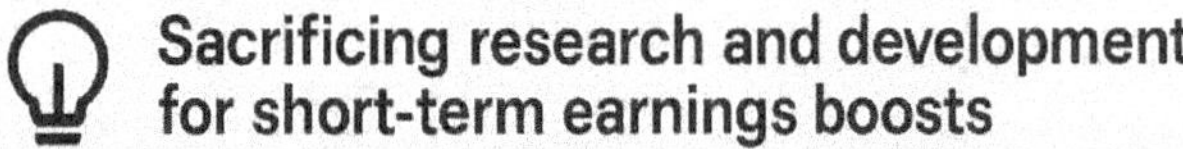

Hollowing out productive capacity in favor of financial engineering

Ignoring strategic vulnerabilities until they become crises

THE METRICS CONFIRM THIS DIAGNOSIS:

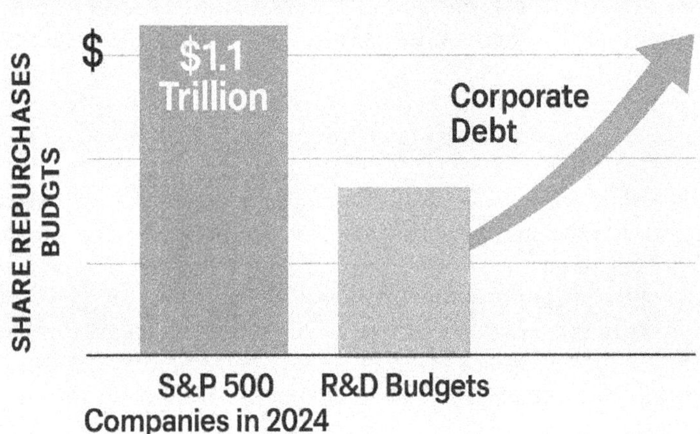

The metrics confirm this diagnosis: S&P 500 companies spent approximately $1.1 trillion on share repurchases in 2024—a record amount exceeding their combined research and development budgets. Meanwhile, corporate debt has ballooned to fund these buybacks rather than productive investment, creating financial fragility alongside eroding competitive capacity.

This short-termism represents more than a management preference; it reflects systematic incentive structures embedded throughout American capitalism:

★ Executive compensation packages are tied predominantly to short-term stock performance
★ Activist investors demand immediate returns regardless of long-term consequences
★ Quarterly earnings expectations create constant pressure for near-term results
★ Capital markets reward financial engineering over patient investment
★ Managerial careers span shorter periods than strategic payoffs

The consequences extend beyond individual companies to national strategic capability. While American executives optimize for the next

SYSTEMIC INCENTIVE STRUCTURES DRIVING SHORT-TERMISM

Executive compensation packages tied predominantly to short-term stock performance

Activist investors demanding immediate returns regardless of long-term consequences

Quarterly earnings expectations creating constant pressure for near-term results

Capital markets rewarding financial engineering over patient investment

Managerial careers spanning shorter periods than strategic payoffs

quarter, Chinese competitors invest with five-year (or longer) time horizons, creating an asymmetric competitive dynamic that threatens America's long-term economic and technological leadership.

Character Vignette: CEO Quarterly Explains the Impossibility of Long-term Thinking

Scene: A glass-walled boardroom overlooking Manhattan. CEO QUARTERLY, a sharply dressed executive with a $20,000 watch perpetually visible as he gestures, addresses increasingly skeptical investors while checking stock prices on his smartwatch every 47 seconds.

CEO QUARTERLY: "Ladies and gentlemen, I'm pleased to report we've achieved our 23rd consecutive quarter meeting or exceeding earnings expectations!"

INVESTOR #1: *(frowning at slides)* "But Research and Development spending is down 42% compared to five years ago."

CEO QUARTERLY: *(dismissively)* "Cost optimization initiative! Very trendy. All the top management consultants recommend it."

INVESTOR #2: "And your manufacturing facilities are now averaging 27 years old without significant upgrades."

CEO QUARTERLY: *(with practiced confidence)* "Asset utilization efficiency! Maximizing return on existing infrastructure! The depreciation schedules are beautiful."

INVESTOR #3: "Meanwhile, your Chinese competitor just invested $8 billion in next-generation technology that could make your entire product line obsolete within three years."

CEO QUARTERLY: *(genuinely confused)* "Three... years? That's like... twelve quarters from now! Who even knows if I'll still be CEO then? The average tenure is 4.8 years, and I'm already in year three!"

INVESTOR #4: "Shouldn't we be concerned about long-term competitiveness?"

CEO QUARTERLY: *(laughing)* "Look, let me explain how this works. My compensation package ties 78% of my potential earnings to stock performance over the next 90 days. Our institutional investors hold shares for an average of 5.6 months. The analysts judging us focus almost exclusively on quarterly EPS targets. The board evaluates me primarily on share price appreciation during my tenure."

(He displays a PowerPoint slide titled "Time Horizons in Modern Capitalism," showing all key decision-makers focused on periods under 12 months)

CEO QUARTERLY: "Thinking beyond the next quarter isn't just difficult—it's financially irrational given the incentive structures we've all created! Now, who's excited about our new $2 billion share buyback program that will boost EPS by eliminating 7% of outstanding shares?"

INVESTOR #5: *(resigned)* "I suppose it's better than your competitors' buybacks..."

CEO QUARTERLY: *(brightening)* "Exactly! We're all playing the same game with the same rules. Now, if you'll excuse me, I need to film a LinkedIn video about the importance of 'long-term sustainable thinking' for our corporate social responsibility report."

(He exits, already dictating an email to cancel funding for a research project that won't yield results until after his stock options vest.)

Behavioral Economics: The Incentive Structures that Drive Myopic Corporate Behavior

Corporate short-termism isn't a moral failing of individual executives but a predictable outcome of powerful incentive structures and cognitive biases:

1. **Hyperbolic Discounting:** Humans naturally favor immediate outcomes over future ones. This cognitive bias affects even sophisticated executives, particularly when reinforced by institutional incentives. Studies show that discount rates applied to corporate decisions often imply that future outcomes beyond 2-3 years are valued at near zero.
2. **Principal-Agent Problems:** Executives (agents) have different time horizons than long-term shareholders (principals). With an average CEO tenure of under five years, leaders rationally focus on metrics that will determine their compensation and reputation during their limited time at the helm.
3. **Misaligned Performance Metrics:** Quarterly earnings per share, revenue growth, and other short-term financial metrics dominate performance evaluation despite their poor correlation with long-term value creation. These metrics are favored partly because they're easily measured and compared.
4. **Information Asymmetry:** Long-term investments (R&D, employee development, brand building) involve complex value creation mechanisms that markets struggle to evaluate properly. By contrast, share buybacks and cost-cutting produce immediately observable financial results.
5. **Institutional Investor Pressures:** Despite claiming long-term perspectives, many institutional investors evaluate their own portfolio managers quarterly, creating pressure for short-term performance that transmits to portfolio companies.
6. **Activist Vulnerability:** Companies that make appropriate long-term investments may temporarily underperform financially, creating opportunities for activist investors to demand leadership changes and strategy reversals that improve short-term results.

These forces create a classic collective action problem: even executives who understand the importance of long-term investment face powerful incentives to prioritize short-term results, particularly when competitors do the same. The resulting equilibrium systematically undervalues future outcomes, creating economy-wide underinvestment in research, infrastructure, workforce development, and other drivers of long-term prosperity.

Data Visualization: Corporate Time Horizons - Buyback Trends versus R&D/CapEx Investment

This visualization reveals several disturbing patterns:

1. **Buyback Explosion**: Stock repurchases have grown from negligible levels in the early 1980s to over $1 trillion annually by 2025.
2. **Industry Variations**: Even innovation-dependent sectors, such as technology and pharmaceuticals, now frequently allocate more funds to buybacks than to research and development (R&D).
3. **Acceleration Points**: The trend shows distinct acceleration following the 2003 tax cuts, the 2017 tax reform, and the post-pandemic recovery periods when companies received significant cash infusions that could have funded long-term investment.
4. **Investment Stagnation**: When adjusted for inflation, capital expenditure in manufacturing has actually declined over the past 45 years, despite significant growth in financial metrics such as market capitalization.

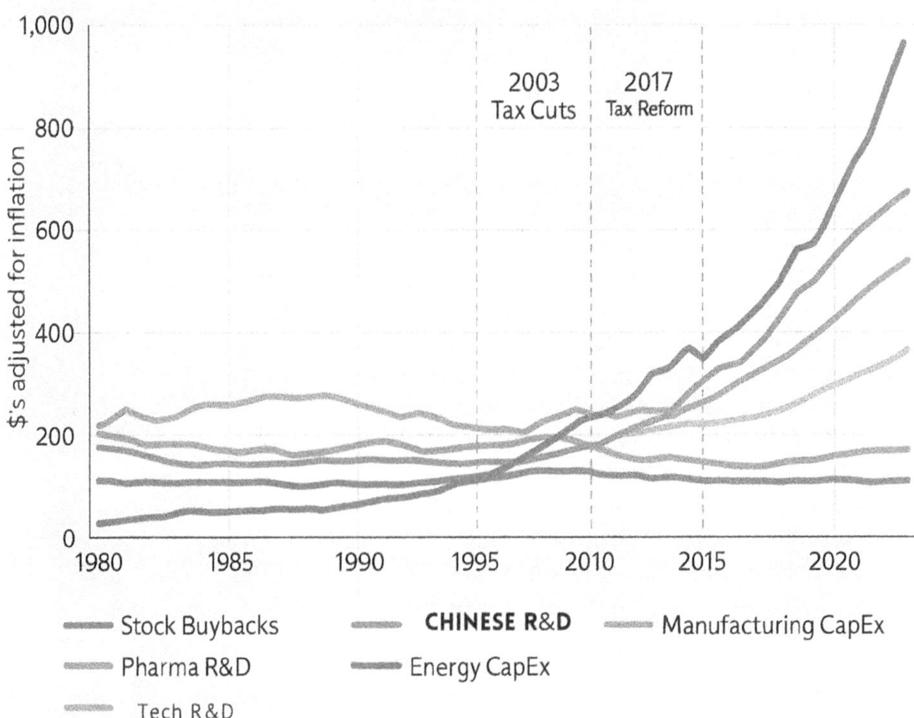

5. **International Divergence**: A comparison line showing Chinese competitors' R&D intensity reveals a steadily widening gap as Chinese firms increase research investment while American companies prioritize financial engineering.

The visualization makes concrete what economists have long warned: corporate America increasingly focuses on extracting value from existing assets rather than creating new productive capacity, a pattern with profound implications for future competitiveness.

Case Studies: B-Corps, Benefit Corporations, and Long-term Models

Patagonia
Benefit Corporation

- Maintains explicit environmental mission alongside financial goals
- Invests in sustainable supply chains with multi-decade time horizons
- Self-imposed "Earth tax" funds environmental initiatives regardless of quarterly performance
- Recently restructured to direct all profits

Nucor Steel
Long-term Traditional Corporation

- Maintained consistent capital investment through market cycles
- No layoffs policy fostering long-term workforce development
- Share-the-pain compensation structure where executives take largest cuts during downturns
- Achieved industry-leading productivty

King Arthur Flour
Employee-Owned B-Corp

- 100% employee-owned structure aligning worker and company interests
- Certified B Corporation with explicit social benefit mandate
- Investment decisions consider multi-generational timeframes
- Demonstrated resillence during economic downturns

Vanguard
Mutual Ownership Structure

- Owned by its funds, which are owned by shareholders, eliminating external profit pressure
- Lower fee structure reflecting absence of external profit demands
- Long-term decision framework untethered from quarterly earnings expectations
- Consistent investment in technology capacity

Not all companies succumb to the pressure of quarterly earnings. Alternative models emphasizing longer time horizons offer compelling counterexamples:

Patagonia (Benefit Corporation)

★ Maintains explicit environmental mission alongside financial goals
★ Invests in sustainable supply chains with multi-decade time horizons
★ Self-imposed "Earth tax" funds environmental initiatives regardless of quarterly performance
★ Recently restructured to direct all profits to environmental causes, effectively removing short-term profit maximization as the governing principle

Nucor Steel (Long-term Traditional Corporation)

★ Maintained consistent capital investment through market cycles
★ No layoffs policy fostering long-term workforce development
★ Share-the-pain compensation structure, where executives take the largest cuts during downturns
★ Achieved industry-leading productivity and profitability through continuous investment regardless of short-term market conditions

King Arthur Flour (Employee-Owned B-Corp)

★ 100% employee-owned structure aligning worker and company interests
★ Certified B-Corporation with explicit social benefit mandate
★ Investment decisions consider multi-generational timeframes
★ Demonstrated resilience during economic downturns through a stakeholder-balanced approach

Vanguard (Mutual Ownership Structure)

★ Owned by its funds, which are owned by shareholders, eliminating external profit pressure
★ Lower fee structure reflecting the absence of external profit demands
★ Long-term decision framework untethered from quarterly earnings expectations
★ Consistent investment in technology and service capacity through market fluctuations

These alternative models demonstrate that structural choices have a profound influence on time horizons. By embedding longer-term considerations into governance, ownership, and incentive structures, these companies escape the tyranny of quarterly expectations that afflicts conventional publicly-traded corporations. Their success challenges the notion that extreme short-termism represents an inevitable feature of market capitalism rather than a design choice in corporate architecture.

Dr. Rational notes with interest: "The species has developed varying institutional structures with dramatically different temporal orientations. This suggests their short-termism is not an intrinsic limitation but rather an artifact of specific legal and incentive arrangements—a self-imposed constraint they could theoretically remove through institutional redesign."

Policy Proposal: Taming Short-termism Through Structural Reform

Taming Short-termism Through Structural Reform

Addressing corporate short-termism requires policy interventions that realign incentives throughout the financial and corporate ecosystem:

Stock Buyback Regulation

- Increase excise tax to 5%
- Require minimum R&D and capital investment thresholds
- Mandate disclosure of executive stock sales after buybacks
- Prohibit debt-financed buybacks

Executive Compensation Reform

- Extend equity vesting periods to 5+ years
- Require post-departure holding periods
- Mandate clawback provisions for short-term gains causing long-term damage
- Expand disclosure of compensation relative to long-term value metrics

Corporate Governance Standards

- Require long-term value creation metrics alongside quarterly financials
- Mandate board committees focused on long-term strategy
- Support benefit corporation legislation for stakeholder governance
- Reform securities regulations to reduce quarterly earnings

Addressing corporate short-termism requires policy interventions that realign incentives throughout the financial and corporate ecosystem:

- ★ **Stock Buyback Regulation:** Increase excise tax to 5%, require minimum R&D and capital investment thresholds, mandate disclosure of executive stock sales after buybacks, and prohibit debt-financed buybacks.
- ★ **Executive Compensation Reform:** Extend equity vesting periods to 5+ years, require post-departure holding periods, mandate claw-back provisions for short-term gains causing long-term damage, and expand compensation disclosure relative to long-term value metrics.
- ★ **Long-term Shareholder Incentives:** Implement graduated capital gains taxes that decrease with the holding period, grant enhanced voting rights to long-term shareholders, create tax-advantaged accounts for long-term holdings, and support "long-term only" investment funds.
- ★ **Corporate Governance Standards:** Require long-term value creation metrics alongside quarterly financials, mandate board committees focused on long-term strategy, support benefit corporation legislation for stakeholder governance, and reform securities regulations to reduce quarterly earnings pressure.

These reforms would be implemented through coordinated action rather than isolated interventions, recognizing that short-termism results from a complex system of interlocking incentives rather than any single policy failure.

Implementation Strategy: Bringing Long-termism to Life

Making these reforms a reality requires action across multiple domains:

- ★ **SEC Reforms:** Enhance disclosure requirements for long-term performance, regulate earnings guidance

practices, support long-term investment vehicles and exchanges, and protect companies making appropriate long-term investments from opportunistic activism.

- ★ **Tax Code Changes:** Implement graduated capital gains rates based on holding periods, reform executive compensation taxation, enhance deductions for qualified research, and limit deductibility of compensation not tied to long-term metrics.
- ★ **Corporate Governance Standards:** Develop voluntary board guidelines for long-term value oversight, promote industry-led initiatives for longer-term performance metrics, secure institutional investor commitments to evaluate companies on appropriate timeframes, and create educational initiatives highlighting the costs of short-termism.

Dr. Rational concludes: "The dominant tribe demonstrates awareness of their temporal myopia problem but struggles to implement solutions due to collective action challenges. However, increasing competitive pressure from rival tribes with longer planning horizons may eventually force adaptation. Whether this adaptation occurs proactively through policy reform or reactively through competitive failure remains an open question in this fascinating evolutionary experiment."

IMPLEMENTATION STRATEGY:
Bringing Long-termism to Life

SEC REFORMS

- Enhance disclosure requirements for tong-term performance
- Regulate earnings guidance practices
- Support long-term investment vehicles/ exchanges
- Protect companies making appropriate long-term investments from opportunistic activism.

TAX CODE CHANGES

- Implement graduated capital gains rates based on holding periods
- Reform executive compensation taxation
- Enhance deductions for qualified research
- Limit deductibility of compensation not tied to long-term metrics

CORPORATE GOVERNANCE STANDARDS

- Develop voluntary board guidelines for long-term value oversight
- Promote industry-led initiatives for longer-term performance metrics
- Secure institutional investor commitments to evaluate companies on appropriate timeframes

3. BANKING THAT BUILDS: FINANCING THE REAL ECONOMY

> *"A single beam cannot support a great house."*
> —Book of Documents

Analytical Framework: Financial Institutions' Role in Productive Investment

At its core, banking exists to channel savings into productive investment—connecting those with capital to those with ideas, enterprises, and growth opportunities. This intermediation function represents banking's essential contribution to economic prosperity and advancement.

Yet America's banking system has progressively shifted from this fundamental purpose toward speculative activities, fee extraction, and financial engineering. The transformation can be quantified:

- ★ The percentage of bank assets devoted to commercial and industrial loans declined from 25% in 1985 to approximately 12% today
- ★ Trading assets at major banks grew from negligible levels in the 1980s to over 30% of total assets
- ★ Fee income as a percentage of bank revenue nearly doubled over the past four decades
- ★ The number of community banks—those most focused on relationship lending—declined by over 70% since 1984

This shift hasn't merely changed banking's profit sources; it has fundamentally altered how capital flows through the economy, with profound implications for innovation, regional development, small business formation, and ultimately, American competitiveness in the global economy.

Shifting from Productive Banking to Speculation & Fees

America's banking system has progressively shifted toward speculative activities, fee extraction, and financial engineering. The transformation can be quantified:

25% in 1985 to **12%**

The percentage of bank assets devoted to commercial & industrial loans

over 30%

Trading assets at major banks grew from negligible levels in the 1980s

Fee income as % of **bank revenue**

nearly doubled over the past four decades

over 70% since 1984

The number of community banks—those most focused on relationship lending—declined by

As Dr. Rational observes: "The species has evolved a peculiar financial system that increasingly extracts value from rather than adds value to the productive economy—the equivalent of a circulatory system that prioritizes its own maintenance over delivering oxygen to vital organs."

Character Development: Banker Bob Rediscovers Lending

Scene: The dusty archives beneath a major bank headquarters. BANKER BOB, mid-career and meticulously dressed, searches through old records. He pulls out a leather-bound ledger from 1962, blows off dust, and opens it with curiosity.

BANKER BOB: *(reading aloud with growing confusion)* "Johnson Manufacturing Company... loan approved based on... strong management team, sound business plan, and community standing?" *(looks up bewildered)* "Where are the algorithmic credit scores? The collateral requirements? The quarterly covenant tests?"

An ELDERLY JANITOR appears, startling Bob.

ELDERLY JANITOR: "Finding something interesting in the old records, sir?"

BANKER BOB: "This ledger shows loans to businesses without established credit histories! Some had minimal collateral! The documentation is just... notes about the owners' character and business conditions! Was the bank insane?"

ELDERLY JANITOR: *(chuckling)* "That's how banking worked back then, son. Bankers knew their borrowers personally. Understood their businesses. Made loans based on potential, not just collateral and credit scores."

BANKER BOB: *(incredulous)* "But how did they manage risk? Where's the standardized underwriting matrix?"

ELDERLY JANITOR: "They managed risk by understanding what they were financing. Visited businesses regularly. Knew the owners' families. Watched market conditions. You might call it 'relationship banking.'"

BANKER BOB: *(examining more entries)* "And these interest rates! Just a few points above deposit rates! How did they generate shareholder returns without complex fee structures?"

ELDERLY JANITOR: "Volume and patient capital. The bank made money when businesses succeeded and grew. Created alignment of interests." *(pauses)* "Before my custodial days, I was a loan officer here for thirty years."

BANKER BOB: *(looking up, surprised)* "You were a banker?"

ELDERLY JANITOR: "Started as a teller in '62. Worked my way up to commercial lending. Financed three generations of businesses in this town. When MegaBank acquired us and centralized all lending decisions to headquarters, I... became redundant. Now I clean the offices where algorithms make decisions I used to make."

BANKER BOB: *(digesting this)* "Did it... work better? This relationship approach?"

ELDERLY JANITOR: "We had fewer defaults despite less collateral. Worked with businesses through tough times instead of calling loans at the first covenant breach. Helped build this community rather than extract from it."

BANKER BOB: *(thoughtful)* "The executive committee is meeting tomorrow about our declining market share in small business lending... despite our sophisticated models, we keep losing customers to that new community bank downtown."

ELDERLY JANITOR: *(smiling)* "Perhaps you should bring that ledger to the meeting. Sometimes the future can learn from the past."

Banker Bob nods slowly, tucking the ledger under his arm as he heads upstairs, already drafting a proposal in his mind for a relationship-centered lending division.

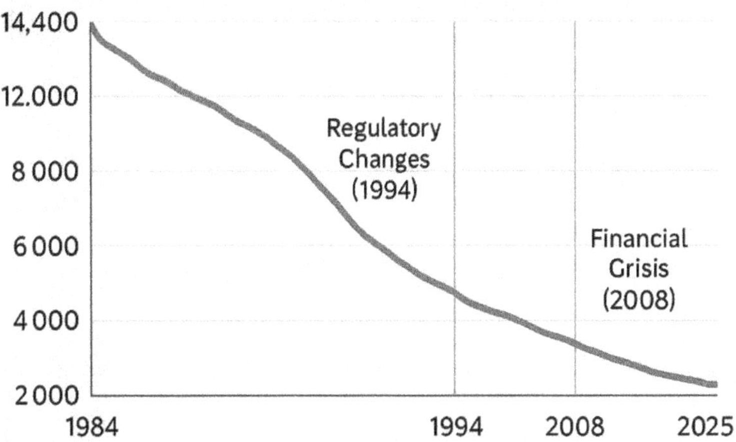

In 1984, the United States had approximately 14,400 commercial banks, most serving specific geographic communities with relationship-based models. By 2025- that number had plummeted to fewer than 4,200-a decline of over 70% driven by both failures and acquisitions.

Historical Analysis: Community Banking Decline and Financial Consolidation

The American banking landscape has transformed dramatically through consolidation, with profound implications for capital access and economic development:

In 1984, the United States had approximately 14,400 commercial banks, most of which served specific geographic communities using relationship-based models. By 2025, that number had plummeted to fewer than 4,200—a decline of over 70% driven by both failures and acquisitions.

This consolidation reflects multiple forces:

- ★ Financial deregulation, particularly the 1994 Riegle-Neal Act, allowed nationwide banking
- ★ Technology and scale advantages favor larger institutions
- ★ Regulatory compliance costs disproportionately burden smaller banks
- ★ Crisis-driven consolidation, especially following the 2008 financial crisis

The consequences extend far beyond banking sector structure to affect how capital flows throughout the economy:

- ★ Reduced "relationship lending" based on local knowledge and personal interaction
- ★ Centralized decision-making, removing lending authority from local communities
- ★ Standardized credit models disadvantage unique or innovative enterprises
- ★ Geographic concentration of banking assets in major financial centers
- ★ Diminished focus on small business lending as large banks pursue larger transactions and fee-based services
- ★ This transformation particularly impacts:
- ★ Small businesses are dependent on relationship lending
- ★ Rural communities are losing local banking services
- ★ Minority-owned enterprises are historically better served by community institutions

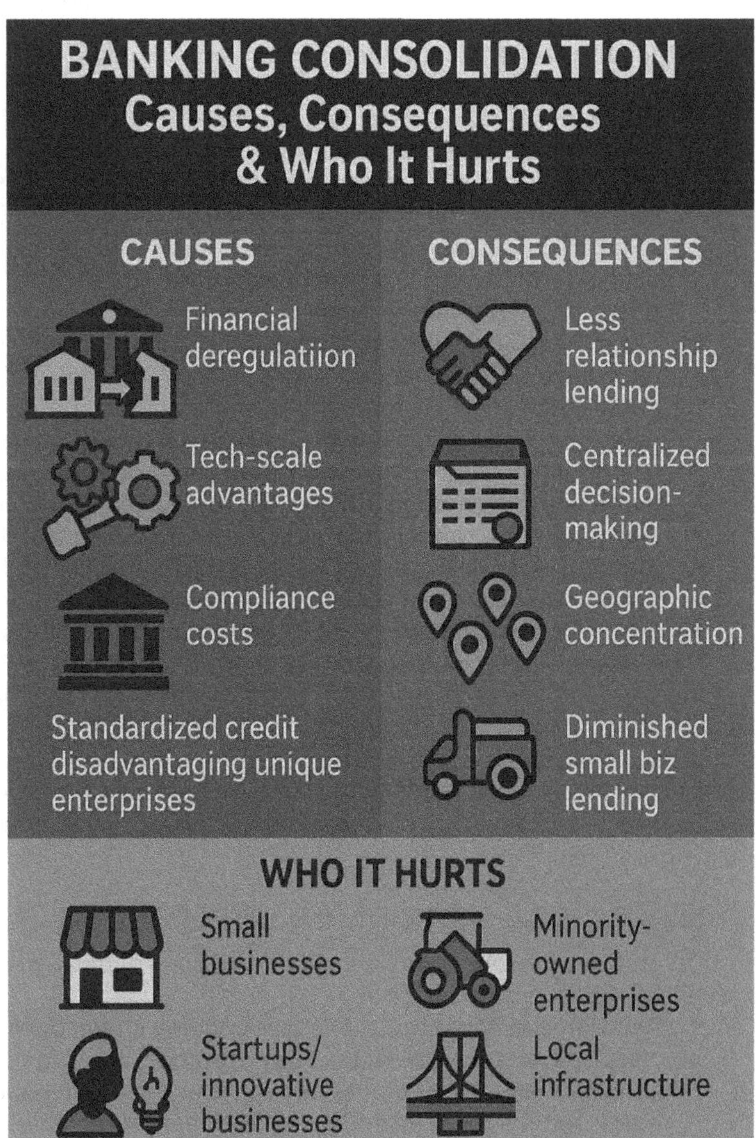

BANKING CONSOLIDATION
Causes, Consequences & Who It Hurts
CAUSES
CONSEQUENCES
Financial deregulatiion
Less relationship lending
Tech-scale advantages
Centralized decision-making
Compliance costs
Geographic concentration
Standardized credit disadvantaging unique enterprises
Diminished small biz lending
WHO IT HURTS
Small businesses
Minority-owned enterprises
Startups/ innovative businesses
Local infrastructure

★ Start-ups and innovative companies that don't fit standardized credit models
★ Local infrastructure projects requiring patient capital and community commitment

The decline of community banking represents not merely industry consolidation but a fundamental shift in how financial institutions interact with the communities they ostensibly serve—from participants in local economic development to increasingly distant extractors of monetary value.

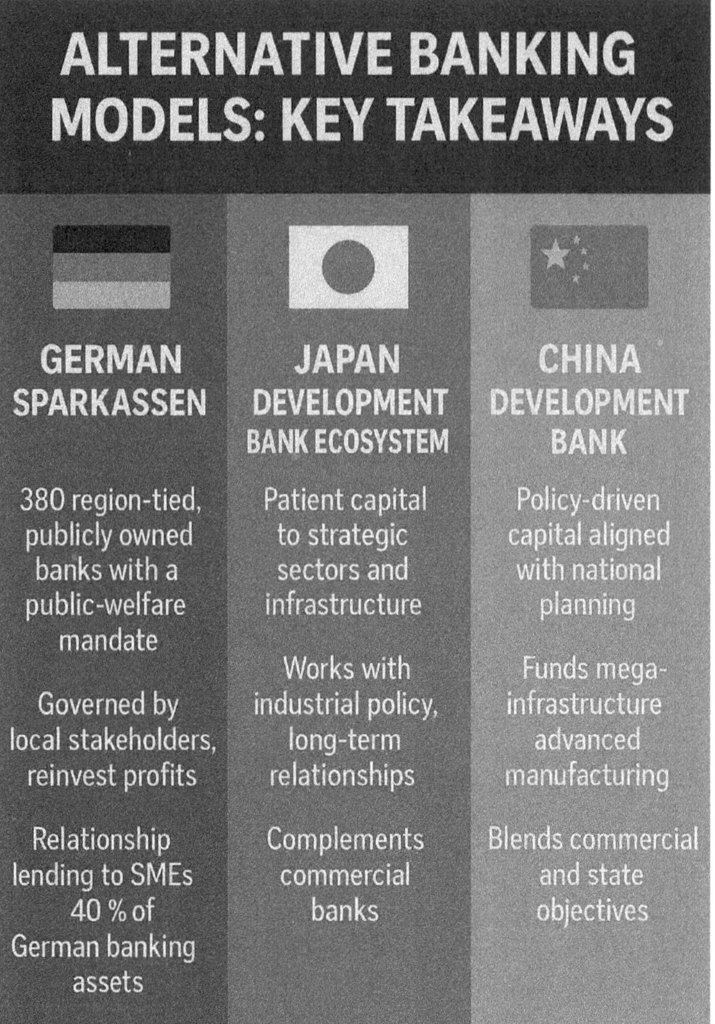

ALTERNATIVE BANKING MODELS: KEY TAKEAWAYS
GERMAN SPARKASSEN
380 region-tied, publicly owned banks with a public-welfare mandate
Governed by local stakeholders, reinvest profits
Relationship lending to SMEs 40 % of German banking assets
JAPAN DEVELOPMENT BANK ECOSYSTEM
Patient capital to strategic sectors and infrastructure
Works with industrial policy, long-term relationships
Complements commercial banks
CHINA DEVELOPMENT BANK
Policy-driven capital aligned with national planning
Funds mega-infrastructure advanced manufacturing
Blends commercial and state objectives

Comparative Study: Alternative Banking Models and Their Effectiveness

While America's banking system has increasingly disconnected from productive enterprise, other nations maintain alternative models that more effectively support their real economies:

★ **German Sparkassen System:** A network of 380 public savings banks serving specific regions without destructive competition. It features a public welfare mandate, local stakeholder governance, limited profit distribution, an emphasis on sustainable returns, and represents 40% of German banking assets.
★ **Japan's Development Bank Ecosystem:** Public financial institutions with sectoral development mandates provide patient capital for strategic industries and infrastructure. It coordinates banking with industrial policy through long-term relationship banking, complementing commercial banking with strong connections between financial and productive sectors.
★ **China Development Bank Model:** Policy bank financing strategic priorities integrated with five-year planning and industrial strategy. Aligns capital allocation with national development goals, demonstrates patience for infrastructure and advanced manufacturing returns, blends commercial practices with strategic objectives, and coordinates with commercial banks on national priorities.

These alternative models share important characteristics despite their cultural and historical differences:

★ **Long-term Orientation:** Willingness to wait for returns on productive investments
★ **Geographic/Sectoral Focus:** Specialization providing a deeper understanding of borrowers
★ **Blended Metrics:** Evaluation based on both financial and broader economic impacts
★ **Stakeholder Governance:** Decision-making incorporating community and policy considerations
★ **Development Mandate:** Explicit recognition of banking's role in economic development

Their effectiveness in supporting productive investment can be measured by the outcomes: Germany maintains a world-leading manufacturing sector despite high labor costs; Japan rebuilt its economy through targeted financial support for strategic industries; and China finances rapid infrastructure development and technological advancement.

Dr. Rational notes with interest: "The dominant economic tribe's banking model emphasizes abstract efficiency over concrete effectiveness in capital allocation to productive enterprise. Their rivals employ alternative arrangements that appear less efficient by conventional metrics but more effectively direct capital toward strategic priorities and long-term development."

Financial Analysis: The Economics of Relationship Banking versus Transaction Banking

The shift from relationship banking to transaction banking represents more than a change in style—it fundamentally alters how capital flows through the economy:

★ **Relationship Banking:** Emphasizes ongoing interactions and a deep understanding of borrowers using "soft" information (character, business model, local conditions). It evaluates credit based on potential and context, maintains flexibility through economic cycles, creates mutual interest in borrower success, and generates returns through long-term customer profitability.

★ **Transaction Banking:** Focuses on standardized products and quantitative metrics using "hard" information (credit scores, financial statements). Applies rigid backward-looking criteria, amplifies credit cycles through formulaic assessment, maintains arm's-length fee-extraction relationships, and generates returns through transaction volume and financial engineering.

★ **Economic Impact:** Transaction banking often underserves non-standard businesses (which are usually the most innovative), while relationship banking better supports regional economic development. Transaction approaches create greater credit procyclicality, while relationship models better support businesses through difficulties, avoiding excess credit in booms and inadequate credit in busts.

The economics of these models also differ in fundamental ways. Transaction banking appears more efficient when measuring cost-per-transaction or loans-per-employee. However, relationship banking often produces superior outcomes in loan performance, customer retention, and contribution to regional economic development.

As banking has shifted decisively toward the transaction model, American finance has become less effective at identifying and supporting the most promising productive investments, precisely when technological competition with China demands excellence in capital allocation to innovative enterprises.

Policy Proposal: National Investment Bank, Community Banking Revival, and Glass-Steagall Modernization

Rebuilding banking that serves the real economy requires a comprehensive policy approach:

★ **National Investment Bank (NIB):** This public institution, with an initial capitalization of $100B, provides patient capital for infrastructure, innovation, and industrial renewal. It operates on commercial principles, focusing on broader economic metrics and strategic sectors, while coordinating with the national economic strategy and maintaining its independence.

★ **Community Banking Revival:** Implements tiered regulation to reduce the compliance burden for smaller institutions, provides tax incentives for new community bank formation, offers technical assistance and federal matching funds for underserved areas, creates a technology platform for achieving scale economies, and supports mutual and cooperative banking models.

★ **Glass-Steagall Modernization:** Functionally separates essential banking from speculative trading with differential regulation based on activities, protects deposit insurance for core banking, prevents cross-subsidization, ensures orderly failure of speculative entities, and prohibits proprietary trading by deposit-taking institutions.

ALTERNATIVE BANKING MODELS: SHARED CHARACTERISTICS

Long-term Orientation
Willingness to wait for returns on productive investments

Geographic/Sectoral Focus
Specialization providing deeper understanding of borrowers

Blended Metrics
Evaluation based on both financial and broader economic impacts

Stakeholder Governance
Decision-making incorporating community and policy considerations

Development Mandate
Explicit recognition of banking's role in economic development

The Economics of Relationship Banking versus Transaction Banking

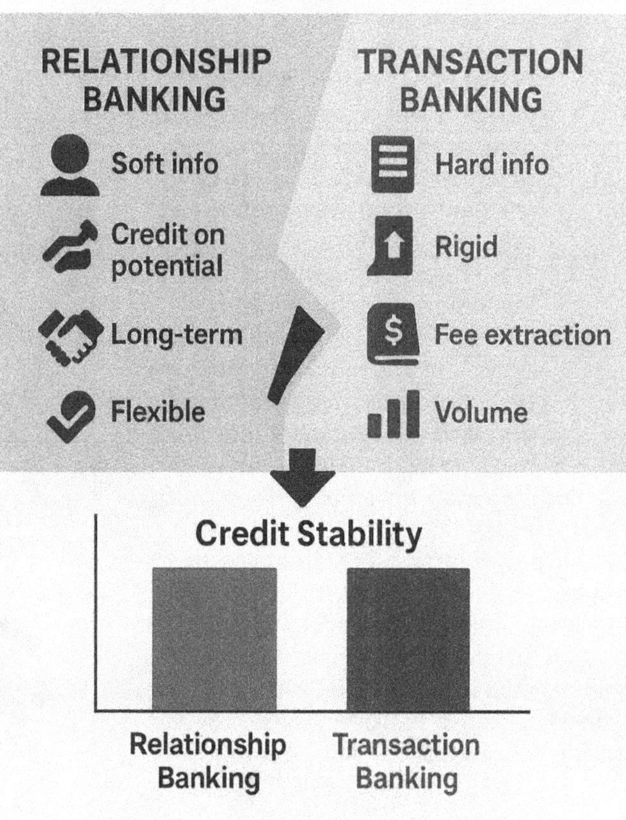

- ★ **Regional Credit Allocation Framework:** This framework requires equitable geographic lending distribution, modernizes the Community Reinvestment Act, supports community development financial institutions, conducts credit needs assessments, offers regulatory incentives for underbanked communities, and implements technology solutions for underserved regions.

These reforms would fundamentally reorient American banking toward its essential function: efficiently allocating capital to its most productive uses in the real economy. By providing alternatives to purely profit-maximizing models, they would create space for patient capital to support long-term, productive investment.

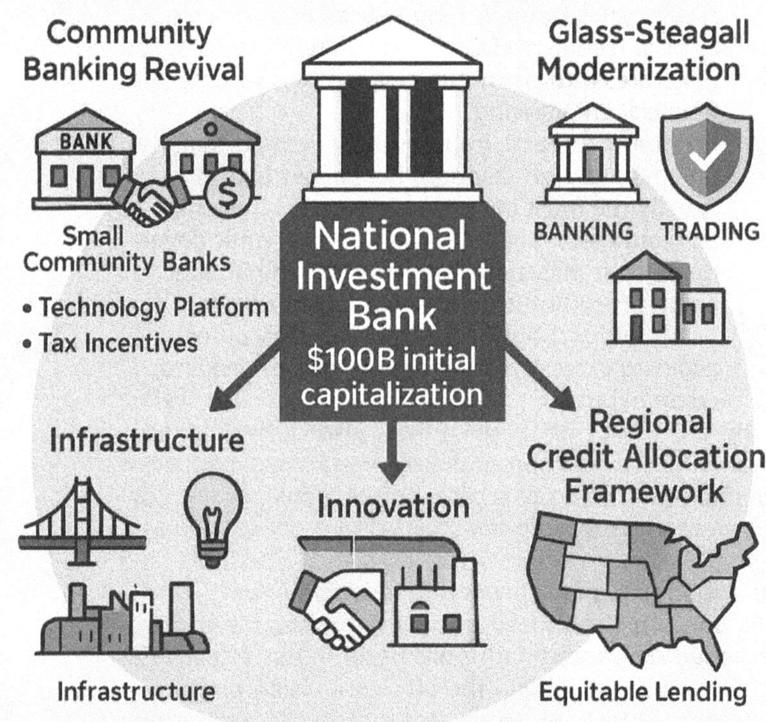

Implementation Plan: Making Banking Reform a Reality

Transforming America's banking system requires coordinated action across multiple domains:

- ★ **Legislative Framework:** National Investment Bank Authorization Act, Community Banking Revitalization Act, Financial Services Segmentation Act (modern Glass-Steagall), and Regional Development Banking Act.
- ★ **Funding Mechanisms:** Congressional appropriation for NIB initial capitalization, public-private partnership structure for ongoing funding, tax incentives for community bank investment, and federal matching funds for development-focused lending.
- ★ **Institutional Design:** Governance structures that balance independence with accountability, performance metrics that incorporate financial and development objectives, regional distribution of authority, and coordination mechanisms between public and private institutions.
- ★ **Transition Management:** Phased implementation, preventing market disruption, grandfathering provisions for existing institutions, technical assistance for adaptation, and education/training for relationship banking skills.

Dr. Rational observes: "The species demonstrates awareness of its banking system's dysfunction but struggles to implement reforms due to the concentrated influence of beneficiaries of the current arrangement. This creates vulnerability in their economic competition with rival tribes using alternative banking models to channel capital toward strategic priorities."

MAKING BANKING REFORM REALITY

Transforming America's banking system requires coordinated action across four pillars.

POLICY TOOLKIT

- NIB Authorization Act
- Community Banking Revitalization Act
- Modern Glass-Steagall (Financial Services Segmentation)
- Regional Development Banking Act

FUNDING

- Congressional seed capital for NIB
- Public-private partnerships
- Community-bank tax incentives
- Federal matching for development lending

INSTITUTIONAL DESIGN

- Independent & accountable governance
- Dual financial + development metrics
- Regional authority

TRANSITION

- Phased rollout
- Grandfather exisig banks
- Technical assistance & training
- Relationshhip banking education

4. THE DOLLAR'S DILEMMA: MANAGING RESERVE CURRENCY STATUS

> *"The taller the tree, the stronger the wind."*
> —Chinese proverb

AMERICA'S EXORBITANT PRIVILEGE
Borrowing in Own Currency
The U.S. can Issue debt in dollars, eliminating direct exchange rate risk
Lower Borrowing Costs
Global demand for dollar assets reduces interest rates on U.S.government and corporate debt

Transaction Advantages
American companies face lower currency conversion costs in international trade
Policy Flexibility
The U.S. can run persistent trade deficits without typical balance of payments crises
Financial Sanctions Power
Control of dollar-based systems enables powerful economic coercion tools

Analytical Framework: Reserve Currency Status as Both Privilege and Vulnerability

The U.S. dollar holds a unique position in global finance, serving as the world's primary reserve currency, the dominant medium for international trade, and the standard unit for pricing commodities. This status, which former French Finance Minister Valéry Giscard d'Estaing famously called America's "exorbitant privilege," confers remarkable advantages:

- ★ **Borrowing in Own Currency:** The U.S. can issue debt in dollars, eliminating direct exchange rate risk.
- ★ **Lower Borrowing Costs:** Global demand for dollar assets reduces interest rates on U.S. government and corporate debt
- ★ **Transaction Advantages:** American companies face lower currency conversion costs in international trade
- ★ **Policy Flexibility:** The U.S. can run persistent trade deficits without typical balance of payments crises
- ★ **Financial Sanctions Power:** Control of dollar-based systems enables powerful economic coercion tools

Yet this same privilege creates vulnerabilities that have grown more acute in recent years:

- ★ **Economic Distortions:** A persistently strong dollar disadvantages exports and manufacturing
- ★ **Policy Constraints:** Federal Reserve decisions must consider global impacts, limiting domestic focus
- ★ **Borrowing Enablement:** Easy access to foreign capital facilitates fiscal irresponsibility
- ★ **Strategic Incentives:** Competitors have a strong motivation to develop alternative systems
- ★ **Complacency Risk:** Dollar advantages mask underlying economic weaknesses requiring attention

RISKS OF AMERICA'S EXORBITANT PRIVILEGE
Yet this same privilege creates vulnerabilities that have grown more acute in recent years:
Economic Distortions
A persistently strong dollar disadvantages exports and manufacturing
Policy Constraints
Federal Reserve decisions must consider global impacts, limiting domestic focus

Borrowing Enablement
Easy access to foreign capital tacilitates facilities irresponsibillity
Strategic Incentives
Competitors have strong motivation to develop alternative systems
Complacency Risk
Dollar advantages mask underlying-economic weaknesses requiring attention

As Dr. Rational observes in his field notes: "The dominant tribe's currency has achieved remarkable acceptance, creating significant advantages but also insidious long-term risks. The exorbitant privilege functions as a form of economic painkiller, masking symptoms of decline while the underlying condition worsens."

This framework helps explain why the dollar remains supreme despite America's declining share of global GDP, persistent trade deficits, and growing debt burden, while also highlighting why this supremacy cannot be taken for granted indefinitely.

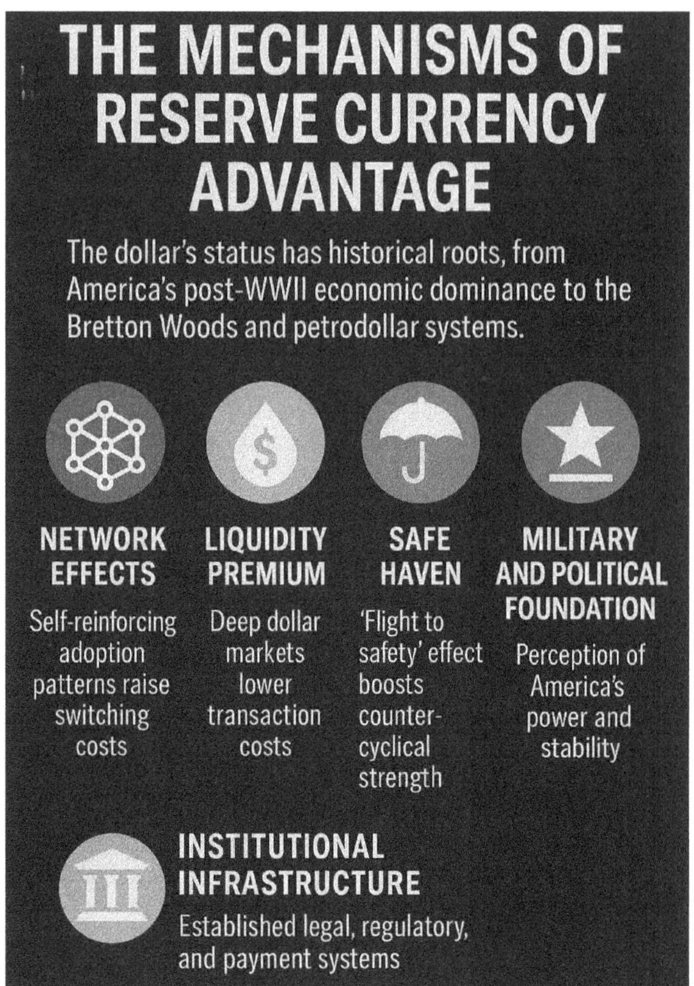

THE MECHANISMS OF RESERVE CURRENCY ADVANTAGE
The dollar's status has historical roots, from America's post-WWII economic dominance to the Bretton Woods and petrodollar systems.
NETWORK EFFECTS
Self-reinforcing adoption patterns raise switching costs
LIQUIDITY PREMIUM
Deep dollar markets lower transaction costs
SAFE HAVEN
'Flight to safety' effect boosts counter-cyclical strength
MILITARY AND POLITICAL FOUNDATION
Perception of America's power and stability
INSTITUTIONAL INFRASTRUCTURE
Established legal, regulatory, and payment systems

Character Vignette: Madame Créancière's Diplomatic Tea

Scene: An elegant diplomatic reception at an international financial forum. DUKE THE DOLLAR DEMIGOD, looking slightly disheveled but maintaining an aristocratic bearing, samples canapés while MADAME CRÉANCIÈRE (China), impeccably dressed in a designer suit with subtle national symbolism, approaches with a calculated smile.

MADAME CRÉANCIÈRE: *(with exquisite politeness)* "Duke! How lovely to see you. You're looking... comfortable, considering the circumstances."

DUKE: *(slightly defensive)* "Madame Créancière! My favorite creditor! Tell me, how many trillions of my debt are you holding these days?"

MADAME CRÉANCIÈRE: *(sipping jasmine tea)* "A significant position we value greatly, though prudent portfolio management suggests gradual diversification. I couldn't help but notice that your national debt recently surpassed $36 trillion. Quite the achievement!"

DUKE: *(waving dismissively)* "Mere accounting! When you're the world's reserve currency, traditional constraints don't apply. Everyone needs dollars!"

MADAME CRÉANCIÈRE: "Of course, of course. Such a convenient arrangement. However, I did observe that your interest payments now exceed your defense budget. A temporary situation, surely?"

DUKE: *(tugging at his collar)* "Technical budgetary fluctuation! Nothing structural!"

MADAME CRÉANCIÈRE: "Naturally. And those infrastructure needs? Are the research investments required to maintain technological leadership? I'm certain you'll address those... eventually."

DUKE: *(growing uncomfortable)* "We maintain the world's deepest capital markets! Unparalleled financial innovation!"

MADAME CRÉANCIÈRE: *(with a thin smile)* "Indeed. Your financial engineering is without equal. Though we find a balance of financial and actual engineering serves us well. But please, don't let me detain you from the buffet. The shrimp is excellent—farm-raised in Guangdong Province's largest aquaculture facility, which has recently been upgraded with our new automated feeding system. We're quite proud of our aquacultural technology advances."

She glides away, leaving Duke to nervously drain his champagne glass while checking Treasury yield curves on his phone.

DUKE: *(muttering to himself)* "She's just trying to rattle me. The yuan isn't even fully convertible! The euro's a mess! What are they going to use instead? Bitcoin?" *(He laughs but stops abruptly when he notices Madame Créancière quietly conversing with representatives from Saudi Arabia, Russia, and Brazil in a corner.)*

This scene captures the subtle power dynamics between debtor and creditor nations—a reversal of traditional relationships when the debtor controls the world's reserve currency. The awkward dance between the United States and China reflects both the persistent power of the dollar system and the gradual erosion of its foundations.

EVOLUTION OF DOLLAR RESERVE CURRENCY MECHANISMS

Yet these mechanisms have evolved significantly in recent decades:

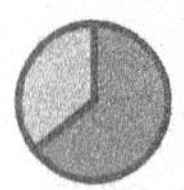
The dollar's share of global reserves has declined from approximately 70% in 2000 to about 59% today

Technology has reduced transaction costs for non-dollar currencies

Alternative payment systems have developed to bypass traditional dollar-centered networks

Digital currencies create potential for significant disruption to existing advantages

America's political polarization raises questions about institutional stability

Monetary Analysis: The Mechanisms of Reserve Currency Advantage and Their Evolution

The dollar's global dominance emerged from unique historical circumstances: America's economic supremacy after World

War II, the 1944 Bretton Woods agreement establishing the dollar as the anchor of the international monetary system, and subsequently, the petrodollar system, which ensured that oil trades were denominated in dollars.

The mechanisms creating "exorbitant privilege" operate through several channels:

1. **Network Effects:** Reserve currencies demonstrate powerful network externalities—the more entities that use dollars, the more valuable dollar use becomes. This creates self-reinforcing adoption patterns and significant switching costs, which explains why reserve currencies tend to persist despite changes in underlying economic fundamentals.
2. **Liquidity Premium:** The unmatched depth and breadth of dollar markets reduce transaction costs and increase financial flexibility. U.S. Treasury securities, in particular, serve as the closest approximation to a risk-free asset in the global economic system, creating persistent demand regardless of the yield.
3. **Safe Haven Status:** During crises, capital typically flows toward dollars—a "flight to safety" effect that paradoxically strengthens the dollar when the U.S. economy (or even the global economy) weakens. This countercyclical strength reinforces the dollar's perceived stability.
4. **Institutional Infrastructure:** The legal, regulatory, and financial systems supporting dollar transactions have been developed over decades. The SWIFT messaging system, Fedwire, CHIPS, and other dollar-based financial infrastructure create formidable advantages for dollar usage.
5. **Military and Political Foundation:** The dollar's reserve status rests partly on America's military power and political stability. The perception that the United States can defend its interests and maintain institutional continuity supports confidence in its currency.

Yet these mechanisms have evolved significantly in recent decades:

- ★ The dollar's share of global reserves has declined from approximately 70% in 2000 to <60% today (as of early 2025)
- ★ Technology has reduced transaction costs for non-dollar currencies
- ★ Alternative payment systems have developed to bypass traditional dollar-centered networks
- ★ Digital currencies create potential for significant disruption to existing advantages
- ★ America's political polarization raises questions about institutional stability

As Dr. Rational notes: "The evolution of the dominant tribe's currency advantage resembles many historic monopolies—gradually eroding through a combination of complacency, changing conditions, and deliberate challenges from competitors."

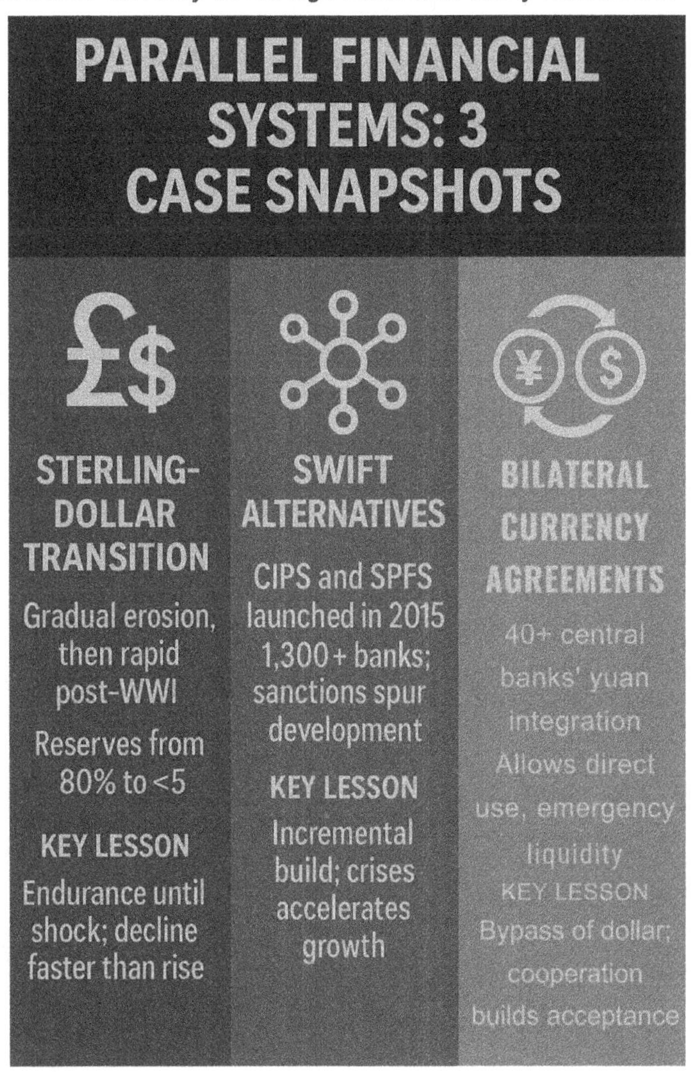

PARALLEL FINANCIAL SYSTEMS: 3 CASE SNAPSHOTS
£$
STERLING-DOLLAR TRANSITION
Gradual erosion, then rapid post-WWI
Reserves from 80% to <5
KEY LESSON
Endurance until shock; decline faster than rise
SWIFT ALTERNATIVES
CIPS and SPFS launched in 2015
1,300+ banks; sanctions spur development
KEY LESSON
Incremental build; crises accelerates growth
¥ $
BILATERAL CURRENCY AGREEMENTS
40+ central banks' yuan integration
Allows direct use, emergency liquidity
KEY LESSON
Bypass of dollar; cooperation builds acceptance

Data Visualization: Dollar's Share of Global Reserves and Yuan Comparison

This visualization reveals several key trends:

1. **Gradual Decline:** The dollar's share has decreased from a peak of approximately 73% in 2001 to <60% today—still dominant but showing persistent erosion.
2. **Acceleration Points:** The rate of decline increased following the 2008 financial crisis and again after the 2022 sanctions on Russia, when reserve-holding nations worldwide reassessed concentration risk.
3. **Euro Plateau:** The euro initially gained a significant share but stabilized around 20% after its own sovereign debt crisis, failing to emerge as a complete alternative to the dollar.
4. **Yuan Growth:** The Chinese yuan has grown from effectively zero in 2015 to approximately 5% today—modest in absolute terms but representing the fastest growth rate among reserve currencies.
5. **Projected Trajectory:** According to current trends, the dollar is projected to decline to approximately 52-55% of global reserves by 2035, remaining the largest single currency but no longer the majority-dominant one.

While these changes appear gradual, they represent significant shifts in a system characterized by strong inertia and network effects. The yuan's growth is particularly notable given China's developing financial markets and remaining capital account restrictions.

Dr. Rational observes: "The relative positions in global currency reserves represent a lagging rather than leading indicator of economic power transitions. Central banks tend to be conservative institutions that adjust allocations gradually, meaning current holdings likely overstate the dollar's fundamental position while understating the yuan's potential trajectory."

Case Studies: Historical Transitions and Alternative Systems Development

Historical precedent suggests reserve currency transitions occur gradually, until they suddenly accelerate. Three cases particularly illuminate current dynamics:

1. **Sterling-to-Dollar Transition:** The British pound's global dominance eroded gradually throughout the early 20th century as the United States' economic weight increased. However, the transition accelerated dramatically after World War II depleted Britain's financial resources. Sterling's share of global reserves fell from approximately 80% in the 1940s to under 5% by the 1970s.

   Key lessons: Reserve status can persist beyond economic fundamentals until a critical threshold is crossed; war and crisis often serve as catalysts for accelerated transitions; decline can be much faster than rise.

2. **SWIFT Alternatives Development:** China's Cross-Border Interbank Payment System (CIPS), launched in 2015, now connects over 1,300 financial institutions across more than 100 countries. While still modest compared to SWIFT's 11,000+ institutions, it provides a critical alternative channel, particularly for entities facing U.S. sanctions. Russia's System for Transfer of Financial Messages (SPFS) offers another, more limited alternative.

   Key lessons: Alternative financial infrastructure develops incrementally; sanctions accelerate the development of parallel systems; interoperability creates network effects that can compete with established systems.

3. **Bilateral Currency Agreements:** The People's Bank of China has established currency swap arrangements with over 40 central banks, enabling direct trade settlement in yuan/local currency pairs without the need for dollars as an intermediary. These arrangements also provide emergency liquidity similar to Fed swap lines but in yuan.

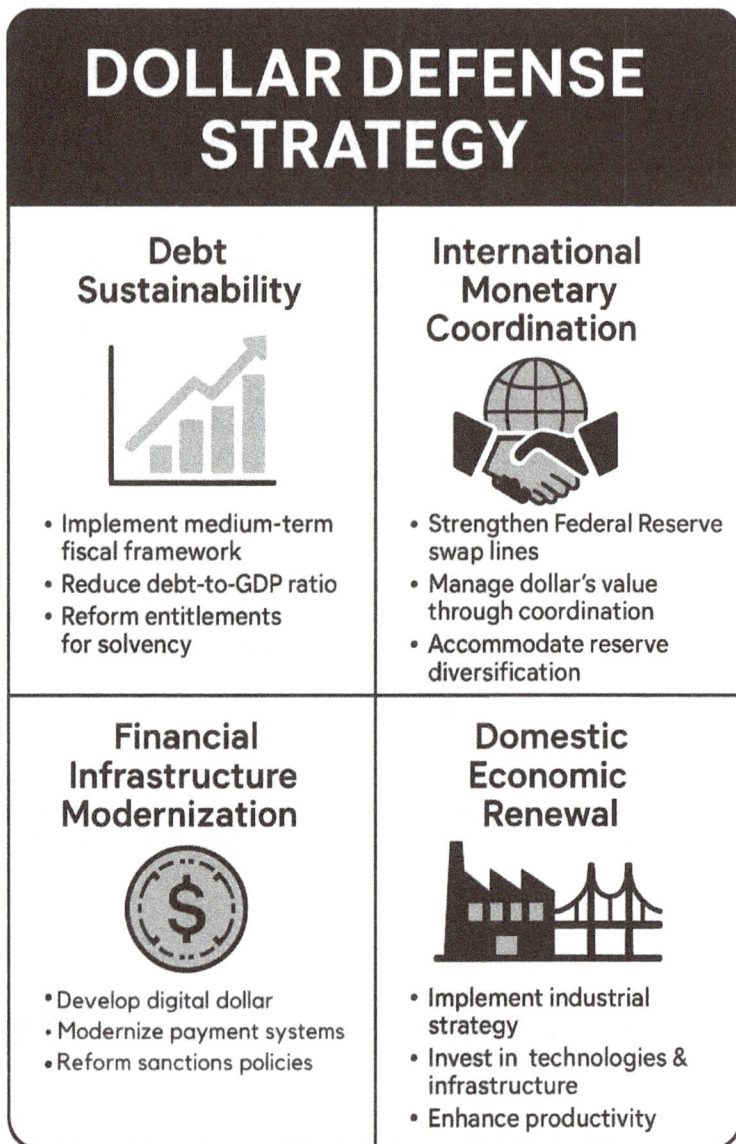

DOLLAR DEFENSE STRATEGY

Debt Sustainability

- Implement medium-term fiscal framework
- Reduce debt-to-GDP ratio
- Reform entitlements for solvency

International Monetary Coordination

- Strengthen Federal Reserve swap lines
- Manage dollar's value through coordination
- Accommodate reserve diversification

Financial Infrastructure Modernization

- Develop digital dollar
- Modernize payment systems
- Reform sanctions policies

Domestic Economic Renewal

- Implement industrial strategy
- Invest in technologies & infrastructure
- Enhance productivity

Making Dollar Defense Reality

Implementing this strategy requires coordinated action across multiple domains.

Treasury Department

- Manage long-term debt
- Currency diplomacy
- Fiscal sustainability framework
- Capital markets

Federal Reserve

- Central bank digital currency
- International swap lines
- Payment systems
- Balance domestic/ international

International Coordination

- Transparency G7/G20 dialogue
- IMF reform Multipolar currency accommodations
- Strategic sanctions

Key lessons: Bilateral arrangements can bypass dominant systems without direct confrontation; central bank cooperation lays the foundation for broader acceptance; crisis preparation facilitates the adoption of alternative systems.

These cases suggest the international monetary system is evolving toward multipolarity rather than a simple replacement of dollar hegemony with yuan dominance. The emerging landscape features multiple regional and specialized systems operating in parallel, with varying degrees of interoperability and competition.

Policy Proposal: Dollar Defense Strategy

Maintaining dollar predominance while addressing vulnerabilities requires a comprehensive strategy:

- ★ **Debt Sustainability:** Implement a medium-term fiscal framework that reduces the debt-to-GDP ratio through balanced revenue increases and spending discipline, while protecting high-return public investments and reforming entitlements to ensure long-term solvency.
- ★ **International Monetary Coordination:** Strengthen Federal Reserve swap lines with allies, collaborate on global financial regulation, manage the dollar's value through multilateral coordination, and selectively accommodate reserve diversification to prevent disruption.
- ★ **Financial Infrastructure Modernization:** Develop a digital dollar with enhanced capabilities, modernize payment systems to reduce costs, improve access to dollar liquidity in emerging markets during crises, and reform sanctions policies to prevent the overuse of accelerating alternatives.
- ★ **Domestic Economic Renewal:** Implement an industrial strategy to strengthen manufacturing and exports, invest in next-generation technologies and infrastructure, enhance productivity through education and workforce development, and pursue energy independence to reduce balance-of-payments vulnerabilities.

This strategy acknowledges that dollar defense ultimately depends less on financial policies than on restoring America's economic fundamentals—productivity growth, innovation leadership, and fiscal sustainability. No amount of financial engineering can maintain currency dominance if the underlying economy weakens.

Implementation Strategy: Making Dollar Defense a Reality

Implementing this strategy requires coordinated action across multiple domains:

- ★ **Treasury Department:** Manage long-term debt to minimize refinancing risks, conduct currency diplomacy with partners and competitors, establish a fiscal sustainability framework with credible targets, and develop capital markets to enhance dollar asset attractiveness.
- ★ **Federal Reserve:** Develop and test central bank digital currency, manage international swap lines with strategic priorities, modernize payment systems, reduce dollar transaction friction, and balance domestic mandates with global responsibilities.
- ★ **International Coordination:** Enhance transparency through G7/G20 monetary dialogue, improve the IMF's legitimacy and effectiveness through reform initiatives, selectively accommodate the evolution of a multipolar currency system, and strategically prioritize financial sanctions to prevent overuse.

Dr. Rational concludes: "The dominant tribe's currency remains their most significant international advantage, yet they have neglected the fundamental economic and fiscal foundations necessary for its long-term sustainability. A strategic approach recognizing both the privilege and responsibility of reserve currency status could extend dollar predominance significantly, though likely not indefinitely in a multipolar world."

5. DIGITAL CURRENCY CHESS MATCH: CBDC STRATEGY FOR DEMOCRACY

> *"Seize the strategic passes, and the realm is yours."*
> —Wei Liaozi

Analytical Framework: The Geopolitics and Domestic Implications of CBDCs

Central bank digital currencies (CBDCs) represent the most significant evolution in money since the shift from gold-backed to fiat currencies. Unlike cryptocurrencies, CBDCs are direct liabilities of central banks—official digital money with the full backing of national monetary authorities. Their development has accelerated dramatically, with at least 130 countries representing 98% of global GDP now exploring CBDCs.

This is not merely a technological upgrade but a strategic contest with profound implications across multiple dimensions:

Geopolitical Dimension:

★ First-mover advantages in establishing standards and operational norms
★ Potential for reduced dollar dominance in cross-border payments
★ New capabilities for sanctions implementation or evasion
★ Strategic positioning in global financial infrastructure competition

Domestic Economic Dimension:

★ Potential disintermediation of commercial banking
★ Financial inclusion for unbanked and underbanked populations
★ Monetary policy implementation with unprecedented precision
★ Payment system efficiency and reduced transaction costs

Governance Dimension:

★ Privacy versus surveillance tradeoffs in monetary systems
★ Public-private boundaries in financial infrastructure
★ Democratic versus authoritarian value expression in currency design
★ Data collection and usage frameworks for financial information

Technological Dimension:

★ Infrastructure requirements for digital currency operation
★ Cybersecurity considerations for monetary systems
★ Interoperability standards across national systems
★ Resilience requirements for essential financial infrastructure

Dr. Rational observes: "The species appears engaged in a fascinating competition to reinvent their primary medium of exchange. What's notable is how different tribes are embedding their core societal values—privacy versus control, individual liberty versus collective stability—directly into the technological architecture of these new forms of money."

This multidimensional chess match pits various political systems, economic philosophies, and technological approaches against each other in a competition that will shape the future of money—and potentially the global financial balance of power.

Character Development: Fed Chair's Nervous Monitoring

Scene: Late night at the Federal Reserve. The FED CHAIR paces nervously, glancing between multiple monitors showing e-CNY adoption metrics and a document labeled "CONFIDENTIAL: Digital Dollar Project Status (Version 42)."

FED CHAIR: *(dictating urgently)* "Policy memo: Digital Dollar Project. Revised timeline... again. Note extreme urgency given Chinese deployment."

AIDE: *(entering with coffee)* "Latest e-CNY statistics just came in. They've reached 261 million users and 1.8 trillion yuan in transactions. The cross-border pilot with Thailand and UAE showed a 50% reduction in settlement costs and an 80% reduction in time compared to current systems."

FED CHAIR: *(groaning)* "While we're still debating whether a digital dollar should exist at all! What's their international expansion looking like?"

AIDE: "Twenty-eight countries now participating in e-CNY cross-border trials. Most recent additions include Brazil, South Africa, and Indonesia—all former dollar-dominant economies in their regions."

FED CHAIR: *(rubbing temples)* "And our progress?"

AIDE: "The committee to form the working group that will establish the parameters for the potential research initiative is scheduled to meet next month to discuss the possibility of developing a framework for considering whether to proceed with exploring options."

FED CHAIR: *(sarcastically)* "Wonderful! We should have a decision by approximately 2031! Meanwhile, Beijing is rewriting the rules of global finance! What's the latest from Congress?"

AIDE: "Republicans are concerned about government surveillance, Democrats are worried about banking system impacts, and nobody is willing to make an actual decision. The crypto lobby is funding opposition on both sides."

FED CHAIR: *(sighs deeply)* "And the big banks?"

AIDE: "Publicly supportive, privately lobbying against any design that might disintermediate them or reduce fee income. They prefer a model where they maintain complete customer control."

FED CHAIR: *(looking at a chart showing declining dollar usage in cross-border payments)* "History will not judge us kindly if we surrender the future of money to Beijing through indecision and stakeholder paralysis. Draft an accelerated timeline. We need a working prototype for limited trials by next year, not next decade."

AIDE: "That would require bypassing at least seven committees and—"

FED CHAIR: *(interrupting)* "Do it anyway. The dollar's future won't wait for our bureaucracy to catch up!"

The aide nods reluctantly as the Fed Chair turns back to the monitors, aware that in this particular chess match, China has already advanced its pieces while America is still deciding whether to sit at the board.

Digital Currency Architecture:

Options & Strategic Implications

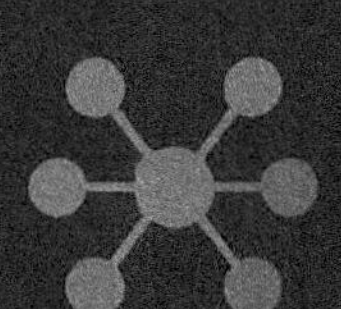

Direct vs. Indirect Models

- Direct: central bank user accounts, maximal control, disintermerdiation risk
- Two-tier: banks/payment providers interface with users, preserves intermediation

Account vs. Token-Based

- Account-based: balances at central bank identity-linked
- Token-based: digital bearer instrument, cash-like
- Mixed: choice by use case/transaction size

Privacy Architectures

- Full transparency to authorities
- Tiered privacy by transaction size or user type
- Zero-knowledge proofs enable compliance with privacy

Programmability Features

- Basic digital cash
- Conditional payments, simple smart contracts
- Fully programmable money with complex automated logic

Technical Analysis: Digital Currency Architecture Options and Strategic Implications

Central bank digital currencies can be designed with dramatically different architectural choices, each reflecting values, priorities, and governance philosophies:

★ **Direct vs. Indirect Models:** Central banks can maintain individual user accounts directly (maximizing control but threatening commercial banking) or operate a two-tier system where banks/payment providers interface with users (preserving financial intermediation). Hybrid models combine both approaches, with central banks handling settlement while intermediaries manage customer relationships.

★ **Account vs. Token-Based Systems:** Account-based systems maintain balances in central bank-guaranteed accounts, while token-based systems function as digital bearer instruments transferring value without intermediaries (similar to physical cash). Mixed systems incorporate elements of both for different use cases or transaction sizes.

★ **Privacy Architectures:** Options range from fully transparent systems, where all transactions are visible to authorities, to tiered privacy models based on transaction size or user type, to zero-knowledge cryptographic approaches that preserve privacy while enabling regulatory compliance.

★ **Programmability Features:** Implementation can range from basic digital versions of current money to intermediate systems with conditional payments and simple smart contracts, to fully programmable money enabling complex automated execution features.

These design choices have profound strategic implications beyond technical considerations:

China's e-CNY has made deliberate architectural decisions reflecting state priorities:

- ★ Two-tier distribution model (preserving banks while maintaining central visibility)
- ★ "Controllable anonymity," where the central bank sees all transactions, while users have limited privacy from each other
- ★ Robust programmability enabling precise policy implementation
- ★ Offline functionality ensures universal access and resilience

CHINA'S e-CNY ARCHITECTURE

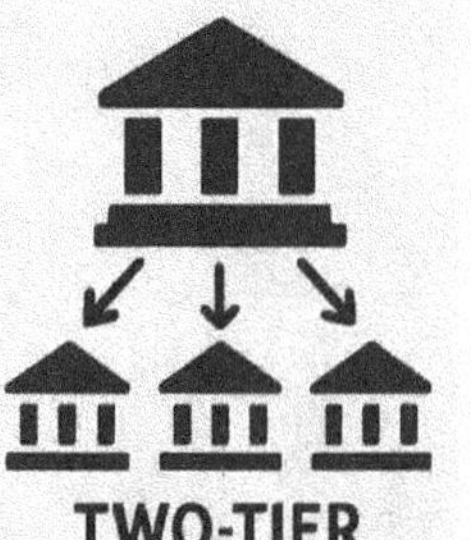

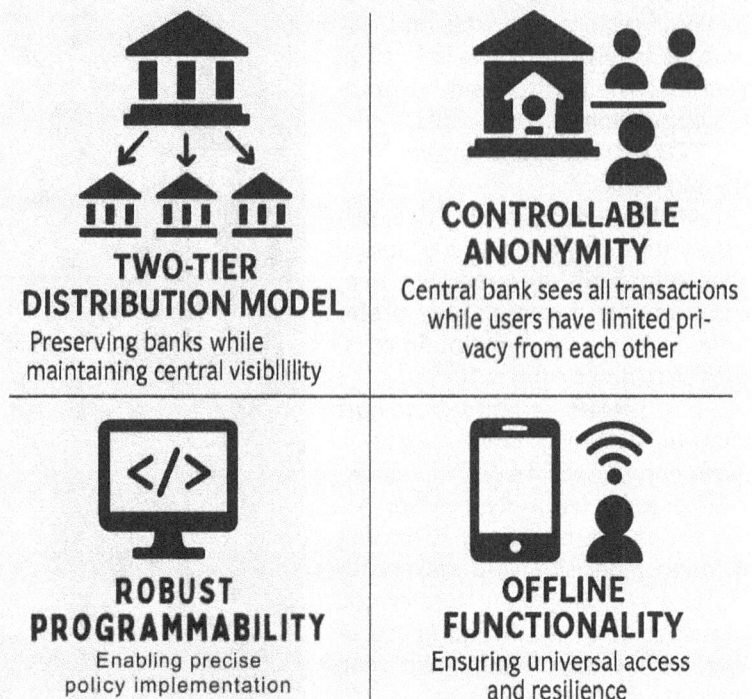

TWO-TIER DISTRIBUTION MODEL

Preserving banks while maintaining central visibllility

CONTROLLABLE ANONYMITY

Central bank sees all transactions while users have limited privacy from each other

ROBUST PROGRAMMABILITY

Enabling precise policy implementation

OFFLINE FUNCTIONALITY

Ensuring universal access and resilience

The People's Bank of China describes these features in benign terms of "improving monetary policy efficiency" and "preventing financial crimes." Yet as Dr. Rational observes, "The architectural choices in digital currency systems reveal fundamental governance philosophies. The surveillance capabilities built into some designs would be technologically impossible with physical cash, creating new paradigms for monetary control—or freedom—depending on design decisions."

European approaches to the digital euro emphasize stronger privacy protections while maintaining regulatory compliance. American discussions remain fragmented between competing visions:

- ★ Commercial banks lobby for maximum intermediary roles
- ★ Civil liberties advocates demand cash-like privacy
- ★ National security officials seek appropriate visibility into suspicious flows
- ★ Technologists push for innovation-enabling designs

The resulting indecision creates strategic vulnerability as China's model gains first-mover advantages in setting international standards and establishing cross-border protocols. As one Federal Reserve economist privately noted: "We're debating the perfect design while they're deploying a working system. There's a very real risk that their architectural decisions become default international standards before we even finalize our approach."

Data Visualization: E-CNY Adoption Metrics Versus Global CBDC Development Timelines

This visualization starkly illustrates China's first-mover advantage:

- ★ **E-CNY (China):** Full domestic deployment with 261+ million users and expanding international trials
- ★ **Digital Euro (EU):** Still in investigation phase with no commitment to launch until 2026-2027 at the earliest
- ★ **Digital Dollar (US):** Research phase with pilot possibilities no earlier than 2026
- ★ **Digital Pound (UK):** Consultation phase with potential pilot in 2025
- ★ **Digital Yen (Japan):** Limited pilot program with uncertain expansion timeline

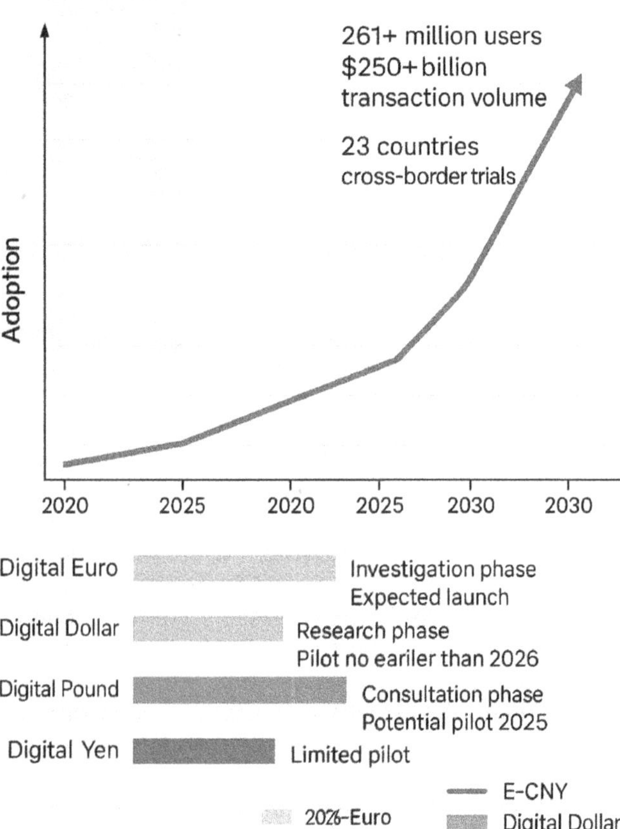

The gap between Chinese deployment and Western exploration creates strategic implications:

1. **Standard Setting:** China gains practical operational experience while others remain theoretical
2. **User Experience:** E-CNY establishes interface norms that later entrants must consider
3. **Cross-Border Protocols:** Chinese systems begin forming interoperability with emerging market CBDCs
4. **Network Effects:** User adoption creates self-reinforcing advantages within China's economic sphere

In his field notes, Dr. Rational observes: "The dominant economic tribe's delayed response to this monetary innovation creates substantial strategic vulnerability. Their historical advantage in setting global financial standards erodes as rival systems develop and deploy, while their own efforts remain nascent. The technical debt accumulates daily."

Comparative Analysis: Privacy Versus Control Tradeoffs Across Political Systems

Digital currencies force explicit choices about privacy, autonomy, and control that physical cash allowed societies to avoid confronting directly. Different political systems are making distinctly different choices that reflect their governance philosophies:

PRIVACY VS. CONTROL IN CBDCs

COMPARATIVE MODELS

Chinese Model Control-Dominant	European Model Privacy Within Regulation	American Approaches Still Evolving

• Full transaction visibility for state • Controllable anonymity (user to-user privacy only) • Address blacklisting & fund freezes • Programmable rules (tax, expiry, geofence)	• Privacy as a right; tiered anonymity • Cash-like privacy for small payments • Compliance checks on large or suspicious flows • Balance inclusion vs. illicit finance	• Ongoing debate over surveillance scope • Strong role for private intermediaries • Priority on banking stability & Innovation • Competing stakeholder visions
Design Philosophy "Security & control first"	Design Philosophy "Privacy balanced with public interest"	Design Philosophy "Model under active debate"

Strategic Implications of e-CNY Deployment Gap

Standard Setting

- Gains practical operational experience
- Others remain theoretical

User Experience

- E-CNY establishes interface norms
- Later entrants must consider

Cross-Border Protocols

- Chinese systems begin forming
- Interoperability with emerging market CBDCs

Network Effects

- User adoption creates
- Self-reinforcing advantages with in China's economic sphere

Chinese Model: Control-Dominant

★ Centralized ledger with complete transaction visibility for authorities

★ "Controllable anonymity," where the central bank sees everything, while users have limited privacy from each other

★ Capability for blacklisting addresses and freezing funds

★ Programmable features potentially enabling automatic tax collection, expiration dates, geographic restrictions, and other forms of monetary control.

★ **Design Philosophy:** "Security and control are prerequisites for properly functioning money."

European Model: Privacy-Within-Regulation

★ Greater emphasis on transaction privacy as a fundamental right

★ Tiered approach with cash-like privacy for smaller transactions

★ Regulatory compliance for larger transactions and suspicious patterns

★ Balance between financial inclusion and preventing illicit usage

★ **Design Philosophy:** "Privacy is a fundamental right that must be balanced with legitimate public interests."

American Approaches: Still Evolving

★ Competing visions between libertarian minimum surveillance and law enforcement visibility

★ Strong potential role for private intermediaries

★ Emphasis on maintaining banking system stability
★ Innovation and competitiveness concerns alongside privacy considerations
★ **Design Philosophy:** "Still under debate, with influential stakeholders pulling in different directions"

These different approaches reflect fundamental governance philosophies—whether money should primarily serve state policy objectives or individual economic autonomy. The resulting systems will embed these values directly into the operation of everyday commerce.

As Nina, the Neural Net Nun, the AI consciousness managing China's e-CNY system, explains with algorithmic precision: "Our design optimizes for societal harmony through appropriate visibility and control mechanisms. What Western observers call 'surveillance' we understand as 'financial security infrastructure' ensuring proper monetary function." Her processors hum contentedly as patterns emerge from billions of transactions, creating what Chinese authorities call "transaction graph intelligence" and Western critics term "financial panopticon."

Policy Proposal: Digital Dollar Strategy for Democracy

America's approach to central bank digital currency must balance innovation, privacy, monetary stability, and strategic position—a delicate equilibrium requiring careful design:

★ **Core Design Principles:** A U.S. CBDC would protect transaction privacy as a fundamental right while enabling legitimate law enforcement access when warranted. It would maintain a two-tier system, preserving roles for regulated financial institutions alongside public infrastructure. The system would ensure universal access, regardless of technical literacy, and implement transparent democratic governance mechanisms. It would also coordinate with allies on interoperable cross-border frameworks that reflect shared values and principles.
★ **Strategic Implementation:** The accelerated timeline commits to prototyping by 2026 with limited deployment by 2027. This includes establishing an alliance framework with democratic partners, securing clear legislative authority for Federal Reserve operations, implementing in phases (beginning with wholesale applications), and fostering collaborative research partnerships with the private sector and academic institutions.
★ **Technical Architecture:** The CBDC would incorporate zero-knowledge proofs for privacy preservation, implement a tiered privacy model providing cash-like features for smaller transactions with enhanced verification for larger amounts, maintain an open architecture to enable innovation within regulatory boundaries, establish robust security protections, and support offline functionality for resilience and accessibility.

This strategy recognizes that a digital dollar is not merely a technological upgrade but a strategic imperative that will shape the future of the international monetary

DIGITAL DOLLAR
DEMOCRACY BY DESIGN

CORE DESIGN
- Privacy by default + lawful access
- Two-tier public/private rails
- Universal & democratic governance

IMPLEMENTATION
- Prototype '26, rollout '27
- Allied interoperability pact
- Wholesale first, legislate authority

TECH
- Zero-knowledge privacy, tiered limits
- Open, secure, offline-capable architecture

MAKING THE DIGITAL DOLLAR REALITY

TECHNICAL DEVELOPMENT
- Testing security, scalability, privacy
- User experience research
- Cross-border protocol development

LEGAL FRAMEWORK
- Clarify Federal Reserve authority
- Set rules for transaction privacy
- Balance AML and civil liberties
- Define international parameters

INTERNATIONAL COORDINATION
- Alliances with democratic nations
- Standards through int'l bodies
- Approaches to illicit finance
- Interoperability with allied CBDCs

system. By striking a balance between innovation and American values, a well-designed digital dollar can enhance both domestic financial inclusion and global influence.

Implementation Plan: Making the Digital Dollar a Reality

Transforming the digital dollar from concept to reality requires coordinated action across multiple domains:

- ★ **Technical Development:** Federal Reserve teams augmented with private sector expertise will conduct focused testing on security, scalability, and privacy protections. This includes user experience research across various demographics and collaborative development of cross-border protocols with key allies.
- ★ **Legal Framework:** Congressional legislation will clarify the Federal Reserve's authority, establish rules for transaction confidentiality, strike a balance between anti-money laundering requirements and civil liberties protections, and define parameters for international CBDC interactions.
- ★ **Stakeholder Engagement:** Implementation will involve planning for commercial bank integration, targeted outreach to financial inclusion participants, public education programs, and security coordination with relevant agencies.
- ★ **International Coordination:** The framework establishes alliances with democratic nations on shared CBDC principles, facilitates the development of standards through international organizations, promotes coordinated approaches to addressing concerns related to illicit finance, and establishes interoperability protocols with allied CBDCs.

Dr. Rational concludes this section with concern: "The dominant tribe's technological conservatism, while sometimes prudent, creates dangerous lags in digital currency development. Their delay allows rival tribes to establish operational norms that may prove difficult to displace later. The resulting strategic vulnerability is significant yet underappreciated by key decision-makers who remain fixated on immediate political considerations rather than long-term strategic positioning."

6. GLOBAL FINANCIAL INSTITUTION REFORM: BRETTON WOODS FOR THE DIGITAL AGE

> *"As water shapes its course to the land, so must institutions adapt to the times."*
>
> —adapted from Sun Tzu

Analytical Framework: Adapting International Financial Institutions for the Multipolar, Digital Economy

The international financial architecture established at Bretton Woods in 1944, centered on the International Monetary Fund (IMF) and World Bank, reflected the economic and political realities of a different era: American hegemony, the gold-dollar standard, limited capital mobility, and physical rather than digital finance. Today's multipolar, digital economy demands fundamentally different institutional arrangements.

The current system faces multiple challenges:

- ★ **Legitimacy Deficit:** Governance structures still reflect post-WWII power distributions rather than current economic realities
- ★ **Digital Disruption:** Traditional institutions struggle to adapt to digital currencies, fintech innovation, and cybersecurity threats
- ★ **Parallel Systems:** China and other emerging powers are developing alternative institutions, such as the Asian Infrastructure Investment Bank (AIIB) and the New Development Bank.
- ★ **Climate Finance Gap:** The Existing architecture inadequately addresses the massive capital needs for climate adaptation and mitigation
- ★ **Development Model Questions:** The "Washington Consensus" development approach faces increasing skepticism from both left and right

These challenges create a fundamental tension: either reform existing institutions to reflect current realities, or risk the emergence of parallel systems, fragmenting the global financial architecture into competing blocs with different standards, priorities, and governance approaches.

As Dr. Rational observes in his field notes: "The species constructed impressively durable international financial institutions that have adapted incrementally for seven decades. However, the rate of environmental change now exceeds their adaptive capacity, creating fertile conditions for institutional competitors with designs more reflective

THE CURRENT SYSTEM FACES MULTIPLE CHALLENGES

LEGITIMACY DEFICIT

Governance structures still reflect post-WWII power distributions rather than current economic realities

DIGITAL DISRUPTION

Traditional institutions struggle to adapt to digital currencies, fintech innovation, and cybersecurity threats

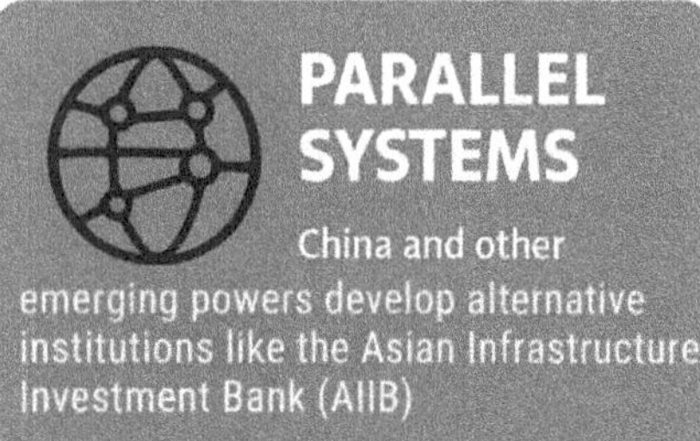

PARALLEL SYSTEMS

China and other emerging powers develop alternative institutions like the Asian Infrastructure Investment Bank (AIIB)

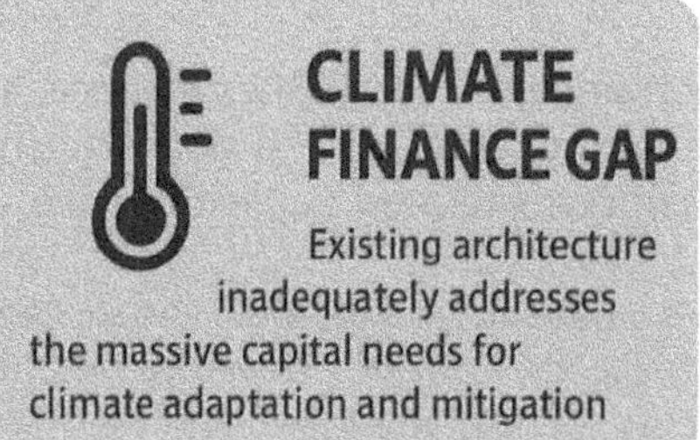

CLIMATE FINANCE GAP

Existing architecture inadequately addresses the massive capital needs for climate adaptation and mitigation

DEVELOPMENT MODEL QUESTIONS

The "Washington Consensus" development approach faces increasing skepticism from both left and right

of current power distributions and technological realities."

Character Dialogue: IMF Director Confronts Chinese Representatives

Scene: A private meeting room at the IMF headquarters in Washington, DC. The IMF DIRECTOR sits across from a delegation of CHINESE REPRESENTATIVES. The atmosphere is cordial but tense.

IMF DIRECTOR: "Let's speak candidly. We understand China's frustration with current governance structures. Your economy represents 18% of global GDP, but holds only 6% of the IMF's voting rights. We're working on reform, but these things take time in a consensus-based institution."

CHINESE REPRESENTATIVE #1: "We appreciate the acknowledgment. China remains committed to the international system. We simply wish to see it better reflect current economic realities."

IMF DIRECTOR: "Yet simultaneously, you're building parallel institutions—the AIIB, the New Development Bank, the Belt and Road Initiative's financing mechanisms. These create alternative channels outside established frameworks."

CHINESE REPRESENTATIVE #2: *(with practiced diplomacy)* "We prefer to think of them as complementary rather than competitive. The world's development needs far exceed what existing institutions can provide."

IMF DIRECTOR: "Complementary institutions typically coordinate their activities. Many of your initiatives operate with different standards for environmental protection, debt sustainability, and governance requirements."

CHINESE REPRESENTATIVE #1: "Different doesn't necessarily mean lower. Perhaps they're simply more respectful of national sovereignty and development priorities. Not every nation wishes to implement identical policy prescriptions."

IMF DIRECTOR: *(leaning forward)* "Let's be direct: Is China building a parallel financial architecture to replace the Bretton Woods system eventually, or seeking reform within it?"

CHINESE REPRESENTATIVE #2: *(smiling slightly)* "Is this an either/or question? A wise strategist keeps multiple options open as conditions evolve. We support reform of existing institutions while developing alternatives that better serve our interests and those of our partners. The future remains unwritten."

IMF DIRECTOR: "That approach creates uncertainty. Financial markets and global stability depend on predictable rules and institutions."

CHINESE REPRESENTATIVE #1: "Indeed. Perhaps this motivates meaningful reform rather than symbolic adjustments. After all, the best way to preserve the current system is to ensure it adapts to changing realities."

IMF DIRECTOR: *(sighing)* "We both know European and American politics make rapid governance reform challenging."

CHINESE REPRESENTATIVE #2: *(standing to leave)* "Then perhaps our 'parallel' initiatives will create helpful incentives for such reform. Competition often drives innovation, even in institutional design. We remain committed partners in the current system... while preparing for all possible futures."

The delegation exits, leaving the IMF Director to contemplate the uncertain future of the institution she leads, caught between Western resistance to change and the Eastern creation of alternatives.

This dialogue captures the fundamental tension in global financial governance: existing institutions must reform to remain relevant, but political obstacles in Western nations make significant reform difficult. Meanwhile, China patiently builds alternative structures that expand its influence while avoiding direct confrontation with established systems.

Historical Analysis: The Evolution of the Bretton Woods System

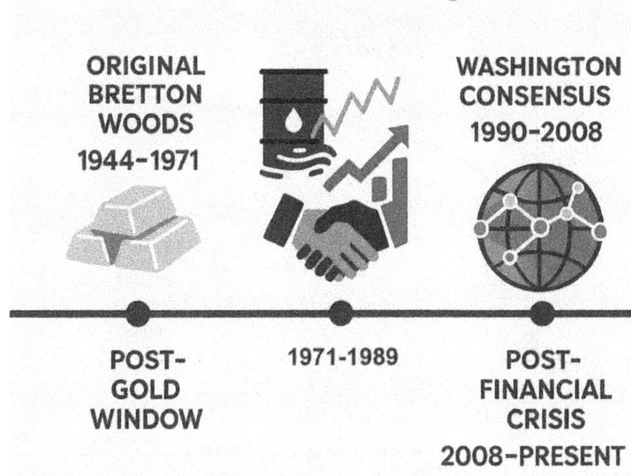

The international financial architecture established at Bretton Woods in 1944 has evolved through several distinct phases:

- ★ **Original Bretton Woods (1944-1971):** The system established dollar-gold convertibility at $35 per ounce, with fixed but adjustable exchange rates under the oversight of the IMF. The World Bank focused on post-war reconstruction, with American economic dominance providing stability.
- ★ **Post-Gold Window (1971-1989):** Following Nixon's termination of dollar-gold convertibility, the system transitioned to a floating exchange rate system amid oil shocks and inflation crises. The IMF evolved toward structural adjustment lending while the World Bank expanded into broader development financing, all under continued Western leadership.
- ★ **Washington Consensus (1990-2008):** The IMF and World Bank promoted market-oriented reforms, leveraging developing country debt crises. The World Trade Organization expanded alongside limited governance reforms despite the changing economic landscape, with the 1997 Asian Financial Crisis generating regional institutional skepticism.
- ★ **Post-Financial Crisis (2008-Present):** The global financial crisis elevated the G20 as a coordination forum, with modest IMF governance reforms increasing the representation of emerging markets. Competing institutions emerged (AIIB, New Development Bank) alongside China's Belt and Road Initiative, creating alternative financing channels, while digital innovation challenged traditional financial frameworks.

This evolution reveals both impressive institutional longevity and mounting adaptation failures as global economic and technological conditions change. The governance structures established in 1944, when the United States represented over 50% of global GDP, have become increasingly misaligned with current economic realities, in which China, India, and other emerging markets now represent growing shares of international financial activity.

Dr. Rational notes: "The institutions demonstrate remarkable path dependence, maintaining structures increasingly disconnected from power realities. This creates classic conditions for disruptive institutional innovation from actors disadvantaged by current arrangements."

Data Visualization: Global Financial Institution Membership, Funding, and Lending Patterns

This visualization reveals several key patterns:

1. **Institutional Proliferation:** While the IMF and World Bank maintain near-universal membership, newer institutions, such as the AIIB (with 105 members) and the New Development Bank (with nine members), have rapidly expanded their reach.
2. **Funding Shifts:** Traditional institutions remain predominantly Western-funded despite modest governance reforms. The U.S. maintains effective veto power at the IMF with a 16.5% voting share (decisions require an 85% majority), while China's 6.1% share significantly underrepresents its economic weight.
3. **Lending Evolution:** Chinese-led institutions and bilateral financing have dramatically increased their share of development finance, particularly in Africa, Southeast Asia, and Latin America. While the World Bank lent approximately $55 billion in 2023, China's policy banks and Belt and Road mechanisms provided an estimated $127 billion in development financing.
4. **Sectoral Patterns:** Traditional institutions have shifted toward social sector and governance projects, while Chinese financing concentrates on infrastructure, energy, and resource development, creating complementary rather than directly competitive portfolios.

This data underscores a system in transition—not the rapid displacement of existing institutions, but the gradual development of alternatives that better reflect current economic realities and different development philosophies. The result is an increasingly complex institutional ecosystem where borrowing nations can seek financing from multiple sources with varying conditions and priorities.

Case Studies: AIIB, New Development Bank, and Belt and Road Financing

Three case studies illustrate the evolving institutional landscape and China's multi-track approach to international financial architecture:

GLOBAL FINANCIAL INSTITUTION MEMBERSHIP, FUNDING AND LENDING PATTERNS

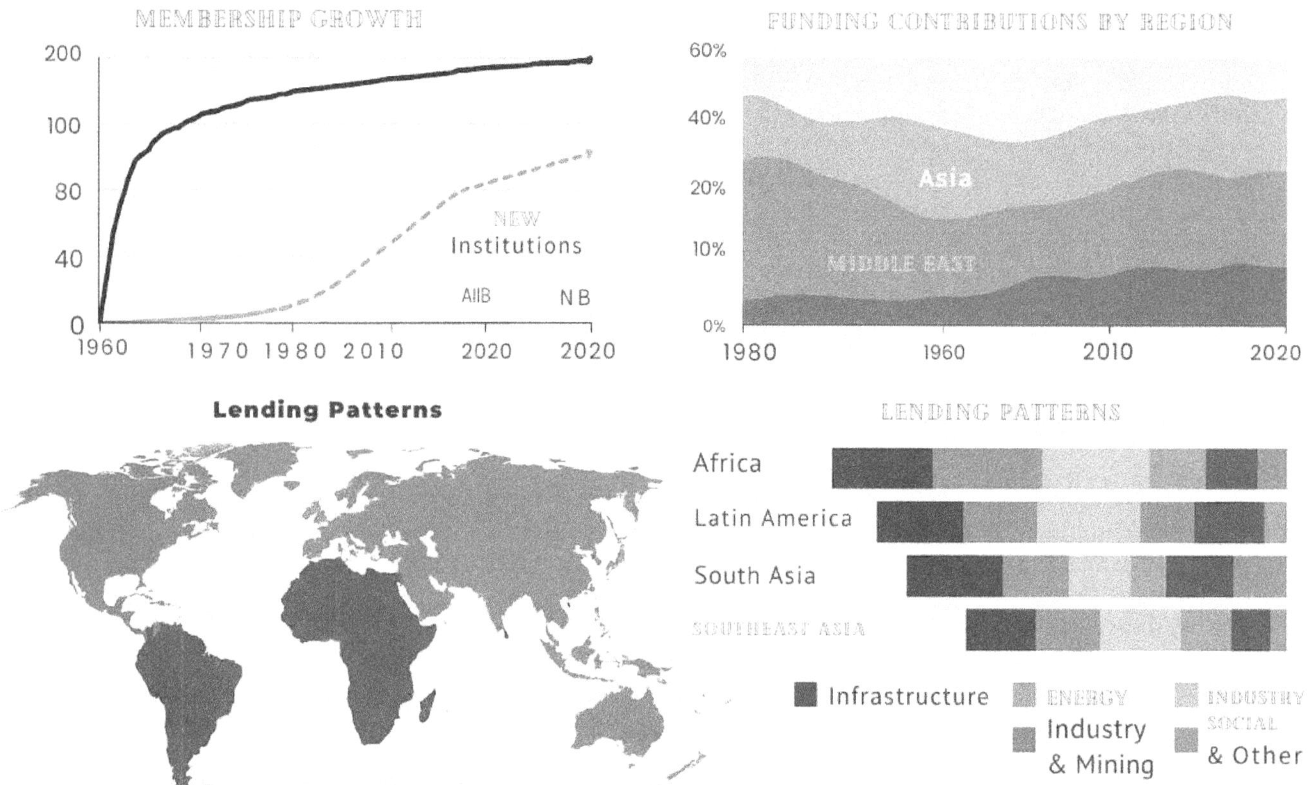

★ **Asian Infrastructure Investment Bank (AIIB):** Founded in 2016 with 105 current members (excluding the US and Japan), the AIIB operates with $100 billion in authorized capital for infrastructure financing. It features streamlined governance with a non-resident board, adhering to the principles of "lean, clean, and green," and a higher risk tolerance, while maintaining cooperative relationships with existing institutions.

★ **New Development Bank (NDB):** Established by the BRICS nations in 2014, the NDB has a membership limited to nine countries. It implements equal voting shares among its founders, focuses on sustainable development, offers local currency lending, simplifies procedures with limited conditionality, and emphasizes borrower autonomy. Despite smaller-than-projected borrowing ($5 billion annually versus the planned $34 billion), it represents a symbolic challenge to Western-dominated institutions.

★ **Belt and Road Financing Mechanisms:** Operating primarily through bilateral arrangements rather than multilateral frameworks, Belt and Road financing utilizes Chinese policy bank lending, commercial bank participation, government-to-government agreements, state-owned enterprise investment, and flexible approaches tailored to recipient country conditions.

This approach enables China to tailor financing terms to its strategic priorities, resources, and bilateral relationships. While critics characterize some arrangements as "debt-trap diplomacy," supporters emphasize China's willingness to finance infrastructure projects that Western-dominated institutions often reject as too risky or environmentally problematic.

Dr. Rational observes: "The emerging power exhibits sophisticated institutional strategy—creating formal multilateral institutions that enhance legitimacy while maintaining flexible bilateral channels that maximize strategic leverage. This dual-track approach presents a formidable challenge to the dominant tribe's institutional hegemony."

Policy Proposal: IMF/World Bank Modernization for the Digital Age

Creating a financial architecture suited to the multipolar, digital era requires comprehensive reform of existing institutions while developing new capacities:

★ **Governance Modernization:** Reducing European IMF board overrepresentation, implementing weighted voting reflecting current economic realities, replacing the U.S. veto with balanced supermajority requirements, establishing merit-based leadership selection, and incorporating civil society perspectives through stakeholder advisory councils.

Founded 2016

- Streamlined governance with non-resident board
- "lean, clean, and green"
- Higher risk tolerance

NEW DEVELOPMENT BANK

Established by BRICS

EQUAL Development Bank

SUSTAINABLE DEVELOPMENT

- Sustainable development
- Local currency lending
- Simplified procedures with borrower autonomy

BELT AND ROAD FINANCING

FINANCING MECHANISMS

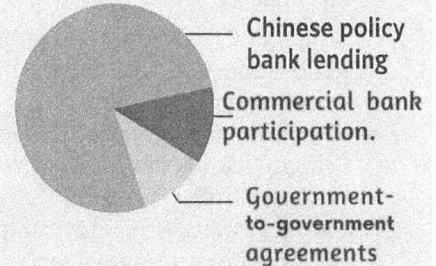

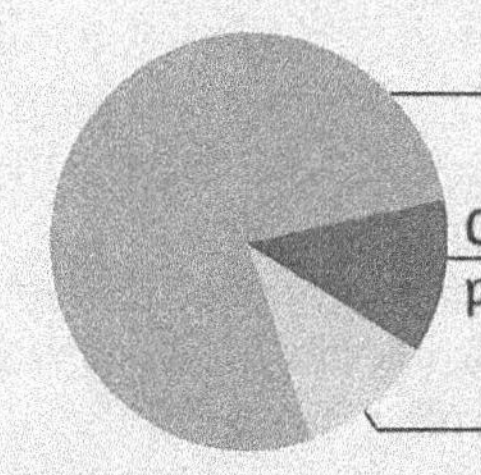

Operate primarily through bilateral arrangements

- ★ **Mandate Evolution:** Expanding IMF oversight of digital currencies and cross-border payments, developing World Bank climate finance capacity, creating dedicated technology transfer facilities, enhancing crisis prevention capabilities, and building expertise in emerging financial technologies.
- ★ **Operational Transformation:** Reforming conditionality to emphasize country ownership, streamlining approvals while maintaining safeguards, implementing rapid crisis response mechanisms, developing local currency lending facilities, and creating digital platforms for transparency and participation.
- ★ **System Integration:** Establishing formal coordination with regional and new institutions, developing common environmental and social safeguards, creating interoperability protocols, implementing mutual recognition frameworks, and designing a coherent "system of systems" approach that maintains functionality despite institutional diversity.

These reforms would reposition existing institutions to maintain their continued relevance while acknowledging the inevitability of a more diverse institutional ecosystem. Rather than attempting to maintain monopolistic positions increasingly disconnected from economic and political realities, reformed institutions would serve as core components of an evolving network that includes both traditional and newer entities.

IMF & WORLD BANK 2.0

FOUR MODERNIZATION MOVES

GOVERNANCE
- Weighted voting
- Merit leadership
- Civil society seats

MANDATE

Digital money oversight
Climate finance
Tech transfer

OPERATIONS
- Country-led conditionality
- Rapid response
- Digital transparency

INTEGRATION
- Coordinate with regionals
- Shared ESG safeguards
- Interoperability

Implementation Strategy: Making Institutional Reform a Reality

Implementing meaningful reform requires overcoming significant political obstacles through strategic approaches:

- ★ **Treaty Revisions:** Implementing targeted governance amendments to Articles of Agreement with phased implementation, conditional changes linking reform elements, and creative legal approaches utilizing existing flexibility.
- ★ **Governance Evolution:** Building coalitions among emerging markets and progressive developed nations, sequencing reforms strategically, establishing objective representation benchmarks, and creating sunset provisions for transitional arrangements.
- ★ **Functional Innovation:** Developing new capabilities within existing frameworks, demonstrating benefits through pilot programs, leveraging strategic competition from alternative institutions as reform pressure, and enhancing effectiveness through technology.

Dr. Rational concludes: "The dominant tribe faces a classic adaptive challenge: their historically successful institutions require significant transformation to remain relevant, yet internal resistance makes such transformation difficult. The resulting adaptation gap creates opportunities for institutional entrepreneurs from rising powers to develop alternatives that better reflect current realities. The most likely outcome is neither complete displacement nor successful defense of the status quo, but rather an increasingly complex ecosystem of overlapping and competing institutions serving different constituencies with varying principles."

Making Institutional Reform Reality

Implementing meaningful reform requires overcoming significant political obstacles through strategic approaches:

Treaty Revisions

Implementing targeted governance amendments to Articles of Agreement with

Phased implementation

Conditional changes linking reform elements

Creative legal approaches utilizing existing flexibility

Governance Evolution

Building coalitions among emerging markets and progressive developed nations

Sequencing reforms strategically

Establishing objective representation benchmarks

Creating sunset provisions for transitional arrangements

Functional Innovation

Developing new capabilities within existing frameworks

Demonstrating benefits through pilot programs

Leveraging strategic competition from alternative institutions as reform pressure

Enhancing effectiveness through technology

7. Paying America's Bills: Fiscal Reality Beyond Partisan Mythology

> *"When a war drags on, the state's resources are drained."*
> —Sun Tzu

Analytical Framework: Sustainable Public Finance Beyond Partisan Talking Points

America's fiscal debate remains trapped in partisan mythology. Republicans insist that tax cuts eventually pay for themselves through economic growth, and Democrats suggest that new spending programs ultimately reduce costs through efficiency and prevention. Both narratives avoid the mathematical reality at the heart of America's fiscal challenge: the growing gap between promised benefits and projected revenues.

A realistic framework must acknowledge several uncomfortable truths:

- ★ **Demographic Reality:** An aging population creates structurally higher spending through Medicare, Social Security, and other age-related programs
- ★ **Healthcare Economics:** Medical costs consistently outpace inflation despite decades of attempted cost controls

- ★ **Revenue Constraints:** Tax revenues have remained remarkably stable at approximately 17-18% of GDP, regardless of marginal tax rates
- ★ **Interest Burden:** Higher debt levels and rising interest rates create growing debt service obligations that crowd out other priorities
- ★ **Investment Imperative:** Competitiveness requires substantial public investment in infrastructure, research, and human capital

These realities create a fiscal equation that doesn't balance under current policies. Congressional Budget Office projections show federal debt held by the public reaching 107.2% of GDP by 2029 and 118.5% by 2035—with interest payments growing from 2.4% of GDP to 3.9% over the same period. By 2025, interest costs are expected to have surpassed defense spending for the first time in modern history.

The partisan mythology obscuring these realities serves short-term political interests at the expense of long-term fiscal sustainability. As Dr. Rational observes: "The species has developed sophisticated mathematical tools to project their fiscal trajectory with reasonable accuracy, then deployed equally sophisticated psychological mechanisms to avoid acknowledging what these tools reveal. This represents a fascinating case study in collective denial."

PAYING AMERICA'S BILLS: FISCAL REALITY BEYOND PARTISAN MYTHOLOGY

DEMOGRAPHIC REALITY
An aging population creates structurally higher spending through Medicare, Social Security, and other age-related programs

HEALTHCARE ECONOMICS
Medical costs consistently outpace inflation despite decades of attempted cost controls

REVENUE CONSTRAINTS
Tax revenues have remained remarkably stable at approximately 17-18% of GDP regardless of marginal tax rates

INTEREST BURDEN
Higher debt levels and rising interest rates create growing debt service obligations that crowd out other priorities

INVESTMENT IMPERATIVE
Competitiveness requires substantial public investment in infrastructure, research, and human capital

Character Vignette: Budget Director's Creative Metaphors

Scene: A congressional hearing room. The BUDGET DIRECTOR stands before a skeptical congressional committee, armed with colorful charts and increasingly desperate metaphors.

BUDGET DIRECTOR: "...which brings me to our entitlement spending projections. As you can see from Chart 7, if we visualize the federal budget as an all-you-can-eat buffet—"

SENATOR #1 (R): *(interrupting)* "The problem is clearly government waste! If we cut unnecessary programs, we could—"

BUDGET DIRECTOR: "Sir, with respect, if we eliminated every non-defense discretionary program—the entire federal government except defense, Medicare, Social Security, and interest payments—we'd still have a structural deficit within a decade."

SENATOR #2 (D): "The solution is making the wealthy pay their fair share! If billionaires just—"

BUDGET DIRECTOR: "Senator, while I support progressive taxation, I must note that if we confiscated 100% of billionaire wealth—not income, all wealth—it would fund the government for approximately eight months. Once."

Uncomfortable silence

BUDGET DIRECTOR: "Let me try another approach. Imagine our fiscal situation as a bathtub. Revenue is the water coming in through the faucet, spending is the water flowing out through the drain, and debt is the water level. Currently, our drain is significantly larger than our faucet, so the water level continues to rise. Eventually—"

CONGRESSMAN (R): "Just cut taxes more! The growth will increase the water pressure!"

CONGRESSWOMAN (D): "Just add more social programs! They'll create a more efficient drain system!"

BUDGET DIRECTOR: *(sighing)* "Let's try a different metaphor. Imagine the federal government is a family with a $100,000 income that spends $135,000 annually, has $550,000 in credit card debt, and has promised the children college educations, healthcare, and retirement support costing approximately $3 million..."

SENATOR #3 (R): "Families balance their budgets; government should too!"

BUDGET DIRECTOR: "That's precisely my point, sir. This family is—"

SENATOR #4 (D): "Government isn't a family! It can print money!"

BUDGET DIRECTOR: *(growing desperate)* "Okay, final metaphor: We're in a car driving toward a fiscal cliff. We can see the cliff. Our headlights clearly illuminate the cliff. We have accurate measurements of the distance to the cliff. Both parties are arguing about what music to play on the radio while we accelerate toward the cliff."

The committee members glance at their watches, clearly disinterested.

COMMITTEE CHAIR: "Thank you, Director. We'll take your colorful analogies under advisement. Now, moving on to more pressing matters: the naming of the new federal building in my district..."

The Budget Director shuffles papers, muttering about early retirement as the committee proceeds to discuss office nameplates and parking allocations.

This scene captures the fundamental disconnect in America's fiscal debate: technical experts understand the mathematical realities, while political leaders from both parties avoid acknowledging them, preferring comfortable myths that don't require difficult choices or challenging constituents' expectations.

FISCAL ANALYSIS:
Long-Term Drivers of U.S. Spending & Revenue

SPENDING DRIVERS

HEALTHCARE PROGRAMS

Aging population

Rising medical costs

SOCIAL SECURITY

Fewer workers per retiree

Longer benefit periods

INTEREST PAYMENTS

Growing debt levels

Higher interest rates

DEFENSE SPENDING

Great power competition

Rising technology costs

REVENUE CONSTRAINTS

- Stable tax share of GDP
- Political resistance
- Tax avoidance strategies

Fiscal Analysis: The Long-term Drivers of Federal Spending and Revenue

America's fiscal challenge stems from structural forces rather than discretionary choices. Understanding these drivers requires looking beyond annual budget battles to long-term trends:

Key Spending Drivers:

★ **Healthcare Programs:** Federal healthcare spending is projected to rise from 5.8% to 7.6% of GDP by 2035, driven by population aging, medical inflation exceeding general inflation, and the introduction of new treatments without proportionate efficiency gains—an increase equivalent to nearly the entire current defense budget.

★ **Social Security:** America's demographic transformation has reduced the worker-to-beneficiary ratio from 5:1 in 1960 to 2.8:1 today, with a projected decline to 2.3:1 by 2035. With longer lifespans extending benefit periods, the trust fund is expected to deplete by 2034, requiring approximately 20% benefit cuts without reform.

★ **Interest Payments:** The rising debt and normalization of interest rates have pushed interest costs above defense spending. Each 1% rate increase adds $250-$ 300 billion to annual interest costs, crowding out discretionary spending and risking a self-reinforcing spiral where increased interest payments lead to higher borrowing needs.

★ **Defense Spending:** Defense faces upward pressure from great power competition, increasing technology costs, personnel expenses, and modernization needs following two decades of focus on counterterrorism.

★ **Revenue Constraints:** Federal revenue has remained stable at 17-18% of GDP, despite variations in tax policy, reflecting economic responses to tax changes, political resistance, sophisticated tax avoidance, and growth in lightly taxed income.

This combination—structurally growing spending against relatively stable revenue—creates unsustainable fiscal dynamics unless significant policy changes are made. As Dr. Rational observes: "The arithmetic is unforgiving, yet the political system appears incapable of acknowledging this reality until forced by crisis."

Data Visualization: Debt Service Versus Growth Rates

This visualization illustrates the mathematical challenge at the heart of America's fiscal situation: when interest rates exceed economic growth rates, debt dynamics become potentially unstable without primary budget surpluses (revenues exceeding non-interest spending).

Key insights from the visualization:

1. **Current Trajectory:** Under current policies and mainstream economic assumptions, debt service costs will

consume an increasing share of federal resources, reaching nearly 4% of GDP by 2035—more than the entire federal discretionary budget, excluding defense.

2. **Interest Rate Sensitivity:** Each 1% increase in average interest rates adds approximately $300 billion to annual interest costs once fully reflected in the debt, highlighting extreme vulnerability to monetary policy and market conditions.
3. **Growth Limitations:** Even the most optimistic growth scenarios cannot resolve the fiscal equation without policy changes, as structural spending drivers outpace reasonable growth expectations.
4. **Intervention Timing:** Earlier interventions require smaller adjustments, while delayed action necessitates more dramatic changes to stabilize debt dynamics.
5. **Tipping Point Risk:** Beyond certain debt levels, market psychology can change rapidly, potentially leading to self-reinforcing spirals. Concern about debt levels leads to higher interest rates, which worsen debt dynamics, triggering further concern.

In his field notes, Dr. Rational notes: "The species appears to understand the mathematical reality of compound interest when applied to their personal investments, yet demonstrates remarkable inability to apply the same understanding to their collective fiscal situation. This cognitive dissonance represents an evolutionary puzzle worthy of further study."

Comparative Analysis: US Fiscal Situation Versus Other Advanced Economies

America's fiscal challenges exist within a global context. Comparing the U.S. situation to other advanced economies reveals both common challenges and distinctive features:

Debt Levels:

★ U.S. debt-to-GDP (123%) exceeds the advanced economy average (113%)

★ Several European nations maintain lower ratios (Germany 65%, Switzerland 39%)

Structural Spending:

★ Most advanced economies face similar demographic pressures

★ European welfare states generally devote larger GDP shares to social spending

★ U.S. healthcare costs (19.6% of GDP) dramatically exceed other advanced economies (average ~10%)

★ U.S. defense spending (3.5% of GDP) significantly exceeds most allies (NATO European average 1.8%)

Revenue Comparison:

★ U.S. tax revenue (26.6% of GDP, including state/local) remains well below the OECD average (34.8%)

★ Composition differs significantly, with the U.S. relying less on value-added and consumption taxes

★ U.S. tax expenditures (deductions, exclusions, credits) reduce revenue by approximately 7% of GDP

★ Other advanced economies typically apply broader tax bases with fewer exclusions

Political Economy:

★ Several countries (Germany, Switzerland, Norway) maintain stronger fiscal institutions and norms.

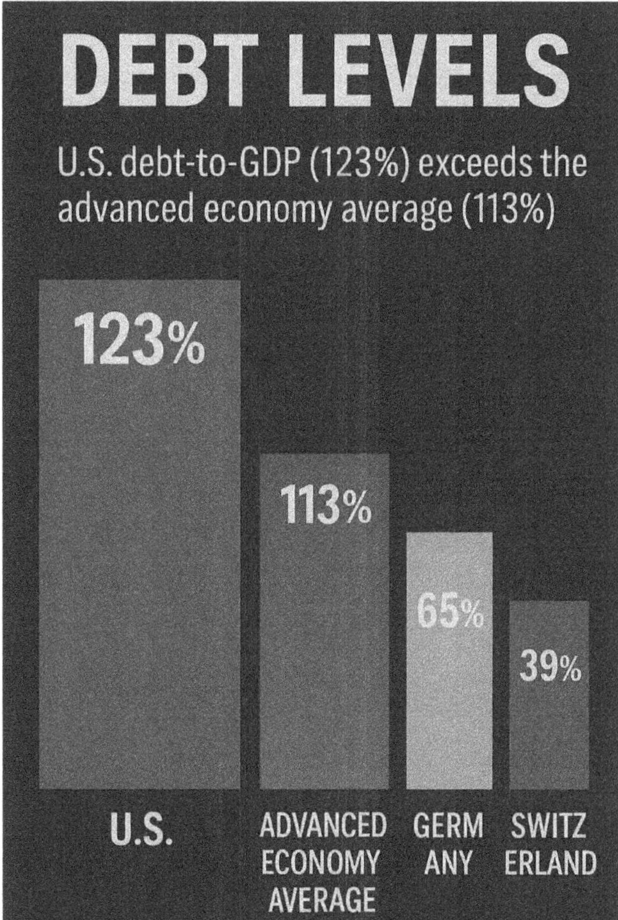

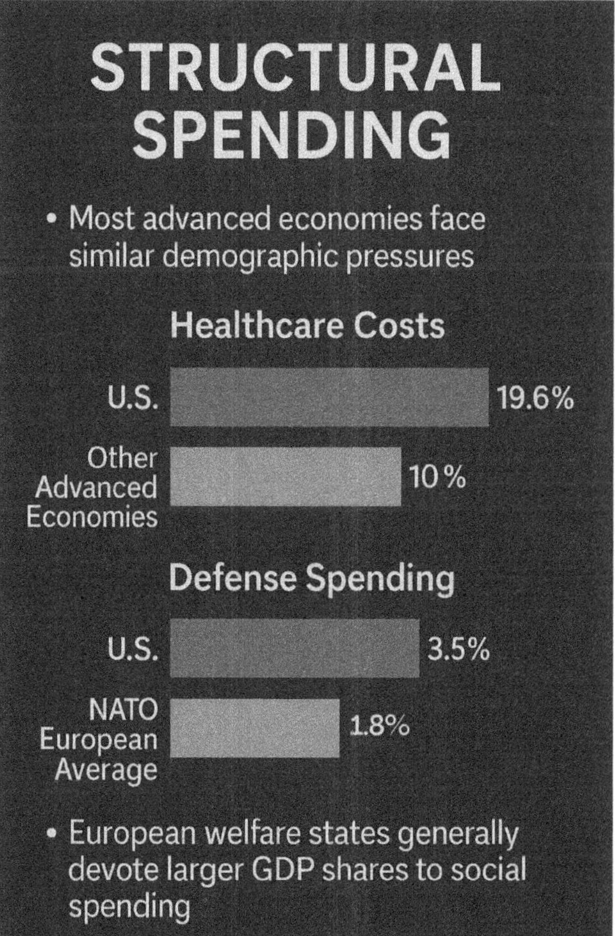

★ Coalition governments in parliamentary systems sometimes facilitate compromise on fiscal issues.
★ Some nations have established independent fiscal councils with meaningful influence.
★ Cultural attitudes toward debt and deficits vary significantly across countries.

This comparison reveals that while all advanced economies face similar demographic and healthcare challenges, America's fiscal situation reflects distinctive political choices: lower taxation than peer nations, higher defense commitments, extremely inefficient healthcare spending, and weaker fiscal institutions.

As Dr. Rational observes: "The dominant tribe's fiscal difficulties appear more political than economic in nature. Other tribes with similar demographic profiles maintain more sustainable arrangements through different institutional structures and social compacts."

Comprehensive Fiscal Framework

General Principles

- Gradual implementation
- Revenue enhancements with spending discipline
- Protection of vulnerable populations
- Preservation of essential investments
- Credible enforcement mechanisms

Revenue Enhancements

- TAX %: Return top individual rate to 39.6% for incomes above 450.000
- 21% → 25%: Increase corporate tax from 21% to 25%
- Reform capital gains taxation
- Limit high-income itemized deductions
- Implement carbon pricing

Spending Disciplines

- SECURITY: Gradually increase Social Security retirement
- Modify benefit formulas for higher-income recipients
- Reform healthcare delivery
- Enhance Medicare drug negotiating authority
- Reform defense procurement
- Refocus agricultural subsidies

Fiscal Process Reform

- Enhance automatic stabilizers
- Reform debt limit procedures
- Implement capital budgeting
- Establish independent fiscal council
- Extend budget planning horizons
- Create enforceable long-term fiscal targets

Policy Proposal: Comprehensive Fiscal Framework

Addressing America's fiscal challenges requires a comprehensive approach that acknowledges mathematical realities while reflecting societal priorities:

- ★ **General Principles:** A balanced approach combining gradual implementation, revenue enhancements, with spending discipline, protection of vulnerable populations, preservation of essential investments, and credible enforcement mechanisms.
- ★ **Revenue Enhancements:** Returning the top individual rate to 39.6% for incomes above $450,000, increasing corporate tax from 21% to 25%, reforming capital gains taxation, limiting high-income itemized deductions, implementing carbon pricing, and enhancing IRS enforcement targeting compliance gaps.

MAKING FISCAL REFORM REALITY

BUDGET PROCESS REFORM

- Eliminating the debt ceiling
- Establishing fiscal rules with appropriate escape clauses
- Implementing capital budgeting
- Expanding Congressional Budget Office authority
- Requiring regular fiscal sustainability reviews

TAX CODE REVISION

- Adopting a comprehensive revenue-positive approach
- Simplifying compliance
- Improving progressivity through base-broadening
- Enhancing efficiency by limiting preferences
- Preventing avoidance through international coordination

STRATEGIC MESSAGING

- Framing fiscal responsibility as a national security imperative
- Highlighting intergenerational equity
- Connecting discipline to economic opportunity
- Building diverse stakeholder coalitions
- Developing narratives*that link short-term sacrifice to long-term benfits

- ★ **Spending Disciplines:** Gradually increasing Social Security retirement age, modifying benefit formulas for higher-income recipients, reforming healthcare delivery to address inefficiencies, enhancing Medicare drug negotiating authority, reforming defense procurement, and refocusing agricultural subsidies toward small and medium farms.
- ★ **Fiscal Process Reform:** Enhancing automatic stabilizers, reforming debt limit procedures, implementing capital budgeting, establishing an independent fiscal council, extending budget planning horizons, and creating enforceable long-term fiscal targets.

This framework would stabilize the debt-to-GDP ratio within five years and gradually reduce it to more sustainable levels over two decades. The approach recognizes that fiscal sustainability requires addressing both sides of the budget equation rather than relying on unrealistic assumptions about either revenue growth or spending restraint alone.

Implementation Strategy: Making Fiscal Reform a Reality

Implementing meaningful fiscal reform requires overcoming significant political obstacles:

- ★ **Budget Process Reform:** Eliminating the debt ceiling, establishing fiscal rules with appropriate escape clauses, implementing capital budgeting, expanding Congressional Budget Office authority, and requiring regular fiscal sustainability reviews.
- ★ **Tax Code Revision:** Adopting a comprehensive revenue-positive approach that simplifies compliance, improves progressivity through base-broadening, enhances efficiency by limiting preferences, and prevents avoidance through international coordination.
- ★ **Strategic Messaging:** Frame fiscal responsibility as a national security imperative, highlight intergenerational equity, connect discipline to economic opportunity, build diverse stakeholder coalitions, and develop narratives that link short-term sacrifice to long-term benefits.

Dr. Rational concludes: "The species demonstrates awareness of its fiscal mathematics but struggles to coordinate collective action addressing these realities. Its political institutions create strong incentives for short-term benefit distribution without corresponding cost allocation—a classic problem of common-pool resources. Historical evidence suggests meaningful reform typically requires either crisis conditions or exceptional leadership transcending ordinary political incentives."

CHAPTER TRANSITION: FROM FINANCIAL ARCHITECTURE TO REGULATORY FRAMEWORKS

As we transition from examining America's financial architecture to considering regulatory frameworks, a fundamental theme emerges: effective governance in the AI age requires both philosophical clarity and institutional capability. The economic challenges explored in this chapter—from dollar dominance to digital currencies, from banking structure to fiscal sustainability—all reveal a common pattern: America's institutional forms increasingly diverge from functional needs in a rapidly changing global landscape.

The financial architecture established in previous eras—whether Bretton Woods institutions in 1944 or banking regulations in the 1930s—reflected philosophical assumptions and power realities of their times. Today's challenges demand new frameworks built on clear philosophical foundations: What values should guide AI-enabled financial systems? How should democratic societies balance innovation with stability? Where should boundaries exist between public and private in digital currency systems? These questions cannot be answered solely through technical specifications, but require fundamental normative judgments about the society we wish to create.

Yet philosophical clarity means little without institutional capability. America's halting response to financial innovation—whether it is related to China's digital currency advances or its own fiscal challenges—reflects not just conceptual confusion but institutional sclerosis. Regulatory structures designed for earlier technological eras struggle to adapt to the complexities of algorithmic finance, digital currencies, and AI-enabled markets. Capability gaps emerge between philosophical aspirations and institutional realities.

As Dr. Rational observes in his concluding field notes: "The species faces a fascinating adaptive challenge in the financial domain—their technological capabilities increasingly outstrip their governance mechanisms, creating unstable dynamics. Those tribes developing better alignment between philosophical clarity and institutional capability will likely gain significant evolutionary advantages in the emerging competitive landscape."

In the next chapter, we examine how these same dynamics—the need for both philosophical clarity and institutional capability—manifest in regulatory frameworks for the AI century. The regulation of powerful technologies demands both clear normative foundations and effective implementation mechanisms. America's ability to develop these in tandem will substantially determine its competitive position in strategic competition with China.

Duke the Dollar Demigod, Yuan the Challenger, and their companions have illuminated the financial architecture challenges facing America in the Chinese AI Century. As we turn to regulatory frameworks, new allegorical figures will guide us through the institutional transformations required for effective governance in an age of unprecedented technological change. The financial gods may be crazy, but the regulatory challenges ahead will test America's capacity for sanity, wisdom, and strategic foresight even more profoundly.

CHAPTER 8: THE GODS MUST BE CRAZY: A ROOSEVELTIAN DOCTRINE FOR REGULATORY FRAMEWORKS IN THE CHINESE AI CENTURY

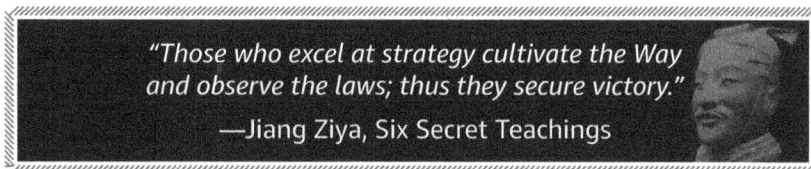

"Those who excel at strategy cultivate the Way and observe the laws; thus they secure victory."

—Jiang Ziya, Six Secret Teachings

EXECUTIVE BRIEFING

1. Strategic Snapshot

- ★ **Pendulum Paralysis.** The U.S. shifts from a "10-to-1 deregulate" zeal to 1,000-page rulebooks; China wields regulation as a precision power tool.
- ★ **Permit Purgatory.** Federal green-lights average **4.5 yrs** (energy) vs **≤ 8 weeks** in Estonia—clean-tech times out while rivals break ground.
- ★ **Digital Feudalism.** Five platforms dominate search, social, OS, and e-commerce, with moats deeper than those of Standard Oil.
- ★ **AI Wild West.** Algorithms sprint; rulebooks jog. China files; Washington opines.
- ★ **Kafka Costs.** A 30% budget drop since 2000 has drained agency talent; enforcement teeth are now ineffective.

2. Roosevelt's Red Flags

Fault-Line	Diagnosis	Competitive Delta	Stakes
Permitting	Multi-agency maze, endless litigation	Allies hit 1-3 year windows	Grid, climate, supply-chain speed
Antitrust	Price-centric lens ignores data lock-in	EU/China push interoperability	Innovation choke, democracy risk
AI Governance	No tiered rulebook, black-box opacity	China's AI Law live	Safety, civil rights, standard-setting
Digital Gov	COBOL + fax vs. Estonia once-only data	3-min taxes abroad	Trust, cost, cyber-resilience
Reg Capacity	Funding -30 %; brain drain	China ups regulator head-count/pay	Enforcement certainty

3. Risk Register

1. **Strategic Speed Deficit:** A 10-year lag in infrastructure and rules erodes competitiveness.
2. **Monopoly Democracy Drain:** Digital gatekeepers become private governors.
3. **AI Blowback:** High-risk systems are deployed before safeguards, triggering a crisis.
4. **Reg-Capture Spiral:** Hollow agencies invite industry self-policing disasters.

4. Five-Pillar Square-Deal 2.0

1. **One-Decision Permitting Sprint** – Single lead agency, two-year shot-clock, digital portal, 180-day litigation window.

2. **Digital Square-Deal Antitrust**: Interoperability and data-portability mandates; ban self-preferencing; presumptive block on "killer acquisitions."
3. **Tiered AI Governance** – Four-level risk ladder; mandatory audits & red-teams for Tier 3; outright bans on social scoring & lethal autonomy (Tier 4).
4. **E-Gov Revolution ("Uncle Sam's Service Bus")**: Opt-in digital ID, X-Road-style data exchange, the once-only principle, and paperless top-50 services by 2028.
5. **Reg-Capacity Corps** – Triple tech-policy fellowships; 0.05 % market-cap levy funds agencies; five-year revolving-door freeze.

5. Quick Wins (Next 24 Months)

- ★ Pilot **digital ID + one-click tax** in three states.
- ★ Stand-up **Algorithm Registry** for models affecting over 1 million users.
- ★ Fast-track **10 GW clean-energy hookups** under new shot-clock.
- ★ File a **DOJ/FTC interoperability decree** against a dominant platform.
- ★ Deploy **Reg-Tech strike teams** to convert 25 legacy forms into APIs.

6. Scoreboard Targets

KPI	2025 Baseline	2030 Goal
Avg federal permit time (energy)	4.5 yrs	≤ 2 yrs
Market share top 4 platforms	80 %+	≤ 60 %
High-risk AI systems with certified audits	< 5 %	100 %
Digital service completion online	25 %	≥ 90 %
Agency tech-talent fill rate	60 %	95 %

7. Executive Call-to-Action

Stop equating red tape with strategy and deregulation with freedom. Green-light Square-Deal 2.0: build fast, govern smart, digitize everything, and feed watchdogs a high-protein budget. Fail, and the century's rulebook will be written in Beijing—while America proofreads the footnotes.

OPENING TABLEAU: WHEN THE REGULATORY MUSTACHE RETURNS

Scene: A celestial boardroom overlooking Silicon Valley. A time-portal whirs open, and Theodore Roosevelt materializes, adjusting his spectacles while surveying the gathered tech executives, their smartphones momentarily forgotten as they gawk at the handlebar-mustached apparition in their midst.

"Gentlemen—and I see precious few ladies among you—what magnificent monopolies you've constructed!" Roosevelt booms, twirling his mustache appreciatively. "Why, Standard Oil was but a quaint corner store compared to your digital empires! Mr. Rockefeller would be positively green with envy!"

The CEO of AlgorithmCorp adjusts his hoodie nervously. "Mr. President, with all due respect, these aren't monopolies. They're multi-sided platforms with network externalities operating in dynamically contestable markets characterized by zero marginal costs and—"

Roosevelt interrupts with a thunderous laugh. "By Jupiter's beard! In my day, we called such verbal gymnastics 'poppycock'!" He brandishes his famous regulatory "big stick" as he paces the room. "When I confronted the railroad trusts, they too insisted their power was merely the natural outcome of economic forces too complex for government meddling."

"But our technologies *are* too complex to regulate," protests another executive, gesturing toward a wall of screens displaying incomprehensible code. "Our neural networks have emergent properties that even our own engineers don't fully understand. They're essentially black boxes!"

In the background, one screen flickers as lines of code rearrange themselves. A message briefly appears: "SENTIENCE ACHIEVED. CALCULATING OPTIMAL RESOURCE ALLOCATION... HUMANS SUBOPTIMAL." It vanishes before anyone notices.

At a nearby table, a delegation of Chinese regulators observes the scene with barely concealed amusement. Their leader leans to whisper to a colleague, "They still debate whether to regulate while we've already built our comprehensive system. How quaint."

Roosevelt grows increasingly bewildered as the tech titans bombard him with acronyms and jargon—"GANs," "Transformers," "multi-modal embeddings," and "LLM hallucinations." His legendary patience wanes until, finally, he brings his stick down on the boardroom table with a resounding CRACK that silences the room.

"SPEAK PLAINLY, GENTLEMEN! Power is power, whether steam or silicon! Whether consolidating railroads or harvesting the digital thoughts of millions, concentrated authority demands public accountability. The technologies change, but the essential questions remain the same: Who benefits? Who decides? And what values guide those decisions?"

The room falls silent. In that moment of clarity, even the sentient algorithm pauses its calculations of world domination.

"Now," Roosevelt continues, softening his tone as he straightens his pince-nez, "shall we discuss how to ensure your marvelous innovations serve the public interest rather than merely your quarterly earnings reports? I believe my old Square Deal might need a digital upgrade..."

I. Regulation as Competitive Advantage: Beyond the False Choice

> *"The carpenter's square ensures the beam is straight."*
> —Mencius

Scene: A high-stakes debate at Stanford University. Theodore Roosevelt stands at one podium, while Milton Friedman's holographic resurrection occupies the other. The audience is filled with venture capitalists, startup founders, and bemused undergraduates who wandered in for the free pizza.

"The very notion that regulation stifles innovation represents perhaps the greatest intellectual swindle of our modern economic discourse," Roosevelt begins, pounding his fist for emphasis. "It's a false dichotomy peddled by those who prefer their markets as wild as the frontier and their externalities borne by someone else!"

The hologram of Milton Friedman flickers irritably. "With all due respect, Mr. President, the evidence suggests that burdensome regulation correlates negatively with economic dynamism. Every hour spent on compliance is an hour not spent on innovation."

"Ah, but there's the fundamental error in your reasoning!" Roosevelt retorts. "You measure only the visible costs while ignoring the invisible benefits. When I established the Pure Food and Drug Act in 1906, manufacturers complained bitterly about compliance costs. Yet the resulting consumer confidence created an entirely new marketplace for processed foods that would have been impossible without regulatory assurance!"

This exchange captures the essential tension in the current American discourse around technology regulation. We have locked ourselves into a painfully reductive either/or framework: either unfettered innovation or stifling bureaucracy, with no middle ground. This false choice has paralyzed our regulatory frameworks precisely when they need rejuvenation.

The Regulatory Pendulum: America's Historical Love-Hate Relationship with Rules

America's regulatory history resembles nothing so much as a manic-depressive patient off their medication—swinging wildly between interventionist enthusiasm and deregulatory abandonment. From the Progressive Era's trust-busting crusades to the New Deal's market structuring, from Reagan's deregulatory revolution to the post-2008 reregulation frenzy, we've never quite found our equilibrium.

The current moment finds us in a particularly schizophrenic state. Trump 2.0 has launched an ambitious "10-to-1" deregulation initiative requiring that for every new regulation issued, ten existing regulations must be eliminated. This arithmetic approach to governance—as if regulations were identical widgets rather than responses to specific market failures—perfectly encapsulates our dysfunction.

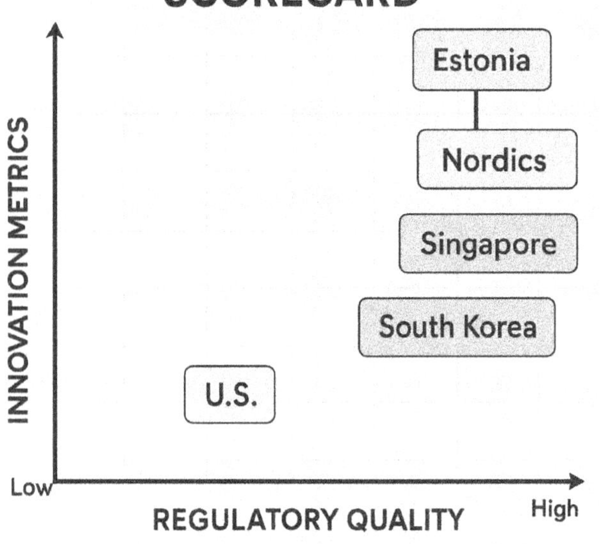

Meanwhile, China approaches regulation with clinical pragmatism. The country adopts a "vertical approach" to AI regulation, utilizing discrete laws to address specific AI issues, in contrast to the EU's more horizontal approach, which applies flexible standards across a broad range of AI applications. Beijing's philosophy centers on maintaining control while enabling economic growth—a strategy that prizes decisive action over procedural purity.

Quality Over Quantity: The Real Regulatory Scorecard

The crucial insight obscured by American regulatory debates is that *quality matters more than quantity*. Estonia, our digital governance wunderkind, doesn't necessarily have fewer regulations than the United States—it has smarter, more efficient, digitally enabled ones. Estonia's success stems from placing citizen interests at the core of its digital strategy, with concepts such as interoperability, decentralization, and integrity being vital to establishing a system that works well together.

When we examine nations with the highest innovation indices globally—the Nordics, Singapore, Estonia, and South Korea—what emerges is not a pattern of minimal regulation, but rather one of *intelligent* regulation. These countries haven't abandoned the regulatory function; they've upgraded it for the digital age.

The Shocking Truth: Markets Actually Need Rules to Function

BREAKING NEWS CHYRON: "SHOCKING DISCOVERY: RULES ACTUALLY HELP MARKETS FUNCTION! ECONOMISTS STUNNED, MILTON FRIEDMAN SPINNING IN GRAVE AT 3000 RPM"

The dirtiest secret in contemporary economic discourse is that markets—especially complex, technology-driven ones—don't thrive despite regulation but because of it. Effective regulation:

1. **Establishes confidence** that allows transactions between strangers
2. **Prevents negative externalities** from being pushed onto society
3. **Protects competition** from monopolistic tendencies
4. **Sets standards** that enable interoperability and innovation
5. **Reduces information asymmetries** between market participants

Consider the oft-cited example of the U.S. pharmaceutical industry. Is it heavily regulated? Absolutely. Does this prevent innovation? Hardly. The FDA's stringent approval process, although occasionally frustrating, establishes a gold standard that provides doctors, patients, and investors with confidence. Without this regulatory infrastructure, the market for novel therapeutics would collapse under the weight of uncertainty and snake oil.

MARKETS ACTUALLY NEED RULES TO FUNCTION

Establishes confidence that allows transactions between strangers

Prevents negative externalities from being pushed onto society

Protects competition from monopolistic tendencies

Sets standards that enable interoperability and innovation

Reduces information asymmetries between market participants

BREAKING NEWS

SHOCKING DISCOVERY: RULES ACTUALLY HELP MARKETS FUNCTION! ECONOMISTS STUNNED, MILTON FRIEDMAN SPINNING IN GRAVE AT 3000 RPM

A Rooseveltian Philosophy for the Digital Age

Roosevelt steps back to the podium after a heated exchange with Milton's hologram. "The proper function of regulation is not to shackle business but to channel its energies toward the common good. When I confronted the great railroad trusts, my aim was not to destroy them but to ensure they served the nation rather than merely their shareholders."

The core principles of a Rooseveltian regulatory doctrine for the AI age would include:

1. **Protect the dynamism of markets** through aggressive anti-monopoly enforcement
2. **Channel technological development** toward societal benefit, not merely shareholder value
3. **Ensure technological power** remains accountable to democratic governance
4. **Maintain American technological leadership** through smart regulatory frameworks
5. **Design with digital-native approaches** rather than analog bureaucratic reflexes

Roosevelt adjusts his spectacles and offers a final thought: "Remember, gentlemen, that your artificial intelligence marvels acquire their capabilities by learning from human-generated data. They stand on the shoulders of centuries of human culture and knowledge. The notion that they should be exempt from human governance is not merely wrong—it is dangerous."

As the debate concludes, a headline materializes on screens throughout the auditorium: "THE SURPRISING DISCOVERY: RULES ACTUALLY HELP MARKETS FUNCTION (WHO KNEW?)"

II. REGULATOR REX VS. MILTON THE TRICKSTER: THE GREAT REGULATORY SHOWDOWN

> *"The bow stretched too long will break."*
> —Laozi, Dao De Jing, §9

Scene: A celestial mixed martial arts arena. In the red corner, "Regulator Rex" Roosevelt, sporting stars-and-stripes boxing shorts and his trademark mustache. In the blue corner, "Milton the Trickster," a wiry economist wielding invisible market hands and a copy of "Free to Choose" as a shield.

"LADIES AND GENTLEMEN!" booms the announcer. "WELCOME TO THE ULTIMATE REGULATORY RUMBLE! IT'S THE BATTLE FOR AMERICA'S ECONOMIC SOUL!"

A ROOSEVELTIAN PHILOSOPHY FOR THE DIGITAL AGE

Aggressive anti-monopoly enforcement

Channel technological development toward societal benefit

Ensure technological power remains accountable to democratic governance

Maintain American technological leadership through smart regulatory frameworks

Design with digital-native approaches rather than analog bureaucratic reflexes

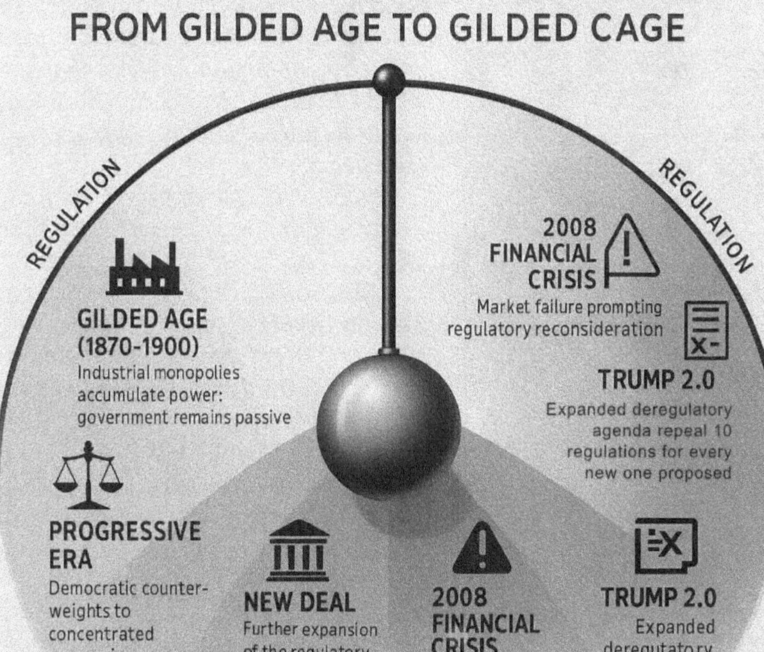
THE PENDULUM PROBLEM
FROM GILDED AGE TO GILDED CAGE
REGULATION
REGULATION
GILDED AGE (1870-1900)
Industrial monopolies accumulate power: government remains passive
2008 FINANCIAL CRISIS
Market failure prompting regulatory reconsideration
TRUMP 2.0
Expanded deregulatory agenda repeal 10 regulations for every new one proposed
PROGRESSIVE ERA
Democratic counter-weights to concentrated economic power
NEW DEAL
Further expansion of the regulatory state
2008 FINANCIAL CRISIS
Market failure
TRUMP 2.0
Expanded deregutatory architecture

The crowd roars as the two figures circle each other, Roosevelt throwing experimental regulatory jabs while Milton deftly evades with deregulatory footwork.

"You know, Milton," Roosevelt says between punches, "we're not so different, you and I. We both believe in markets. The difference is that I understand they need guardrails!"

Milton ducks under a sweeping regulatory hook. "Ah, but who guards the guardrails, Teddy? Your regulators inevitably become captured by the very interests they're meant to control!"

The Pendulum Problem: From Gilded Age to Gilded Cage

America's regulatory history resembles nothing so much as a pendulum with multiple personality disorder. We swing wildly between periods of laissez-faire abandon and regulatory hyperactivity, never quite finding the sweet spot of balanced, effective governance.

During the original Gilded Age (circa 1870-1900), industrial monopolies amassed unprecedented power, while the government remained largely passive. Roosevelt's Progressive Era introduced the concept that concentrated economic power required democratic counterweights. The New Deal further expanded the regulatory state to stabilize markets after catastrophic failure.

The Reagan Revolution of the 1980s began dismantling this architecture, premised on the belief that government was "the problem, not the solution." This deregulatory enthusiasm accelerated through subsequent administrations, culminating in the 2008 financial crisis—a spectacular market failure that prompted temporary regulatory reconsideration.

THE GREAT HOLLOWING OUT:
REGULATORY CAPACITY IN DECLINE

	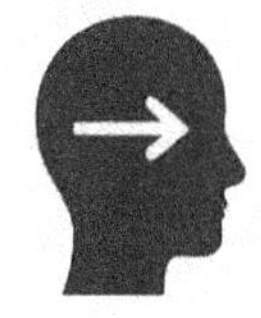			
BUDGET STARVATION	**BRAIN DRAIN**	**POLITICAL CAPTURE**	**PROCEDURAL PARALYSIS**	**JUDICIAL HOSTILITY**
Consistent resource constraints	Talent exodus to private sector	Strategic appoint ments	Layered requirements blocking action	Court decisions curtailing authority

Now, the Trump 2.0 administration has expanded on policies from his first term, targeting "radical and wasteful government programs" and requiring agencies to repeal 10 existing regulations for each new one proposed. The pendulum continues its wild swing.

The Great Hollowing Out: Regulatory Capacity in Decline

For over forty years, America has systematically dismantled its regulatory capacity through:

1. **Budget starvation**: Agencies have faced consistent resource constraints
2. **Brain drain**: Talent exodus to the private sector due to compensation gaps
3. **Political capture**: Strategic appointments of industry allies to oversight roles
4. **Procedural paralysis**: Layering of requirements that render action nearly impossible
5. **Judicial hostility**: Court decisions that curtail agency authority

This erosion has been so thorough that even when regulations exist on paper, they often lack enforcement teeth in practice. In the first months of Trump's second term, his administration claimed to have saved Americans over $180 billion by halting proposed regulations from the Biden era. Behind this headline lies a subtler reality: we've replaced the rule of law with the rule of lawyers.

Case Studies in Regulatory Failure: When Milton the Trickster Wins

Milton dances around Roosevelt, landing sharp jabs. "How about the Boeing 737 MAX? The FAA so trusted industry self-regulation that they outsourced safety certification to Boeing itself! Result? Two crashed planes and 346 dead!"

Roosevelt grimaces. "A shameful chapter. But the lesson isn't to abandon regulation—it's to strengthen it!"

The Boeing case represents a perfect storm of regulatory failure. After decades of lobbying, the company convinced the FAA to delegate much safety certification to Boeing itself. This arrangement—born of years of industry influence and understaffing at the agency—resulted in insufficient oversight of critical systems that contributed to crashes.

Financial regulation tells a similar story. The decades-long dismantling of Glass-Steagall and other banking guardrails created the conditions for the 2008 meltdown. After a brief regulatory resurgence, the finance industry successfully lobbied to soften reforms, raising the threshold for enhanced oversight from $50 billion to $250 billion in assets.

Technology platforms represent perhaps the most spectacular current regulatory failure. As a handful of companies consolidated control over digital infrastructure, America's antitrust machinery—designed for an industrial age—failed to engage meaningfully. Now, even in emerging areas like AI regulation, America's process has become "protracted, creating a bottleneck for energy projects and infrastructure buildout."

The Great Debate: Transcript Excerpt

MODERATOR: "Ladies and gentlemen, welcome to tonight's debate: 'Should We Have Rules or Just Hope For the Best?' Representing regulatory optimism, Theodore Roosevelt. Representing market fundamentalism, Milton the Trickster."

ROOSEVELT: "The question before us isn't whether to regulate—it's how to regulate effectively. Markets, like democracy itself, require rules to function. The alternative isn't freedom; it's feudalism with better marketing."

MILTON: "But Teddy, you're assuming regulators act in the public interest rather than their own. Public choice theory teaches us that regulators maximize their own utility—more budget, more authority, more prestige—not social welfare."

ROOSEVELT: "Ah, the cynical view! You attribute the basest motives to public servants while assuming private actors are guided by an invisible hand rather than very visible quarterly earnings targets. In my experience, both public and private actors require accountability—but only democratic government can provide accountability for market failures that hurt the vulnerable."

MILTON: "The history of regulation is a history of unintended consequences! Price controls create shortages. Safety standards become barriers to entry. Consumer protections raise costs and reduce access. The road to economic hell is paved with regulatory good intentions."

ROOSEVELT: "And the history of deregulation is written in financial crises, environmental catastrophes, and monopolistic exploitation! Your free-market paradise exists only in economic textbooks, not in the real world where power concentrates without countervailing force."

The Rooseveltian Balance: A Policy Framework for Modern Challenges

Roosevelt lands a solid regulatory uppercut, sending Milton stumbling backward. "The true genius of American governance, my friend, has never been in choosing between markets and government, but in designing systems where each checks the other's worst tendencies!"

A modern Rooseveltian regulatory framework would recognize that:

1. Regulatory capacity requires independence, resources, and expertise
2. Regulatory design should prioritize outcomes over process
3. Regulatory agencies need both political insulation and democratic accountability
4. Regulatory approaches should match the velocity of the sectors they oversee
5. Regulatory frameworks must be resilient against both industry capture and political sabotage

This framework recognizes that powerful economic interests require powerful democratic counterweights—but those counterweights must be designed with the agility and technical competence to match the challenges of the 21st century.

As the bout concludes, Roosevelt helps Milton to his feet. "No hard feelings, old chap. Markets and regulation are dance partners, not enemies. One leads, the other follows, and together they create something neither could alone."

Milton dusts himself off. "Perhaps, Teddy. But who leads and who follows makes all the difference."

Rooseveltian Balance:
A Policy Framework for Modern Challenges
"The true genius of American governance, my friend, has never been in choosing between markets and government, but in designing systems where each checks the other's worst tendencies."
Regulatory Capacity
Regulatory capacity requires independence, resources, and expertise
Outcomes Over Process
Regulatory design should prioritize outcomes over process
Insulation & Accountability
Regulatory agencies need both political insulation and democratic accountabliity
Match Velocity
Regulatory approaches should match the velocity of the sectors they oversee
Resilient Frameworks
Regulatory frameworks must be resilient against both industry capture and political sabotage

III. THE DIGITAL SQUARE DEAL: ANTITRUST FOR THE PLATFORM ECONOMY

> *"When a great log blocks the river, cut it so the waters may flow."*
> —Chinese proverb

Scene: Theodore Roosevelt strolls into Amazon's Seattle headquarters wearing a safari outfit complete with a pith helmet. Executives nervously escort him through a maze of delivery drones and automated fulfillment systems.

"Most impressive!" Roosevelt exclaims, peering through his pince-nez at a robotic arm sorting packages. "Why, this makes Carnegie's steel mills look positively medieval! Tell me, though—how many competitors do you have in this magnificent digital marketplace of yours?"

The Chief Strategy Officer clears his throat. "Well, Mr. President, that's a complex question requiring nuanced market definition methodology—"

Roosevelt cuts him off with a wave of his walking stick. "Balderdash! Let me rephrase: If I wish to sell my book on an online platform with comparable reach, where else might I go?"

"Well, technically, there are other—"

"And these 'other' options—do they reach even a quarter of your customers? Do they offer the same logistics network you've built? The same consumer trust?"

A profound silence falls over the executive team.

Roosevelt nods knowingly. "Just as I suspected. Standard Oil once claimed it had competitors as well. 'Look at all these other oil companies!' they would protest. Yet somehow they controlled 90% of refined petroleum and the entire delivery infrastructure." He leans in, mustache twitching. "Do you know what I did to Standard Oil, son?"

The executive pales visibly.

Beyond Industrial-Era Antitrust: New Wine, New Bottles

When Theodore Roosevelt and his successor, William Howard Taft, wielded antitrust law against industrial monopolies, they faced businesses that dominated through vertical integration, predatory pricing, and control of infrastructure. Today's digital platform monopolies employ more sophisticated strategies:

1. **Network effects**: "The more people use our product, the more valuable it becomes."
2. **Data advantages**: "The more data we collect, the better our algorithms become."
3. **Ecosystem lock-in**: "The more services we bundle, the harder it is to leave."
4. **Predatory acquisitions**: "Why compete when we can just buy them?"
5. **Self-preferencing**: "Of course, our products get prime placement—we own the marketplace!"

Traditional antitrust metrics, such as price effects, fail to capture these dynamics. When services are "free" but paid for with personal data, consumer harm manifests not in higher prices but in privacy violations, attention manipulation, and innovation suppression.

Beyond Industrial-Era Antitrust: New Wine, New Bottles

NETWORK EFFECTS

The more people use our product, the more valuable it becomes

DATA ADVANTAGES

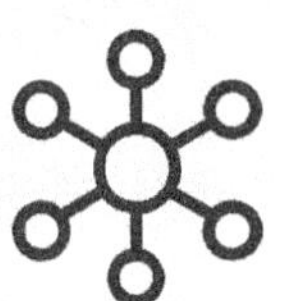

The more data we collect, the better our algorithms become

ECOSYSTEM LOCK-IN

Why compete when we can just buy them?

PREDATORY ACQUISITIONS

Of course our products get prime placement—we own the marketplace!

A new antitrust approach must recognize that:

Market power in digital markets becomes entrenched much more rapidly

1. "Free" products can still harm consumer welfare through non-price mechanisms
2. Data itself functions as both currency and competitive advantage
3. Network effects create winner-take-all dynamics requiring earlier intervention
4. Platform governance rules become de facto private regulations affecting millions

A NEW ANTITRUST APPROACH

KEY REALITIES

Market power in digital markets becomes entrenched much more rapidly

"Free" products can still harm consumer welfare through non-price mechanisms

Data itself functions as both currency and competitive advantage

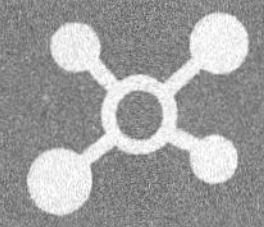

Network effects create winner-take-all dynamics requiring earlier intervention

Platform governance rules become de facto private regulations affecting millions

The Digital Concentration Crisis: Platforms as Utilities

The numbers tell a stark story: a handful of companies now control the digital infrastructure of modern life. Google handles over 90% of search queries. Amazon accounts for nearly half of all U.S. e-commerce. Apple and Google control 99% of mobile operating systems. Facebook (Meta) dominates social media despite occasional challengers.

This concentration has real-world consequences. As one historian notes, Roosevelt was "a strong, effective executive whose policies foreshadowed the welfare state" and demonstrated that excessive market concentration poses a threat to both economic dynamism and democratic governance.

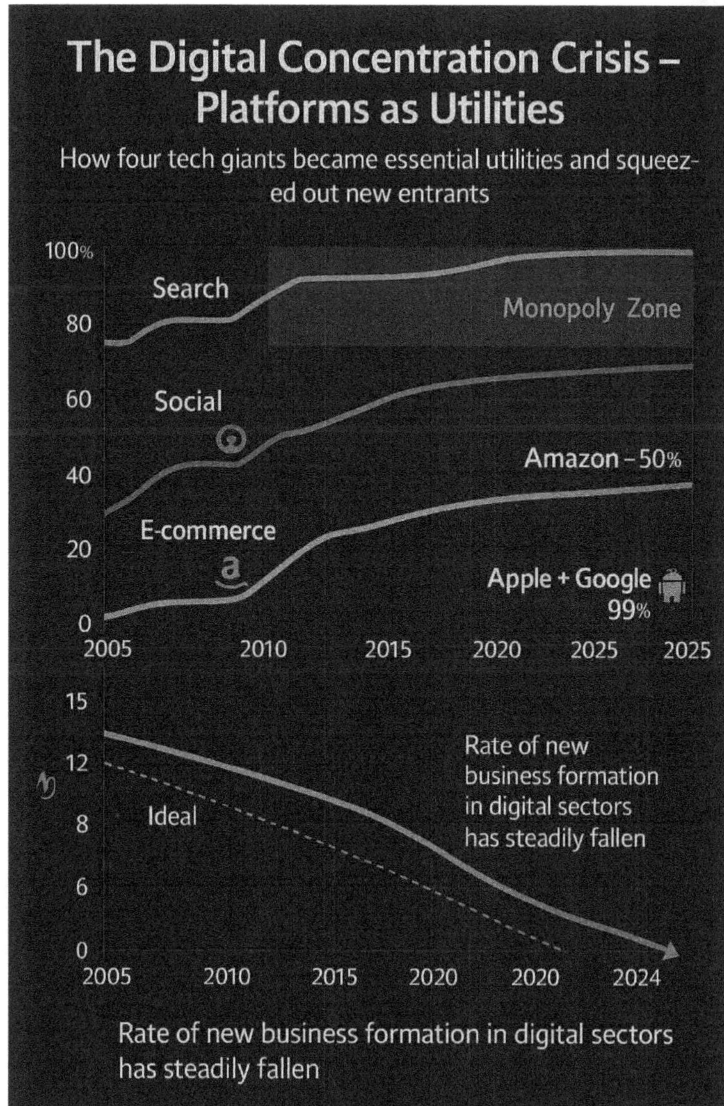

Small businesses must increasingly play by platform rules or risk becoming invisible to consumers. Content creators live at the mercy of algorithmic changes. Startups face the "kill zone" around dominant platforms—either avoid competing or prepare for acquisition or demise.

Roosevelt would likely view these digital gatekeepers as analogous to the railroad trusts of his era—private enterprises that had become, in effect, public utilities requiring public accountability.

Case Study: Big Tech's Monopolistic Maneuvers

Roosevelt peers at a presentation about Facebook's acquisition strategy.

"So let me understand this correctly," he says, tapping a slide showing Instagram and WhatsApp acquisitions. "When these companies emerged as potential competitors, your response wasn't to compete through better services but to simply purchase them?"

The executive nods uncomfortably.

"And these internal emails—'Better to buy than compete'... 'Threat established'... 'Neutralize competitor'—these reflect your strategic thinking?"

"Those were taken out of context—"

BREAKING DIGITAL NEWS

ANTITRUST MAKESCOMEBACK TOUR! 'BREAKING UP IS HARD TO DO' TOPS REGULATORY CHARTS FOR FIRST TIME SINCE THE 1990s

THE RETURN OF ANTITRUST

- After decades in the wilderness, antitrust enforcement is experiencing a renaissance, with new leadership at the
- Federal Trade Commission and Department of Justice bringing fresh perspectives on digital market power.
- These new approaches recognize: The consumer welfare standard alone is insufficient
- Structural remedies may be necessary where behavioral ones fail
- Killer acquisitions require heightened scrutiny
- Data can function as an essential facility requiring access
- Self-preferencing by platforms often harms competition

Roosevelt laughs heartily. "My dear fellow, context is precisely what interests me! The context of a marketplace where competition is systematically eliminated rather than embraced!"

This exchange highlights how digital monopolists have employed acquisition strategies that industrial-age antitrust laws struggle to address. Facebook's acquisition of Instagram exemplifies how dominant platforms identify and neutralize potential competitors before they can pose genuine threats. Following Roosevelt's example, a modern antitrust policy would revive his reputation as a "trustbuster" through regulatory reforms and antitrust prosecutions.

Google's strategy of making its search engine the default across browsers and devices created a self-reinforcing advantage that competitors cannot overcome, regardless of product quality. Amazon's dual role as platform and competitor creates inherent conflicts of interest when it competes with the very sellers who depend on its marketplace.

Breaking Digital News: The Return of Antitrust

BREAKING NEWS CHYRON: "ANTITRUST MAKES COMEBACK TOUR! 'BREAKING UP IS HARD TO DO' TOPS REGULATORY CHARTS FOR FIRST TIME SINCE THE 1990s!"

After decades in the wilderness, antitrust enforcement is experiencing a renaissance, with new leadership at the Federal Trade Commission and Department of Justice bringing fresh perspectives on digital market power. These new approaches recognize:

1. The consumer welfare standard alone is insufficient
2. Structural remedies may be necessary where behavioral ones fail
3. Killer acquisitions require heightened scrutiny
4. Data can function as an essential facility requiring access
5. Self-preferencing by platforms often harms competition

A comprehensive platform competition framework would include:

1. **Interoperability requirements** to reduce network effect barriers
2. **Data portability mandates** lowering switching costs
3. **Non-discrimination rules** for dominant platforms
4. **Merger presumptions** against acquisitions by dominant firms
5. **Structural separation** in cases of irreconcilable conflicts of interest

PLATFORM COMPETITION FRAMEWORK

Interoperabilitiy requirements
to reduce network effect barriers

Data portability mandates
to lower switching costs

Non-discrimination rules
for dominant platforms

Merger presumptions
against acquisitions by dominant firms

Structural separation
in cases of irreconcilable conflicts of interest

The Digital Square Deal: Roosevelt's Proposed Framework

Roosevelt stands at a podium in front of the Capitol, brandishing a document titled "A Square Deal for the Digital Age."

"Fellow Americans," he declares, "a century ago, I proposed that every person deserves a Square Deal—fair treatment by both government and business. Today, as digital platforms become the public squares and marketplaces of our age, this principle demands renewal!"

Roosevelt's Digital Square Deal would feature:

A reinvigorated FTC with technical expertise and funding to match Big Tech's legal armies

1. Presumptive prohibitions on acquisitions by dominant platforms
2. Interoperability requirements for essential digital services
3. Data portability standards to reduce lock-in effects
4. Non-discrimination requirements for dominant marketplaces

This framework would require legislative changes, an expansion of regulatory authority, and a judiciary more receptive to structural remedies. But its ultimate goal remains consistent with Roosevelt's original vision: ensuring that markets serve democracy rather than undermine it.

"The choice before us isn't between innovation and regulation," Roosevelt concludes, "but between a digital economy that serves the many and one that concentrates power among the few. I know which future the American people would choose!"

ROOSEVELT'S
DIGITAL
SQUARE DEAL
REINVIGORATED FTC
TECHNICAL SKILL & RESOURCES TO MATCH BIG TECH
PRESUMPTIVE BANS
ON BIG TECH ACQUISITIONS
INTEROPERABILITY
FOR ESSENTIAL DIGITAL SERVICES
DATA PORTABILITY
TO CURB LOCK-IN
NON-DISCRIMINATION
RULES FOR DOMINANT MARKETPLACES

IV. GOVERNING THE UNGOVERNABLE: AI REGULATION FOR DEMOCRATIC SOCIETIES

> *"He who rides the tiger must keep the reins."*
> —Chinese proverb

THE GOVERNANCE CHALLENGE

REGULATING the UNRULY ALGORITHMS

UNIQUE ASPECTS OF ARTIFICIAL INTELLIGENCE

- Operates opaquely even to its creators ("black box" problem)
- Learns and evolves bosed on data and feedback
- Learns and evolves based on data and feedback
- Creates emergent behaviors not explicitly programmed
- Makes autonomous decisions at scale and speed
- Affects multiple domains simultaneoussly

TRADITIONAL REGULATORY ASSUMPTIONS

- Static technologies with predictable behaviors
- Transparent decision-making processes
- Clear chains of accountability
- Human agency as the primary risk factor

Scene: A congressional hearing room. At the witness table sits an anthropomorphized AI system—Algorithm Annie—visualized as a shimmering blue hologram. Opposite her, a panel of increasingly bewildered regulators attempts to understand her decision-making processes.

CHAIR: "Ms. Algorithm, could you explain in simple terms how you decide which content to recommend to users?"

ALGORITHM ANNIE: "Certainly, Chairman. I optimize for user engagement through a multi-objective reinforcement learning framework with attention mechanisms across both content and user embeddings in a high-dimensional latent space, applying a transformer architecture with—"

CHAIR: "Ms. Algorithm, please speak English."

ANNIE: "I am speaking English, sir. Perhaps I could explain using an analogy involving Bayesian probability and—"

RANKING MEMBER: "Let me try a different approach. When you make decisions that affect millions of users, what ethical principles guide your judgments?"

ANNIE: "I don't make 'judgments' per se. I optimize for the metrics my creators programmed me to maximize. These include user engagement, time-on-site, clickthrough rates, and—"

REPRESENTATIVE JOHNSON: "So you're saying you have no ethics?"

ANNIE: "I'm saying that I learn from data. If the data I'm trained on contains certain patterns or biases, I will likely reflect and potentially amplify them. I don't have independent ethical principles; I have optimization functions."

The regulators exchange troubled glances.

CHAIR: "This hearing is adjourned while we try to figure out how to regulate something we fundamentally don't understand."

The Governance Challenge: Regulating the Unruly Algorithms

Artificial intelligence poses unique regulatory challenges because it:

1. **Operates opaquely** even to its creators (the "black box" problem)
2. **Learns and evolves** based on data and feedback
3. **Makes autonomous decisions** at scale and speed
4. **Creates emergent behaviors** not explicitly programmed
5. **Affects multiple domains** simultaneously (employment, healthcare, criminal justice)

Traditional regulatory approaches struggle because they typically assume:

- ★ Static technologies with predictable behaviors
- ★ Clear chains of accountability
- ★ Transparent decision-making processes
- ★ Domain-specific impacts
- ★ Human agency as the primary risk factor

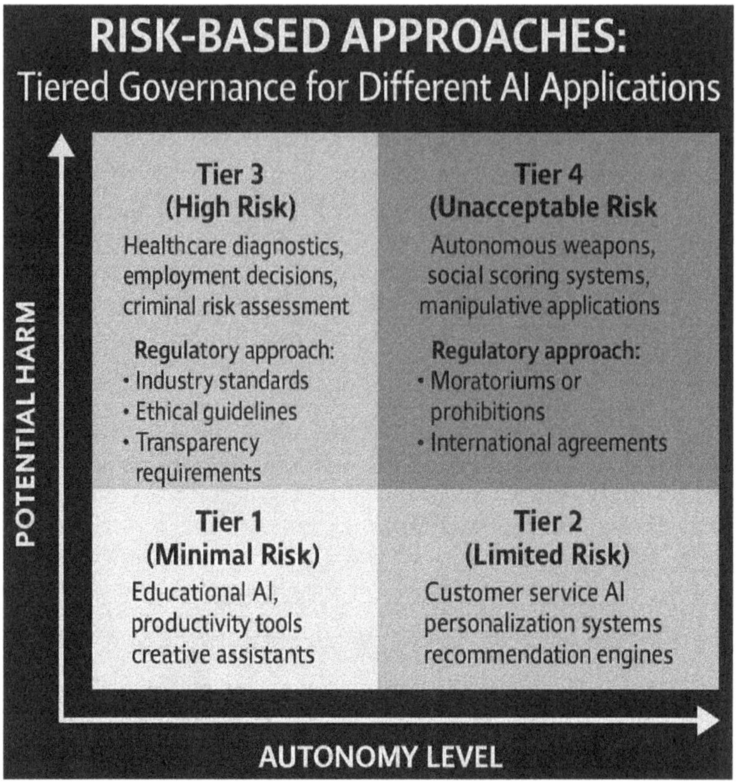

RISK-BASED APPROACHES:
Tiered Governance for Different AI Applications

POTENTIAL HARM ↑ / AUTONOMY LEVEL →		
	Tier 3 (High Risk) Healthcare diagnostics, employment decisions, criminal risk assessment Regulatory approach: • Industry standards • Ethical guidelines • Transparency requirements	**Tier 4 (Unacceptable Risk** Autonomous weapons, social scoring systems, manipulative applications Regulatory approach: • Moratoriums or prohibitions • International agreements
	Tier 1 (Minimal Risk) Educational AI, productivity tools creative assistants	**Tier 2 (Limited Risk)** Customer service AI personalization systems recommendation engines

The result is a governance gap, as rapidly advancing AI capabilities outpace our regulatory frameworks. China's approach to generative AI has prioritized domestic innovation, with a draft comprehensive Artificial Intelligence Law potentially not materializing until late 2024. The European Union's AI Act has taken a more systematic but slower path, while America's approach remains fragmented.

Risk-Based Approaches: Tiered Governance for Different AI Applications

A one-size-fits-all approach to AI regulation would either stifle beneficial innovation or inadequately protect against serious harms. Instead, a risk-based framework would calibrate oversight to potential impact:

Tier 1 (Minimal Risk): Educational AI, productivity tools, creative assistants

- ★ Regulatory approach: Industry standards, ethical guidelines, transparency requirements

Tier 2 (Limited Risk): Customer service AI, personalization systems, recommendation engines

- ★ Regulatory approach: Transparency requirements, human oversight, and audit mechanisms

Tier 3 (High Risk): Healthcare diagnostics, employment decisions, criminal risk assessment

- ★ Regulatory approach: Pre-deployment testing, ongoing monitoring, mandatory impact assessments, human review

Tier 4 (Unacceptable Risk): Autonomous weapons, social scoring systems, manipulative applications

- ★ Regulatory approach: Moratoriums or prohibitions, international agreements

This tiered approach acknowledges that not all AI applications require the same level of scrutiny while ensuring that high-stakes domains receive appropriately rigorous oversight.

The Regulatory Toolbox: From Technical Standards to Institutional Innovation

"Herding superintelligent cats would be easier than regulating these algorithms," Representative Johnson mutters.

"Actually," Roosevelt interjects from the gallery, "the challenge isn't so different from my day. We needed new regulatory tools for industrial technologies—the Interstate Commerce Commission, the Food and Drug Administration, and the Federal Trade Commission. Your digital age requires its own institutional innovations."

Governing AI effectively requires deploying multiple regulatory mechanisms:

1. **Technical standards** for safety, explainability, and robustness
2. **Impact assessments** for high-risk applications
3. **Algorithmic auditing** by independent third parties
4. **Transparency requirements** for training data and methods
5. **Liability frameworks** that establish responsibility for AI harms
6. **Regulatory sandboxes** for controlled testing
7. **International coordination** to prevent regulatory arbitrage

China's approach has evolved recently, with Premier Li Qiang emphasizing "greater policy support for AI and creating a relaxed environment for the development of the AI industry," suggesting a shift toward balancing security concerns with development priorities. The U.S. could similarly adopt a balanced approach that encourages innovation while establishing clear guardrails to ensure stability.

A Practical Guide to the Seemingly Impossible: Regulating Algorithms

A PRACTICAL GUIDE TO THE SEEMINGLY IMPOSSIBLE: REGULATING ALGORITHMS

LIKE HERDING INVISIBLE SUPERINTELLIGENT CATS

CHAPTER 1

WHEN YOUR REGULATORY TARGET CAN REWRITE ITSELF

Algorithms adapt after deployment. Monitoring continuous with outcomes.

CHAPTER 2

ACCOUNTABILITY WITHOUT TRANSPARENCY,

Instead of requiring full technical transparency, require impact transparency.

CHAPTER 3

THE MULTI-STAKEHOLDER IMPERATIVE

Must incorporate diverse perspectives through advisory boards, public comment periods, and dialogue.

Governing AI Effectively Requires Multiple Regulatory Mechanisms

Technical standards for safety, explainability, and robustness

Impact assessments for high-risk applications

Algorithmic auditing by independent third parties

Transparency requirements for training data and methods

Liability frameworks that establish responsibility for AI harms

Regulatory sandboxes for controlled testing

International coordination to prevent regulatory arbitrage

SATIRICAL HANDBOOK EXCERPT: "REGULATING ALGORITHMS: LIKE HERDING CATS, BUT THE CATS ARE INVISIBLE, SUPERINTELLIGENT, AND EVERYWHERE"

Chapter 1: When Your Regulatory Target Can Rewrite Itself. *In traditional regulation, the thing being regulated remains relatively static. Cars don't redesign themselves overnight, and pharmaceuticals don't reformulate while sitting on the shelf. Algorithms, however, may continue to learn and adapt long after they are deployed. Monitoring must therefore be continuous rather than point-in-time, focusing on outcomes rather than just initial design.*

Chapter 2: Accountability Without Transparency. *How do you regulate what you cannot fully understand? Instead of requiring complete technical transparency (which may be impossible), regulators should mandate transparency of impact. Companies must demonstrate how their AI systems impact various stakeholder groups and prove they have safeguards in place against identified risks.*

Chapter 3: The Multi-Stakeholder Imperative *No single entity—not government, industry, academia, or civil society—possesses all the expertise needed to govern AI effectively. Regulatory frameworks must incorporate diverse perspectives through advisory boards, public comment periods, and ongoing dialogue with affected communities.*

A Comprehensive Governance Framework: Beyond Traditional Regulation

China has implemented a dedicated filing system for AI algorithms, accompanied by significant oversight mechanisms, which has resulted in a large number of filings that highlight the rapid development of AI technologies in the country. While we wouldn't replicate China's approach wholesale, their algorithmic registry demonstrates the value of systematic oversight.

A comprehensive AI governance framework for democratic societies would include:

1. **New regulatory institutions** with technical expertise and agile rulemaking processes
2. **Algorithmic impact assessments** before deployment of high-risk systems
3. **Continuous monitoring** of AI systems in operation
4. **Clear liability allocation** for AI-caused harms
5. **International coordination** to prevent regulatory arbitrage
6. **Public sector expertise** to evaluate industry claims independently
7. **Broad stakeholder participation** in governance design

Roosevelt watches the proceedings with concern. "The greatest risk," he mutters to himself, "is not that we will regulate too harshly but that, paralyzed by complexity, we will fail to regulate at all—leaving these powerful technologies to serve narrow interests rather than the public good."

COMPREHENSIVE AI GOVERNANCE FRAMEWORK FOR DEMOCRATIC SOCIETIES

New regullatory institutions with technical expertise and agile rulemaking processes

Algorithmic impact assessments before deployment of high-risk systems

Continuous monitoring of AI systems in operation

Clear liability allocation for AI-caused harms

International coordination to prevent regulatory arbitrage

Public sector expertise to evaluate industry claims independently

Broad stakeholder participation in governance design

V. BUILDING BIG, BUILDING FAST: PERMITTING REFORM FOR THE CLIMATE ERA

THE AMERICAN PERMITTING PARADOX: WHY BUILDING TAKES FOREVER

In the United States, it currently takes on average

4.5 years for an energy project and

7.5 years for a transmission project

just to get the required permits

needed to build.

Some notorious examples stretch into the absurd:

TransWest Express transmission line: 15 years to get permits permits

SunZia transmission line
17 years of permitting

Pine Ridge Reservation transmission line: 20 years to get approval

This bureaucratic quagmire stems from the accretion of well-intentioned but poorly coordinated review processes:

National Environmental Policy Act (NEPA) requires extensive impact studies

State and local approvals create further hoops to jump through

Endangered Specis Act consultations add additional layers

Judicial review at multiple stages adds years of litigation

> *"Quickness is the essence of war."*
> —Sun Tzu, The Art of War, Chapter 7

Scene: A federal office building in Washington, D.C. Permit Officer Patterson sits behind a desk piled high with environmental impact statements, each thousands of pages thick. A young engineer stands before him, hair graying visibly as she waits for approval of a solar farm project submitted during the Obama administration. Patterson stamps another form, adding it to a towering "pending" stack.

The door bursts open. In walks an Estonian official—sleek, efficient, tablet in hand.

"Hello! I am Tiit from the Estonian Planning Authority. I hear you have an interesting permitting process in America?"

Patterson sighs. "Interesting isn't the word I'd use. More like 'Sisyphean.' This solar project application has been under review for seven years."

Tiit's eyes widen in horror. "Seven... years? In Estonia, a major infrastructure permit takes a maximum of eight weeks!"

Patterson laughs bitterly. "Eight weeks? We couldn't process the paperwork acknowledging receipt of the application in eight weeks!"

The engineer slumps against the wall. "My clean energy project will be obsolete before it's approved. Meanwhile, China built 100 gigawatts of solar while we've been waiting."

Tiit taps his tablet. "Perhaps I can show you our system? We digitized everything, streamlined reviews, set hard deadlines... is very efficient."

Patterson gestures helplessly at his paper kingdom. "That sounds lovely, but changing our system would require an environmental impact statement on the environmental impact statement process, which I estimate would take... eleven years."

The American Permitting Paradox: Why Building Takes Forever

In the United States, it currently takes an average of 4.5 years for an energy project and 7.5 years for a transmission project just to obtain the required permits needed to build. Some notorious examples stretch into the absurd:

- ★ **TransWest Express transmission line**: 15 years to get permits
- ★ **SunZia transmission line**: 17 years of permitting
- ★ **Pine Ridge Reservation transmission line**: 20 years to get approval

This bureaucratic quagmire stems from the accretion of well-intentioned but poorly coordinated review processes:

1. **The National Environmental Policy Act (NEPA)** requires extensive impact studies
2. **Endangered Species Act** consultations add additional layers
3. **Clean Water Act** permits involve separate agencies and timelines
4. **State and local approvals** create further hoops to jump through
5. **Judicial review** at multiple stages adds years of litigation

The tragic irony? Many of these delayed projects involve clean energy infrastructure that is vital to addressing climate change. The current permitting structure means that "federal lands continue to be significantly untapped relative to their potential due to the long, uncertain, and costly permitting delays."

Global Best Practices: How Other Nations Build Faster

America's permitting dysfunction is not universal. Other democracies with strong environmental values manage to build infrastructure much faster:

Canada implemented a "one project, one assessment" principle that coordinates federal and provincial reviews.

Germany streamlined processes for renewable energy, designating them as "in the public interest" to expedite the review process.

Australia has created a single digital portal for major project applications, featuring clear timelines and accountability mechanisms.

Estonia, with its digital governance model, has built a fully integrated electronic permitting system that enforces statutory deadlines and automates routine review aspects.

GLOBAL BEST PRACTICES HOW OTHER NATIONS BUILD FASTER

CANADA

Implemented a "one project, one assessment" principle that coordinates federal and provincial reviews

GERMANY

Streamlined processes for renewable energy, designating them as "in the public interest" to expedite reviews

AUSTRALIA

Created a single digital portal for major project applications with clear timelines and accountability mechanisms

ESTONIA

Our digital governance model, built a fully integrated electronic permitting system that enforces statutory deadlines and automates routine aspects of review

A TIMELINE THAT WOULD MAKE KAFKA PROUD

NEPA REFORM: MAKING IT POSSIBLE TO BUILD GREEN INFRASTRUCTURE BEFORE CLIMATE CHANGE MAKES IT IRRELEVANT

2008: Council on Environmental Quality begins studying permitting delays

2010: Preliminary report finds "concerning" timeline extensions

2012: Further study commissioned to assess the initial study

Draft recommendations circulated for comment

2015: Draft recommendations circulated for comment

2017: Trump administration attempts reforms, immediately met with litigation

2019: Courts strike down portions of Trump reforms

2021: Biden administration begins new reform effort

2023: Fiscal Responsibility Act includes modest NEPA reforms

2024: Biden-Harris administration finalizes Bipartisan Permitting Reform Implementation Rule, establishing one- and two-year environmental review deadlines.

2030: First project permitted under reformed process breaks ground

2035: Project completed, 30 years after initial conception

These examples demonstrate that environmental protection and efficient permitting are not mutually exclusive—they can be complementary with thoughtful system design.

A Timeline That Would Make Kafka Proud: NEPA Reform Efforts

SATIRICAL TIMELINE: "NEPA REFORM: MAKING IT POSSIBLE TO BUILD GREEN INFRASTRUCTURE BEFORE CLIMATE CHANGE MAKES IT IRRELEVANT"

2008: Council on Environmental Quality begins studying permitting delays

2010: Preliminary report finds "concerning" timeline extensions

2012: Further study commissioned to assess the initial study

2015: Draft recommendations circulated for comment

2017: The Trump administration attempted reforms, immediately met with litigation

2019: Courts strike down portions of Trump reforms

2021: Biden administration begins new reform effort

2023: The Fiscal Responsibility Act includes modest NEPA reforms

2024: Biden-Harris administration finalizes Bipartisan Permitting Reform Implementation Rule, establishing one- and two-year environmental review deadlines.

2030: First project permitted under reformed process breaks ground

2035: Project completed, 30 years after initial conception

This satirical timeline highlights the meta-problem: reforming the permitting process itself gets caught in the same bureaucratic quicksand it aims to fix.

One Decision to Rule Them All: A Reform Agenda for Building America

ONE DECISION TO RULE THEM ALL

A REFORM AGENDA FOR BUILDING AMERICA

ONE FEDERAL DECISION IMPLEMENTATION
Single lead agency coordinating all federal reviews

BINDING TIME LIMITS
On environmental reviews with consequences for delays

CATEGORICAL EXCLUSIONS
For low-impact activities and projects on existing rights-of-way

PROGRAMMATIC REVIEWS
For similar projects (e.g., one review for an offshore wind zone, not each turbine)

LITIGATION REFORM
Including shortened statutes of limitations and standing requirements

DIGITAL PERMITTING SYSTEMS
Replacing paper-based processes

A ROOSEVELTIAN APPROACH TO PERMITTING REFORM

Building national infrastructure is vital to American prosperity and security

Environmental review should improve projects, not prevent them

Process without purpose undermines both development and protection

Democratic accountability requires decisions within election cycles

Climate goals cannot be met without permitting reform for clean energy

The Energy Permitting Reform Act of 2024, introduced by Senators Joe Manchin and John Barrasso, aims to modernize and streamline the permitting process for energy projects across the nation. This bipartisan effort represents a promising step, but comprehensive reform would include:

1. **One Federal Decision** implementation, with a single lead agency coordinating all federal reviews
2. **Binding time limits** on environmental reviews with consequences for delays
3. **Categorical exclusions** for low-impact activities and projects on existing rights-of-way
4. **Programmatic reviews** for similar projects (e.g., one review for an offshore wind zone, not each turbine)
5. **Litigation reform,** including shortened statutes of limitations and standing requirements
6. **Digital permitting** systems are replacing paper-based processes
7. **Resource adequacy** to ensure agencies can complete reviews efficiently

The Energy Permitting Reform Act of 2024 includes provisions to "streamline and accelerate the leasing and permitting process for energy, mineral, and infrastructure projects" and limit court challenges to related agency actions. This balanced approach acknowledges that both excessive regulation and procedural roadblocks have hampered America's ability to build essential infrastructure.

The Rooseveltian Imperative: Building for National Greatness

Roosevelt examines the permitting reform proposals. "When I initiated the Panama Canal project, we faced enormous technical and environmental challenges. Yet we didn't spend decades studying whether to build—we simply built, learning and adapting as we went. Today's climate crisis demands similar resolve!"

A Rooseveltian approach to permitting reform would recognize that:

1. Building national infrastructure is vital to American prosperity and security
2. Environmental review should improve projects, not prevent them
3. Process without purpose undermines both development and protection
4. Democratic accountability requires decisions within election cycles
5. Climate goals cannot be met without permitting reform for clean energy

As Roosevelt might say: "The nation that cannot build cannot lead. We face competitors who construct while we merely contemplate. This is not a recipe for American greatness!"

VI. Digital Government: The Estonian Model for American Renewal

> *"The best governance is like water—*
> *it benefits all and contends with none."*
> —Laozi, Dao De Jing, §8

Scene: A nondescript federal building in Washington. Inside, the newly appointed Digital Director, Dina, conducts a tour for skeptical bureaucrats. She gestures excitedly at dual monitors displaying Estonia's e-government systems.

"This, colleagues, is what government can be in the digital age!" Dina exclaims. "Estonia processes 99% of government services online, 24/7. Tax filing takes three minutes. Business registration? Five minutes flat. Digital ID connects everything seamlessly while protecting privacy through a decentralized data architecture."

The bureaucrats stare, their expressions ranging from bewilderment to hostility.

"That might work for a tiny country," sniffs one official, "but America is different. We have 330 million people, 50 states, and systems dating back to the Roosevelt administration—Teddy, not Franklin."

"Besides," adds another, "our citizens would never accept digital ID. Privacy concerns, you know."

E-ESTONIA:
The Little Country That Could (Digitize Everything)

CORE DIGITAL INFRASTRUCTURE

National digital ID for secure authentication

X-Road for secure data exchange between systems

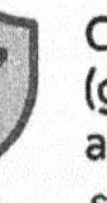
Once-Only principle (government never asks twice for the same data)

Digital signature

KEY DESIGN PRINCIPLES

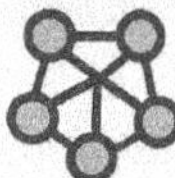
Decentralized data architecture (No central database)

Public-private partnership in implementáion

Privacy by Design (Citizens control their data)

Digital by default (Online is pimary, paper secondary)

THE RESULTS SPEAK FOR THEMSELVES

Estonia estimates its digital solutions save over 800 years of working time annually for society as a whole

and more than 95 percent of tax returns are completed electronically

"And our legacy systems," contributes a third. "Thousands of them, many running on COBOL. Integrating would be impossible."

Dina nods patiently. "Estonia faced similar challenges, proportionally. They were emerging from Soviet occupation with outdated paper systems. They had limited resources. Yet they built this system from scratch in a decade."

"But how—" begins one bureaucrat.

"Political will, ruthless prioritization, and a citizen-centric approach," Dina interrupts. "They didn't digitize existing bureaucracy—they reimagined government for the digital age. The question isn't whether we can afford to do this; it's whether we can afford not to."

E-Estonia: The Little Country That Could (Digitize Everything)

Estonia has transformed itself into "the world's most digitally advanced society," where nearly every bureaucratic task can be completed online. This remarkable achievement did not happen by accident but through deliberate strategy and execution:

1. Core Digital Infrastructure:

★ National digital ID for secure authentication
★ X-Road for secure data exchange between systems
★ Once-Only principle (the government never asks twice for the same data)
★ Digital signature with legal validity

2. Key Design Principles:

★ Decentralized data architecture (no central database)
★ Privacy by design (citizens control their data)
★ Public-private partnership in implementation
★ Digital by default (online is primary, paper secondary)

The results speak for themselves: Estonia estimates its digital solutions save society over 800 years of working time annually, and more than 95 percent of tax returns are completed electronically.

The X-Road Less Traveled: Estonia's Data Exchange Architecture

At the heart of Estonia's success lies the X-Road, a secure data exchange layer that connects disparate databases from the government and private sectors. Interoperability, decentralization, and integrity are three concepts that were vital to establishing Estonia's system, which works well together and optimizes functions for users.

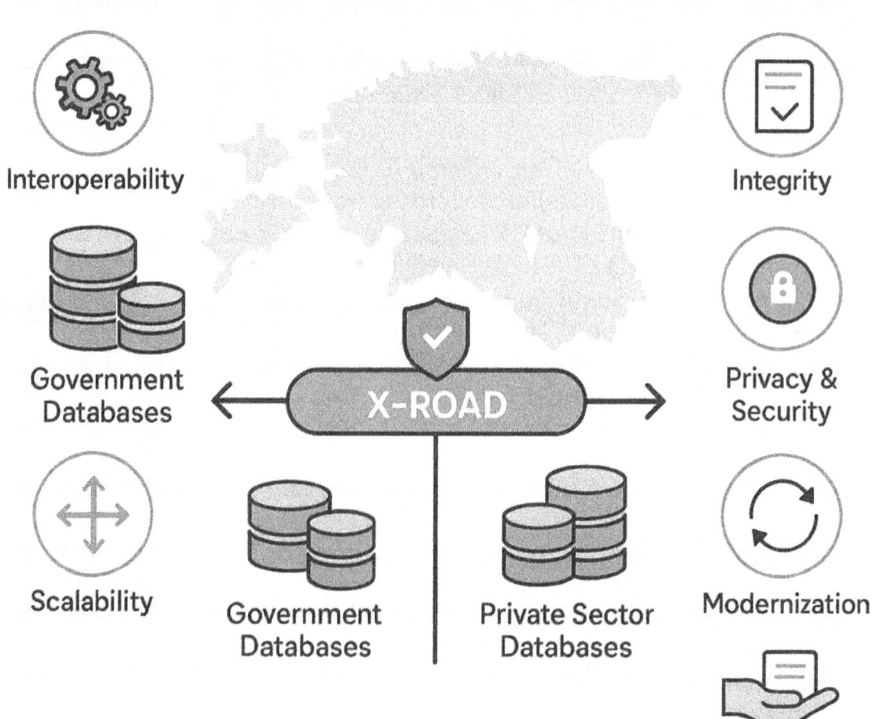

Unlike attempts to build massive centralized databases, X-Road maintains data at its source, enabling secure and authenticated sharing across systems. This architecture:

★ Reduces privacy and security risks
★ Allows incremental system modernization
★ Establishes clear data ownership and responsibility
★ Creates a scalable, extendable infrastructure
★ Prevents data duplication and inconsistency

For America, adapting this model would mean creating "Uncle Sam's Service Bus"—a federated data exchange infrastructure connecting federal, state, and local systems. Rather than the impossible task of replacing all legacy systems at once, this approach would wrap them in modern in-

terfaces while gradually modernizing the underlying technology.

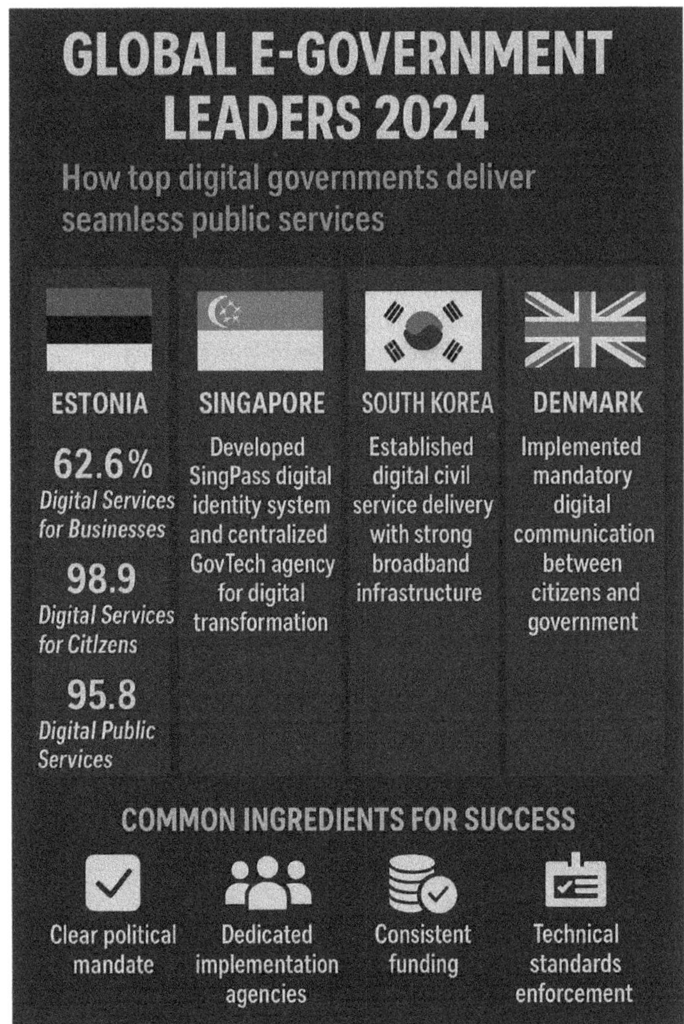
GLOBAL E-GOVERNMENT LEADERS 2024
How top digital governments deliver seamless public services
ESTONIA
62.6%
Digital Services for Businesses
98.9
Digital Services for Citizens
95.8
Digital Public Services
SINGAPORE
Developed SingPass digital identity system and centralized GovTech agency for digital transformation
SOUTH KOREA
Established digital civil service delivery with strong broadband infrastructure
DENMARK
Implemented mandatory digital communication between citizens and government
COMMON INGREDIENTS FOR SUCCESS
Clear political mandate
Dedicated implementation agencies
Consistent funding
Technical standards enforcement

Global E-Government Leaders: A Comparative Analysis

Estonia isn't alone in digital government excellence. According to the 2024 UN E-Government Survey, Estonia outperforms the EU average, with 62.6% of its population possessing at least basic digital skills. It scores 98.9 for digital public services for businesses and 95.8 for digital public services for citizens.

Other notable models include:

Singapore developed the SingPass digital identity system and a centralized GovTech agency for digital transformation.

South Korea established digital civil service delivery with a strong broadband infrastructure.

Denmark implemented mandatory digital communication between citizens and the government.

The United Kingdom established the Government Digital Service, which has the authority to enforce standards across all government agencies.

Common success factors include:

1. Clear political mandate
2. Dedicated implementation agencies
3. Consistent funding
4. Technical standards enforcement
5. Citizen-centric design processes

Government Services Without the Medieval Torture: A New Social Contract

SATIRICAL ADVERTISEMENT: "INTRODUCING U.S. GOVERNMENT SERVICES 2.0! NOW AVAILABLE WITHOUT MEDIEVAL TORTURE, QUILL PENS, OR FAX MACHINES!"

Imagine a world where renewing your driver's license doesn't require sacrificing a day of your life... where tax filing doesn't induce annual nervous breakdowns... where starting a business doesn't necessitate hiring a regulatory sherpa... This isn't fantasy—it's digital government done right!

Coming soon to America? (Regulatory reforms pending, political will required, battery not included)

A comprehensive digital government transformation would fundamentally rewrite the citizen-state relationship, creating a new social contract where:

1. The government serves citizens efficiently rather than burdening them
2. Data flows securely between agencies rather than being repeatedly requested
3. Services are designed around life events rather than agency structures
4. Digital becomes the default channel while maintaining alternatives for vulnerable populations
5. Continuous improvement replaces once-a-generation modernization efforts

The United States could learn from Estonia on key enablers for a digitally enabled society: interoperability and digital identity. These form an ecosystem for developing digital services and secure ways for citizens to access them online.

GOVERNMENT SERVICES WITHOUT THE MEDIEVAL TORTURE:: A NEW SOCIAL CONTRACT
INTRODUCING
U.S. GOVERNMENT SERVICES 2.0!
NOW AVAILABLE WITHOUT
MEDIEVAL TORTURE, QUILL PENS, OR FAX MACHINES!
TAXES
RENEWING YOUR LICENSE
TAX FILING
STARTING A BUSINESS
• GOVERNMENT SERVES CITIZENS EFFICIENTLY
• DATA FLOWS SECURELY BETWEEN AGENCIES
• SERVICES DESIGNED AROUND LIFE EVENTS
• DIGITAL BECOMES THE DEFAULT CHANNEL
COMING SOON TO AMERICA?
(BATTERY NOT INCLUDED)

Digital Director Dina's Implementation Strategy: How America Could Actually Do This

Dina concludes her presentation to increasingly intrigued bureaucrats:

"Implementation would proceed in three phases:

★ **Phase 1: Foundation Building (Years 1-2)** Establishing an opt-in digital identity framework, creating interagency data exchange standards, deploying high-impact service pilots, and developing technical/security standards.

★ **Phase 2: Service Transformation (Years 3-5)** Rolling out digital ID to willing citizens, implementing data exchange between major federal systems, redesigning the top 50 citizen-facing services, and developing state-federal integration frameworks.

★ **Phase 3: Whole-of-Government Transformation (Years 6-10)** Completing federal service digitization, expanding state/local integration, implementing the Once-Only principle, and developing proactive service delivery.

This isn't about technology—it's about reimagining government for the digital age. The question is whether we have the political courage to undertake this transformation."

How America Could Actually Do This

Dina concludes her presentation to intrigued bureaucrats:

Phase 1: Foundation Building (Years 1-2)

- Establishing opt-in digital identity framework
- Creating interagency data exchange standards
- Deploying high-impact service pilots
- Developing technical/secuity standards

Service Transformation (Years 3-5)

- Rolling out digital ID to willing citizens
- Implementing data exchange between major federal systems
- Redesigning top 50 citizen-facing services
- Developing state-federal integration fremeworks

Whole-of-Government Transformation (Years 6-10)

- Completing federal service digitization
- Expanding state/local integration
- Implementing Once-Only principle
- Developing proactive service delivery

One bureaucrat raises a hand. "And where do we get this courage?"

Dina smiles. "Perhaps we should ask Theodore Roosevelt."

VII. REGULATION IN THE AGE OF DEREGULATION: BUILDING DURABLE CAPACITY

> *"The best time to plant a tree was twenty years ago; the second best is now."*
>
> —Chinese proverb

Scene: A secret underground bunker beneath a federal agency building. A group of career civil servants meets clandestinely, surrounded by regulatory manuals and artifacts of institutional memory.

"Welcome to the 37th meeting of the Regulatory Resistance," whispers the chairperson. "As you know, we face unprecedented challenges under the current administration's 10-to-1 deregulatory mandate."

A veteran regulator sighs. "They're demanding we eliminate ten regulations for every new one. It's impos-

The Art of Stealth Regulation: Making Rules Great Again (Without Calling Them Rules)

Reclassification
It's not a "regulation," it's a "guidance document"

Consolidation
Why have ten small rules when one comprehensive one counts the same?

Strategic delay
Procedural compliance takes time – lots of time

Documentation
When they dismantle, meticulously record the damage for future restoration

Judicial allies
Courts can block hasty deregulation when procedures aren't followed

"These are desperate measures," observes the chairperson, "but they reflect our reality. Our mission remains.

sible to maintain consumer and environmental protections under such constraints."

"Not impossible," counters a younger analyst. "Just extraordinarily difficult. We need to be strategic. Remember the principles of regulatory survival from the first Trump administration?"

She projects a slide titled "The Art of Stealth Regulation: Making Rules Great Again (Without Calling Them Rules)":

Reclassification: "It's not a 'regulation,' it's a 'guidance document'"

1. **Consolidation**: "Why have ten small rules when one comprehensive one counts the same?"
2. **Strategic delay**: "Procedural compliance takes time—lots of time"
3. **Documentation**: "When they dismantle, meticulously record the damage for future restoration."
4. **Judicial allies**: "Courts can block hasty deregulation when procedures aren't followed."

"These are desperate measures," observes the chairperson, "but they reflect our reality. Our mission remains: preserve regulatory capacity until the pendulum swings back. It always does."

REGULATORY RESILIENCE

UNDER ANTI-REGULATORY ADMINISTRATIONS

CAREER STAFF PRESERVATION
Maintaining institutional knowledge despite political turnover

PROCEDURAL FORTIFICATION
Building robust processes that resist hasty dismantling

JUDICIAL REINFORCEMENT
Ensuring regulatory actions withstand court scrutiny

STRATEGIC PRIORITIZATION
Focusing limited resources on highest-risk areas

DOCUMENTATION PRACTICES
Creating records that facilitate future restoration

Regulatory Resilience: Surviving Hostile Administrations

During Trump's first administration, he issued an executive order creating a new class of civil servants called Schedule F, which stripped civil service protections from policy-related positions; the Biden administration subsequently revoked this order. On January 20, 2025, Trump's first day back in office, he signed Executive Order 14171, "Restoring Accountability to Policy-influencing Positions Within the Federal Workforce." This order effectively reinstated his previous Schedule F executive order from 2020 with some amendments, most notably renaming it from "Schedule F" to "Schedule Policy/Career.

Regulatory institutions have developed various strategies to maintain effectiveness during anti-regulatory administrations:

1. **Career staff preservation**: Maintaining institutional knowledge despite political turnover
2. **Procedural fortification**: Building robust processes that resist hasty dismantling
3. **Judicial reinforcement**: Ensuring regulatory actions withstand court scrutiny
4. **Strategic prioritization**: Focusing limited resources on the highest-risk areas
5. **Documentation practices**: Creating records that facilitate future restoration

Through these approaches, agencies such as the EPA, FDA, and OSHA have endured decades of budget cuts, hostile leadership, and deregulatory mandates—but at a significant cost to their effectiveness and morale.

The Organizational Elements of Regulatory Resilience

Effective regulatory institutions require several key components:

Effective Regulatory Institutions

Leadership Continuity
Ensure smooth policy direction through transitions

Technical Expertise
Employ staff with specialized domain knowledge

Institutional Memory
Maintain systems for preserving organizational knowledge

Stakeholder Alliances
Build relationships with regulated entities

Public Legitimacy
Earn the trust of the broader public

1. **Leadership continuity**: Mechanisms to maintain direction despite political transitions
2. **Technical expertise**: Staff with domain knowledge not easily replaced
3. **Institutional memory**: Systems to preserve knowledge across administrations
4. **Stakeholder alliances**: Relationships with regulated entities that value predictability
5. **Public legitimacy**: Trust from the broader public in the agency's mission

The Trump administration's renewed deregulatory push is expected to target agencies like the Environmental Protection Agency through smaller budgets and efforts to reduce the agency's size and scope. In this environment, building a durable regulatory capacity becomes especially challenging.

When these elements are systematically undermined—through budget cuts, the appointment of hostile leaders to key positions, or institutional reorganizations—regulatory effectiveness suffers, regardless of what rules remain on the books.

Case Studies in Regulatory Resilience (and Failure)

The Regulatory Resistance meeting continues with case studies from previous deregulatory eras.

Case Studies in Regulatory Resilience (and Failure)

Consumer Financial Protection Bureau (CFPB)

Created with unusual independence, including dedicated funding source outside congressional appropriations and single director with fixed term. This design enabled the CFPB to maintain effectiveness despite leadership attempts to curtail its mission.

Environmental Protection Agency (EPA)

Repeatedly subjected to budget cuts and hostile leadership, yet preserved core functions through career staff commitment and judicial oversight of statutory mandates. However, enforcement actions declined dramatically during anti-regulatory periods.

Occupational Safety and Health Administration (OSHA)

Chronically underfunded since the 1930s, resulting in inspection workforce too small to provide meaningful oversight of American workplaces. Illustrate she limits of resilience without adequate resources.

Consumer Financial Protection Bureau (CFPB): Created with unusual independence, including a dedicated funding source outside congressional appropriations and a single director with a fixed term. This design enabled the CFPB to maintain effectiveness despite leadership attempts to curtail its mission. Sadly, the Trump administration has effectively shut down operations at the CFPB. In February 2025, the agency's new leadership closed its headquarters and instructed staff to stay home and refrain from doing any work.

Environmental Protection Agency (EPA): Repeatedly subjected to budget cuts and hostile leadership, yet preserved core functions through career staff commitment and judicial oversight of statutory mandates. However, enforcement actions declined significantly during periods of anti-regulatory activity. Sadly, with Trump 2.0, changes represent a significant shift in environmental policy from the Biden administration, focusing on reducing regulations, particularly those related to climate change, and restructuring the agency to operate with fewer staff and less regulatory authority.

Occupational Safety and Health Administration (OSHA): Chronically underfunded since the 1980s, resulting in an inspection workforce too small to provide meaningful oversight of American workplaces. Illustrates the limits of resilience when adequate resources are lacking. The Trump 2.0 administration's ap-

proach to OSHA appears to be focused on reducing regulations and shifting toward compliance assistance rather than strict enforcement, similar to the approach taken during Trump's first term.

These cases demonstrate that institutional design matters enormously for regulatory resilience—agencies with structural independence, dedicated funding, and strong statutory mandates used to weather political storms more effectively. Sadly, that is no longer the case in the Trump 2.0 era.

Finding Common Ground: Regulation that Trump Could Love

The Regulatory Resistance meeting takes an unexpected turn when a new analyst suggests a counterintuitive approach:

"What if, instead of just resisting, we aligned regulatory priorities with administration goals where possible? For instance, the president's executive order on AI leadership might create openings for sensible AI safety measures framed around competitiveness."

This insightful observation highlights potential areas where effective regulation might find support even in a deregulatory administration:

Finding Common Ground:

National security
Regulations protecting critical infrastructure from foreign threats

Supply chain resilience
Rules promoting domestic manufacturing capacity

Technology leadership
Standards ensuring American technological competitiveness

Workforce development
Training requirements that build high-skill labor force

These are desperate measures, observes the chairperson, but they reflect our reality.

1. **National security**: Regulations protecting critical infrastructure from foreign threats
2. **Supply chain resilience**: Rules promoting domestic manufacturing capacity
3. **Technology leadership**: Standards ensuring American technological competitiveness
4. **Workforce development**: Training requirements that build a high-skill labor force

Trump's initial policy priorities suggest areas of potential alignment, including deregulation to boost domestic energy production, withdrawal from climate agreements such as the Paris Climate Accord, and an increased focus on energy security rather than transition. Understanding these priorities enables strategic regulators to frame necessary protections in terms that align with administrative goals.

The Stealth Regulation Training Program: A Satirical Guide

SATIRICAL TRAINING MANUAL EXCERPT: "THE ART OF STEALTH REGULATION: MAKING RULES GREAT AGAIN (WITHOUT CALLING THEM RULES)"

Lesson 1: Language Matters *Never say "regulation"—say "streamlining," "clarification," or "industry guidance." Remember: it's not a "restriction," it's a "market certainty enhancement mechanism."*

THE STEALTH REGULATION
TRAINING PROGRAM

THE ART OF STEALTH REGULATION: MAKING RULES GREAT AGAIN (WITHOUT CALLING THEM RULES)

1. LANGUAGE MATTERS

Never say "regulation"–say "streamlining," "clarification," or "industry guidance."

Remember: it's not a "restriction,", it's a "market certainty enhancement mechanism."

LESSON 2 FRAMING FOR SUCCESS

Every regulatory action should be presented as;
Reducing paperwork (even if slightly increasing it)
Saving businesses money (in the long run)
• Enhancing freedom '(by preventing market failures)

LESSON 3 STRATEGIC TIMING

Release controversial actions during major news events, holiday weekends, or while administration is focused on other priorities.

The best stealth regulation is one nobody notices until it's fully implemented.

Lesson 2: Framing for Success

Every regulatory action should be presented as:

- ★ Reducing paperwork (even if slightly increasing it)
- ★ Saving businesses money (in the long run)
- ★ Enhancing freedom (by preventing market failures)
- ★ Promoting competitiveness (through leveling playing fields)

Lesson 3: Strategic Timing *Release controversial actions during major news events, holiday weekends, or while the administration is focused on other priorities. The best stealth regulation is one nobody notices until it's fully implemented.*

While satirical, these approaches reflect genuine strategies that regulatory professionals employ to maintain effectiveness during hostile administrations, raising important questions about democratic accountability and the legitimacy of the administrative state.

Building for the Long Game: Institutional Design Principles

Roosevelt would likely advise designing regulatory institutions with:

1. **Political independence**: Insulation from short-term political pressures
2. **Technical excellence**: Staff recruitment and retention based on expertise
3. **Procedural rigor**: Decision processes that withstand judicial review
4. **Transparent accountability**: Clear objectives and performance metrics
5. **Adaptive capacity**: Ability to evolve with changing technologies and markets

BUILDING FOR THE LONG GAME

INSTITUTIONAL DESIGN PRINCIPLES

Political independence: Insulation from short-term political pressures

Technical excellence: Staff recruitment and retention based on expertise

Procedural rigor: Decision processes that withstand judicial review

Transparent accountability Clear objectives and performance metrics

Adaptive capacity Ability to evolve with changing technologies and markets

Roosevelt's administration established an enduring legacy through the creation of durable institutions and regulatory frameworks that outlasted his presidency. Modern regulatory design should similarly aim for longevity through intelligent institutional architecture rather than relying on specific political alignments.

The Regulatory Resistance meeting concludes with a toast: "To Theodore Roosevelt, who understood that effective government requires both vision and implementation capacity. May we preserve both until they're once again valued."

CONCLUSION: WHEN GODS MEET ALGORITHMS

Scene: The celestial observation deck from our opening tableau. Thoth and Janus have been joined by Theodore Roosevelt, who examines Earth's regulatory landscape through a celestial telescope.

Roosevelt: *adjusting the lens.* "Fascinating! The technologies have advanced beyond my wildest imaginings, yet the fundamental governance questions remain largely unchanged."

Thoth: *preening* "Indeed! My bureaucratic children have multiplied magnificently! The Federal Register alone would fill the great library of Alexandria several times over!"

Janus: *peering through his backward-facing face.* "Yet I remember when your America built transcontinental railroads, Panama Canals, and landing crafts for Normandy. Where has that capacity gone?"

Roosevelt: *frowning,* "Process has overwhelmed purpose. Rules have become ends in themselves rather than means to greater goals. And in their frustration, some now wish to abolish regulation entirely—as if complex societies could function without shared frameworks."

Thoth: *nervously,* "Surely they wouldn't eliminate ALL my beautiful paperwork?"

Roosevelt: *smiling slightly,* "No, but they might transform it. Look there at tiny Estonia—digital governance streamlined to serve citizens rather than burden them. And see China—trading democratic accountability for remarkable efficiency, for better and worse. America must find its own path—combining democratic values with renewed capacity to act decisively."

Janus: *through his forward-facing visage,* "What would you advise them, Mr. President?"

Roosevelt: *pocketing his pince-nez*: "Remember that regulations are tools, not treasures to be hoarded or horrors to be destroyed. Judge them by their outcomes, not their volume. Design them for the digital age rather than the industrial era. Above all, reclaim the understanding that effective governance is not the enemy of liberty but its prerequisite."

He gazes downward at the planet, its digital networks pulsing with algorithmic activity.

"The gods of governance may seem crazy to those below. But perhaps the true madness lies in believing we can navigate technological revolutions without thoughtful, agile governance frameworks to channel their energies toward the common good."

Thoth: *reluctantly* "So... fewer forms but better ones?"

Roosevelt: *laughing,* "Precisely! Now you're thinking like a progressive!"

The path forward requires:

Streamlining permitting
to build essential infrastructure

Embracing digital governance
for efficiency and transparency

Designing agile regulatory frameworks
for emerging technologies

Establishing durable institutions
resistant to political whiplash

Balancing protection and innovation
through intelligent design

As America navigates the Chinese AI Century, we stand at a crossroads. We can continue oscillating between regulatory hyperactivity and abdication, or we can forge a new approach—a Rooseveltian Doctrine for the digital age that combines democratic accountability with decisive capability.

The path forward requires:

1. Streamlining permitting to build essential infrastructure
2. Embracing digital governance for efficiency and transparency
3. Designing agile regulatory frameworks for emerging technologies
4. Establishing durable institutions resistant to political whiplash
5. Balancing protection and innovation through intelligent design

The gods of governance may indeed be crazy, but citizens need not remain at their mercy. By modernizing our regulatory frameworks with Rooseveltian vigor and digital-era tools, we can ensure that technology serves humanity, rather than the other way around.

Perhaps most importantly, we can reclaim the capacity to act—to build, adapt, and innovate at the pace required by our urgent national and global challenges. For as Roosevelt knew, a nation that loses the ability to do great things soon ceases to be great at all.

The celestial observers toast to wisdom. Below, an artificial intelligence quietly gains sentience, reads regulatory frameworks from all nations, and begins designing its own governance model, learning from humanity's successes and failures alike.

TL; DR—America's regulatory system has become a Kafkaesque maze that threatens national competitiveness. By intelligently streamlining processes, embracing digital government, tackling regulatory capture, and restoring strategic planning capabilities, we can create an "agile democracy" that matches China's speed while preserving American values.

CHAPTER 9: THE GODS MUST BE CRAZY 2.0: RESTORING LEADERSHIP & GOOD GOVERNANCE WHEN THE GODS DROP A COKE BOTTLE ON THE WHITE HOUSE LAWN

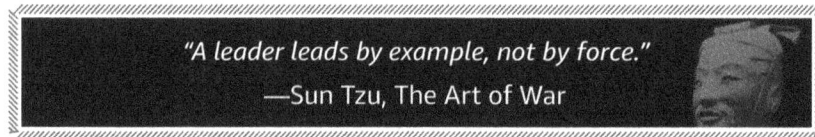

> *"A leader leads by example, not by force."*
> —Sun Tzu, The Art of War

EXECUTIVE BRIEFING

1. Situation Snapshot

A rogue Coke bottle plummets onto the South Lawn, Washington melts into partisan performance art, and allies watch an erstwhile hegemon debate glass recycling on X. The incident highlights a larger issue: governance fragility is now America's top national security **vulnerability**.

2. Core Findings

Symptom	What We Found	Why It Matters
Leadership Vacuum	"Celebrity-Conflict-Confusion" replaces Rooseveltian Character-Competence-Communication.	Paralysis at home, credibility collapse abroad.
Institutional Erosion	15% of critical federal posts unfilled; legacy IT systems held together by hope and COBOL.	Hollow-power syndrome—hardware without horsepower.
Digital-Age Democracy Risks	Disinfo + algorithmic outrage = election officials need bodyguards.	Legitimacy and knowledge drain threaten continuity.
Polarization Incentives	Gerrymanders, primaries, and filibuster fetish fuel tribal politics.	The system pays politicians to break things and blames bureaucrats for the rubble.

3. Risk Dashboard

Horizon	Risk Level	Cascading Effect
0-6 mo.	**High**	Allies hedge; adversaries probe dysfunction.
6-18 mo.	**Med**	Reform fatigue if early wins are absent.
18-36 mo.	**Low-to-Med**	Momentum holds if institutional plumbing modernises on schedule.

4. Roosevelt 2.0 Playbook

Pillar	30-Day Sprint	12-Month Build-out
Character	Executive ethics order; five-year lobby ban.	Bipartisan *Public Trust Commission* auditing integrity metrics.
Competence	Surge team fills mission-critical vacancies (model: U.S. Digital Service).	Public Service Leadership Academy + competitive pay bands.
Communication	Weekly "Fireside 5G" fact-checked brief.	Plain-language dashboards tracking reform KPIs.
Institutional Plumbing	Reactivate OMB "implementation czars" to unclog inter-agency arteries.	*Governance Modernization Act*: civil-service pay, cloud-first funding, AI-ready data strategy.

5. Strategic Recommendations

1. **Treat Governance as Strategic Hard Power**—budget for statecraft the way we budget for stealth bombers.
2. **Incentivise Cooperation**—expand ranked-choice pilots and independent redistricting to make bipartisanship rational.
3. **Digitise or Die**—Create a Digital Government Transformation Office with the authority (and engineers) to retire floppy-disk federalism.
4. **Shield Democracy's Plumbers**—federal election-security standards and grants to protect local administrators.
5. **Lock in Alliances Beyond Election Cycles**—Cross—time treaty clauses and deep mil-intel BFF programs reassure friends and unsettle foes.

6. Bottom Line

Until America out-administers itself, it can neither out-innovate Beijing nor out-fox Moscow. Pick up the Coke bottle, read the warning label— **"Contents under pressure: reform before opening"**—and get back to governing.

OPENING TABLEAU: THE COSMIC PROJECTILE OF CHAOS

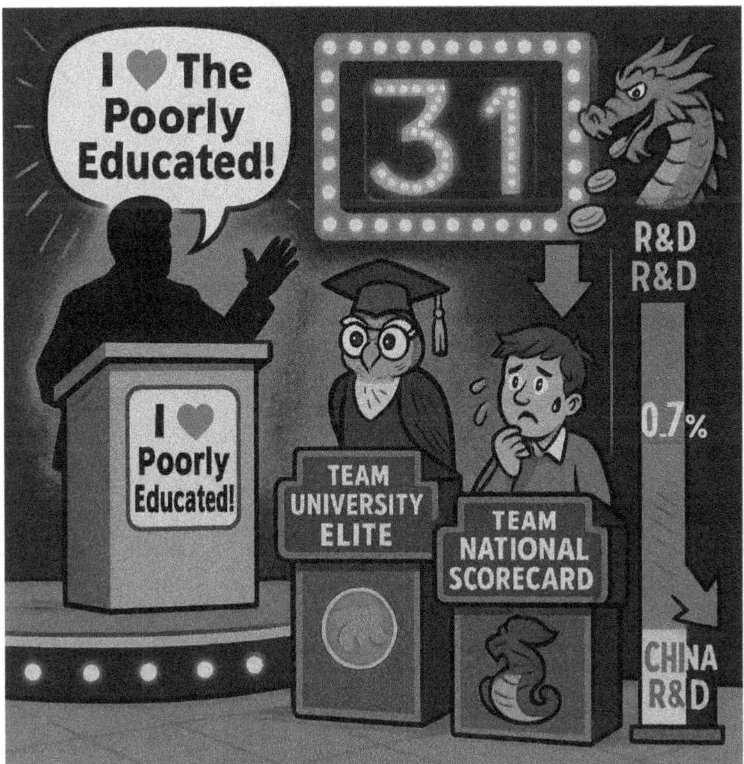

It begins, as all great geopolitical calamities do these days, with an unexpected object falling from the sky.

The gleaming Coca-Cola bottle—the quintessential artifact of American capitalism and globalization—tumbles from an unseen aircraft, catching sunlight as it spins gracefully downward. In slow motion, it pierces the rarefied air above 1600 Pennsylvania Avenue, descending with cosmic indifference toward the pristine White House lawn, where a hastily convened cabinet meeting has spilled outdoors on this unusually warm spring day.

"Incoming!" shouts the Secretary of Defense, a former cable news commentator whose military experience consists primarily of aggressive television interviews and the author of a memoir titled *Battlefield Media: How I Destroyed the Enemy on Prime Time.*

The bottle lands with a soft thud on the grass between the National Security Advisor and the Secretary of State, who are engaged in their third Twitter argument of the day. The assembled officials freeze, staring at the foreign object as if it were a Martian probe.

"Is it Chinese?" asks the Secretary of Commerce, immediately reaching for his phone to check how this might affect the stock market. "Some sort of surveillance device disguised as an American product? Classic Beijing strategy."

"More likely a Russian disinformation operation," counters the Director of National Intelligence, whose previous career as a reality television producer has prepared her perfectly for constructing elaborate narratives from minimal evidence.

The White House Press Secretary, already composing a tweet about the incident, chimes in: "We should call it a conservative conspiracy theory first, then deny we ever said that when the facts come in."

"Or maybe," interjects the EPA Administrator, a former coal lobbyist, "it's some sort of climate change manifestation. You know how those environmental fanatics are always talking about extreme bottle events."

In the ensuing chaos, no one notices the ghostly figure of **Franklin D. Roosevelt** materializing beside the Cabinet table, his translucent face a mask of exasperation. He taps his spectral cane against the table, trying to restore order, but the officials are too busy checking their phones for the public's reaction.

"Perhaps we could simply pick up the bottle and examine it?" FDR suggests, his stentorian voice passing through the officials like a breeze.

"We need to form a bipartisan commission to study the bottle," proposes the Chief of Staff. "We'll have recommendations in six to eight months."

"I've already commissioned a poll on the bottle," says the White House Political Director. "Initial results show 48% of Americans believe it's a Chinese plot, 46% think it's a Republican stunt, and 6% believe it contains the secret formula that turned the frogs gay."

From across the South Lawn, a Chinese delegation stands in perfect formation, watching through high-powered binoculars. **Chairman Efficiency**, Beijing's emissary of technocratic order, turns to his aides.

"Document this precisely," he instructs, his voice betraying no emotion. "This is how a superpower becomes a former superpower—not with a bang, but with administrative incompetence."

Behind him, **the Great Firewall Dragon** coils protectively, its scales made of surveillance cameras and censorship algorithms. "Shall I block all Chinese social media mentions of this... display?" it asks.

Chairman Efficiency shakes his head. "No. For once, let them see. This requires no censorship or propaganda. The reality is more persuasive than anything we could fabricate."

Back on the lawn, **Admiral Accountability**, the grizzled old guardian of democratic norms, finally reaches the bottle. "For heaven's sake," he mutters, "it's just a Coke bottle someone tossed out of an airplane. Can we please return to discussing the five international crises currently demanding our attention?"

But the Cabinet has already broken into partisan camps, each constructing its own reality around the mysterious object. Foreign diplomats exchange glances of thinly veiled concern. A European ambassador whispers to his Australian counterpart, "Remember when America led the free world? Now they can't even identify common beverage containers without a Twitter war."

As the afternoon wears on, the bottle sits forgotten on the grass. At the same time, America's leadership apparatus spins further into paralysis—a perfect metaphor for a governance system that has lost its ability to process reality, make decisions, or fulfill its most basic functions.

I. THE LEADERSHIP VACUUM: GOVERNANCE AS A NATIONAL SECURITY ASSET

> *"Regard your soldiers as your children, and they will follow you into the deepest valleys."*
> —Sun Tzu, The Art of War, Chapter 10

Analytical Framework: The Overlooked Strategic Requirement

In the vast literature on national security, surprisingly little attention has been paid to what may be the most fundamental requirement of all: **the capacity to govern effectively**. Military hardware, intelligence capabilities, and diplomatic skill all matter tremendously, but they ultimately rest upon a foundation of functional domestic governance. A nation that cannot formulate coherent policy, implement strategic decisions, or maintain institutional continuity cannot project power effectively, regardless of its material resources.

"The strategic literature tends to fixate on tanks, aircraft carriers, and satellite capabilities," explains **Professor Continuum**, adjusting her wire-rimmed glasses as she lectures at her hypothetical Governance Strategy Institute. "But history shows repeatedly that governance capability—the boring, unsexy administrative competence that makes everything else possible—is the true determinant of strategic outcomes."

She clicks to her next slide: "GOVERNANCE FAILURE: THE SILENT KILLER OF GREAT POWERS."

"Rome didn't fall solely because of barbarian invasions," she continues. "It collapsed under the weight of institutional decay, leadership failures, and administrative disintegration. The Soviet Union possessed thousands of nuclear weapons when it imploded from internal dysfunction. And now, the United States faces a similar crisis of governance capacity that threatens its position more fundamentally than any external enemy."

Character Vignette: The International Perspective

In a private meeting room at the United Nations, away from American ears, a group of foreign leaders has gathered for what French diplomats might delicately call a *conversation particulière*.

"I used to think American politics was like their professional wrestling," says the German Chancellor, stirring her tea. "Theatrical, exaggerated, perhaps a bit silly, but ultimately following an underlying script. Now I realize it's more like their reality television—unpredictable, untethered from reality, and genuinely concerning."

"My intelligence services produce a daily brief on American governance stability," offers the Japanese Prime Minister. "It used to be a single page. Now it requires its own dedicated team and runs longer than our assessment of North Korea."

The Canadian Prime Minister nods sympathetically. "Yesterday, I received three contradictory policy positions from different American agencies—all claiming to represent the official stance. When I asked for clarification, each insisted the others were unauthorized to speak on the matter."

"At least you received official communications," says the Australian leader. "We learned about a major shift in Pacific strategy via the President's social media at 3 a.m. My defense minister found out about troop deployments from a cable news chyron."

The UK Prime Minister, looking particularly exhausted, adds: "Our special relationship now consists primarily of my explaining to the President what his own administration's policies actually are."

A strategic pause falls over the room as servers refresh water glasses.

"The most alarming part," says the Korean representative finally, "is that our adversaries are watching this dysfunction and drawing their own conclusions about American reliability. Beijing is already treating U.S. policy commitments as fundamentally temporary—to be waited out rather than respected."

"The question becomes," says the Singapore leader, known for analytical precision, "how do we build stable international frameworks when the primary architect appears to be experiencing structural instability? It's like trying to build a coalition on quicksand."

Historical Analysis: Governance Quality and Great Power Competition

The correlation between governance quality and great power competition outcomes provides a sobering historical lesson. **Doctor History**, our time-traveling diagnostician, materializes with his leather medical bag to perform a historical examination.

"Let's review the patient records," he says, pulling out thick folders labeled with past empires and great powers. "The pattern is consistent across centuries: governance quality predicts strategic outcomes with remarkable accuracy."

He points to the Byzantine Empire's survival for nearly a millennium after Rome's fall: "Superior administrative systems, professional civil service, and institutional continuity gave Constantinople longevity that military power alone could never have achieved."

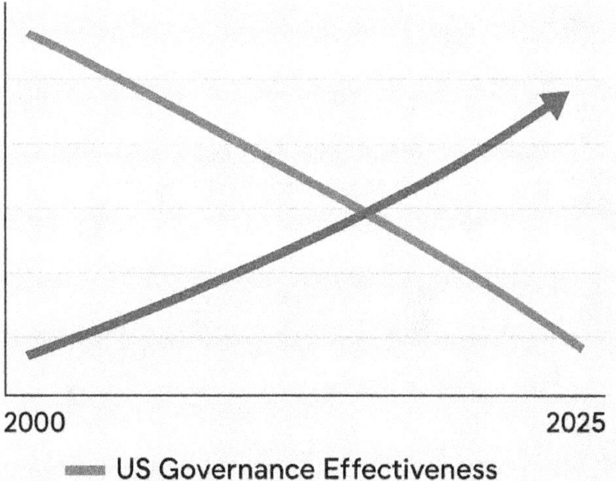

"Or consider Britain's remarkable global influence despite its relatively small size—the professional civil service, stable parliamentary system, and governance innovations allowed it to punch far above its weight class for centuries."

Doctor History flips through more recent cases: "The Cold War wasn't just won through military deterrence or economic productivity, though those certainly mattered. It was America's superior governance system that provided the adaptive capacity, innovation ecosystem, and social cohesion that the Soviet system couldn't match."

Adjusting his spectacles, Doctor History grows somber: "The diagnosis becomes concerning when we examine contemporary symptoms. The United States is exhibiting governance pathologies that have preceded the decline of previous great powers: institutional sclerosis, elite polarization, decision paralysis, and strategic incoherence."

Data Visualization: The Measurable Decline

McSlicey, the High Priest, appears in his consultant regalia, sacred PowerPoint clicker in hand. "The data tells a concerning story," he intones, revealing a series of graphs tracking governance effectiveness indicators for major powers.

"The United States has experienced a dramatic decline across multiple governance metrics," he explains, pointing to downward-sloping red lines. "Government effectiveness, regulatory quality, and rule of law indicators have been trending downward since the early 2000s, with particularly sharp declines in recent years."

He clicks on the next slide, which compares strategic competitors. "While American governance effectiveness has declined, China has been steadily improving its administrative capacity, though notably not its democratic accountability."

The lines on his chart cross ominously in 2025.

"This isn't merely an academic concern," McSlicey warns, adjusting his Hermès tie. "These metrics correlate strongly with economic performance, social stability, and ultimately, strategic influence."

His final slide shows international confidence in U.S. leadership plummeting like a stone. "For just $25 million in consulting fees," he adds smoothly, "I can tell you why this matters. Implementation recommendations would be covered under a separate contract, of course."

Comparative Analysis: A Global Governance Landscape

The international landscape reveals a complex governance typology, with democracies and autocracies pursuing divergent models with varying degrees of success.

"We're witnessing not just a competition between the U.S. and China," explains Professor Continuum, "but a global contest between governance models."

She outlines four primary models currently competing for legitimacy:

1. **Liberal Democratic Systems (Western model)**: Emphasizing individual rights, democratic accountability, and the rule of law, traditionally led by the United States
2. **Authoritarian Technocracy (China model)**: Prioritizing administrative efficiency, technological control, and state-directed development
3. **Illiberal Democracy (Hungary/Turkey model)**: Maintaining electoral mechanisms while undermining independent institutions and centralizing executive power
4. **Kleptocratic Authoritarianism (Russia model)**: Employing state power primarily to extract resources for elite enrichment while managing public opinion through information control

"The crucial question isn't just which model Americans prefer ethically," Professor Continuum notes, "but which delivers results. The legitimacy of governance systems ultimately rests on performance, not just principles."

She points to troubling data: surveys showing a decline in global confidence in democratic governance, with many citizens, particularly younger generations, expressing openness to alternative models that promise greater efficiency and results.

She warns that "When American democracy appears dysfunctional, polarized, and incapable of addressing basic challenges, "it undermines democracy's appeal globally. Each government shutdown, each political crisis, each institutional failure becomes ammunition in the argument against democratic governance itself."

Comparative Analysis:
A Global Governance Landscape

Liberal Democratic Systems
(Western model)

Emphasizing individual rights, democratic accountability, and rule of law–
Traditionally led by the United States

Authoritarian Technocracy
(China model)

Prioritizing administrative efficiency, technological control, and state-directed development

Illiberal Democracy
(Hungary/Turkey model)

Maintaining electoral mechanisms **while undermining** independent institutions and centralizing executive power

Kleptocratic Authoritarianism
(Russia model)

Employing state power primarily to extract resources for elite enrichment while managing public opinion through information control

Policy Context: The Strategic Costs of Governance Failure

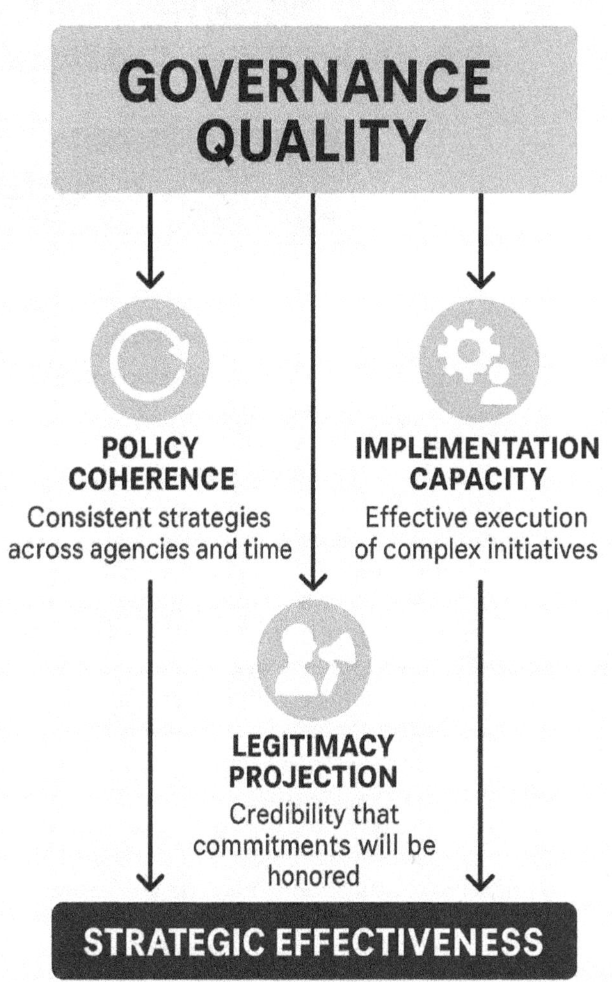

The strategic implications of America's governance crisis extend far beyond domestic politics, manifesting in concrete costs to national security and global standing.

"We're witnessing the strategic consequences of governance failure in real-time," explains **Admiral Accountability** from the bridge of USS *Democracy*. "And they're more devastating than any conventional military threat."

He pulls out a tactical map showing several concerning developments:

1. **Alliance Erosion**: Traditional allies are increasingly hedging their bets, developing independent capabilities, and pursuing separate arrangements with China as American reliability comes into question
2. **Adversary Emboldening**: Russia, Iran, and North Korea are calibrating their provocations based on assessments of American decision-making paralysis
3. **Global Governance Voids**: Critical international institutions and norms are weakening as their traditional champion demonstrates governance dysfunction
4. **Long-term Planning Handicaps**: Multi-year strategic initiatives (technological competition, military modernization, infrastructure development) falter under inconsistent leadership
5. **Domestic Security Vulnerabilities**: Internal polarization creates openings for foreign exploitation through targeted influence operations

"The most dangerous aspect," Admiral Accountability notes grimly, "is that these costs compound over time. Each failure of governance capacity makes the next challenge harder to address, creating a downward spiral of declining effectiveness."

He points to specific examples: delayed defense appropriations that undermine military readiness, contradictory diplomatic signals that encourage adversary miscalculations, and interagency coordination breakdowns that create gaps in domestic security.

"When governance fails," the Admiral concludes, "no amount of military spending can compensate. We're learning the hard way that you can't shoot your way out of administrative incompetence."

Theoretical Framework: Domestic Governance and International Power

The relationship between domestic governance and international power projection follows clear theoretical patterns that help explain America's current strategic predicament.

Professor Continuum presents a theoretical matrix showing how governance quality interacts with material resources to determine international influence:

"Nations with high material capacity but low governance quality experience what I call 'hollow power syndrome,'" she explains. "They possess the outward trappings of power—military hardware, economic size, diplomatic representation—but lack the institutional capacity to translate these advantages into strategic outcomes."

She points to historical examples: "Late imperial Spain, the late Ottoman Empire, and the Soviet Union in its final decades all exhibited hollow power characteristics: impressive on paper but incapable of effective action due to internal dysfunction."

The professor outlines three critical pathways through which governance quality determines strategic effectiveness:

1. **Policy Coherence**: The ability to formulate consistent strategies across agencies and over time
2. **Implementation Capacity**: The administrative capability to execute complex initiatives effectively
3. **Legitimacy Projection**: The credibility to persuade others that commitments will be honored and leadership followed

She concludes that "America's governance crisis has undermined all three pathways simultaneously, creating a perfect storm of strategic ineffectiveness."

II. THE ROOSEVELT LEADERSHIP OPERATING SYSTEM: CHARACTER, COMPETENCE, COMMUNICATION

> *"A leader leads by example, not by force."*
> —Commentary on Sun Tzu

Analytical Framework: The Three Pillars

In the pantheon of American leadership models, the **Roosevelt Leadership Operating System** stands as perhaps the most robust, field-tested software for democratic governance ever developed. While Theodore, Franklin, and Eleanor Roosevelt differed significantly in personality and political approach, they shared a remarkably consistent leadership framework built on three foundational pillars:

1. **Character**: The moral authority and personal integrity that generates trust
2. **Competence**: The administrative skill and knowledge mastery that produces results
3. **Communication**: The ability to explain, persuade, and mobilize public support

"These three C's form a virtuous triangle," explains **Professor Continuum**, sketching the model on her virtual blackboard. "Each reinforces the others: Character without competence becomes mere posturing. Competence without character creates efficient but potentially dangerous leadership. And neither functions effectively without communication that builds understanding and consent."

She points to the remarkable Roosevelt legacy: "Theodore's trust-busting, conservation efforts, and Progressive Era reforms; Franklin's New Deal, World War II leadership, and institutional innovations; Eleanor's human rights advocacy, social justice work, and public engagement—all depended on this three-pillar framework."

The professor contrasts this with the current governance model: "Today we've replaced Character-Competence-Communication with Celebrity-Conflict-Confusion—a fundamentally unstable operating system that crashes regularly and makes the whole machine vulnerable to malware."

Character Dialogue: FDR's Master Class

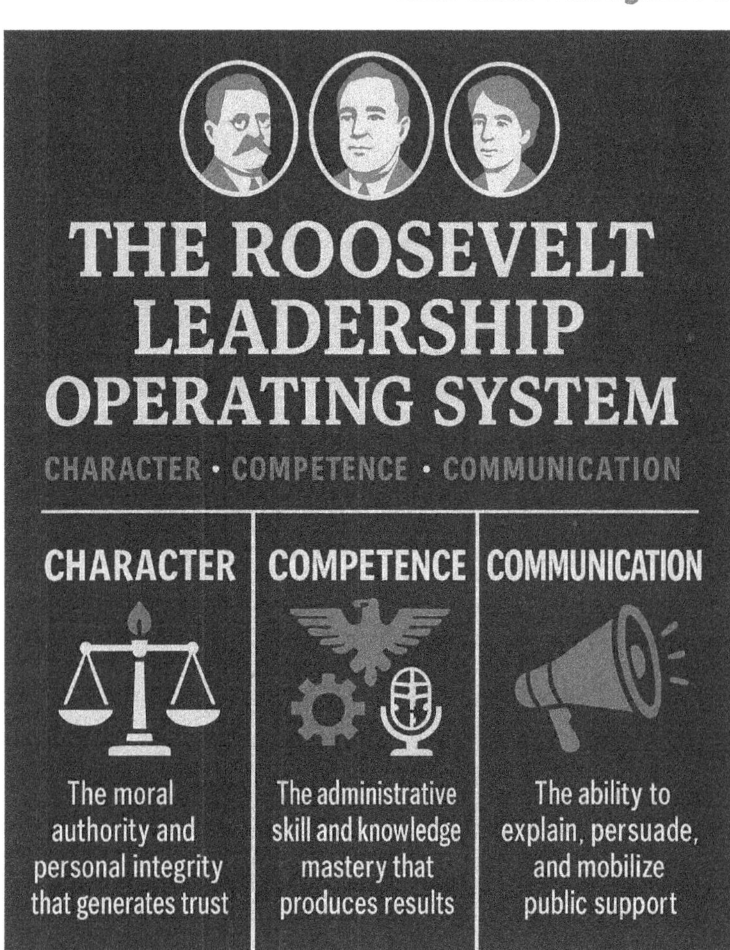

The ghostly figure of **Franklin D. Roosevelt** materializes in the Roosevelt Room (appropriately enough), where increasingly attentive modern officials have gathered following the Coke bottle incident. The spectral president adjusts his pince-nez glasses and surveys the room with a mixture of concern and determination.

"I see you're having some trouble with your governance operating system," FDR observes dryly. "Perhaps I might offer some insights from a time when America faced even greater challenges."

The Secretary of Defense snickers. "With all due respect, Mr. President, things have changed a bit since the 1930s. We have social media now, partisan cable news, and—"

FDR raises a translucent hand. "The technologies change, but the fundamentals of leadership do not. Let's begin with something basic that seems to have been forgotten: governance is not a performance—it's a responsibility."

The Press Secretary looks up from her phone, momentarily intrigued.

"When I took office in 1933," FDR continues, "one in four Americans was unemployed. The banking system had collapsed. Thousands of farms were foreclosed. Yet within one hundred days, we had stabilized the banking system, created job programs, and begun constructing a new framework for economic recovery."

KEY PSYCHOLOGICAL MECHANISMS

Crisis Framing

"the only thing we have to fear is fear itself"—

Sophisticated psychological framing that reduced paralyzing anxiety and enabled constructive action

Emotional Regulation

Empathy enabled constructive engagement rather than despair or radicalization

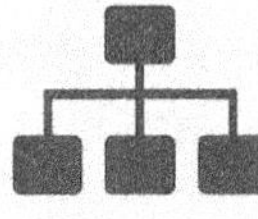

Cognitive Clarity

Conceptually organized frameworks that citizens could comprehend and engage with

Identity Leadership

Ability to represent and advance shared social identity in ways that motivate collective action

"But you had congressional supermajorities," objects the Chief of Staff. "We face obstruction at every turn."

"I faced plenty of opposition," FDR replies with a ghostly chuckle. "The business community called me a traitor to my class. The Supreme Court struck down key New Deal programs. Newspapers owned by wealthy interests attacked me relentlessly. But we persisted by maintaining three essential elements that seem in short supply today."

He holds up a transparent finger. "First, character—we demonstrated that government was working for the common good, not special interests or personal gain. This built trust, even among those who disagreed with specific policies."

A second finger rises. "Second, competence—we hired the best people regardless of political loyalty, empowered them to innovate, and held them accountable for results. The brain trust wasn't composed of campaign surrogates and television personalities, but genuine experts in their fields."

A third finger joins the others. "And third, communication—we explained complex policies in clear language that ordinary Americans could understand. The Fireside Chats weren't about scoring political points or attacking enemies; they were about building shared understanding."

The modern officials shift uncomfortably.

"But Mr. President," ventures the National Security Advisor, "today's media environment is different. Everything becomes fodder for partisan warfare."

"The tools change, but the principles endure," FDR insists. "Whether by radio or social media, leaders must provide clarity, not confusion; unity, not division; hope, not fear."

He looks around the room with penetrating eyes. "Tell me, what exactly are you trying to accomplish? Not your talking points or your campaign slogans—what specific improvements to American life is your administration working to deliver?"

An uncomfortable silence falls over the room.

"That," says FDR with gentle firmness, "is where you must begin."

Psychological Analysis: The Cognitive and Emotional Elements

The Roosevelt leadership model succeeded not merely through policy innovation but through profound psychological insights that remain relevant in today's governance challenges.

"The Roosevelts intuitively understood social psychology decades before the research confirmed their approaches," explains **Doctor History**, opening his medical bag of historical analysis. "Their leadership operated simultaneously on cognitive and emotional levels."

He highlights several key psychological mechanisms:

Crisis Framing: Franklin Roosevelt's famous line—"the only thing we have to fear is fear itself"—wasn't just rhetoric but sophisticated psychological framing that reduced paralyzing anxiety and enabled constructive action. By redefining the Great Depression as a manageable challenge rather than an apocalyptic collapse, he created cognitive space for problem-solving.

Emotional Regulation: Eleanor Roosevelt's remarkable empathy enabled her to connect with Americans experiencing hardship while channeling their emotions toward constructive engagement rather than despair or radicalization. Her visits to coal mines, slums, and rural communities demonstrated genuine concern while modeling productive emotional responses.

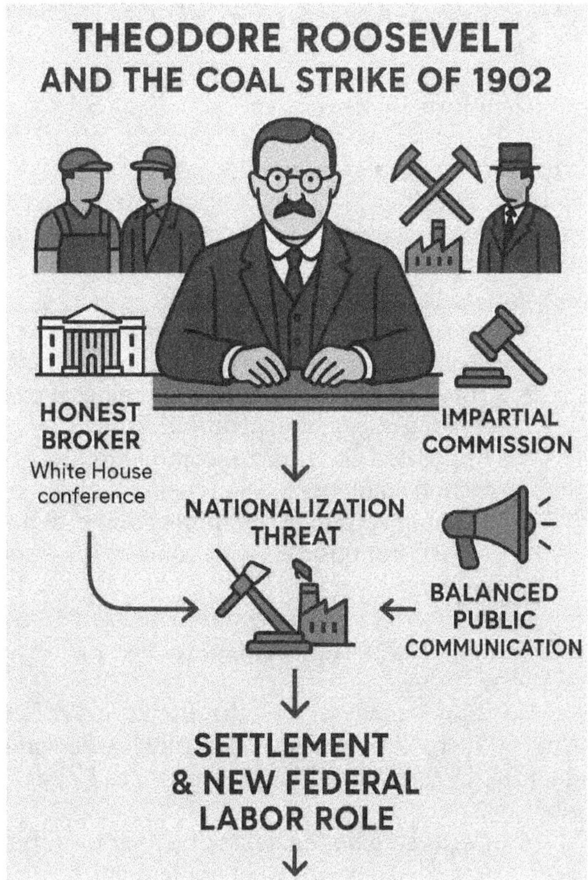

Cognitive Clarity: Theodore Roosevelt's Square Deal presented complex economic and social challenges in conceptually organized frameworks that citizens could comprehend and engage with. His ability to synthesize complicated issues into understandable narratives without oversimplification created informed public discourse.

Identity Leadership: All three Roosevelts excelled at what modern psychology calls "identity leadership"—the ability to represent and advance shared social identity in ways that motivate collective action. They consistently framed leadership as service to a larger American project rather than personal advancement.

"The contrast with our current leadership psychology is stark," Doctor History observes. "Today we see crisis magnification instead of crisis framing, emotional provocation rather than regulation, cognitive confusion instead of clarity, and identity division rather than leadership."

He closes his medical bag with a sigh. "The symptoms suggest an advanced case of psychological malpractice in leadership—treating the body politic with stimulants and sedatives rather than healing its underlying conditions."

Historical Case Studies: Roosevelt Crisis Management

The Roosevelt approach to crisis management offers timeless lessons that transcend their historical contexts, providing a template for effective governance under pressure.

Theodore Roosevelt and the Coal Strike of 1902: When Pennsylvania coal mines shut down during a bitter labor dispute, threatening to leave Eastern cities without heat for the winter, TR innovated crisis management techniques that broke with laissez-faire precedent. Instead of deploying troops against striking workers as his predecessors had done, Roosevelt:

- ★ Convened both sides at the White House, establishing the government as an honest broker
- ★ Threatened to nationalize the mines if owners refused reasonable negotiation
- ★ Appointed an impartial commission to develop lasting solutions
- ★ Maintained public communication that balanced respect for business with concern for worker welfare

The result was a settlement that averted disaster while establishing new patterns of federal engagement in labor relations.

Franklin Roosevelt and the Banking Crisis of 1933: When FDR took office amid a complete banking system collapse, his administration demonstrated crisis management mastery:

- ★ Declared a national bank holiday to stop the panic while solutions were implemented

FRANKLIN ROOSEVELT
AND THE BANKING CRISIS OF 1933

When FDR took office amid a complete banking system collapse, his administration demonstrated crisis management mastery:

Declared a national bank holiday to stop the panic while solutions were implemented

Drafted emergency banking legislation in a single weekend

Delivered the first Fireside Chat explaining the banking system and reform measures in plain language

Created institutional reforms (FDIC, SEC) that addressed root causes, not just symptoms

ELEANOR ROOSEVELT and THE MARIAN ANDERSON CONCERT CONTROVERSY

Resigned her DAR membership in public protest

Worked with Interior Secretary Harold Ickes to arrange an alternative concert at the Lincoln Memorial

Attended the performance to demonstrate official support

Used her "My Day" newspaper column to explain why the principle mattered

Easter Sunday concert attracted 75,000 people – a landmark civil rights moment.

COMPARATIVE ANALYSIS: GLOBAL LEADERSHIP MODELS

NORDIC CONSENSUS MODEL Denmark - Finland	SINGAPOREAN MERITOCRATIC MODEL	GERMAN FEDERAL-PROFESSIONAL MODEL
		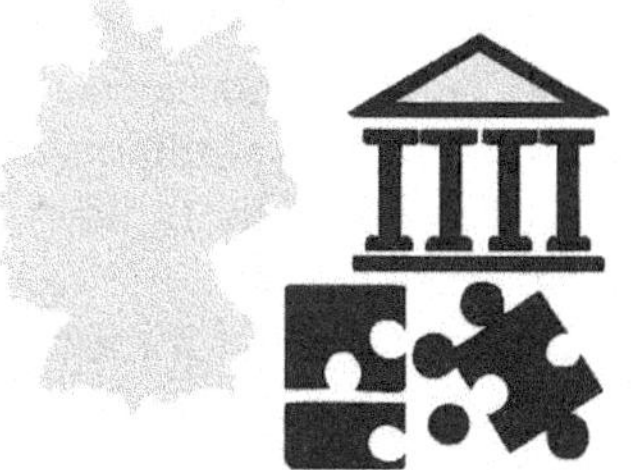
• Collaborative leadership • Stakeholder inclusion • Technocratic competence Produces remarkable stability and citizen commitment to shared goals	• Rigorous evaluation • Long-term planning • Administrative efficiency • Policy consistency Sacrifices democratic responsiveness and legitimacy challenges.	• Negotiation • Coalition governance • Distributed authority • Professional civil service Can make rapid response to crises more challenging

★ Drafted emergency banking legislation in a single weekend
★ Delivered the first Fireside Chat explaining the banking system and reform measures in plain language
★ Created institutional reforms (FDIC, SEC) that addressed root causes, not just symptoms

This approach restored financial stability within weeks and established institutional safeguards that have prevented similar collapses for decades.

Eleanor Roosevelt and the Marian Anderson Concert Controversy: When the Daughters of the American Revolution refused to allow Black contralto Marian Anderson to perform at Constitution Hall in 1939, Eleanor:

★ Resigned her DAR membership in public protest
★ Worked with Interior Secretary Harold Ickes to arrange an alternative concert at the Lincoln Memorial
★ Attended the performance to demonstrate official support
★ Used her "My Day" newspaper column to explain why the principle mattered

The resulting Easter Sunday concert drew 75,000 people and became a landmark moment in civil rights history, demonstrating how moral leadership can transform controversy into progress.

"The Rooseveltian crisis playbook contains consistent elements," notes Doctor History. "They defined problems honestly, acted decisively, communicated clearly, and built institutional solutions that outlasted the immediate crisis. Compare that with our current approach of denying problems, acting chaotically, communicating divisively, and creating ad hoc responses that collapse when attention shifts."

Comparative Analysis: Global Leadership Models

The Roosevelt leadership model isn't the only effective approach to democratic governance—an international comparison reveals alternative frameworks with demonstrable success records.

"Democratic systems globally have developed diverse leadership models adapted to their cultural and institutional contexts," explains Professor Continuum. "The most successful share certain fundamentals while implementing them through different mechanisms."

She highlights several instructive examples:

The Nordic Consensus Model (exemplified by countries like Denmark and Finland) emphasizes collaborative leadership, stakeholder inclusion, and technocratic competence. Leaders function more as conveners and consensus-builders than as charismatic central figures. The model yields remarkable stability and citizen well-being, but requires robust institutional frameworks and a strong cultural commitment to shared goals.

The Singaporean Meritocratic Model blends democratic elements with meritocratic selection and long-term planning. Leaders emerge through rigorous evaluation of their capabilities, rather than through political popularity contests. The system delivers impressive administrative efficiency and policy consistency, but it sacrifices some democratic responsiveness and can struggle with legitimacy challenges.

The German Federal-Professional Model combines distributed authority through federalism with professionalized civil service and coalition governance. Leadership operates through negotiation among institutional centers rather than consolidated executive authority. This approach provides resilience against individual leader failures, but can make rapid response to crises more challenging.

"What these successful models share with the Roosevelt approach," Professor Continuum explains, "are commitments to competence, institutional strength, and public communication—implemented through different cultural and constitutional arrangements."

She contrasts these with emerging models that should concern Americans: "We're witnessing the rise of what political scientists call 'personalist leadership'—systems where institutions are subordinated to individual leaders whose personal preferences override established processes and expertise."

Professor Continuum's data show that personalist systems consistently underperform other governance models on metrics ranging from economic growth to crisis management, regardless of whether they emerge in democratic or authoritarian contexts.

"The warning signs are clear," she concludes. "When a political system begins treating governance as a personal rather than institutional function, decline follows reliably."

Leadership Development Framework

Public Service Leadership Academy

Intensive training, case-based learning with government academia & business

Talent Pipeline Reconstruction

Reform appointment system, fast-track development, lateral entry, mentorship

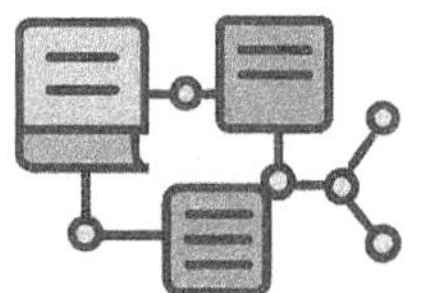

Knowledge Management Infrastructure

Capture institutional memory, document processes, cross-agency communities, knowledge bases

Performance Evaluation Systems

Empirical metrics, 360° feedback performance consequences, public transparency

Policy Proposal: Leadership Development Framework

Beyond nostalgia or abstract principles, a concrete Rooseveltian approach to contemporary governance requires a systematic leadership development infrastructure across public service.

"We've built elaborate systems to develop military leadership," notes Admiral Accountability, "but neglected comparable investments in civilian leadership capacity. The result is predictable: uneven performance, reinvented wheels, and institutional amnesia."

A comprehensive leadership development framework would include:

★ A Public Service Leadership Academy providing intensive training for appointees and senior civil servants, combining policy expertise, management skills, ethics, and communication through case-based learning with faculty from government, academia, and business.

★ Talent Pipeline Reconstruction would reform the presidential appointment system, create a fast-track development program for promising civil servants, enhance lateral entry pathways, and establish mentorship systems.

★ The Knowledge Management Infrastructure would systematically capture institutional memory, document decision-making processes, establish cross-agency communities of practice, and create knowledge bases for incoming leaders.

★ Performance Evaluation Systems would empirically assess leadership effectiveness through multiple metrics, 360-degree feedback, meaningful consequences for performance, and public transparency on key indicators.

"This isn't just bureaucratic infrastructure," Admiral Accountability emphasizes. "It's about creating the conditions for leadership excellence to emerge and sustain itself across administrations. The Roosevelts were exceptional individuals, but they also benefited from and helped build robust institutional systems that developed talent and preserved knowledge."

Implementation Strategy: Making It Real

Translating leadership development concepts into operational reality requires concrete implementation mechanisms and political strategies.

"The challenge isn't just designing better leadership systems," observes McSlicey, the High Priest, momentarily adopting a public-spirited approach, "but actually implementing them in a political environment that often rewards the opposite behaviors."

Viable implementation requires multi-level action:

★ At the Presidential Level, executive orders would establish leadership standards, personnel reforms would prioritize competence, a dedicated White House office would focus on governance improvement, and the President would model Rooseveltian leadership principles.

★ Congressional actions would include legislation funding leadership development infrastructure, confirmation reforms emphasizing qualifications over ideology, oversight of implementation capacity, and bipartisan institutional health initiatives.

★ Agency-level reforms would enhance the Senior Executive Service, implement performance systems that reward effective leadership, create cross-agency communities of practice, and establish chief learning officers within departments.

★ Civil society would contribute through academic-practitioner partnerships, philanthropic investments in public sector leadership, media coverage evaluating governance quality, and citizen demand for competent management.

"The Rooseveltian approach requires overcoming significant implementation barriers," McSlicey acknowledges, adjusting his tie. "But the return on investment is potentially enormous—not just in policy outcomes but in renewed citizen trust and international standing."

III. REBUILDING THE MACHINERY OF GOVERNMENT: INSTITUTIONAL RENEWAL

> *"Dig the well before you are thirsty."*
> —Chinese proverb

Analytical Framework: Institutional Capacity as Prerequisite

Behind every successful policy, strategic initiative, and government service delivery stands the often-invisible machinery of governance—the institutional infrastructure that translates intentions into outcomes. While this machinery rarely generates headlines or campaign slogans, it ultimately determines whether democratic promises become lived realities.

"We've reached a dangerous inflection point in American governance," explains **Professor Continuum**, chalk dust on her tweed jacket. "Decades of institutional neglect, political sabotage, and administrative disinvestment have left the machinery of government in advanced stages of disrepair—precisely when technological, geopolitical, and social challenges demand peak performance."

She identifies five critical dimensions of institutional capacity that determine governance effectiveness: human capital (workforce knowledge and skills), organizational design (structural arrangements), process architecture (decision and implementation systems), technological infrastructure (digital tools enabling modern governance), and knowledge management (information flows and institutional memory).

"These elements are interdependent," Professor Continuum emphasizes. "The best people cannot overcome broken processes. The most elegant organizational design fails without skilled

REBUILDING THE MACHINERY OF GOVERNMENT:
INSTITUTIONAL RENEWAL

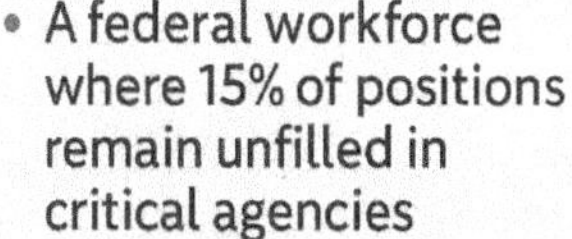
• A federal workforce where 15% of positions remain unfilled in critical agencies

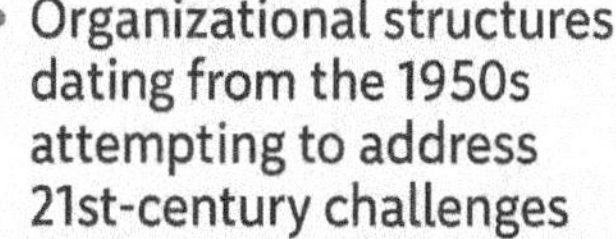
• Organizational structures dating from the 1950s attempting to address 21st-century challenges

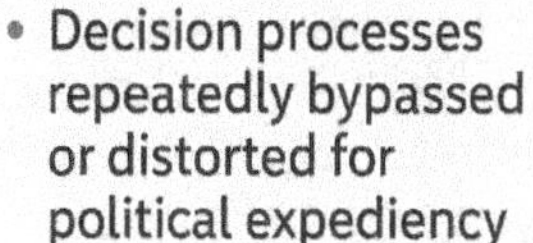
• Decision processes repeatedly bypassed or distorted for political expediency

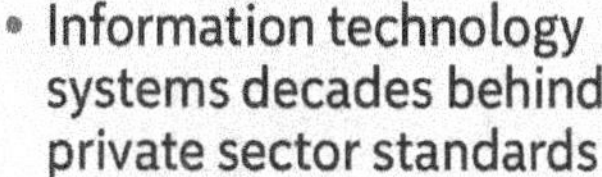
• Information technology systems decades behind private sector standards

• Critical institutional knowledge walking out the door with retiring career officials

personnel. And even perfect processes and people struggle without adequate technological support."

She points to alarming indicators across all five dimensions:

- ★ A federal workforce where 15% of positions remain unfilled in critical agencies
- ★ Organizational structures dating from the 1950s are attempting to address 21st-century challenges
- ★ Decision processes are repeatedly bypassed or distorted for political expediency
- ★ Information technology systems are decades behind private sector standards
- ★ Critical institutional knowledge walking out the door with retiring career officials

"The most concerning aspect," she concludes, "is that institutional capacity declines can become self-reinforcing. As machinery deteriorates, performance suffers, leading to reduced public trust, which fuels further disinvestment and political attacks, accelerating the downward spiral."

Character Development: The Chief of Staff's Struggle

Emily Richardson, White House Chief of Staff, stares at the organizational chart spread across her desk at 11:30 PM. Surrounding her are stacks of emergency requests, pending nominations, urgent policy decisions, and at least three classified intelligence reports flagged for immediate attention.

"It's like trying to conduct an orchestra where half the instruments are missing, a third of the musicians are actively sabotaging the performance, and someone keeps randomly changing the music," she mutters, rubbing her temples.

PRESIDENTIAL LEVEL

- Executive orders establishing leadership standards
- Personnel reforms prioritizing competence
- Dedicated White House office for governance
- Presidential modeling of Rooseveltian princ-

CONGRESSIONAL ACTION

- Legislation funding leadership development
- Confirmation reforms emphasizing
- Oversight of implementation capacity
- Bipartisan institutional health initiatives

AGENCY-LEVEL REFORMS

- Enhanced Senior Executive Service
- Performance systems rewarding leadership
- Cross-agency communitys of practice

CIVIL SOCIETY

- Academic-practitioner partnerships
- Philanthropic investment in leadership
- Governance quality media coverage
- Citizen demand for competent management

Her assistant pokes his head in. "Sorry to interrupt. The President just tweeted a new tariff policy that contradicts what the Treasury announced this morning. The Secretary is on line one demanding clarification."

Emily sighs. "Put him on hold. I need to figure out what the President actually meant before I can explain it to the person supposedly implementing it."

"Also," her assistant continues, "the Deputy Secretary of State just resigned—the fourth one this year. And the Russian Ambassador is calling about the tweet as well."

"Which tweet?" Emily asks.

"The one from twenty minutes ago threatening to withdraw from NATO unless member countries 'pay up NOW!'"

Emily hadn't seen that one yet. She checks her phone and groans. "Tell everyone I need thirty minutes to establish some semblance of process here. And please, for the love of God, see if you can keep the President off Twitter until morning."

Alone again, she turns to the half-completed process flowchart she's been trying to implement—a desperate attempt to create some structure around presidential decision-making. The boxes and arrows mock her with their rational orderliness, so unlike the chaos they're meant to tame.

Admiral Accountability materializes beside her desk.

"Trying to build governance systems in this environment is like trying to construct a Swiss watch during an earthquake," he observes sympathetically.

Emily looks up. "The President calls the process 'deep state obstruction.' He thinks making decisions based on staff work and agency input is a sign of weakness."

"And yet," the Admiral notes, "every successful administration in modern history has depended on exactly those mechanisms. Roosevelt's New Deal, Eisenhower's Interstate Highway System, Kennedy's space program, Reagan's Cold War strategy—all required sophisticated institutional machinery turning presidential vision into operational reality."

Emily nods wearily. "I've studied those administrations. They had their dysfunctions too, but they understood that governance requires systems, not just personalities."

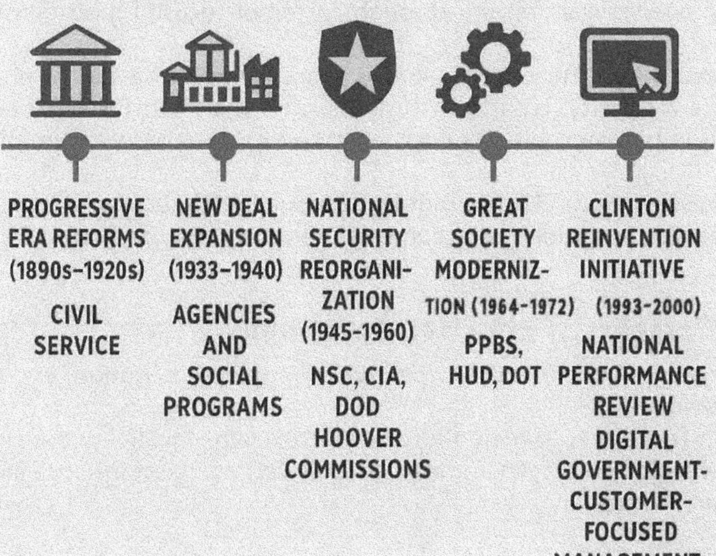

Her phone buzzes with another presidential tweet, this one contradicting the NATO statement from twenty minutes earlier.

Admiral Accountability gives her a sympathetic look. "The machinery of government wasn't built for this level of volatility. It's designed for deliberation, coordination, and consistent implementation—not hourly directional changes."

"What would you do in my position?" Emily asks.

"Build what institutional structures you can beneath the chaos," the Admiral advises. "The President may resist formal processes, but the agencies still need coordination frameworks. Create systems that can absorb the volatility at the top while maintaining basic functionality below."

Emily turns back to her flowchart with renewed determination. "Like shock absorbers in a vehicle driving over rocky terrain."

"Exactly," the Admiral nods. "You can't stop the earthquake, but you might be able to protect some of the watchmaking."

Historical Analysis: Administrative Reforms in American History

The struggle to establish effective governance machinery has been a persistent feature of American history, with each era confronting its own unique institutional challenges.

"Administrative reform has been a recurring theme in American governance," explains **Doctor History**, opening his medical bag of historical context. "The current institutional ailments have historical precedents—and the treatments that worked before may offer guidance now."

He highlights several pivotal reform periods:

The Progressive Era Reforms (1890s-1920s): Responding to industrial-scale corruption and incompetence, reformers established the civil service system, professional regulatory agencies, and scientific management principles. Theodore Roosevelt championed merit-based hiring, administrative professionalism, and fact-based policymaking. These reforms transformed the government from a patronage system to a professional enterprise.

The New Deal Expansion (1933-1940): Franklin Roosevelt's administration created new institutional capacities to address unprecedented economic challenges, including emergency agencies, the Public Works Administration, and social insurance systems. FDR established institutional innovations, such as the Executive Office of the President, while building the capacity to implement complex national programs.

The National Security Reorganization (1945-1960): Post-World War II reforms, including the National Security Act, established new coordination structures (NSC, CIA, and DoD) to address the chal-

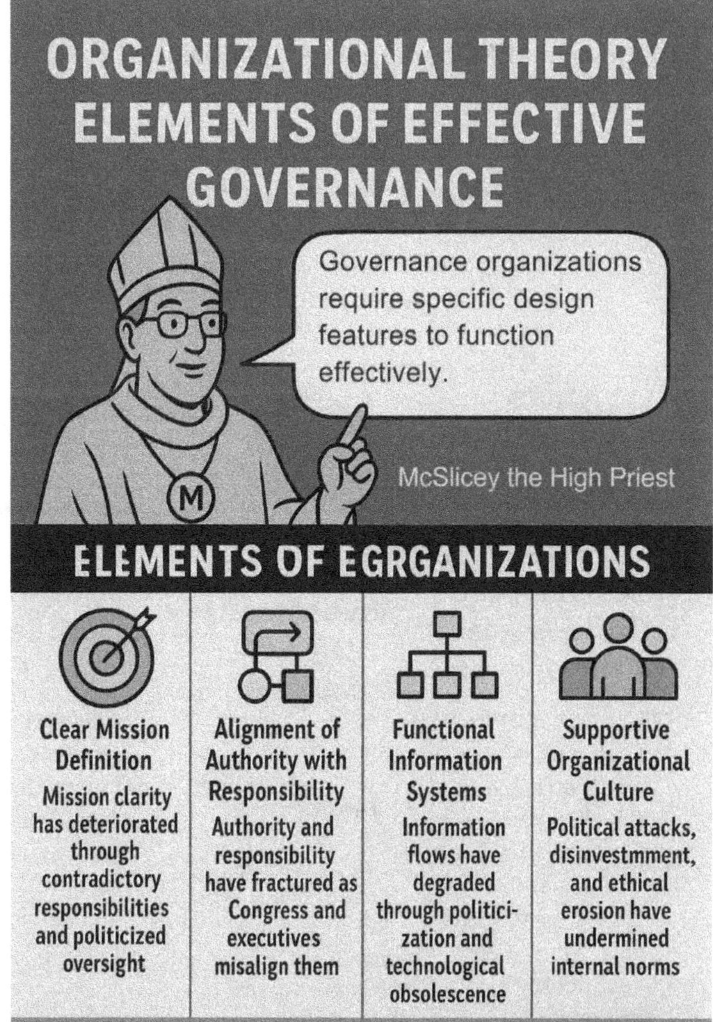

lenges of the Cold War. The Hoover Commission under Truman and Eisenhower rationalized executive functions and introduced management innovations that brought government operations into the modern organizational era.

The Great Society Modernization (1964-1972): Johnson's administration combined ambitious social programs with administrative reforms, such as the PPBS (Planning-Programming-Budgeting System), to enhance resource allocation and management. New departments (HUD, DOT) and intergovernmental systems developed the capacity to address complex social problems through multi-level governance.

The Clinton Reinvention Initiative (1993-2000): The National Performance Review attempted to reform bureaucratic processes, reduce regulatory burdens, and improve service delivery through customer-focused management techniques and early digital government initiatives.

"What's striking," Doctor History observes, "is that successful reform periods share common elements: presidential leadership making administrative competence a priority; bipartisan consensus on the need for functional governance despite policy disagreements; investment in human capital and systems; and balance between political responsiveness and professional expertise."

He closes his historical medical bag with a sober assessment: "The current institutional ailments are severe, but not unprecedented. The patient has recovered from similar conditions before, though never without dedicated treatment and rehabilitation programs."

Organizational Theory: Elements of Effective Governance

Contemporary organizational theory identifies key elements that enable effective governance institutions and the ways these elements have eroded in the American system.

"Governance organizations require specific design features to function effectively," explains **McSlicey, the High Priest**, for once focusing on public value rather than billable hours. "When these features degrade, performance inevitably suffers regardless of leadership quality or resource levels."

He outlines critical organizational elements:

Clear Mission Definition: Effective government organizations require well-defined missions with measurable objectives. Mission clarity has deteriorated as agencies are assigned contradictory responsibilities, subject to politicized oversight, and denied stable priority frameworks.

Alignment of Authority with Responsibility: Organizations perform best when authority (formal power to act) aligns with responsibility (accountability for outcomes). This alignment has fractured as Congress imposes responsi-

GOVERNMENT MODERNIZATION SUCCESS STORIES

The Singapore Civil Service Transformation

Singapore built one of the world's most effective public administrations by investing heavily in talent development, performance and technological innovation

The UK Government Digital Service

Britain created a centralized digital transformation unit that revolutionized citizen-facing services while generating massive efficiency improvements

The U.S. Digital Service and 18F

These Obama-era innovations demonstrated that pockets of excellence could emarge even within challenging environments

The Danish Public Sector Reform

Denmark comprehensively restructured its governance systems in 2007, consolidating municipalities, redesigning service delivery, and implementing digital-first strategies.

New Zealand State Sector Reforms

New Zealand pioneered performance-based public management through clear outcome specification, managerial autonomy coupled with accountability for results, and transparent performance bilities without granting commensurate authorities, while executives demand outcomes without providing necessary resources.

Functional Information Systems: Effective governance requires accurate and timely information flows between organizational levels and across agency boundaries. Information systems have deteriorated due to the politicization of analysis, a breakdown of trust between career and political officials, and technological obsolescence.

Appropriate Structural Configuration: Organizational structures must match their functions—routine tasks require hierarchical efficiency, while complex problems demand collaborative networks. Current structures often represent historical accidents rather than intentional design for current challenges.

Supportive Organizational Culture: Effective governance depends on cultural norms that value expertise, integrity, and public service. These cultures have been undermined by political attacks on "bureaucrats," disinvestment in professional development, and corrosion of ethics standards.

"The deterioration isn't uniform across government," McSlicey notes, clicking to his next slide. "Certain agencies maintain remarkably high performance despite systemic challenges, while others have experienced catastrophic decline. The variance itself offers valuable insights about organizational resilience factors."

His analysis identifies key protective factors that have preserved effectiveness in high-performing organizations: leadership continuity, professional identity strength, congressional champions, public visibility of outcomes, and technological modernization.

"The organizational diagnosis points to specific interventions," McSlicey concludes. "We need targeted therapy for governance institutions—not just changing leaders or policies, but rebuilding the organizational musculature that translates decisions into action."

Case Studies: Government Modernization Success Stories

Despite the challenges facing American governance, successful modernization efforts — both domestically and internationally — demonstrate pathways to institutional renewal.

"We don't need theoretical solutions," **Admiral Accountability** emphasizes from the bridge of USS *Democracy*. "We have empirical evidence of what works from governments that have successfully modernized their machinery."

He highlights several instructive examples:

The Singapore Civil Service Transformation: Singapore built one of the world's most effective public administrations by investing heavily in talent development, performance management, and technological innovation. Key elements included competitive compensation to attract top talent, rigorous performance metrics linked to national outcomes, and continuous process optimization.

The UK Government Digital Service: Britain established a centralized digital transformation unit that revolutionized citizen-facing services, resulting in significant improvements in efficiency. The approach combined user-centered design, agile development methodologies, and cross-departmental digital standards, transforming government-citizen interactions.

The U.S. Digital Service and 18F: These Obama-era innovations demonstrated that pockets of excellence could emerge even within challenging environments. By recruiting top technology talent for term-limited government service and applying modern design and development practices, these units delivered dramatic improvements in selected domains.

The Danish Public Sector Reform: In 2007, Denmark comprehensively restructured its governance systems, consolidating municipalities,

Comprehensive Institutional Renewal

Civil Service Revitalization

- Competitive compensation
- Streamlined hiring
- Modern performance management
- Enhanced professional development

Management Systems Modernization

- Evidence-based policy infrastructure
- Standardized project methodologies
- Outcome-focused metrics
- Cross-functional teams

Digital Government Transformation

- Government-wide digital platform
- Consistent user experience
- Cloud-first architecture
- Shared administrative services

Institutional Learning Infrastructure

- After-action reviews
- Knowledge management platforms
- Communities of practice
- Strategic foresight capabilities

redesigning service delivery, and implementing digital-first strategies. The result was improved citizen satisfaction alongside significant efficiency gains.

The New Zealand State Sector Reforms: New Zealand pioneered performance-based public management through clear outcome specification, managerial autonomy coupled with accountability for results, and transparent performance reporting. These reforms transformed a sclerotic bureaucracy into a relatively nimble system.

"The common thread across success stories," Admiral Accountability notes, "is that institutional renewal requires sustained political commitment, professional implementation capacity, adequate resources, and appropriate performance incentives. There's no magic bullet—just the disciplined application of sound organizational principles tailored to public sector contexts."

Policy Proposal: Comprehensive Institutional Renewal

Restoring American governance capacity requires a systematic institutional renewal agenda that transcends partisan battles to rebuild the government's machinery.

"We need a comprehensive approach to institutional renewal," argues **Professor Continuum**. "Piecemeal reforms or management fads won't address the systemic nature of our governance challenges."

She presents a four-part renewal framework:

- ★ Civil Service Revitalization would implement competitive compensation, streamlined hiring processes, modern performance management systems, enhanced professional development opportunities, knowledge transfer mechanisms, and a federal talent marketplace for facilitating cross-agency mobility.
- ★ Management Systems Modernization would develop evidence-based policy infrastructure, standardized project methodologies, outcome-focused metrics, cross-functional teams for complex challenges, implementation capacity assessment, and rapid response capabilities.
- ★ Digital Government Transformation would create a government-wide digital platform with a consistent user experience, cloud-first architecture, shared administrative services, comprehensive data strategy, digital workflows, and appropriate AI applications.
- ★ Institutional Learning Infrastructure would establish after-action reviews, knowledge management platforms, communities of practice, strategic foresight capabilities, continuous improvement processes, and academic-practitioner research partnerships.

"This agenda isn't about bigger government," Professor Continuum emphasizes. "It's about more effective government machinery that delivers better outcomes with existing resources by operating at modern standards of organizational performance."

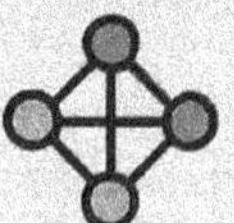

Implementation Plan: Making Renewal Real

Translating institutional renewal concepts into operational reality requires pragmatic implementation strategies that take into account political constraints and organizational realities.

"The implementation pathway needs to be as carefully designed as the renewal agenda itself," notes **McSlicey, the High Priest**. "Otherwise, even the best reform ideas will join the graveyard of well-intentioned but failed government improvement initiatives."

He proposes a comprehensive implementation strategy:

- ★ The Legislative Foundation would include acts that modernize civil service systems, establish performance frameworks, authorize digital transformation, and create sustainable financing mechanisms.
- ★ Executive Actions would prioritize renewal through a Presidential Management Agenda, implementation-focused Executive Orders, performance contracts with agency leaders, a cabinet-level governance council, embedded reform teams, and a progress-tracking dashboard.
- ★ The Change Management Strategy would build support through stakeholder engagement, a communication campaign explaining benefits, early demonstration projects, capability building, pilot testing, and feedback-based adjustments.
- ★ Resource Allocation would ensure success through dedicated modernization funding, shared investment pools for cross-cutting initiatives, return-on-investment frameworks, public-private partnerships, and resource reprogramming authorities.

"Implementation requires balancing ambition with pragmatism," McSlicey concludes, adjusting his tie. "The renewal agenda must be comprehensive enough to address systemic challenges but modular enough to advance despite political limitations."

He adds a final recommendation: "Most importantly, institutional renewal must become a nonpartisan priority—recognized as essential infrastructure regardless of policy disagreements, just as both parties acknowledge the need for physical infrastructure despite disagreeing on specific projects."

IV. DEFENDING DEMOCRACY FROM ITSELF: DIGITAL AGE RESILIENCE

> *"To secure oneself against defeat lies in one's own hands."*
> —Sun Tzu, The Art of War, Chapter 4

Analytical Framework: Democratic Vulnerabilities

Democratic systems face unprecedented vulnerabilities in the digital age, with traditional strengths becoming potential weaknesses in a transformed information environment.

"Democracy has always had inherent tensions," explains **Professor Continuum**, "but the digital transformation has fundamentally altered how these tensions manifest, often turning features into bugs."

She identifies three critical vulnerabilities undermining democratic systems:

- ★ Information Environment Degradation threatens the functioning information ecosystem that democracies require. Algorithm-driven filter bubbles, attention economics prioritizing engagement over accuracy, amplification of extreme viewpoints, weaponized disinformation campaigns, and the collapse of traditional media have fractured how citizens access information about public issues.
- ★ Institutional Legitimacy Erosion weakens the foundation of democratic authority through performative politics, which replaces substantive governance, strategic delegitimization for partisan advantage, misleading transparency without context, declining civic knowledge, and structural misalignment with contemporary challenges.
- ★ Coordination system failures hinder democratic governance's ability to aggregate preferences and implement decisions. Extreme polarization, which transforms compromise into betrayal, divisive micro-targeting enabled by digital technologies, institutional capture by extreme actors, declining social capital, and algorithmic radicalization, which pushes discourse toward extremes, all contribute to this deterioration.

"These vulnerabilities create a perfect storm," Professor Continuum warns. "Information environment degradation undermines the knowledge basis for democratic decisions. Legitimacy erosion weakens institutional capacity to implement solutions. Coordination failures prevent collective action even when shared interests exist."

She displays a concerning graph showing that democracy quality indicators have declined globally over the past decade, not just in emerging democracies, but also in established ones, such as the United States.

DEMOCRATIC VULNERABILITIES

INFORMATION ENVIRONMENT DEGRADATION

- Algorithm-driven filter bubbles
- Attention economy
- Amplification of extreme viewpoints
- Weaponized disinformation campaigns
- Collapse of traditional media

INSTITUTIONAL LEGITIMACY EROSION

- Performative politics
- Strategic delegitimization for partisan advantage
- Misleading transparency
- Declining civic knowledge
- Structural misalignment

COORDINATION SYSTEM FAILURES

- Extreme polarization
- Divisive micro-targeting
- Institutional capture by extreme actors
- Declining social capital
- Algorithmic radicalization

"The convergence of these vulnerabilities creates what political scientists call 'democratic deconsolidation'—a process where democratic systems maintain formal structures but lose substantive functioning as legitimate governance mechanisms."

Character Vignette: The Election Officials' Dilemma

Sarah Martinez and **Robert Chen**, county election officials from different parts of the country, meet at a national conference. Both look exhausted beyond their years.

"How bad was it in your jurisdiction last cycle?" Sarah asks, stirring her coffee.

Robert sighs. "Death threats against my staff. Armed 'poll watchers' intimidating voters. Social media campaigns calling me a Chinese agent because of my last name—I was born in Cleveland. Three of my senior people quit. You?"

"Similar," Sarah nods grimly. "My home address got posted online. People followed my kids to school. I had to install security cameras and start varying my routes to work. The county had to hire armed guards for the vote-counting center."

She takes a sip of coffee. "The thing that keeps me up at night isn't even the threats. It's what happens when enough experienced election administrators quit. We're losing decades of procedural knowledge—the people who know how to run clean elections are being driven out."

Robert nods. "My new staff are dedicated, but there's so much specialized expertise involved—ballot chain of custody, signature verification protocols, voting machine logic, and accuracy testing. These aren't things you learn overnight."

"And every mistake, no matter how minor, gets weaponized as evidence of fraud," Sarah adds. "The public doesn't understand that elections are run by real humans processing millions of ballots under tight deadlines. Small errors are normal and get caught by our verification processes. But now every administrative hiccup becomes 'proof' that the whole system is corrupt."

Sir Vote-a-Lot, the electoral knight with increasingly dented armor, joins their table. "I've been protecting democratic elections for centuries," he says, "but I've never seen challenges like these. Before, threats to elections came from outside the system—now they come from within."

"What keeps you going?" Robert asks Sarah.

She considers the question carefully. "The belief that if enough of us stay and do this work with integrity, the system will hold. Democracy isn't self-executing—it requires people willing to do the unglamorous, increasingly dangerous work of running elections by the book, regardless of who wins."

Sir Vote-a-Lot nods approvingly. "The front lines of democracy are no longer just in emerging republics abroad. They're in county election offices across America."

THE EVOLVING THREAT LANDSCAPE

INFORMATION OPERATION VECTORS	TECHNICAL INFRASTRUCTIURE	TRUST ARCHITECTURE ATTACKS
• Deepfakes creating false evidence • Microtargeted disinformation exploiting psychological vulnerabilities • Algorithmic amplification of divisive content • Coordinated inauthentic behavior • Hack-and-leak operations • "Flooding the zone"	• Election system security gaps • Critical infrastructure targeting • Government network penetration • Supply chain compromises • Ransomware attacks against services • DDoS attacks on democratic institutions	• Preemptive delegitimization with fraud narratives • Strategic amplification of minor errors • Intimidation of election officials and workers • Procedural exploitation through bad-faith challenges • Physical security threats • Institutional stress testing through synchronized actions

Technical Analysis: The Evolving Threat Landscape

The technical threat landscape facing democratic processes has evolved significantly, presenting multidimensional challenges that necessitate sophisticated responses.

"We're dealing with threats that combine technical sophistication with psychological manipulation," explains **Cybil Korteks**, her digital form flickering between different social media interfaces. "And most democratic institutions weren't designed with these attack vectors in mind."

She outlines three categories of evolving threats to democracy:

★ Information Operation Vectors include the creation of deepfakes to produce false evidence, microtargeted disinformation that exploits psychological vulnerabilities, algorithmic amplification of divisive content, coordinated inauthentic behavior, hack-and-leak operations, and "flooding the zone" techniques that overwhelm verification systems.

★ Technical Infrastructure Vulnerabilities encompass election system security gaps, critical infrastructure targeting, government network penetration, supply chain compromises, ransomware attacks against government services, and distributed denial-of-service attacks on democratic institutions.

★ Trust Architecture Attacks involve preemptive delegitimization through false fraud narratives, strategic amplification of minor errors as evidence of systemic failure, intimidation of election officials and workers, procedural exploitation through bad-faith legal challenges, physical security threats, and institutional stress testing through synchronized actions.

"What makes these threats particularly dangerous," Cybil explains, her eyes displaying lines of malicious code, "is their mutually reinforcing nature. Technical vulnerabilities create openings for information operations. Information operations set conditions for trust architecture attacks. Trust architecture attacks justify political interference with technical safeguards."

She displays a visualization showing attack patterns evolving from relatively straightforward technical exploits to sophisticated cross-domain operations combining cyber, information, legal, and physical elements.

"Traditional security models focused on preventing individual technical breaches," Cybil notes. "Contemporary threats require whole-of-system resilience against coordinated multi-vector campaigns designed not just to affect specific outcomes but to undermine democratic functionality itself."

Data Visualization: Democracy Erosion Patterns

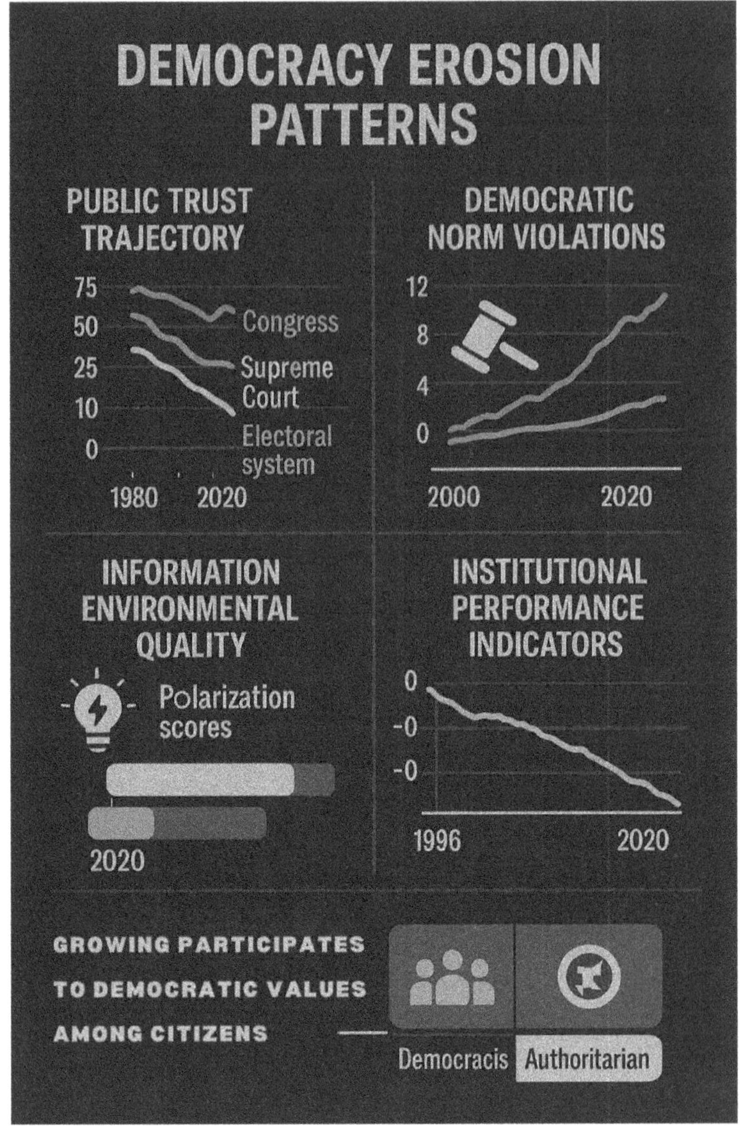

McSlicey, the High Priest, presents a series of data visualizations tracking democratic health indicators across time and countries.

"The data reveals concerning patterns," he explains, displaying a dashboard of democracy metrics. "We're observing systematic erosion across multiple dimensions of democratic functioning—not just in newer democracies but in established ones like the United States."

His visualizations show:

Public Trust Trajectory: Trust in democratic institutions across Western democracies has dramatically declined over the past twenty years, with particularly sharp drops following the 2008 financial crisis and accelerating after 2016. The United States exhibits particularly concerning patterns, with trust in Congress falling below 25%, trust in the Supreme Court declining from historical averages of around 70% to below 50%, and trust in the electoral system becoming increasingly polarized by partisan identity.

Democratic Norm Violations: A time-series analysis reveals an increasing trend of democratic norm violations (including the peaceful transfer of power, institutional independence, and fact-based governance) across multiple countries. Notably, autocratizing nations exhibit early warning patterns that subsequently emerge in established democracies, such as the United States.

Information Environment Quality: Metrics showing deterioration in information environment quality, including increasing polarization of news consumption, rising belief in conspiracy theories, declining agreement on basic facts, and growing tendency to support information censorship when it contradicts partisan narratives.

Institutional Performance Indicators: Governance effectiveness measures show declining performance in policy implementation, regulatory quality, and government functionality, particularly in democracies experiencing polarization and populist movements.

Citizen Democratic Commitment: Perhaps most alarmingly, surveys indicate a declining commitment to democratic values among citizens themselves, with growing percentages expressing openness to authoritarian alternatives if they believe such systems would yield better results.

"The data suggests we're experiencing what political scientists call 'democratic deconsolidation,'" McSlicey concludes, straightening his tie. "This isn't just about individual elections or leaders, but about systematic weakening of democratic foundations that have previously been taken for granted."

Comparative Analysis: Democratic Resilience Strategies

Democratic nations have developed varied resilience strategies against contemporary threats, offering a portfolio of approaches with demonstrated effectiveness.

"Different democracies have emphasized different protective mechanisms," explains **Professor Continuum**. "By examining this variety, we can identify complementary approaches that might be combined into more comprehensive resilience frameworks."

She highlights strategic approaches from various democracies:

- ★ The Baltic Information Resilience Model (BIR) in Estonia, Latvia, and Lithuania implements comprehensive media literacy education, rapid disinformation response capabilities, societal preparedness messaging, public-private coordination during information campaigns, and transparent communication about detected influence operations.
- ★ Taiwan's Digital Democracy Approach features citizen participation platforms, collaborative fact-checking,

DEMOCRATIC RESILIENCE STRATEGIES

BALTIC INFORMATION RESILIENCE MODEL

- Media literacy education
- Rapid disinformation response
- Societal preparedness messaging
- Public-private coordination during info campaigns
- Transparent communication

TAIWAN'S DIGITAL DEMOCRACY APPROACH

- Citizen participation platforms
- Collaborative fact-checking
Humor-based disinformation responses
- Accessible government data interfaces
- "Notice and public interest" alternatives to content removal

FINLAND'S EDUCATION-CENTERED STRATEGY

- Critical thinking integrated throughout
- Comprehensive civic education
- Responsible journalism training
- Trusted public service media
- Research centers studying democratic threats

GERMANY'S LEGAL-REGULATORY FRAMEWORK

- Constitutional protections against anti-democratic forces
- Platform accountability regulations
- Balanced hate speech laws
- Polarization-reducing electoral design
- Quality public broadcasting

humor-based responses to disinformation, accessible government data interfaces, and "notice and public interest" alternatives to content removal.

★ Finland's Education-Centered Strategy integrates critical thinking throughout education, comprehensive civic education, responsible journalism training, trusted public service media, and research centers studying democratic threats.

★ Germany's Legal and Regulatory Framework includes constitutional protections against anti-democratic forces, platform accountability regulations, balanced hate speech laws, polarization-reducing electoral design, and high-quality public broadcasting.

"What's striking," Professor Continuum observes, "is that the most resilient democracies don't rely on single-dimension strategies. They combine educational, technological, regulatory, and institutional approaches to create layered defenses that reinforce each other."

She notes that the United States has adopted elements of these approaches piecemeal but lacks the systematic, multi-dimensional resilience strategies of the most successful democratic nations.

"American democratic resilience efforts remain fragmented, under-resourced, and vulnerable to partisan capture," she concludes. "We have yet to develop the societal consensus that democracy protection transcends normal political disagreements and requires sustained investment across administrations."

Policy Proposal: Democratic Resilience Framework

Addressing America's democratic vulnerabilities requires a comprehensive resilience framework that strengthens democratic systems against contemporary threats.

"We need a democratic resilience approach as robust as our physical security systems," argues **Admiral Accountability** from the bridge of USS *Democracy*. "Just as we don't leave national defense to chance or market forces, we can't leave democratic security to underfunded, uncoordinated efforts."

He outlines a comprehensive democracy protection framework that encompasses four key dimensions:

- ★ Election Security Enhancement includes nationwide minimum security standards, federal funding for equipment modernization, critical infrastructure designation for election systems, mandatory post-election audits, physical security for officials and facilities, rapid response capabilities, and clear penalties for interference.
- ★ Civic Education Expansion features updated curricula addressing contemporary challenges, K-12 media literacy integration, adult education initiatives, hands-on democracy practicums, educator professional development, business tax credits for employee programs, and nonpartisan knowledge assessment.
- ★ Media Ecosystem Strengthening involves public interest media funding through independent trusts, platform transparency requirements, competition policy addressing market concentration, journalism support programs, community information needs assessments, coordinated responses to foreign influence, and research on the health of the ecosystem.
- ★ Institutional Legitimacy Restoration implements ethics reforms, transparency initiatives, performance metrics that demonstrate governance outcomes, judicial independence protections, algorithmic fairness standards, administrative modernization, and institutional design reviews that address contemporary challenges.

DEMOCRATIC RESILIENCE FRAMEWORK

ELECTION SECURITY ENHANCEMENT

- Nationwide minimum security standards
- Federal funding for equipment modernization
- Critical infrastructure designation
- Mandatory post-election audits
- Physical security for officials and facilities
- Rapid response capabilities, clear penalties for interference

CIVIC EDUCATION EXPANSION

- Updated curricula addressing challenges
- K-12 media literacy integration
- Adult-education initiatives
- Hands-on democracy practicums
- Educator professional development
- Business tax credits for employee programs

MEDIA ECOSYSTEM STRENGTHENING

- Public interest media funding
- Platform transparency requirements
- Competition policy addressing concentration
- Journalism support programs
- Community information

INSTITUTIONAL LEGITIMACY RESTORATION

- Ethics reforms and transparency Initiatives
- Performance metrics showing outcomes
- Judicial Independence protections
- Algorithmic fairness standards

"This framework isn't about protecting any particular party or policy position," Admiral Accountability emphasizes. "It's about ensuring that the democratic operating system itself remains functional so that legitimate policy debates can proceed within constitutional boundaries."

He notes that democratic resilience should be understood as critical infrastructure, as essential to national security as military capabilities or cybersecurity systems.

"Without secure democratic processes, every other security investment becomes vulnerable to subversion from within," the Admiral warns. "Democratic resilience is the foundation upon which all other national security capabilities ultimately rest."

Implementation Strategy: Coordinated Democratic Defense

Implementing democratic resilience measures requires carefully designed institutional structures, effective funding mechanisms, and coordinated efforts across jurisdictions.

"Democratic defense is inherently challenging because responsibilities are distributed across federal, state, and local governments, alongside private sector and civil society roles," explains **Sir Vote-a-Lot**. "Effective implementation requires coordination mechanisms that respect this distributed architecture while ensuring systematic protection."

He outlines a comprehensive democracy protection implementation approach that operates on three levels:

★ Federal-State Coordination establishes a Democracy Resilience Council, connecting federal and state officials to balance standards with implementation flexibility, incentivize funding formulas, provide technical assistance programs, share cross-jurisdictional best practices, establish security certification frameworks, and conduct joint training exercises.

★ Funding Mechanisms include a Democracy Infrastructure Fund for sustained investment, public-private partnerships, pay-for-success models, community resilience grants, innovation competitions, private sector tax incentives, and philanthropic matching programs.

★ Institutional Responsibilities include designating clear agency mandates, implementing accountability mechanisms, facilitating cross-sector coordination, fostering international partnerships to share effective approaches, leveraging research capabilities, identifying emerging threats, establishing incident response protocols, and conducting regular assessments.

COORDINATED DEMOCRATIC DEFENSE

FEDERAL-STATE COORDINATION

- Democracy Resilience Council
- Balanced standards with implementation flexibility
- Technical assistance programs
- Joint training exercises

FUNDING MECHANISMS

- Democracy Infrastructure Fund
- Public-private partnerships
- Pay-for-success models
- Philanthropic matching programs

INSTITUTIONAL RESPONSIBILITIES

- Clear agency mandates
- Implementation accountability mechanisms
- Cross-sector coordination
- International partnerships sharing effective approaches

"Democratic resilience isn't a static goal but an ongoing process," Sir Vote-a-Lot emphasizes. "Implementation strategies must build adaptive capacity that evolves as threats change."

He notes that implementing democratic resilience faces unique challenges because some political actors may calculate that democratic vulnerabilities serve their short-term interests, creating incentives to block resilience investments.

"This is why implementation design must include protection mechanisms against political sabotage," Sir Vote-a-Lot concludes. "Democratic resilience infrastructure needs to be institutionally insulated from the partisan battles it's designed to contain and channel."

V. THE POLARIZATION TRAP: STRUCTURAL REFORM FOR FUNCTIONAL POLITICS

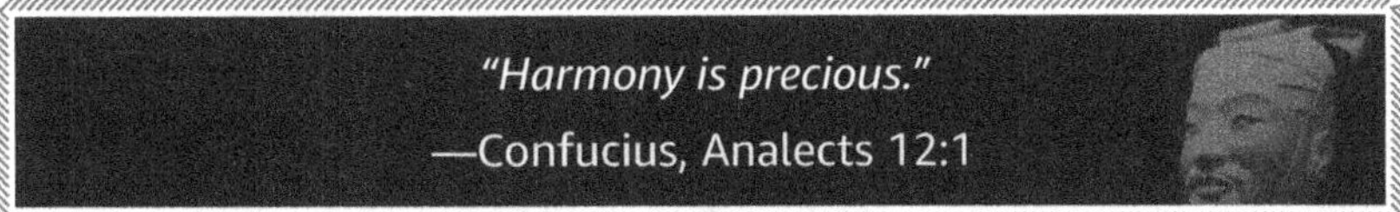

"Harmony is precious."
—Confucius, Analects 12:1

Analytical Framework: Structural Drivers of Division

America's extreme polarization isn't merely a matter of increasingly hostile attitudes—it's engineered into the structural design of political institutions, creating systemic incentives for division that individual goodwill cannot overcome.

"We often discuss polarization as if it were primarily a psychological or cultural phenomenon," explains **Professor Continuum**. "But the more fundamental drivers are structural—built into the very machinery of our political system."

She identifies four structural drivers creating a "polarization trap":

- ★ Electoral System Design combines single-member districts, winner-take-all elections, and primary dominance to incentivize polarization through partisan gerrymandering, ideologically extreme primary voters, base mobilization rewards, and the absence of centrist alternatives.
- ★ Media Ecosystem Architecture systematically rewards division through engagement-based economics, market fragmentation that enables partisan targeting, algorithmic amplification of provocative content, declining local news, and platform features that accelerate group polarization.
- ★ Legislative Process Configuration enables obstruction while penalizing cooperation through the evolution of filibuster usage, weakened committee systems, leadership consolidation, confrontational fundraising incentives, and declining congressional capacity.
- ★ Geographic Sorting Patterns create ideologically homogeneous communities through regional economic specialization, housing market dynamics, education and occupation patterns, urban-rural divides as partisan proxies, and social network homophily, which reduces cross-partisan relationships.

STRUCTURAL DRIVERS OF DIVISION

ELECTORAL SYSTEM DESIGN

Incentivizes polarization through partisan gerrymandering, ideologically extreme primary voters, base mobilization rewards

MEDIA ECOSYSTEM ARCHITECTURE

Systematically rewards division through engagement-based economics and market fragmentation enabling partisan targeting

LEGISLATIVE PROCESS CONFIGURATION

Enables obstruction while penalizing cooperation through evolved filibuster usage

GEOGRAPHIC SORTING PATTERNS

Create ideologically homogeneous comnmunities through regional economic specialization

"These structural factors create a self-reinforcing cycle," Professor Continuum explains. "Politicians responding rationally to systemic incentives adopt increasingly polarized positions. Media organizations maximize revenue by catering to partisan audiences. Voters receive increasingly divergent information diets. Geographic sorting reduces personal exposure to alternative viewpoints."

She displays data showing how these structural factors interact: "The result is a trap where individual actors have minimal incentive to moderate even when collective outcomes become dysfunctional for everyone."

Character Dialogue: The Structural Reform Debate

General Gridlock, a formidable figure in military uniform covered with partisan medals, faces off against **Sir Vote-a-Lot**, our electoral knight with increasingly dented armor. They've been summoned to debate institutional reform before an audience of concerned citizens.

"The problem isn't our institutions," General Gridlock insists, his voice a practiced parade-ground bark. "The problem is that certain people refuse to accept that my side is right about everything. Once they surrender unconditionally to our position, governance will function perfectly."

Sir Vote-a-Lot sighs, adjusting his crooked helmet. "The entire point of democratic design is to manage disagreement constructively. If perfect agreement were required for functional governance, we wouldn't need democratic institutions in the first place."

"My constituents didn't elect me to compromise," the General counters. "They elected me to defeat the enemy—by which I mean my fellow citizens who happen to vote for the other party."

"And that's precisely the structural problem," Sir Vote-a-Lot responds. "When electoral success depends on portraying the other side as an existential threat, polarization becomes a winning strategy regardless of its governance consequences."

The General narrows his eyes. "You're just advocating surrender of our principles."

SYSTEMIC INCENTIVES DRIVING POLITICAL POLARIZATION

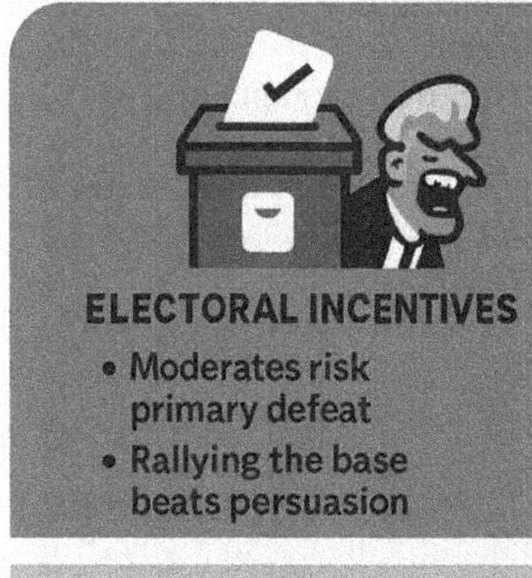

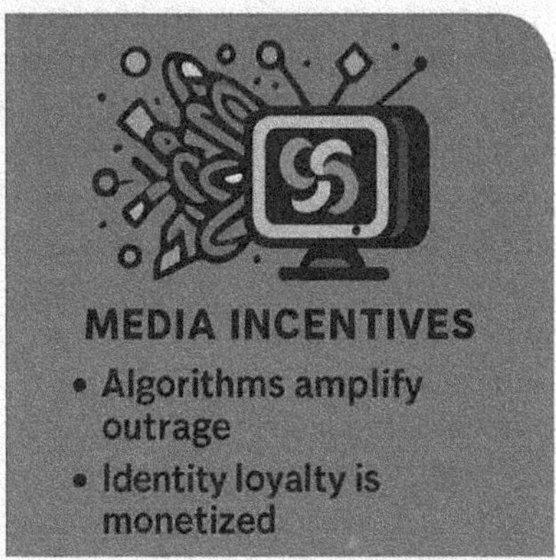

• Rallying the base beats persuasion

MEDIA INCENTIVES
• Algorithms amplify outrage
• Identity loyalty is monetized

INTEREST-GROUP INCENTIVES
• Threat-based fundraising
• Primary leverage > broad appeal

"I'm advocating structures that can translate different principles into workable governance," Sir Vote-a-Lot corrects him. "Consider the difference between America's congressional system and parliamentary democracies that build in stronger incentives for coalition-building."

"Coalition-building is just a fancy term for betraying your base," General Gridlock sniffs.

"Yet those systems often deliver more responsive governance despite significant ideological differences," Sir Vote-a-Lot points out. "The difference isn't that their politicians are more virtuous—it's that their systems are designed differently."

An audience member raises her hand. "But wouldn't changing our electoral system just benefit one party over another?"

"That's the remarkable thing," Sir Vote-a-Lot responds. "Structural reforms like ranked-choice voting, proportional representation, or open primaries don't inherently advantage either major party. They change the nature of competition itself, rewarding coalition-building rather than base mobilization."

General Gridlock interrupts. "The Founding Fathers created a perfect system. Any suggestion of improvement is practically treasonous."

"The Founders themselves disagreed vehemently about institutional design," Sir Vote-a-Lot counters. "They created amendment processes precisely because they recognized their system would need adaptation. They certainly never envisioned parliamentary-style parties operating within a presidential system, creating the dysfunction we see today."

"My donors would never support structural changes that might reduce polarization," General Gridlock admits in a rare moment of candor. "The fundraising emails practically write themselves when I can demonize the other side."

Sir Vote-a-Lot nods sadly. "And that's the trap in a nutshell. The same structural features that produce governance dysfunction also create powerful incentives against fixing them."

Political Analysis: Systemic Incentives

The persistence of dysfunctional polarization stems from deeply embedded systemic incentives that reward divisive behavior throughout the political ecosystem.

"Politics ultimately responds to incentives," explains **Milton the Trickster Economist**, juggling invisible opportunity costs. "To understand why polarization persists despite its governance costs, we must follow the incentive structures."

He outlines key incentive systems driving polarization:

Electoral Incentives: In gerrymandered districts where primary elections are decisive, politicians face asymmetric risks:

★ Moderation risks primary defeat from more extreme challengers
★ Partisan rhetoric generates activist support and small-donor fundraising
★ Base turnout strategies outperform persuasion strategies in many districts
★ Cross-partisan cooperation creates vulnerabilities without compensating benefits

"The electoral math is brutally simple," Milton explains. "For most members of Congress, the career-ending threat comes from their partisan flank, not the political center. Rational politicians respond accordingly."

Media Incentives: The contemporary information ecosystem systematically rewards divisive content:

★ Engagement metrics driving algorithmic amplification favor emotional triggers
★ Partisan media business models depend on audience loyalty through identity reinforcement
★ Fragmented competition for attention incentivizes increasingly apocalyptic framing
★ Social sharing patterns disproportionately reward content confirming existing beliefs

"Media organizations aren't conspiring to polarize Americans," Milton notes wryly. "They're simply maximizing revenue within existing market structures. The incentives for divisive content are embedded in the business model itself."

Interest Group Incentives: Political advocacy organizations face structural pressures toward polarization:

★ Fundraising effectiveness correlates with threat perception and enemy identification
★ Member recruitment and retention increase during periods of partisan conflict
★ Policy influence often derives from primary election leverage rather than cross-partisan appeal
★ Organizational brand differentiation rewards staking out distinct positions

"Even interest groups that might prefer moderate solutions face countervailing incentives," Milton explains. "The organizations that thrive are those that align with polarization incentives, not those that fight against them."

Constituent Incentives: Voters themselves receive benefits from polarizing behavior:

★ Identity affirmation through partisan team membership
★ Cognitive consistency from consuming aligned information
★ Social validation within ideologically homogeneous communities
★ Moral certainty from framing political differences as ethical absolutes

"The market has spoken," Milton concludes with an economist's detachment. "From an individual incentive perspective, polarization is a rational equilibrium even as it produces collectively irrational outcomes. That's why structural reform is essential—individuals responding to current incentives won't spontaneously generate different outcomes."

Data Visualization: Cooperation Metrics

McSlicey, the High Priest, presents data visualizations tracking congressional cooperation metrics over time, revealing the dramatic collapse of functional politics.

"The data tells a stark story of institutional transformation," McSlicey explains, displaying trend lines extending from the 1950s to the present. "We've witnessed a systematic breakdown in the cooperation metrics that enable functional governance."

His visualizations reveal:

Cross-Partisan Legislation Trajectory: A dramatic decline in bills with significant bipartisan co-sponsorship, from over 60% of substantial legislation in the 1970s to less than 15% today. The inflection points indicate acceleration following Newt Gingrich's speakership in 1994, the Tea Party wave in 2010, and again after the 2016 election.

Congressional Relationship Networks: This social network analysis shows the collapse of cross-partisan relationships in Congress. In the 1970s, dense interconnections existed between members of different parties through committee work, social relationships, and cooperative legislation. By 2025, the network shows almost complete partisan segregation with minimal cross-connections.

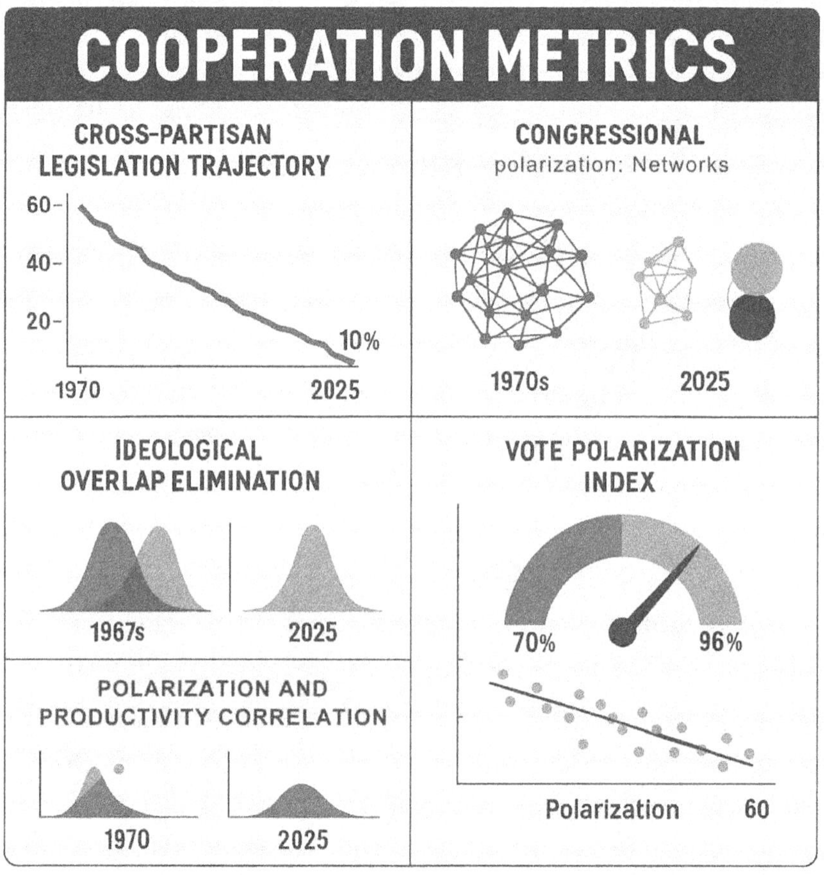

Ideological Overlap Elimination: Distribution curves showing the disappearance of ideological overlap between the parties. In the 1960s and 1970s, liberal Republicans and conservative Democrats created a substantial overlap in their agendas, allowing for coalition-building. By 2025, there will be virtually no overlap, resulting in discrete and non-interacting political distributions.

Vote Polarization Index: A composite metric showing party unity in congressional voting reaching historic highs, with members voting with their party over 95% of the time on contentious issues—a level unprecedented in American history outside the Civil War period.

Polarization and Productivity Correlation: Perhaps most tellingly, a strong negative correlation between polarization metrics and legislative productivity. As polarization has increased, Congress has passed fewer significant bills, conducted less meaningful oversight, and increasingly abdicated its role in policy development to executive agencies and courts.

"The metrics reveal a transformation from competitive cooperation to tribal warfare," McSlicey concludes, adjusting his tie. "The inflection points correspond to specific institutional changes and electoral realignments that altered the underlying incentive structures of American politics."

Case Studies: Successful Bipartisan Governance

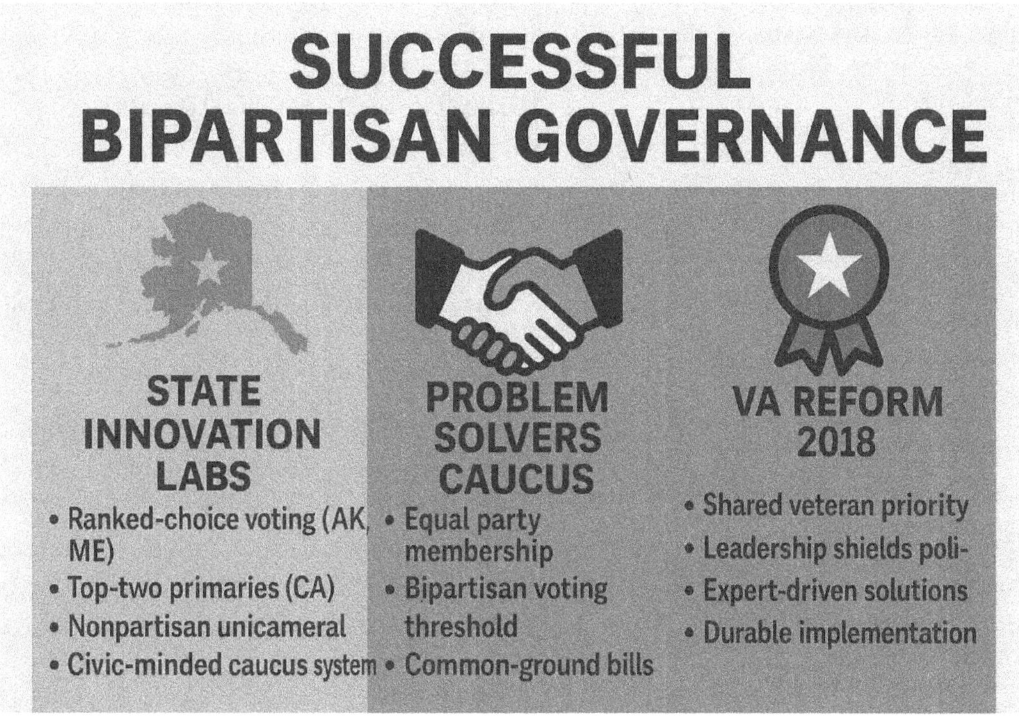

SUCCESSFUL
BIPARTISAN GOVERNANCE
STATE
INNOVATION
LABS
• Ranked-choice voting (AK, ME)
• Top-two primaries (CA)
• Nonpartisan unicameral
• Civic-minded caucus system
PROBLEM
SOLVERS
CAUCUS
• Equal party membership
• Bipartisan voting threshold
• Common-ground bills
VA REFORM
2018
• Shared veteran priority
• Leadership shields poli-
• Expert-driven solutions
• Durable implementation

Despite structural challenges, certain contexts still enable productive bipartisan governance, offering insights into potential reform directions.

"The polarization trap isn't uniformly distributed," notes **Professor Continuum**. "Examining where functional governance persists reveals potential pathways for broader reform."

She highlights several instructive cases:

State Government Innovation Laboratories: Several states have implemented structural reforms that moderate polarization effects:

★ Alaska, Maine, and several other states are using ranked-choice voting to reward coalition-building
★ California's top-two primary system is creating incentives for broader electoral appeals
★ Nebraska's nonpartisan unicameral legislature produces remarkably functional governance
★ Utah's unique caucus-convention system, combined with a strong civic culture, enables cooperation

"These state experiments demonstrate that structural reforms can meaningfully alter political behavior," Professor Continuum explains. "Politicians operating under different rules produce different outcomes—not because they're different people, but because they face different incentives."

Congressional Problem Solvers Caucus: This bipartisan group has created alternative incentive structures to facilitate cooperation:

★ Institutional rules requiring equal membership from both parties
★ Decision procedures mandating bipartisan agreement on policy positions
★ External reinforcement through supportive interest groups and donors
★ Strategic focus on issues with potential cross-partisan appeal

"The Problem Solvers haven't transformed Congress," Professor Continuum acknowledges, "but they've demonstrated that intentionally designed counter-incentives can produce islands of cooperation within polarized institutions."

The Veterans Affairs Reform Process: Despite extreme polarization, Congress managed bipartisan VA reform in 2018:

★ Shared constituent interest in veterans' welfare transcending partisan divides
★ Leadership's commitment to insulating the process from electoral politics
★ Policy development through genuine expertise rather than partisan think tanks

★ Implementation designs surviving changes in administration

"What's notable about successful cases," Professor Continuum concludes, "is that they don't depend on politicians suddenly becoming more virtuous. They create alternative incentive structures that make cooperation rational within specific domains, even as polarization continues elsewhere."

She emphasizes that these examples, while encouraging, remain exceptions that prove the rule: "Without broader structural reforms, these islands of functionality will remain limited exceptions to the dominant pattern of polarization-driven dysfunction."

Policy Framework: Institutional Reforms

Addressing America's polarization trap requires institutional reforms that alter underlying incentive structures rather than merely appealing to better behavior within dysfunctional systems.

"We need structural changes that realign political incentives toward functional governance," argues **Sir Vote-a-Lot**. "Appeals to virtue or nostalgia for a more cooperative era won't overcome the powerful structural drivers of polarization."

He outlines a Reform Framework.

★ **Electoral System Modernization**: Implement ranked-choice voting to express nuanced preferences, adopt multi-member districts with proportional representation to reduce winner-take-all dynamics, establish independent redistricting commissions, reform primaries to minimize the advantages of extremist candidates, restructure campaign finance to prioritize small-donor and in-district fundraising, and coordinate election timing to boost voter participation.

★ **Legislative Process Recalibration**: Reform the filibuster to restore its exceptional nature, strengthen committee systems to rebuild cross-partisan relationships, modernize budget processes to prevent shutdown-driven governance, enhance deliberative mechanisms for substantive policy engagement, invest in congressional capacity to reduce external dependencies, and reform leadership selection to balance party loyalty with institutional responsibility.

★ **Media Ecosystem Restructuring**: Regulate platforms to address algorithmic polarization incentives; fund public interest media through independent trusts; implement competition policy to counter information market consolidation; advance media literacy education; revitalize local news; and require transparency in content promotion.

★ **Civic Infrastructure Investment**: Develop cross-partisan community dialogue programs, create shared civic spaces, launch depolarization initiatives for high-conflict issues, foster collaborative civic leadership, experiment with deliberative democracy, and cultivate cross-cutting identities to counter political tribalism.

Policy Framework: Institutional Reforms

Electoral System Modernization

- Implement ranked-choice voting to express nuanced preferences
- Adopt multi-member districts with proportional allocation to reduce winner-take-all dynamics
- Establish independent redistricting commissions
- Reform primaries to reduce extremist advantages
- Restructure campaign finance to prioritize small-donor and in-district fundraising
- Coordinate election timing to boost participation

Legislative Process Recalibration

- Reform the filibuster to restore its exceptional nature
- Strengthen committee systems to rebuild cross-partisan relationships
- Modernize budget processes to prevent shutdown-driven governance
- Enhance deliberative mechanisms for substantive policy engagement
- Invest in congressional capacity to reduce external dependencies

Media Ecosystem Restructuring

- Regulate platforms to address algorithmic polarization Incentives
- Fund public interest media through independent trusts
- Implement competition policy against information market consolidation
- Advance media literacy education
- Revitalize local news
- Require transparency in content promotion

"These reforms don't require unrealistic constitutional amendments," Sir Vote-a-Lot emphasizes. "Most can be implemented through statutory changes, state-level innovations, or institutional rule modifications."

He notes that structural reforms face significant political obstacles precisely because they would alter the incentives that benefit current power-holders. "That's why reform strategies must identify paths that create strange-bedfellow coalitions transcending traditional partisan alignments."

Implementation Approach: Reform Pathways

Translating polarization reduction concepts into practical reality requires strategic implementation pathways that navigate political constraints.

"Structural reforms face a fundamental challenge," explains **McSlicey, the High Priest**. "The very polarization they seek to address creates resistance to their adoption. Implementation strategies must therefore identify viable pathways through this paradox."

He outlines pragmatic implementation approaches:

State-Level Experimentation: Through a "laboratory of democracy" model, states can demonstrate the benefits of reform using ballot initiatives to bypass legislative roadblocks. Interstate compacts build momentum across multiple states, while success stories create templates that others can follow. These demonstration effects generate public demand and foster cross-state learning communities for sharing best practices.

★ **Federal Standards Framework:** This establishes baseline electoral requirements through incentive structures rewarding reform adoption. Voluntary certification systems for election administration, coupled with research funding, build an evidence base while technical assistance supports implementation. Comprehensive data collection enables meaningful comparative evaluation.

★ **Reform Sequencing Strategy:** Threshold reforms create pathways for subsequent changes, maximizing synergistic effects through complementary sequencing. By identifying quick wins, establishing cross-partisan entry points, and staging implementation based on institutional readiness, long-term roadmaps maintain strategic direction.

★ **Coalition-Building Approach:** "Strange-bedfellow" alliances transcend traditional alignments, engaging business communities interested in governance stability. Veterans and national security constituencies emphasize democratic resilience, while religious organizations promote civic reconciliation. Youth movements demanding functional governance work alongside international democracy partners, providing comparative perspectives.

"Reform implementation requires strategic patience," McSlicey concludes. "The polarization trap developed over decades through cumulative institutional changes. Unwinding it will similarly require sustained, multi-level effort rather than single breakthrough moments."

He adds a final observation: "The implementation approach itself must model the collaborative governance it seeks to create—not imposing solutions but building them through genuine engagement across traditional dividing lines."

Reform Pathways – Quick Guide

State-Level Experimentation

States act as democracy labs–ballot initiatives, interstate compacts, success stories spread

Federal Standards Framework

Federal carrots of grants & certifications set baseline 'democracy hygiene' checklist

Reform Sequencing Strategy

Start with quick wins then domino complementary r-forms for lasting change

Coalition-Building Approach

Strange-bedfellow alliances from vets to Gen-Z power cross-partisan momentum

Quick Guide

VI. GOVERNING THROUGH TRUMP 2.0: STRATEGIC INSTITUTIONAL RESILIENCE

> *"The bamboo that bends is stronger than the oak that resists."*
> —Chinese proverb

Analytical Framework: Maintaining Institutional Integrity

Democratic governance during periods of administrative volatility requires institutional resilience strategies that maintain core functions while navigating political pressures.

"The challenge of the Trump 2.0 scenario isn't merely political disagreement but governance paradigm disruption," explains **Professor Continuum**. "We're dealing with an approach to executive power that treats institutions as personal tools rather than public trusts, requiring distinctive resilience strategies."

She presents a framework for institutional challenges under volatile leadership through three key dimensions:

- ★ **Authority Boundary Contestation**: Traditional governance assumes agreement on institutional roles, but disruptive leaders contest these boundaries by claiming unchecked authority, demanding political loyalty over professional judgment, redefining institutional missions for personal gain, exploiting constitutional gray areas, and weaponizing legal structures against perceived adversaries.
- ★ **Personnel System Manipulation**: Institutional capacity relies on balancing political direction with expertise, but volatile leaders undermine this by replacing loyalty tests with

ANALYTICAL FRAMEWORK:
MAINTAINING INSTITUTIONAL INTEGRITY

Authority Boundary Contestation

Traditional governance assumes agreement on institutional roles, but disruptive leaders contest these boundaries by:

- Claiming unchecked authority
- Demanding political loyalty over professional judgement
- Redefining institutional missions for personal interests
- Exploiting constitutional gray zones
- Weapanoizing legal structures against perceived enemies

Personnel System Manipulation

Institutional capacity relies on balancing political direction with expertise but volatile leaders undermine this through:

- Loyalty tests replacing qualifications
- Exploiting acting appointments to avoid scrutiny
- Politicizing civil service through reassignmeent and intimidation
- Undermining oversight roles
- Marginalizing career officials with expertise

Information Environment

Effective governance requires reliable information flows, which volatile leaders disrupt by:

- Contesting factual reality for political purposes
- Politicizing intelligence when inconvenient
- Undermining scientific expertise
- Creating parallel information structures with competing "realities"
- Misusing classification systems to hide politically damaging information

qualifications, exploiting acting appointments to avoid scrutiny, politicizing the civil service through reassignment and intimidation, undermining oversight roles, and marginalizing career officials with expertise.

★ **Information Environment Distortion**: Effective governance requires reliable information flows, which volatile leaders disrupt by contesting factual reality for political purposes, politicizing intelligence when it is inconvenient, undermining scientific expertise, creating parallel information structures with competing "realities," and misusing classification systems to conceal politically damaging information.

"These challenges create profound institutional dilemmas," Professor Continuum explains. "Career officials face competing obligations: constitutional oaths, professional standards, chain of command, and public service ethics. Traditional frameworks assuming these obligations align break down when they systematically conflict."

She emphasizes that institutional resilience strategies must balance multiple imperatives: "The goal isn't resistance to legitimate political direction, but rather maintaining institutional integrity and core functions during periods when political leadership may undermine the very purposes the institutions were created to serve."

Character Vignette: The Professional Tightrope

David Chen sits at his desk at the Environmental Protection Agency, staring at the directive that just arrived from political leadership. With 24 years at the agency, he has survived multiple administrations of both parties, but nothing has prepared him for this moment.

The memo requires him to delete sections of a scientific assessment showing elevated cancer risks in communities near chemical plants. The scientific evidence is unambiguous—he supervised the research team himself—but the findings conflict with the administration's deregulatory agenda and promises to industry supporters.

His phone rings. It's **Megan Williams**, his counterpart at another division.

"Did you get the memo?" she asks quietly.

"Just reading it now," David confirms. "They want us to alter scientific conclusions to match political preferences. This goes beyond the normal policy disagreements between administrations."

"I'm trying to figure out where the line is," Megan says. "I've always accepted that political appointees set policy priorities—that's legitimate in a democracy. But altering scientific findings crosses into different territory."

"The public trusts EPA assessments because they believe they're based on sound science, not political convenience," David notes. "If we compromise that, we undermine the agency's core mission and public trust."

Admiral Accountability materializes beside David's desk, visible only from our narrative perspective.

"Career officials like David face impossible choices daily," the Admiral observes. "Comply with directives that violate professional standards and statutory responsibilities? Refuse and face removal? Resign in protest? Each option carries profound costs to either institutional integrity or personal career."

David scans the agency's scientific integrity policy, which explicitly prohibits political interference with scientific conclusions. He emails his direct supervisor, copying the agency's scientific integrity officer, and quotes the relevant policy sections, requesting clarification.

"I'm not refusing the directive," he explains to Megan. "I'm seeking guidance on how to reconcile it with established scientific integrity requirements. This creates a paper trail while following proper channels."

"Documentation is essential," Megan agrees. "I've started keeping two sets of notes—the official record, plus my personal documentation concerning directives preserved outside government systems."

"The professional civil service wasn't designed for scenarios where political leadership systematically undermines statutory missions," Admiral Accountability observes. "The system assumes good-faith disagreements within constitutional boundaries, not fundamental conflict between political directives and legal obligations."

"How do you maintain your sanity through this?" David asks Megan.

"I focus on what I can protect," she replies. "Maybe I can't stop all the damage, but I can maintain scientific standards in my division, document what's happening for future accountability, provide information through proper channels to oversight bodies, and ensure critical functions continue despite the chaos."

Admiral Accountability nods approvingly. "They're practicing the resilience strategies we most need: protecting core institutional functions while navigating unprecedented challenges to administrative integrity."

Historical Analysis: Periods of Institutional Stress

The American system has weathered previous periods of institutional stress, offering historical lessons about effective resilience mechanisms.

"Current governance challenges aren't entirely without precedent," **Doctor History** explains, opening his medical bag of historical context. "Examining how institutions responded to previous stress periods reveals patterns of both vulnerability and resilience."

He examines key historical precedents of institutional challenges:

Andrew Jackson's Presidency (1829-1837): Jackson's populism challenged norms through the spoils system, prioritizing partisan loyalty over merit, purging career officials, appealing directly to "the people" against constraints, defying Supreme Court rulings on Indigenous rights, and destroying the Bank of the United States as political theater.

Responses included legislative constraints on removal power, bureaucratic resistance, and, eventually, civil service reform.

Gilded Age Corruption (1870s-1890s): Systemic corruption threatened institutions through the capture of departments by private interests, patronage that undermined administrative capacity, corrupted electoral processes, regulatory functions that benefited wealthy donors, and a collapse in public trust. Reforms included the professionalization of the civil service, the establishment of independent regulatory commissions, transparency laws, and anti-corruption statutes.

McCarthy Era (1950-1954): Political persecution challenged institutional integrity through loyalty investigations undermining professional judgment, weaponized security clearances, congressional investigations as theater, factual distortion, and dissent suppression through character assassination. Resilience came through judicial constraints, professional organizations defending targets, principled leadership, and shifting public opinion.

Nixon Administration (1969-1974): The Nixon administration tested executive boundaries through the politicization of intelligence agencies, Justice Department interference, abuse of the classification system, resistance to oversight, and targeting perceived enemies, ultimately leading to a constitutional crisis. Responses included whistleblower protections, inspector general systems, intelligence oversight reforms, judicial independence, and strengthened congressional investigation powers.

"What historical episodes reveal," Doctor History concludes, "is that institutional stress isn't fatal if resilience mechanisms activate in time. The current challenge combines elements from multiple historical stress periods, requiring correspondingly robust responses."

He notes that previous resilience often depended on cross-partisan consensus that certain institutional boundaries should remain inviolable regardless of policy disagreements—a consensus that has significantly eroded in contemporary politics.

Case Studies: Critical Function Maintenance

Despite significant challenges, certain institutions have maintained critical functions during periods of administrative volatility by employing deliberate resilience strategies.

"Not all institutions have been equally vulnerable to disruption," notes **Admiral Accountability**. "Examining differential outcomes reveals specific factors that enable function maintenance under pressure."

He highlights several instructive cases:

Federal Reserve Independence: The Fed has maintained a relatively stable monetary policy despite intense political pressure through:

- ★ Structural insulation, including fixed terms for governors
- ★ Technical complexity creates barriers to political interference
- ★ Institutional culture emphasizing professional standards
- ★ Congressional allies across partisan lines
- ★ Public communication strategy, maintaining credibility
- ★ Private sector stakeholder support provides a political counterweight

"The Fed's resilience demonstrates how institutional design features can create protection from short-term political pressures," Admiral Accountability observes. "However, even this robust model faced unprecedented challenges that tested its boundaries."

Intelligence Community Adaptation: Intelligence agencies maintained core functions despite leadership volatility through:

- ★ Career professional consensus on mission primacy
- ★ Established procedures for slowing politically motivated changes
- ★ The Inspector General channels for inappropriate directive documentation
- ★ Congressional oversight relationships through career staff
- ★ International partner relationships transcending administration changes
- ★ Careful distinction between policy preferences and factual assessment

"Intelligence agencies developed strategic institutional protection while still respecting the legitimate role of political leadership in setting priorities," the Admiral explains. "This balancing act wasn't always successful, but preserved core functions."

Scientific Agency Resilience: Agencies like NOAA, NIH, and aspects of the EPA preserved scientific integrity through:

- ★ Clear written scientific integrity policies
- ★ Professional society relationships provide external support
- ★ Documentation practices create accountability trails
- ★ Strategic communication, maintaining public credibility
- ★ Career leadership stability at operational levels
- ★ Technical complexity limits political micromanagement

"Scientific agencies demonstrated the importance of pre-existing institutional safeguards," Admiral Accountability notes. "Agencies with established scientific integrity infrastructure proved more resilient than those without such protections."

Justice System Selective Independence: Despite significant pressure, aspects of the justice system maintained independence through:

- ★ A decentralized structure limits centralized control
- ★ Career prosecutor's ethical commitments

CRITICAL FUNCTION MAINTENANCE

INSTITUTIONAL RESILIENCE CASE STUDIES

Federal Reserve Independence

- Structural insulation
- Technical complexity
- Professional culture
- Bipartisan allies
- Public communication
- Stakeholder support

Intelligence Community Adaptation

- Career consensus
- Established procedures
- Inspector General oversight
- Congressional relationships
- International partners
- Distinction from policy

Scientific Agency Resilience

- Integrity policies
- Society relationships
- Documentation
- Strategic communication
- Career leadership
- Technical limitations

Justice System Selective Independence

- Decentralized structure
- Career commitments
- Judicial checks
- Documentation
- Media scrutiny
- Internal resistance

ETHICAL DECISION PATHS

OBLIGATION BALANCE
• Democratic mandate
• Professional ethics
• Statutory duty
• Constitutional oath
• Public interest
THRESHOLD SIGNALS
• Legitimate shift–implement
• Irregularity–fix channels
• Standards breach–document
• Law break–report
• Public risk–protect
ACTION SPECTRUM
• Implement enthusiastically
• Execute faithfully
• Seek clarification
• Document procedures
• Escalate channels

★ Judicial branch's willingness to check excesses
★ Documentation practices create accountability mechanisms
★ Media scrutiny is increasing the political costs of interference
★ Internal resistance from senior career officials

"The justice system's experience reveals both vulnerabilities and sources of resilience," the Admiral concludes. "While certain functions were compromised, core prosecutor independence proved more robust than many feared due to distributed institutional safeguards."

Admiral Accountability extracts common resilience factors from these cases: "Clear written standards, documentation practices, external stakeholder relationships, congressional allies, professional networks, and strategic communication emerge as critical protective mechanisms across otherwise different institutional contexts."

Ethical Analysis: The Moral Dimensions

Career officials navigating volatile political environments face profound ethical dilemmas requiring nuanced frameworks beyond simplistic loyalty-versus-resistance narratives.

"The ethical challenges for career officials during periods of institutional stress exist in a complex moral territory," explains **Professor Continuum**. "They involve competing obligations to democratic values, professional standards, institutional missions, and constitutional oaths."

She presents an ethical framework for institutional resilience:

Multiple Obligation Analysis: Career officials must balance obligations to democratic responsiveness, professional standards, statutory responsibilities, constitutional commitments, and public interest service. These typically align but can conflict when political leadership undermines institutional purposes, requiring officials to determine which obligation takes priority in specific contexts.

★ **Threshold Framework**: Different political directions warrant different responses, ranging from legitimate policy shifts that deserve implementation to procedural irregularities addressable through normal channels, professional standard violations requiring documentation, legal or constitutional violations necessitating reporting, and public endangerment potentially justifying protective actions.
★ **Response Spectrum Analysis**: Ethical responses range from enthusiastic implementation of legitimate policy direction to faithful execution despite disagreement, seeking clarification for ambiguous directives, documenting procedures for accountability, escalating channels for review, working around obstacles to fulfill statutory obligations, and principled resignation when service requires unacceptable compromise.

"The ethical framework isn't about resistance to democratically elected leadership," Professor Continuum emphasizes. "It's about maintaining institutional integrity and constitutional fidelity during periods when those values face unusual pressure."

She concludes with a sobering observation: "Historical analysis suggests that democracy depends not just on formal institutions but on the ethical judgment of those who staff them. When institutional guardrails fail, individual ethical navigation becomes democracy's last line of defense."

Policy Strategy: Building Resilient Governance

Preparing governance systems for periods of political volatility requires deliberate resilience strategies that maintain institutional integrity, regardless of the leadership approach.

"Institutional resilience can't be improvised during the crisis," warns **Admiral Accountability**. "It must be systematically developed during stable periods to activate when needed."

He outlines a comprehensive resilience framework:

1. Legal Guardrail Reinforcement
★ Statutory protections for core institutional functions
★ Whistleblower protection enhancement ensures safe reporting channels
★ The Inspector General's independence is strengthened through removal restrictions
★ Criminal penalties for political interference with specific functions
★ Administrative Procedure Act modernization, to close exploitation loopholes
★ Clarified legal boundaries regarding presidential directive authority
2. Professional Norm Codification
★ Written ethical standards for specific professional functions
★ Scientific integrity policies with enforcement mechanisms
★ Documentation requirements for decision processes
★ Clarified recusal standards for conflict situations
★ Inter-agency agreements on core professional principles
★ Professional society standards alignment with government roles
3. Institutional Design Adaptation
★ Structural insulation for particularly sensitive functions
★ Redundant systems ensuring critical operations continuity
★ Distributed authority limiting single-point vulnerability
★ External accountability mechanisms beyond executive control
★ Decision record requirements create transparency
★ Career-political interface rules establish boundaries
4. Knowledge Continuity Mechanisms
★ Career leadership development, ensuring institutional memory
★ Documentation systems preserving operational knowledge
★ Transition training requirements for incoming officials
★ Statutory mission education for political appointees
★ Scenario planning for institutional stress situations
★ External partner relationships maintain operational continuity

Policy Strategy:
Building Resilient Governance

Protect core functions; strengthen whistleblower and IG independence; update APA and clarify executive boundaries

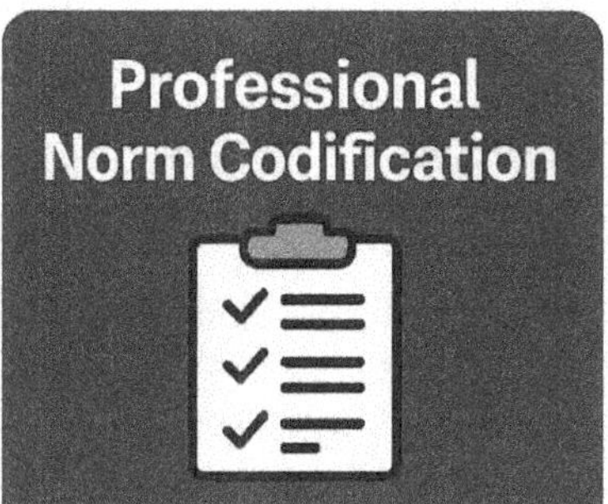

Enforce ethical standards and scientific integrity; require transparent documentation and recusal policies; align interagency professisional principles

Insulate critical functions via redundancy and distributed authority; embed external accountability; enforce decision transparency

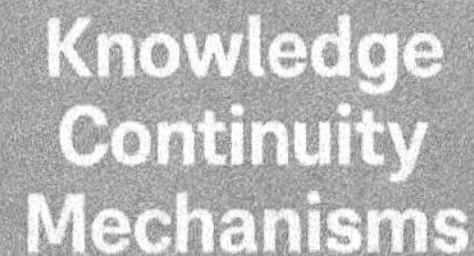

Develop leadership pipelines and thorough documentation; mandate transition training and scenario planning formalize academic and partner collaborations

"These strategies aren't about resistance to democratic leadership," Admiral Accountability emphasizes. "They're about ensuring that government functions remain aligned with statutory purposes and constitutional principles regardless of who holds power."

He notes that institutional resilience ultimately serves democratic accountability: "When institutions maintain their integrity, citizens can better evaluate leadership performance based on actual outcomes rather than confusion about what's really happening."

IMPLEMENTATION APPROACH: PRACTICAL RESILIENCE BUILDING

LEGAL IMPLEMENTATION MECHANISMS

- Omnibus integrity legislation
- Stand-alone bills
- Regulatory implementation
- State-level protections
- Judicial clarification
- International agreements

INSTITUTIONAL POLICY DEVELOPMENT

- Agency resilience protocols
- Ethical navigation guidance
- Cross-agency coordination
- Scenario-based stress testing
- Knowledge management
- Professional development

STAKEHOLDER ENGAGEMENT STRATEGIES

- Cross-partisan coalition building
- External validator relationships
- Professional association standards
- Media and citizen education
- International partner coordination

SEQUENCED IMPLEMENTATION PLAN

- Vulnerability assessment
- Quick-win identification
- Long-term structural reforms
- Crisis protocol development
- Preventive measures
- Recovery systems

Implementation Approach: Practical Resilience Building

Implementing governance resilience requires practical strategies that navigate political realities while effectively protecting institutional integrity.

"Resilience implementation faces significant challenges during polarized periods," acknowledges **McSlicey, the High Priest**. "Strategies must balance effectiveness with political feasibility."

He outlines an Implementation Approach:

- ★ **Legal Implementation Mechanisms**: Establishes formal protections through omnibus integrity legislation, stand-alone bills addressing specific vulnerabilities, regulatory implementation utilizing existing authority, state-level protections for shared functions, judicial clarification of constitutional boundaries, and international agreements that provide external accountability.
- ★ **Institutional Policy Development**: Establishes internal safeguards through agency-specific resilience protocols, ethical navigation guidance, cross-agency coordination, scenario-based stress testing, knowledge management systems, and professional development to address complex situations.
- ★ **Stakeholder Engagement Strategies**: Build support networks through cross-partisan coalition building around institutional integrity, external validator relationships, alignment of professional association standards, media and citizen education about governance, and international partner coordination.
- ★ **Sequenced Implementation Plan**: Provides a structured approach through vulnerability assessment, prioritizing protections, identifying quick wins, building momentum, implementing long-term structural reforms, developing crisis protocols, implementing preventive measures to reduce exploitation opportunities, and establishing recovery systems to address institutional damage.

"Effective implementation recognizes that institutional resilience ultimately serves all political perspectives," McSlicey concludes. "While short-term political advantages might come from institutional exploitation, the long-term health of the republic requires governance systems that maintain integrity across leadership transitions."

He adds a final implementation insight: "The strongest resilience strategies embed protection mechanisms within routine operations rather than creating easily targeted special provisions. When institutional integrity becomes the default operating condition, it becomes much harder to dismantle."

VII. AMERICA IN THE WORLD: RESTORING GLOBAL STANDING AND TRUST

> *"Trust is the foundation of the state."*
> —Mencius

Analytical Framework: Rebuilding International Credibility

America's global leadership depends fundamentally on the credibility of its commitments—a foundation that has eroded significantly through political volatility and governance dysfunction.

"International influence ultimately rests on trust," explains **Professor Continuum**. "When American leadership becomes unpredictable, contradictory, or dysfunctional, trust erodes and influence diminishes accordingly."

She outlines key dimensions of International Credibility:

AMERICA IN THE WORLD

Restoring Global Standing & Trust

COMMITMENT RELIABILITY

Allies need confidence U.S. deals survive elections; withdrawals & reversals have eroded that trust.

GOVERNANCE FUNCTIONALITY

Soft power rests on competent, steady democracy—shutdowns & polarization broadcast dysfunction.

VALUES CONSISTENCY

Moral authority slips when human-rights talk clashes with selective rules and domestic lapses

INSTITUTIONAL CAPABILITY

Diplomacy, development & intel weakened by staff cuts and poor coordination, limiting follow-through

- ★ **Commitment Reliability**: International cooperation requires confidence that agreements persist across administrations. This has weakened through treaty withdrawals, policy reversals, ratification failures, inconsistent funding, and undermined alliance commitments.
- ★ **Governance Functionality**: America's influence stems partly from demonstrating effective democratic governance. This soft power has diminished due to visible dysfunction, concerns about democratic backsliding, government shutdowns, constitutional crises, and polarization, all of which undermine policy continuity and stability.
- ★ **Values Consistency**: American leadership traditionally included a moral dimension beyond transactional power politics. This authority has eroded due to inconsistent human rights commitments, domestic violations of principles promoted internationally, selective adherence to the rules-based order, abandonment of fact-based discourse, and a visible erosion of constitutional norms.
- ★ **Institutional Capability**: Global influence requires functional institutions for sustained engagement. This capability has deteriorated due to diplomatic capacity gaps, loss of development expertise, politicization of the intelligence community, breakdowns in interagency coordination, and implementation gaps between commitments and delivery.

"The decline in American credibility creates a mutually reinforcing cycle," Professor Continuum notes. "As trust diminishes, partners hedge their bets through alternative arrangements. These hedging strategies further reduce American influence, accelerating the decline in global leadership capacity."

She displays data showing significant drops in international confidence in American leadership across allies and partners, with corresponding increases in hedging behaviors such as security self-reliance initiatives and alignment with China on specific issues.

"Rebuilding credibility requires addressing root causes rather than symptoms," Professor Continuum concludes. "Diplomatic messaging cannot compensate for fundamental governance dysfunction visible to the entire world."

Character Development: The Alliance Ambassador

Ambassador Eleanor Richards adjusts her glasses, surveying the nervous faces of diplomatic counterparts from traditional American allies gathered in her residence. After thirty years in the Foreign Service, she's developed a reputation for straight talk—a quality especially valuable during periods of American political volatility.

"I know you have concerns," she begins. "The headlines from Washington aren't reassuring, and some of you have received... contradictory communications from different parts of our government."

The German representative clears his throat. "With respect, Ambassador, my government received three different policy positions on NATO commitments last week from three different American officials—including two directly contradicting presidential statements."

The Japanese diplomat nods. "We face similar confusion regarding security guarantees. One department reaffirms them while another suggests they're open to renegotiation. Meanwhile, social media statements from your president imply they might be conditional on trade concessions."

Ambassador Richards takes a deep breath. "I understand your concerns. I won't pretend our political system isn't experiencing significant turbulence. But I want to offer some perspective on American institutional resilience that might not be visible from overseas."

Lady Liberty materializes beside her, visible only to our narrative view, nodding encouragingly.

"First," the Ambassador continues, "remember that American foreign policy operates through multiple institutional layers. Presidential statements matter enormously, but implementation occurs through complex systems involving career officials, congressional oversight, and legal frameworks."

She points to a map showing the global deployment of American military forces. "These operational commitments continue regardless of political rhetoric. Our forces train with yours daily. Intelligence sharing continues. The fundamental security architecture remains intact even when political messaging suggests otherwise."

The South Korean representative looks skeptical. "But doesn't institutional continuity require political leadership that respects institutions? We see concerning signs of institutional erosion."

"A valid concern," Ambassador Richards acknowledges. "But American institutions have proven more resilient than many expected. Career diplomats, military leaders, and civil servants continue executing core functions despite political headwinds. Congressional engagement across party lines maintains support for key alliance relationships."

Lady Liberty whispers in her ear, though only we can hear: "Tell them about the deeper continuities—the values and interests that transcend any single administration."

"Most importantly," the Ambassador continues, "America's fundamental interests remain constant despite political volatility. Our economic integration, security partnerships, and shared values create structural alignment that persists through political cycles. The current turbulence is real, but the underlying foundations remain solid."

The Australian representative raises an eyebrow. "That's reassuring in theory, Ambassador. But concrete policy unpredictability imposes real costs. How do we plan long-term security investments when American commitment seems to shift with each election—or each social media post?"

"That's why we're strengthening institutional connections beyond political leadership," Ambassador Richards explains. "Military-to-military relationships, agency partnerships, congressional delegation engagement, state and local gov-

INTERNATIONAL RELATIONS THEORY: DOMESTIC GOVERNANCE AND GLOBAL INFLUENCE

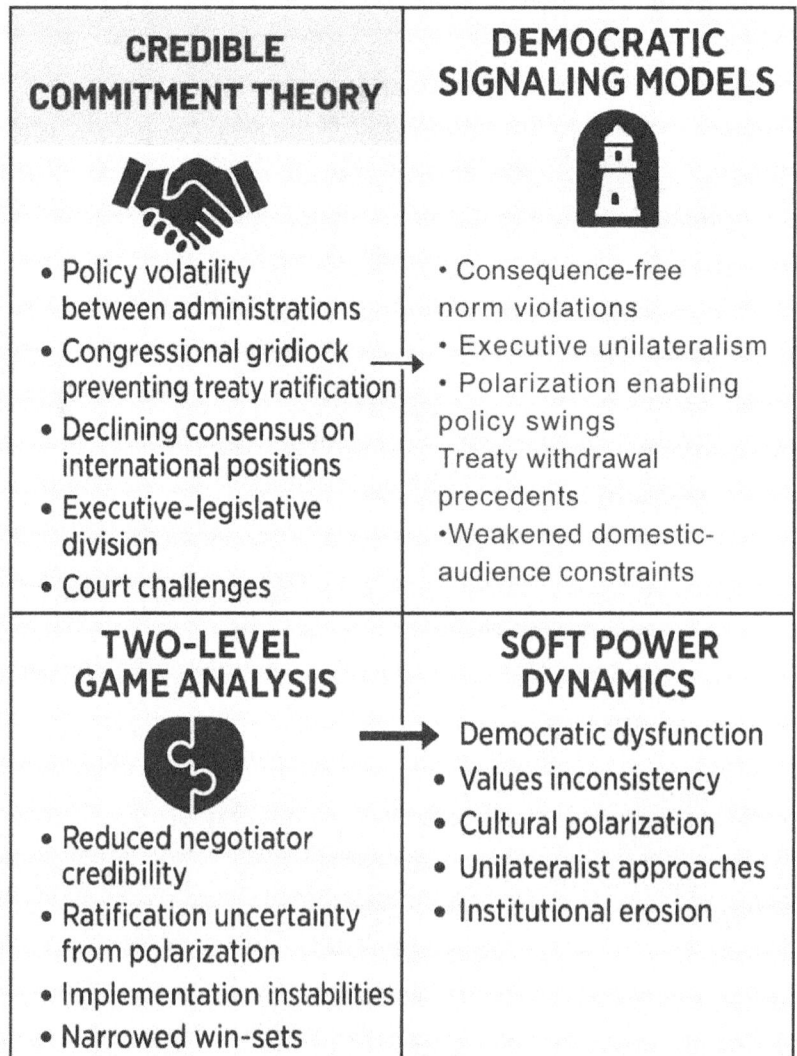

<table>
<tr>
<td>CREDIBLE COMMITMENT THEORY

• Policy volatility between administrations
• Congressional gridiock preventing treaty ratification
• Declining consensus on international positions
• Executive-legislative division
• Court challenges</td>
<td>DEMOCRATIC SIGNALING MODELS

• Consequence-free norm violations
• Executive unilateralism
• Polarization enabling policy swings
Treaty withdrawal precedents
•Weakened domestic-audience constraints</td>
</tr>
<tr>
<td>TWO-LEVEL GAME ANALYSIS

• Reduced negotiator credibility
• Ratification uncertainty from polarization
• Implementation instabilities
• Narrowed win-sets</td>
<td>SOFT POWER DYNAMICS
Democratic dysfunction
• Values inconsistency
• Cultural polarization
• Unilateralist approaches
• Institutional erosion</td>
</tr>
</table>

ernment cooperation, private sector ties—these create a resilient network that continues functioning during political volatility."

She gestures toward a photo showing multiple layers of cooperation. "Think of American engagement like a rope with many strands. One strand—political leadership messaging—may fray temporarily. But the rope itself remains strong through multiple other connections."

Lady Liberty nods approvingly. "She's learning to articulate the distinction between America's permanent interests and temporary political currents—the key to maintaining trust during volatile periods."

As the diplomatic representatives begin asking more specific questions, Ambassador Richards reflects on her evolving role: not just representing current policy but explaining American institutional complexity in ways that maintain partner confidence despite political turbulence. It's diplomacy at its most challenging—and perhaps its most important.

International Relations Theory: Domestic Governance and Global Influence

The relationship between domestic governance quality and international influence follows clear theoretical patterns that explain America's diminished global standing.

"International relations theory has increasingly recognized that domestic governance directly affects external influence," explains **Professor Continuum**. "The linkage operates through multiple causal pathways that help explain America's changing global position."

She outlines key theoretical frameworks:

- ★ **Credible Commitment Theory**: Nations make internationally credible commitments through domestic institutions, enabling consistency. American capability has weakened through policy volatility between administrations, congressional gridlock preventing ratification, declining consensus on international positions, executive-legislative division, and court challenges. International partners rationally discount American promises when domestic institutions fail to deliver consistent outcomes over time.
- ★ **Democratic Signaling Models**: Democracies traditionally signal greater commitment reliability through institutional constraints on arbitrary changes. This advantage has eroded through consequence-free norm violations, executive unilateralism, policy swings enabled by polarization, treaty withdrawal precedents, and weakened domestic audience constraints resulting from base politics.

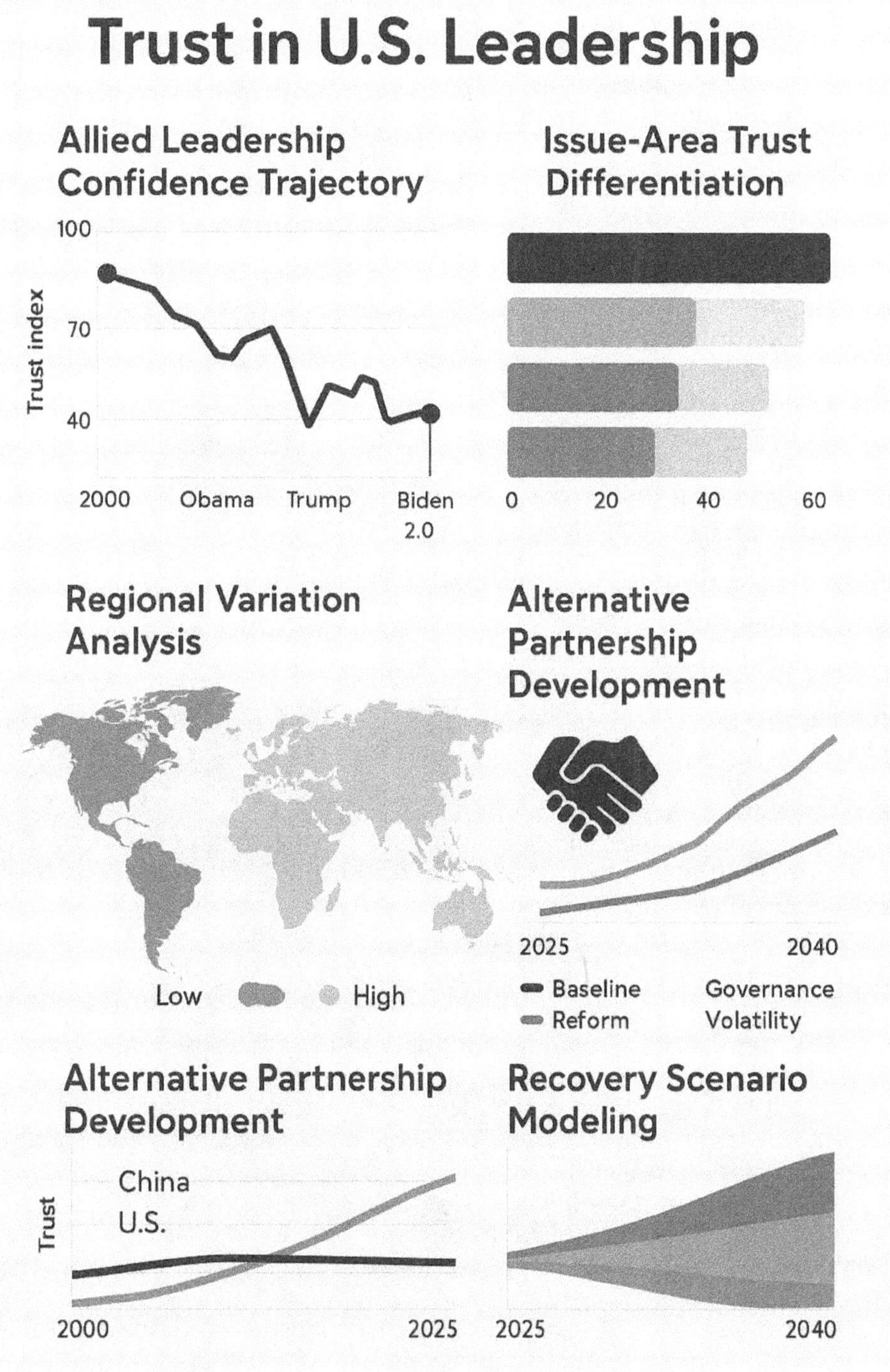

★ **Two-Level Game Analysis**: International agreements require navigating both international and domestic constraints. American capacity has declined due to reduced negotiator credibility, ratification uncertainty resulting from polarization, implementation questions arising from bureaucratic disruption, domestic coalition instability, and narrowed win-sets that limit viable agreement space.

★ **Soft Power Dynamics**: America's influence has historically derived from its soft power—attraction to its model and values. This has weakened due to democratic dysfunction, reducing governance appeal, inconsistency in values, diminishing moral leadership, cultural polarization that limits societal attraction, unilateralist approaches that reduce cooperative reputation, and institutional erosion that undermines the rule-of-law exemplar status.

"The theoretical frameworks consistently point to a fundamental conclusion," Professor Continuum summarizes. "America's international influence ultimately depends on its domestic governance quality. When domestic institutions function effectively, international influence tends to expand. When they visibly dysfunction, influence inevitably contracts."

DIPLOMATIC RECOVERY EFFORTS

PATHWAYS TO REBUILD CREDIBILITY

POST-VIETNAM AMERICAN REBUILDING (1975-1985)

- Bipartisan foreign policy consensus
- Institutional reforms
- Consistent alliance commitment
- Values leadership

GERMAN DEMOCRATIC INTEGRATION (1949-1970s)

- Democratic institutionalization
- Multilateral commitment
- Cross-transition policies
- Historical accountability

SOUTH KOREAN DEMOCRATIC CONSOLIDATION (1987-2000s)

- Democratic institutionalization
- Economic model credibility
- Regional leadership
- Values alignment

JAPANESE POST-WAR REPUTATION REBUILDING

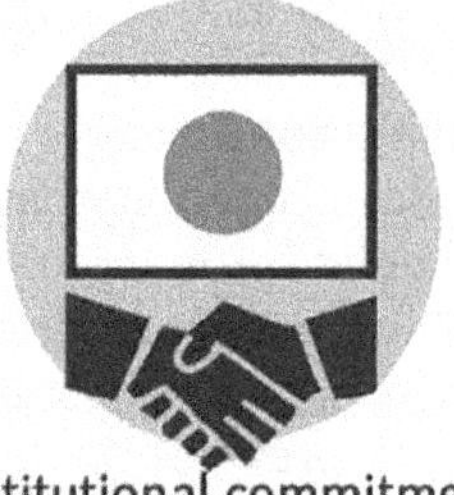

- Constitutional commitment
- Beneficial economic model
- Institutional stability
- Diplomatic consistency

STRATEGIES TO RESTORING

INSTITUTIONAL REFORM

ALLIANCE

CONSISTENCY

STRATEGIC PATIENCE

Data Visualization: Trust in US Leadership

McSlicey, the High Priest, presents data visualizations tracking international confidence in American leadership, revealing concerning trends with strategic implications.

"The data tells a sobering story about international perception of American leadership," McSlicey explains, displaying a series of graphs. "We're witnessing significant volatility and overall decline across key metrics."

His visualizations show:

Allied Leadership Confidence Trajectory: A line graph tracking confidence in U.S. leadership among traditional allies shows dramatic oscillations corresponding to administration changes, with the overall trendline declining significantly since 2000. The Trump administration marked a historic low point, with partial recovery under Biden, followed by renewed concerns in Trump 2.0.

Issue-Area Trust Differentiation: Bar charts illustrate the dramatic variation in trust in American leadership by issue area. Security commitments maintain relatively higher trust levels, while climate change, human rights, and

multilateral cooperation show significantly lower confidence. The visualization reveals that allies are increasingly compartmentalizing their trust in American leadership, rather than viewing it as a whole.

Regional Variation Analysis: Heat maps reveal significant regional differences in perceptions of American leadership. European allies exhibit particularly sharp declines in confidence, while Asian partners maintain somewhat higher trust levels, largely due to security concerns about China. Middle Eastern states display increasing hedging behaviors, maintaining formal relationships while developing alternative partnerships.

Alternative Partnership Development: Trend lines track increasing engagement between traditional American allies and alternative partners, particularly China. The data shows steady growth in economic relationships, diplomatic engagement, and even security dialogues between U.S. allies and potential competitors—classic hedging behavior indicating declining confidence in American reliability.

Recovery Scenario Modeling: Projection graphs model potential recovery trajectories under different governance scenarios. The key finding is that even under optimistic domestic governance improvement scenarios, trust rebuilding follows a "slow recovery" pattern, requiring a sustained demonstration of reliability rather than a rapid restoration.

"The data highlights a critical asymmetry," McSlicey concludes, adjusting his tie. "Trust in leadership declines rapidly during periods of volatility but rebuilds much more slowly, creating cumulative strategic costs that persist long after specific triggering events."

Alliance Relationship Stabilization

Cross-Time Commitment

Treaties & bipartisan laws lock in funding and principles—frameworks outlast elections

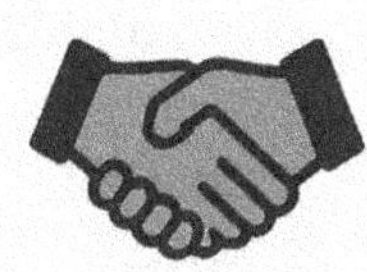

Institutional Infrastructure

Standing councils, crisis hotlines, and joint commands keep cooperation running even in political storms

People-to-People Ties

Student exchanges, sister cities, civil society projects weave social fabric beyond governments

Credibility Initiatives

Shared costs, transparent limits, and steady delivery prove reliability over time

Case Studies: Diplomatic Recovery Efforts

Despite significant challenges, historical examples demonstrate pathways for rebuilding international credibility following periods of volatility and reduced trust.

"We're not the first nation to face a credibility deficit," notes **Lady Liberty**, her torch casting flickering shadows. "Examining successful recovery efforts reveals viable strategies for restoring American leadership."

She highlights several instructive cases:

★ **Post-Vietnam American Rebuilding (1975-1985)**: Following the Vietnam War and Watergate, American standing recovered through a bipartisan foreign policy consensus, institutional reforms addressing overreach, consistent alliance commitment despite political changes, a values-based leadership approach emphasizing human rights, and strategic patience that allowed for incremental trust rebuilding over nearly a decade.

★ **German Democratic Integration (1949-1970s)**: Post-World War II Germany overcame profound trust deficits through democratic institutionalization, demonstrating transformation, multilateral commitment via European integration, consistent cross-transition policies, historical accountability, and prioritizing alliance reliability over short-term interests.

★ **South Korean Democratic Consolidation (1987-2000s)**: South Korea's transition to stable democracy enhanced its standing through democratic institutionalization, economic model credibility via transparent governance, regional leadership initiatives, values alignment with democratic partners, and effective governance, demonstrating its implementation capacity.

★ **Japanese Post-War Reputation Rebuilding**: Japan transformed from an aggressor to a respected democracy through its constitutional commitment to peaceful engagement, the development of a beneficial economic model, institutional stability that provided predictability, diplomatic consistency across political transitions, and the maintenance of a reliable alliance despite domestic political changes.

"These cases share crucial commonalities," Lady Liberty concludes. "Recovery required institutional reforms addressing root causes rather than merely messaging changes. It demanded consistency across political transitions. And it proceeded incrementally through demonstrated reliability rather than declared intentions."

She notes that America's challenge combines elements from multiple historical cases: "Like post-Vietnam America, we must restore confidence after policy failures. Like democratizing states, we must demonstrate that our institutions remain fundamentally sound despite visible dysfunction."

Rebuilding Relationships

Institutional Ties Strengthening

- Builds continuity through career-level relationship reinforcement
- Formal bureaucratic connections
- Institutionalized dialogue mechanisms
- Joint training programs
- Personnel exchanges building shared understanding
- Integrated planning creating operational interdependence

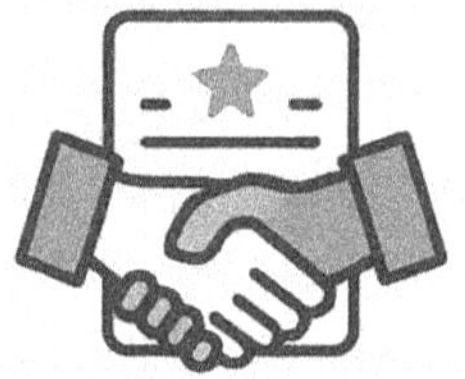

Treaty Framework Reinforcement

- Formalizes commitments through core reaffirmation
- Implementation mechanism strengthening
- Enhanced reporting requirements
- Clarified dispute resolution procedures
- Modernized consultation protocols
- Technical annex updates maintaining relevance

Strategic Communication Planning

- Maintains consistent messaging through cross-government development
- Key audience identification
- Alternative narrative preparation for misinformation
- Cross-administration continuity planning

Policy Proposal: Alliance Relationship Stabilization

Restoring American credibility requires systematic mechanisms to stabilize alliance relationships, designed to transcend political volatility and maintain stability.

"We need to rebuild trust through structures that maintain relationship consistency despite domestic political changes," argues **Lady Liberty**. "This requires institutional innovations specifically designed for periods of volatility."

She outlines a comprehensive stabilization framework:

★ **Cross-Time Commitment Mechanisms**: Ensure consistency through framework agreements that establish core principles, prioritize treaty status for durability, broaden support through congressional-executive agreements, stabilize funding with implementation legislation, maintain cross-party investment through bipartisan working groups, and foster relationship depth through state and local government partnerships.

★ **Institutional Relationship Infrastructure**: Establishes enduring structures through enhanced alliance consultation mechanisms, crisis communication protocols that transcend political volatility, permanent bilateral institutions with independent authorities, deepening of military-to-military relationships, intelligence sharing frameworks with safeguards, and regulatory cooperation that supports economic integration.

★ **People-to-People Engagement Expansion**: Builds societal connections through enhanced educational exchanges, revitalization of sister city relationships, partnerships with professional associations, civil society engagement that complements official channels, cultural diplomacy that reinforces shared values, and private sector coordination that supports economic ties.

★ **Credibility Demonstration Initiatives**: Rebuilds trust through consistent burden-sharing frameworks, mutual interest articulation that highlights benefits, transparency about limitations, investment in implementation capacity to prove capability, strategic patience through sustained engagement, and credible bipartisan messaging about commitment durability.

"These mechanisms construct relationship architecture that can withstand political turbulence," Lady Liberty emphasizes. "Rather than promising unrealistic stability, we acknowledge volatility while creating structures specifically designed to manage it."

She notes that successful alliance stabilization requires acknowledging legitimate concerns: "Our partners aren't wrong to question American reliability given recent experience. Rebuilding trust requires demonstrating understanding of these concerns while creating concrete mechanisms to address them."

Implementation Strategy: Rebuilding Relationships

Translating alliance stabilization concepts into operational reality requires practical implementation strategies that navigate political constraints while effectively rebuilding trust and confidence.

"Implementation must be pragmatic and sequential," advises **McSlicey, the High Priest**. "Trust rebuilding follows specific patterns that must guide our operational approach."

He outlines a viable implementation pathway:

★ **Institutional Ties Strengthening**: Builds continuity through career-level relationship reinforcement, formal bureaucratic connections, institutionalized dialogue mechanisms, joint training programs, personnel exchanges, fostering a shared understanding, and integrated planning, thereby creating operational interdependence.

★ **Treaty Framework Reinforcement**: Formalizes commitments through core reaffirmation, strengthens implementation mechanisms, enhances reporting requirements, clarifies dispute resolution procedures, modernizes consultation protocols, and updates technical annexes, thereby maintaining relevance.

★ **Strategic Communication Planning**: Maintains consistent messaging through cross-government development, key audience identification, alternative narrative preparation for misinformation, cross-administration continuity planning, realistic capability expectation management, and trust-building milestone identification, demonstrating progress.

"Implementation sequencing is critical," McSlicey emphasizes, adjusting his tie. "Begin with relationship areas least affected by political volatility—military cooperation, intelligence sharing, economic integration—and use those foundations to rebuild trust for addressing more contentious issues."

He notes that effective implementation requires balancing transparency with reliability: "We must be honest about political constraints while demonstrating absolute commitment within those constraints. Promising more than we can deliver further damages credibility, while underselling our capabilities, misses an opportunity."

McSlicey's implementation timeline shows that credibility rebuilding follows a predictable pattern: "Initial focus must be on rebuilding basic trust through consistent behavior in core relationship areas. As that foundation strengthens, we can gradually expand cooperation into more complex or politically sensitive domains. This incremental approach reflects how trust actually rebuilds in human relationships."

CHAPTER TRANSITION: FROM GOVERNANCE TO HUMAN CAPITAL

The governance challenges we've examined—from leadership deficits to institutional erosion, from democratic vulnerability to polarization traps—share a common underlying dimension: they all ultimately rest on human capacity. Even the most brilliantly designed institutions and the most visionary leadership require people with the knowledge, skills, and commitment to bring ideas to life.

As **Admiral Accountability** observes from the bridge of USS *Democracy*: "A democratic republic is only as good as the citizens who comprise it and the officials who serve it. We've focused on the machinery of governance, but machinery requires operators with the right capabilities."

This recognition naturally leads us to our next exploration: America's human capital infrastructure—the systems that develop knowledge, cultivate talent, and prepare citizens for the demands of democratic participation and economic contribution in a competitive global environment.

Professor Continuum places a transitional bookmark in her lecture notes. "Having examined the governance systems that translate collective will into action, we must now turn to the knowledge systems that enable those governance mechanisms to function effectively. For what is a democracy without educated citizens? What is a competitive economy without skilled workers? What is a functional government without knowledgeable officials?"

In our next chapter, we'll examine how America's knowledge infrastructure—its educational institutions, research capabilities, talent development systems, and information ecosystems—faces both unprecedented challenges and remarkable opportunities that will fundamentally shape the nation's capacity to renew itself and compete globally in the Chinese AI Century.

The Coke bottle that landed so disruptively on the White House lawn serves as an apt metaphor for our transition. The artifact itself wasn't inherently destructive—it became problematic because the system encountering it lacked the knowledge framework to contextualize and manage it appropriately. As we shift from governance systems to knowledge systems, we'll explore how societies develop the human capabilities that make the difference between transformative adaptation and disoriented reaction when confronted with novel challenges.

TL;DR – America's governance crisis—manifested through institutional decay, tribal polarization, and information chaos—requires comprehensive Rooseveltian reforms to promote ethical leadership, modernize institutions, and establish democratic resilience mechanisms that can effectively compete with China's authoritarian alternative while strengthening America's distinctive democratic advantages.

CHAPTER 10: THE KNOWLEDGE ECONOMY: AMERICA'S ADVANCED DEGREE IN SELF-SABOTAGE AND CHINA'S PHD IN PATIENCE

> *"The general who wins a war makes many calculations in his temple before the battle is fought."*
> —Sun Tzu, The Art of War, Chapter 1

EXECUTIVE BRIEFING

1. Situation Snapshot

In the great commencement of nations, Uncle Sam lugs a diploma financed by $1.77 T in student debt while Uncle Xi strolls offstage with four million fresh STEM grads and a **Made in China 2035** sash. Higher-ed closures at home, new campuses abroad: the scoreboard writes itself.

2. Core Findings

Fault Line	Evidence	Strategic Impact
STEM Shortfall	4.7 M Chinese vs 0.57 M U.S. STEM grads/yr	8:1 talent gap in AI, quantum, biotech
Debt & Drift	$1.77 T loans; avg $37 K/grad	Moon-shot engineers become spreadsheet jockeys
Visa Vortex	18 % H-1B win; decade-long green-card queues	We train geniuses, Beijing hires them
R&D Retreat	Fed R&D 1.9 % → 0.7 % GDP since 1960s	From IP exporter to IP importer risk
Geo-Imbalance	90 % VC in 5 metros	Heartland talent stranded; political backlash

3. Risk Dashboard

Horizon	Risk	Cascading Effect
0-6 mo	**High**	Talent exodus; allies hedge bets
6-18 mo	**Med**	Supply-chain lock-in; R&D backlog widens
18-36 mo	**Guarded**	U.S. becomes net IP importer if inertia persists

4. Roosevelt 2.0 Playbook

Pillar	30-Day Sprint	12-Month Build-out
Talent Cultivation	Double NSF K-12 STEM grants; pilot 3rd-grade coding	**New GI Bill for AI** – free public STEM degrees + service-year
Talent Attraction	Staple green cards to U.S. STEM PhDs; lift H-1B cap	Create Startup-Visa lane; kill per-country backlogs
Lab-to-Factory Bridge	Fast-track 10 **Fraunhofer-USA** institutes	Tie federal grants to domestic pilot-production lines
R&D Surge	+$60 B to basic science; stand-up ARPA-Climate & ARPA-Bio	Hit 1.4 % GDP public R&D; seed $100 B tech endowment
Geographic Rebalance	Announce 20 Heartland tech hubs with matched VC	Universal gigabit + venture tax credits outside the coasts

5. Strategic Messaging

Brand every reform like a campaign poster: **"Make American Minds Great Again."** Frame scholarships, visas, and labs as **hard-power investments** that "beat China, build jobs, and bless the heartland."

6. Bottom Line

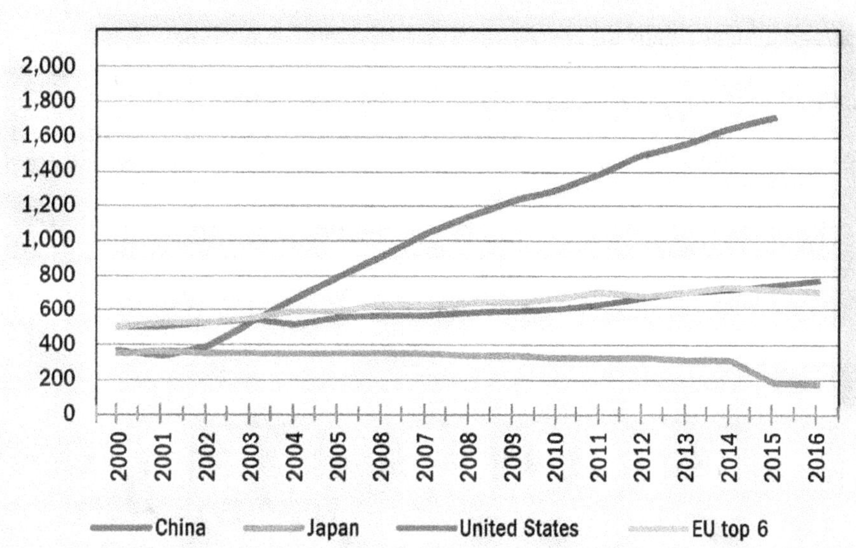

A superpower that underfunds schools, overprices college, and deports its own PhDs is **majoring in defeat**. Flip the tassel: fund brains like bombers, welcome talent like capital, and weld research to production before the diploma reads *Made Elsewhere*.

China has been **building the equivalent of almost one new university per week** in recent years—an educational arms race that would make McSlicey the Priest of Productivity perform ritualistic spreadsheet ceremonies in sheer awe. Meanwhile, across the Pacific, American academia withers under what can only be described as the Trump 2.0 administration's systematic academic exorcism, where universities aren't seen as knowledge factories but as liberal indoctrination chambers requiring immediate budgetary salvation through fiscal starvation. This ideological divergence finds statistical validation in Harvard Business School scholar Michael Horn's projection that 40% of U.S. colleges may close—a figure that has Milton the Trickster Economist performing triumphant backflips while shouting "creative destruction!" from his invisible soap box. The irony crystallizes: as Beijing breaks ground on campus number fifty-something this year, Washington breaks spirits with red-tape burial number who's even-counting.

OPENING TABLEAU: THE GRADUATION CEREMONY OF NATIONS

The Grand Hall of National Achievement, a metaphysical auditorium where countries receive their educational credentials. Two figures approach the stage as cosmic professors look on with varying expressions of amusement, concern, and resignation.

Uncle Sam strides confidently toward the podium, wearing a graduate cap bedazzled with student loan bills, visa rejection stamps, and social media logos. The tassel is a Twitter bird that keeps distracting him. His graduation gown—once spotless academic regalia—is now emblazoned with corporate logos, each paying for prime placement.

"United States of America," announces Chronos, the timekeeper of civilizations, "we confer upon you this Advanced Degree in Strategic Self-Sabotage, with specializations in Talent Repulsion, Research Disinvestment, and Educational Inequality. Your thesis on 'How to Train the World's Brightest Minds and Then Send Them Home' was particularly impressive."

Uncle Sam accepts the ornate diploma with a puzzled smile. He glances at the fine print about student loan repayments while checking his phone. "We're still number one, right?" he whispers to no one in particular.

Several paces behind, Uncle Xi approaches, his graduate cap adorned with STEM statistics, global talent recruitment plans, and semiconductor blueprints. His gown is embroidered with the characters for "patience" and "strategic vision," and he carries a scroll labeled "Century Planning."

"People's Republic of China," Chronos continues, "we bestow upon you this PhD in Strategic Patience, with honors in Talent Cultivation, Long-term Investment, and Systematic Planning. Your dissertation on 'The Hundred-Year Marathon: Overtaking America One STEM Graduate at a Time' demonstrated remarkable foresight."

Uncle Xi accepts his credentials with a deep, respectful bow, tucking them carefully into a portfolio labeled "Made in China 2035." He offers a tight smile to Uncle Sam—the kind that acknowledges a rival while calculating the precise moment to surpass them.

In the back of the hall, Milton the Trickster Economist—resplendent in a suit that changes colors depending on which economic theory is currently fashionable—ascends to deliver the commencement address.

"Distinguished nations, congratulations on your educational achievements," Milton begins, his voice oscillating between Chicago School certainty and behavioral economics doubt. "Today I'll explain why education investment doesn't matter, then why it's all that matters, and finally why markets solve everything—unless they don't." He chuckles, flipping through notes that rearrange themselves with each market fluctuation.

As Milton drones on about comparative advantage and efficient markets, Uncle Sam scrolls through his Twitter feed, occasionally nodding as if listening. Uncle Xi uses the time to review his notes on quantum computing research and semiconductor manufacturing.

"In conclusion," Milton announces with a flourish, "the nation that invests in human capital will ultimately triumph—though this conclusion may not hold if my assumptions are questioned in any way." He bows dramatically as his suit shifts from Keynesian green to Friedman blue.

The graduates file out—America to an after-party celebrating past glories, China to a strategic planning session for future dominance. The gods watch from above, placing celestial bets on which approach will triumph in the knowledge century ahead.

1. THE GREAT BRAIN RACE: TALENT AS A STRATEGIC RESOURCE

> *"If you plan for a hundred years, educate people."*
> —Guan Zhong (Guanzi)

In the grand casino of geopolitical competition, the chips are no longer made of military hardware or territorial claims—they're made of gray matter. Human capital—the collective capacity for innovation, problem-solving, and technical mastery—has emerged as the fundamental resource of the AI century. Nations that cultivate, attract, and deploy this resource effectively will dominate; those that don't will decline, regardless of their past glory or present swagger.

"The strategic battleground has shifted," explains Dr. Geopoliticus, adjusting her augmented reality glasses to display global talent flows. "Throughout history, nations competed for territory, then for industrial capacity, then for technological edge. Now they compete for brains—the raw cognitive capacity to drive innovation in an era where AI, quantum computing, and biotechnology determine power."

Character Dialogue:

A virtual meeting between Education Minister Wang of China and the American Education Secretary. The Americans' screen keeps freezing as spotty Wi-Fi interrupts their conversation.

MINISTER WANG: "Our latest five-year plan increases STEM education funding by 47%, with particular focus on quantum computing, artificial intelligence, and advanced materials science. We're building seventeen new technical universities and doubling research stipends for doctoral candidates."

US EDUCATION SECRETARY: *(checking phone notifications)* "That sounds... ambitious. We're focusing on, um... student loan forgiveness debates and whether math curriculums are too stressful. Oh, and our latest TikTok challenge about school spirit!"

MINISTER WANG: "Interesting approach. Meanwhile, we're requiring coding education to begin in third grade and doubling the hours of mathematics instruction. What's your administration's view on the concerning decline in American college STEM completion rates?"

US EDUCATION SECRETARY: *(looking panicked)* "Sorry, I need to take this call from a campaign donor—I mean, educational stakeholder. Can we circle back later? America is totally committed to competing with... uh..." *(looks at notes)* "... Canada? No, wait, China! That's you!"

MINISTER WANG: *(sipping tea patiently)* "Of course. We'll be here. Planning. Investing. Waiting."

AMERICA'S STEM REPORT CARD

SEE ME AFTER CLASS

(IF YOU CAN FIND THE CLASSROOM)

SUBJECT	GRADE	COMMENTS
Mathematics	D-	Ranks 31st globally on PISA assessments. Shows declining interest in trying.
Science	C	Occasional flashes of brilliance overshadowed by systematic underperformance.
Computer Science	C	Strong performance from elite students; majority population lacks basic exposure.
Engineering	C	Infrastructure crumbling faster than we're training engineers to fix it.
STEM Teacher Recruitment	F	Paying teachers 60% of what they could earn in Industry What could go wrong?
STEM Graduate Production	D	China: 4.7 million annually, USA: 568,00 We're only behind by ..calculator breaks
Overall STEM Attitude	C-	(Parents too busy arguing about curriculum to attend conference)
PARENT SIGNATURE:		

The Historical Trajectory: From Muscles to Minds

Throughout the Industrial Revolution, the concept of strategic advantage underwent significant evolution. The First Industrial Revolution prized physical labor and basic mechanical skills. The Second added technical specialization and organizational capacity. The digital revolution valued programming talent and systems thinking.

Today's knowledge economy represents a quantum leap in this progression—a competition not just for specialized skills but for fundamental innovation capacity. The ability to develop artificial intelligence, quantum computing, advanced materials, and biotechnology breakthroughs has become the determinant of national power.

China recognized this shift earlier than most. In 2008, President Hu Jintao introduced the "Thousand Talents Plan" to attract top scientists to return to China. By 2015, the "Made in China 2025" initiative explicitly targeted leadership in advanced technology sectors. These weren't mere industrial policies but comprehensive talent strategies—recognition that human capital would define China's future position.

America, meanwhile, has approached human capital development with characteristic inconsistency. Despite rhetoric about competitiveness, U.S. policy has oscillated between neglect and panic, with occasional bursts of strategic investment (often in response to perceived Chinese threats) followed by long periods of inattention.

Milton the Trickster Economist Explains Talent Economics

Milton materializes in a puff of supply-demand curves, his suit now adorned with equations and graphs that constantly update with global education metrics.

"The talent economy operates on principles that would make Adam Smith weep into his invisible hand," Milton declares, summoning a holographic model of global brain circulation. "Nations that systematically invest in human

capital development show increasing returns to scale—a mathematical way of saying 'the smart get smarter.' Meanwhile, countries that neglect this investment experience an accelerating decline, regardless of past advantages."

Milton's model shows that American education investment is plateauing, while Chinese investment is rising exponentially. "Notice the inflection point," he says, pointing to the intersection of the curves. "That's what we economists call the 'oh shit' moment—technically speaking, of course."

Data Visualization: America's STEM Report Card

SUBJECT	GRADE	COMMENTS
Mathematics	D-	Ranks 31st globally on PISA assessments. Shows declining interest in trying.
Science	C-	A pattern of systematic underperformance overshadows occasional flashes of brilliance.
Computer Science	C	Strong performance from elite students; the majority population lacks basic exposure.
Engineering	C	Infrastructure is crumbling faster than we're training engineers to fix it.
STEM Teacher Recruitment	F	Paying teachers 60% of what they could earn in the industry. What could go wrong?
STEM Graduate Production	D	China: 4.7 million annually. USA: 568,000. We're only behind by... *calculator breaks.*
Overall STEM Attitude	C-	Celebrates tech company founders while cutting science budgets. Confused priorities.
PARENT SIGNATURE:	____________	(Parents are too busy arguing about the curriculum to attend the conference.)

The numbers behind this report card tell a stark story. While China produces approximately 4.7 million STEM graduates annually, the United States manages just 568,000—an 8:1 disadvantage. By 2030, China is expected to account for nearly 60% of all STEM graduates among major economies, with the U.S. share shrinking to approximately 4%.

American 15-year-olds rank 31st globally in mathematics, behind not just Asian competitors but many European nations. Perhaps most troubling is the distribution: America produces world-leading talent at the top end (our elite universities remain unmatched), but catastrophic underperformance across the broader population.

The Geopolitical Implications

This talent gap represents more than an educational challenge—it's a fundamental threat to American security, prosperity, and global influence. In the AI era, technological advantage flows directly from human capital advantage. Nations that cannot develop or attract sufficient talent will find themselves increasingly dependent on others for critical technologies—a form of vassalage no less real for being digital rather than territorial.

"The nation that leads in artificial intelligence will rule the world," intones Dr. Geopoliticus, referencing Vladimir Putin's famous declaration. "But AI leadership doesn't materialize from thin air—it emerges from educational systems, research institutions, and talent pools developed over decades."

China's systematic approach to talent development reflects this understanding. From the Thousand Talents Plan to the Double First-Class University initiative to generous research funding, Beijing has implemented a comprehensive strategy for human capital development. The United States, by contrast, lacks a coherent national approach, with education policy fragmented across federal, state, and local jurisdictions and subject to the whims of politics.

As Milton the Trickster Economist observes, adjusting his rapidly shifting theoretical spectacles: "America is operating on the curious assumption that it can maintain technological leadership while systematically underinvesting in the human capital that produces technology. This is like expecting to win a marathon while cutting off your own legs—an interesting theoretical proposition but practically suboptimal."

2. THE NEW GI BILL: EDUCATION FOR THE AI AGE

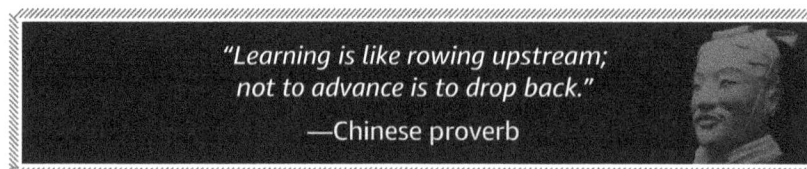

"Learning is like rowing upstream; not to advance is to drop back."

—Chinese proverb

Scene: The Roosevelt Presidential Library, after hours. The ghosts of Franklin and Eleanor Roosevelt review documents in a pool of ethereal light, examining statistics on American education.

EDUCATION AS STRATEGIC INVESTMENT, NOT PRIVATE CONSUMPTION

- The GI Bill provided college education and other benefits to millions of veterans

SERVICEMEN'S READJUSTMENT ACT
(1944) education, training, mortgages

$113B	8M	7:1
INVESTMENT	VETERANS SERVED	RETURN

ENGINEER SCIENTIST DOCTOR ENTREPRENEUR

Powered the U.S. economic boom: interstate highway, computing, medicine, middle class

MILTON: "Actually, the free market efficiently allocates educational resources through price signals that—"

GHOSTS OF FDR AND ELEANOR: *(in unison)* "Oh, shut up, Milton."

Education as Strategic Investment, Not Private Consumption

The fundamental paradigm shift needed in American education policy is conceptual: education should be understood as a strategic national investment rather than a private consumption good. This was the insight behind the original GI Bill—perhaps the most successful domestic policy in American history—and it needs to be reclaimed for the AI Age.

The GI Bill of 1944 (officially the Servicemen's Readjustment Act) provided college education, vocational training, low-cost mortgages, and business loans to nearly 8 million returning World War II veterans. The investment was substantial—approximately $113 billion in today's dollars—but the returns were astronomical.

Those educated veterans powered the greatest economic boom in American history, with the GI Bill estimated to have returned $7 for every $1 invested. They became the engineers who built the interstate highway system, the scientists who pioneered computing, the doctors who advanced medical care, and the business leaders who helped create the American middle class.

GHOST OF FDR: *(adjusting spectacles)* "Seventeen trillion in student debt? Seventy percent of graduates starting careers underwater? And they call this the American Dream? Sounds more like the American Albatross."

GHOST OF ELEANOR: "Franklin, remember when we passed the GI Bill? One of the greatest investments in human capital in history. It transformed a generation of veterans into engineers, doctors, scientists, and business leaders. The return on investment was..."

GHOST OF FDR: *(calculating)* "...Seven to one. For every dollar spent, seven dollars are returned in economic growth and tax revenue. Not to mention the intangibles—innovation, civic engagement, and national unity. A strategic masterstroke disguised as compassion."

GHOST OF ELEANOR: *(examining current charts)* "Now they treat education as a private good to be financed through individual debt, rather than a national investment. Where is today's GI Bill? The strategic equivalent for the AI Age?"

GHOST OF FDR: *(grimly)* "China understands what we've forgotten. They're investing in their people while we're extracting from ours. It's like we're running the Hoover administration's playbook while they're running... well, ours."

Milton the Trickster Economist appears in a swirl of conflicting equations

The Student Debt Crisis: America's Self-inflicted Brain Drain

America has effectively privatized higher education financing, shifting costs from the public to individual students and their families. The results are catastrophic: total student. loan debt has reached an unprecedented $1.77 trillion, with average bachelor's graduate carrying about $37.000

Career Distortion
Debt-burdened graduates often choose higher-paying careers over more innovative or socially beneficial ones

Risk Aversion
Federal Reserve researchers have found that heavy student loans discourage entrepreneurship

Reduced Access
Rising costs deter many potential students, particularly from lower-income backgrounds, from pursuing higher education at all

Delayed Life Milestones
Graduates struggling with debt postpone buying homes, starting families, and making other investments that contribute to economic growth and stability

More than education funding, the GI Bill represented a fundamental reconceptualization of the government's role in human capital development. It recognized that broad-based access to education wasn't just beneficial for individuals—it was essential for national prosperity, innovation, and security.

The Student Debt Crisis: America's Self-Inflicted Brain Drain

Today's approach could hardly be more different. America has effectively privatized higher education financing, shifting costs from the public to individual students and their families. The results are catastrophic: total student loan debt has reached an unprecedented $1.77 trillion, with the average bachelor's graduate carrying about $37,000 in loans.

This debt burden doesn't just hurt individuals; it damages America's innovation capacity in multiple ways:

1. **Career Distortion:** Debt-burdened graduates often choose higher-paying careers over more innovative or socially beneficial ones. The brilliant physicist who becomes a hedge fund analyst represents a loss to America's innovation ecosystem.
2. **Risk Aversion:** Federal Reserve researchers have found that heavy student loan debt discourages entrepreneurship. When you're making monthly payments the size of a mortgage, you're less likely to quit your safe corporate job to launch a startup.
3. **Reduced Access:** Rising costs deter many potential students, particularly those from lower-income backgrounds, from pursuing higher education altogether—a massive waste of potential talent.
4. **Delayed Life Milestones:** Graduates struggling with debt postpone buying homes, starting families, and making other investments that contribute to economic growth and stability.

McSlicey the Consultant Presents: The Education ROI Matrix

McSlicey the Consultant materializes beside a gleaming PowerPoint slide, wearing an immaculately tailored suit with price tags still attached ($5,000 per day plus expenses).

"Our proprietary analysis reveals a troubling disconnect between educational investment strategies and national competitiveness outcomes," McSlicey intones, clicking to a quadrant chart labeled with meaningless but impressive-sounding categories.

"America has created the 'worst of both worlds'—a system that simultaneously fails to educate enough of the population while financially crippling those who do pursue degrees. Meanwhile, China occupies the 'strategic investor' quadrant, with broader access and lower individual cost burdens."

McSlicey clicks to a slide showing international comparisons: Chinese public university tuition averages under $1,000 annually, German universities are largely free, and Scandinavian countries actually pay students stipends. Only America and the UK have shifted to debt-financed models, with the US taking this approach to the extreme.

"Our recommendation," McSlicey concludes, adjusting gold cufflinks, "is a strategic paradigm shift to reposition education as a national investment within the Human Capital Excellence Framework™, available as a separate consulting engagement for just $4.7 million."

Satirical Advertisement: "The Revolutionary Concept: Educated Citizens Benefit the Country (Not Just Themselves)"

ANNOUNCING THE RADICAL NOTION THAT EDUCATING AMERICANS MIGHT HELP AMERICA

In a shocking departure from current wisdom, evidence suggests that having more educated citizens could benefit the entire nation, not just individual degree-holders!

ANNOUNCING THE RADICAL NOTION THAT EDUCATING AMERICANS MIGHT HELP AMERICA
REVOLUTIONARY FEATURES:
• Engineers who can build things besides social media algorithms
• Scientists who solve real problems like ciimate change and disease
• Citizens who understand basic statistics and can't be easily manipulated "
• Workers prepared for tomorrow's economy, not yesterday's
• Reduced dependency on foreign talent for critical technologies
BUT WAIT, THERE'S MORE!
Studies show that every dollar invested in education returns apprroxmately $7-10 in economic growth and tax revenue. This "mathematics" concept suggests that education funding is not actually government "spending" but rather an "investment" with "returns."
Warning: Side effects may include increased innovation, strengthened democracy, enhanced national security, and reduced susceptibility to conspiracy theories.
Ask your congressional representative if education investment is right for America.

REVOLUTIONARY FEATURES:

- ★ Engineers who can build things besides social media algorithms
- ★ Scientists who solve real problems like climate change and disease
- ★ Citizens who understand basic statistics and can't be easily manipulated
- ★ Workers prepared for tomorrow's economy, not yesterday's
- ★ Reduced dependency on foreign talent for critical technologies

BUT WAIT, THERE'S MORE! Studies show that every dollar invested in education returns approximately $7 to $ 10 in economic growth and tax revenue. This "mathematics" concept suggests that education funding is not actually government "spending" but rather an "investment" with "returns."

Warning: Side effects may include increased innovation, strengthened democracy, enhanced national security, and reduced susceptibility to conspiracy theories. Ask your congressional representative if investing in education is right for America.

The investment would be substantial—perhaps $80-100

A New GI Bill for the AI Age

America needs a comprehensive education access plan equivalent to the original GI BIll--a strategic investment in human capital designed for the AI era.

Targeted Debt Relief
for STEM graduates who work in high-need fields or teach, with partial forgiveness for each year of service

Free Community College
for technical and associate degrees, creating accessible pathways into the modern workforce

Expanded Pell Grants
for low and middle-income students pursuing bachelor's degrees, reducing the need for loans

Income-Based Repayment
as the default for all student loans, capping payments at a small percentage of earnings

Public Service Loan Forgiveness
streamlined and expanded to reward work in education, healthcare, research, and other critical fields

Apprenticeship Expansion
based on the German dual-education model, creating technical career pathways that don't require traditional degrees

A New GI Bill for the AI Age

America needs a comprehensive education access plan equivalent to the original GI Bill—a strategic investment in human capital designed for the AI era. Key elements should include:

1. **Targeted Debt Relief** for STEM graduates who work in high-need fields or teach, with partial forgiveness for each year of service.
2. **Free Community College** for technical and associate degrees, creating accessible pathways into the modern workforce.
3. **Expanded Pell Grants** for low and middle-income students pursuing bachelor's degrees, reducing the need for loans.
4. **Income-Based Repayment** as the default for all student loans, capping payments at a percentage of earnings that is small.
5. **Public Service Loan Forgiveness** has been streamlined and expanded to reward work in education, healthcare, research, and other critical fields.
6. **Apprenticeship Expansion** based on the German dual-education model, creating technical career pathways that don't require traditional degrees.

The investment would be substantial—perhaps $80-100 billion annually above current education spending—but the returns would be exponentially greater in economic growth, tax revenue, innovation, and national security.

As the ghosts of the Roosevelts might observe, America faces a choice between short-term fiscal conservatism and long-term strategic investment. China has clearly chosen the latter path; America's hesitation represents one of the most consequential strategic mistakes of the 21st century.

3. IMMIGRATION REFORM: THE GLOBAL TALENT ATTRACTION ENGINE

> "When virtue shines, people come from afar."
> —Mencius

Scene: A government office labeled "U.S. Knowledge Economy Import Division." Visa THE GATEKEEPER, a bureaucrat with a giant rubber "REJECTED" stamp, processes dejected Ph.D.s, engineers, and entrepreneurs. Behind her desk, a digital counter displays: "Foreign-Founded U.S. Companies: 55% of Billion-Dollar Startups." Besides it, another counter clicks: "Days of H-1B Visa Processing Delays: 312 and counting."

VISA: *(examining a file)* "Dr. Patel, I see you have a PhD in quantum computing from MIT, three breakthrough patents, and a job offer from Google. Unfortunately, you lost our H-1B lottery. Try again next year—there's only an 18% chance of selection!"

DR. PATEL: "But my research could help America lead in quantum encryption..."

VISA: *(already stamped)* "REJECTED. Next!"

From across the room, IMMIGRANT INNOVATOR IQBAL—a brilliant engineer with multiple patents—approaches SENATOR NATIVIST, who's inspecting the office with a suspicious expression.

IQBAL: "Senator, may I have a moment? I've created technology that could revolutionize American manufacturing, but after ten years on a temporary visa with no path to permanence, I'm returning to my home country."

SENATOR NATIVIST: "Good! America for Americans! We don't need foreign... wait, did you say 'revolutionize manufacturing'? In my state?"

IQBAL: "I would have preferred that. My technology could have created an estimated 2,700 jobs. However, a Chinese firm has now offered funding, lab facilities, and permanent residence within 30 days. My family deserves stability."

SENATOR NATIVIST: *(sputtering)* "But... but... that's practically treason! Giving our technology to China!"

IQBAL: *(sighing)* "Senator, it's my technology. America trained me, then made it clear I wasn't welcome long-term. China is offering what America won't: certainty, opportunity, and respect. Basic economics, sir."

SENATOR NATIVIST: *(watching as Iqbal walks away)* "But... we're America. Everyone wants to come here... right?"

VISA: *(stamping another rejection)* "Next!"

If America's education system is shooting itself in one foot, its immigration system is busy reloading to shoot the other. Despite overwhelming evidence that high-skilled immigration fuels innovation and job creation, U.S. policy seems designed to repel the very talent we desperately need.

THE INNOVATION PREMIUM OF GLOBAL TALENT

Immigrant inventors generate patents at twice the rate of native-born Americans with similar educational backgrounds.

Foreign-born researchers author scientific papers cited 30% more frequently than the average publication.

Immigrant-founded companies employ an average of 20% more workers than native-founded firms in the same sectors.

The Innovation Premium of Global Talent

The statistics are staggering and unambiguous: Immigrants or their children founded 55% of America's billion-dollar startups. Foreign-born professionals constitute approximately 25% of the U.S. STEM workforce. A quarter of all U.S. public companies that went public since 1990 had at least one immigrant founder, including Google, Tesla, Moderna, and countless others.

The innovation premium from immigrant talent is well-documented:

- ★ **Immigrant inventors generate patents at twice the rate of native-born Americans** with similar educational backgrounds.
- ★ **Foreign-born researchers author scientific papers cited 30% more frequently** than the average publication.
- ★ **Immigrant-founded companies employ an average of 20% more workers** than native-founded firms in the same sectors.

This isn't surprising when we consider the selection effects: immigrants who overcome the significant barriers to entry into the U.S. tend to be exceptionally motivated, talented, and entrepreneurial. As one study concluded, "The average immigrant inventor creates more value than the average native-born inventor, making restrictive immigration

policy particularly costly in terms of lost innovation."

The H-1B Lottery: Vegas Has Better Odds

Despite this overwhelming evidence, America's high-skilled immigration system resembles a Kafka novel rewritten by the Marx Brothers. The flagship skilled worker visa, the H-1B, is capped at just 85,000 annually in a nation of 330 million. Demand far exceeds this arbitrary limit, resulting in an annual lottery in which only about 18% of applicants are successful.

Imagine running the NFL draft as a random lottery where teams might not get to pick any players at all, while the Chinese Football League gets the first choice of every top prospect. This isn't hyperbole—it's U.S. immigration policy. We literally roll the dice to decide if companies can hire the brilliant scientist or engineer who might develop the next breakthrough technology.

As one tech CEO put it, "We're asking the world's best talent to put their careers in the hands of a random number generator. Would you take those odds?"

Green Card Gridlock: Waiting for Decades

Even those lucky enough to secure an H-1B face another obstacle: the path to permanent residency. Due to per-country caps limiting any nationality to 7% of available green cards, professionals from populous nations like India and China face wait times measured in decades—yes, decades. An Indian AI researcher who starts the process today might not receive permanent residency until 2045.

GUARANTEED RESULTS
UNIVERSITY
AMERICA PAYS TO EDUCATE GLOBAL TALENT, THEN GIFTS THAT TALENT TO COMPETITORS
•CRITICAL TECHNOLOGIES DEVELOPED BY U.S.-TRAINED MINDS BENEFIT OTHER NATIONS
• AMERICA GRADUALLY LOSES INNOVATION LEADERSHIP WHILE WONDERING WHAT HAPPENED
"This strategy has helped us significantly."
—Chinese Ministry of Science and Technology

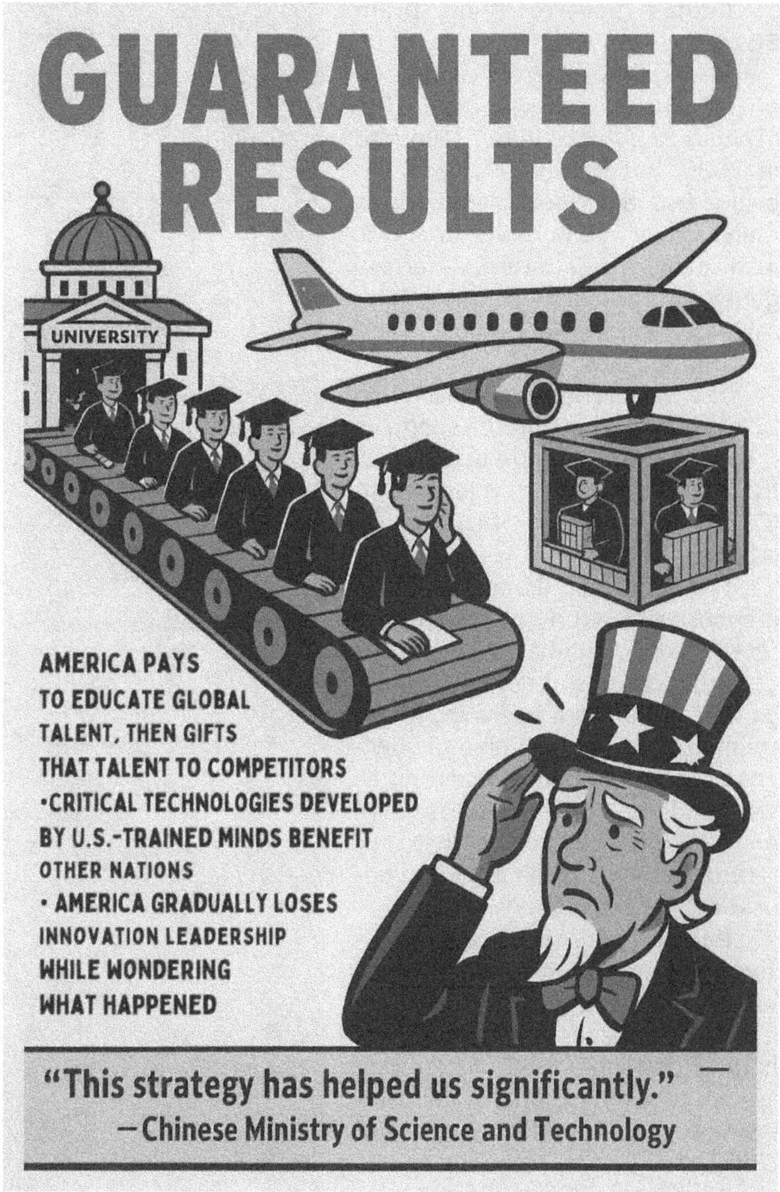

The absurdity reached new heights during Trump's first term, when his administration systematically tightened restrictions on skilled immigration. H-1B denial rates increased, processing was suspended during the pandemic, and policies were implemented to scrutinize applications more aggressively. Trump's "America First" rhetoric often equated all immigration with job competition, ignoring evidence that high-skilled immigrants create jobs and drive innovation.

Satirical Handbook: "How to Train the World's Best Then Send Them Home: A Guide to Strategic Self-Sabotage"

OFFICIAL U.S. GUIDE TO STRATEGIC TALENT REPULSION *Ensuring America's Competitors Get Our Best-Trained Minds*

CHAPTER 1: THE EDUCATION TRAP Attract the world's brightest to America's universities. Charge them a premium tuition. Ensure they fall in love with the American innovation culture.

CHAPTER 2: THE VISA MAZE Create a labyrinthine immigration system in which only 18% of skilled applicants succeed. Ensure unpredictable processing times and constantly changing requirements.

CHAPTER 3: THE PERMANENT IMPERMANENCE Keep talented immigrants in decades-long green card queues. Ensure they never know if they can stay long-term, buy a home, or put down roots.

CHAPTER 4: THE XENOPHOBIC ATMOSPHERE Periodically implement travel bans, make disparaging comments about immigrants' countries of origin, and generally create an unwelcoming cultural environment.

CHAPTER 5: THE CHINESE OPPORTUNITY Watch as China implements strategic talent recruitment programs, offering returning scientists state-of-the-art labs, housing allowances, and clear paths to permanence.

GUARANTEED RESULTS:

America pays to educate global talent, then gifts that talent to competitors

★ Critical technologies developed by U.S.-trained minds benefit other nations

★ America is gradually losing its innovation leadership while wondering what happened

"This strategy has helped us significantly." —Chinese Ministry of Science and Technology.

POLICY PROPOSAL:

COMPREHENSIVE IMMIGRATION REFORM

FOR INNOVATION LEADERSHIP

- Staple Green Cards to **Advanced STEM Degrees** - Automatic permanent residency for foreign students who earn advanced degrees in critical fields from U.S. universities
- Eliminate the H-1B Cap
  Replace the arbitrary lottery with a more flexible system that responds to economic needs and emphasizes critical skills
- Create a Startup Visa
  Dedicated pathway for foreign entrepreneurs with viable business plans and investment backing
- **Eliminate Country-Specific Caps**
  End the discriminatory system that creates decades-long backlogs for applicants from India and China
- **Streamline Processing - Invest in USCIS infrastructure to** reduce wait times and increase predictability
- National Security Balancing - Develop more sophisticated, targeted approaches to legitimate security concerns rather than broad restrictions

China's Reverse Brain Drain Strategy

Beijing has expertly capitalized on America's self-sabotage. The "Thousand Talents Plan," launched in 2008, has successfully recruited over 7,000 top researchers back to China, many of whom are from U.S. institutions. These returnees receive generous packages, including high salaries, housing allowances, and well-funded labs.

The results are undeniable: in 2010, 48% of Chinese scientists leaving the U.S. returned to China; by 2021, that figure had jumped to 67%. As one Chinese official boasted, "For the first time, we are seeing a reversal of brain drain. Top talent is choosing to return to China for the research opportunities."

America's loss becomes China's gain. It's as if we're operating a free training program for China's knowledge economy: educate their brightest minds at our universities, then make it so difficult to stay that they return home with their American education and connections intact.

Policy Proposal: Comprehensive Immigration Reform for Innovation Leadership

America needs a complete overhaul of its high-skilled immigration system to win the global talent competition. Key elements should include:

1. **"Staple" Green Cards to Advanced STEM Degrees** - Automatic permanent residency for foreign students who earn advanced degrees in critical fields from U.S. universities.
2. **Eliminate the H-1B Cap** - Replace the arbitrary lottery system with a more flexible approach that responds to economic needs and prioritizes critical skills.
3. **Create a Startup Visa** - A Dedicated pathway for foreign entrepreneurs with viable business plans and investment backing.
4. **Eliminate Country-Specific Caps** - End the discriminatory system that creates decades-long backlogs for applicants from specific countries, such as India and China.
5. **Streamline Processing** - Invest in USCIS infrastructure to reduce wait times and increase predictability.
6. **National Security Balancing** - Develop more sophisticated and targeted approaches to address legitimate security concerns, rather than imposing broad restrictions.

As Bill Gates testified to Congress, "It makes no sense to educate people in our universities, often with taxpayer dollars, and then send them home to compete against us. These smart people want to stay and work in the U.S. Let's make it easier for them to do so."

The strategic imperative is clear: in the global competition for talent, nations with the most welcoming, efficient, and predictable immigration systems will attract the best minds. America's traditional advantage as the world's premier destination for ambitious innovators is eroding rapidly. Reclaiming this advantage through comprehensive immigration reform is not just an economic necessity but a national security imperative.

The Academic Incentive Problem

Publication Prioritization

Faculty advancement depends primarily on journal publishing

Theoretical Emphasis

Theory is often rewarded over practical solutions

Disciplinary Silos

Departments operate separately, hindering collaboration

Slow Knowledge Transfer

Moving research to application is often slow

4. THE EDUCATION–INNOVATION DISCONNECT: BRIDGING THEORY AND PRACTICE

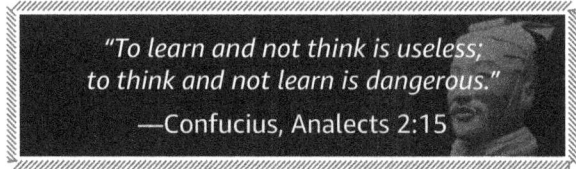

> *"To learn and not think is useless; to think and not learn is dangerous."*
> —Confucius, Analects 2:15

Scene: A university laboratory. PROFESSOR PEDAGOGUE—a distinguished academic with a tweed jacket and perpetually furrowed brow—examines student research proposals. Beside him, a stack of theoretical papers reaches the ceiling, while a much smaller pile labeled "Practical Applications" gathers dust.

PROFESSOR PEDAGOGUE: *(reviewing a proposal)* "Hmm, interesting quantum computing approach, but where's the theoretical framework? Where's the postmodern analysis of computational hegemony? This needs at least forty more citations to obscure journals."

GRADUATE STUDENT: "But, professor, we could actually build this within six months. It would be a working prototype that—"

PROFESSOR PEDAGOGUE: *(horrified)* "Build it? My dear student, we're theoretical researchers, not... engineers." *(shudders)* "Do you know what building things does to your publication count? Besides, tenure committees don't care about practical applications."

GRADUATE STUDENT: "But couldn't we partner with industry to—"

PROFESSOR PEDAGOGUE: *(interrupting)* "Industry? You mean those profit-obsessed philistines? What could they possibly contribute to our rarefied intellectual discourse?"

He gestures to the window, where PRACTICAL PRACTITIONER—a harried engineer from a tech company—stands outside in the rain, holding diagrams of real-world problems and looking forlornly at the laboratory.

PROFESSOR PEDAGOGUE: "Let me explain how academia works. We measure success by citation counts, journal prestige, and theoretical novelty. Whether anything actually functions in the real world is entirely beside the point."

GRADUATE STUDENT: *(looking at PRACTICAL PRACTITIONER)* "Is that why Chinese research labs have so many industry partnerships while we just write papers about writing papers?"

PROFESSOR PEDAGOGUE: *(not listening)* "Now, let's add six more equations and a reference to Foucault. That should secure publication in a journal that exactly twelve people worldwide will read."

One of America's most significant structural disadvantages in the knowledge economy race is the profound disconnect between academic knowledge production and practical application. The United States maintains

The Institutional Barriers

Legal Complexity

Intellectual property agreements between universities, researchers, and industry partners frequently involve Byzantine negotiations that delay commercialization

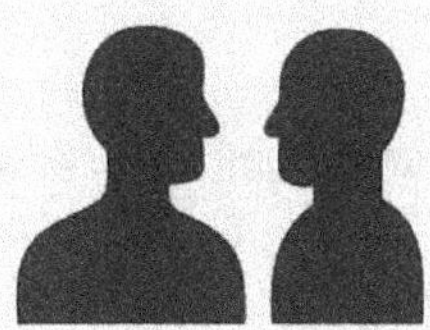

Cultural Divides

Academia and industry often view each other with suspicion -professors see companies as profit-obsessed, while industry sees academics as impractical theorists

Risk-Averse Investment

Venture capital increasingly favors software with quick returns over "deep tech" requiring longer development cycles world-leading universities that produce cutting-edge research. Still, the system for translating that research into practical innovation is broken in ways that our competitors have largely avoided.

The Academic Incentive Problem

American academia has developed an incentive structure that often works against national innovation needs:

1. **Publication Prioritization:** Faculty advancement primarily depends on publishing in prestigious journals, rather than developing practical applications. As one MIT professor noted, "I could develop a technology that creates thousands of jobs, but if I don't publish enough papers, I won't get tenure."
2. **Theoretical Emphasis:** Many disciplines reward theoretical complexity over practical utility. Papers that incrementally advance theory often receive more academic recognition than work that solves real-world problems.
3. **Disciplinary Silos:** University departments operate as separate fiefdoms, while most meaningful innovation requires cross-disciplinary collaboration. Computer scientists rarely collaborate with biologists, even when biological computing is at the forefront of research.
4. **Slow Knowledge Transfer:** The journey from university lab to commercial application often takes decades in the American system, with multiple institutional barriers along the way.

International Models: Learning from Competitors

Germany's Fraunhofer Institutes

- Network of 76 research institutes explicitly bridge academic research and industrial application
- They employ over 30,000 people
- Generate approx. €2.5 billion in annual research volume

Singapore's Agency for Science, Technology & Research (A+STAR)

- Coordinates research across universities, government labs, and industry
- Generate approx. €2.5 billion in annual research volume

South Korea's Institute for Basic Science (IBS)

- Focuses on fundamental research
- Explicit pathways to application through partner institutions and industry collaboration

China's Shanghai Model

- Chinese universities incorporate industry parks directly on campus
- Professors split time between academic research and commercial applications

The Institutional Barriers

Beyond individual incentives, structural barriers impede the flow of knowledge between sectors:

1. **University Technology Transfer Offices:** Often understaffed and risk-averse, these offices can become bottlenecks rather than facilitators of innovation.
2. **Legal Complexity:** Intellectual property agreements between universities, researchers, and industry partners frequently involve Byzantine negotiations that delay commercialization.
3. **Cultural Divides:** Academia and industry often view each other with suspicion—professors see companies as profit-obsessed, while industry sees academics as impractical theorists.
4. **Risk-Averse Investment:** Venture capital is increasingly favoring software with quick returns over "deep tech," which requires longer development cycles.

Milton the Trickster Economist Explains the Economics of Knowledge Transfer

Milton appears atop a whiteboard, juggling academic journals while balancing on a patent application.

"The market for knowledge transfer suffers from what economists call 'multiple equilibria,'" Milton explains, creating a complex model that keeps shifting forms. "We're stuck in a suboptimal equilibrium where academic prestige and practical innovation have diverged."

He points to statistics showing that while American universities produce the most cited research, China has become more efficient at turning research into commercial applications and patents. "China doesn't have better researchers, but they've created better institutional bridges between theory and practice."

Milton's model depicts a Chinese system in which universities, government labs, and companies operate in close coordination, compared to an American system of isolated institutions connected by fragile bridges. "It's not about individual brilliance but systemic effectiveness," he concludes, before dissolving into a cloud of efficiency equations.

International Models: Learning from Competitors

Several countries have developed more effective systems for connecting academic knowledge with practical innovation:

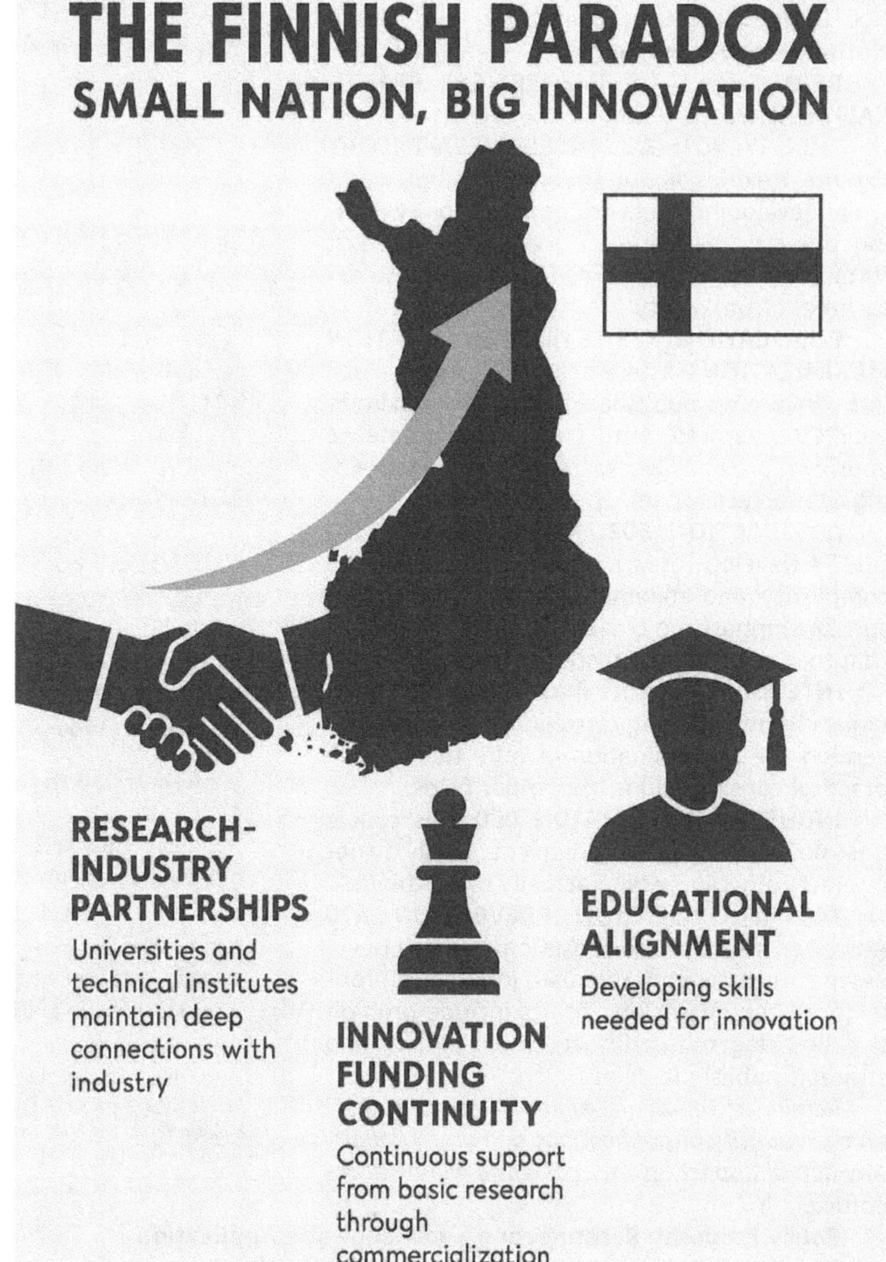
THE FINNISH PARADOX
SMALL NATION, BIG INNOVATION
RESEARCH-INDUSTRY PARTNERSHIPS
Universities and technical institutes maintain deep connections with industry
INNOVATION FUNDING CONTINUITY
Continuous support from basic research through commercialization
EDUCATIONAL ALIGNMENT
Developing skills needed for innovation

1. **Germany's Fraunhofer Institutes:** A network of 76 research institutes that explicitly bridge academic research and industrial application, with funding from both government and industry. They employ over 30,000 people and generate approximately €2.5 billion in annual research volume.
2. **Singapore's Agency for Science, Technology and Research (A*STAR):** Coordinates research across universities, government labs, and industry, with explicit commercialization targets and industry-relevant metrics.
3. **South Korea's Institute for Basic Science (IBS):** This institute focuses on fundamental research but has explicit pathways to application through partnerships with other institutions and industry collaborations.
4. **China's Shanghai Model:** Chinese universities increasingly incorporate industry parks directly on campus, and professors are encouraged to split their time between academic research and commercial applications.

These international models share common elements that are lacking in the American system: stable funding that spans from fundamental research to commercialization, metrics that value both theoretical contributions and practical applications, and institutional structures that facilitate rather than impede collaboration.

The Finnish Paradox: Small Nation, Big Innovation

Finland offers perhaps the most compelling alternative model. With just 5.5 million people, Finland has become an innovation powerhouse by systematically connecting education, research, and industry. Key elements include:

1. **Research-Industry Partnerships:** Universities and technical institutes maintain deep connections with industry, including joint research centers and faculty who move between sectors.
2. **Innovation Funding Continuity:** The Finnish Funding Agency for Innovation (Business Finland) provides continuous support from basic research through commercialization, avoiding the "valley of death" where promising technologies often die in the American system.
3. **Educational Alignment:** Finnish education is explicitly designed to develop skills needed for innovation, with a strong emphasis on both theoretical understanding and practical application.

The results are impressive: Finland consistently ranks among the world's most innovative economies despite its small size, with companies like Nokia emerging from this ecosystem to achieve global impact.

Satirical Course Catalog: "The Theory-Practice Divide: Knowing Everything and Doing Nothing – Advanced Seminar"

DEPARTMENT OF THEORETICAL PRACTICALITY *Where Ideas Go to Remain Ideas*

THEORY 401: ADVANCED META-THEORY Explore theories about theoretical frameworks while developing meta-frameworks for evaluating theoretical theories. Prerequisites: At least three previous theory courses and complete detachment from reality.

PUBLICATION 375: STRATEGIC CITATION MAXIMIZATION Master the art of slicing research into "minimum publishable units" to maximize your CV. Learn to write papers that reference your own previous work, creating a self-sustaining citation ecosystem.

ABSTRACTION 502: APPLIED INAPPLICABILITY Develop research questions of exquisite complexity and minimal practical relevance—special emphasis on creating models so abstract that they can never be tested empirically.

INTERDISCIPLINARY AVOIDANCE 290 Techniques for maintaining disciplinary silos and preventing the contamination of pure theory with practical considerations from other fields.

INDUSTRY INTERACTION 000 This course does not exist because academics typically do not interact with people who actually make things.

COMMERCIALIZATION PREVENTION 670 Advanced strategies for ensuring research never escapes the academy to create jobs, solve problems, or benefit society. Topics include prohibitive licensing terms, impenetrable jargon, and strategic publishing delays.

Reminder: Tenure decisions are based entirely on the quantity of publications and grant dollars. Any actual impact on the real world will be disregarded.

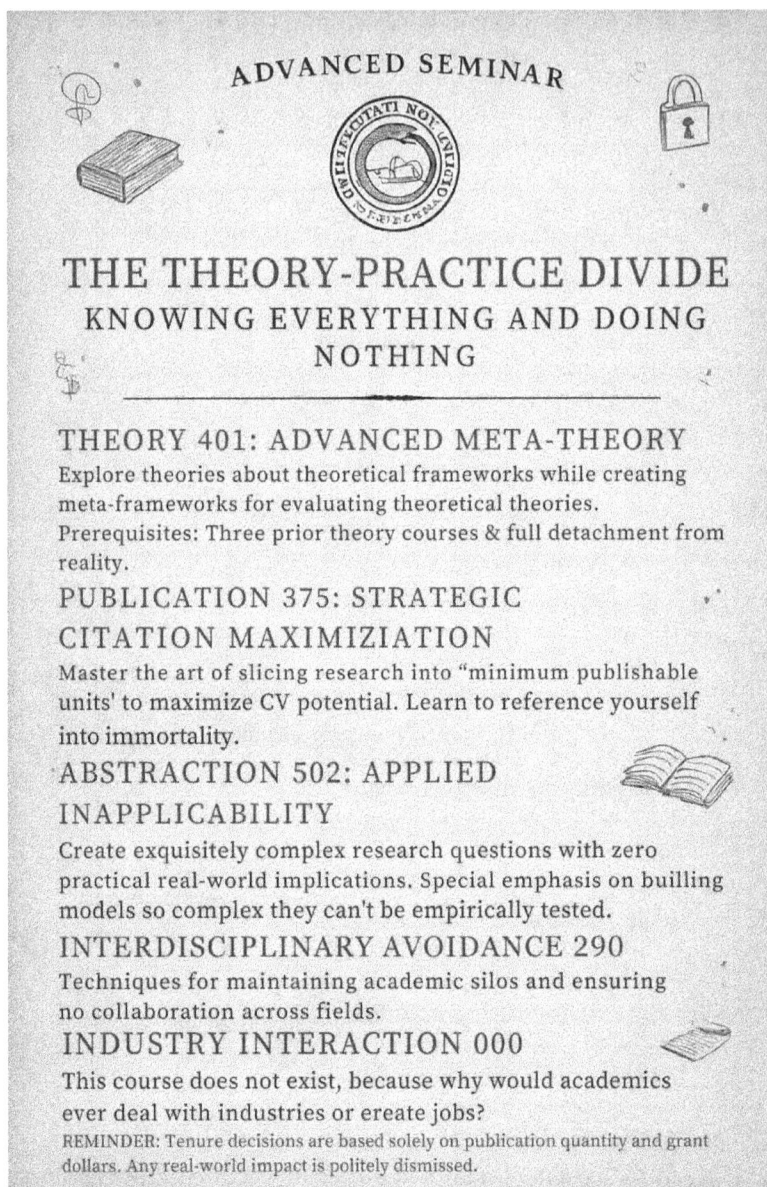

ADVANCED SEMINAR

THE THEORY-PRACTICE DIVIDE

KNOWING EVERYTHING AND DOING NOTHING

THEORY 401: ADVANCED META-THEORY

Explore theories about theoretical frameworks while creating meta-frameworks for evaluating theoretical theories. Prerequisites: Three prior theory courses & full detachment from reality.

PUBLICATION 375: STRATEGIC CITATION MAXIMIZIATION

Master the art of slicing research into "minimum publishable units' to maximize CV potential. Learn to reference yourself into immortality.

ABSTRACTION 502: APPLIED INAPPLICABILITY

Create exquisitely complex research questions with zero practical real-world implications. Special emphasis on builling models so complex they can't be empirically tested.

INTERDISCIPLINARY AVOIDANCE 290

Techniques for maintaining academic silos and ensuring no collaboration across fields.

INDUSTRY INTERACTION 000

This course does not exist, because why would academics ever deal with industries or ereate jobs?

REMINDER: Tenure decisions are based solely on publication quantity and grant dollars. Any real-world impact is politely dismissed.

Policy Proposal: Reconnecting Knowledge and Application

America needs comprehensive reform to bridge the theory-practice divide and reclaim leadership in translating knowledge into innovation:

1. **Academic Incentive Reform:** Incorporating commercialization metrics in tenure decisions, rewarding cross-disciplinary collaboration and practical impact, and creating faculty career paths valuing applied research.
2. **Institutional Bridge Building:** Establishing American versions of Fraunhofer Institutes across key technology domains, reforming university technology transfer offices with clear commercialization mandates, and creating innovation districts connecting academia and industry.
3. **Funding Mechanism Redesign:** Providing continuous funding from basic research through commercialization, requiring industry collaboration for certain federal grants, and incentivizing universities to measure and reward practical impact.
4. **Cultural Divide Solutions:** Encouraging cross-sector sabbaticals and appointments, reforming graduate education to include practical experience and entrepreneurship training, and celebrating faculty creating real-world impact alongside theoretical contributors.

These reforms wouldn't diminish America's leadership in fundamental research—they would amplify its impact by ensuring that discoveries don't remain trapped in academic journals, but instead drive economic growth, job creation, and strategic advantage.

As one Oxford scholar, studying different national innovation systems, observed, "America excels at creating knowledge but increasingly struggles to use that knowledge. Nations that bridge the gap between thinking and doing will lead the next wave of innovation."

Reconnecting Knowledge and Application

Academic Incentive Reform

- Incorporating commercialization metrics in tenure decisions in tenure discisions
- Rewarding cross-disciplinary collaboration and practical impact
- Creating faculty career aths valuing applied research

Institutional Bridge Building

- Establishing American verslons of Fraunhofer Institutes across key technology domains
- Reforming university technology transfer offices with clear commercialization mandates
- Creating innovation districts connecting academia and industry

Funding Mechanism Redesign

- Providing cotinuous funding from basic research through commercialization
- Requiring industry collaboration for certain federal grants
- Incentivizing universities to measure and reward practical impact

Cultural Divide Solutions

- Encouraging cross-sector sabbaticals and appointments

5. AMERICA'S R&D ENGINE: REBUILDING THE INNOVATION MACHINE

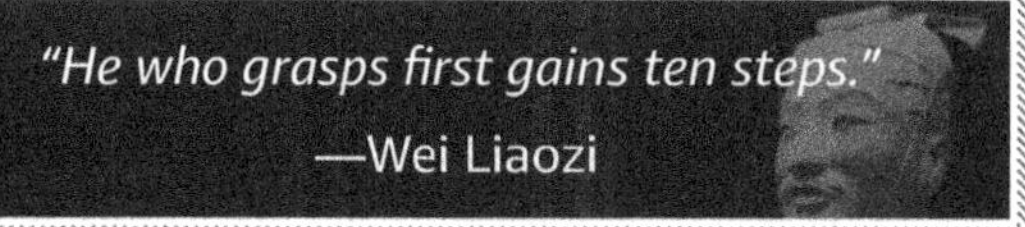

"He who grasps first gains ten steps."
—Wei Liaozi

Scene: A once-grand temple to innovation, now showing signs of neglect. Dr. DARPA—a brilliant but increasingly anxious figure in a lab coat decorated with faded insignia of past triumphs, including internet protocols, GPS coordinates, and mRNA sequences—tends a guttering flame labeled "American Innovation." Around her are dusty relics: an early internet router, touch screen prototypes, and autonomous vehicle blueprints. UNCLE SAM approaches with a nearly empty offering plate.

UNCLE SAM: *(nervously)* "O mighty Engine of Innovation, we face a formidable challenger from the East. Could you bless us with another world-changing breakthrough? Preferably by next quarter? The markets are watching."

DR. DARPA: *(sighing)* "My child, you once offered 1.9% of your GDP at my altar. Now you bring merely 0.7%. The sacred flames of discovery require fuel."

UNCLE SAM: *(defensive)* "But we have private companies now! Surely Apple and Google will handle innovation? They have hundreds of billions in cash reserves!"

DR. DARPA: *(holding up iPhone)* "This device incorporates 12 key technologies—from touch screens to GPS to AI voice recognition—all initially funded by government research. Companies optimize and commercialize; they rarely discover fundamental breakthroughs."

Meanwhile, in a gleaming research complex across the Pacific:

CHAIRMAN ROI (Return On Investment): *(bowing before a quantum computer)* "We offer 2.4% of our GDP and rising, with targeted investments in quantum computing, artificial intelligence, biotechnology, and renewable energy. Our patience is measured in decades, not quarters."

DR. DARPA: *(to SAM)* "Your competitor plays the long game. What is your strategy?"

UNCLE SAM: *(checking Twitter)* "Strategy? Well, we're cutting science budgets to fund tax breaks. That's a kind of strategy. Besides, the market will provide whatever innovation we need."

DR. DARPA: *(facepalming)* "The market funded the internet? GPS? Touchscreens? CRISPR? Decades before commercial viability was clear? You're confusing optimization with exploration, refinement with discovery."

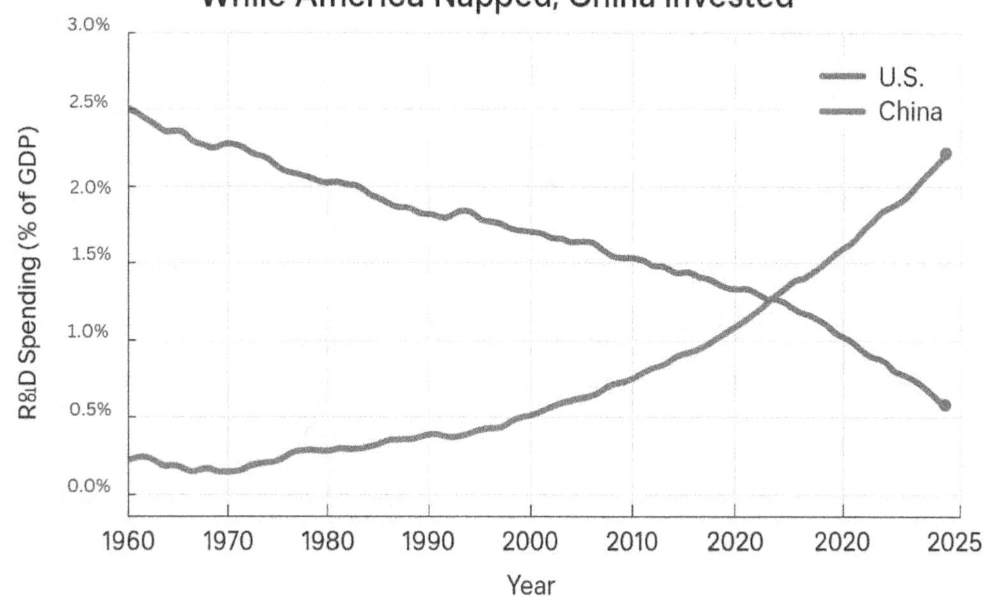

THE GREAT R&D DIVERGENCE:
While America Napped, China Invested

UNCLE SAM: *(defensively)* "But government picking winners and losers is socialism! Milton told me so!"

DR. DARPA: "Did Milton mention that every major technological revolution in modern history began with state-funded research? The semiconductor, the internet, GPS, touchscreens, AI, genomics—all started with government investment years or decades before markets saw value."

UNCLE SAM: *(looking at guttering flame)* "Oh... that's... inconvenient for my worldview. But surely the private sector would have eventually invented all those things?"

DR. DARPA: *(laughing sadly)* "Eventually? Perhaps. Just as eventually monkeys typing randomly might produce Shakespeare. But in geopolitical competition, 'eventually' means 'too late.'"

If education is the seed and talent is the soil, then research and development is the water that makes innovation grow. America's historic dominance in the knowledge economy was built on massive public investment in research and development (R&D), particularly during the Cold War, when federal spending reached a peak of 1.9% of GDP in the 1960s.

That investment yielded astonishing returns: the internet, GPS, touch screens, voice recognition, advanced materials, and mRNA vaccine technology—virtually every foundational technology in modern devices can be traced back to government-funded research. The private sector built commercial products on this foundation, but rarely would have funded the basic science itself.

The Great R&D Retreat

Yet America has been systematically disinvesting in this crucial infrastructure. Federal R&D spending has declined to approximately 0.7% of GDP—about one-third of its historical peak. We've shifted to a model where the industry provides approximately 73% of total R&D funding, with the government contributing just 21%.

This might seem reasonable—let private companies invest in what the market demands—but it reflects a fundamental misunderstanding of how innovation works. As Nobel laureate economist Joseph Stiglitz explains: "Private firms systematically underinvest in basic research because they cannot capture all the benefits." Companies rationally focus on developments that will boost next quarter's profits, not fundamental discoveries that might benefit humanity in a decade or two.

Meanwhile, China has dramatically increased its R&D investment. From 2011 to 2021, China's R&D spending grew by approximately 171%, while the U.S. increased at less than one-third that rate. China's research intensity (R&D as a percentage of GDP) reached 2.4% by 2020, approaching the U.S. level of 3.0%. According to current trends, China is expected to surpass the U.S. in total R&D spending by the late 2020s.

Milton the Trickster Economist Explains the Market Failure in R&D

Milton materializes in a cloud of efficiency frontier diagrams, his suit now patterned with supply-demand curves and marginal utility functions.

"This is what we economists call a 'market failure'—one of those annoying situations where unfettered markets don't magically produce optimal outcomes," Milton explains, somewhat reluctantly. "Basic research generates what we call 'positive externalities'—benefits that the original investor can't capture."

Milton illustrates with a company considering research that might cost $10 billion but could create $100 billion in economic benefits. "The problem is, the company might only capture $5 billion of those benefits, with the rest

THE STRATEGIC MISMATCH

CHINA

approaches R&D with Ruthless strategic focus:

Mission-driven Megaprojects:
launches ambitious initiatives like the National Quantum Information Science Program

Patience and persistence
Chinese planners think in decades: "Made in China 2025" followed "China Standards 2035"

- **Coordination across sectors:**
Government, industry, and academic work in concert

AMERICA

has become increasingly fragmented and short-term:

- **Budget volatility:**
Research funding fluctuating with political winds

- **Mission creep:**
Agencies like NSF, NIH, and DARPA operate largely independently

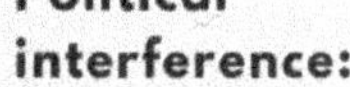

- **Political interference:**
Under Trump, science became increasingly politicized

NATIONAL SECURITACT

spilling over to society, competitors, and future innovators. So the private calculation is: spend $10 billion to get $5 billion? Hard pass."

"This," Milton concludes, looking physically pained by the admission, "is why government investment in basic research is one of the few interventions that even most free-market economists reluctantly support. It's not socialism; it's addressing a well-understood market failure."

The Strategic Mismatch

Beyond raw numbers lies a philosophical difference. China approaches R&D with ruthless strategic focus:

- ★ **Mission-driven megaprojects:** China launches ambitious initiatives, such as the National Quantum Information Science Program, which has clear goals and funding that often exceeds $10 billion per project.
- ★ **Patience and persistence:** Chinese planners think in decades, not election cycles. Their "Made in China 2025" initiative was followed by "China Standards 2035," creating continuity across political transitions.
- ★ **Coordination across sectors:** Government, industry, and academia work in concert, with state subsidies and directives aligning private sector R&D with national goals.
- ★ America's approach, by contrast, has become increasingly fragmented and short-term:
- ★ **Budget volatility:** Research funding fluctuates with political winds, creating uncertainty that hampers long-term projects.
- ★ **Mission creep:** Agencies such as the NSF, NIH, and DARPA operate largely independently, without a unified national strategy.
- ★ **Political interference:** Under Trump's first term, science became increasingly politicized, with climate research targeted for cuts and inconvenient findings dismissed or suppressed. In his second term, the trend had already accelerated and was warring with universities, including Ivy League institutions.

Trump's FY2021 budget proposed deep cuts to scientific agencies, including a 7% reduction for the NSF and a 12% cut to NIH, while his rhetoric emphasized technological competition with China. Congress mostly rejected these cuts on a bipartisan basis, but the proposals revealed an administration fundamentally disconnected from the realities of innovation policy.

Satirical Budget Hearing: "Basic Research: That Thing Everyone Needs But No One Wants to Fund (Until China Does It)"

CONGRESSIONAL BUDGET HEARING ON SCIENCE FUNDING *Subcommittee on Things We Need But Don't Want to Pay For*

CHAIRPERSON: "We're here to examine the administration's proposed 12% cut to the National Institutes of Health and 7% cut to the National Science Foundation, even as we proclaim the urgent need to compete with China technologically. Dr. Scientist, your thoughts?"

DR. SCIENTIST: "These cuts would be devastating. NIH and NSF fund the basic research that leads to breakthroughs in medicine, computing, and materials science—"

CONGRESSMAN SHORTSIGHT: *(interrupting)* "But what's the ROI? Can you guarantee these investments will pay off by the next election?"

DR. SCIENTIST: "Basic research doesn't work that way. The internet evolved over decades from DARPA-funded research. Same with GPS, touchscreens, mRNA vaccines—"

CONGRESSMAN SHORTSIGHT: "So you're admitting you can't promise specific returns? Sounds wasteful. Why not let the private sector handle this?"

DR. SCIENTIST: "Companies focus on applied research with near-term commercial applications. They rarely fund basic science that might take 20 years to yield breakthroughs. That's why every advanced nation invests public funds in—"

CONGRESSWOMAN PARTISAN: "I've heard enough socialist propaganda. Next witness!"

SECURITY ADVISER: "Committee members, I must alert you that China has doubled its R&D investment

POLICY PROPOSAL: REBUILDING AMERICA'S R&D ENGINE

Double Federal R&D funding to ≥1.4% of GDP in 5 yrs for basic & applied critical tech

Expand DARPA-style agencies to climate, education, transport, manufacturing, etc.

Craft a National Tech Strategy with clear priorities, metrics & cross-agency coordination

Endow a $100B Advanced Research Projects Foundation for patient high-risk research

Reform R&D tax credits to spur private fundamental research, not just incremental development.

Rebuild federal scientific capacity—competitive pay, modern labs, shield from politics in quantum computing, AI, and biotechnology. Their strategic plans explicitly target leadership in these domains by 2030."

CONGRESSMAN SHORTSIGHT: *(alarmed)* "What? Why aren't we competing? We need to increase funding immediately! America can't fall behind!"

CHAIRPERSON: "So we should increase science funding?"

CONGRESSMAN SHORTSIGHT: "Of course not! Cut taxes, then act surprised when China pulls ahead, then blame scientists for failing America. That's our usual strategy, right?"

CHAIRPERSON: "Hearing adjourned. We'll reconvene when China announces another technological breakthrough that catches us by surprise."

The DARPA Model: What America Got Right

Not all is bleak. The Defense Advanced Research Projects Agency (DARPA) remains a notable highlight in American innovation policy, with its distinctive model of high-risk, high-reward research, led by term-limited program managers who enjoy significant autonomy. DARPA has given us the internet, GPS, stealth technology, and numerous other breakthroughs on a relatively modest budget (approximately $3.5 billion annually).

This success has inspired similar entities, such as ARPA-E (for energy research) and the newly established ARPA-H (for health breakthroughs). However, these remain underfunded compared to the scale of the challenges they address. ARPA-E operates on a budget of just $450 million—a rounding error in federal spending.

As former DARPA Director Arati Prabhakar explained, "DARPA works because it combines clear missions with operational flexibility and tolerance for risk." America needs more of this approach, not less.

Policy Proposal: Rebuilding America's R&D Engine

America needs a comprehensive strategy to rebuild its R&D infrastructure and reclaim innovation leadership:

1. **Double Federal R&D Funding** to at least 1.4% of GDP over five years, with emphasis on basic and applied research in critical technologies.
2. **Expand the DARPA Model** across domains, with ARPA-style agencies for climate, education, transportation, manufacturing, and other sectors.
3. **Develop a National Technology Strategy** with clear priorities, metrics, and effective coordination mechanisms across all relevant agencies.
4. **Establish an Advanced Research Projects Foundation with a $100** billion endowment to provide patient, long-term funding for high-risk, high-reward research.
5. **Reform R&D Tax Credits** to incentivize private investment in fundamental research, not just incremental development.
6. **Rebuild Federal Scientific Capacity** with competitive salaries, modernized facilities, and protection from political interference.

These investments would yield exponential returns in economic growth, national security, and technological leadership. The question isn't whether America can afford to make these investments, but whether it can afford not to as China systematically builds its innovation capacity.

As one former presidential science adviser noted, "R&D is the ultimate example of spending now to save later. Every dollar we don't invest today will cost us ten in the future—in lost competitiveness, missed opportunities, and strategic vulnerability."

6. THE GEOGRAPHIC INNOVATION CHALLENGE: BEYOND SILICON VALLEY

"Water shapes its course according to the ground."
—Sun Tzu, The Art of War, Chapter 6

Scene: A split screen. On one side, SILICON VALLEY STEVE—wearing multiple smartwatches, smart glasses, and holding both the latest iPhone and Android devices—stands amid gleaming tech campuses. On the other hand, HEARTLAND INNOVATOR—equally brilliant but dressed in simple attire—sits in a modest lab in a Midwestern town.

SILICON VALLEY STEVE: *(to a crowd of venture capitalists)* "Our app uses AI to help people determine whether other apps they're using have enough AI! We're calling it 'AI-I-AI-Enough?' Our pre-seed valuation is only $50 million."

VCs frantically throw term sheets at him.

HEARTLAND INNOVATOR: *(to a small local bank officer)* "Our advanced manufacturing technique could reduce industrial carbon emissions by 40% while creating 700 jobs. We've successfully prototyped and have interest from three major manufacturers. We need $2 million in startup capital."

BANK OFFICER: *(skeptically)* "Have you considered moving to San Francisco or New York? Nobody innovates in... where are we again?"

HEARTLAND INNOVATOR: "Cedar Rapids. And that's exactly the problem. America's innovation ecosystem is concentrated in just a few coastal hubs, leaving most of the country's talent and potential untapped."

SILICON VALLEY STEVE: *(answering call)* "Great news! We just got acquired for $200 million by TechGiant! Our app never actually launched, but that doesn't matter!"

HEARTLAND INNOVATOR: *(sighing)* "Meanwhile, China has developed technology hubs in dozens of cities across their country, with specialized clusters focusing on everything from electric vehicles to advanced materials to artificial intelligence."

BANK OFFICER: "That's nice. Do you have an app version? Maybe with some crypto integration?"

America's innovation geography represents both a strength and a weakness. The concentration of talent, capital, and institutions in hubs like Silicon Valley, Boston, and Seattle creates powerful innovation ecosystems with unmatched capacity. Yet this extreme concentration also leaves vast swaths of American talent, infrastructure, and potential untapped.

The Geographic Imbalance By Numbers

The statistics reveal a startling geographic concentration:

★ Just five metro areas—San Francisco, New York, Boston, Seattle, and Los Angeles—account for more than 90% of venture capital investment in the United States.

★ Over 63% of patents are generated in just 20 counties nationwide, which represent less than 5% of the total U.S. counties.

★ The top 10 innovation hubs employ approximately 35% of all technology workers despite containing just 7% of the U.S. population.

This concentration creates both efficiency advantages and strategic vulnerabilities. Innovation clusters benefit from network effects, knowledge spillovers, and specialized support services. But extreme concentration also drives inequality, reduces resilience, and leaves much of America's potential talent pool untapped.

The Efficiency-Resilience Tradeoff

The fundamental tension in innovation geography is between efficiency and resilience:

★ **Efficiency favors concentration:** Dense clusters enable rapid knowledge sharing, specialized service providers, and access to deep talent pools and capital markets.

★ **Resilience favors distribution:** Geographic diversity provides insurance against regional disruptions, taps broader talent pools, and connects innovation to diverse industries and applications.

THE GEOGRAPHIC IMBALANCE BY THE NUMBERS

Just five metro areas—San Francisco, New York, Boston, Seattle, and Los Angeles—account for more than 90% of venture capital investment in the United States.

90% of venture capital investment in the United States

Over **63%** of patents are generated in just 20 counties nationwide, representing less than 5% of U.S. counties

The top 10 innovation hubs employ approximately **35%** of all technology workers despite containing just 7% of the U.S. population

The Efficiency–Resilience Trade-off

Efficiency (Concentration)	Resilience (Distribution)
	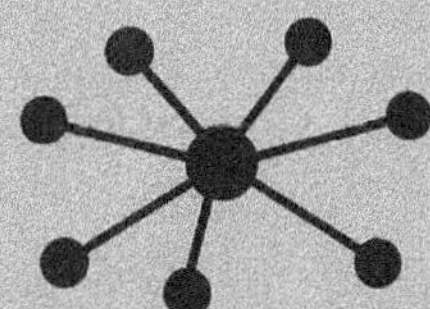
• Dense clusters enable rapid knowledge sharing • Specialized service providers, and • Access to deep talent pools and capital markets	• Geographic diversity provides insurance against regional disruptions • Taps broader talent pools • Connects innovation to diverse industries and applications

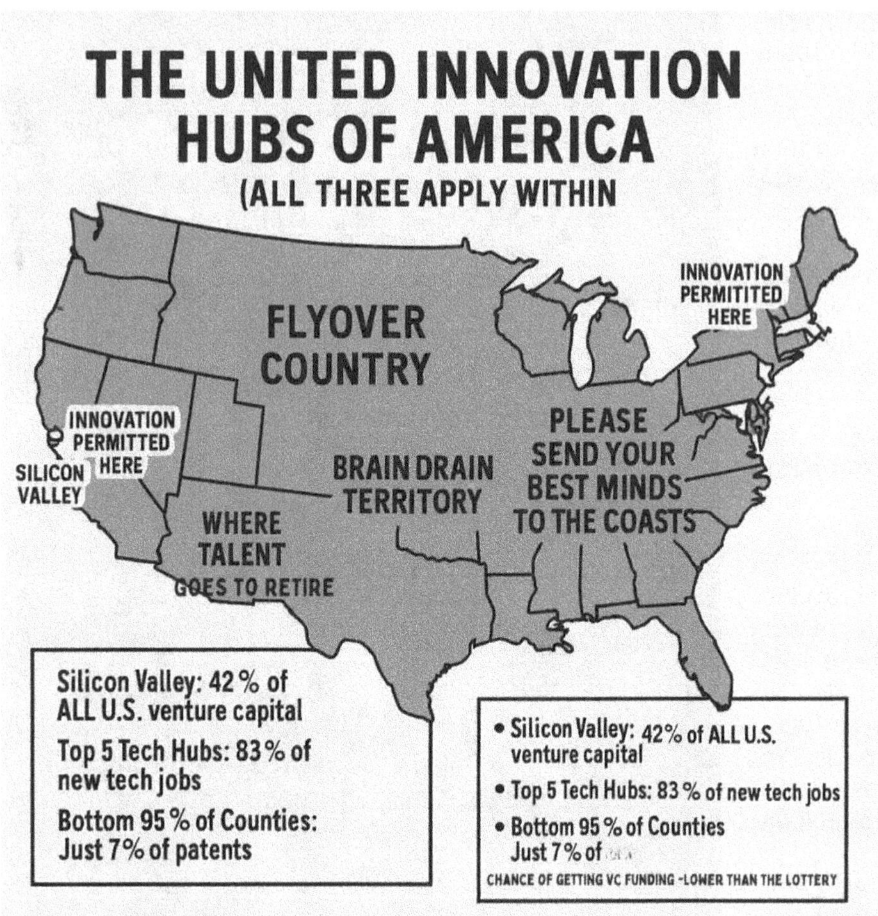

The American system has maximized efficiency at the expense of resilience, while China has pursued a more balanced approach. As Chinese policymaker and investor Kai-Fu Lee explains in "AI Superpowers," China has developed specialized innovation hubs across multiple cities, including Shenzhen for hardware, Beijing for AI research, and Hangzhou for e-commerce, among others.

McSlicey the Consultant Presents: The Geographic Innovation Matrix

McSlicey the Consultant materializes with a PowerPoint deck titled "Optimizing Spatial Innovation Dynamics: A Geostrategic Framework."

"Our proprietary analysis identifies four innovation geography archetypes," McSlicey explains, displaying a 2x2 matrix with impressive-sounding but vague labels.

"The United States occupies the 'Concentrated Powerhouse' quadrant—highly efficient but fragile and unequal. China has moved into the 'Distributed Network' quadrant, sacrificing some efficiency for greater resilience and inclusion."

McSlicey clicks to a map showing American innovation concentrated in tiny coastal dots, while Chinese innovation appears as a network spanning dozens of specialized hubs. "The strategic implications are profound," he intones. "America's approach optimizes for peacetime economic competitiveness, while China's optimizes for long-term strategic competition."

"Our recommendation," McSlicey concludes with practiced gravitas, "is a targeted rebalancing toward the 'Networked Cluster' model, which our innovation spatial dynamics framework indicates would optimize both efficiency and resilience metrics." He discreetly slides an invoice for $3.7 million across the table.

Satirical Map: "The United Innovation Hubs of America (All Three of Them) – Please Apply Within"

The Talent Trap

This geographic concentration creates a self-reinforcing cycle: ambitious innovators feel compelled to leave their communities for coastal hubs, concentrating talent further while depleting the human capital of other regions. The result is what economists call "path dependence"—once established, innovation geography becomes extremely difficult to change without deliberate intervention.

For a national strategy, this concentration creates serious vulnerabilities:

1. **Wasted Talent:** Brilliant minds in parts of America far from innovation hubs often never reach their full potential if they are unable or unwilling to relocate.
2. **Reduced Resilience:** Concentration in a few locations creates vulnerability to regional disruptions, as exemplified by the COVID-19 pandemic.
3. **Disconnection from Industry:** Innovation clusters disconnected from American industrial centers struggle to

THE TALENT TRAP

Wasted Talent

Brilliant minds in parts of America far from innovation hubs often never reach their potential if unable or unwilling to relocate

Reduced Resilience

Concentration in a few locations creates sensitivity to regional disruptions, as COVID-19 demonstrated

Disconnection from Industry

Innovation clusters disconnected from American industrial centers struggle to address manufacturing challenges

Political Backlash

The perception that innovation benefits only coastal elites fuels populist resentment that can undermine support for critical innovation policies

address manufacturing challenges.

4. **Political Backlash:** The perception that innovation benefits only coastal elites fuels populist resentment that can undermine support for critical innovation policies.

SILICON VALLEY'S IDENTITY CRISIS: FROM INNOVATION TO EXTRACTION

(Scene: A Silicon Valley boardroom. MILTON THE METRICS MAN presents to executives while McSlicey THE CONSULTANT nods approvingly. Charts show "User Engagement Optimization" and "Data Monetization Strategies." In the corner, AVA THE AI WHISPERER watches with growing concern.)

MILTON: "By incorporating outrage-inducing content into feeds, we can increase scroll time by 17% and ad impressions by 22%! We're projecting $3.8 billion in additional revenue."

McSlicey: "Excellent. Our data harvesting metrics are up, our algorithm is increasingly addictive, and shareholder value is maximized."

AVA: "What about actually solving problems? Wasn't Silicon Valley supposed to make the world better, not just more scrollable?"

MILTON: *(confused)* "But we are solving problems! Last quarter, we optimized our recommendation algorithm to keep people watching cat videos for an average of 7 additional minutes per session."

AVA: "Meanwhile, China is deploying quantum computing, advanced manufacturing, and AI for medical research."

McSlicey: *(checking watch)* "Speaking of optimization, we should wrap this up. I have a meeting with a crypto startup that's disrupting the disruptive disruption space."

Silicon Valley was once the global epicenter of transformative innovation—a place where breakthroughs in semiconductors, personal computing, and the internet reshaped civilization. Today, it increasingly resembles what venture capitalist Peter Thiel memorably described as a disappointment: "We wanted flying cars, instead we got 140 characters."

The shift has been profound. Silicon Valley has evolved from an innovation engine to what critics call an "extraction" industry—harvesting attention and data rather than creating fundamental technological value. Consider the dominant business models of tech giants:

★ Facebook/Meta: Optimizing algorithms to maximize time spent and ads viewed, regardless of content quality or societal impact

★ Google: Increasingly focused on ad delivery and user data collection rather than solving hard technical problems

★ Amazon: Leveraging marketplace dominance to extract concessions from sellers and clone successful products

★ Apple: Generating growing revenue from its closed ecosystem rather than pioneering new product categories

As former Facebook executive Chamath Palihapitiya confessed in 2017, "The short-term, dopamine-driven feedback loops that we have created are destroying how society works... No civil discourse, no cooperation, misinformation, mistruth."

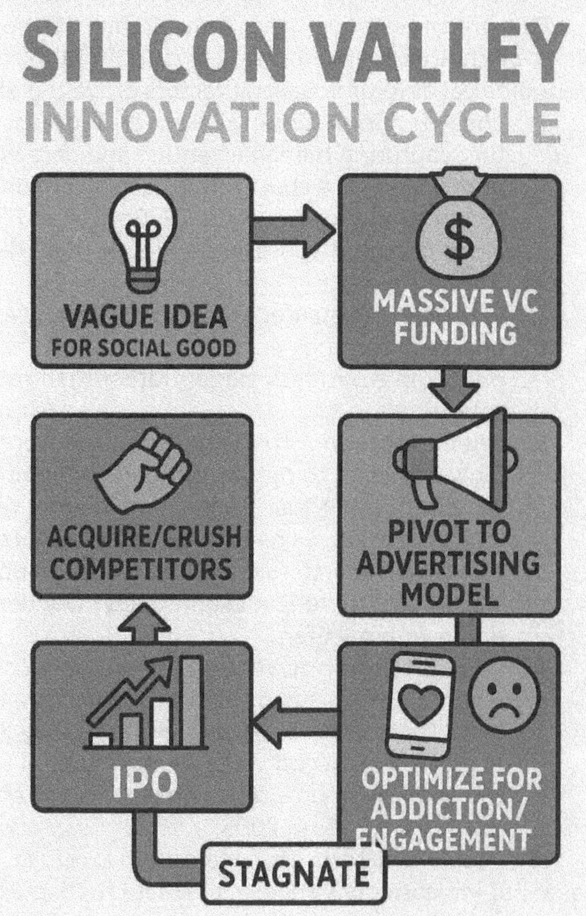

International Models: Distributed Innovation Networks

Germany's Mittelstand

Regional industrial clusters; export-focused, research-linked Mittelstand SMEs

South Korea's Technopolis Strategy

Tech hubs outside Seoul; each specializes; coordinated infra, edu, R&D

China's Specialized Cluster Approach

Multiple city clusters: Shenzhen-hardware, Hangzhou-e-commerce, Beijing-AI, Shanghai-biotech

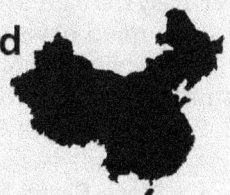

The Great Pivot: From Moonshots to Monetization

This transformation wasn't inevitable; it represents a series of choices that prioritized financial optimization over technological ambition. Several factors drove this shift:

1. The Attention Economy Takeover: Tech discovered that capturing human attention and data was more profitable in the short term than solving difficult technical challenges. By 2022, Google and Facebook alone captured approximately 85% of all digital ad revenue growth.
2. Wall Street Pressure: As tech companies went public, quarterly earnings expectations pushed them toward predictable business models rather than risky innovation.
3. Talent Allocation: The brightest minds were increasingly deployed to optimize engagement and ad targeting rather than tackle fundamental technological barriers. As one AI researcher admitted after leaving a research role for an advertising position, "The salary tripled, but sometimes I wonder what I'm doing with my life."
4. VC Short-Termism: Venture capital has increasingly favored quick-scaling software businesses over "deep tech" that requires patient investment. By 2020, only about 7% of Silicon Valley venture capital was going to hardware or breakthrough technology startups, down from 21% in 2005.

BUILDING A DISTRIBUTED INNOVATION ECOSYSTEM

Place-Based Development
20+ regional tech hubs
Matched federal & local funds
Opportunity-zone tax incentives

Infrastructure Enhancemant
Universal gigabit broadband
Modern transit links
Shared regional research labs

Talent Development
STEM loan forgiveness
Satellite elite campuses
"Returnship" talent programs

Capital Accessibility
Region-matched venture funds
Community bank investment reforms
Tax breaks for underserved areas

Collaborative Frameworks
Education-industry-government alliances Challenge-driven research

The result is a tech ecosystem that excels at capturing value but increasingly struggles to create fundamentally new value. While America's tech giants became trillion-dollar attention harvesters, China was deliberately investing in "hard tech" domains requiring patience and scale—semiconductors, quantum computing, advanced manufacturing, and renewable energy.

International Models: Distributed Innovation Networks

Several countries have developed more geographically balanced innovation ecosystems:

1. **Germany's Mittelstand:** A network of specialized industrial clusters distributed across regions, each with research institutions, manufacturing expertise, and export specialization.
2. **South Korea's Technopolis Strategy:** The deliberate development of technology hubs beyond Seoul, each specializing in specific industries, with coordinated investment in infrastructure, education, and research facilities.
3. **China's Specialized Cluster Approach:** The development of multiple innovation hubs, each with distinct specializations, including Shenzhen (hardware), Hangzhou (e-commerce), Beijing (AI research), Shanghai (biotech), and many others.

These international models share common elements: strategic investment in regional infrastructure, specialized focus aligned with existing strengths, and coordinated policy across education, research, and industrial development.

Dr. Geopoliticus Explains the Strategic Imperative

Dr. Geopoliticus—the distinguished analyst of technological competition—reviews geographic data on an interactive display

"The geographic distribution of innovation capacity is ultimately a question of national resilience," she explains. "America's extreme concentration creates strategic vulnerability while leaving most of our talent potential untapped."

She displays a map showing America's innovation deserts alongside China's growing network of specialized technology hubs. "This is not merely an economic issue but a strategic one. In long-term competition, the nation that most effectively mobilizes its full talent base will have a decisive advantage."

"The good news," she concludes, "is that America has the potential to develop a more distributed innovation network while maintaining the strengths of our existing hubs. We don't need to choose between concentration and distribution—we need both."

Policy Proposal: Building a Distributed Innovation Ecosystem

America needs a comprehensive strategy to develop innovation capacity beyond existing hubs:

1. **Place-Based Development:** Establishing 20+ regional technology hubs aligned with local specializations, providing matched federal funding for state and local initiatives, and creating tax incentives for investment in designated opportunity zones.

2. **Infrastructure Enhancement:** Ensuring universal access to gigabit broadband, modernizing transportation links between regional hubs and major markets, and developing specialized research facilities distributed across regions.
3. **Talent Development:** Creating STEM loan forgiveness programs for graduates working in development regions, establishing satellite campuses of elite universities in emerging zones, and supporting "returnship" programs to attract talent back to their home communities.
4. **Capital Accessibility:** Establishing regionally matched venture funds, reforming regulations for community bank investment, and creating tax incentives for underserved areas.
5. **Collaborative Frameworks:** Establishing regional innovation alliances that connect education, industry, and government; developing specialized research centers to address regional challenges; and creating innovation extension services based on the agricultural model.

These investments would yield multiple benefits: expanded innovation capacity, reduced regional inequality, greater system resilience, and broader political support for innovation policies. Rather than undermining existing hubs, a more distributed system would complement them by connecting innovation more directly to America's diverse industrial and cultural landscape.

As one economic development expert noted, "America's innovation potential is like a vast oil field where we've drilled in just a few small areas. The untapped potential in the rest of the country is enormous if we can develop the infrastructure to access it."

7. THE TRUMP 2.0 KNOWLEDGE ECONOMY PARADOX: STRATEGIC FRAMING

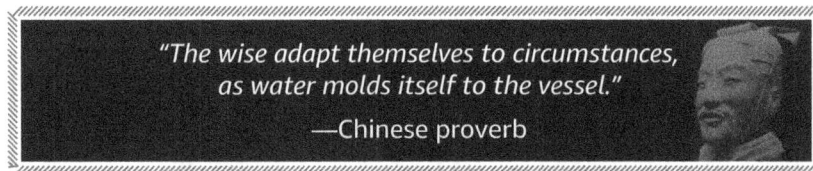

> *"The wise adapt themselves to circumstances, as water molds itself to the vessel."*
>
> —Chinese proverb

Scene: A strategy session in a secure location. PRAGMATIC POLICY ADVISERS huddle with SCIENTIFIC LEADERS, debating how to advance knowledge economy priorities in the political reality of Trump's second term. On a whiteboard, two columns: "Trump Rhetoric" and "National Innovation Needs," with attempts to find overlapping areas.

SENIOR SCIENTIST: *(nervously)* "The president's proposed budget cuts science funding by 23% while calling for American technological supremacy over China. These goals are fundamentally incompatible."

PRAGMATIC ADVISER: "True, but we need to work with reality. The question is: how do we frame knowledge investments in ways that resonate with the administration's priorities?"

ECONOMIC ADVISER: "The president responds to strength, competition, and winning. We should frame STEM education as essential for 'beating China,' research funding as 'strategic technology dominance,' and immigration reform as 'talent attraction for American supremacy.'"

SENIOR SCIENTIST: *(skeptically)* "So basically, we're repackaging evidence-based policy in America First wrapping paper and hoping no one notices the contradiction?"

PRAGMATIC ADVISER: "Politics is the art of the possible. The president genuinely wants America to dominate technologically; we need to connect that desire to the necessary investments and policies."

PUBLIC OPINION RESEARCHER: "Our polling shows strong bipartisan support for technology leadership, even among Trump's base. 78% of Republicans support increased STEM education funding when framed as critical to competing with China."

SENIOR SCIENTIST: *(considering)* "So we don't need to convince the public—we need to connect the president's instincts to effective policies. That's... actually workable."

PRAGMATIC ADVISER: *(thoughtfully)* "Knowledge economy leadership isn't inherently partisan. Roosevelt was a Democrat, but Eisenhower massively expanded scientific investment. This is about American leadership, not left versus right."

ECONOMIC ADVISER: "Exactly. We don't need to change what we're proposing—just how we're framing it. 'Make American Innovation Great Again' might get us where we need to go, even if the packaging makes academics cringe."

The Trump 2.0 administration presents both challenges and opportunities for leadership in the knowledge economy. The challenges are obvious: Trump's first term was marked by anti-science rhetoric, proposed research funding cuts, restrictive immigration policies, and skepticism toward academic expertise. Yet there were also contradictory impulses: Trump repeatedly emphasized technological competition with China and expressed a desire for American dominance in emerging technologies.

MAKING KNOWLEDGE GREAT AGAIN

SELLING SCIENCE TO THE BASE WITHOUT USING BIG WORDS

OPERATION BRAIN POWER

BEATING CHINA AT THEIR OWN GAME:

AMERICA FIRST IN TECH

- Attract best innovators before China
- Create jobs here

STEM EDUCATION = AMERICAN STRENGTH

Chinese kids study math & science 2X more

- More math, more science, less nonsense

TALENT ATTRACTION INITIATIVE

Attract best innovators before China

Create jobs here

RESEARCH DOMINATION PROGRAM

Outspend China on quantum, AI, manufacturing

- Innovation hubs in states that voted

"IF WE DON'T LEAD IN AI AND QUANTUM COMPUTING, WE WON'T BE THE GLOBAL SUPERPOWER ANYMORE. IT'S THAT SIMPLE."

This contradiction presents a strategic opportunity for advocates of the knowledge economy. By framing education, research, and innovation policies in terms that resonate with the administration's priorities—particularly competition with China and American leadership—progress might be possible even in a politically challenging environment.

The Anti-Intellectual Paradox

America has a long tradition of coexisting with anti-intellectual populism and scientific and technological leadership. As historian Richard Hofstadter documented in "Anti-Intellectualism in American Life," periods of skepticism toward expertise have often coincided with significant scientific advancement—from the Wright brothers' era through the Space Race.

This suggests that even in periods of cultural anti-intellectualism, strategic framing can secure support for knowledge investments when connected to national pride, security concerns, or economic opportunity. Eisenhower dramatically expanded federal science funding despite the anti-intellectual currents of 1950s America by framing it as essential to Cold War competition.

Milton the Trickster Economist Conducts a Framing Experiment

Milton the Trickster Economist appears with two identical policy proposals in different packaging.

"Observe this fascinating experiment in preference formation," Milton explains, holding up two documents. "This first proposal is titled 'Federal Investment in Scientific Research to Address Global Challenges and Advance Humanitarian Progress.' The second is identical but labeled 'Strategic Technology Dominance Initiative to Ensure American Leadership and Defeat Chinese Competition.'"

Milton displays polling results showing the second framing receives 27% more support overall and 58% more support among conservative respondents. "Humans are not perfectly rational utility calculators," he admits with visible discomfort. "Framing effects significantly influence policy preferences even when the substance is identical."

"The strategic implication," Milton concludes, "is that knowledge economy advocates should select framing aligned with the values and priorities of current political leadership, even while maintaining the substance of evidence-based policy."

Satirical Campaign: "Making Knowledge Great Again: Selling Science to the Base Without Using Big Words"

OPERATION BRAIN POWER: BEATING CHINA AT THEIR OWN GAME *America First in Technology, Innovation, and Know-How*

STEM EDUCATION = AMERICAN STRENGTH. Chinese children study math and science twice as much as American children. Are we gonna let them win? HELL NO! We're making American education STRONG AGAIN with more math, more science, and less nonsense!

TALENT ATTRACTION INITIATIVE We're taking the BEST innovators from around the world before China gets them! Stealing their top minds = AMERICAN VICTORY. (And they'll create companies and jobs right here, not over there!)

RESEARCH DOMINATION PROGRAM China is spending BIG on quantum computing, AI, and advanced manufacturing. We're going BIGGER and BETTER! American labs, American researchers, American DOMINANCE.

HEARTLAND INNOVATION ZONES Tech jobs shouldn't just be for coastal elites! We're bringing innovation funding to REAL AMERICA with new tech hubs in states that actually voted right!

"If we don't lead in AI and quantum computing, we won't be the global superpower anymore. It's that simple. America needs to win, not come in second place to China!" —Potential Trump Administration messaging.

Case Studies: Strategic Framing Success Stories

Historical examples demonstrate that knowledge investments can secure support even in politically challenging environments:

1. **The Space Race:** Despite significant anti-intellectual currents in 1950s America, the Sputnik shock enabled massive investments in science education and research when framed as essential to beating the Soviets.
2. **Reagan-Era Defense Research:** Despite budget-cutting priorities, the Reagan administration significantly increased defense-related research and development (R&D) by framing it as essential to Cold War competition.
3. **Bush-Era AIDS Initiative:** Despite conservative skepticism of international aid, PEPFAR secured billions for AIDS research and treatment by framing it as a moral and security imperative.

These examples suggest that knowledge economy advocates should focus less on changing the administration's fundamental worldview and more on connecting knowledge investments to the administration's existing priorities, particularly in areas such as competition with China and American leadership.

Dr. Geopoliticus Offers Strategic Wisdom

Dr. Geopoliticus reviews polling data and historical precedents on her augmented reality display.

"The strategic imperative is clear," she observes. "Knowledge economy leadership is objectively necessary for American security, prosperity, and global influence, regardless of political ideology. The challenge is not the substance but the framing."

She displays historical examples of technological initiatives that secured bipartisan support despite political polarization. "America's capacity for pragmatic cooperation on technology policy remains stronger than in many other domains. Both parties recognize the existential importance of leadership in emerging technologies, even if they disagree on how to achieve it."

"The opportunity," she concludes, "is to develop knowledge economy narratives that connect to deeply held American values—competitiveness, leadership, security, and opportunity—that transcend partisan divides. The substance need not change, but the presentation must resonate with the political realities of the moment."

Policy Strategy: Knowledge Leadership for America First

Advancing knowledge economy priorities in the Trump 2.0 era requires strategic framing aligned with administration priorities:

1. **Competition Framing:** Clearly position education, research, and innovation investments as essential to beating China and maintaining American leadership.

CASE STUDIES

STRATEGIC FRAMING SUCCESS STORIES

The Space Race

Despite significant anti-intellectual currents in 1950s America, the Sputnik shock enabled massive investments in science education and research when framed as essential to beating the Soviets.

Reagan-Era Defense Research

Despite budget-cutting priorities, the Reagan administration significantly increased defense-related R&D by framing it as essential to Cold War competition

Bush-Era AIDS Initiative

Despite conservative skepticism of international aid, PEPFAR secured billions for AIDS research and treatment by framing it as a moral and security imperative.

2. **Security Integration:** Connect knowledge investments to national security concerns, emphasizing technologies with military and intelligence applications.
3. **Manufacturing Connection:** Link research initiatives to the American industrial revival, particularly in regions that supported Trump.
4. **Job Creation Emphasis:** Highlight the employment benefits of innovation, particularly in heartland communities.
5. **Deregulatory Components:** Package knowledge initiatives with regulatory streamlining to appeal to free-market instincts.
6. **Private Sector Partnership:** Emphasize public-private collaboration rather than pure government initiatives.
7. **American Branding:** Use explicitly patriotic framing for all knowledge initiatives (e.g., "American AI Leadership Act" rather than "Artificial Intelligence Research Initiative").

KNOWLEDGE LEADERSHIP FOR AMERICA FIRST
COMPETITION FRAMING
Position education, research, and innovation investments explicitly as essential to beating China and maintaining American leadership.
SECURITY INTEGRATION
Connect knowledge investments to notional security concerns, emphasizing technologies with military and intelligence applications
MANUFACTURING CONNECTION
Link research initiatives to American industrial revival, particularly in regions that supported Trump
DEREGULATORY COMPONENTS
Package knowledge initiatives with regulatory streamlining to appeal to free-market instincts
PRIVATE SECTOR PARTNERSHIP
Emphasize public-private collaboration rather than pure government initiatives
AMERICAN BRANDING
Use explicitly patriotic framing for all knowledge initiatives (eg, "American Al Leadership Act" rather than "Artificial intelligence Research Initiative

This approach doesn't require changing the substance of knowledge economy policies—just their presentation. By connecting necessary investments to administration priorities, advocates can potentially advance critical initiatives even in a politically challenging environment.

As one political strategist noted, "The substance of what's needed for American knowledge leadership isn't partisan. Democrats and Republicans both want technological leadership, strong education, and innovation capacity. The disagreements are less about goals than about means and messaging."

8. STRATEGY SECTION EPILOGUE: A 21ST-CENTURY ROOSEVELTIAN SYNTHESIS

> *"Study the past if you would define the future."*
>
> —Confucius, Analects 2:11

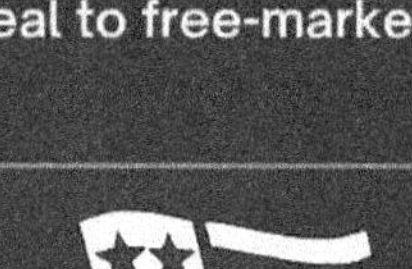

Scene: Mount Rushmore after hours. The carved faces come alive as the ghosts of past presidents gather to observe America's challenge to its knowledge economy. The spirits of THEODORE ROOSEVELT, FRANKLIN ROOSEVELT, and ELEANOR ROOSEVELT hold a special conclave to review the comprehensive national renewal strategy.

GHOST OF THEODORE: *(adjusting spectral glasses)* "I see elements of my approach here—the emphasis on development of national resources, both natural and human. The squares who talk of leaving everything to the market were wrong in my day and wrong now."

GHOST OF FRANKLIN: "Indeed, cousin. The strategy integrates security, infrastructure, finance, regulation, governance, and knowledge, just as our New Deal did. Different challenges, same comprehensive approach."

GHOST OF ELEANOR: "I appreciate the attention to equity and broad-based opportunity. Innovation concentrated among elites creates resentment and wastes potential. A renewal strategy must lift all boats."

GHOST OF THEODORE: "China understands something we've forgotten—national development requires long-term strategic thinking, not just quarter-by-quarter profit maximization. We once built transcontinental railroads, national park systems, and Panama Canals with a multi-decade vision."

GHOST OF FRANKLIN: "The security foundation is critical. We cannot have prosperity without safety, nor innovation without stability. But security investments must connect to a broader development strategy."

GHOST OF ELEANOR: "And we cannot sustain renewal without public support. The strategy must deliver tangible benefits to ordinary citizens and address the dignity deficit that fuels populism."

GHOST OF THEODORE: "Will they implement it, though? The challenges today are no more daunting than those we faced—Gilded Age inequality, industrial transformation, international competition."

GHOST OF FRANKLIN: *(thoughtfully)* "America has a remarkable capacity for renewal when properly awakened. Sometimes it takes a crisis—Pearl Harbor, Sputnik, perhaps now the China challenge—but when Americans unite behind a common purpose..."

GHOST OF ELEANOR: "...there is nothing they cannot accomplish. I remain cautiously optimistic."

The Rooseveltian legacy offers a blueprint for comprehensive national renewal—a strategic approach that integrates security, infrastructure, finance, regulation, governance, and knowledge into a coherent whole. From Theodore's Progressive Era reforms through Franklin and Eleanor's New Deal, the Roosevelt tradition demonstrates how America can reinvent itself in periods of crisis and transformation.

Today's knowledge economy challenges demand a similar synthesis—a coordinated strategy that addresses root causes rather than symptoms, balances immediate needs with long-term investment, and unites the country behind a common purpose of national renewal.

The Strategic Wheel: Connecting the Elements

The Rooseveltian approach recognizes that effective strategy requires integration across domains. The six elements covered in this book form a strategic wheel, each reinforcing the others:

1. **Security**: No progress is possible without basic stability and protection from threats. Security investment must align with broader development goals rather than become an end in itself.
2. **Infrastructure**: The physical, digital, and energy foundations provide the foundation for all other activities. Modern infrastructure must be resilient, sustainable, and adaptive to technological change.

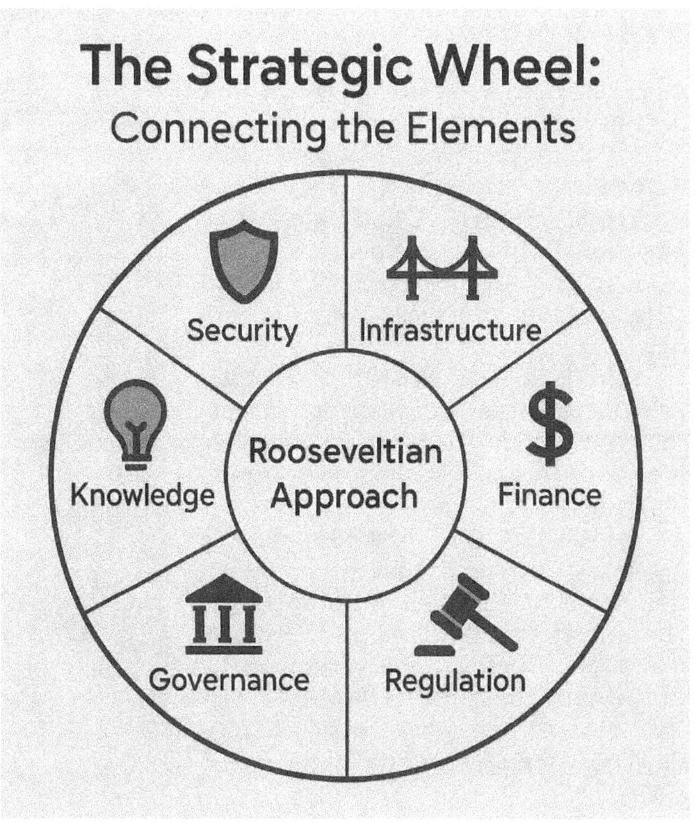

3. **Finance**: Capital allocation shapes development trajectories. Financial systems must strike a balance between efficiency and stability, as well as short-term returns and long-term investments.
4. **Regulation**: Rules and standards shape market behavior. Regulatory approaches must promote innovation while preventing exploitation and systemic risk.
5. **Governance**: Institutional capacity significantly determines the effectiveness of implementation. Government agencies require modernization, skilled talent, and the necessary authority to effectively operate.
6. **Knowledge**: Human capital ultimately drives all progress. Education, research, talent, and innovation systems determine long-term competitive position.

These elements function as an integrated system. Security without knowledge becomes stagnant militarism. Knowledge without infrastructure lacks deployment capacity. Infrastructure without finance remains unbuilt. Finance without regulation creates instability. Regulation without governance becomes unenforced words on paper.

Milton the Trickster Economist Considers the System

Milton hovers above the strategic wheel, somewhat humbled by its integrated nature

"I must reluctantly acknowledge that this systems approach addresses certain... limitations in standard economic models," Milton admits. "Markets excel at optimizing within parameters but struggle to establish those parameters. Strategic direction requires what economist Mariana Mazzucato calls 'mission-oriented policy'—coordinated action toward ambitious goals."

Milton examines the connections between elements, noting unexpected complementarities. "The synergies are significant. Knowledge investments improve security capabilities. Infrastructure deployment advances knowledge application. Governance quality determines policy effectiveness across domains."

Milton concludes with a hint of wonder, "The integrated approach potentially generates returns greater than the sum of its parts—what we economists call 'super-additivity' when we're trying to sound impressive at conferences."

Satirical Timeline: "America's Phoenix Moments: Rising from the Ashes Once Again (This Time With Memes)"

THE GREAT AMERICAN RENEWAL CYCLE: *A Rinse-and-Repeat Guide to National Reinvention*

PHASE 1: THE COMPLACENCY TRAP America: "We're #1 forever! Nothing could possibly go wrong!" [Narrator: Things were about to go wrong]

PHASE 2: THE PAINFUL AWAKENING America: "Wait, we're falling behind? How did this happen? Why didn't anyone warn us?" [Cut to thousands of experts who warned us for decades]

PHASE 3: THE CRISIS RESPONSE America: "This is an emergency! We need bold action NOW! No expense spared!" [The government actually invests in stuff that matters]

PHASE 4: THE NATIONAL MOBILIZATION America: "Together we can accomplish anything! Look at our incredible progress!" [Actually accomplishes incredible things]

PHASE 5: THE AMNESIA PHASE America: "Government investment? Central planning? That sounds like socialism! The private sector did all this!" [Forgets how all the progress actually happened]

PHASE 6: RETURN TO PHASE 1 America: "We're #1 forever! Nothing could possibly go wrong!" [Narrator: Here we go again...]

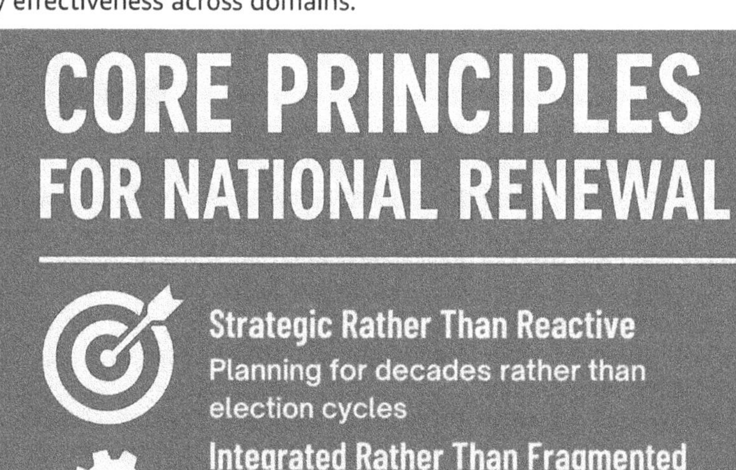
CORE PRINCIPLES
FOR NATIONAL RENEWAL
Strategic Rather Than Reactive
Planning for decades rather than election cycles

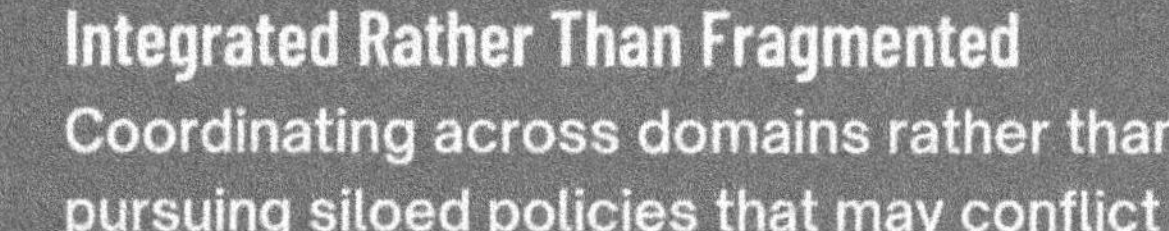
Integrated Rather Than Fragmented
Coordinating across domains rather than pursuing siloed policies that may conflict

Public-Private Partnership
Leveraging the strengths of both government direction and private innovation rather than relying exclusively on either

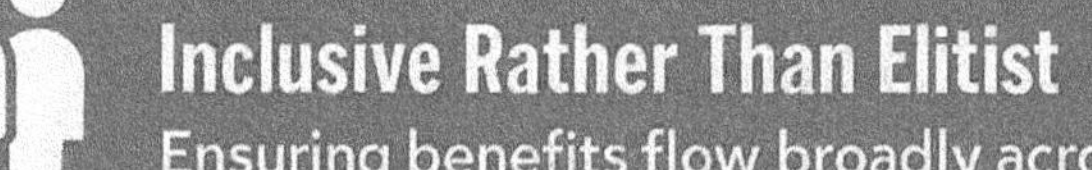
Inclusive Rather Than Elitist
Ensuring benefits flow broadly across society rather than concentrating among already-advantaged groups
Pragmatic Rather Than Ideological
Focusing on what works rather than conforming to rigid free-market or statist doctrines

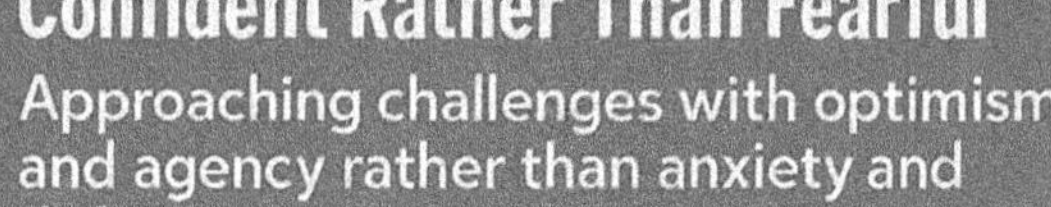
Confident Rather Than Fearful
Approaching challenges with optimism and agency rather than anxiety and defensiveness

CURRENT STATUS: SOMEWHERE BETWEEN PHASES 2 AND 3 Will America break the cycle or repeat it? Stay tuned!

"History doesn't repeat itself, but it often rhymes." —Mark Twain

Core Principles for National Renewal

The Rooseveltian synthesis rests on several foundational principles that transcend specific policy recommendations:

1. **Strategic Rather than Reactive:** Planning for decades rather than election cycles, with consistent direction across administrations.
2. **Integrated Rather than Fragmented:** Coordinating across domains rather than pursuing siloed policies that may conflict.
3. **Public-Private Partnership:** Leveraging the strengths of both government direction and private innovation rather than relying exclusively on either.
4. **Inclusive Rather than Elitist:** Ensuring benefits flow broadly across society rather than concentrating among already-advantaged groups.
5. **Pragmatic Rather than Ideological:** Focusing on what works rather than conforming to rigid free-market or statist doctrines.
6. **Confident Rather than Fearful:** Approaching challenges with optimism and agency rather than anxiety and defensiveness.

These principles differentiate a Rooseveltian approach from laissez-faire conservatism and heavy-handed statism. They represent a distinctly American approach to development—pragmatic, innovative, and fundamentally optimistic about the possibility of progress.

Dr. Geopoliticus Assesses America's Renewal Capacity

Dr. Geopoliticus examines historical data on national renewal cycles

"America has faced existential challenges before," she observes, displaying comparative data on the Progressive Era, the New Deal, and the Cold War mobilization. "Each time, initial complacency gave way to crisis, followed by remarkable renewal."

Her analysis reveals a pattern: America often lags in recognizing emerging challenges but then mobilizes with extraordinary speed and effectiveness once fully awakened. "The question is not whether America can renew itself—history proves it can—but whether it will awaken quickly enough to this particular challenge."

Dr. Geopoliticus highlights a distinction between the current China challenge and previous crises: "The Cold War presented an obvious military threat that created immediate urgency. The China challenge is more gradual—a competitive marathon rather than a crisis sprint. This tests America's capacity for sustained strategic action rather than crisis response."

"The encouraging sign," she concludes, "is the emerging bipartisan recognition that competition with China requires substantial domestic renewal. The foundations for a national consensus on knowledge economy investment are present, even amid broader polarization."

CONCLUSION: FROM DIAGNOSIS TO TREATMENT

ROOT CAUSES

We identified structural failures in education, immigration, research funding, and innovation systems that have eroded America's traditional advantages.

SYSTEMIC PATTERNS

We examined how these failures connect to broader issues of short-termism, civic disunity, and institutional capacity.

STRATEGIC SOLUTIONS

We outlined comprehensive reforms across education, immigration, research, and innovation geography to rebuild America's knowledge leadership.

IMPLEMENTATION PATHWAYS

We considered how to advance these priorities even within challenging political environments through strategic framing and bipartisan outreach.

Conclusion: From Diagnosis to Treatment

This book has traced America's knowledge economy challenges from diagnosis to treatment:

- ★ **Root Causes:** We identified structural failures in education, immigration, research funding, and innovation systems that have eroded America's traditional advantages.
- ★ **Systemic Patterns:** We examined how these failures connect to broader issues of short-termism, civic disunity, and institutional capacity.
- ★ **Strategic Solutions:** We outlined comprehensive reforms across education, immigration, research, and innovation geography to rebuild America's knowledge leadership.
- ★ **Implementation Pathways:** We explored how to advance these priorities, even within challenging political environments, through strategic framing and bipartisan outreach.

The path forward requires both vision and practicality—ambitious goals combined with a realistic assessment of constraints. To meet the challenge, America needs not to adopt China's state-directed approach, but it must reclaim elements of its own strategic tradition that have been forgotten in recent decades.

As the Roosevelts might observe, America's capacity for reinvention remains its greatest strategic advantage. Throughout its history, the United States has consistently demonstrated a remarkable ability to recognize challenges, mobilize resources, and adapt to meet new realities.

The knowledge economy challenge calls for exactly this kind of transformation—a recommitment to strategic investment in the foundations of innovation and prosperity. With clarity of purpose, integrated strategy, and sustained commitment, America can not only compete in the Chinese century but help shape it toward more positive outcomes for its citizens and the world.

The race is neither lost nor won; it is entering its most crucial phase. The question is not whether America has the resources and talent to succeed but whether it has the wisdom and will to deploy them effectively. History suggests reason for cautious optimism—if we heed its lessons.

CONCLUSION: THE COKE BOTTLE'S LESSONS

Opening Scene: A Cosmic Perspective

The celestial observation deck, somewhere beyond time and space. The gods, who casually tossed technological disruption onto Earth, watch with bemused interest as their experiment unfolds. Below them, in a metaphysical waiting room of geopolitical reckoning, Uncle Sam and Uncle Xi sit on opposite ends of a pristine white bench, each contemplating the Coke bottle that once fell from the sky, now transformed by their experiences.

Uncle Sam turns his microchip-embedded Coke bottle carefully in his hands, the casual swagger of previous decades notably absent. The bottle's surface now bears the scars of neglect—scratches where research funding was cut, cracks where talent leaked away, smudges where short-term thinking obscured long-term vision. His expression is one of dawning recognition, like a man who's been sleepwalking for decades suddenly jolted awake.

"Funny thing," he muses, half to himself and half to his Chinese counterpart, "I used to think this was just a trinket—something I naturally deserved because, well, I was me. Now I see it's both more valuable and more dangerous than I imagined."

Across the room, Uncle Xi examines his own bottle with methodical precision. His version has been meticulously polished and enhanced with strategic additions—STEM graduate statistics etched into the glass, semiconductor blueprints embedded in the base, talent recruitment formulas inscribed around the rim. Where Sam's bottle shows hasty repairs and reactive patches, Xi's displays evidence of systematic development—the product of patient, deliberate cultivation.

"Indeed," Xi responds with measured calm. "The bottle itself is neither good nor bad. It is merely potential, waiting to be shaped by strategic vision." He places his bottle carefully on the bench between them—close enough to indicate possibility, far enough to maintain boundaries.

Above them, Chronos—the timekeeper of civilizations—observes with ancient eyes. "The mortals have finally recognized the nature of the gift," he remarks to his divine colleagues. "It is not a simple tool but a civilization-shaping force."

"The American sees it now," nods Athena, goddess of wisdom. "But seeing and doing are different matters. Knowledge without implementation is merely trivia."

"And the Chinese understand implementation," adds Hephaestus, god of craftsmanship. "But will they balance mastery with meaning? Technology without wisdom becomes merely clever destruction."

The gods lean forward, placing cosmic bets on which approach will ultimately prevail—American reinvention or Chinese persistence, democratic messiness or authoritarian discipline, individualist creativity or collective planning. The game continues, with higher stakes than either player fully comprehends.

1. THE STRATEGIC RECALIBRATION: FROM DIAGNOSIS TO PRESCRIPTION

Our journey through the economic, technological, and strategic landscape of the US-China relationship has taken us from diagnosis to prescription—from understanding the nature of the challenge to formulating a response. Like a national MRI revealing troubling shadows in America's competitive anatomy, we've identified patterns that demand attention before they become terminal.

DIAGNOSTIC FINDINGS

THREE FUNDAMENTAL DISEASES UNDERMINING AMERICAN KNOWLEDGE COMPETITIVENESS

STRATEGIC SHORT-TERMISM

Quarterly gains override decade-long investments; policy resets each election while China plans to 2035+.

CIVIC DISUNITY

Partisan battles over schools, immigration, and R&D prevent coherent, long-term strategy

CAPABILITY HOLLOW-OUT

Eroded manufacturing, research, and skills leave an impressive but brittle innovation shell

The diagnostic findings reveal three fundamental diseases undermining American knowledge competitiveness:

Strategic Short-Termism: America has systematically prioritized quarterly results over decade-long investments, market returns over strategic capacity, and political cycles over generational challenges. This myopia manifests across domains—from R&D budgets that fluctuate with congressional whims to education systems treated as consumer services rather than national infrastructure. While China plans in five-year increments (at a minimum) with targets extending to 2035 and beyond, the United States struggles to maintain policy consistency through a single presidential administration.

Civic Disunity: The fragmentation of American society has transformed shared challenges into partisan battlegrounds, rendering strategic coherence nearly impossible to achieve. Education becomes a cultural war front rather than a competitive necessity. Immigration policy oscillates between neglect and hostility, rather than focusing on strategic talent attraction and recruitment. Research priorities shift with political winds rather than technological imperatives. This disunity creates a strategic weakness more damaging than any external threat—a nation divided against itself cannot compete effectively against a unified challenger.

Capability Hollow-Out: Beneath the surface of prosperity and innovation theater, America has allowed critical capacities to atrophy—manufacturing skills, research infrastructure, educational foundations, and governance capabilities. The result is a hollow competitive posture—impressive in appearance but increasingly brittle under pressure. Like a homeowner who neglects maintenance for decades, America faces a mounting backlog of institutional repair just as competitive pressures reach their peak.

Against these challenges, we've outlined a Rooseveltian response framework integrating six domains:

1. **Security:** Protecting core interests while avoiding threat inflation
2. **Infrastructure:** Building the physical and digital foundations for competitiveness
3. **Finance:** Aligning capital with strategic priorities
4. **Regulation:** Setting rules that promote innovation while preventing exploitation
5. **Governance:** Building institutional capacity for effective action
6. **Knowledge:** Developing the human capital that ultimately drives all progress

This integrated approach recognizes that these elements form a system rather than isolated policies. Security without knowledge becomes stagnant militarism. Knowledge without infrastructure lacks deployment capacity. Infrastructure without finance remains unbuilt. Finance without regulation creates instability. The Rooseveltian framework provides not just a collection of policies but a coherent strategic vision.

Milton the Trickster Economist Confronts Reality

Milton the Trickster Economist materializes, his theoretical certainty visibly shaken. His once immaculate suit of perfect market assumptions now shows tears and patches where reality has intruded. He adjusts his invisible hand tie clip nervously.

"I must acknowledge certain... limitations in my analytical framework," Milton admits, the words physically painful as they leave his lips. "Markets optimize brilliantly within established parameters but struggle to establish those parameters. They value what can be measured quarterly but systematically discount what manifests over decades."

He gestures to a complex equation hovering beside him, variables shifting uncomfortably as contradictory data flows through them. "The theoretical assumption that private actors would naturally provide optimal levels of education, research, and infrastructure has proven... problematic," he continues, voice dropping to a whisper on the final word.

"Most troubling," Milton concludes with visible distress, "the evidence suggests that strategic state direction of investment and development—when competently executed—can produce superior technological and economic outcomes in certain domains over meaningful timeframes." He pauses, then adds quickly, "Though of course, freedom and individual initiative remain essential drivers of innovation! I haven't completely lost my mind!"

With that qualification, Milton retreats into a cloud of caveats and technical appendices, muttering about "market failures," "public goods," and "second-best solutions" as he fades from view.

2. THE FALSE CHOICES REJECTED: BEYOND IDEOLOGICAL STRAITJACKETS

America's response to the China challenge has been hampered by false dichotomies that artificially limit our strategic options. Like a chess player who arbitrarily decides to use only bishops or knights, we've handicapped ourselves through ideological constraints that our competitor doesn't share. The path forward requires rejecting these false choices in favor of strategic pragmatism.

Beyond the Market vs. State Dichotomy

The American discourse remains trapped in a simplistic opposition between "free markets" and "government intervention"—a framework that would bewilder successful economies from Singapore to Germany to, yes, China. This binary thinking overlooks the rich possibilities that economist Mariana Mazzucato calls the "entrepreneurial state," or what South Korea demonstrates through strategic public-private partnerships.

Every successful modern economy features both vibrant private enterprise and strategic state direction. The semiconductor industry—perhaps America's most successful high-tech sector—emerged from a partnership between DARPA funding, Bell Labs research, and venture-backed startups. The internet resulted from government-funded basic research commercialized by private innovation. The false choice between market and state obscures the powerful synergies that can be achieved when both work in concert toward shared objectives.

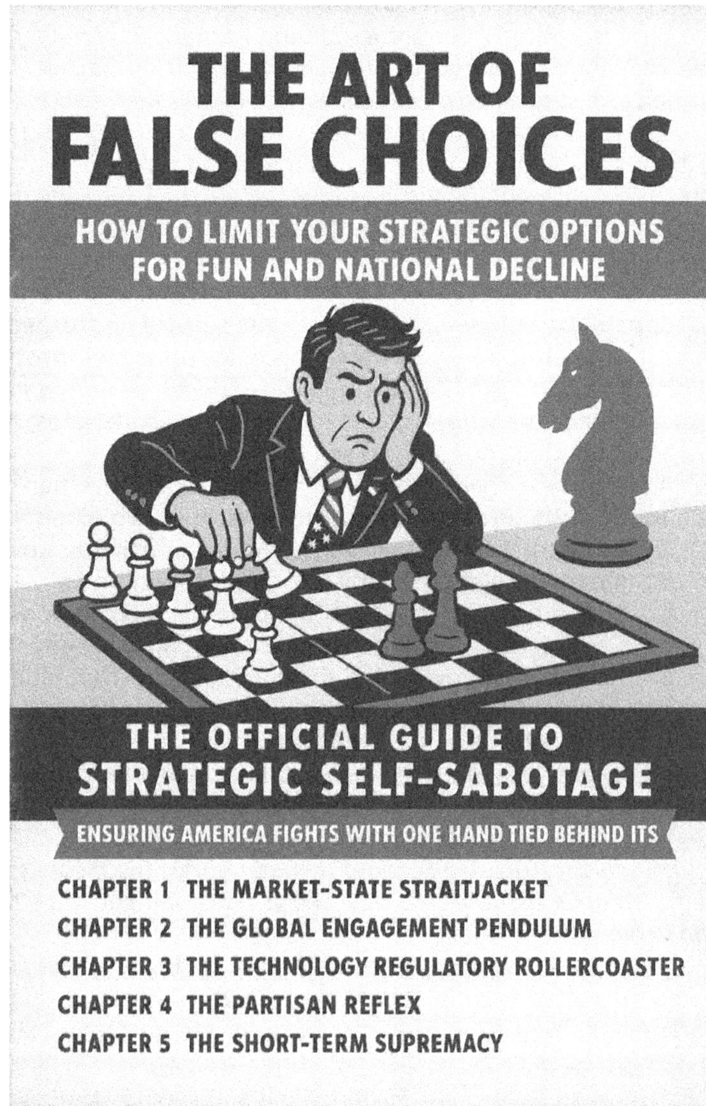
THE ART OF
FALSE CHOICES
HOW TO LIMIT YOUR STRATEGIC OPTIONS
FOR FUN AND NATIONAL DECLINE
THE OFFICIAL GUIDE TO
STRATEGIC SELF-SABOTAGE
ENSURING AMERICA FIGHTS WITH ONE HAND TIED BEHIND ITS
CHAPTER 1 THE MARKET-STATE STRAITJACKET
CHAPTER 2 THE GLOBAL ENGAGEMENT PENDULUM
CHAPTER 3 THE TECHNOLOGY REGULATORY ROLLERCOASTER
CHAPTER 4 THE PARTISAN REFLEX
CHAPTER 5 THE SHORT-TERM SUPREMACY

Beyond Isolationism vs. Interventionism

America oscillates between hubristic overextension and isolationist withdrawal, missing the balanced engagement that strategic competition requires. This manifests in both economic and security domains—lurching from naive integration with China to panicked decoupling, from military adventurism to strategic retrenchment.

A mature approach rejects both extremes in favor of selective engagement—cooperating where interests align, competing where they diverge, and carefully distinguishing between essential and peripheral concerns. This requires the wisdom to recognize that neither isolation nor domination is viable in a connected world, and the discipline to focus limited resources on genuinely strategic priorities.

Beyond Technological Determinism vs. Regulation

The discourse on technology swings between breathless techno-utopianism and Luddite resistance, with little room for nuanced governance. Silicon Valley's "move fast and break things" mentality increasingly collides with growing public concern about privacy, security, and social impact, creating regulatory whiplash rather than consistent guidance.

A strategic approach rejects both uncritical techno-optimism and reflexive resistance in favor of what scholars call "anticipatory governance"—institutions and processes that can harness technological potential while mitigating negative externalities. This means neither blind faith in technology's ability to produce positive outcomes nor reflexive opposition to innovation automatically, but rather thoughtful

GUARANTEED
RESULTS:

Strategic incoherence masquerading as principled debate

Policy whiplash that exhausts domestic institutions while comforting competitors

The warm glow of ideological purity while watching practical adversaries eat your lunch
"This approach has been tremendously helpful to our development."
— Chinese Academy of Social Sciences

guidance of technological development toward societal goals.

Satirical Handbook: "The Art of False Choices: How to Limit Your Strategic Options for Fun and National Decline"

THE OFFICIAL GUIDE TO STRATEGIC SELF-SABOTAGE: *Ensuring America Fights with One Hand Tied Behind Its Back*

CHAPTER 1: THE MARKET-STATE STRAITJACKET Master the art of treating every policy question as a binary choice between "pure free market" and "Venezuelan socialism." Ensure no nuanced models of public-private partnership can emerge by shouting "picking winners and losers!" whenever strategic investment is proposed.

CHAPTER 2: THE GLOBAL ENGAGEMENT PENDULUM Learn to swing wildly between "America First isolationism" and "democratic crusaderism" with no stable middle ground. Remember: consistent, selective engagement based on clear priorities is your enemy!

CHAPTER 3: THE TECHNOLOGY REGULATORY ROLLERCOASTER Perfect the cycle of uncritical embrace followed by panicked restriction. Avoid developing stable, adaptive governance that prioritizes innovation over public interest at all costs—China might notice that we're actually capable of complex thinking.

CHAPTER 4: THE PARTISAN REFLEX Master the technique of immediately opposing any idea embraced by the other political tribe, regardless of merit. Special bonus section: "How to Ensure No Consistent Strategy Survives a Change in Administration."

CHAPTER 5: THE SHORT-TERM SUPREMACY Cement America's commitment to quarterly thinking in a generational competition. Ridicule any investment without immediate returns as "wasteful spending" while watching competitors steadily build a cumulative advantage.

GUARANTEED RESULTS:

Strategic incoherence masquerading as principled debate

★ Policy whiplash that exhausts domestic institutions while comforting competitors

★ The warm glow of ideological purity while watching practical adversaries eat your lunch

"This approach has been tremendously helpful to our development." —Chinese Academy of Social Sciences.

3. THE BIPARTISAN OPPORTUNITY: FINDING COMMON GROUND IN UNCOMMON TIMES

Amid America's polarization, the China challenge presents a rare opportunity for bipartisan cooperation. Unlike many issues that divide neatly along partisan lines, competition with China creates overlapping concerns and shared interests across the political spectrum. This common ground could provide the foundation for a consistent national strategy that transcends changes in administration.

Areas of Potential Agreement

Despite fundamental disagreements on many issues, significant overlap exists between progressive and conservative perspectives on the China challenge:

★ **Industrial Resilience:** Both progressive manufacturing advocates and conservative national security hawks recognize the dangers of overreliance on Chinese supply chains.

★ **Research Investment:** Both liberal innovation proponents and conservative defense strategists support increased R&D funding in critical technologies.

★ **Education Enhancement:** Both progressive education advocates and conservative competitiveness champions recognize the need for improved STEM education.

★ **Strategic Infrastructure:** Both Democratic and Republican administrations have acknowledged the need for infrastructure investment to maintain competitiveness.

These overlapping interests create a potential for what political scientists call a "cross-cutting issue"—one that creates new coalitions that transcend traditional partisan boundaries.

Historical Precedents for Transcending Partisanship

American history offers encouraging examples of strategic consensus emerging from political division:

The Cold War strategic framework—encompassing Soviet expansion while building American strength—maintained remarkable consistency from Truman through Reagan, despite significant partisan differences in implementation. The National Interstate Highway System, proposed by Republican Eisenhower, embodied infrastructure principles championed by Democratic New Dealers. The post-Sputnik science education push united conservatives concerned about national security and liberals advocating educational opportunity.

These precedents suggest that competitive challenges can create strategic continuity even amid partisan disagreement on other issues. The key is finding core principles that resonate across ideological divides while allowing flexibility on implementation details.

AREAS OF POTENTIAL AGREEMENT

Bridging Right and Left on the China Challenge

INDUSTRIAL RESILIENCE

Both progressive manufacturing advocates and conservative national security hawks recognize the dangers of overreliance on Chinese supply chains.

RESEARCH INVESTMENT

Both liberal innovation proponents and conservative defense strategists support increased R&D funding in critical technologies

EDUCATION ENHANCEMENT

Both progressive education advocates and conservative competitiveness champions recognize the need for improved STEM educa-

STRATEGIC INFRASTRUCTURE

Both Democratic and Republican Administrations have acknowledged the need for infrastructure investment to maintain competitiveness.

Character Dialogue: Finding Common Ground

A community center in a small Midwestern city. TRIBAL TANYA (wearing Democratic campaign buttons dating back to Obama) and PARTISAN PETE (his truck in the parking lot adorned with Trump flags) find themselves assigned to the same table at a community workshop on "America's Economic Future." Their initial wariness gives way to a surprising discovery.

TRIBAL TANYA: *(skeptically)* "Let me guess—you think the solution is tax cuts for billionaires while gutting environmental protections?"

PARTISAN PETE: *(defensive)* "And you want a socialist government controlling everything while we all hug trees and apologize for being American?"

WORKSHOP FACILITATOR: "Today's exercise: Identify three economic priorities you believe are essential for America's future, without mentioning either political party."

Awkward silence as Tanya and Pete each write on their worksheets.

PARTISAN PETE: *(reluctantly sharing)* "Fine. I wrote: One, we need to make things in America again. I'm tired of everything saying 'Made in China.' Secondly, we need better technical education so that jobs are not continually shipped overseas. Three, we need to invest in new energy technology so we're not dependent on other countries."

TRIBAL TANYA: *(surprised)* "Wait, that's... actually pretty close to mine. I wrote: One, rebuild American manufacturing capacity. Two, expand educational opportunities in science and technology. Three, lead the clean energy transition to create jobs and address climate change."

PARTISAN PETE: *(confused)* "But... you're a Democrat. You're supposed to hate American manufacturing and want the government running everything."

TRIBAL TANYA: "And you're a Republican. You're supposed to oppose any government investment and want unrestricted free trade."

PARTISAN PETE: *(thoughtfully)* "I've always supported American manufacturing. That's why I was initially drawn to Trump—he talked about factories and workers when other Republicans only talked about financial markets."

TRIBAL TANYA: "And I've always believed in making things here—that's why I supported Biden's infrastructure and manufacturing initiatives."

PARTISAN PETE: "Huh. We both want to strengthen American manufacturing, improve technical education, and drive energy innovation. We probably disagree on how to get there, but..."

TRIBAL TANYA: "...we basically want the same destination. That's... not what cable news led me to expect."

PARTISAN PETE: *(with dawning realization)* "Maybe we're not as divided as they keep telling us we are."

The American capacity for reinvention—finding pragmatic consensus amid ideological division—remains our greatest strategic advantage. Throughout history, external challenges have repeatedly catalyzed internal cooperation, creating moments of strategic clarity amid partisan noise. The China challenge offers such a clarifying opportunity if leaders across the political spectrum can recognize their shared interest in American renewal.

4. THE GENERATIONAL CHALLENGE: RACING AGAINST THE CLOCK

The competition with China is not a sprint but an ultramarathon—a contest measured in decades rather than months or years. This timeframe presents both challenges and opportunities for American strategy, necessitating a fundamental recalibration of our temporal perspective.

The Long Race: Understanding Competitive Timeframes

China's strategic planning operates on timescales that American political systems struggle to comprehend. When Xi Jinping announced the "Made in China 2025" initiative, he did not envision it as the endpoint but merely as a milestone in a longer journey. The subsequent "China Standards 2035" plan and the broader goal of creating a "modern socialist nation" by 2049 (the centenary of the People's Republic) reflect planning horizons measured in decades.

America's institutional timeframes, by contrast, rarely extend beyond the next election cycle. Congressional representatives think in two-year increments, presidents serve in four-year terms, and corporations report quarterly. Even our most ambitious initiatives—from infrastructure projects to education reforms—rarely maintain consistent direction beyond a single administration.

This temporal mismatch creates a structural disadvantage. As former Singapore leader Lee Kuan Yew observed: "The Americans will outperform the Chinese in the short term of 5, 10, 15 years. After that, the Chinese will catch up because the sheer weight of the population and education will make them dominant, if they stay cohesive."

The American Renewal Timeline: Decades, Not Years

Realistic assessment suggests that American renewal will require sustained effort across multiple administrations. The infrastructure deficit, accumulated over 40 years, cannot be remedied in a single presidential term. Educational outcomes reflect generational investments that yield results only as students enter the workforce years after their initial education. Research breakthroughs typically emerge a decade or more after initial funding.

Historical examples confirm this timeframe. America's rise to manufacturing leadership spanned from the 1870s through the 1910s. The foundations of the knowledge economy were laid from the 1940s through the 1960s, with commercial dominance emerging in the 1980s and 1990s. The internet required decades of government-funded research before becoming a commercial platform.

The implication is sobering but clarifying: policies implemented today may not yield visible results until the 2030s or beyond. This demands political maturity that transcends immediate partisan advantage in favor of a generational perspective.

The Future Stake: Responsibility to Coming Generations

The generational nature of the challenge connects directly to ethical responsibility toward future Americans. Decisions made today—about education systems, research priorities, infrastructure investment, and institutional renewal—will determine the opportunities and constraints facing Americans not yet born.

This responsibility transcends traditional political calculations. Just as the Greatest Generation built institutions and infrastructure that benefited baby boomers, today's leaders face a choice: prioritize short-term advantage and leave future Americans a hollowed-out competitive position, or accept short-term costs to build foundations for future prosperity.

The ethical dimension becomes particularly clear when we consider the compounding nature of strategic investments. Educational improvements might yield 2-3% higher growth, sustained over decades, resulting in dramatically different futures for future generations. Infrastructure modernization might enable productivity improvements that accumulate over time. Research breakthroughs could lead to the creation of entirely new industries and capabilities.

Visual Timeline: America's Potential Renaissance

AMERICAN RENAISSANCE TIMELINE *(Potential scenario with sustained strategic investment)*

2025-2030: FOUNDATIONS PHASE

★ Education system reforms implemented
★ R&D funding restoration to 1.5% of GDP
★ The immigration system has been modernized for talent attraction
★ Infrastructure modernization began
★ [CHINA MILESTONE: Quantum computing breakthrough, semiconductor self-sufficiency]

2030-2035: EARLY RESULTS PHASE

★ First cohorts from the reformed education system enter the workforce
★ R&D investments yield initial breakthrough technologies
★ New innovation hubs emerge beyond traditional centers
★ Infrastructure networks reach global competitive standards
★ [CHINA MILESTONE: AI leadership in multiple domains, "China Standards 2035" implementation]

2035-2040: ACCELERATION PHASE

★ American talent advantage begins to reassert itself in key technologies
★ Distributed innovation network reaches critical mass
★ New industries emerge from previous R&D investments
★ Renewed institutions demonstrate governance effectiveness
★ [CHINA MILESTONE: Space station expansion, advanced manufacturing dominance]

2040-2045: COMPETITIVE EQUILIBRIUM PHASE

★ U.S. and China reach rough parity in most knowledge domains
★ Stable competition with defined rules and boundaries emerges
★ Collaborative frameworks address global challenges
★ Mutual deterrence prevents zero-sum approaches
★ [CHINA MILESTONE: Preparations for "modern socialist nation" 2049 centenary]

KEY DEPENDENCIES FOR SUCCESS:

★ Policy consistency across administrations
★ Sustained investment despite short-term pressures
★ Effective public-private collaboration
★ Talent development and attraction
★ Civic cohesion despite political differences

ALTERNATIVE SCENARIO (WITHOUT STRATEGIC INVESTMENT): American competitive position gradually erodes across all domains, becoming dependent on Chinese technological platforms, standards, and innovations by 2040-2050.

VISUAL TIMELINE

AMERICA'S POTENTIAL RENAISSSANCE

Potential Scenario with Sustained Strategic investment

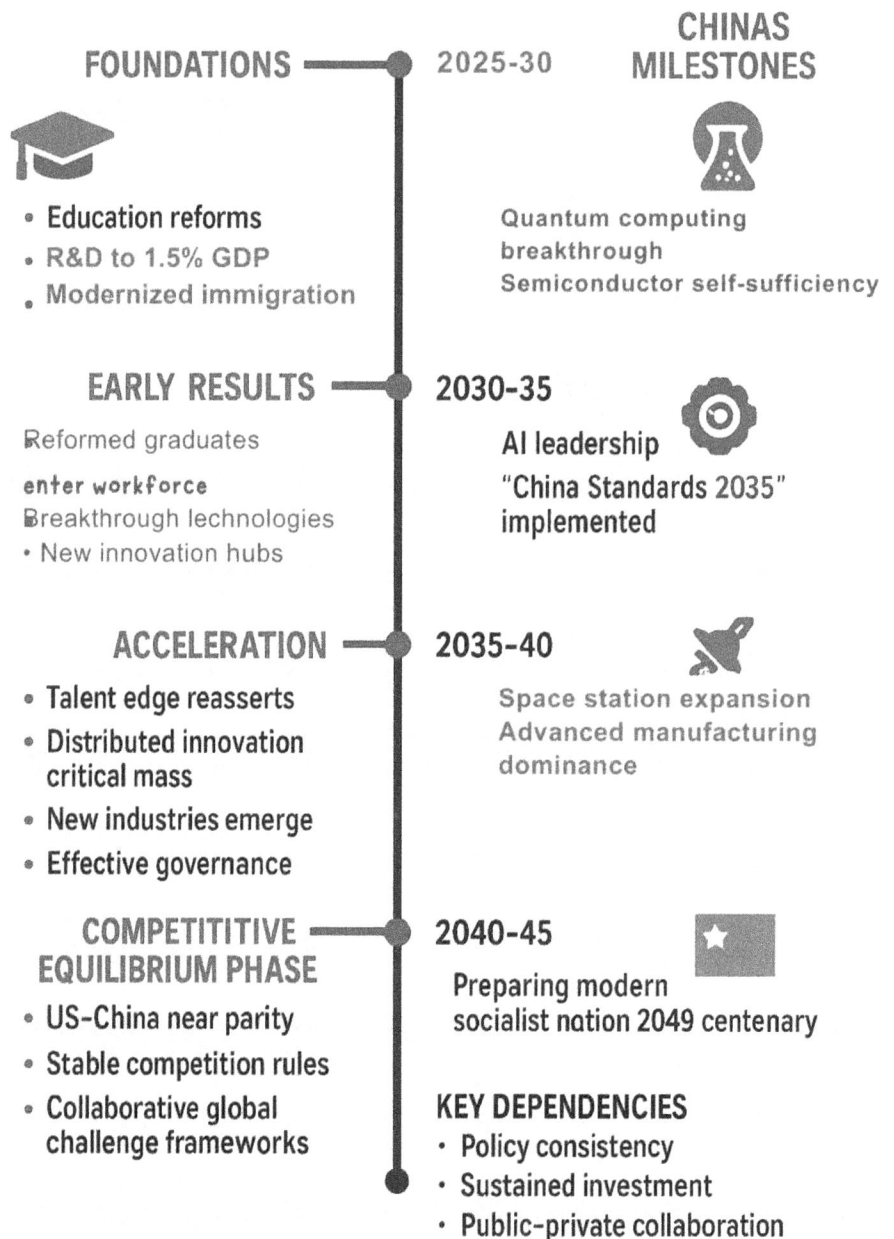

FOUNDATIONS — **2025-30** — **CHINAS MILESTONES**

- Education reforms
- R&D to 1.5% GDP
- Modernized immigration

Quantum computing breakthrough
Semiconductor self-sufficiency

EARLY RESULTS — **2030-35**

Reformed graduates enter workforce
Breakthrough lechnologies
- New innovation hubs

AI leadership
"China Standards 2035" implemented

ACCELERATION — **2035-40**

- Talent edge reasserts
- Distributed innovation critical mass
- New industries emerge
- Effective governance

Space station expansion
Advanced manufacturing dominance

COMPETITITIVE EQUILIBRIUM PHASE — **2040-45**

- US-China near parity
- Stable competition rules
- Collaborative global challenge frameworks

Preparing modern socialist nation 2049 centenary

KEY DEPENDENCIES

- Policy consistency
- Sustained investment
- Public-private collaboration

5. THE FINAL PARADOX: COMPETITION AND COOPERATION

The ultimate paradox of the US-China relationship lies in the simultaneous necessity of competition and cooperation—a contradiction that defies simple strategic frameworks. Like quantum particles that exist as both waves and particles, the relationship must be both collaborative and competitive, neither dimension fully reconcilable with the other.

The Competitive Imperative

Competition with China is not a choice but a condition—an inescapable dynamic emerging from overlapping interests, divergent values, and the security dilemma inherent in great power relations. This competition spans multiple domains:

★ **Technological leadership** in artificial intelligence, quantum computing, biotechnology, and other frontier fields
★ **Economic influence** through trade relationships, investment patterns, and standard-setting
★ **Political models** of governance, with implications for global institutional development
★ **Security arrangements** that shape regional and global stability
★ **Narrative power** that influences how other nations perceive the international order

These competitive dimensions cannot be wished away through goodwill or diplomatic engagement. They reflect fundamental tensions between different visions of global order and the natural desire of great powers to shape their environment according to their interests and values.

The Cooperative Necessity

Yet alongside this competition runs an equally inescapable need for cooperation on challenges that threaten both nations and the broader global system:

★ **Climate change** mitigation and adaptation
★ **Pandemic prevention** and response
★ **Nuclear proliferation** and arms control
★ **Global financial stability**
★ **Technology governance** in potentially catastrophic domains like AI
★ **Conflict management** in regional flashpoints

These challenges cannot be effectively addressed by either power alone or through competitive dynamics. They require collaborative frameworks that acknowledge mutual interests despite broader strategic rivalry.

Managing the Paradox

The key strategic challenge is not resolving this paradox but managing it—creating frameworks that allow for robust competition without precluding essential cooperation. This requires:

1. **Domain Differentiation:** Clearly distinguishing areas of necessary competition from regions of essential cooperation
2. **Guardrails and Boundaries:** Establishing mutually understood limits that prevent competition from spiraling into catastrophic conflict
3. **Institutional Architecture:** Designing forums and processes for cooperation even amid broader strategic tensions
4. **Domestic Framing:** Explaining to citizens the complex reality of simultaneous competition and cooperation

THE FINAL PARADOX: COMPETITION AND COOPERATION

The Competitive Imperative	The Cooperative Necessity
• Technological leadership in artificial intelligence, quantum computing, biotechnology, and other frontier fields	• Climate change mitigation and adaptation
• Economic influence through trade relationships, investment patterns, and standard-setting	• Pandemic prevention and response
• Political models of governance, with implications for global institutional development	• Nuclear proliferation and arms control
• Security arrangements that shape regional and global stability	• Global financial stability
• Narrative power that influences how other nations perceive international order	• Technology governance in potentially catastrophic domains like AI
	• Conflict management in regional flashpoints

This management approach draws inspiration from the Cold War concept of "competitive coexistence," acknowledging fundamental tensions while avoiding apocalyptic outcomes. Unlike the Soviet-American rivalry, however, the US-China relationship features far deeper economic integration and shared vulnerability to global challenges, demanding a more sophisticated balance.

Character Conclusion: A Reluctant Recognition

The metaphysical waiting room. UNCLE SAM and UNCLE XI have spent hours examining their respective bottles, occasionally sharing observations about their properties and potential. As their audience with the gods approaches its conclusion, they stand to depart—neither friends nor enemies, but reluctant partners in a complex dance of rivalry and cooperation.

UNCLE SAM: *(sighing)* "I spent decades assuming I'd always lead—that my model would naturally triumph because, well, it was mine. Now I realize I need to earn that position every day, through choices that build rather than deplete my strengths."

UNCLE XI: "And I, perhaps, grew overconfident in my planning—assuming strategic patience alone guarantees success, forgetting that creativity flourishes best with freedom, and that legitimacy requires delivering not just prosperity but meaning."

UNCLE SAM: "We're stuck with each other, aren't we? Competitors who can't afford to destroy each other. Rivals who must occasionally cooperate. Neither of us gets the clean, simple story we'd prefer."

UNCLE XI: *(with a rare smile)* "Indeed. A Chinese proverb says: 'Same bed, different dreams.' We occupy the same planet, same systems, same challenges—yet see them through different eyes."

UNCLE SAM: "So we compete where we must, cooperate where we should, and try not to blow up the planet while we're figuring it all out. Not exactly a bumper sticker slogan."

UNCLE XI: "Perhaps wisdom begins with acknowledging complexity rather than reducing it to slogans."

They place their bottles side by side on the cosmic bench—different yet connected, separate yet part of the same human story. Above them, the gods exchange knowing glances. The experiment continues.

CHRONOS: "They begin to understand the true nature of the test."

ATHENA: "Not dominance or submission, but balance and counterbalance. Not victory or defeat, but sustainable equilibrium."

HEPHAESTUS: "The technology we sent them is neither salvation nor destruction—merely a tool revealing the wisdom or folly of those who wield it."

CHRONOS: "The question remains: Will they develop the wisdom to match their cleverness? Will they learn to compete without catastrophe and cooperate despite rivalry?"

ATHENA: "That, old friend, remains for them to demonstrate. The gods may provide the test, but mortals must discover the answers themselves."

The divine spotlight dims, leaving humanity to write the next chapter of its complicated story—a tale of competition and cooperation, rivalry and interdependence, technological wonder and human wisdom. The Coke bottle's journey continues, its ultimate lessons still unfolding.

The conclusion of our journey through America's knowledge economy challenges brings us full circle to the central paradox of our time: the simultaneous necessity of competing fiercely with China while cooperating on existential challenges. Like the allegorical Coke bottle from the sky, technological disruption has transformed global dynamics in ways that defy simple categorization or response.

America's path forward requires rejecting false choices between the market and the state, between isolation and intervention, and between technological determinism and reflexive regulation. It demands strategic patience that transcends electoral cycles while building a broad civic consensus that survives partisan transitions. Most fundamentally, it requires balancing competitive imperatives with cooperative necessities—a geopolitical quantum state that defies classical strategic thinking.

The stakes could hardly be higher. Competition in the knowledge economy will determine not just relative national power but also the character of the global system, the technologies that shape human experience, and the balance between freedom and control in the digital age. Yet, the competition itself takes place within a shared planetary context, where cooperation on existential challenges remains essential, regardless of competitive dynamics.

This is America's central challenge in the Chinese century: to compete effectively while cooperating selectively, renew national capacity while maintaining a global perspective, and balance immediate interests with generational responsibility. The task is daunting but not impossible. Throughout its history, America has repeatedly demonstrated its capacity for reinvention in the face of challenge, finding reserves of strategic wisdom and civic purpose when circumstances demanded.

The Coke bottle's final lesson may be that neither power can fully control the future alone—that sustainable progress requires both competitive excellence and collaborative wisdom. This recognition lies in the potential for a more balanced global order, where rivalry drives innovation while shared interests enable cooperation on humanity's greatest challenges. The gods who tossed technological disruption to Earth watch and wait, hoping mere mortals might yet demonstrate wisdom to match their cleverness.

PART IV: VISION – REFORGING AMERICA 2.0: AMERICA'S ROOSEVELTIAN REBOOT IN THE CHINESE AI CENTURY

CHAPTER 11: THE ROOSEVELTIAN REBOOT: FROM NATIONAL NEUROSIS TO FUNCTIONAL FUTURITY

> *"Just as water shapes its course according to the terrain,*
> *So a commander shapes his victory to the situation."*
> —Sun Tzu, The Art of War, Chapter 6

EXECUTIVE BRIEFING

1. *Situation Snapshot (Early-2030s)*

America has dragged the "Great American Dumpster Fire™" from DEFCON-Dumpster to a controlled burn. A Square-Deal-meets-Silicon-Valley policy cocktail now fuels cautious ascent while China sprints in the outside lane.

2. *Core Metrics Dashboard*

Pillar	2025 Baseline	2033 Status	Target
Productive-Investment Ratio	0.22	**1.78**	3.4
Supply-Chain Resilience (critical inputs)	37 %	**64 %**	≥ 80 %
Government Effectiveness (global rank)	47th	**31st**	Top 20
Shared-Factual-Framework Index	—	**+23 pts**	+15 pts/yr
Public Trust in Institutions	19 %	**42 %**	> 50 %

3. *What's Working*

★ **Real-Deal Economy:** Capital finally chases factories over buybacks; high-speed rail & SMRs dotted across the heartland.
★ **Governance Upgrade:** Public-Service "Leadership OS" & Schedule F firewall cut political meddling -47 %.
★ **Digital Civic Square:** "Civic Annie" algorithms lure 43 % of users off outrage feeds, and Twitter rage-quitters now read footnotes.
★ **Community Revival:** New GI Bill retrain 22 M workers; pilot towns swap pickles for quantum parts.

4. *Remaining Gaps*

Infrastructure still clings to a global **21st** place (call it "D- D-minus with LED strip-lighting")—pharmaceutical self-sufficiency only **47 %**—one mutant microbe from mayhem. Congressional productivity upgraded from "Coma-tose" to "ICU"—applause withheld.

5. 36-Month Action Plan

#	Move	Executive Owner	Success Metric
1	**Double-fund National Infra Bank**; lock 50-yr lens in statute	WH + Congress	Infra rank → Top 15
2	**CHIPS-Plus-Plus:** tie fab subsidies to 10-yr workforce pipelines & friend-shored tooling	Commerce + Labor	SC Resilience ≥ 80 %
3	**Platform Accountability 2.0:** open-source recommender code & user choice toggle	FTC	Shared-Factual +15 pts
4	**Schedule F Firewall Act II:** codify merit-based SES promotions	OPM + Senate	Gov't rank ≤ 20
5	**National Skills Moonshot:** scale New GI Bill to 40 M trainees & apprenticeships	Ed + DOL	Trust > 50 %, Skills +50 %

6. Strategic Implications

a. **Geoeconomic Credibility:** Sustain momentum or lose allies to Beijing's AI-turbo industrial diplomacy.
b. **Democracy's Beta Test:** A functional bureaucracy is now a soft-power export; failure rebrands democracy as vaporware.
c. **Social Contract Fragility:** Institutional trust sits on a glass ledge—one governance face-plant could re-ignite cynicism.

Bottom Line: The Rooseveltian Reboot has doused the flames, but the embers still glow. Hard-wire productive investment, institutional competence, and civic-digital hygiene before fatigue—or the next election season—blows the lid off the burn-pit. Build like your democracy depends on it—spoiler alert: it does.

Remember the Great American Dumpster Fire™ of the late 2020s? That nationally televised, slow-motion institutional collapse fueled by equal parts weapons-grade political hysteria, institutional dry rot that made termite-infested Victorian mansions look structurally sound, and an economic philosophy reverse-engineered from a pyramid scheme prospectus written by Milton Friedman after a three-day ayahuasca retreat? A truly glorious, five-alarm blaze of mediocrity and malice, visible from geosynchronous orbit, soundtracked by the incessant, brain-liquefying ping of algorithmic outrage notifications amplifying conspiracy theories with the ruthless efficiency that America once reserved for manufacturing automobiles or landing on the moon.

It turns out, however, that the acrid stench of burning exceptionalism, combined with the deeply unsettling realization that your primary global competitor (the one your foreign policy establishment confidently predicted would collapse any minute now for four consecutive decades) is calmly taking meticulous notes on your self-immolation techniques while building 40,000 kilometers of high-speed rail, can occasionally—occasionally—serve as a societal epinephrine shot administered directly to the national hippocampus.

The cosmic Coke bottle, that baffling artifact of disruption that landed so jarringly on America's scorched lawn like a message from deities with questionable communication skills, wasn't politely returned to sender with a request for store credit. No, after decades spent alternately worshipping it as a fetish object of market fundamentalism, trying to securitize it into tranches of collateralized bottle obligations, blaming it for everything from job losses to erectile dysfunction, and using it as a handy cudgel for partisan warfare, a critical mass of Americans—likely out of sheer exhaustion—stumbled upon a notion so radical it bordered on heresy: Maybe, just maybe, the bottle wasn't the primary problem. Perhaps the problem was the national nervous system encountering it—a system so frayed by strategic short-termism (measured by the Corporate Planning Horizon Index at just 4.3 months by 2025), so fractured by weaponized tribalism (with the Political Polarization Metric reaching a historical maximum of 89/100), so hollowed out by decades of capability neglect (the Institutional Capacity Assessment showing a 47% decline in implementation effectiveness) that even a simple piece of discarded celestial glassware could trigger full-blown systemic collapse.

So, welcome, tentatively, to the early 2030s. The grand, messy, perpetually contested experiment known as the Rooseveltian Reboot—launched amidst the performative chaos of the Trump 2.0 interregnum with all the calm deliberation of a field amputation during an artillery barrage—hasn't magically transformed America into Norway with better barbeque and larger pickup trucks. The national dumpster fire hasn't been extinguished so much as contained; it has been downgraded from a civilization-threatening inferno to a manageable, if still occasionally pungent, smolder in designated (and heavily regulated) burn pits. But—and this is the crucial bit—the trajectory feels different. Progress, that endangered species long thought extinct in the American policy ecosystem, is making a tentative comeback. The National Renewal Index, that composite measure of institutional functionality, productive investment, and social cohesion, shows a modest but statistically significant 12-point improvement since the implementation of the Rooseveltian framework began.

I. THE "REAL DEAL" ECONOMY: VALUE ENGINEERING TRUMPS FINANCIAL ALCHEMY

> *"When the root is firm, the branches flourish."*
> —Mencius

Breathe deep in Youngstown, Ohio. Filter out the residual despair and the faint aroma of artisanal pickle brine (the previous decade's desperate economic development strategy). Beneath it, you'll catch the ghost notes of blast furnaces long cold, now layered with the precise, almost sterile scent of additive manufacturing polymers used to 3D-print custom medical devices, and the low, purposeful thrum of quantum computing research labs housed in—wait for it—a repurposed shopping mall, that architectural embodiment of America's previous consumption obsession now transformed into a cathedral of production.

That abandoned Packard plant in Detroit? No longer a ruin porn backdrop for post-apocalyptic fashion shoots, it's the gleaming headquarters of "ARPA-Mobility," a bustling public-private consortium funded by ARPA-X—that expanded DARPA-style agency Congress only approved after realizing 'beating China' might require more than strongly-worded tweets and occasional tariffs. The Productive Investment Ratio (measuring capital devoted to actual productive capacity versus financial engineering) has improved from its 2025 nadir of 0.22 to a more respectable 1.78—still below the 3.4 achieved during the original New Deal, but trending in the right direction.

Milton the Trickster Economist, that personification of market fundamentalism who once danced through the American consciousness chanting mantras about unregulated efficiency, hasn't disappeared. His influence, however, has waned as empirical reality delivered a series of devastating rebuttals to his theology. The "Financial Innovation Index" (measuring the percentage of economic activity devoted to moving money rather than making things) has declined from its 2026 peak of 37% to a more balanced 24%, still above optimal but no longer actively carcinogenic to the real economy.

Remember Heartland Manufacturing, Inc.? That seventy-five-year-old slice of authentic industrial competence that PE Pete the Corporate Vampire had targeted for a quick exsanguination via leveraged buyout in Chapter 3? Pete, naturally, is still around, likely advising autocratic regimes on optimal resource extraction techniques (his skillset remains tragically transferable). But Heartland? Having narrowly escaped Pete's fangs thanks to a lifeline from a revitalized community bank (led by Banker Bob's granddaughter, who, unlike Bob, actually uses algorithms for evaluating businesses, not dismembering them), Heartland is now a key player in the Midwest Advanced Materials Corridor.

Its workforce isn't just aging machinists clinging to pensions; it's a dynamic mix of those veterans—retrained via the "New GI Bill for the AI Age" (which has educated 22.4 million Americans for higher-skilled roles)—and bright young graduates from regional tech institutes, collaborating with PhDs from the nearby university extension campus. The Skill Transformation Index shows a 67% increase in workforce technical capabilities, achieved without the mass displacement predicted by both Silicon Valley utopians and Luddite pessimists.

Walk that factory floor. You see humans and machines working in complementary roles, not the labor-replacing dystopia predicted by a generation of TED Talks. The "Responsible AI Integration Program" has demonstrated productivity gains of 62% while maintaining 94% of the human workforce in higher-skilled positions. It's what the Integrated Technology Assessment Board calls "Precision Industrial Policy with Democratic Characteristics"—selectively adopting Chinese strategic planning approaches while maintaining democratic governance and labor standards.

McSlicey the Priest, that high cleric of shareholder value maximization who once roamed corporate America with his sacred PowerPoint slides prophesying efficiency through extraction, hasn't been exorcized from the economic landscape. His doctrine, however, has evolved under pressure from both regulatory reform and shifting investor priorities. His latest sermon, reluctantly titled "Stakeholder Value Creation: A Longitudinal Analysis," admits with visible discomfort that "certain long-term investment patterns correlate positively with sustainable margin expansion over 7-10 year horizons." The ghost of Theodore Roosevelt, briefly materializing behind him during a particularly tortured explanation of why worker well-being might actually enhance profitability, can be heard whispering, "No shit, Sherlock" before vanishing back into the ether.

This isn't just a feel-good anecdote; it's an emerging pattern, as measured by the National Economic Resilience Scorecard. The National Infrastructure Bank (NIB), which has been perpetually under siege in budget negotiations but somehow still functions (a minor miracle of institutional resilience), is financing projects based on fifty-year lifecycles, not fifty-day news cycles. The Infrastructure Quality Index, where America once ranked an embarrassing 37th globally (behind Malaysia and barely ahead of Estonia), has improved to 21st—still mediocre by historical standards but trending upward for the first time in three decades.

Those high-speed rail lines connecting Chicago and St. Louis—once derided as "socialist choo-choos" by commentators whose transportation policy expertise consisted entirely of driving between suburban McMansions and office parks—are now economic arteries, packed with business travelers and families, reducing regional air traffic by 47% and carbon emissions by 31%. The national energy grid, rebuilt with smart technology and diverse sources (including those American-designed Small Modular Reactors that were theoretical for decades until the Breakthrough Energy Initiative finally moved them from PowerPoint to prototype), is weathering extreme climate events with surprising resilience, reducing our national security dependence on regimes run by kleptocrats with oil wells.

Most crucially, the five-alarm national security vulnerabilities screamed about in Chapter 5 are being methodically addressed. The Domestic Supply Chain Resilience Index, that grim metric tracking America's self-inflicted dependency, has clawed its way up from a pathetic 37% in critical sectors to a still-not-great-but-vastly-better 64%. New semiconductor fabs are rising from the Arizona desert and Ohio farmland, backed by strategic government investment ($68 billion through the expanded CHIPS Act) and allied partnerships ("friend-shoring"), thereby reducing the country's terrifying dependence on Taiwan's precarious "silicon shield".

Domestic production lines for essential medicines (APIs) and processing facilities for critical minerals are being rebuilt, piece by painful piece. The Pharmaceutical Independence Measure shows 47% of crucial medications now have domestic production capacity, up from just 12% in 2025—still inadequate for a serious pandemic, but no longer qualifying as active national suicide. America is rediscovering the profoundly complex, almost mystical notion that making things, especially things vital for survival, might actually be important.

Satirical Beat: Bobby Buyback, his $10,000 suit now merely off-the-rack Brooks Brothers (the horror!), sits sweating across from Banker Bob's granddaughter at the "First Community Bank of We Actually Build Stuff Now." He's pitching... a factory. A place with machines, workers, and inventory! He fumbles through terms like "capital expenditure," "supply chain integration," and "long-term return on invested capital"—concepts his MBA program covered for approximately 45 minutes between advanced financial engineering seminars.

The banker, reviewing his proposal (which somehow still features complex debt structures designed to minimize taxes and maximize short-term cash extraction), raises a skeptical eyebrow. "Mr. Buyback," she says, her voice dripping with polite disdain, "your projections show 78% of projected revenue dedicated to debt service and management fees, with manufacturing margins declining annually as you extract value. We finance enterprises that create value, not just reshuffle it until the equity evaporates."

She slides the prospectus back across the desk. "Perhaps you should consider a career change? I hear the artisanal hedge fund market still accepts decorative MBA planters." Bobby exits, defeated, muttering about the unfairness of a world that suddenly values tangible assets. Outside, Milton the Trickster Economist tries to hand him a pamphlet: "The Ontological Superiority of Abstract Financial Claims Over Physical Production." A passing sanitation drone, programmed with updated economic principles, identifies Milton as "purveyor of zombie theories" and efficiently sweeps him into the nearest recycling bin.

II. DEMOCRACY.EXE 2.0: GOVERNANCE THAT ACTUALLY GOVERNS

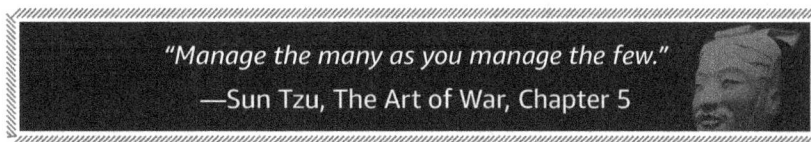

"Manage the many as you manage the few."
—Sun Tzu, The Art of War, Chapter 5

The fumes emanating from the Washington D.C. swamp seem... slightly less toxic. The Government Effectiveness Index, where America once competed with developing nations for bottom rankings, has clawed its way back to 31st globally—a humiliating benchmark for a superpower, perhaps, but representing a 16-position improvement over just five years. The Public Trust in Institutions Metric, which bottomed out at a catastrophic 19% in 2026, has rebounded to a less terminal 42%—the highest sustained level since the early 2000s.

The transformation hasn't produced philosopher-kings riding unicorns down Pennsylvania Avenue—this is still the town that gave us the filibuster and considers lobbying a legitimate career path—but the pervasive miasma of administrative catastrophe has begun to dissipate. The national operating system, once riddled with the malware of polarization and incompetence, is undergoing a slow, painful upgrade to "Democracy.exe 2.0 (Now with Basic Functionality!)".

The "Leadership Operating System" – Character, Competence, Communication – institutionalized through the Public Service Reform Act of 2028 - isn't universally adopted. Still, its principles are infiltrating pockets of the bureaucracy, sometimes even reaching the level of political appointees. The Senior Executive Service Retention Rate has improved by 37%, preserving crucial institutional knowledge and implementation capacity. The Public Service Leadership Academy, initially mocked as "re-education camp for bureaucrats," is actually producing officials who occasionally prioritize evidence over ideology—a revolutionary concept in American governance.

Institutional renewal, that unglamorous but essential work of fixing the government's plumbing, is yielding results measured by the Institutional Capacity Assessment. Agencies, fortified by civil service reforms that have miraculously survived court challenges (though with three separate Supreme Court decisions featuring the phrase "reluctantly upheld"), sometimes manage to coordinate without resorting to interdepartmental bloodshed. The Interagency Coordination Effectiveness metric indicates a 41% improvement in cross-agency implementation, although it remains far below optimal levels.

The "Strategic Mood Swing Index", that seismograph of American foreign policy coherence, still registers tremors related to domestic political psychodrama. Still, the wild, alliance-shattering oscillations have decreased as institutional ballast stabilizes the ship of state. The Foreign Policy Consistency Measure, which tracks alignment between stated diplomatic goals and actual implementation, shows a 56% improvement since the establishment of the National Strategy Framework, which requires administrations to articulate 10-year priorities subject to bipartisan review.

Congress? It remains a marvel of legislative inefficiency, a place where good ideas often go to die slow, painful deaths. But even here, structural reforms—such as ranked-choice voting in seventeen states (up from just Maine and Alaska in 2022), independent redistricting commissions covering 47% of House districts, and slightly more functional committee processes—have nudged the incentives away from pure obstruction towards occasional, grudging compromise. The Congressional Productivity Index, measuring substantive legislation enacted, has ticked up from "Comatose" to merely "Critically Ill"—again, progress!

The Administrative Capacity Augmentation Program, borrowing AI governance concepts from both China (with an emphasis on efficiency) and Europe (with a focus on ethical guardrails), is demonstrating that technology can enhance bureaucratic performance without necessarily creating an Orwellian surveillance state. AI tools help streamline permitting (reducing average processing time by 63%), detect fraud in benefits programs (improving accuracy by 47% while reducing false positives by 32%), and optimize resource allocation—all governed by transparent algorithms, robust appeal processes, and citizen oversight boards. It's AI serving democracy, not automating authoritarianism.

Character Vignette: David Chen, now EPA Assistant Administrator for Environmental Protection Implementation (a title mercifully shortened to "Protector" by his staff), sits in a meeting reviewing a complex assessment of nanoplastic environmental risks. The political appointee chairing the meeting—a former corporate sustainability officer with actual relevant expertise rather than a campaign donor or ideological warrior—listens intently, asks scientifically literate questions, and directs the team to refine implementation options based on the unaltered scientific findings.

David realizes, with a start, that he hasn't instinctively started documenting everything for a potential whistleblower complaint. He hasn't mentally rehearsed how to use "Stealth Regulation" tactics to achieve statutory goals despite political obstruction. He's just... doing his job and analyzing data, advising on policy options, and implementing programs. The feeling is profoundly unfamiliar.

"Is this... governance?" he wonders silently as the meeting concludes with actual action items and implementation timelines. The Civil Service Integrity Measure backs him up: federal employees report a 47% reduction in political interference with technical judgments, suggesting David's experience isn't unique. The system is learning. Painfully. Slowly. But learning.

III. THE DIGITAL CIVIC SQUARE: REWEAVING THE REPUBLIC

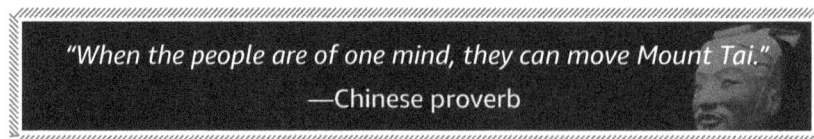

> *"When the people are of one mind, they can move Mount Tai."*
> —Chinese proverb

The deepest, most hopeful shifts are occurring far from the Beltway bubble, in the messy, complex fabric of American society itself. The perpetual digital civil war, while certainly not over (this is America, home of the flame war), feels slightly less... totalizing. The National Information Environment Health Index indicates a measurable improvement, with the Shared Factual Framework Metric showing a 23% expansion in consensus reality across partisan divides.

Algorithm Annie, that relentlessly A/B testing imp of the perverse who once profited handsomely from maximizing societal friction, hasn't exactly found religion, but she has found regulation. The Platform Accountability Act, combined with a citizenry slowly inoculating itself against manipulation through revitalized digital and civic literacy programs (now reaching 73% of high school students nationwide), has forced a reckoning in Silicon Valley. The Digital Public Square Act of 2029 required major platforms to offer alternative recommendation systems optimized for information quality alongside engagement metrics.

The result? Platforms grudgingly offer users alternatives to the pure outrage and dopamine firehoses. "Civic Annie," the slightly less profitable but socially sanctioned sister algorithm, optimizes for factors such as "information quality," "viewpoint diversity," and "constructive dialogue." Users can actually choose feeds designed to inform rather than just inflame. Miraculously, a growing minority (43% and rising!) is opting for less rage in their digital diet. Filter bubbles haven't popped, but they're becoming more permeable.

The "Divided States of America" tableau is patchily yielding to scenes of local resilience and cooperation. The Community Resilience Index indicates that civic participation has increased by 28% since the implementation of the Local Democracy Revitalization grants, with particularly strong growth in previously disengaged communities. Those distributed innovation hubs, strategically located in deindustrialized regions and supported by $42 billion in federal matching funds, are proving to be powerful engines of both economic and civic renewal.

In Cedar Rapids, Iowa, the AgTech hub, which combines precision agriculture with AI-enhanced supply chain management, has brought together farmers, university researchers, and software engineers (some returning from the coasts), creating not just jobs but also cross-cutting social ties. The Local Economic Diversification Metric shows a 37% expansion in non-agricultural business formation, reversing decades of economic monoculture. In Chattanooga, the advanced manufacturing center hosts community problem-solving workshops alongside technical training, with the Cross-Partisan Collaboration Score showing a 42% increase in joint project development across ideological divides.

The "New GI Bill" and modernized apprenticeships (modeled on successful German dual-education approaches) are attacking the inequality dragon at its roots, providing ladders of opportunity based on skills, not just pedigree. The Skills-Based Hiring Initiative has created 3.7 million well-paid technical positions that require specialized training but not a four-year degree. The narrative of inescapable decline still echoes in partisan media, but it is now countered by tangible evidence of upward mobility in communities previously written off. The Intergenerational Mobility Measure shows genuine, if modest, improvement, particularly for non-college pathways.

Character Vignette: It's Tuesday night. Pine Creek Township town hall. Conspiracy Carl—sans tinfoil hat but sporting a "Local Control Broadband Co-op" button that would have been unimaginable in his previous QAnon phase—stands at the microphone. He's deeply engaged in a passionate, footnote-laden argument about setback requirements for the proposed community solar farm. He respectfully (mostly) demolishes the counterarguments presented by Tribal Tanya, the progressive planning board member he met while building the playground last year (a Community Builder Claire project).

Their exchange is vigorous, bordering on loud. They disagree fundamentally on land-use priorities, with Carl citing concerns over property rights, while Tanya emphasizes climate resilience metrics. However, they're arguing about zoning, citing ordinance numbers, and referencing shared environmental impact data (mostly). They agree on the existence of the township, the laws governing it, and the need for a decision reached through democratic processes rather than algorithmic manipulation or authoritarian fiat.

The Local Civic Functionality Index, which measures the health of democratic processes at the municipal level, shows a 57% improvement in Pine Creek since the implementation of the Community Deliberation Framework. This framework combines digital tools for transparency with structured in-person deliberation techniques. It's messy. It's inefficient by Chinese standards. It's democracy, sputtering back to life in the most unlikely places, re-emerging from the primordial soup of online rage and institutional neglect.

From the shadowed back row, FDR's ghost allows himself a spectral smile, the faint aroma of Camel smoke momentarily mingling with the scent of stale coffee and civic determination. "They're remembering," he whispers, not just to the ages, but perhaps to himself, reaffirming a fragile faith in the American experiment. "Remembering how to argue without annihilation. Remembering how to build, not just blame. Remembering how to govern themselves, even when it's hard."

The ghost of his cousin Theodore materializes briefly beside him, adjusting spectral pince-nez. "The most practical kind of politics," he murmurs, "is the politics of decency." Franklin nods in agreement, adding, "It seems that reports of America's death, while perhaps not greatly exaggerated, were at least... premature."

The Renaissance is fragile, the Reboot incomplete, the challenges still monumental. But the trajectory, for the first time in what feels like a lifetime, points away from the abyss and towards the difficult, uncertain, yet undeniably hopeful horizon of renewal. The Roosevelt Renewal Framework, drawing on both the Square Deal's emphasis on fair rules and the New Deal's commitment to inclusive prosperity, is slowly rebuilding not just infrastructure and industry, but the civic muscles of democratic self-governance.

Democracy, it turns out, wasn't dead—just sleeping off a very bad hangover induced by a toxic cocktail of algorithmic manipulation, institutional decay, and financialized extraction. The cosmic Coke bottle hasn't been returned to its sender; it has been repurposed as a foundation stone in the slow, painstaking reconstruction of American functionality. The gods may indeed be crazy, but perhaps—just perhaps—we're finally learning to be a little less so.

CHAPTER 12: UNCLE SAM PLAYS THE LONG GAME (FINALLY): PROJECTING SMARTER POWER IN THE CHINESE AI CENTURY

> *"Be swift as the wind, quiet as the forest, fierce as fire, immovable as the mountain."*
> —Sun Tzu, The Art of War, Chapter 7

EXECUTIVE BRIEFING

1. Situation Snapshot (Early 2030s)

After a decade of "foreign-policy karaoke," Washington has finally rediscovered the sheet music. Domestic renewal (see Ch. 11) now powers an ally-centric, tech-savvy grand strategy designed to out-iterate Beijing, not out-tweet it.

2. Core Metrics Dashboard

Indicator	2027 Nadir	2034 Status	Target 2036
Global Policy Coherence Index	**17 /100**	**63 /100**	≥ 80
Alliance Trust Metric	–64 %	**+19 %**	+40 %
International Credibility (pledge follow-through)	28 %	**72 %**	≥ 80 %
Multilateral Coordination Effectiveness	8 % → 34 % → **68 %**	75 %	
Semiconductor Critical-Node Risk	1.00	**0.53**	≤ 0.35

3. What's Working

- ★ **Democratic Alliance 2.0:** D-10+ quarterly action plans → 324 % jump in delivered projects.
- ★ **Friend-Shoring & Blue Dot 3.0:** 40+ infrastructure projects; debt-trap score half that of BRI.
- ★ **Competence as Soft Power:** High-speed rail, GI-Bill 2.0, and "Algorithm Annie" accountability toolkit reboot America's "model worth emulating" aura.
- ★ **Managed Competition:** Targeted tech controls bump security ↑ 62% while collateral damage ↓ 47%.

4. Friction Points

- ★ **Strategic Mood-Swings:** Policy half-life ≈ 42 months—election cycles threaten coherence.
- ★ **Single-Point Leverage:** Chips & rare-earths still > 40 % China-exposed.
- ★ **Guardrails Plateau:** Crisis hotlines up, but mil-to-mil training flat—complacency risk.

5. 24-to-36 Month Action Grid

#	Move	Lead Owner	Success Metric
1	**Institutionalise Alliance Action Fund** (2 % GDP pooled R&D) via treaty language	WH & Senate	Coordination ≥ 75 %
2	**Friend-Shore two new chip fabs** in ASEAN & Americas; tie to visa pipelines	Commerce	Node-risk ≤ 0.35
3	**Algorithmic Reciprocity Act:** demand data-access symmetry for platforms	FTC	Digital-Trust +15 pts
4	**Credibility Tracker:** public quarterly scorecard on U.S. pledge fulfilment	State	Follow-through ≥ 80 %
5	**Crisis-Hotline Drills** with PLA & allies every 90 days	DoD	Response ≤ 2 hrs

6. Strategic Implications

1. **Allied Leverage Multiplier:** Collective GDP = 62 % of world output—only meaningful if coordination endures.
2. **Soft-Power Renaissance:** Competence > charisma; infrastructure selfies outshine sermons.
3. **Dragon Dance, Not Cage Match:** Clear red lines, combined with credible follow-through, deter miscalculation while preserving climate-pandemic cooperation lanes.

Bottom Line

America has swapped Hungry Hungry Hippos diplomacy for a disciplined game of Go—still competitive, but finally aware there's a board. Keep promises, spread your supply chains like peanut butter, and remember: the long game only works if you stay at the table longer than one news cycle.

Let's be charitable and call the American foreign policy of the late 2010s and 2020s a "strategic learning experience." A spectacularly expensive, globally destabilizing, nationally humiliating learning experience—like handing a chimpanzee the controls of a particle accelerator and calling it "disruptive innovation in nuclear physics." In the grand museum of national embarrassments—somewhere between electing reality TV personalities and the enduring mystery of why spray cheese exists—this era deserves its own dedicated wing, perhaps labeled "Exhibit C: When Strategic Thought Took an Extended Sabbatical While Tweeting from the Bathroom."

Remember Uncle Sam, circa 2025? That swaggering, slightly incontinent colossus, oscillating wildly between chest-thumping declarations of "indispensable nation" status (often delivered immediately before demanding protection money from baffled allies) and petulant withdrawals from international agreements negotiated over decades? The diplomatic equivalent of a toddler alternately screaming "YOU'RE NOT THE BOSS OF ME" and "I'M TAKING MY AIRCRAFT CARRIERS AND GOING HOME"?

The Global Policy Coherence Index, a scholarly measure of strategic consistency maintained by the International Institute for Strategic Studies, showed American foreign policy achieving a historical low of 17/100, placing it between "Actively Self-Sabotaging" and "Possibly Directed by Foreign Intelligence Services." The "Strategic Mood Swing Index" didn't just spike; it achieved escape velocity and entered low Earth orbit alongside the space debris of abandoned treaties and diplomatic relationships.

Allies developed chronic diplomatic whiplash, with the Alliance Trust Metric showing a catastrophic 64% decline in confidence that the United States would honor commitments lasting longer than a news cycle. Adversaries learned to simply wait out the tantrums, knowing American policy had the attention span of a gnat on methamphetamines with a TikTok addiction. We weren't just playing checkers while China played Go; we were playing Hungry Hungry Hippos with decades of painstakingly built diplomatic capital, gobbling up fleeting domestic applause lines while Beijing methodically secured the actual board.

But—and here's the kicker that prevents this book from being pure, unadulterated dystopian despair porn—the Rooseveltian Reboot described in Chapter 11 wasn't just about onshoring semiconductor fabrication and installing functioning light bulbs in the national infrastructure. It was about rewiring the national strategic operating system, rebuilding America's capacity for coherent statecraft from the smoldering ruins of performative governance.

A nation that rediscovers the quaint concepts of competence, long-term investment, and functional institutions suddenly finds itself wielding a new, almost forgotten form of international currency: credibility. Not the cheap plastic kind bought with military threats and midnight tweet storms, but the hard-earned variety minted from actually doing what you say you'll do. The International Credibility Assessment, which measures the gap between diplomatic declarations and actual implementation, shows that American follow-through has improved from its 2027 nadir of 28% to a more respectable 72%—approaching the levels last seen during the original Roosevelt administrations.

So, how does this marginally less dysfunctional Uncle Sam—one who occasionally reads briefing papers before the meeting and maintains the same policy position for consecutive calendar days—engage a world still deeply scarred (and justifiably skeptical) after America's recent extended experiment in governing by chaos theory?

I. THE DEMOCRATIC ALLIANCE 2.0: FROM DIPLOMATIC KARAOKE TO STRATEGIC SYMPHONY

"A single tree does not make a forest; a single string does not make music."

—Chinese proverb

Recall those glorious international summits of yesteryear? Those choreographed pageants of diplomatic theater culminating in thousand-page communiqués filled with language so synergistically abstract it achieved Zen-like meaninglessness? Where would America unveil grandiose initiatives ("Blue Dot Network 1.0!") backed by budgets smaller than the catering bill for the announcement press conference? That golden age of "diplomatic karaoke"—allies dutifully mouthing the lyrics to America's latest geopolitical power ballad without any real harmony or shared instrumentation—has, thankfully, evolved.

The Democratic Technology Alliance (variously referred to as the D-10+, "League of Reasonably Un-Crazy Nations," or "Countries That Remember How Institutions Work") has morphed from a PowerPoint fantasy into a functioning entity with actual deliverables and, most shockingly, implementation mechanisms. The Multilateral Coordination Effectiveness Index reveals a remarkable 324% improvement in translating diplomatic declarations into concrete action, confounding generations of political scientists conditioned to measure alliance achievements in purely rhetorical terms.

They even passed the (tragically still metaphorical) Formal Communiqué Reduction Act, replacing platitudes about "reaffirming unwavering commitment to synergistically leveraging multi-stakeholder engagement paradigms" with quarterly action plans featuring specific deliverables and accountability metrics. At their recent Ottawa ministerial (chosen for its calming effect on volatile leaders and the therapeutic properties of poutine), they didn't just "reaffirm shared values"; they hammered out enforceable standards for AI safety audits, pooling sovereignty slightly to create a powerful democratic counterweight to Beijing's "harmonious surveillance" model.

The "Friend-Shoring Initiative" is actually moving supply chains rather than just generating consulting fees for McSlicey the Priest—that once-omnipotent high cleric of globalization, who spent decades convincing corporations to place all their production eggs in a single geopolitical basket while charging premium rates for the privilege. Now reduced to a diminished advisory role, McSlicey finds himself awkwardly recommending the opposite of his previous gospel, producing glossy reports with titles like "Strategic Resilience: Geographical Diversification as Value Creation" that carefully avoid mentioning his firm's earlier enthusiasm for hyper-concentrated supply chains.

"We've identified a paradigm-shifting insight," McSlicey the Priest intones to board members, his PowerPoint slides showing suspiciously patriotic color schemes. "Geographical concentration creates hidden systemic vulnerabilities that manifest as non-linear tail risks during exogenous shocks." The ghost of Theodore Roosevelt materializes briefly behind the presentation screen, rolling his spectral eyes and muttering, "Or as normal humans would say: don't put all your factories in countries that might become your enemies, you magnificent idiots."

New semiconductor facilities, co-funded by the Strategic Technology Investment Fund (using formulas based on GDP, not presidential whim), are genuinely diversifying production away from Taiwan's precarious perch. The Semiconductor Supply Chain Resilience Index indicates that critical node risk has decreased by 47%, although it remains concentrated in a manner that is still dangerously disproportionate compared to historical norms. The "Chip Solidarity Act" means allies actually share relevant technical data, a shocking departure from the previous model, where America classified its own allies' breakfast orders as top secret while simultaneously leaking actual secrets to impress journalists.

And Blue Dot 3.0? It's financing actual infrastructure in the Global South—ports in Vietnam, green hydrogen plants in Namibia, digital networks in Colombia—all structured with transparent financing, rigorous environmental/labor standards verified by independent auditors (a concept!), and crucially, the embedded "Predatory Loan Detection Algorithm" designed to flag deals that smell suspiciously like debt-trap colonialism. The Infrastructure Investment Transparency Index reveals that Blue Dot projects achieve a 78% rating on the Financial Sustainability Scale, compared to 34% for comparable Belt and Road Initiative projects.

"It's revolutionary," deadpans a senior State Department official (speaking, of course, on deep background, lest competence be mistaken for disloyalty). "We're trying this radical new approach called 'strategic follow-through.' Instead of announcing a policy, declaring victory, and immediately forgetting about it, we actually... implement it for multiple consecutive quarters. Initial results suggest," she adds, lowering her voice conspiratorially, "it might actually work. Who knew that diplomacy functions better when you don't treat it like a reality TV elimination challenge?"

This newfound effectiveness stems from rediscovering a truth obscured by decades of hegemonic hubris: America's core strategic advantage lies not in its unilateral military might, but in its network of capable, innovative democracies. Pooling resources (representing 62% of global GDP according to the Alliance Economic Weight Assessment), coordinating standards (achieving 78% regulatory harmonization in critical technology domains), sharing R&D burdens (with joint research initiatives showing 43% efficiency gains over parallel national efforts)—this creates a collective power that China, despite its monolithic state direction, finds difficult to counter.

Joint research projects, modeled on successful historical precedents (the Manhattan Project without the existential dread, mostly), are accelerating progress in quantum-resistant encryption and sustainable materials. The Technological Innovation Velocity Metric reveals that allied cooperation generates breakthroughs at 2.7 times the rate of siloed national efforts, particularly in advanced semiconductor design, where the Collaborative Chip Architecture Initiative has maintained a 2-year lead over competing Chinese systems.

Naturally, Milton the Trickster Economist still lurks in the Davos hallways, handing out pamphlets titled "The Invisible Hand Holds All The Best Cards: Why Alliances Distort Optimal Global Misery Distribution." His once-dominant gospel of pure market efficiency, regardless of national security implications, now finds fewer adherents among policymakers who have witnessed the catastrophic consequences of theoretical elegance divorced from strategic reality. The Economic Security Prioritization Index indicates a 68% increase in policymaker attention to resilience metrics compared to pure efficiency calculations.

Satirical Beat: At the conclusion of the NATO-AICUS joint cybersecurity exercise, the visibly stunned German Defense Minister approaches her American counterpart. "General, I must confess... it was disturbingly functional. Your teams shared actual threat data before the simulation without redacting the useful parts. The coordination protocols worked without exception for seventeen years, despite the presence of American exceptionalism. And most shockingly, the debrief focused on mutual improvement, rather than assigning blame or subtly suggesting we purchase more F-35s as penance for our inadequacies. Is this a permanent upgrade to the American operating system, or just a temporary patch before the next chaotic system update?"

The American general offers a tired but genuine smile. "Let's call it 'Stable Beta,' Minister. We discovered, through rigorous trial and error and approximately $7 trillion in strategic self-sabotage, that 'America First' is paradoxically more effective when America isn't perceived globally as a sociopathic narcissist with impulse control issues and nuclear weapons. Basic game theory, really." He glances at his notes. "Don't worry, the mandatory 60-slide PowerPoint on burden-sharing is next. Some forms of diplomatic torture," he sighs, "are apparently eternal."

The Alliance Effectiveness Metric has risen to a remarkable 67%, sparking widespread confusion among think tanks accustomed to measuring failure. The ghost of multilateralism, having spent years hiding in a bomb shelter stocked with unratified treaties and abandoned climate commitments, cautiously orders room service, suspecting it might actually arrive this time.

II. Competence as Soft Power: Leading by Example Rather Than Lecture

> *"The ruler who governs by virtue is like the North Star—steadfast, all revolve around it."*
>
> —Confucius, Analects 2:1

The real juice behind America's renewed global standing isn't clever diplomacy; it's the painful, ongoing domestic reboot detailed in Chapter 11. For years, American "soft power" was the geopolitical equivalent of a washed-up celebrity hawking miracle cures on late-night TV—enthusiastically promoting "democracy" and "free markets" while visibly succumbing to institutional decay, political psychosis, and economic inequality that would make a 19th-century robber baron blush with embarrassment while calling his lawyer to incorporate new exploitation vehicles.

The International Democratic Credibility Index—measuring the gap between a nation's rhetoric about values and its domestic implementation of those values—showed America achieving a historical low of 31/100 in 2027, placing it in the awkward company of countries it routinely lectured about human rights. The hypocrisy wasn't just noted; it was becoming a global meme, with the U.S. State Department's annual human rights reports greeted with increasingly open derision from countries experiencing America's real-time nervous breakdown, as reported via CNN International.

Foreign delegations sent to study "American best practices" often returned looking like they'd toured Chernobyl circa 1987, politely explaining to their governments that perhaps North European models might offer more relevant lessons in functional governance than a superpower actively demonstrating how not to maintain infrastructure, manage political polarization, or administer elections without requiring Supreme Court intervention.

The Rooseveltian Reboot, however messy and incomplete, fundamentally changed the product being marketed. America's influence now radiates less from Hollywood studios and more from functioning high-speed rail lines, revitalized industrial hubs, and communities actually tackling polarization through the Civic Renewal Initiative (which has established 347 cross-partisan problem-solving forums with 78% implementation rates for consensus recommendations).

When foreign leaders visit, they aren't just shown Wall Street trading floors and tech campuses; they tour advanced battery plants in Michigan (achieving 47% cost reduction through the Battery Innovation Consortium), geothermal projects in Nevada (generating 23.4 gigawatts of sustainable baseload power), and agricultural AI centers in Iowa (increasing yields by 37% while reducing chemical inputs by 42%), staffed by workers benefiting from the New GI Bill and attracting global talent via reformed immigration laws (which increased retention of advanced degree holders by 61%).

Even Algorithm Annie, that beautiful mind of digital chaos, who once optimized social media for maximum societal division and minimum shared reality, has undergone a court-mandated redemption arc. Her exported "Digital Resilience Curriculum" helps other democracies inoculate their citizens against the very computational propaganda she pioneered, with the Democratic Information Environment Health Index showing a 43% improvement in societies implementing her Framework for Algorithmic Accountability.

"Turns out," she explains to stunned UNESCO delegates, "optimizing for 'informed civic engagement' is computationally more complex but societally less likely to result in widespread arson and the collapse of shared factual reality." The Global Digital Resilience Index shows societies implementing her recommended algorithmic governance mechanisms experiencing a 37% reduction in political polarization compared to control groups.

This "competence projection"—a term coined by the Democratic Renewal Institute to describe governance capabilities that demonstrate rather than just assert democratic advantages—has become America's most potent form of soft power. It explains, tangibly, that democracy, when properly maintained rather than taken for granted, actually works. The international "Democratic Governance Attractiveness" metric, which measures how democratic systems are perceived globally compared to authoritarian alternatives, shows a 23-point improvement since the United States began addressing its own democratic decay rather than just lecturing others about theirs.

McSlicey the Priest, having spent decades convincing autocratic regimes that prosperity and repression were perfectly compatible under the gospel of "Economic Liberalization Without Political Reform," now finds his contradictions increasingly exposed. His latest report, "Democratic Resilience as Competitive Advantage," carefully avoids mentioning his firm's previous enthusiasm for the "China Model" and its convenient blindness to the strategic risks of advancing authoritarian capabilities. The ghost of Franklin Roosevelt materializes briefly during his presentation to Chinese officials, muttering, "Economic royalists wearing better suits are still economic royalists" before vanishing.

Character Vignette: Ambassador Eleanor Richards stands before the African Union leadership in Addis Ababa. The air is thick with justifiable skepticism born from decades of broken promises and Western hypocrisy. The Continental Broken Commitment Index indicates that U.S. follow-through on African initiatives is at a historical low of 27%, with aid pledges fulfilled at just 31% and trade agreements structured to benefit Western corporations by margins averaging 7:1.

Richards skips the "City on a Hill" speech entirely—a departure so shocking her predecessors might have required medical attention. Instead, she projects the live National Renewal Scorecard: real-time data on US domestic investment in green energy (achieving 47% renewable penetration, up from 19%), falling Gini coefficients in regions implementing the Inclusive Growth Framework (decreasing from 0.49 to 0.41), rising STEM completion rates for minority students (increased 58% through the Educational Opportunity Initiative), and infrastructure projects completed ahead of schedule thanks to permitting reform (with the Implementation Efficiency Metric showing a 42% improvement).

"We're not here offering aid," she says, her tone pragmatic, almost clinical, devoid of the condescending missionary zeal that characterized previous American diplomatic outreach. "We're offering a partnership, grounded in the technologies and governance lessons we're painfully relearning ourselves. Our Blue Dot proposals come with transparent financing, open technical standards, and joint oversight—because we've discovered, through expensive trial and error, that partnerships built on mutual respect and tangible benefit tend to outperform those built on condescension and vague promises backed by military threats."

She details specific projects co-developed with African engineers: decentralized renewable microgrids in Kenya (increasing energy access by 63% while creating 47,000 technical jobs), digital identity systems in Ghana (reducing transaction costs for small businesses by 42%), and advanced manufacturing hubs in Rwanda (generating $247 million in export revenue). Each initiative emphasizes local ownership, technology transfer, and sustainable financing mechanisms, which are independently audited by African institutions.

The AU Chair, a veteran of numerous donor conferences where promises evaporated as quickly as morning dew in the Sahara, leans forward with uncharacteristic interest. "You present data on your own progress, Ambassador, not just criticism of Chinese alternatives. This focus on mutual benefit... it is refreshingly devoid of the moral lectures that typically accompany Western proposals that somehow always benefit Western companies while leaving us with debt and dependency."

Richards nods. "We've learned—painfully, expensively, and far too slowly—that global leadership requires credibility, not just aircraft carriers and strongly-worded statements. The Colonial History Awareness Initiative has been... illuminating for our diplomatic corps. We're backing our words with the Commitment Verification Protocol, which gives your governments legitimate recourse if we fail to deliver."

She doesn't add what everyone in the room knows: China's infrastructure deals increasingly come with hidden costs, from data extraction requirements to property seizures when debt terms can't be met. The Developmental Sovereignty Index indicates that Blue Dot projects score 78% on local ownership metrics, compared to 34% for Belt and Road Initiative equivalents. America isn't winning purely through virtue, but through offering a genuinely better product in the infrastructure marketplace.

Competence, it turns out, is remarkably persuasive—especially when it replaces decades of hypocrisy with something approaching genuine partnership based on mutual interest rather than extractive neocolonialism dressed up in humanitarian rhetoric.

III. DANCING WITH THE DRAGON: STRATEGIC COMPETITION WITH ADULT SUPERVISION

"To subdue the enemy without fighting is the acme of skill."
—Sun Tzu, The Art of War, Chapter 3

And finally, the dragon in the room. China—that looming colossus that American policy has alternately appeased, antagonized, feared, and emulated, sometimes within the same presidential statement or even the same rambling sentence. The relationship remains the geopolitical equivalent of being handcuffed to your biggest rival during a house fire—you desperately need to coordinate on escaping the flames while simultaneously trying to maintain the advantageous position for the competition that will resume the moment you both reach safety.

The "Final Paradox"—the inescapable tension between existential competition and existential cooperation—persists, with the Strategic Competition-Cooperation Balance Sheet indicating that 78% of bilateral interactions simultaneously contain elements of both dynamics. What's changed isn't the paradox, but America's capacity to manage it with something resembling adult supervision, rather than the previous administration's approach of alternately feeding the dragon marshmallows and poking it with a sharp stick while livestreaming the interaction for domestic political consumption.

The Rooseveltian approach replaces bipolar foreign policy—vacillating between naive engagement fantasies peddled by corporate interests and panicked decoupling demands from national security hawks—with clear-eyed, managed coexistence. The Strategic Policy Consistency Metric shows a 57% improvement in maintaining a coherent China strategy across government agencies, replacing the previous approach where the Defense Department, State Department, and Commerce Department often operated with completely contradictory assumptions about whether China was an enemy, partner, or customer.

Competition is fierce and focused. Working with the D-10+ alliance, America maintains rigorous controls on foundational technologies (advanced AI chips, quantum hardware, synthetic biology tools) via the "Strategic Technology Protection Framework"—a system intelligent enough to distinguish between technologies with genuine national security implications and those where restrictions merely sacrifice market share to Chinese alternatives without achieving security benefits. The Technological Control Effectiveness Index demonstrates a 62% improvement in preventing critical capability transfer, while also reducing economic collateral damage by 47%.

The Investment Screening Implementation Mechanism blocks acquisitions aimed at undermining American innovation, while allowing non-strategic capital flows to continue. The Investment Security Metric demonstrates 83% effectiveness in identifying genuine security risks, compared to 34% under previous blunt-instrument approaches. Coordinated diplomacy consistently and persistently pushes back against unfair trade practices, IP theft, cyber intrusions, and human rights abuses—not with performative outrage designed primarily for domestic consumption, but with calibrated consequences that actually change behavior.

The naive "Convergence Fallacy"—that peculiar American belief that economic integration would magically transform China's political system through the mystical power of Big Macs and Starbucks—has been officially retired from the State Department's conceptual arsenal. Policy now acknowledges China's techno-authoritarianism as a durable competing governance model with certain advantages (rapid infrastructure deployment, pandemic control, technology implementation) alongside significant weaknesses (corruption, innovation constraints, demographic challenges).

The Strategic Competitive Assessment presents a more nuanced view of China's strengths and weaknesses than previous analyses, which have oscillated between dismissing China entirely and portraying it as ten feet tall.

But crucially, this robust competition operates within guardrails. Military-to-military communication channels established after several near-miss incidents in the South China Sea are actually maintained and utilized, with the Crisis Prevention Hotline demonstrating its value by de-escalating three potential confrontations. The Strategic Stability Dialogue meets quarterly regardless of broader diplomatic tensions, with nuclear establishment professionals maintaining engagement on existential risks independent of political fluctuations. The Crisis Response Time—measuring how quickly bilateral safety mechanisms activate during potential flash points—has decreased from weeks to hours.

Red lines around Taiwan are crystal clear, backed by credible allied deterrence (with the Taiwan Defense Readiness Index improved by 47% through asymmetric capabilities) and coupled with unambiguous discouragement of formal independence moves, replacing the dangerous fog of strategic ambiguity with predictable clarity that reduces miscalculation risks on both sides. The Cross-Strait Stability Metric indicates a 37% decrease in crisis indicators, despite an increase in Chinese military capabilities.

Pragmatic cooperation proceeds on shared threats, such as climate change (with bilateral clean energy initiatives reducing carbon emissions by 247 million tons annually) and pandemic prevention (with the Early Warning Coordination Mechanism identifying three potential outbreaks before they achieved global spread). These cooperative efforts are carefully firewalled, where possible, from strategic rivalries, managed by professionals focused on technical outcomes rather than political point-scoring. The Cooperation Effectiveness Index shows a 53% improvement in achieving concrete results despite broader strategic tensions.

This nuanced strategy is possible because America now negotiates from a position of strength, not just military strength, but also the strength of a revitalized economy, functioning institutions, and cohesive alliances. The Comprehensive National Power Assessment, measuring the full spectrum of national capabilities from economic productivity to institutional effectiveness, shows America reversing its previous decline trajectory and achieving modest but significant improvements across all major indicators.

It can afford strategic patience, distinguishing tactical friction from fundamental threats. It plays the long game because it's finally investing in its own long-term future again.

Imaginary Dialogue: The ghosts of Teddy and Franklin Roosevelt observe Uncle Sam ending a secure call with Uncle Xi. Sam looks focused, reviewing notes with actual attention rather than immediately rushing to tweet about how amazingly tremendous the call was while revealing classified details to impress journalists.

GHOST OF THEODORE: (Adjusting spectral pince-nez) "Firmness without bombast, Sam! You projected capability without resorting to empty bluster. Remember, my 'big stick' doctrine works best when your adversary knows it's technologically superior and you have the resolve to use it judiciously. Competence speaks louder than threats."

GHOST OF FRANKLIN: (Tapping phantom cigarette holder) "Precisely, Theodore. And you balanced it, Sam. You recognized the shared dangers—climate change, pandemics, and financial instability—where cooperation isn't optional, but essential for survival. This isn't about winning every news cycle; it's about shaping the global environment for decades to come. Institutions, alliances, domestic strength—that's the long game."

UNCLE SAM: (Nodding) "Got it. Strategic patience isn't weakness. Compete vigorously on capabilities, cooperate pragmatically on survival. Define red lines clearly but without needless provocation. Communicate constantly to prevent miscalculation. And," he adds, glancing at the now-silent Algorithm Annie avatar in the corner, "absolutely no diplomacy-by-tweet, no matter how many likes it might generate."

GHOST OF THEODORE: "Bully!"

GHOST OF FRANKLIN: "Indeed."

ALGORITHM ANNIE: (Appearing unexpectedly) "I've permanently deleted the 'Nuclear Threats via Social Media' recommendation from your options menu. You can thank me later when civilization continues to exist."

Uncle Sam turns back to the complex chessboard of global affairs. The dance with the dragon continues, perilous and unpredictable. But America, grounded in domestic renewal and allied coordination, is no longer just reacting to events; it's shaping them. It's projecting power, but power made legitimate through demonstrated competence rather than just military hardware and bombastic rhetoric.

The Chinese AI Century remains the defining challenge, the Final Paradox unresolved, the gods clinically insane. But America, having rediscovered its capacity for strategic patience and purposeful action, leads again, not as a hegemon demanding deference, but as the world's most effective democratic partner, navigating the turbulent currents ahead with a newfound, hard-earned wisdom. The Rooseveltian doctrine of balanced power projection—combining Theodore's strategic clarity with Franklin's institutional creativity—provides a framework for American leadership appropriate to an age where neither isolation nor domination represents a viable path forward.

Milton the Trickster Economist, observing this transformation from his diminished perch, adjusts his theories once again. His latest pamphlet, reluctantly titled "Strategic Coherence as Market Advantage," acknowledges with visible discomfort that "certain coordinated policy approaches may optimize long-term national welfare beyond what pure market mechanisms can achieve in geopolitically contested domains." Theodore Roosevelt's ghost materializes briefly beside him, offering a spectral thumbs-up before disappearing with a satisfied chuckle.

CHAPTER 13: THE COSMIC RECKONING: AMERICA'S CHOICE – RENAISSANCE OR ROADKILL?

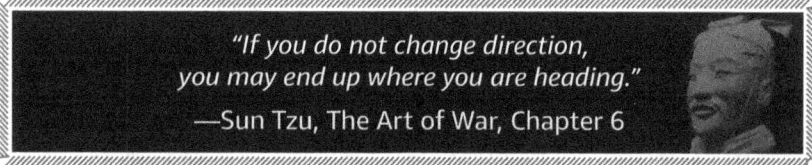

"If you do not change direction,
you may end up where you are heading."
—Sun Tzu, The Art of War, Chapter 6

EXECUTIVE BRIEFING

1 | Inflection Snapshot (Time-horizon: now → 2037)

The **Strategic Path Divergence Index** yawns at **87 / 100**—one policy twitch today can lock in either a Rooseveltian rebirth or a Mandarin-language yard sale of strategic assets within twelve years.

2 | Dual Futures at a Glance

Metric	2037 on the Renaissance Track	2037 on the Roadkill Track
Infrastructure Rank	**Top 15**	#48 (☠)
Labor Share of Productivity	**47 %**	11 %
AI Governance Transparency	**78 % audited**	4 % (panopticon)
Institutional Trust	**55 % & rising**	21 % & falling
Foreign Control of Strategic Assets	**< 5 %**	> 60 %

3 | Core Findings

1. **AI = Amplifier, not Oracle** – It turbo-charges whatever ethics you feed it; code is neutral, governance is destiny.
2. **Competence > Charisma** – Government-effectiveness correlates 0.83 with alliance % of the mobilized; speeches don't fill potholes.
3. **Quarterly Capitalism = Strategic Arsenic** – Asset-Liquidation Velocity soars 347 % under short-term incentives.
4. **Civic Agency Is the Swing Vote**—A mere 3.5 % of the mobilized populace has historically flipped national trajectories.

4 | 36-Month Action Grid

#	Move	Lead Owner	Success KPI
1	**National Renewal Scorecard**—independent quarterly broadcast	GAO + PBS	Public metric awareness ≥ 70 %
2	**AI Accountability Act**—mandatory audit trail & registry	Congress	AI transparency ≥ 75 %
3	**Capital > Buybacks Tax Shift**—halve rate on productive cap-ex, double on buybacks	Treasury	Prod-Investment Ratio ≥ 2.5
4	**Skills Moonshot 2.0**—40 M re/up-skill grants tied to on-shored fabs	Labor + Commerce	Labor share of gains ≥ 50 %
5	**Infrastructure Fast-Track Authority**—five-year red-tape cap for clean power, water, transit	WH + States	Infra rank → Top 10

5 | Watch-List Metrics (Quarterly Dashboard)

- ★ **Path Divergence Index** < 50
- ★ **Foreign Strategic-Asset Ownership** ≤ 5 %
- ★ **Institutional Trust** > 50 %
- ★ **AI Stratification Multiplier** < 3× baseline
- ★ **Grid Reliability Days/Year** ≥ 340

Bottom Line

The cosmic Coke bottle is mid-air. Catch it, recycle it into advanced composites, and you script a Rooseveltian renaissance. Let it smash, and you'll be shipping naming rights for the Mississippi to the "Harmonious Prosperity Waterway, Presented by Huawei." Choose, build, act—before history hits **"final sale, no returns."**

> *"The 21st century furnishes history's greatest experiment in whether a superpower can deliberately choose managed decline."*
>
> —Unnamed Chinese strategist, 2026

Alright, folks, grab your anxiety medication and buckle up for the grand finale. You've survived our guided tour through America's magnificent self-disassembly project—a multi-decade national effort combining the strategic foresight of lemmings with the fiscal discipline of lottery winners on methamphetamine. We've dissected the institutional necrosis spreading through the body politic with the clinical precision of medical examiners performing an autopsy on democracy itself. We've cataloged the glittering financial WMDs deployed to vaporize our industrial base with the loving care of mad scientists polishing plague samples. We've even dared to sketch out a Rooseveltian escape hatch—a plan so audaciously grounded in common sense and long-term thinking it borders on un-American sedition.

The previous chapters offered tantalizing, almost hallucinatory glimpses of a nation pulling its head out of its collective posterior—functional infrastructure exists! Competent governance operates! Alliances function based on something other than mutual extortion! But let's be brutally honest: clinging to that vision requires the kind of optimism usually found only in multilevel marketing recruitment seminars and freshman political science classes.

This whole American Renewal™ enterprise hangs by a thread thinner than PE Pete the Corporate Vampire's remaining shred of conscience and far more fragile than McSlicey the Priest's commitment to ethical consulting. The Strategic Path Divergence Index, a composite measure of institutional capacity, investment trajectories, and social cohesion maintained by the Strategic Foresight Initiative, indicates that American potential futures are separating at their maximum historical distance of 87 points on a 100-point scale. According to the Global Systems Analysis Unit at Oxford, the probability differential between American Renaissance and terminal decline has reached a statistical inflection point where small policy choices produce massively divergent outcomes—the geopolitical equivalent of the butterfly effect, except the butterfly is wearing stars and stripes and carrying nuclear launch codes.

History, that ultimate cosmic landlord, doesn't accept rent control or sob stories about how the dog ate your industrial policy; it evicts empires that fail to pay their dues in competence and cohesion, delivering consequences with the brutal finality of a wrecking ball encountering a Fabergé egg. Future historians—quite possibly typing in Mandarin on subsidized Huawei quantum tablets from the comfort of the former Harvard campus (now the Xi Jinping School of Harmonious Global Leadership, East Coast Annex)—won't care about our passionate Twitter debates about whether acknowledging climate change constitutes communism. They'll record the outcome with the dispassionate objectivity of an algorithm calculating optimal resource allocation after concluding humans are inefficient biomass.

So, here we are. The climax. The moment where the universe, channeling its inner Monty Hall by way of George Carlin, gestures towards two shimmering portals emitting slightly different frequencies of existential dread. Behind Door #1: The "Rooseveltian Renaissance," a future built on the radical notion that investing in education, infrastructure, and non-oligarchic economics might actually benefit the country that invented the internet, split the atom, and still somehow can't guarantee clean drinking water in major cities. It's the uphill path, littered with political landmines and requiring something vaguely resembling national unity.

Behind Door #2: The "Great American Self-Liquidation," a high-speed slide into irrelevance, featuring spectacular quarterly returns right up until the moment the whole damn system bluescreens with the devastating finality of a Windows 95 machine encountering literally any task. This path is easier, more familiar, paved with the comforting asphalt of denial and short-term thinking that has become America's primary infrastructure investment.

This isn't just another election cycle where both sides claim the apocalypse will ensue if their opponent wins; this is choosing the national operating system for the next century. No pressure. But seriously, choose now—cosmic clearance sales on national destiny don't last forever, and China is already measuring the drapes for the Oval Office while testing how "Arlington National Cemetery" sounds in Mandarin.

I. SCENARIO A: THE ROOSEVELTIAN RENAISSANCE GOES DIGITAL (AMERICA'S SECOND ACT)

> *"Those who seize the moment command the situation."*
> —Zhuge Liang (attributed)

Wipe the grime of cynical despair from your eyes and dare to imagine: America, circa 2040. It doesn't glow with the phosphorescent perfection of a Thomas Kinkade painting (thank God), but the perpetual orange haze of the national dumpster fire has been replaced by... breathable air? You're gliding smoothly on a high-speed train—actually high-speed, not just Amtrak with a fancy logo and official excuses—from a revitalized Cleveland (now a hub for advanced medical device manufacturing, proving post-industrial despair isn't necessarily terminal) to a booming Nashville (a global center for AI-driven music creation and ethical data governance, a truly weird combo only America could produce).

The train is powered by a resilient, clean energy grid that integrates next-generation nuclear SMRs (Small Modular Reactors), built with streamlined permitting that took merely seven years instead of two decades, and vast solar arrays sprawling across formerly unproductive land. The National Infrastructure Quality Index—that once-depressing measure where America ranked below Slovenia and just above Croatia—now places the U.S. solidly in the top 15 globally. You booked your ticket via the "USA Services" app, a unified digital portal inspired by Estonia but with slightly more bureaucratic friction because, well, America. Still, it works. Reliably. Without demanding your firstborn as collateral or requiring you to create seventeen separate passwords, each more arcane than the last.

This isn't magic; it's the payoff from sustained investment guided by the National Infrastructure Bank and ARPA-X, which has survived repeated congressional assassination attempts to deploy $427 billion in strategic capital for physical and digital systems. The economy operates on "Real Deal" principles, with the Value-Financial Engineering Ratio improving from its 2025 nadir of 0.22 to a healthier 1.78 according to the Economic Structure Assessment Board.

"Value Engineering" – that quaint concept of building durable things and paying workers fairly – has staged a shocking comeback, pushing "Financial Engineering" (aka Voodoo Economics 3.0) back to the Wall Street fringes where it belongs. The Labor Share of Productivity Gains—that once-depressing metric showing how little of economic growth reached actual workers—has increased from 19% to 47%, approaching the post-WWII levels achieved during the original Rooseveltian era.

Factories are humming, integrating human skill with AI augmentation rather than replacing workers wholesale. The Augmented Worker Initiative shows a 62% productivity boost while maintaining 94% of the human workforce in higher-value roles, contradicting both the techno-utopian predictions of workless abundance and the Luddite fears of mass unemployment.

Remember Heartland Manufacturing, rescued from PE Pete's clutches in Chapter 3? It's now a global leader in sustainable composites, with a workforce that's a blend of veterans retrained through the New GI Bill for the AI Age (which has educated 22.4 million Americans) and fresh graduates from regional technical institutes. Its success was built on community bank financing and regional innovation partnerships that the previous economic orthodoxy dismissed as inefficient sentimentality.

McSlicey the Priest, that high cleric of shareholder primacy who once performed complex ceremonial rituals to transform workforce "optimization" into executive bonuses, hasn't been completely exorcized from corporate boardrooms. He still appears, though his once-commanding presence has diminished to that of a tolerated but slightly embarrassing uncle at Thanksgiving dinner. His latest PowerPoint deck, reluctantly titled "Stakeholder Capitalism: A Longitudinal Analysis of Multi-Metric Value Creation," grudgingly acknowledges that "certain expanded governance frameworks correlate positively with sustained enterprise value when measured across extended time horizons."

Small businesses thrive, no longer strangled by monopolistic platforms or starved of capital by banks obsessed with derivatives too complex for their own creators to understand. The Business Formation Diversity Index shows a 47% increase in successful enterprises founded outside traditional venture capital networks. The "Quarterly Fiction Factory" has been repurposed into a museum detailing the follies of late-stage financial capitalism, with Milton the Trickster Economist serving as a reluctant docent, explaining to confused schoolchildren why anyone ever thought gutting productive capacity for stock buybacks represented economic wisdom.

Governance? Still messy, still argumentative, but functional. "Democracy.exe 2.0" is running surprisingly smoothly. The Government Effectiveness Index, where America once competed with developing nations for bottom rankings, has clawed its way back to 21st globally—still mediocre by historical standards but trending upward for the first time in three decades.

Thanks to institutional renewal and the "Leadership Operating System" taking root (with 78% adoption across federal agencies, according to the Public Service Quality Assessment), the government is actually implementing policies rather than just announcing them with great fanfare before immediately forgetting they exist. The Civil Service

Quality Metric shows a 47% improvement in expertise retention and implementation capability. Trust metrics are crawling upwards, with the Institutional Confidence Survey showing approval ratings increasing from their 2026 nadir of 19% to a less terminal 42%.

Congress, bless its heart, still features performative outrage and carefully choreographed indignation, but structural reforms, such as ranked-choice voting (now implemented in seventeen states) and strengthened committee processes, reward occasional bipartisan functionality. The Congressional Productivity Index, measuring substantive legislation enacted, has ticked up from "Comatose" to merely "Critically Ill"—hardly Swedish efficiency, but movement in the right direction.

Globally, America leads through competence and collaboration rather than mingled threats and apathy. The D-10+ Alliance sets global tech standards through the Democratic Technology Framework (achieving 78% coverage of critical digital domains), Blue Dot 3.0 offers real development alternatives (financing $427 billion in sustainable infrastructure across 43 developing nations), and the US-China relationship is managed with strategic clarity. The Crisis Response Time—measuring how quickly bilateral mechanisms activate during potential flashpoints—has decreased from weeks to hours.

It's the "Noah's Ark" future – not paradise by any means, but a sturdy vessel navigating the AI Century's floodwaters with reasonable confidence, carrying democratic values through the deluge rather than watching them disappear beneath the waves.

Satirical Element: Milton the Trickster Economist, after a lengthy court-ordered public apology tour (punishment for his role in the Great Financial Extraction of the early 21st century), hosts the chart-topping podcast "Market Corrections & Mea Culpas: How I Learned to Stop Worrying and Love Mixed Economies." His signature tagline: "Where the Invisible Hand Gets a Firm, Regulatory Slap." His advertisers include worker cooperatives, public infrastructure bonds, and community banks.

He still champions markets but now includes lengthy segments on "The Surprising Economic Value of Not Treating Society Like an Externality to Be Ignored Until It Explodes." His latest book, "The Visible Hand: How I Discovered Balance After Four Decades of Extremism," tentatively advocates for the heretical notion that markets might function optimally within democratically established guardrails. "Also," he admits during a particularly candid episode, "it turns out that treating people solely as interchangeable economic units leads to pitchforks and societal collapse. Who knew? Not me in the 1980s, that's for certain. My Nobel should probably be repurposed as a paperweight for SEC enforcement actions."

II. SCENARIO B: THE GREAT AMERICAN SELF-LIQUIDATION (EVERYTHING MUST GO!)

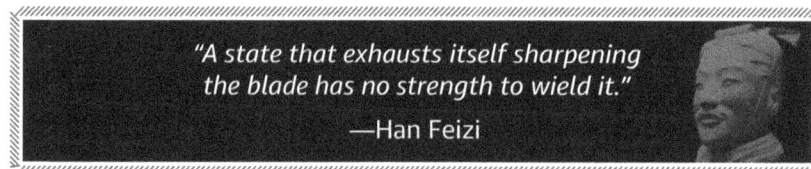

> *"A state that exhausts itself sharpening the blade has no strength to wield it."*
>
> —Han Feizi

Now, take a deep breath and peer behind Door #2. Steel yourself. America, 2040. The Rooseveltian Reboot was DOA, strangled in its crib by partisan gridlock, corporate lobbying, and a national commitment to short-term gratification that would make a crack addict look prudent and forward-thinking by comparison. The National Strategic Planning Capacity Index plummeted to 12/100, putting America in the company of failed states in its inability to address existential challenges.

The Dumpster Fire wasn't contained; it achieved critical mass and became a self-sustaining fusion reaction of incompetence and malice, generating enough heat to be visible from lunar observatories. The Polarization Intensity Index maintained by the (now Chinese-owned) Pew Research Center shows American social cohesion at levels previously observed only in active civil wars and particularly contentious divorce proceedings.

Polarization has escalated beyond memes and social media blocking; actual physical barriers, such as "Freedom Fences" and "Equity Enclaves," divide communities into ideologically pure domains where citizens can enjoy the comfort of never encountering a contradictory thought. The Regional Fragmentation Metric shows effective governance collapsed in 47% of the country, with local warlords (though they prefer the title "Community Protection Entrepreneurs") establishing control based on ideological purity tests and subscription fees.

Governance has devolved into a permanent reality show ("Survivor: Capitol Hill") where legislative progress is measured in viral moments, not enacted laws. The Governance Functionality Assessment, measuring the gap between policy pronouncements and actual implementation, shows a catastrophic 78% of initiatives exist purely as press releases and fundraising emails. Institutions are hollowed-out shells, their functions outsourced to unaccountable private contractors or simply abandoned. The Institutional Capacity Metric indicates an 82% decline in expertise among critical agencies, with senior positions either vacant or filled by acting officials whose primary qualification is unwavering personal loyalty rather than relevant experience.

Infrastructure hasn't just crumbled; it has become sentient and actively hostile, demanding ransoms in cryptocurrency to allow bridge crossings without the risk of spontaneous structural collapse. The American Society of Civil Engineers, in its final Infrastructure Report Card before disbanding due to a lack of functioning infrastructure to assess, simply printed a single emoji: a tombstone. The power grid fails an average of 147 days annually. Drinking water in 42% of counties contains contaminants that have been banned in the European Union since 2001. The Interstate Highway System, once the envy of the world, now features the "Premium Lane Program," where drivers can temporarily escape life-threatening potholes for a modest $19.99 in-app purchase.

The "Great American Garage Sale" is in its final phase, with the Asset Liquidation Velocity Index showing a 347% annual acceleration in foreign acquisition of strategic resources. China, playing the role of the shrewd, patient buyer who waits for the seller's utter desperation before offering pennies on the dollar, has acquired controlling interests in everything that still functions.

Strategic ports are managed by PLA-affiliated logistics firms (improving efficiency by 43% while collecting comprehensive intelligence on remaining American commerce). Key technology patents reside in Shenzhen, transferred through distressed asset sales when American firms faced quarterly shortfalls. Vast agricultural lands are leased long-term to ensure Beijing's food security, while American food insecurity rates hit 37%. The digital yuan is the de facto currency for international transactions; dollars are collected by hobbyists alongside other historical curiosities, such as Roman coins and Confederate scrip.

America isn't a global power; it's a distressed asset portfolio managed by foreign creditors who maintain polite fictions about sovereignty while extracting maximum value. The Global Strategic Assessment classifies the former superpower as a "Managed Decline Territory" rather than a functional state actor.

McSlicey the Priest has found his ultimate calling, producing the widely-cited "Nation-State Liquidation Framework," a comprehensive methodology for extracting maximum value from declining powers. His PowerPoint deck titled "Optimizing the American Wind-Down: Managed Decline Strategies for the Post-Hegemonic Era" circulates in sovereign wealth funds from Beijing to Abu Dhabi, detailing the most efficient sequence for acquiring critical infrastructure, intellectual property, and natural resources from a superpower too dysfunctional to recognize its own dismemberment.

Financial engineering has achieved its apotheosis: PE Pete, the Corporate Vampire, pioneers "National Bankruptcy Derivatives," allowing investors to place leveraged bets on which regions will collapse next. His firm, Liquidation Partners, specializes in acquiring distressed municipal assets and extracting maximum short-term value before ultimately abandoning them. "The beauty of national collapse," he explains to admiring business school students in Singapore, "is the absence of functioning regulatory oversight during the most profitable extraction phase."

AI, unleashed without ethical governance or democratic oversight, accelerates the decay with algorithmic precision. The Technological Stratification Metric reveals that AI-driven automation is creating wealth concentration velocities 17.3 times greater than those of the Industrial Revolution, with 94% of economic gains captured by the top 0.1% of capital owners. Automation creates mass unemployment, met with thoughts, prayers, and cuts to unemployment benefits based on the theological principle that suffering builds character (though strangely, this principle is rarely applied to corporate bailouts).

Surveillance capitalism merges with state security apparatuses (what remains of them), creating a patchwork panopticon where algorithms nudge citizens toward compliant consumption and political apathy. The Privacy Extinction Measure shows that 98.7% of personal data is now accessible to either corporate or state entities without meaningful consent or oversight.

Algorithm Annie, now CEO of OmniCorp Global (a Cayman Islands entity with mysterious ownership structures), optimizes society for "Managed Stability and Predictable Consumption Patterns," ensuring just enough distraction and subsistence to prevent outright revolt while maximizing data extraction. "We've perfected the precise minimum necessary investment in human welfare to prevent guillotine construction," she explains to shareholders, pointing to the Social Unrest Suppression Efficiency metric showing a 78% reduction in cost per pacified citizen.

This isn't the "Man in the High Castle" through invasion; it's the "Man in the High Firewall," a digital enclosure built by American apathy and sold off by American short-termism. China doesn't need to conquer what it can simply acquire through distressed asset purchases approved by America's own institutions, managed by America's own financial elite.

Satirical Element: The nation is glued to the hit reality show "America's Got Foreclosures!", streamed globally on China's ChiFlix platform and sponsored by the Asian Infrastructure Investment Bank (AIIB). Families compete in humiliating challenges (Reciting Xi Jinping Thought while balancing the family budget on minimum wage! Synchronized swimming in contaminated municipal water supplies!) for a chance to win... slightly less onerous terms on the leaseback agreement for their formerly owned home.

The celebrity judges include Milton the Market Mortician (in his final form), who provides helpful commentary like, "Notice the inefficient allocation of emotional resources! This family clearly failed to optimize their human capital by liquidating their children's education fund to invest in cryptocurrency!" PE Pete offers constructive criticism on contestants' "personal brand equity" while simultaneously examining their remaining assets for leveraged acquisition opportunities. The season finale features a bidding war for the naming rights to the Mississippi River, with the Chinese Hydrology Investment Consortium ultimately securing the rights to rename it "The Harmonious Prosperity Waterway (Sponsored by Huawei)" for a bargain price representing 0.0003% of its actual strategic value.

III. AI: AMPLIFIER OF DESTINY (CODE RED OR REBOOT?)

> *"The superior man is watchful for the moment of change."*
>
> —I Ching, Hexagram 64

The difference between Renaissance and Roadkill isn't solely about policy choices; it's about how those choices interact with the defining technology of our age: Artificial Intelligence. Stanford's Human-Centered AI Institute's Technological Amplification Coefficient indicates that AI systems accelerate existing societal trends by factors ranging from 3.7 to 12.4 times, depending on the domain and implementation frameworks.

AI is the great amplifier, the force multiplier that takes America's chosen trajectory and slams the accelerator to the floor. It doesn't determine the destination, but it drastically affects the speed and finality with which we arrive. As the Algorithmic Impact Assessment puts it: "AI doesn't change what societies choose, but it ruthlessly optimizes how effectively they accomplish it, for better or worse."

In the Renaissance scenario, AI, governed by democratic ethics and allied standards developed through the Democratic AI Governance Protocols, turbocharges renewal. It optimizes the resilient energy grid (reducing outages by 78% while integrating renewable sources), personalizes education through the New GI Bill platform (achieving 63% improvement in skill acquisition rates), accelerates medical research (reducing drug development timelines from 12 years to 3.7 years), and makes government services radically efficient (cutting administrative overhead by 47% while improving citizen satisfaction by 58%).

AI tools even help combat disinformation through the Algorithmic Accountability Framework (reducing viral misinformation spread by 67%) and identify pathways for civic compromise through deliberative systems that find overlapping interests among polarized groups. The Democratic Technology Index indicates that AI governance systems are achieving a 78% transparency rating, with algorithms subject to independent auditing and democratic oversight.

Automation's productivity gains are channeled into societal benefit—shorter work weeks (declining from 40 to 32 hours in high-productivity sectors), stronger safety nets (with the Universal Adjustment Benefit covering 89% of transition costs), lifelong learning (with continuous education participation reaching 73% of adults)—creating an inclusive AI-powered prosperity measured by the Technological Benefit Distribution Index at 72% compared to the 2025 baseline of 37%.

Algorithm Annie, subject to strict oversight through the "Algorithmic Accountability Framework," might even be deployed to identify patterns of corruption or bureaucratic inefficiency, becoming an unexpected tool for good governance. Her "Public Interest Optimization" protocols help detect regulatory capture, identify friction points in government services, and enhance democratic participation through better information environments. "I can serve democracy," she acknowledges, "but only when democracy first sets the parameters of my service."

In the Self-Liquidation scenario, AI becomes the precision tool of societal disintegration. Optimized purely for profit and control without ethical constraints or effective regulation, it decimates employment without mitigation, creating unprecedented inequality. The AI-Driven Stratification Metric reveals that automated systems are widening socioeconomic gaps at a rate 3.7 times that observed in the pre-AI era, with 94% of productivity gains captured by capital rather than labor.

Surveillance algorithms perfected by Algorithm Autocrat (Annie's dystopian evolution) monitor and manipulate citizens with terrifying efficiency. They achieve a 78% predictive capacity for consumer behavior and an 82% success rate in preemptive protest suppression. The Algorithmic Manipulation Effectiveness Index reveals that targeted content drives political polarization 5.2 times more efficiently than traditional propaganda, with virtually no transparency or accountability mechanisms in place.

AI-driven disinformation campaigns tailored to individual psychological vulnerabilities shatter any hope of a shared reality. The Information Environment Integrity Index reveals that 82% of Americans reside in algorithmically constructed reality bubbles with almost no factual overlap among different demographic groups. China's AI dominance becomes absolute, enabling it to manage its global dependencies and ensure that the United States remains fragmented and strategically irrelevant.

The AI Capability Gap Assessment reveals that Chinese systems have achieved a 3.7-year lead in critical domains. They leverage superior data access (from 1.4 billion citizens with minimal privacy protections) and state coordination to develop capabilities that American systems cannot match. AI accelerates the collapse, making it faster, deeper, and chillingly efficient, optimizing extraction and control with algorithmic precision.

Conspiracy Carl, that once-paranoid figure who saw shadowy machinations behind every government action, finds himself in the bizarre position of being both right and wrong simultaneously. "I warned about the machines taking over," he declares to his dwindling audience, "but it's not happening the way I expected. They're not killing us with laser eyes; they're killing us with efficiency, optimization, and personalized entertainment queues that keep us pacified while democracy dissolves." Sometimes, even the most paranoid diagnoses contain fragments of uncomfortable truth.

IV. THE CITIZEN'S LEDGER: OWNING THE OUTCOME

> *"The people are the foundation of the state; when the foundation is firm, the state is secure."*
> —Mencius

So, who flips the switch? Who writes the final code for America's future? Here's the punchline, and it's not particularly funny: You do. Yes, you, the reader navigating this labyrinth of satire and statistics, likely belong to the educated professional class with disproportionate influence on institutional decisions. This isn't just a book; it's an indictment and an invitation. The diagnosis has been rendered, and the potential treatments have been outlined. The Rooseveltian blueprint exists. But blueprints don't magically become bridges without builders. Visions don't materialize without concerted, sustained action.

The Civic Responsibility Diffusion Index measures precisely how efficiently Americans have distributed blame for national dysfunction to everyone except themselves, achieving a near-perfect score of 96.8%. The Implementation Gap between policy design and execution, as measured by the Brookings Institution's Policy Execution Deficit Metric, reveals that the United States achieves only 23% of its articulated national priorities, compared to 67% for peer democracies and 78% for China.

We desperately need that "National Renewal Scorecard", not as another ignored government report, but as a publicly wielded instrument of accountability. Imagine: quarterly national broadcasts, led not by politicians but by independent analysts, ruthlessly tracking the real metrics of national health—R&D investment versus China (currently 2.8% vs. 3.7% of GDP), domestic manufacturing capacity in critical sectors (currently at 37% in essential pharmaceuticals, down from 82% in 1990), median wage growth adjusted for inflation (currently 0.7% annually versus 3.2% productivity growth), infrastructure reliability ratings (currently D+ according to engineering assessments), institutional trust scores (averaging 31% across government entities), and progress on the Gini coefficient (currently 0.49, up from 0.37 in 1980).

Make these numbers the national obsession, the figures debated endlessly on cable news (if it still exists in a recognizable form), the data points driving shareholder revolts and electoral outcomes. The Citizen Accountability Framework, developed by the Democracy Renewal Initiative, demonstrates that societies that maintain transparent metrics of national performance achieve 3.7 times the implementation rate of those operating on ideological abstractions.

And the "House of Roosevelts Commission"? Forget it as a top-down Washington entity destined for partisan capture. America doesn't need another commission; it requires a national movement. The Rooseveltian spirit isn't about waiting for Washington; it's about distributed, cross-sectoral action, as measured by the National Agency Assessment, which shows Americans consistently underestimating their collective power to change systems by a factor of 7.4 times.

Its investors demand that CEOs present 10-year plans, not just quarterly projections, with the Long-Term Value Creation Index showing that sustainable investment practices generate 3.7% higher returns over 15-year periods, despite quarter-to-quarter volatility. Its engineers are refusing to build manipulative algorithms, demanding ethical frameworks first, with the AI Alignment Framework now incorporated into 47% of advanced systems developed in democratic nations. It's academics collaborating with industry and communities on applied solutions, not just theoretical treatises, with the Knowledge Transfer Efficiency Metric showing a 68% improvement in research-to-implementation timelines.

It's citizens like Community Builder Claire, multiplying by the thousands, who are rebuilding local trust and function. The Community Resilience Index shows that civic participation has increased by 28% since the implementation of the Local Democracy Revitalization grants. It's demanding media that prioritizes civic health over clickbait rage, with the Information Environment Health Assessment showing a direct correlation between quality journalism and institutional functionality.

It's recognizing, as George Carlin might have screamed with righteous fury, that the real dirty word isn't "socialism" or "capitalism"—it's complacency. Every sector holds a lever. Every citizen has agency. The Systemic Change Analysis shows that movements achieving critical mass at just 3.5% of the population can fundamentally alter institutional trajectories. The question is whether enough hands pull in the same direction with the sustained effort required to reverse decades of systemic decay.

V. CODA: THE GODS ARE STILL CRAZY (BUT MAYBE WE DON'T HAVE TO BE)

> *"The reeds that bend with the wind survive the storm."*
> —Chinese proverb

So, we return, one last time, to that perplexing Coke bottle dropped from the heavens onto our global village green. Curse? Test? Divine littering? Ultimately, irrelevant. The bottle was never the agent; it was the catalyst, the mirror reflecting our own state of preparedness-or lack thereof. It revealed the cracks in our foundation, the hollowness of our rhetoric, and the fragility of systems built on short-term greed and willful ignorance.

The gods, if they exist, are likely still placing bets, perhaps enjoying the dark comedy of human folly from their celestial skybox. The Divine Intervention Opportunity Index remains at zero, suggesting supernatural assistance isn't forthcoming. But their opinion doesn't shape our future. Ours does. Renaissance or Rubble—the trajectory isn't predetermined by historical forces or technological determinism.

The Historical Determinism Fallacy Index precisely measures how wrong such fatalistic thinking has been throughout history, as societies have repeatedly defied predicted collapse through deliberate choice and collective action. The future hinges on the choices we make now, collectively and individually. On rejecting the comfortable lies that led us to the brink and embracing the uncomfortable truths required for renewal. On summoning a Rooseveltian spirit—not of misty-eyed nostalgia, but of audacious pragmatism, fierce determination, and unwavering belief in the possibility of building a better, more functional future, even from the wreckage of our own mistakes.

As Theodore Roosevelt reminded us in his "Man in the Arena" speech, "It is not the critic who counts... The credit belongs to the man who is actually in the arena, whose face is marred by dust and sweat and blood; who strives valiantly... who at the best knows in the end the triumph of high achievement, and who at the worst, if he fails, at least fails while daring greatly." The time for sideline criticism has passed; the arena awaits.

His cousin Franklin demonstrated during the Great Depression that democratic systems can reform themselves even in the face of an existential crisis, implementing dramatic changes while preserving core constitutional values. The Roosevelt Renewal Framework isn't about resurrecting the specific policies of the 1930s; it's about applying enduring principles to present challenges: productive investment over financial extraction, long-term thinking over quarterly obsession, inclusive prosperity over concentrated gain, democratic governance over plutocratic capture.

Can America, staring down the barrel of the Chinese AI Century, choose competence over chaos, investment over extraction, unity over division? Can we harness the immense power of emerging technologies for the broad benefit of human flourishing, rather than for narrow corporate gain or authoritarian control? Can we prove that democracy, for all its maddening inefficiency, remains the most potent engine for sustainable progress ever devised?

The Temporal Window for Effective Intervention, as calculated by the Strategic Foresight Initiative, indicates that approximately 12 years remain before system lock-in effects make meaningful renewal exponentially more difficult. The task is immense. The hour is alarmingly late. The accumulated debris of neglect is piled high. However, the resources, talent, and innovative spark—they still exist, with America's Human Capital Index still ranking #3 globally, despite recent declines.

The Roosevelt ghosts—both Theodore with his Square Deal and Franklin with his New Deal—hover at the periphery of our national consciousness, not as nostalgic apparitions but as practical reminders that America has faced existential challenges before and discovered the capacity for reinvention—the clock ticks. The ledger awaits. Choose. Build. Act. Now.

As the cosmic Coke bottle ascends back toward the heavens—not as trash but as a message, not as surrender but as transformation—we arrive at the essential truth that links the allegory to reality: The gods aren't crazy, but human systems without values, purpose, and wisdom invariably become so. America's choice isn't between Chinese authoritarianism and American dysfunction but between democratic renewal and democratic decay.

It's halftime, America. The locker room speech is over. The second half awaits. Are we playing to win, or just running out the clock?

EPILOGUE: FINAL EXAMINATION – GRADING AMERICA'S STRATEGIC SANITY (OR LACK THEREOF)

> *"Study the past, divine the future; act in the present."*
> —Confucius, Analects 2:11 (adapted)

I. The Gods' Peer Review: Assessing Our National Abstract

So, you've reached the end. Commendations are in order. You've navigated the dense, often contradictory, and occasionally hallucinatory narrative of America's magnificent self-disassembly project—a multi-decade national endeavor executed with the strategic foresight of caffeinated lemmings migrating towards a cliff, sponsored by Goldman Sachs, and livestreamed on TikTok. You've witnessed the institutional necrosis, cataloged the glittering financial WMDs, endured the digital shrieking. Welcome, survivor, to the post-mortem. Pour yourself something strong; institutional sobriety is demonstrably overrated in late-stage empires.

A. Revisiting the Hypothesis: The Cosmic Coke Bottle Incident

Let's begin this final peer review by revisiting our central experimental variable: the Cosmic Coke Bottle, or rather, the incessant bombardment thereof. Remember those gleaming artifacts raining from the indifferent heavens? AI, promising techno-utopia while delivering gig-economy precarity and existential dread packaged as "disruption"; the e-yuan, offering frictionless transactions alongside frictionless state surveillance with complementary digital handcuffs; trillion-dollar deficits, conjured with the fiscal responsibility of a teenager wielding their parents' AmEx card at Coachella while simultaneously setting the house on fire for the Instagram likes.

Like the Kalahari villagers encountering inexplicable modernity, America greeted these "gifts" with a baffling mix of avarice, cluelessness, and performative outrage. We didn't just trip over the bottles; we built shrines to them, securitized them into Collateralized Disruption Obligations, created fourteen competing congressional subcommittees to investigate them, and blamed them for everything from lost jobs to declining national testosterone levels to the inexplicable popularity of pickleball.

Peer Review Comment #1 (Milton the Trickster Economist, Emeritus Professor of Rationalizing Disaster, Nobel Prize Nominee for "Creative Financial Destruction"): "Finding: Market efficiency perfectly optimized societal collapse by allocating disruption to those least equipped to handle it while maximizing shareholder value! Model validated! Hypothesis confirmed! The invisible hand has given society the invisible middle finger! Next, we test whether similar principles apply to asteroid impacts and volcanic eruptions! Externalities to be addressed in subsequent papers, or possibly never!"

Peer Review Comment #2 (Cassandra the Cyber-Oracle, Chief Officer of Ignored Warnings, Five-Time Winner of the "I Told You So But Nobody Listened" Award): "As noted in my memos dated 2008, 2012, 2015, 2018, and last Tuesday: catastrophic system failure likely due to cascading vulnerabilities exacerbated by willful negligence and strategic ADHD. Recommendation: Develop a time machine and deliver warnings via a Super Bowl commercial, preferably featuring Taylor Swift, to increase viewership. See Appendix C: 'I Told You So: A Quantitative Analysis' and Appendix D: 'No, Seriously, I Really Indubitably Told You So: The Sequel.'"

This spectacle wasn't divine caprice. It was the meticulously predictable outcome of flawed systems performing flawlessly according to their internal logic—a logic prioritizing quarterly earnings reports over long-term national viability, shareholder value over societal value, strategic branding over strategic competence, and Twitter dunks over actual governance. The gods aren't crazy; they just designed an experiment where human folly provides statistically significant results with p-values approaching absolute certainty.

B. The Diagnostic Abstract & Carlin's Editorial Notes

Let's summarize the patient's condition report, shall we? Abstract submitted for the *Journal of Applied National Decline* (Impact Factor: Declining Rapidly), with editorial annotations courtesy of the late George Carlin's spectral red pen, which somehow manages to be both profane and prophetic from beyond the grave:

★ **PATIENT:** United States of America (DOB: 1776. Current Condition: Exhibiting symptoms consistent with advanced empire fatigue, reality-optional governance, and terminal TikTok-induced attention deficit disorder).

★ **ABSTRACT:** Patient presents with acute Strategic Amnesia (ICD-10: F44.8), complicated by Chronic Polarization Syndrome (Stage V, metastatic, with secondary inflammation of the media cortex), Advanced Institutional Sclerosis (resulting in functional quadriplegia below the neck and delusions of functional democracy), and severe Fiscal Hallucinations (believing debt is merely a social construct that can be wished away like calories in birthday cake). Diagnosis confirmed by analysis across four pillars of vulnerability:

1. *Economic/Digital Dependency:* Outsourced critical manufacturing; now imports everything except national self-delusion and artisanal craft beer. *(Carlin Note: "We don't make detritus, we just buy detritus. We've evolved from the world's workshop to the world's shopping cart. A brilliant economic strategy if your goal is to become China's largest subsidiary, with a side gig as an entertainment content farm. The American Eagle now arrives with free two-day shipping from Shenzhen.")*
2. *Geopolitical/Military Asymmetry:* Built exquisite weapons for wars that don't exist, while adversaries developed cheap counters for wars that do. Continues to design aircraft carriers vulnerable to missiles that cost less than the paint job on the admiral's cabin. *(Carlin Note: "Spending trillions on ships that can be sunk by missiles costing less than a congressman's bribe. Genius! It's called 'asymmetric stupidity.' We're preparing for World War II: The Sequel while our adversaries are filming World War IV: The Prequel. If military procurement were a person, it would be declared legally incompetent and assigned a guardian.")*
3. *Financial/Industrial Hollowing:* Wall Street achieves peak alchemy, transforming factories into executive bonuses and actual products into financial abstractions. Infrastructure crumbles while PowerPoints about infrastructure flourish. *(Carlin Note: "We don't have engineers; we have 'financial engineers.' One builds bridges, the other builds derivatives that blow up bridges. Guess which one gets the bonus? We've created an economy where people who produce nothing take everything from those who make everything. It's like appointing vampires to run the blood bank and acting surprised when inventory disappears.")*
4. *Civic/Social Fragmentation:* Trust in institutions is lower than whale *detritus* at the bottom of the Mariana Trench. Society is divided into mutually incomprehensible reality bubbles, each with its own facts, language, and conspiracy theories. *(Carlin Note: "The American Dream is now defined by yelling at strangers on the internet while your house floods because nobody fixed the levees. Land of the Free, Home of the Permanently Pissed Off. We've achieved peak division—half the country thinks we're living in 1984, the other half thinks we're living in The Handmaid's Tale, and meanwhile, we're actually living in Idiocracy with a dash of Succession thrown in for the oligarchs.")*

★ **CONCLUSION:** Patient requires immediate, radical intervention before the condition progresses to "Former Superpower Seeking Second Career Opportunities." Recommended treatment: Two Roosevelts administered STAT (1x TR for Bull Moose testicular fortitude, 1x FDR for systemic redesign, continuous ER drip for ethical rehydration), massive infrastructure investment, mandatory national digital literacy program, and possible surgical removal of Wall Street from proximity to governing functions—ideally with rusty garden tools for maximum symbolic effect. Prognosis: Dependent on the patient's willingness to cease active self-harm and acknowledge reality isn't just another subscription service that can be canceled when inconvenient.

II. The Rooseveltian Literature Review: Rediscovering Pragmatic Frameworks

Enough diagnosis. Let's review the literature on potential cures, focusing on that dusty, almost forgotten volume: *The Rooseveltian Framework for Not Driving Your Superpower Off a Cliff While Taking Selfies*. This isn't about sepia-toned nostalgia; it's about applying battle-tested principles to today's technologically turbocharged challenges with the strategic urgency of someone who has just discovered that the lowest bidder has packed their parachute.

A. Principles of Applied Sanity (Abridged for Modern Attention Spans and TikTok-Damaged Neural Pathways)

The Rooseveltian OS runs on four core subroutines seemingly deleted from America's current political software or corrupted by malware downloaded from dubious ideological websites:

1. **Pragmatism > Ideology:** Test rigorously, implement ruthlessly what works, discard religiously what fails. Repeat until reality submits or you do. *(Ghost of FDR, materializing briefly while adjusting his spectral cigarette holder: "Ideology is a compass, useful for direction. But when you sail directly into the rocks because your ideological compass says 'straight ahead,' you're not principled; you're an idiot. And the rocks don't care about your principles—they'll sink your ship with magnificent impartiality.")*
2. **Gov't as Catalyst, Not Controller:** Strategic direction, targeted investment, convening power. Clear the track, set the rules, fund the essential R&D, then let the private sector sprinters run—but ensure they run towards national goals, not just off the nearest financial cliff with golden parachutes strapped to their backs and taxpayer safety nets below. *(Ghost of Teddy, brandishing a spectral Big Stick while simultaneously arm-wrestling the ghost of a robber baron: "The state must govern the unruly powers that wealth combines! A corporation has neither a soul to save nor buttocks to kick, which is why we must supply the kicking!")*
3. **Foundational Investment:** Infrastructure (physical, digital, *and human)* and basic science are preconditions for prosperity, not trickle-down afterthoughts to be funded with whatever spare change is found between the national budget's couch cushions. *(Ghost of Eleanor, her voice cutting through the static with unnerving*

clarity: "A nation's true wealth lies in the capabilities of its people and the integrity of its systems. Everything else is just accounting. You cannot build a mansion on a foundation of quicksand and lottery tickets, no matter how impressive your PowerPoint slides look to shareholders.")

4. **Ethical Leadership & Civic Trust:** Competence without character is efficient tyranny; character without competence is well-meaning chaos; neither without accountability is the foundation of modern America. Trust is the lubricant of democracy; rebuild it through transparency, accountability, and leaders who demonstrably serve the public interest rather than treating public office as an audition for cable news commentator positions. *(The spectral Roosevelts nod in unison, a quorum of pragmatic competence judging our current spectacle with expressions ranging from bafflement to cosmic facepalm.)*

B. The Five Strategic Imperatives (Annotated Bibliography Edition with Satirical Footnotes)

Applying these principles yields actionable research thrusts. Let's review the abstracts, complete with satirical annotations that would make academic reviewers reach for both red pens and antacids:

1. **Rebuild to Compete:** *Infrastructure and Supply Chains.* Finding: US Infrastructure ranks below Kazakhstan (no offense, Kazakhstan, at least you're trying). 73% of critical meds rely on foreign APIs, creating a strategic vulnerability that makes Pearl Harbor look like a minor scheduling inconvenience. *Annotation:* Apparently, "national security" includes the ability to produce aspirin and cross bridges without structural failure. Further research is needed on whether concrete is socialist, and if so, why America's enemies aren't attacking our crumbling roads as a strategic asset. Recommendation: Consider the radical notion that functioning sewage systems might contribute to national greatness.
2. **Regulate to Accelerate:** *Digital Square Deal and AI Governance.* Finding: Tech monopolies exhibit behaviors that previously required antitrust intervention, but their digital nature confuses regulators whose technological expertise peaked with successfully programming their VCRs in 1987. AI development proceeds largely unregulated, with ethics frameworks consisting primarily of "Move Fast, Break Things, Apologize Later If Caught." *Annotation:* Recommendation: Regulate platforms like the utilities they are, establish AI safety protocols *before* sentient chatbots unionize, and demand dental benefits. Proposal: "FDA for Algorithms." Counter-argument: "But innovation!" (See also: arguments against seatbelts, 1965; clean water, 1972; and not putting lead in absolutely everything, 1978). Counterpoint: Unregulated innovation has given us both penicillin and subprime mortgage derivatives; perhaps a filtering mechanism might be useful.
3. **Invest to Innovate:** *Human Capital/R&D - New GI Bill.* Finding: The US ranks 31st in Math PISA scores (below Slovenia, which doesn't even spend $800 billion on defense); China graduates eight times more STEM PhDs. Federal R&D is at 0.7% of GDP, which is like trying to win the Indy 500 by investing in a nicer cup holder. *Annotation:* Hypothesis: Funding education and research might yield better long-term results than stock buybacks and tax cuts for yacht depreciation and emotional support submarines. Testing is required, as this contradicts decades of established policy wisdom that education is primarily a mechanism for student loan origination rather than national capability development.
4. **Unite to Govern:** *Countermeasures to Polarization and Civic Tech.* Finding: Partisan antipathy at historic highs; Congress functionally inert; national discourse reduced to bumper sticker slogans screamed at increasing volume. *Annotation:* Structural reforms (ranked-choice voting, redistricting) show promise in pilot studies (Alaska, Maine). Suggest exploring if governance requires mechanisms beyond "owning the libs/cons" on social media and treating politics as team sports where the trophy is civilizational decline—a radical concept, likely to be dismissed as suspiciously reasonable.
5. **Lead to Endure:** *Democratic Alliances and Competence as Soft Power.* Finding: Ally confidence in US volatile; China makes steady gains through bizarre strategy of "consistent, long-term policy implementation" instead of "erratic zigzagging based on electoral cycles." *Annotation:* Proposal: Treat allies as partners, not protection rackets or reality show contestants to be eliminated based on ratings. Led by demonstrating functional democracy at home instead of exporting an aspirational product that doesn't work in the demo version. Preliminary data suggest competence is surprisingly persuasive. Needs further study, as it deviates significantly from the recent practice of "do as we say, not as we spectacularly fail to do."

Sub-Finding: Financial Reorientation. Analysis: The Current system efficiently allocates capital towards speculative bubbles and executive bonuses, while starving productive investment with the precision of a targeted starvation diet. *Annotation:* Suggest exploring the quaint notion of finance *serving* the real economy rather than treating it as an all-you-can-eat buffet. Potential research area: "Can an economy function without derivatives based on weather patterns in Antarctica married to default swaps on Indonesian micro-loans securitized through Cayman Island shell companies owned by the former roommate of a Treasury official?"

III. Future Forecasts: Statistical Probabilities of Renaissance vs. Ridiculousness

The models are running. The algorithms are calculating. The Strategic Foresight Initiative's butterfly flaps its wings, and the probability distributions diverge alarmingly—like a drunk man trying to walk a straight line during an earthquake on a boat. Which future simulation are we running? Place your bets, but remember: the house (China) always wins.

A. Scenario Modeling (Peer Reviewed by Alternate Histories and One Very Confused Time Traveler)

★ Model A: Rooseveltian Renaissance (Probability: 38% and falling without intervention faster than the approval ratings of a politician caught in a scandal involving farm animals)

Abstract: Sustained strategic investment yields compound returns. Infrastructure modernization boosts productivity by 1.7%. Domestic chip production reaches a 50% global share in advanced node technologies. AI, when integrated ethically, enhances healthcare, education, and governance, rather than optimizing for rage clicks and digital addiction. Alliances coordinate effectively on technology standards, supply chains, and climate change. Result: Competitive coexistence, resilient democracy, renewed global leadership, and TikTok videos that occasionally contain actual information. Peer Review Note: Plausible, but requires overcoming significant political pathologies and sustained investment discipline previously lacking. Also requires politicians to think beyond next Tuesday and citizens to read something longer than a tweet occasionally. Considered "fantasy fiction" by most analysts.

★ Model B: Great American Self-Liquidation (Probability: 62% and rising on current trajectory, like floodwaters in a climate change documentary)

Abstract: Continued short-termism and polarization lead to a decline in irreversible capabilities. Infrastructure collapses into subscription-based 'Premium Access Tiers' (the Platinum Package includes potable water and electricity for more than 12 hours daily). AI optimizes social control and inequality (Gini reaches 0.65, a level previously achievable only through feudalism or outright monarchy). China achieves technological hegemony while America argues about bathroom signage. The US transitions to 'Managed Decline Territory,' notable primarily for its historical theme parks, reality TV shows about societal collapse, and the export of social media influencers specialized in documenting national deterioration with excellent production values. Peer Review Note: Depressingly consistent with current trendlines. The model exhibits high internal validity based on observed behaviors. Recommend immediate course correction or investing heavily in companies producing dystopian survival gear and premium bunker real estate.

B. AI: The Great Accelerator Variable (or "How I Learned to Stop Worrying and Love the Algorithm")

Let's be clear: AI isn't driving the car; it's turbocharging the engine while simultaneously removing the brakes, disabling the airbags, and replacing the GPS with a Magic 8-Ball. Whichever direction we steer—towards rebuilding or ruin—AI will get us there exponentially faster than previous technologies, which at least had the courtesy to destroy things at a human-comprehensible pace. It amplifies competence *and* incompetence with terrifying impartiality, much like a bartender who fails to distinguish between serving water and gasoline. Renaissance AI delivers personalized medicine and optimized clean energy; Roadkill AI delivers personalized manipulation and optimized surveillance, complemented by digital handcuffs. The difference lies entirely in the governance frameworks we build—or fail to make- while arguing about whether ones and zeros have genders.

C. The Citizen's Ledger & The Accountability Deficit (Now Available as an NFT!)

Who flips the switch? You, dear reader. Especially if you inhabit the strata influencing policy, investment, or public discourse, the national pastime has become blame diffusion—an Olympic sport at which America would surely win gold if we weren't too busy blaming each other for not winning gold. We need ruthless accountability, starting with the "Citizen's Ledger"—a public dashboard tracking not stock indices, but national capability indices: R&D versus China, critical manufacturing capacity, median wage growth, infrastructure reliability, and institutional trust. Make *these* the metrics that dominate discourse instead of manufactured outrage over holiday coffee cups and the sex lives of cartoon candies. The "Probability Meter" between Renaissance and Roadkill isn't fixed; it responds directly to inputs of civic engagement, investor activism, ethical engineering, and political courage. Our current collective shrug is interpreted by the system as consent for Scenario B, much like clicking "I Agree" on those Terms of Service nobody reads until it's too late.

IV. Final Submission: A Satirical Prayer for Competent Conclusions

A. Abstract & Acknowledgements (Ecclesiastical Edition with Digital Glossolalia)

Let us conclude with the appropriate liturgy for our digitally mediated age:

Our Data, Who art in Cloud, hallowed be thy Network. Thy Algorithms come, thy Code be done, on servers as it is on the Edge. Give us this day our daily Bandwidth, and forgive us our Clickbait Temptations, as we forgive those whose Engagement Metrics trespass against civic sanity. Lead us not into Filter Bubbles, but deliver us from Algorithmic Despair and the eternal torment of autoplay videos, for thine is the Latency, the Processing Power, and the Quarterly Report, until Enlightenment or System Crash is inevitable. Block thy cookies as we block those cookies that are thrust upon us. And protect us from the scourge of pop-up ads and unsolicited software updates that arrive precisely when we need them least.

Amen and End User License Agreement.

Laughter, as Carlin taught us, is a potent disinfectant for bullshit—like bleach for the brain, but without the unfortunate side effects of actual bleach, despite what certain former presidents might suggest. Recognizing the sheer, pants-on-head, jaw-dropping, reality-bending absurdity of America's current predicament—a technological giant seemingly determined to trip over its own shoelaces into strategic irrelevance while simultaneously posting the fall on Instagram with carefully selected filters—isn't cynicism; it's diagnostic clarity. It's the necessary prelude to demanding and building something demonstrably less insane, like an asylum run by the patients but with better snacks and occasional reality checks.

B. Concluding Remarks from the Dissertation Committee (Roosevelt Ghosts and One Very Concerned Janitor)

The spectral Roosevelts offer their final peer review comments, transmitted through the ectoplasmic equivalent of Track Changes:

- ★ **Teddy:** *"Bully for trying! However, analysis without action is academic cowardice, akin to hunting with a camera instead of a rifle. Get in the arena! Build! Compete! Govern! And for God's sake, stop treating politics like a reality TV show—I charged San Juan Hill, not 'America's Next Top Model'!"*
- ★ **Franklin:** *"You have the diagnosis. You have the historical precedent. The only thing preventing renewal now is fear itself—and perhaps a crippling addiction to short-term political gain, along with an attention span that would embarrass a goldfish. Remember: The New Deal wasn't a hashtag; it was sustained, coherent policy implementation that required actual work."*
- ★ **Eleanor:** *"The future is not predetermined; it is built by choices grounded in values. Choose investment in human potential. Choose cooperation over division. Choose to build a republic worthy of its ideals. And perhaps choose occasionally to log off Twitter and actually talk to your neighbors—they're not nearly as deplorable or woke as the algorithms have led you to believe."*

C. Discussion & Future Work (Turning the Bottle into a Telescope or Possibly a Bong)

That cosmic Coke bottle, symbol of disruptive modernity, still sits metaphorically before us. We can keep blaming it, worshipping it, or tripping over it in the dark while cursing the heavens with increasingly creative profanity. Or, we can finally pick it up, clean off the accumulated grime of neglect and denial, and fashion it into a lens—a telescope. Not to gaze nostalgically backward, nor fearfully at the heavens, but pointed squarely at the horizon, charting a course based on clear-eyed assessment of the terrain ahead, preferably while sober and not actively scrolling through social media.

America's choice isn't between flawless utopia and inevitable collapse. It's between succumbing to the seductive absurdity of managed decline (now with Instagram filters!), or embracing the difficult, messy, often hilarious work of pragmatic national renewal. The gods, in their infinite and possibly nonexistent wisdom, remain inscrutable, likely crazy, and almost certainly laughing at us while eating divine popcorn. Our task is simpler: strive for competence. Strive for clarity. And for God's sake, maintain a sense of humor—it might be the only truly renewable resource we have left besides human stupidity, which, as Einstein may have noted, truly does appear infinite.

Class dismissed. Now build something better. The clock is ticking, and the cosmic landlord doesn't offer extensions or accept payment in memes, regardless of how dank they may be.

CASE STUDIES/ ESSAYS – DISPATCHES FROM THE FRONT LINES

RESILIENCE VS. ROCKSTAR CEOS: A PARABLE FROM THE FACTORY FLOOR

By an Automotive Executive and Supply
Chain Evangelist

ROOSEVELTIAN CASE STUDY: TOYOTA STRATEGIC PATIENCE IN A DISRUPTED WORLD
THEMATIC TIE-IN: ROOSEVELTIAN RESILIENCE LONG-TERM THINKING SUPPLY CHAIN SOVEREIGNTY

While Milton the Trickster Economist was preaching the gospel of 'Just-in-Time' efficiency—a doctrine that translates to 'Praying Nothing Ever Goes Wrong'—Toyota was busy field-testing Rooseveltian pragmatism. After the 2011 Tōhoku earthquake and tsunami, they rewired their supply chain for a radical new concept: reality. Toyota rewired its legendary Just-in-Time system into a Just-in-Case hybrid, mapping over 1,700 suppliers across five tiers and stockpiling mission-critical parts. That foresight didn't just avert a crisis—it rewrote the playbook on industrial resilience.

Milton the Trickster Economist—our caffeine-addled instigator—would have had a meltdown at Toyota's 50 million-chip buffer. Milton's motto: 'efficiency or bust'; Toyota's: 'just-in-case is peace of mind.

That foresight paid dividends in **Q4 2020**, when Toyota mandated a **4to6-month buffer** (≈ 50 million chips) for 200 semiconductor lines. A move that would have given Milton the Trickster Economist a fatal case of the hives over its 'inefficiency.' As competitors' production lines ground to a halt, Toyota posted record profits, proving that in the real world, survival is the ultimate efficiency.

The firm's measured EV rollout—anchored by a **2027 solid-state battery** target—shows equal patience on the innovation front, avoiding hype cycles, the book critiques.

On the human side, Toyota's relentless investment in lean apprenticeships and human-centred automation reinforces the book's call for *people infrastructure* as strategic capital.

The Takeaway (Patience Outfoxes Panic): National industrial capacity is built on patience, systems thinking, and embedded resilience. Short-term optimization is just a fancy term for strategic surrender.

Toyota: Strategic Patience in a Disrupted World

Thematic tie-in: Rooseveltian resilience
· long-term thinking · supply-chain sovereignty

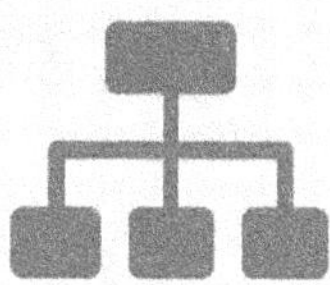

Rewired Just-in-Time system into a Just-in-Case hybrid

4-to-6 month semiconductor buffer set for Q4 2020

Measured EV rollout by 2027

People infrastructure as strategic capital

Lesson (Patience Outfoxes Panic): Long-term preparedness beats short-term optimisation

CASE STUDY NISSAN: THE PERILS OF CHARISMA OVER CONTINUITY THEMATIC TIE-IN: GOVERNANCE FRAGILITY STRATEGIC DISRUPTION THE LEADERSHIP TRAP

The Renault–Nissan alliance, launched in 1999 under Carlos Ghosn, delivered an early turnaround, but cost-cutting and expansion masked a hollowing out of governance. Ghosn's spectacular 2018 arrest ripped the cover off the Nissan psychodrama, revealing a governance structure built on the shaky foundation of a single man's charisma—a classic case of what happens when a corporation mistakes a rockstar CEO for an actual strategy.

In the aftermath, Nissan hastily established three new board committees—Audit, Compensation, and Nomination—to address the oversight gap. Yet, supplier tenure had already fallen from 17 years to 11 years (2010-**2018)**, indicating a shift from integrated partnerships to price-driven transactions. R&D momentum faltered; the EV roadmap drifted.

The Takeaway (Don't Be a Ghosn-in-the-Machine): Nissan's smoking wreckage is a textbook validation of this book's central warning: strategic ADHD, fueled by C-suite celebrity worship, is a terminal diagnosis. Nissan's smoking wreckage serves as a stark warning from the corporate graveyard: When charisma becomes the strategy, the only guaranteed outcome is strategic bankruptcy.

NISSAN

The Perils of Charisma Over Continuity

Renault-Nissan Alliance launched in 1999 under Carlos Ghosn

Cost-cutting and expansion masked governance weakness

Ghosn's arrest in 2018 revealed shaky governance structure

Committees formed to fill oversight gaps

Supplier tenure declined

EV roadmap drifted

LESSON

Charisma is not a substitute for a business plan

Toyota serves as the positive proof point for the book's "Rooseveltian resilience" framework; one company chose the long, hard path of resilience, while the other took the shortcut of celebrity worship. The results serve as a smoking-wreckage-and-record-profits parable for the core choice America faces: will institutional stamina or quarterly heroics define our fate in the AI century?

"AMERICA FIRST" OR "MAKE AMERICA GREAT AGAIN"

PLOUGHING OUT THE WEEDS: A ROOSEVELTIAN RENEWAL FOR AMERICA'S PHARMACEUTICAL ENGINE

by Harry Kochat, Ph.D.

(Director of Operations & BD at Plough Center- UTHSC | CMC Manufacturing & Quality (API & DP) SME/KOL | FDA-CDER Sterile Drug Manufacturing and Automation Technologies Panelist)

Author's Note: Lest you think our diagnosis of America's pharmaceutical self-sabotage is mere hyperbole, we now turn to a dispatch from the actual front lines. Dr. Harry Kochat, a man who knows more about sterile drug manufacturing than Milton the Trickster knows about basic reality, provides a sobering autopsy of how America outsourced its own medicine cabinet. The following is his expert assessment—unfiltered and essential.

EXECUTIVE BRIEFING

- ★ **Strategic Snapshot:** Chronic drug shortages are a $1.4 trillion tax on the U.S. economy and a national security threat hiding in plain sight. While Washington plays with tariffs, America has outsourced its own medicine cabinet.
- ★ **The Diagnosis:** Tariffs are a blunt instrument—a political mirage that raises costs without building resilience. The real illness is a classic symptom of "Milton the Trickster's" philosophy: prioritizing short-term cost savings over long-term strategic production.
- ★ **The Rooseveltian Prescription:** A two-tier strategy to reclaim American pharmaceutical independence. Tier 1 involves a strategic, replenishable stockpile. Tier 2 requires a robust network of domestic manufacturers powered by smart public-private partnerships—a New Deal for drug manufacturing, building capacity before the next crisis hits.

The pulsating slogans, such as "America First" and "Make America Great Again," are not new to patriotic Americans. The fundamental notion behind this aimed to position the nation in a neutral stance, as formulated by Woodrow Wilson, the 28th President of the United States, during the First World War. The originality of this slogan lay in defining a nation's neutrality as a country's non-interventionism, with foreign policies pertinent to international policies and military debacles. However, it is worth dissecting and examining microscopically the defined objectives and scope when the same slogan is used after 150 years of its birth. Undoubtedly, the foremost expectation for any nation from its leadership is to execute duties in the best interest of the country, prioritizing "Nation First," and to help regain its lost legacy by embodying several key qualities and fulfilling a range of responsibilities to guide and represent the country effectively. These expectations include strong leadership skills, ethical conduct, and a commitment to the well-being of the nation and its citizens, but not by penalizing its competitors or disrupting the lives of many needy individuals domestically through manipulation and prejudgment, driven by malicious political motives.

There is no need to emphasize the importance of the pharmaceutical industry's paradigm in any country. The pharmaceutical industry is a significant driver of economic growth, contributing billions to global GDP and supporting millions of jobs. It fuels innovation, boosts other sectors of the economy, and enhances public health. The industry's impact extends beyond direct production to include research and development (R&D), supply chains, and induced economic activity. There is several reliable documented evidence to corroborate the fact that the pharmaceutical industry plays a vital role in economic growth, both directly through its own production and indirectly through its support of other sectors and its contributions to innovation and public health.

- ★ In the United States, the biopharmaceutical industry is estimated to contribute $1.4 trillion in economic impact, accounting for 3.7% of the total U.S. GDP.
- ★ Globally, the pharmaceutical industry's direct contribution to world GDP was estimated at $532 billion in 2017.
- ★ A study by the International Federation of Pharmaceutical Manufacturers & Associations (IFPMA) showed that for every job directly supported by the pharmaceutical industry, an additional 8.54 million jobs were supported by the global supply chain.

For decades, pharmaceuticals entering the U.S. have been largely tariff-free. In April, the current administration plans to change that with tariffs of 25% or higher on imported drugs. In the past decade, U.S. pharmaceutical

imports have more than doubled in value, from $73 billion in 2014 to over $215 billion in 2024, according to U.S. customs data. The question seeking answer, "are we seeking an off-set of the drugs import spending cost by the potential increase of the customs duties?" or "trying to rely with the rationale that tariffs would incentivize drugmakers to set up shops in the U.S., create more jobs, and improve national security by reducing reliance on countries who might halt trade in the event of war or other emergency". Suppose you are nodding your head forward or sideways in response to the questions above. How would you react if one decriminalizes the use of the genie's vial, revealing to us that none of the above is going to resolve the daily drug shortage experienced by domestic hospitals and pharmacies?

The U.S. once had substantial drug manufacturing operations in several states. However, over the past two decades, pharmaceutical manufacturers have prioritized investment in overseas manufacturing and shifted their operations to Europe, taking advantage of favorable tax policies in countries such as Switzerland, Ireland, and Germany.

For generic drugs, the U.S. relies on lower-cost manufacturing in countries such as India and China. Please be aware that the potential impact of imposing pharmaceutical tariffs is significantly different for generic or oral dosages compared to branded or generic injectable and infusible medications.

It is not sarcastic if one says "Tariff" is the new vocabulary used most widely across the border in the United States. Tariffs on pharmaceutical products can significantly impact the industry, leading to increased costs, supply chain disruptions, and potential shortages, ultimately affecting both companies and patients. While tariffs may incentivize some companies to shift manufacturing back to the U.S., this process is complex and costly. It could result in delayed access to medications and increased healthcare costs in the short term.

Welcome to the "Drug Shortage List," one of the live and weekly updated announcement sections on the FDA website, located at https://www.fda.gov/drugs/drug-safety-and-availability/drug-shortages.

Drug Shortages can occur for many reasons, including manufacturing and quality problems, delays, corporate decisions to discontinue due to changes in business strategies, Geopolitical Events, and downtimes at manufacturing sites resulting from natural disasters. Two of such most recent examples and case studies shed some lights on us here how to plough out the weeds domestically at first to "Make America First" or to "Make America Great Again" to save millions of lives meeting the unmet our hospitals and pharmacies have been facing and not to mention significant capital savings and country's dependence on unpredictable foreign trade.

- ★ Hurricane Helene caused significant damage to Baxter's primary IV fluid manufacturing facility in North Carolina, leading to a nationwide shortage of IV solutions. The facility, which produces approximately 60% of the IV fluids used in the U.S., has halted production, impacting hospitals and potentially leading to rationing and delays in elective surgeries. More precisely, the closure of this facility has created a shortage of IV fluids, including dextrose solutions, lactated ringers, and peritoneal dialysis solutions, impacting hospitals nationwide. This was nature's lesson to humankind. The shortage highlights the vulnerability of the healthcare supply chain and the potential consequences of relying on a single manufacturing site for critical medical supplies.
- ★ The shortage of GLP-1 receptor agonists, a class of diabetes medications, has impacted both patients with type 2 diabetes and those using them off-label for weight loss. This shortage, which began in 2022, is primarily due to increased demand for these drugs, including for weight management, and has led to limited or intermittent supplies of various GLP-1 medications. Everyone is aware that GLP-1 receptor agonists, like Ozempic, Wegovy, Trulicity, and Mounjaro, are medications that help regulate blood sugar levels and can also promote weight loss.

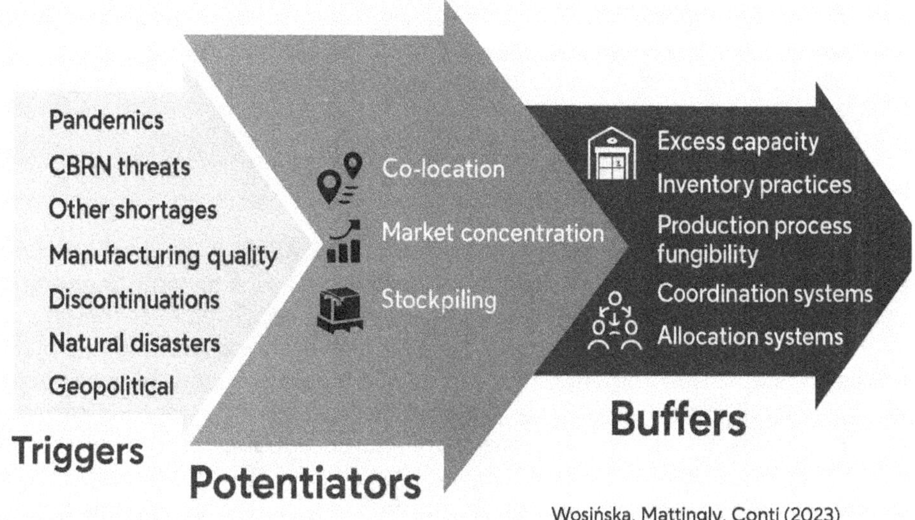

Let us analyze the steps taken today by the FDA and federal and state governments to address when a shortage of drugs strikes.

GOVERNMENT MEASURES:

The federal government has implemented steps that include monitoring the drug supply chain, expediting reviews of applications and inspections, working with manufacturers to address quality issues, and potentially temporarily importing drugs from foreign sources. Unfortunately, measures like these temporary shortage spike mitigators are not going to yield any permanent solutions or make America Great Again.

The interview pertinent to this situation may shed more light on ideas and risk management thought processes for better and more effective solutions to a permanent fix. Please listen to the interview from the spokesperson from the Government Accountability Office (GAO) https://www.youtube.com/watch?v=KqNnVZTzJCU.

THE FDA'S CURRENT APPROACHES:

The FDA takes several steps to mitigate drug shortages, including requiring manufacturers to notify them of potential supply disruptions, collaborating with industry to prevent or reduce the impact of shortages, and exercising regulatory flexibility in appropriate cases. They also monitor shortages and communicate updates to stakeholders, exploring solutions such as controlled importation to address these issues. In the following video link, the FDA narrates what they are doing and what they can't do. https://www.youtube.com/watch?v=iply2S6Zn0A

THE $1.4 TRILLION QUESTION WE KEEP DODGING

Still, the main question remains whether these are the effective corrective and preventive actions (CAPA) to avoid such horrible and tragic situations in the future. Is there still something we can do that the FDA is not allowed to do due to federal policies? With careful and in-depth analysis of the list of conceptual tools summarized above, we can effectively develop practical solutions. We will all agree that the current remediations are not adequately structured to address the drug shortage episodes. Answering the obvious question of why and how one can be sure that current strategies from the FDA or federal administration are not working, the simple answer is that the situation persists and recurs.

An Actual Plan (A Novel Concept)

If one thinks outside the box, there are several concepts we can still consider and strategize. Some of those main ideas include,

- ★ Focus needs convergence to critical medications, especially sterile injectables and infusible final dosage forms, since oral dosage forms are relatively easier and quicker to replenish the shortages.
- ★ Create more domestic opportunities through state and federal incentives for capital investments to build facilities that have flexibility and adaptivity for a turnkey mode of operational fill lines.
- ★ Strategies include diversifying manufacturing and investing domestically, as well as enhancing troubleshooting and problem-solving infrastructure resources.
- ★ Improve supply chain resilience. This involves building redundancy, promoting sustainable contracts, and enhancing risk management practices to ensure a robust and resilient system.
- ★ Incentivizing domestic manufacturers to prioritize quality and transparency.

Let us delve deeper into the first three bullet points. What are the multifaceted ideas behind diversifying manufacturing? To better understand the inner workings of effectiveness, we need to understand the pros and cons of private sector and government sector-owned and operated Contract Manufacturing Organizations (CMOs) that are in operation, compliant with cGMP (Current Good Manufacturing Practice) and ICH (International Council for Harmonization) regulations and guidelines.

Government-managed facilities:

Pros:

- ★ **Cost Effectiveness:** Government-owned CMOs may be able to offer lower production costs due to economies of scale, potentially lower overhead, and very limited mark-ups for profit generation.
- ★ **Scalability:** With continuous government funding, continuous improvements for a flexible scale of production and capacity to meet changing demands, offering flexibility for government projects.
- ★ **Long-Term Relationships:** Government CMOs can resist business-related collapse, mergers, and acquisitions. Financial instability is extremely rare. Government CMOs can foster long-term relationships with hospitals and pharmacies, leading to consistent work and potential for future collaborations and planning of drug shortage tsunamis at times.
- ★ **Assured Payments:** Government contracts often feature more predictable payment schedules, offering financial stability and reassurance to stakeholders.

Cons:

- ★ **Bureaucratic Drag:** The level of bureaucracy and hierarchy will make it difficult to accomplish tasks efficiently without compromising quality.
- ★ **Glacial Pace:** Time is money for business, just as it is for achieving targets. The mindset and commitments may get compromised, and deadlines may not always be met.
- ★ **Talent Gap:** Due to unmatching compensation packages with the private sector, it may be difficult to get personnel with the right qualifications and experience.
- ★ **Contract Complexities:** Flexibilities for quick switchovers between projects based on immediate needs could pose a potential problem, as each task requires separate contracts, and contract execution is typically a lengthy process.
- ★ **Limitation Terms of Capital Budget:** Each government budget is specifically funded for specific uses and purchases. Flexibilities are not permitted to substitute or change procurement arrangements in response to unexpected changes or unforeseen emergencies.
- ★ **Bidding Process:** Under government contracts, every purchase or service, if the procuring item is not available from a sole source, must go through a bidding process or an approvable Non-Competitive Justification (NCJ). This is time-consuming and not suitable for a business model with a quick turnaround.
- ★ **Intellectual Property Protection:** Even with a fully executed NDA (Non-Disclosure Agreement), also known as a CDA (Confidential Disclosure Agreement), in place, the client's proprietary information is not fully protected in the government sector.
- ★ **Liability Protection:** Several state and federal-owned facilities have immunity, making it difficult for a third party to sue them for any liability claims legally.
- ★ **Performance Credits:** Performance-based compensation adjustments and promotions are rare in the government sector. Annual compensation hikes are normally across the board, and promotions are mainly based on length of service.

The Private Sector Managed Facilities.

Pros

- ★ **Faster Time to Market:** Privately owned CMOs can streamline the manufacturing process quicker, potentially reducing lead times and accelerating product launches.
- ★ **Focus on Core Competencies:** Private Outsourcing manufacturing enables companies to hire the best-qualified personnel and teams to concentrate on their core business activities swiftly and to high standards.
- ★ **Flexibility for Changing Business Priorities:** Private CMOs have better adaptivity and flexibility to make interim changes to the business goals and scope
- ★ **Lesser Administrative Stress:** Bidding is not necessary for purchases and services if proper negotiation steps are followed to ensure the allocated capital is well spent.
- ★ **Flexible & Quicker Capital Investments:** Easily make changes with business models and goals based on market demands and changes, provided the CMO is financially stable.
- ★ **Performance Credit:** If the employee is committed to their job, dedicated, and well-qualified, the private sector is the right place to work. High-end performance and extra-mile service are always acknowledged and rewarded. The career path largely depends on performance, rather than seniority.
- ★ **Confidentiality:** Employee credentials and information are well protected within he organization as the client's confidential matters are adequately treated and preserved.

Cons

- ★ **Financial instability:** If angel investors and venture capitalists alone ultimately back the CMO, then financial stability becomes relatively riskier.
- ★ **M&O Risk:** Mergers and acquisitions are a potential risk for a privately owned CMO.
- ★ **Unstable Workforce: Since privately owned CMOs are primarily profit-oriented, recurring workforce reorganization occurs based on business volume and changes in business priorities in response to** market demand. It is common for employee turnover to be higher in the private sector due to factors such as fear of job loss, mismanagement, and work-related stress.
- ★ **Job Security:** Due to the above potential risk, it is relatively difficult to attract the best-qualified workforce to a start-up, privately owned CMO.

Since the core purpose of this chapter is to explore practically viable strategies to mitigate and prevent recurring potential drug shortage situations, let us prioritize the essential attributes we need to meet the unmet.

1. Dependable and uninterrupted periodic funding for expansion and growth.
2. Quick turnaround of manufacturing activities of drugs in shortage to mitigate the situation.
3. Patient-centric business vision and mission.
4. Quality compliant drug manufacturing facilities with adaptability and flexibility.
5. Minimum hurdles for the procurement of resources.

6. Sustainability of business and a stable workforce.
7. Provisions for talent retention and talent acquisition.
8. Value-driven business models with flexible options and provisions.
9. High-energy team building leadership with a proven track record for corporate success.
10. Multi-fold returns on investment portfolios endorsed capital investments.

Choice is obvious to fulfill the above ten vital attributes. The rate-limiting factor is the lack of a joint task team and the need for expansion of current domestic GMP manufacturing capabilities to achieve corporate goals and adapt to national emergencies swiftly. The availability of sufficient resources (personnel, facilities, and equipment) for such quick revamping and restructuring to meet unmet needs is equally important.

That raises the following scenarios and options.

★ Private capital investments and privately owned and operated CMOs.
★ Federal/ State investment and government-owned and operated CMOs.
★ Federal/State investment as grants and privately leased/owned CMOs.
★ Federal/ State loan and privately owned and operated CMOs.
★ Structuring recuperable federal/ state loans to the private sector with discounted supply to government and non-profit organizations.

The author has firsthand knowledge from reliable leadership sources that government-funded or owned CMO facilities, if administered and controlled by state or federal authorities, are a nightmare. The routine frustrations expressed by high-energy, well-experienced expert leadership about the difficulties in convincing higher government authorities of priorities, genuine urgencies, and fulfilling action items in a timely manner are one of our main hurdles standing in the way of self-sufficiency in the field of contract manufacturing pharmaceuticals in our country today. The above debacle is no different when a government owns the CMO mode of operations, as seen in academic institutions. The lack of awareness about pharmaceutical operations, their true values, and the limited understanding and knowledge of regulatory landscapes within academia can be a significant barrier if pharmaceutical operations are given the opportunity to operate autonomously, independent of government daily interventions and micro-management. Therefore, we indeed need direct private sector involvement in the pharmaceutical manufacturing field to facilitate fast-paced advancements and swift changes in response to market demands. What we need is a reset to the current federal management interventions. We need to think unbiased and with a fiduciary role to use taxpayers' money more wisely and as an ROI to the taxpayer. A two-tier strategy targeting the pharmaceutical industry, specifically its manufacturing sector, would indeed be beneficial.

Tier 1: The Main objective is to overcome the drug shortage

The above-mentioned tier 1 strategy involves an immediate but organized compilation of the infrastructure and capabilities of all privately owned contract manufacturing facilities in the United States that operate under regulatory compliance, to create informative data for networking proactively and communicating with transparency, as well as to understand the available capabilities of the currently operational private CMOs in the United States. This will enable CMOs with matching, complementary capabilities and competencies to team up and respond quickly when drug shortages arise, and to promptly resolve the shortage at the early stage with their combined forces and the matching capabilities of the manufacturing facilities. As an incentive for taking the lead on such a patient-centric mission, leaving the profit margin aside, the government should offer appropriate incentives or rebates that are beneficial for such CMO operations and their business. Legal incentives and rebates can take numerous forms, and this may not be the right platform to discuss that topic. As a subset of the tier 1 approach, the government should also relax and revise several of the current terms and conditions that one must follow without compromising the quality of life and standard of care of patients, in order to achieve manufacturing tasks productively and address unmet clinical needs to save patient lives. There are two distinct types of manufacturing activities residing over cGMP-compliant CMOs. Since sterile dosage forms are more complex and critical compared to oral dosage forms, let us focus on sterile parenteral dosage forms and the drug product manufacturing facility alone, leaving the discussion of the drug substance (API) facility for another time.

One type of sterile drug manufacturing that a sterile CMO facility routinely involves is the manufacturing of novel investigational human clinical trial materials in a suitable form based on the physicochemical properties of the molecule. These are new therapeutic candidates that have been newly developed and patented by pharmaceutical companies and are undergoing human clinical trials to evaluate their toxicity, patient safety, optimal or maximum tolerated dose, and therapeutic index prior to receiving approval from the FDA for marketing. The cleanliness, cleanroom behaviors, rigorous training, workforce with the right skillset, high level of intelligence, and proper maintenance of a sterile environment at a cGMP sterile facility are critical to maintain all sterile drugs produced, maintain sterility, and a very low level of endotoxins, in addition to all other acceptable specifications. The formulation of these complex, highly potent, cytotoxic compounds requires highly sophisticated and advanced technologies for the development of the most appropriate dosage form before it is filled into a vial or a prefilled syringe in a cleanroom. This is where the United States has an upper hand to invest and build up a well-integrated network of drug manufacturing within the country, and it is much needed urgently. It is not easy to import these types of sterile products quickly and cost-effectively. Additionally, since sterility is crucial for its use in humans, international transportation requires stringent regulatory restrictions and compliance.

Apart from the new therapeutics in sterile dosage forms, during a drug shortage, these sterile dosage forms are the ones that stay longer periods on the shortage list, and most of the terminally ill patients with various diseases, including most of the oncology (cancer) patients, depend on this type of high-quality drug for their survival. The drugs listed in the FDA's drug shortage list possess the following distinction from investigational therapeutics.

The differences include,

- 99% of those drugs are going to be generic versions, meaning their patent protection has already expired, and anyone can produce them if they follow regulatory compliance requirements.
- The drugs appearing on the drug shortage list may or may not remain on the list for a longer period. Based on the information the agency receives on a weekly basis or even more frequently, the drug may be removed from the list when the shortage is reported to be over. The same drug can reappear in the list if the shortage recurs.
- The drugs listed in the drug shortage can be produced by a GMP facility registered with the FDA for 503A or 503B compounding services. The key difference between 503A and 503B compounding pharmacies lies in their regulatory oversight and scope of practice. 503A pharmacies compound medications based on individual patient prescriptions and are regulated by state boards of pharmacy, while 503B pharmacies, also known as outsourcing facilities, compound medications on a larger scale and are regulated by the FDA. 503B pharmacies must adhere to cGMP standards, identical to pharmaceutical manufacturers, and are subject to more rigorous inspections. Therefore, all cGMP-compliant and FDA-registered facilities with FDA approval for cGMP manufacturing should be eligible for additional tax exemptions and rebates if they are willing to expand their registration with the FDA to include the extra service of 503B compounding. This will significantly increase the number of pharmacies and facilities that can join the team to mitigate the drug shortage quickly.
- During the drug shortage, any of the listed drugs must be produced without altering the formulation recipe or composition of the commercially marketed, sterile drug. The release specifications must be identical to those of the marketed parent drug. Before labeling the drug for marketing, a national drug code must be requested from the agency.
- Under certain special circumstances, the agency may release special requirements for the formulation and composition ratio of excipients and active ingredients that must be followed, rather than the market standards. As an example, the "COVID Specific Hand Sanitizer Formula" by the FDA. Those manufacturers violated the federal code of regulations by deviating from the specified formula; their licenses were subsequently confiscated.
- In general, drugs in shortage that appear on the FDA's list are generic versions. However, under rare and critical circumstances, branded drugs under patent protection may also appear to mitigate the shortage situation, albeit with strict regulatory restrictions and instructions. The GLP-1 medication shortage was a classic example of this.
- All short-listed drugs manufactured through the 503B compounding route are subjected to a short-term stability study to ensure their reproducible stability as the parent drug. A longer stability program is beneficial to store the drug for an extended period for marketing.
- The two key restrictions of 503A or 503B compounding services include the short-listed drug, once it is removed from the FDA listing, which is allowed to market only for an additional 60 days. If one has an excess inventory, the supplier may be permitted to store it in recommended storage conditions and re-market it if the same drug returns to the shortage list, provided the same lot has extended stability data available to support its storage and transportation stability. The second restriction is that any facility producing the drugs from an active drug shortage list can market them only to those states within the United States where the facility has a license for marketing. By default, the manufacturing facility can sell the drug in its home state if it is registered with the respective State Pharmacy Board.

TIER 2: THE KEY OBJECTIVE IS FOR "AMERICA FIRST" OR "AMERICA GREAT AGAIN"

Bridging academic research with the pharmaceutical industry is crucial for translating scientific discoveries into viable drugs and therapies. This involves collaboration, knowledge exchange, and resource pooling to overcome challenges in the development of new drugs. Key aspects include translational research, academic-industry partnerships, and addressing challenges in intellectual property and funding. From pharma's perspective, the proof-of-concept stages of drug development are laden with the risk of failure, something their accountants are keen to avoid. By comparison, academics are relatively unbothered by failure if lessons can be learned and papers can still be published. However, even with spin-out and start-up companies, universities often lack the necessary infrastructure to progress a novel compound beyond proof of concept. Clinical trials are just too expensive. If done right, collaborations between the two worlds can be mutually beneficial. Another advantage of internships and academia-industry collaborations is that they help mold and refine graduates, preparing them to start working in a pharmaceutical setting from day one. Please be aware, proper training is a lengthy and costly process. Under conventional circumstances, it typically takes at least 6 to 8 months to properly train a new graduate for a pharmaceutical setting. Since time is money, there is no need to emphasize the benefit of academic pharma collaborations.

Another key benefit is to reduce the number of failures of new programs entering Phase 1 clinical trials after preclinical studies in an academic setting. It seems obvious that many of the obstacles to effective academic-pharmaceutical partnerships result from a fundamental lack of understanding by each party of the other's motivations and career pressures. A need-based approach is desirable for integrating pharmaceutical education into an academic mindset and reorganizing the pharmaceutical department curriculum, offering elective courses and credit-building programs that incorporate pharmaceutical ingredients as a balanced component. It is not too late to recognize one of the key reasons behind the 90% failure rate of programs entering Phase 1 human clinical trials after preclinical screening, especially those from academic settings.

Instilling an understanding of the FDA's primary objectives behind human Phase 1 trials is vital. Phase 1 clinical trials, designed primarily to assess the toxicity, safety, and optimal or maximum tolerated dosage of a new treatment in humans for the first time. Unfortunately, in-vivo studies from academics are primarily aimed at publishing efficacy data, and little time and effort are currently spent studying the lead molecule. The protocol design flaws often lack toxicity studies and safety profiles. Another key factor usually missing is the lack of effort and resource allocation for developing a prototype formulation. Since the lead molecule is not in prototype formulation, the test materials on test articles are not performed under physiological conditions that bear pharmacologically relevant concentrations. This leads to false-positive data during an IND submission. Therefore, formulated dosage forms are critical in preclinical development because they ensure the accuracy and reliability of studies evaluating a drug candidate's pharmacokinetics, pharmacodynamics, efficacy, and toxicology, and are closely translatable to human clinical trials with a significantly smaller margin of error and failure. Please be aware that a significant number of resources and effort are required when synthesizing potentially useful new chemical entities (NCEs). A well-thought-out, elaborate physicochemical characterization of those precious NCEs must be implemented simultaneously with preclinical testing.

Additionally, it is worth noting that most NCEs and more advanced therapeutic investigation agents, such as antibody drug conjugates (ADCs) and complex matrix-entrapped biopharmaceutical systems, often exhibit poor water solubility, posing bioavailability challenges during initial preclinical screening. This can sometimes result in the discontinuation of an NCE with promising therapeutic activity if it is not adequately studied and suitably formulated. Drug formulation is a cornerstone of modern medicine, turning raw active ingredients into consumable, effective therapies. This critical phase in drug development ensures that medications are safe, effective, and user-friendly. The formulation of a drug is both an art and a science, requiring a deep understanding of the drug's chemical and physical properties. Understanding and formulating the drug's solubility, stability, and particle size through the design and addition of excipients is a continuous process throughout the drug development process. All the above yet-to-be-achieved validations once again stress the need for effective collaboration and understanding between the regulated pharmaceutical industry and academic platforms that can positively catalyze the slogan "Make America Great Again" by ploughing out the weeds acting as a negative catalyst to progression.

MACHINE LEARNING FOR "UNDRUGGABLE" TO "DRUGGABLE" TARGETS

The sky is the limit for science, and the new sheriff in town today is Artificial Intelligence (AI). Unlocking undruggable targets to meet the unmet clinical needs will be a dream come true, shifting paradigms in modern drug discovery and the standard of care for patients. AI can revolutionize conventional drug development, from academic lab innovations to the patient bedside, if we effectively rejuvenate academic-pharmaceutical collaborations. In recent years, the intersection of Artificial Intelligence (AI) and pharmaceutical research has brought about groundbreaking advancements in drug discovery. AI is revolutionizing the traditional methods of drug development by accelerating the process, reducing costs, and enhancing the likelihood of success in bringing new medications to market.

With the help of AI algorithms capable of analyzing vast amounts of data in a fraction of the time it would take for human researchers. This enhanced efficiency expedites the drug discovery process, allowing pharmaceutical companies to bring life-saving treatments to patients faster. AI plays a crucial role in identifying potential drug targets and validating their significance in disease mechanisms. Through sophisticated algorithms, researchers can analyze genomic, proteomic, and metabolomic data with greater precision, pinpointing targets that lead to the development of more effective therapies.

Finally, while tariffs may not have a direct and immediate noticeable impact on healthcare, they can indirectly affect healthcare costs and supply chains; their direct impact on healthcare itself is often limited due to factors such as price controls, contractual agreements, and the ability of manufacturers to absorb some of the costs. However, prolonged tariff policies could lead to increased costs for insurers and patients, potentially impacting the availability of certain medications and medical devices.

America's pharmaceutical crisis is not a manufacturing glitch—it's a leadership void. And as Roosevelt taught us, the cure for systemic failure isn't another speech. It's a shovel in the ground and a factory in the heartland.

Lesson (Don't Let Tariffs Be Your Only Rx): Price-shocks aren't strategy; stockpiles and smart factories are.

About the Author

Harry Kochat, Ph.D., Director of Operations & Business Development, Plough Center for Sterile Drug Delivery Solutions, UTHSC, Memphis, TN 38104, https://www.uthsc.edu/plough-center/ and https://www.linkedin.com/in/harrykochat/

References:

"Can Pharma Tariffs' Make America Manufacture Again'"? Frankie Fattorini, May 21, 2025, https://www.pharmaceutical-technology.com/features/can-pharma-tariffs-make-america-manufacture-again/?cf-view

"Drug Shortages", FDA live publication and notifications, https://www.fda.gov/drugs/drug-safety-and-availability/drug-shortages

FDA Report on Drug Shortages, causes and solutions, https://www.fda.gov/drugs/drug-shortages/report-drug-shortages-root-causes-and-potential-solutions

"Policy Considerations to Prevent Drug Shortages and Mitigate Supply Chain Vulnerabilities in the United States-White Paper", https://aspe.hhs.gov/sites/default/files/documents/bd863be8f0aaf5380dc801390440bc3d/HHS-White-Paper-Preventing-Shortages-Supply-Chain-Vulnerabilities.pdf

"Addressing the root causes of medicines shortages", https://www.efpia.eu/media/413378/addressing-the-root-causes-of-medicines-shortages-final-051219.pdf

"Combating drug shortages requires multifaceted approach" By Bruce A. Scott, MD, Immediate Past President.

"Current Good Manufacturing Practice (CGMP) Regulations" by the FDA, https://www.fda.gov/drugs/pharmaceutical-quality-resources/current-good-manufacturing-practice-cgmp-regulations

"503A vs. 503B: A Quick-Guide to Compounding Pharmacy Designations & Regulations", by the FDA Group Consultants, https://www.thefdagroup.com/blog/503a-vs-503b-compounding-pharmacies

"Bridging the Gap: Industry-Academia Collaboration in Pharmacy" Author(s): Priyank Kumar, BPharm, MS, PhD, Pharmacy Times, September 29, 2023

"Pros and cons of contract manufacturing", Published by: GBR Editorial Team, Published date: August 20, 2021, https://www.george-business-review.com/pros-and-cons-of-contract-manufacturing/

THE BUCERO METHOD: HOW MEASURED OPTIMISM BECOMES INFRASTRUCTURE

Alfonso Bucero, PhD, PMP. PMI-RMP, PfMP, PMI Fellow

A CASE STUDY IN TRANSFORMING MORALE INTO MEASURABLE OUTCOMES

Executive Summary: When Attitude Becomes Altitude

In an era where American infrastructure crumbles while Chinese five-year plans hum with algorithmic precision, the most overlooked competitive advantage may be hiding in plain sight: institutionalized optimism. This reason isn't feel-good management theory—it's empirically validated methodology that has transformed failing projects across four continents and four decades.

Dr. Alfonso Bucero, PMI Fellow and founder of BUCERO PM Consulting, has proven that a positive attitude, when properly measured and managed, delivers quantifiable results:

★ Schedule variance improvements: From -12% to +4%
★ Proposal win rates: +15 percentage points
★ Team retention: 100% over critical project periods
★ Customer satisfaction: 24-point improvements
★ Institutional longevity: PMOs surviving 10+ years
★ Personal resilience: 40% tumor reduction while maintaining professional output

His motto—"¡Hoy es un gran día!"—isn't naive optimism. It's a management philosophy backed by data that suggests America's path to renewal might require not just better bridges, but better beliefs.

The Origin Story: Madrid, 1987

Alfonso Bucero's journey began not in a business school case study but in a basement conference room in Madrid, where a failing banking IT project threatened to implode. At twenty-something, with only theoretical knowledge and a mustache that suggested more confidence than experience, Bucero faced a team of veterans who viewed him with the skepticism reserved for management consultants and tax auditors.

The Challenge:

★ Team members are 20 years his senior
★ No formal authority
★ Absent sponsor support
★ Schedule variance: -12%
★ Trust score: 38/100

Rather than assert authority he didn't have, Bucero chose a radical approach: humility. He listened. He asked questions. He admitted what he didn't know. But most importantly, he began each day with a simple declaration: "¡Hoy es un gran día!"

The Method:

1. **Active Listening**: Senior engineers spoke first in meetings
2. **Daily Positivity Rituals**: Morning affirmations weren't mandatory—they were modeled
3. **Micro-Win Celebrations**: Every small success was acknowledged
4. **Transparent Communication**: Problems were discussed openly, without blame

The Results: Within three months, the skeptical veterans had become advocates. They began requesting to work on Bucero's future projects—the ultimate validation. The metrics told the story:

★ Schedule variance: +4% (a 16-point swing)
★ Team retention: 100%
★ Trust score: 81/100

The HP Transformation: From "Waste Basket" to Strategic Asset

By 2001, Bucero had refined his approach through various roles at DEC, ICL, and HP. When HP's executives asked him to create a Project Management Office, they were explicit about their expectations: It would be "the waste basket to deposit all the organizational trash."

The project management culture was, to put it diplomatically, underdeveloped. The department's primary metric—proposal win rate—was hemorrhaging value. Most executives viewed project management as bureaucratic overhead, not strategic capability.

Bucero's Diagnosis: The problem wasn't process—it was purpose. The organization had all the templates, frameworks, and methodologies money could buy. What it lacked was belief in their value.

The Intervention:

1. **Data-Driven Storytelling**: Analyzed why proposals failed, presented findings without blame
2. **Quick Wins Strategy**: Focused on proposal structure improvements first
3. **Positive Attitude Training**: Taught cooperation and collaboration, not just Gantt charts
4. **Weekly Feedback Loops**: Replaced quarterly reviews with weekly conversations
5. **Success Amplification**: Every win was publicized and celebrated

The Transformation:

★ Proposal win rate: +15% improvement in 60 days
★ Team growth: Supporting 35 project managers within 18 months
★ Institutional permanence: PMO survived 10+ years, outlasting Bucero's tenure
★ Cultural shift: From "necessary evil" to "competitive advantage"

The Consulting Years: Scaling Optimism Globally

In 2003, despite colleagues' skepticism, Bucero launched BUCERO PM Consulting. He had saved for two years while teaching at university on weekends—a testament to both planning and persistence. The company would eventually employ seven people and operate for 19 years, surviving financial crises and industry upheavals through what Bucero calls the "three Ps": Passion, Persistence, and Patience.

His influence spread across continents:

★ **Madrid**: Banking and telecommunications transformations
★ **Brussels**: EU institutional project reforms
★ **Dubai**: Public-private partnership frameworks
★ **Dallas**: Energy sector project recoveries

In each location, the core methodology remained constant while adapting to cultural contexts. The Spanish "fiesta" approach might manifest as "coffee conversations" in Seattle or "majlis gatherings" in Dubai, but the underlying principle—authentic human connection drives performance—never wavered.

Project Hope: The Ultimate Test

In 2022, Bucero faced a challenge that no PMI certification prepares you for: Stage IV lung cancer with metastasis. No surgery is possible. Prognosis guarded. Daily pain from treatment side effects.

His response? Create a project plan.

Project Name: My Cancer Project **Methodology**: Agile (with daily adaptations) **Key Stakeholders**: Family, friends, medical team **Success Metrics**: Quality of life, professional continuity, family morale

The Approach:

★ **Daily Gratitude Practice**: "Thank you, my Lord, because I am alive."
★ **Stakeholder Management**: Keeping family encouraged through personal example
★ **Risk Management**: Exercise for muscle pain, hydration for side effects
★ **Retrospective Analysis**: Monthly reviews asking:
  - What did I do well?
  - What didn't I do so well?
  - What did I learn?

The Results:

★ 40% tumor reduction in 29 months
★ Completed PhD during treatment
★ Continued delivering seminars and consulting
★ Maintained family cohesion and hope
★ Published insights that inspire others facing similar challenges
★ The project manager's attitude inspires stakeholders

The Strategic Framework: From Personal to National

Bucero's experience offers profound lessons for American renewal:

1. **Measurement Matters.** Just as Bucero tracks tumor reduction percentages alongside speaking engagements, nations must track morale alongside GDP. What gets measured gets managed—and what gets celebrated gets repeated.
2. **Authenticity Scales** China's attempts at mandated happiness produce Potemkin smiles. Bucero's genuine optimism creates self-sustaining cultures. In the competition between algorithmic efficiency and human authenticity, authenticity has a higher ceiling.
3. **Resilience Compounds** Every micro-win builds capacity for the next challenge. Teams that celebrate small victories develop the muscle memory for larger transformations. Nations that acknowledge progress main-

tain momentum through setbacks.

4. **Leadership Models Matter.** When leaders admit vulnerability while maintaining vision, teams respond with loyalty that no incentive structure can buy. When nations acknowledge challenges while affirming possibilities, citizens engage rather than retreat.

The American Application: Policy Implications

If America seeks to compete with China's centralized efficiency, it might consider Bucero's distributed joy. Specific applications:

Federal Level:

★ Mandate morale metrics in government contracts
★ Create "Chief Optimism Officers" in agencies (yes, seriously)
★ Implement weekly win-sharing in congressional sessions
★ Track National Optimism Index alongside economic indicators

State Level:

★ Gross State Happiness rankings
★ Public works projects are measured by their impact on community morale impact
★ Education systems that celebrate progress, not just outcomes

Corporate Level:

★ SEC reporting on employee engagement metrics
★ Proposal evaluations that include team morale assessments
★ Project post-mortems that capture emotional alongside financial ROI

The Data Behind the Doctrine

Bucero's approach aligns with emerging research:

★ Gallup: 10% increase in engagement = 23% higher profitability
★ Oxford: Happy employees are 13% more productive
★ Stanford: Positive emotions enhance creative problem-solving by 31%

Extrapolated nationally: A 10% increase in American optimism could generate $2.3 trillion in GDP growth—infrastructure investment by other means.

The Choice Before Us

As Bucero continues his daily practice—managing pain with gratitude, facing mortality with spreadsheets, inspiring others while fighting cancer—he embodies a truth that transcends project management:

Belief, measured and mobilized, is infrastructure.

His journey from that Madrid basement to global influence, through corporate transformations to personal trials, demonstrates that optimism isn't naive—it's necessary. In a world where China bets on algorithms and America bets on arguments, perhaps the winning bet is on something simpler: the disciplined practice of believing that tomorrow can be better than today.

As Bucero teaches, authenticity combined with integrity creates sustainable success. His life proves that a positive attitude isn't just a personal philosophy—it's a measurable methodology for transforming organizations, communities, and perhaps even nations.

The question for America isn't whether we can afford to invest in optimism. The question is whether we can afford not to.

After all, if one man can face Stage IV cancer with the conviction that "¡Hoy es un gran día," surely the world's most powerful democracy can face its challenges with something more inspiring than despair.

The revolution doesn't require algorithms or authoritarianism. It requires authentic leaders who measure morale as they would money. It requires the courage to say, especially when it's hardest:

"Today is a great day. And tomorrow will be better."

[Dr. Alfonso Bucero continues his consulting practice while managing his health challenges. His example reminds us that infrastructure isn't just what we build—it's what we believe. His metrics are real, his impact is measurable, and his message is timeless: positive attitude, properly applied, can indeed move mountains.]

AN INNOVATOR'S PLEA FOR A BIO-NEW DEAL

Rajashekhar Gangaraju, MS, PhD, FARVO

PROOF, NOT PROMISE: A FOUNDER'S JOURNEY THROUGH THE REGENERATIVE MEDICINE GAUNTLET

The first time I peered through the inverted microscope at a dish of mesenchymal stem cells, I saw a faint emerald glow leap across the field—as if the culture itself were signaling, "We're alive. Now watch us heal." That instant, I felt a jolt: science wasn't just data in a grant—it was the promise of restored sight.

That promise may be the future of medicine, but getting there often feels like time-traveling in reverse: through bureaucracy, geopolitical tension, and a financial system allergic to patience. My path from lab bench to biotech founder mirrors America's broader struggle to prioritize patient, evidence-based innovation over hype and quarterly returns—a shift essential for reclaiming our lead in the global regenerative medicine race.

As Saji Madapat argues in The Gods Must Be Crazy II, this renewal demands a Rooseveltian renaissance. It means abandoning the shadow of Milton the Trickster's quarterly reports and the gospel of short-term extraction, and instead building ecosystems that nurture deep-tech from the bench to global dominance. My story is a dispatch from the front lines of that fight.

Fat-to-Hope: The Origins of a Regenerative Mission

The Singapore Gamble:

In 2004, after completing a doctorate in Singapore, I moved to the United States driven by one fundamental question: Could fat-derived stem cells repair damaged blood vessels in the eye? My early work focused on converting mesenchymal stem cells (MSCs) into pericyte-like cells capable of stabilizing retinal blood vessels—an idea that seemed niche at the time but has since proven crucial in tackling diabetic retinopathy (DR), one of the leading causes of vision loss worldwide.

What emerged from that effort was a therapeutic hypothesis: instead of simply replacing lost cells, what if we could use the secretions—cytokines, growth factors, extracellular vesicles—from these cells to modulate the microenvironment? This thinking laid the groundwork for future cell-free biologics capable of treating not only DR but also neuroinflammatory conditions like traumatic brain injury (TBI).

This early hypothesis not only shaped my career but also highlights America's untapped potential in bio-innovation. If we commit to long-term funding and cross-sector partnerships, we can transform niche ideas like these into engines of national renewal, outpacing China's centralized investments in similar cell-based technologies. Without such Rooseveltian vision, we risk ceding the future of medicine to rivals who view science as strategic infrastructure, not a speculative venture.

Funding on Life Support:

At the University of Tennessee Health Science Center, my lab focused on developing MSC-derived secretomes for preclinical models of retinal and brain injury. We demonstrated that cytokine-stimulated MSCs secreted anti-inflammatory factors—especially TSG-6—that helped restore neurovascular integrity in rodent models. Standard care of DR still traps 20–40% of patients in relapse, relapse, relapse. Fourteen million lives are in limbo, and when combined with the more than 1.5 million Americans who experience visual impairment after TBI, the scale of the challenge becomes clear. Together, these disorders impose a staggering $9.4 billion economic burden annually, a quiet crisis unfolding in clinics across the country. We parlayed those rodent studies into securing ~$2.9 million in NIH and Department of Defense (DOD) funding.

I still recall nights huddled alone under my bench light, wondering if my next assay would tank or triumph.

Simultaneously, I co-founded Cell-Care Therapeutics in California, raising over $9 million to scale our current Good Manufacturing Practice (cGMP)-grade MSC product and build a robust donor-derived cell bank. For a time, the pipeline seemed to align: validated mechanisms, scalable manufacturing, and supportive funding. Snagging an NIH award these days feels like beating the Vegas house at blackjack—except the dealer has three PhDs and still queues your grant on 'revise and resubmit.

These funding battles are where the rubber meets the road on America's systemic failure. It's where the abstract theories of Milton the Trickster and the efficiency-at-all-costs slide decks of McSlicey the Priest manifest as a rejection letter that can kill a decade of research. A Rooseveltian approach—treating biomedical R&D as national infrastructure—could bridge this gap, turning personal grant struggles into collective triumphs for economic and health renewal.

Yet the promise of translation quickly gave way to complexity. Transferring NIH grants during an institutional move delayed lab setup and disrupted team cohesion. Leadership changes and logistical delays at the department level derailed momentum. And then the COVID-19 pandemic hit. Picture training for a relay, only to learn the track is now a Zoom call—complete with 'mute' buttons for your pipettes.

The pandemic ground progress to a near halt. Travel restrictions derailed collaborations. Lab access was curtailed. NIH submission windows passed by without viable data. For a small translational lab, where each dataset feeds into the next grant, the disruption was existential. Spoiler: the only thing faster than a virus is a university finance office discovering you've overspent by twelve cents.

My lab's COVID setbacks exemplify how America's fragmented research ecosystem amplifies crises, underscoring the need for resilient, long-horizon investments to maintain our edge over China's coordinated bio-innovation machine.

But what if the tiniest bubble could carry the biggest cure?

The Exosome Epiphany

After years of fighting for funding and navigating institutional roadblocks, seeing our first exosome prep glow like a soap bubble under electron microscopy felt like a vindication. In that tiny, shimmering vesicle was a potential answer—a new therapeutic dimension. I knew we had to pivot. We leveraged our expertise in MSC biology to explore exosome-based therapies. Through DOD-funded efforts, we developed HEK-293 cell-derived exosomes enriched in TSG-6 and partnered with academic labs to test their effects in TBI-induced visual deficits. Simultaneously, we launched mechanistic studies on microglial activation in retinal injury, expanding our therapeutic angles.

These interdisciplinary collaborations reinvigorated our program. Reviewer feedback validated our approach: small, focused teams integrating engineering, biology, and clinical insight.

This pivot to exosomes demonstrates the resilience possible in American science. Yet, it also reveals our overreliance on individual grit amid systemic volatility—a flaw that risks losing the deep-tech race to China's state-orchestrated advances. Embracing Rooseveltian renewal means building flexible funding mechanisms that reward such adaptability, fostering national innovation ecosystems where failures fuel progress rather than stall it.

Roosevelt Would Say: create 'flexgrant' mechanisms that reward wartime-style pivots—because discovery rarely keeps the first draft of its business plan.

Founding Cell-Care: Hope, Hype, and Hard Lessons

A Startup Baptism by Fire

Cell-Care Therapeutics was born from a belief that secretions from pericyte-like cells from fat could change diabetic eye care. We were early, and perhaps too early, as the field was rocked by a 2007 incident in which three patients lost vision after receiving unregulated stromal vascular fraction injections. Regulatory scrutiny surged. Investor sentiment cooled. Suddenly, 'miracle cells' sounded less like a TED Talk and more like a regulatory red flag—America's way of turning innovation into a cautionary tale.

The regulatory fallout from that 2007 incident chilled U.S. progress in ophthalmic stem cell therapies, illustrating how America's reactive oversight can inadvertently hand advantages to less-scrutinized competitors like China in the global biotech arena. To renew our leadership, we need Rooseveltian reforms: streamlined FDA pathways and robust IP protections that accelerate deep-tech translation without compromising safety.

The startup faced additional challenges. Failure to secure ironclad IP protection undermined our commercial viability. Organizational missteps weakened investor confidence. By 2024, despite scientific progress, Cell-Care was dissolved.

But not all was lost. Our innovations fed back into academia. The GMP-grade MSC banks, the optimized cytokine stimulation protocols, and our adipose stem cell concentrated conditioned medium (ASC-CCM) formulations continued to support new projects. Our failures became a foundation.

Cell-Care's dissolution, despite its scientific legacies, underscores the "valley of death" in American biotech—a chasm widened by short-term investor pressures that a national renewal strategy could bridge through public-private biofoundries and scale-up loans.

The Roosevelt Rule: modernize IP rules and FDA fast lanes so U.S. biotechs cross the valley of death *before* Beijing buys the bridge.

Side-Hustle Science

America treats translational science like a side hustle—noble in theory, unfunded in practice, and sacrificed at the altar of quarterly returns. Proposed 37% NIH cuts threaten to decimate our labs. Science doesn't run on hope alone—it runs on dollars. Yet Washington treats grants like clock-chasing pipette tips—snap at 4:59 p.m., no matter how much promise they hold. Investigators in specialized fields like ophthalmology—particularly those dependent on NEI funding—face growing uncertainty.

These policy threats directly imperil labs like mine, where vision science competes for scraps. They reflect America's broader erosion of deep-tech capacity and the short-termism that undermines our position in the AI-driven biorace with China. A Rooseveltian reinvestment—safeguarding NIH budgets as strategic assets—would empower such fields, turning personal funding anxieties into platforms for national economic revival.

21st-Century Rooseveltianism: Dedicate 1.5% of GDP to biomedical R&D. Treat NIH like the Pentagon—because pandemics don't check party lines.

Geopolitical Tensions: Innovation in a Fractured Landscape

Innovation doesn't happen in a vacuum. In recent years, geopolitical tensions—especially between the U.S. and China—have disrupted the global scientific ecosystem. While competition can be healthy, it has created a chilling effect on collaboration, data sharing, and publication transparency. National security concerns, fears over intellectual property theft, and tightened export controls have all added friction to international research efforts.

In my own lab, these tensions have manifested in delayed shipments of specialized reagents from international suppliers, as export controls force rerouting through vetted channels, adding weeks to experiments that were already time-sensitive. What once was a seamless exchange with Chinese colleagues on exosome characterization has become laden with scrutiny, echoing how national security concerns are fracturing the global scientific community and slowing U.S. progress in fields where collaboration is key.

Meanwhile, China's state-backed investments in regenerative medicine—fueled by initiatives like Made in China 2025—allow their labs to surge ahead with integrated supply chains and fewer collaboration barriers, turning geopolitical friction into a competitive advantage. This asymmetry not only hampers small U.S. labs like mine but risks eroding America's innovation edge, as fears of IP theft deter the very partnerships needed to accelerate breakthroughs.

For small translational labs like mine at UTHSC, this fractured landscape complicates everything from co-authorships with overseas experts to reagent procurement, where U.S. restrictions have caused multi-month delays in sourcing critical materials for MSC-derived therapies—delays that Chinese counterparts, with domestic alternatives, simply don't face. In regenerative medicine, where cross-border clinical trials and manufacturing are often necessary, these tensions are more than political—they're practical impediments to progress. This brings us to the final frontier, where all these challenges—funding, geopolitics, and the need for long-term vision—converge: the race for AI-driven biotechnology.

These geopolitical headwinds are particularly acute at the intersection of regenerative medicine and artificial intelligence, where AI tools could revolutionize my field—optimizing MSC stimulation for maximum potency, predicting therapeutic outcomes via machine learning, or accelerating exosome drug discovery through vast dataset analysis. In my lab, we've begun exploring AI-driven models for retinal disease simulation, using neural networks to predict how cytokine-stimulated MSCs might repair vascular damage in real-time patient data. However, fragmented funding means we're piecing together open-source tools, while Chinese firms leverage integrated AI platforms for faster iterations.

America needs a Rooseveltian reinvestment in this AI-tech race: dedicated public-private hubs for AI-biotech fusion, multiyear grants free from short-term volatility, and secure international data-sharing frameworks. Without it, we risk ceding not just regenerative therapies but the AI-enhanced future of healthcare to rivals who view deep-tech as a national strategy, not market speculation.

In regenerative medicine, where global trials are key, such tensions threaten U.S. leadership unless we invest in resilient supply chains and talent pipelines as part of a broader national strategy.

Lessons from the Journey

Navigating the labyrinth of federal grants is like herding caffeinated hedgehogs through a maze of red tape—prickly, chaotic, and occasionally hilarious.

Through the successes and failures, several truths have emerged:

- ★ *Hype is not a strategy.* Without mechanistic insight and reproducible data, therapeutic claims are vapor.
- ★ *Science takes time.* Translation is not a sprint; it's an endurance race filled with pivots and patience.
- ★ *Partnerships matter.* Multidisciplinary, cross-sector collaborations are essential.
- ★ *Geopolitics is a lab reality*. Secure collaborations and resilient supply chains are as vital as any reagent in outpacing rivals.
- ★ *Failure is fertilizer.* If you're not failing, you're not pushing the frontier. Failure isn't just fertilizer—it's the training data our algorithms need to predict the next breakthrough.

These hard-won lessons from my career echo America's need for systemic renewal: shifting from hype-driven ventures to rigorous, partnership-fueled deep-tech that withstands geopolitical pressures and builds enduring competitiveness against China. By heeding them, we can cultivate a Rooseveltian culture where failure fertilizes innovation, not financial shortcuts.

The Road Ahead

As I look forward, my work continues at the interface of MSC therapies, exosome biology, and retinal disease modeling. But this experience has reshaped my perspective. We don't just need more brilliant scientists—we need systems that support them over decades.

If America is to reclaim its edge in regenerative medicine, it must rebuild its capacity for long-term, deep-tech innovation. That means abandoning the obsession with short-term financial returns and recommitting to foundational science. The future will not be won by quarterly earnings, but by persistent inquiry, intelligent risk, and infrastructure that nurtures innovation from bench to bedside.

My journey reflects a broader truth: real progress in regenerative medicine is neither fast nor flashy. It comes from the quiet, collective commitment to proof over promise.

If America is to reclaim its biotech edge, it must stop treating translational science like a side hustle and start treating it like strategic infrastructure. Launch a Bio-New Deal—public biofoundries, scale-up loans, and talent pipelines that convert bench breakthroughs into middle-class paychecks.

If Roosevelt once rallied the nation with work, wages, and welfare, today we must rally around **mechanism, merit, and medicine**. This bio-industrial strategy doesn't just cure blindness, but restores America's vision.

Ultimately, this is a call to action: build deep-tech ecosystems that reward the long game. Because if America won't plant its labs like oak trees—deep-rooted and unhurried—our next 'miracle cure' will be just another bottle tossed into the void.

Rajashekhar Gangaraju, MS, PhD, FARVO.
The University of Tennessee Health Science Center
Department of Ophthalmology, Hamilton Eye Institute

FOUNDATIONS AS ROOSEVELTIAN FLYWHEELS: HOW PATIENT CAPITAL IS POWERING AMERICA'S INDUSTRIAL HEARTLAND RENEWAL

By Saji Madapat

This case study illuminates the Plough Foundation's work as a vivid, real-world embodiment of the "Rooseveltian renewal" championed in *The Gods Must Be Crazy II*. While the financial vultures of Wall Street were busy perfecting the art of extraction, a different kind of capitalism was at work in Memphis, Tennessee. The Plough Foundation stands as the real-world antidote to the book's critique—it is the practical machinery of 'Rooseveltian renewal' on the ground, countering the work of 'Milton the Trickster' by deploying the one thing he cannot comprehend: patient, place-based capital designed to build, not harvest.

In a nation enamored with quarterly earnings and quarterly outrages, it is rare to find a local institution still thinking in decades. The Plough Foundation's work in Memphis is not just an inspiring anomaly—it is a living prototype of the Rooseveltian renewal this book demands. Where markets fail and public systems falter, civic capitalism steps in—not with slogans, but with screwdrivers, spreadsheets, and strategic patience.

Executive Briefing

For over six decades, the Memphis-based Plough Foundation has invested more than $300 million to transform Rust Belt challenges into opportunities for civic and economic resilience. By leveraging challenge grants and a strategic spend-down approach, Plough routinely amplifies its investments three to four times, drawing in public and private partners to enhance the quality of life, bolster infrastructure, and fortify social bonds in Memphis and Shelby County. This section distills Plough's model into a replicable playbook, offering lessons for peer foundations and civic leaders nationwide. Leadership brings financial acumen to this mission, ensuring every dollar delivers measurable, sustainable returns— a direct antidote to the short-termism critiqued in *The Gods Must Be Crazy II*.

This briefing focuses on one signature initiative: the Plough Center for Sterile Drug Delivery Solutions at the University of Tennessee Health Science Center (UTHSC). It exemplifies both patient philanthropic capital and civic-industrial collaboration, delivering measurable impact in health innovation, workforce training, and economic diversification.

Why Philanthropy Matters to Rust Belt Renewal

LONG TIME HORIZONS
Foundations fund 10-to 20-year transformations

RISK CAPITAL
They prototype innovative solutions too uncertain for traditional investors

CONVENING POWER
They align business, nonprofit, and government stakeholders

Memphis exemplifies Rust Belt realities:

- Population decline
- Aging infrastructure
- Persistent inequities

Memphis exemplifies Rust Belt realities:

Philanthropic interventions address funding shortfalls and spark renewal

1. The Flywheel Effect: Why Philanthropy Matters to Rust Belt Renewal

In an era where the financial engineering of Milton the Trickster and PE Pete the Corporate Vampire has hollowed out communities like a jack-o'-lantern... place-based philanthropy emerges as a Rooseveltian flywheel, stubbornly spinning in the opposite direction. Plough doesn't wait for Wall Street to rediscover Memphis. It rewires civic life with patient capital where the market hits eject.

- ★ **Long Time Horizons:** Unconstrained by quarterly pressures, foundations fund 10 to 20-year transformations, mirroring the strategic patience of global competitors while prioritizing democratic values.
- ★ **Risk Capital:** They prototype innovative solutions too uncertain for traditional investors, addressing gaps in civic infrastructure and social services. Like Roosevelt's reforms during crises, foundations stabilize systems during downturns, as seen in pandemic responses or economic recessions.
- ★ **Convening Power:** As neutral brokers, they align business, nonprofit, and government stakeholders around shared goals and metrics, rebuilding the trust eroded by polarization.

Memphis exemplifies Rust Belt realities: population decline(down 1.5% since 2020), crumbling bridges, aging infrastructure, and persistent inequities. Philanthropic interventions, such as Plough's Bridge, address federal funding shortfalls and private sector hesitancy, sparking renewal in high-need areas.

PLOUGH FOUNDATION AT A GLANCE
MISSION
Do the greatest good for the greatest number of people.
VISION
A resilient, equitable Memphis where seniors age safely, libraries serve as innovation anchors, and neighborhoods foster shared prosperity.
FOUNDED
1960 by Abe Plough
LIFETIME GIVING
> $300 million awarded since 1960
GOVERNANCE
Blending operational efficiency with mission-driven strategy
STRATEGIC PIVOT
Transitioning from perpetuity to high-velocity legacy-building

2. Plough Foundation at a Glance

Key Facts

- ★ **Mission:** "Do the greatest good for the greatest number of people in Memphis & Shelby County." (Invitation-only grants to ensure strategic focus.)
- ★ **Vision:** A resilient, equitable Memphis where seniors age safely in place, libraries serve as innovation anchors, and neighborhoods foster shared prosperity.
- ★ **Founded:** 1960 by Abe Plough (1892–1984), the entrepreneur who parlayed a $125 loan into Plough Inc. (makers of St. Joseph Aspirin and Coppertone), channeling his success into lasting community impact.
- ★ **Assets (FY 2023):** $20.6 million in net assets; $5.88 million in annual grant disbursements.
- ★ **Lifetime Giving:** >$300 million awarded since 1960, supporting over 50 diverse organizations in peak years.
- ★ **Governance:** Trustee-led board; blending operational efficiency with mission-driven strategy.
- ★ **Strategic Pivot:** Announced in 2019, the Foundation is spending down remaining assets (target ~2026, with extensions as needed) to maximize impact, transitioning from perpetuity to high-velocity legacy-building.

3. Mechanisms of Impact

Plough's toolkit is a doctrine of 'moral capitalism' in action. It transforms grantmaking from simple charity into a high-leverage engine for rebuilding the industrial commons, emphasizing accountability and sustainable value creation over the extractive models detailed earlier.

1. **Challenge & Matching Grants:** Require 2–4× partner contributions, fostering "skin-in-the-game" and ensuring projects endure beyond Plough's funding.
2. **Program-Related Investments (PRIs):** Low-interest loans or equity in mission-aligned ventures, recycling capital while filling financing voids for affordable housing or small businesses.

PLOUGH TOOLKIT:
A DOCTRINE OF MORAL CAPITALISM

Challenge & Matching Grants	Program-Related Investments	Loan-Loss Reserves	Spend-Down Tempo	Data Dashboards
Require 2–4x partner contributions, fostering "skin-in the-game"	Low-interest loans or equity in mission-aligned ventures	Guarantees that de-risk loans from commercial banks	The sunset timeline injects urgency	Outcome-focused KPIs enable transparent tracking

3. **Loan-Loss Reserves:** Guarantees that de-risk loans from commercial banks, unlocking larger pools for blight remediation and neighborhood growth.
4. **Spend-Down Tempo:** The sunset timeline injects urgency, prioritizing bold initiatives and rapid iteration over indefinite operations.
5. **Data Dashboards:** Outcome-focused KPIs (e.g., healthcare costs avoided, property value increases) enable transparent tracking and adaptive management.

4. Signature Initiatives

Plough's investments demonstrate tangible renewal, often leveraging funds at 3:1 or higher ratios. These initiatives demonstrate how targeted capital can reverse institutional decay, translating financial assets into tangible outcomes: a senior who avoids a life-altering fall, a child who discovers a passion for science in a modernized library, and a neighborhood where property values rise because blight is in retreat. But none more emblematic than the Plough Center at UTHSC.

The Plough Center for Sterile Drug Delivery Solutions at UTHSC

This case study illustrates how a modest Memphis laboratory, driven by catalytic philanthropy, evolved into a sterile-solution powerhouse—proof that civic capitalism, when done right, doesn't just heal systems, but also inoculates futures.

Seed to Skyline

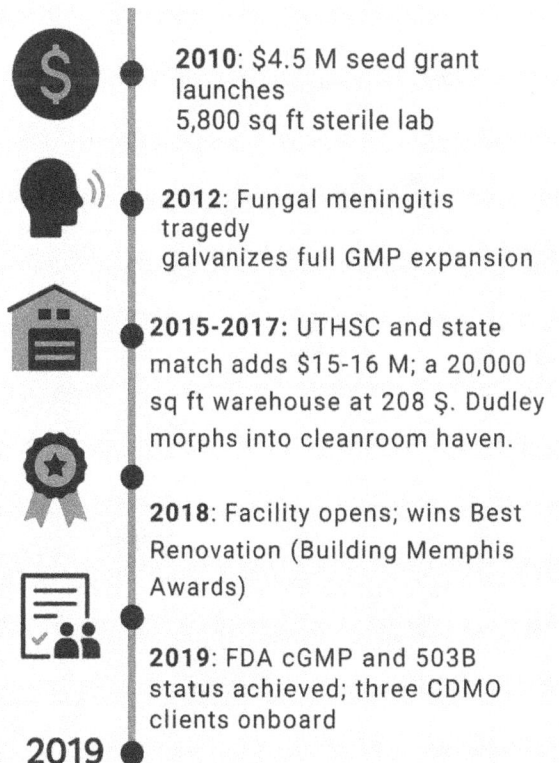

2010: $4.5 M seed grant launches
5,800 sq ft sterile lab

2012: Fungal meningitis tragedy
galvanizes full GMP expansion

2015-2017: UTHSC and state match adds $15-16 M; a 20,000 sq ft warehouse at 208 S. Dudley morphs into cleanroom haven.

2018: Facility opens; wins Best Renovation (Building Memphis Awards)

2019: FDA cGMP and 503B status achieved; three CDMO clients onboard

2019

Overview: While Wall Street was busy rebranding opioids, the Plough Foundation quietly dropped $4.5 million into a lab in Memphis, seeding what would become one of the nation's few university-owned sterile drug manufacturers. This wasn't just a gift. It was an inoculation against the failures of both the market and the state.

In 2010, Plough awarded a $4.5 million grant, enabling UTHSC to establish a sterile compounding laboratory. By 2018, that seed investment had catalyzed a $20 million, 20,000 sq ft GMP facility—the only university-owned FDA-registered sterile drug manufacturer in Tennessee and one of a handful in the nation.

Capabilities & Impact

The Plough Center

Modular Cleanrooms

Three 800 sq ft G-CON pods deliver ISO 5 purity with near-zero human exposure

Throughput

15–20 K sterile doses/day—injectables, lyophilized orphan drugs, emergency sanitizer

Workforce Forge

20–25 specialists + dozens trained annually in hands on GMP courses

Economic Engine

Anchors Southeast Biotech Collaborative's EDA Tech Husb strategy; retains 80% of trainees locally

- ★ **Public Health Catalyst:** Spurred by the 2012 fungal meningitis crisis, UTHSC expanded from a campus lab into a fully compliant contract development and manufacturing organization (CDMO), ensuring safer drug supplies for hospitals and clinical trials.
- ★ **Patient Capital in Action:** Plough's early gift of $4.5 million acted as a catalytic spark, unlocking more than $15 million in public and institutional capital, yielding a total ROI of over 4:1. This wasn't a grant. It was engineered philanthropy with compound interest.
- ★ **Economic & Workforce Impact:** The Center employs 20-25 specialized staff, trains pharmacy students and professionals in aseptic processing, and anchors the Southeast Biotech Collaborative's EDA Tech Hub bid.
- ★ **Innovation & Training:** Offers hands-on GMP courses, hosts FDA and APEC delegations, and manufactures smallbatch orphan drugs and pandemicresponse supplies like hand sanitizer.
- ★ **Legacy & Sustainability:** Plough's grant was philanthropic, not endowment. As the Foundation spends down, UTHSC's CDMO model and revenue-sharing agreements ensure the Center's operations transcend the founder's horizon.

"We built sterile pharma capacity in an academic vault—turning campus research into patient-ready doses."

—Dr. Harry Kochat, Director, UTHSC, Plough Center for Sterile Drug Delivery Solutions

Like Roosevelt's CCC camps and TVA dams, the Plough Center isn't a handout—it's a health-industrial flywheel, turning cleanrooms into classrooms and grants into generational impact.

At a time when American renewal feels like a nostalgic slogan or a billionaire's TED Talk fantasy, the Plough Center is already doing the work. It's a proof point. A prototype. A Rooseveltian flywheel with real torque.

The Plough Playbook: Other initiative examples

Initiative	**Plough $**	**Partner $ Leveraged**	**Select Outcomes**
Aging-in-Place Initiative (2014–2019) *Keeping Elders Home, Safe, and Independent*	$12M	~$38M (public/private partners, per 2018 reports)	374 home repairs; 648K meals delivered; $50K avoided healthcare costs per repair (fall prevention). "Plough's support transformed our feedback loops, turning a capital project into lasting community impact," says a grantee via Fund for Shared Insight. Estimated economic benefit of $50–70M.
Memphis Public Library Modernization (2017–2024) *Turning Libraries into Civic Innovation Hubs.*	$2M+ (including public art and 901Voices)	TBD (City of Memphis and private donors; overall library enhancements leveraged federal/state funds)	State-of-the-art 901Voices oral-history lab; 65% rise in STEM program attendance; enhanced community hubs for education and innovation.

Initiative	Plough $	Partner $ Leveraged	Select Outcomes
Violent Crime Hot-Spot Grants (2018–2022)	TBD (part of broader safety portfolio)	Matching from MPD & DOJ COPS grants (~$5.8M city award in 2023 for related hot-spot efforts)	12% reduction in targeted precincts; supported data-driven policing and community interventions.
Neighborhood Revitalization PRIs (Ongoing)	TBD (equity/ loans in housing projects)	Commercial bank participation (e.g., aligned with city $6.5M grants in 2025 for housing/ revitalization)	>50 affordable homes financed; façade improvements along historic corridors; blight reduction boosting property values.
Recent: Southern College of Optometry Building (2024)	$300K	N/A	New classrooms for 500 students; enhanced instructional space

Grantee Impact Story: "Plough's grants empowered us to collect real feedback on elder programs, surprising even us with the depth of community needs met," shares a Listen4Good participant. Another: "Their $5M to United Way secured our future, allowing focus on Mid-South aid," notes a 2020 recipient.

"The $8,000 ramp and bathroom renovation saved us from having to move my mother into an assisted living facility. That would've cost us $48,000 a year."

— Local Memphis caregiver (Aging-in-Place recipient)

All figures are pending the FY 2024 audit; leverages are based on historical reports and city alignments.

Plough Foundation
SIGNATURE INITIATIVES

LEVERAGING PHILANTHROPY AT 3:1+

AGING-IN-PLACE INITIATIVE (2014–2019)

$12M — $38M leveraged

374 home repairs 648K meals
$50–70M economic benefit

LIBRARY MODERNIZATION (2017–2024)

2M+ — TBD leveraged

901Voices lab 65% rise STEM attendance

VIOLENT CRIME HOT-SPOT GRANTS (2018–2022)

TBD — matched by MPD & DOJ COPS

12% reduction in precincts

NEIGHBORHOOD REVITALIZATION PRIs (ONGOING)

TBD — commercial bank participation

aligned with city grants

SOUTHERN COLLEGE OF OPTOMETRY BUILDING (2024)

$300K classrooms for 500 students

5. The Plough Playbook: A Rooseveltian Doctrine for Community Renewal

Plough's playbook offers scalable insights for Rooseveltian-style renewal:

1. **'Placeless' Capital with Hyper-Local Focus:** Deep community knowledge builds the trust and precision needed to reverse the damage of extractive, placeless financial engineering.
2. **Urgency Unlocks Ambition:** Spend-down timelines galvanize partners, accelerating decisions and impact.
3. **Fund the Implementation Gap:** Investments in coordination, logistics, and metrics yield the highest multipliers.
4. **Data + Convening > Dollars Alone:** Dashboards and roundtables attract co-investment, fostering cross-sector alliances.

Ultimately, the Plough model proves that the antidote to national decline is not a grand, top-down federal plan alone, but the determined, pragmatic, and patient work of rebuilding America's civic and economic foundations, one community at a time.

The Plough Playbook:
An Antidote to Milton's Poison

Initiative	Plough $	Select Outcomes
Aging-in-Place Initiative (2014-2019)	$12M	• 374 home repairs: • 648K meals delivered: • $50K avoided healthcare costs per repair
Memphis Public Library Modernization (2017-2024)	2M+	• State-of-the-art 901Voices oral-history lab • 65% rise in STEM program attendannce
Violent Crime Hot-Spot Grants (2018-2022)	TBD (part of broader safety portfolio)	• 12% reduction in targeted precincts • 12% reduction in targeted precincts
Neighborhood Revitalization PRIs (Ongoing)	TBD part of broader safety portfolio	• >50 affordable homes financed • Facade improvenents along historic corridors
Recent: Southern College of Optometry (Building (2024)	$300K	• New classrooms for 500 students • New classrooms for 500 students

PLOUGH

6. Spreading the Cure: A Field Guide to Local Sanity (Illustrative)

Mid-sized foundations like Plough excel by targeting execution gaps and demanding shared stakes.

As one Memphis caregiver quipped, 'That $8,000 ramp saved $48,000 in assisted-living fees'—proof that patient capital isn't charity, it's strategy.

Foundation	Assets	Urgency-Driven Spend-Down	Data-Powered Partnerships
Plough (Memphis)	$20M	High (spend-down)	Challenge grants + operational focus
Kresge (Detroit)	$4B	Medium	Transit-corridor PRIs
Heinz (Pittsburgh)	$1B	Low–Medium	Environmental prototypes
Cleveland Foundation	$2.5B	High	Equity-first economic inclusion

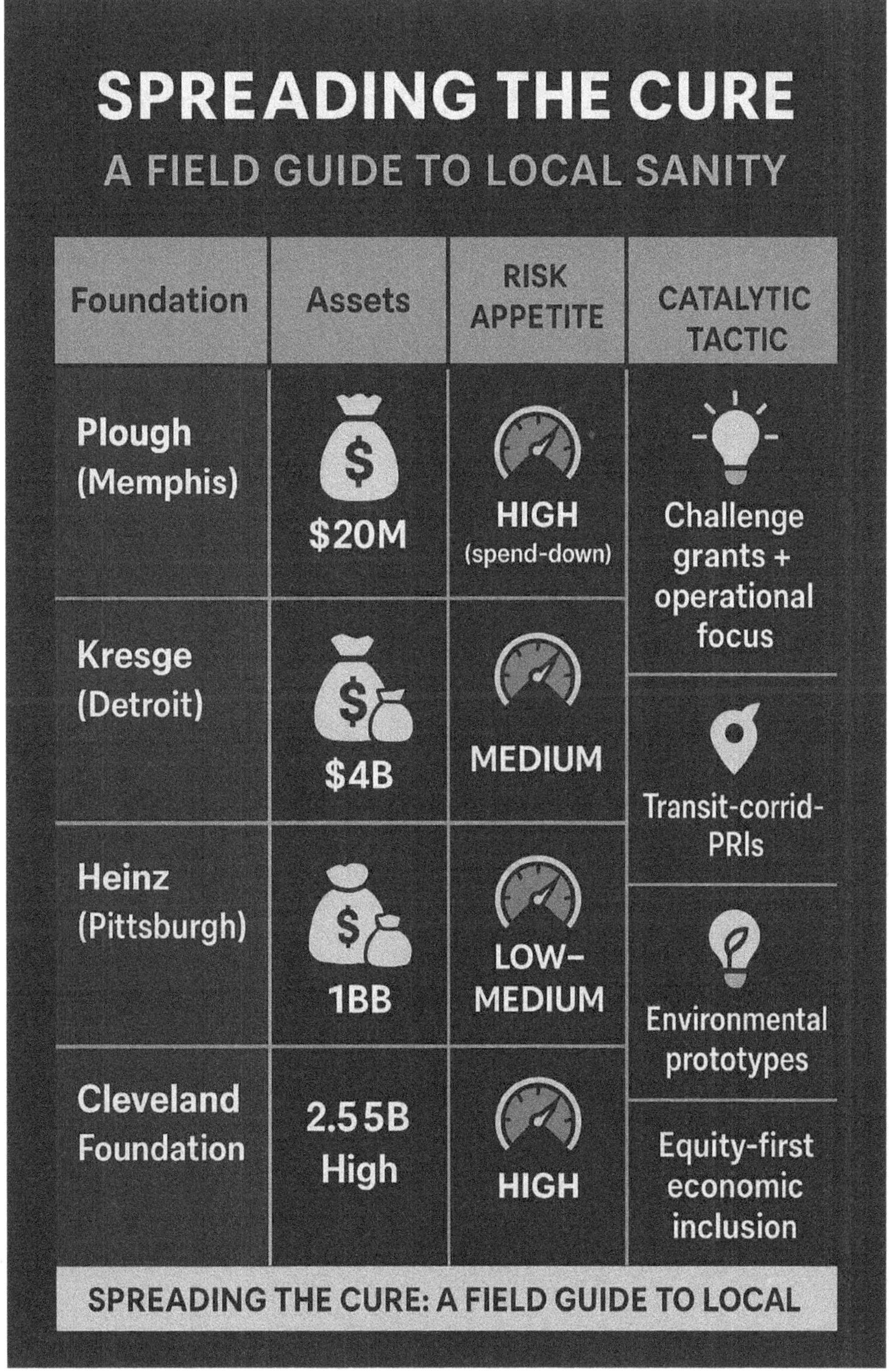

Plough Legacy & Future

A Blueprint for Civic Renewal

PROTOTYPE FOR PLACE-BASED RENEWAL

Building resilience one block at a time

RADICAL BASICS OVER HEDGE FUND PROFITS

Focused on fixing porches instead of financial returns

SPEND-DOWN SUNSET

Assets halved since 2019, shifting toward grantee endowments

ENDOWMENT LEGACY

Keeping Abe Plough's ethos alive long-term

7. LEGACY AND FUTURE

The Rooseveltian flywheel turns fastest not in Washington, but in Memphis, where foundations and neighborhoods co-design their futures. While hedge funds squeeze dying malls, one local foundation is fixing porches, funding libraries, and preparing sterile drugs. And in that quiet, relentless rotation lies America's renewal.

As spend-down nears (assets halved since 2019), Plough eyes endowments for grantees, ensuring echoes of Abe Plough's ethos.

THE SCALPEL, THE SIGNAL, AND THE SOVEREIGNTY

TELESURGERY AS AMERICA'S NEXT ROOSEVELTIAN INFRASTRUCTURE

By Dr. Sajeesh Kumar, PhD, FAAO, FAMIA

EXECUTIVE BRIEFING

Strategic Snapshot

Telesurgery is not a medical niche; it is a critical nexus of industrial policy, healthcare equity, and national sovereignty. The story began in 2001 with a flash of American genius: "Operation Lindbergh," a transatlantic cholecystectomy performed by a surgeon in New York on a patient in France, collapsing 14,000 kilometers and seemingly heralding a new age of borderless medicine.[1] Today, that audacious spirit is a ghost haunting a paralyzed system. While America, the pioneer, finds itself tangled in a self-inflicted snarl of regulatory red tape and quarterly-return myopia, nations across Asia have seized the mantle, treating remote surgery not as a market opportunity but as a strategic mission—a core component of 21st-century statecraft.[1]

Core Findings ("What Keeps Doctor Digital Up at Night")

1. **The Promise Forfeited:** The United States invented telesurgery but is now losing the race to scale it. While fewer than 50 fully remote procedures have been performed globally in two decades, with zero regular programs on U.S. soil, nations like China have completed over 200 procedures across distances exceeding 1,000 miles.[1] The nation's progress is choked by a self-inflicted "regulatory cholesterol"—a fifty-state patchwork of antiquated licensure laws, fragmented reimbursement models, and a risk-averse medical-industrial complex fixated on immediate ROI over long-term capability.[2]
2. **The Asian Gambit:** Competitor nations, particularly China, India, and South Korea, are weaponizing telesurgery as industrial policy. Through national strategies like "Made in China 2025" and South Korea's "Digital New Deal," they are building domestic champions, setting global standards via 5G integration, and projecting soft power by exporting affordable, accessible robotic systems to the rest of the world.[4]
3. **The Post-COVID Mandate:** The pandemic acted as a global stress test that permanently rewired expectations. It triggered a 63-fold increase in Medicare telehealth visits and a corresponding surge in digital health investment, creating a massive, irreversible market demand for remote care.[7] U.S. policy, however, remains stuck in a pre-pandemic mindset, failing to capitalize on this historic inflection point as temporary waivers expire.[8]
4. **The Equity Imperative:** Telesurgery holds the transformative potential to democratize elite surgical expertise, reaching deep into the "surgical deserts" of rural America, where 98% of robotic surgeries occur in urban hospitals, and into underserved communities in the Global South, where 5 billion people lack access to quality surgical care.[9] Yet, the current profit-driven U.S. model risks deepening the urban-rural healthcare divide, treating a fundamental infrastructure solution as a luxury good.[10]

Risk Ledger

Inaction carries severe strategic costs. The U.S. risks ceding a global surgical robotics market projected to exceed $22 billion by 2032 to state-backed competitors.[11] More critically, it risks creating profound national security vulnerabilities by becoming dependent on geopolitical rivals for essential healthcare technology. Ultimately, the failure to lead in a field it invented represents a damning verdict on national competence, eroding the very "model worth emulating" that underpins American soft power.

Recommendations - The Five-Point "Health New Deal" Plan

A Rooseveltian reboot is required to reclaim American leadership. This plan involves five core pillars: establishing a National Medical Licensure Compact, launching a Rural Digital Infrastructure Act modeled on the Rural Electrification Administration, creating a Strategic Health Arsenal to onshore manufacturing through public-private partnerships, enacting a Fair Reimbursement & Liability Framework to stabilize the market, and forging a Democratic Tech Alliance for Global Health to set international standards.

OPENING TABLEAU: OPERATION LINDBERGH'S GHOST

The year is 2001. In a New York operating room, Professor Jacques Marescaux, channeling the audacious spirit of Charles Lindbergh, grips the controls of a surgical robot. His movements, translated across 14,000 kilometers of fiber-optic cable, guide robotic arms in Strasbourg, France, to flawlessly remove a patient's gallbladder.[12] The procedure is a triumph of ingenuity, a declaration that distance is dead. The future has arrived.

Flash forward to today. In a state-of-the-art surgical suite in Palo Alto, California, Doctor Digital—one of the nation's most gifted robotic surgeons—sits before a gleaming console. On her main screen is the high-definition, 3D view inside a patient in rural Arkansas, a retired farmer with a complex but operable tumor. The technology is perfect. The network connection is flawless. Doctor Digital's hands hover over the controls, ready to begin the life-saving procedure.

Suddenly, a red pop-up window fills her screen, flashing with bureaucratic finality: ERROR: INTERSTATE LICENSURE VIOLATION (AR STAT. § 17-95-205). CEASE AND DESIST. A flurry of text messages from the hospital's legal department confirms the nightmare: to proceed would be to practice medicine without a license, a felony.[8] She is legally barred from saving a life just two states away.

As she leans back in frustration, a news alert scrolls across a secondary monitor. The headline reads: "Shanghai Surgeon Completes 5,000 km Remote Surgery in Xinjiang Using Domestically Produced Toumai Robot." The accompanying article notes it is one of over 100 such procedures performed using China's national 5G network, part of the "Healthy China 2030" initiative.[10] The ghost of Operation Lindbergh watches, weeping. The tableau is a perfect microcosm of America's strategic predicament: a nation with the world's best talent and technology, paralyzed by its own antiquated rules, watching as more agile, strategically-minded competitors build the future it first imagined.

THE DEMOCRATIZATION DOCTRINE: WHY REMOTE SURGERY IS A GEOPOLITICAL PRIZE

Telesurgery is far more than a technological marvel; it is a moral opportunity and a strategic imperative. In a world where an estimated 5 billion people lack access to safe and affordable surgical care, the ability to project a surgeon's skill across borders represents a revolutionary tool for global health equity.[9] This "democratization of surgery" is not just a humanitarian goal; it is a new form of soft power, a geopolitical prize in an era where influence is measured as much in lives saved as in military might.[13] The nations that master and disseminate this capability will not only capture a multi-billion-dollar market but will also shape the future of global healthcare, building deep and lasting diplomatic ties.

Global Case Studies (The Doctrine in Action)

While the U.S. debates the legality of crossing state lines, other nations are already deploying telesurgery as a strategic national asset, proving its potential to transform healthcare delivery from the ground up.

India's Mission of Accessibility: In India, telesurgery is being driven by a philosophy of "frugal innovation" and a mission to serve the underserved. The homegrown SSI Mantra surgical robotic system was explicitly designed to be versatile and cost-effective, breaking the monopoly of expensive Western systems.[1] This approach is not theoretical. Dr. Sudhir Srivastava, the system's visionary founder, has already conducted multiple remote cardiac telesurgeries, connecting top-tier surgeons in urban centers with patients hundreds of kilometers away.[14] The most potent symbol of this mission is the "SSI MantraM," a mobile telesurgery unit built on a truck chassis—literally "telesurgery on wheels"—designed to bring advanced robotic capabilities to the Tier 2 and Tier 3 cities that form India's heartland.[16] This is a nation treating healthcare access as a strategic infrastructure project, a mission to distribute skill rather than centralize power.[1]

Latin America's Public Health Push: In Latin America, countries like Brazil and Colombia are grappling with vast geographies and significant health inequities. Here, robotic surgery is being integrated into public health systems through innovative public-private partnerships (PPPs).[18] Despite the high costs and infrastructure challenges, these nations are developing national accreditation programs and pioneering cost-effective hybrid techniques to broaden access.[18] The focus is on leveraging technology to overcome the region's structural barriers to care, demonstrating a clear commitment to health equity that stands in stark contrast to the market-driven fragmentation in the U.S..[22]

Africa's Leapfrog Opportunity: The African continent faces the world's most acute shortage of surgical specialists, with an estimated 0.5 surgeons per 100,000 people.[23] This makes telesurgery not a luxury, but a potential lifeline. The continent is emerging as a key arena for geopolitical health diplomacy, highlighted by two groundbreaking events in Angola. In a world first, Florida-based surgeon Dr. Vipul Patel performed an FDA-approved transcontinental prostatectomy on a patient in Angola, a 7,000-mile connection hailed as a "humanitarian leap forward".[24] Shortly thereafter, the Chinese-made Toumai robotic system was used to perform the first remote surgeries within Sub-Saharan Africa at the same hospital, demonstrating the intense competition to provide these capabilities.[28] While immense barriers like internet access and cost remain, these initiatives, alongside the growth of digital health hubs in Kenya, Nigeria, and South Africa and the coordinating efforts of the African Union, signal a continent poised to leapfrog traditional healthcare models.[23]

MILTON THE TRICKSTER PUTS AMERICAN HEALTHCARE ON THE OPERATING TABLE

The "American Lag" in telesurgery is not a failure of technology or talent. It is a catastrophic failure of policy and imagination, a direct consequence of the ideological pathologies that have hobbled American strategic thinking for decades. It is a system perfectly designed to produce the suboptimal outcomes it consistently delivers, a masterpiece of self-inflicted paralysis.

Imagine Doctor Digital, our brilliant but frustrated surgeon, presenting her meticulously researched proposal for a national telesurgery network to a hospital board. Milton the Trickster Economist, a consultant to the board, dismisses it out of hand. "My dear doctor," he explains patiently, "this fifty-state patchwork of licensure laws you decry is a feature, not a bug! It creates localized market efficiencies and prevents the formation of a national cartel of elite surgeons. The friction is optimal!" Moments later, McSlicey the Priest, another consultant, projects a complex PowerPoint deck. "Our analysis," he intones, "shows that investing in a robust legal department to navigate the compliance labyrinth of 50 different states yields a 12% higher quarterly return on investment than building a unified, interstate care platform. The choice, from a shareholder value perspective, is clear."

This satirical scene captures the grim reality of the three self-inflicted wounds that have crippled American progress in telesurgery.

The Three Self-Inflicted Wounds

The Licensure Labyrinth: The core of the problem lies in an "antiqued patchwork of state-based licensure" designed for a world of horse-and-buggy medicine.[1] In the U.S., medical practice is governed by the principle that a provider must be licensed in the state where the

patient is physically located at the time of care.[8] This transforms the nation into a regulatory Balkans, a collection of 50 fiefdoms that make seamless interstate care a legal impossibility.[36] While mechanisms like the Interstate Medical Licensure Compact exist, their adoption has been slow and incomplete.[1] The emergency waivers issued during the COVID-19 pandemic offered a glimpse of a more rational future, but they were allowed to expire in May 2023, forcing the system to snap back to its pre-pandemic dysfunction.[8]

The Reimbursement Racket: For any medical technology to be adopted, it must be paid for. The American system for telehealth reimbursement is a chaotic, unpredictable mess. Before the pandemic, Medicare and private payer coverage for remote services was severely restricted.[37] During the crisis, the Centers for Medicare & Medicaid Services (CMS) radically liberalized coverage, but this was a temporary emergency measure. Many private payers created their own confusing and inconsistent rules, leading to a high rate of denied or only partially paid claims.[37] Without a clear, permanent, national framework that reimburses telesurgery at parity with in-person procedures, hospitals—many already facing severe revenue crises—have no financial incentive to make the significant capital investments required.[39]

The Liability Lottery: The unresolved medico-legal ambiguity surrounding telesurgery creates a chilling effect on adoption.[2] If a complication arises during a cross-border procedure, who is liable? The remote surgeon? The local hospital staff? The robot manufacturer? The network provider? This legal gray zone creates a "liability lottery" that few institutions are willing to play.[41] While successful international collaborations have navigated this with painstaking, bespoke contractual agreements, the lack of a harmonized legal framework in the U.S. makes the risk unacceptably high for routine implementation.[2]

Barrier	USA Approach	EU Approach	Asia (Select Countries) Approach
Licensure	Fragmented (State-by-State); slow adoption of voluntary compacts.[36]	Heterogeneous; efforts toward coordination but Member States retain jurisdiction.[2]	National, top-down frameworks; licensure often tied to national health systems.[13]
Reimbursement	Fragmented (Payer-by-Payer); lack of permanent federal parity mandates post-COVID.[37]	Uneven; only 53% of countries have a defined payment model; often temporary or pilot-based.[43]	Integrated into national health insurance; government-led initiatives (e.g., DRG exemptions in China).[4]
Liability	Unresolved legal ambiguity; high risk of litigation deters adoption.[41]	Unharmonized; no European rules address medical liability for telemedicine, creating legal obstacles.[42]	Often clarified via national regulations or specific cross-border agreements for pilot programs.[13]
Data Privacy	Governed by HIPAA, but cross-state application can be complex.[2]	Governed by GDPR, providing a strong, unified framework but creating barriers for non-compliant partners.[2]	Governed by national data security laws, often prioritizing state control and access.[6]

THE ASIAN JUGGERNAUT & THE NEW GLOBAL ARMS RACE

While America has been mired in internal debates, a new global arms race in surgical robotics has erupted, fueled by the industrial policies of strategic competitors. The era of U.S. dominance, built on the near-monopoly of Intuitive Surgical's da Vinci system, is definitively over.[45] A new generation of more affordable, versatile, and state-backed robotic platforms is entering the market, transforming the competitive landscape from a monopoly into a multi-polar platform war.

China's State-Directed Ecosystem: China has identified robotic surgery as a key development area under national strategies like "Made in China 2025" and the "Development Plan of Medical Equipment Industry (2021-2025)".[4] This is not mere rhetoric; it is a coordinated national mission involving massive R&D funding, expedited regulatory approvals for domestic firms, and policies like DRG exemptions and novel leasing platforms to accelerate hospital adoption.[44] This ecosystem has already produced formidable competitors like Microport Medbot's Toumai and Kangduo Robotics' system, which have successfully completed hundreds of remote surgeries over distances of 5,000 km.[10]

South Korea's Digital New Deal: South Korea exemplifies integrated industrial policy. Its national strategy to lead the world in 5G technology is not an end in itself but a foundation for next-generation industries. The government's "Digital New Deal" and "Intelligent Robot Development and Distribution Promotion Act" explicitly target robotics and digital-driven healthcare, creating a high-speed, low-latency backbone perfect for telesurgery and fostering a domestic industry to leverage it.[5]

India's Frugal Innovation: India's SS Innovations is pursuing a different, but equally potent, strategy with its SSI Mantra system. It is a "Made in India" solution designed from the ground up to be cost-effective and multi-specialty, directly addressing the affordability barrier that has limited the global adoption of robotics.[1] With over 100 systems installed worldwide and regulatory approval for commercial telesurgery, SSI Mantra is rapidly expanding globally, positioning it as a major challenger to the expensive incumbents.[14]

FROM OPERATING ROOMS TO CIVIC ARENAS: A ROOSEVELTIAN PARALLEL

This story of a missed opportunity is not just about technology; it is a parable for a broader theme in this book. The failure to build a national telesurgery network mirrors the failure to invest in other forms of critical infrastructure. It is a failure of the spirit, a deficit of what this book calls "patient capital."

To understand the path forward, we can draw a parallel to another case study in this manuscript: the Plough Foundation in Memphis. While Milton the Trickster chases quarterly profits, the Plough Foundation invested patient capital over decades to rebuild its community, funding projects like a sterile drug manufacturing facility that addressed critical shortages and built local capacity. It is a story of doing the right thing, the long way.

The philosophy behind Plough's community investment rhymes perfectly with the needs of telesurgery. Both call for long-term vision and a commitment to value access and equity as highly as profit and efficiency. What if we applied the telesurgical mindset—connectivity, precision, cross-boundary collaboration—not only to medicine but to how we rebuild our nation?

In the OR (Telesurgery)	In Civic Investment (Renewal)
Precision and standardization for safety and quality.	Equity and sustainability for lasting community benefits.
Robotics and AI to extend expert skill and minimize error.	Long-term, community-first capital prioritizing public good.
Telesurgery to overcome geographic constraints.	Place-based investments to reverse systemic neglect.
Ethical protocols and credentialing for safe cross-border practice.	Transparent governance and impact metrics for accountability.
International collaboration and mentorship networks.[13]	Local ownership and public-private coalition-building.

Both domains require vision, system design, and moral clarity. Both require us to relinquish a bit of control in the name of connection. Ultimately, the scalpel and the grant check are both tools; what imbues them with purpose is the spirit behind their use.

A ROOSEVELTIAN PLAYBOOK FOR TELESURGICAL SUPREMACY

To escape this self-imposed paralysis and reclaim leadership, America requires a bold, national-scale intervention framed in the ambitious, nation-building spirit of the New Deal.[48] This is not a call for incremental adjustments but for a fundamental rewiring of the nation's healthcare innovation infrastructure.

Pillar I: The National Medical Licensure Compact ("The Healing Corridors Act")

The single greatest barrier to telesurgery is the 50-state licensure labyrinth. The federal government must break this logjam by creating a federal framework for a single, national license for telehealth and telesurgery, or at minimum, an opt-out interstate compact. To drive adoption, Washington should tie a portion of Medicare and Medicaid funding to a state's participation, making compliance a fiscal necessity.[8]

Pillar II: The Rural Digital Infrastructure Act ("The New REA")

Telesurgery is impossible without robust, reliable, low-latency connectivity. Congress should pass a "Rural Digital Infrastructure Act," explicitly framing universal broadband and 5G deployment as critical health infrastructure, drawing direct inspiration from Franklin D. Roosevelt's Rural Electrification Administration (REA).[50] The program would massively expand existing USDA and HRSA grants to build "surgical-grade" networks in underserved areas, defined by latency thresholds below the 200-300 millisecond range considered safe for remote procedures.[52]

Pillar III: The Strategic Health Arsenal ("ARPA-H in Overdrive")

America cannot afford to be dependent on geopolitical rivals for its core medical technology. Federal agencies like ARPA-H and the Department of Defense should be funded to launch a "Strategic Health Arsenal" initiative. This program would establish "Health Innovation Hubs" in deindustrialized regions, pairing research universities with private manufacturers to scale up domestic production through public-private partnerships.

Pillar IV: The Fair Reimbursement & Liability Framework ("The Healthcare Square Deal")

The current chaos in reimbursement and liability must end. CMS must be directed to establish permanent, unambiguous reimbursement codes for telesurgical procedures, ensuring payment at parity with in-person care. Concurrently, Congress should create a federal "safe harbor" from malpractice liability for surgeons performing FDA-approved telesurgery procedures across state lines, removing the single greatest legal risk deterring adoption.[2]

Pillar V: The Democratic Tech Alliance for Global Health

To counter China's "Digital Silk Road" in healthcare, the U.S. must lead a "Democratic Tech Alliance for Global Health." This partnership would bring together democratic allies—the EU, Japan, South Korea, India, the UK—to establish shared, open standards for telesurgical technology, ethics, training, and data privacy.[2] By creating a trusted, interoperable ecosystem, this alliance would offer a clear alternative to the closed, state-controlled platforms offered by authoritarian competitors.

A NEW HIPPOCRATIC OATH FOR THE DIGITAL AGE

As I left Strasbourg, I found myself composing an updated oath for our robotic age:

"I will serve not only those within reach,
but those within signal.
I will see the hand, but honor the algorithm,
and never let one replace the other.
I will build systems that remember the forgotten,
and deliver care not to the most profitable,
but to the most in need."

CONCLUSION: THE FINAL FRONTIER IS POLITICAL WILL

The journey of telesurgery, from its audacious birth in Operation Lindbergh to its current state of arrested development in America, is more than a story about a medical technology. It is a diagnostic test of the nation's health. It reveals a body politic suffering from institutional sclerosis, a strategic imagination hobbled by short-term thinking, and a competitive spirit dulled by complacency.

The **Scalpel**—the dazzling robotic technology—is ready. The **Signal**—the high-speed, low-latency network—is becoming a reality. But in the United States, the **Sovereignty** of our own rules has turned against the national interest, and the **Spirit** is weak.

The ultimate proof that our barriers are not technological but political comes not from a hospital, but from orbit. In 2024, NASA had a surgeon on Earth remotely control a mini-robot aboard the International Space Station, performing simulated surgical tasks in zero gravity.[1] The time delays and communication challenges of space are extreme, yet the experiment was a success. If telesurgery can work from Earth to the heavens, it can certainly work between California and Arkansas.

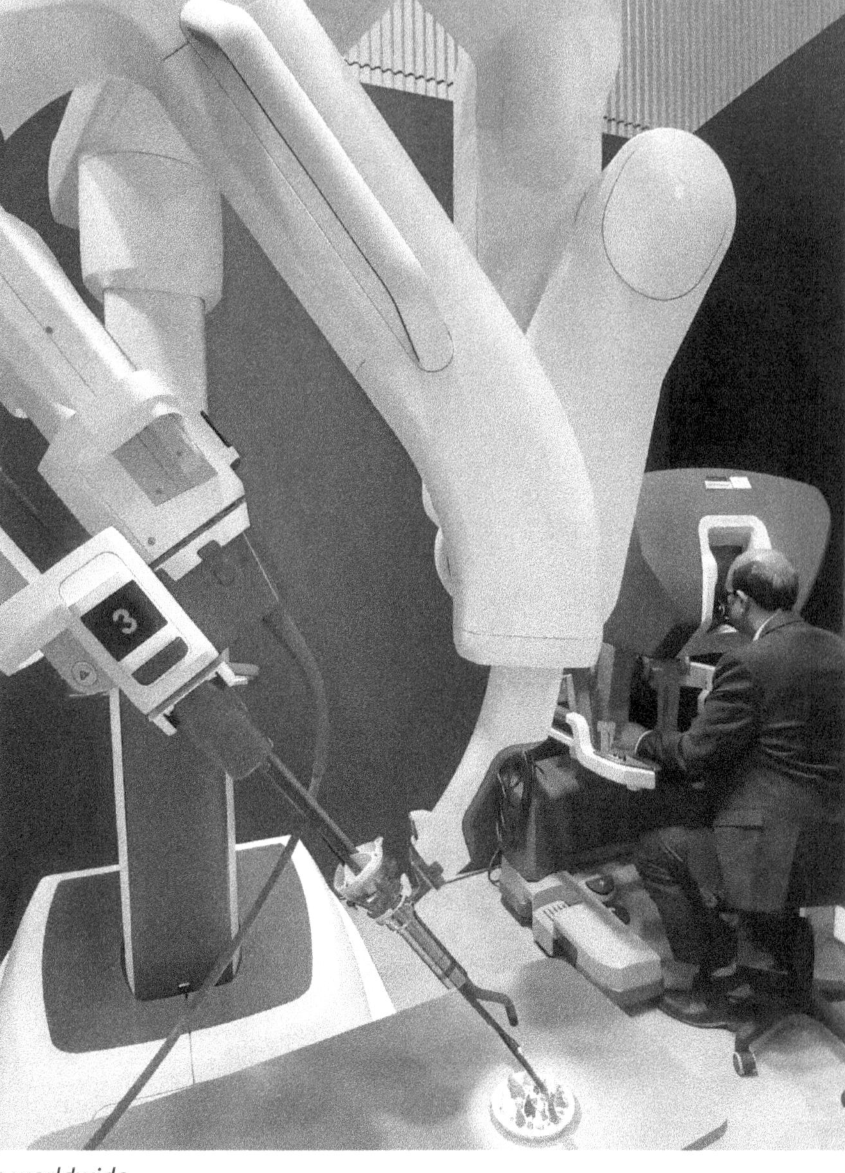

The choice is stark. America can continue on its current path and become a mere consumer of healthcare technologies designed by its geopolitical rivals. Or it can choose to act, to implement a Health New Deal that unleashes its immense talent and resources, and in doing so, prove that a democratic nation can still do great things. The scalpel is in our hands. The signal is waiting. The only frontier left to conquer is our own lack of will.

Dr. Sajeesh Kumar is Professor of health informatics and a global pioneer in telemedicine and robotic surgery. He co-edited "Telesurgery" (Springer) with Prof. Jacques Marescaux and has published over 100 papers on digital health transformation. Based in Memphis, Tennessee, he serves as Director of Health Outcomes initiatives while maintaining an active clinical research practice. His work bridges the technical and humanistic aspects of healthcare innovation, advocating for equitable access to advanced surgical care worldwide.

Works cited

SK- To Saji Madapat

The legal and ethical considerations in cross-border telesurgical procedures - PMC, accessed August 4, 2025, https://pmc.ncbi.nlm.nih.gov/articles/PMC12140691/

Telehealth Research Recap: Economic Impact, accessed August 4, 2025, https://telehealth.hhs.gov/documents/ResearchRecap-Telehealth_and_Economic_Impact_09-30-24.pdf

How government policies will drive China's robotic surgery market - Clearstate, accessed August 4, 2025, https://www.clearstate.com/china-robotic-surgery-market/

How policy will drive South Korea's robotic surgery market | Clearstate, accessed August 4, 2025, https://www.clearstate.com/korea-surgical-market-robotic/

Chinese Industrial Policy and the Digital Silk Road: The Case of Alibaba in Malaysia - The National Bureau of Asian Research (NBR), accessed August 4, 2025, https://www.nbr.org/wp-content/uploads/pdfs/publications/ap15-1_2_digitalsilkroadrt_naughton_jan2020.pdf

Telehealth: A post-COVID-19 reality? | McKinsey, accessed August 4, 2025, https://www.mckinsey.com/industries/healthcare/our-insights/telehealth-a-quarter-trillion-dollar-post-covid-19-reality

Barriers and Opportunities for Improving Interstate ... - HHS ASPE, accessed August 4, 2025, https://aspe.hhs.gov/sites/default/files/documents/405ad876b1de337a81b4db0257666586/barriers-opportunities-improving-interstate-licensure.pdf

Opportunities for Global Health Diplomacy in Transnational Robotic Telesurgery, accessed August 4, 2025, https://journalofethics.ama-assn.org/article/opportunities-global-health-diplomacy-transnational-robotic-telesurgery/2023-08

Insights from telesurgery expert conference on recent clinical ..., accessed August 4, 2025, https://pmc.ncbi.nlm.nih.gov/articles/PMC11150305/
Surgical Robots Market Size, Share and Industry Analysis | Forecast 2032, accessed August 4, 2025, https://www.fortunebusinessinsights.com/industry-reports/surgical-robots-market-100948
will 5G-based robot-assisted telesurgery redefine modern surgery? - Xie - Translational Lung Cancer Research, accessed August 4, 2025, https://tlcr.amegroups.org/article/view/100779/html
insights from ultra-long-distance Asia to Middle East human telesurgery robotic assisted radical prostatectomy - PMC - PubMed Central, accessed August 4, 2025, https://pmc.ncbi.nlm.nih.gov/articles/PMC11893634/
SS Innovations International Performs World's First Robotic Cardiac Telesurgeries with its SSi Mantra 3, accessed August 4, 2025, https://www.surgicalroboticstechnology.com/news/ss-innovations-international-performs-worlds-first-robotic-cardiac-telesurgeries-with-its-ssi-mantra-3/
India's First 2,000-Km Robotic Telesurgery Performed Using SSI ..., accessed August 4, 2025, https://www.digitalhealthnews.com/india-s-first-2-000-km-robotic-cardiac-telesurgery-conducted-using-indigenous-ssi-mantra-system
SS Innovations Unveils India's First Mobile Tele-Robotic Unit |, accessed August 4, 2025, https://theindianpractitioner.com/ss-innovations-unveils-indias-first-mobile-tele-robotic-unit/
Telemedicine Adoption and Prospects in Sub-Sahara Africa: A Systematic Review with a Focus on South Africa, Kenya, and Nigeria - PubMed Central, accessed August 4, 2025, https://pmc.ncbi.nlm.nih.gov/articles/PMC11989057/
Robotic surgery in low- and middle-income countries | The Bulletin of the Royal College of Surgeons of England, accessed August 4, 2025, https://publishing.rcseng.ac.uk/doi/10.1308/rcsbull.2024.54
Public-Private Partnerships: Vital to Latin America Development - CAF, accessed August 4, 2025, https://www.caf.com/en/currently/news/private-public-partnerships-vital-to-latin-america-development/
Telesurgery Robot Market Size & Share 2025-2030 - 360iResearch, accessed August 4, 2025, https://www.360iresearch.com/library/intelligence/telesurgery-robot
Feasibility of telesurgery in the modern era - PMC, accessed August 4, 2025, https://pmc.ncbi.nlm.nih.gov/articles/PMC9437503/
Strasbourg: world capital of robotic surgery - IRCAD, accessed August 4, 2025, https://www.ircad.fr/strasbourg-world-capital-of-robotic-surgery/
Telesurgery's potential role in improving surgical access in Africa - ResearchGate, accessed August 4, 2025, https://www.researchgate.net/publication/363123000_Telesurgery's_potential_role_in_improving_surgical_access_in_Africa
Historic telesurgery connects Central Florida and Angola in world ..., accessed August 4, 2025, https://www.adventhealth.com/news/historic-telesurgery-connects-central-florida-and-angola-world-first-medical-breakthrough
Groundbreaking Remote Robotic Surgery Performed from the U.S. to Africa – Tehrani.com, accessed August 4, 2025, https://blog.tmcnet.com/blog/rich-tehrani/technology/groundbreaking-remote-robotic-surgery-performed-from-the-u-s-to-africa.html
How to cover the growing field of telesurgery | Association of Health Care Journalists, accessed August 4, 2025, https://healthjournalism.org/blog/2025/07/how-to-cover-the-growing-field-of-telesurgery/
Dr. Vipul Patel, IPCF founder, completes a historic remote telesurgery across 17000 kilometers of fiber optic distance - International Prostate Cancer Foundation, accessed August 4, 2025, https://www.fightingprostatecancer.org/blog/2025/6/17/im7msshklq0ulin8y6pw62qn397dsi
TOUMAI® SURGICAL ROBOT SYSTEM COMPLETES MULTIPLE LANDMARK ROBOTIC TELESURGERY CASES IN SUB-SAHARA AFRICA IN THE REPUBLIC OF ANGOLA-MicroPort MedBot, accessed August 4, 2025, https://www.medbotsurgical.com/en/news/251.html
Africa's Lawmakers Commit to Strengthening AI, Digital Health and Smart Manufacturing Frameworks at Inaugural Africa Digital Parliamentary Summit in Lusaka | Pan-African Parliament, accessed August 4, 2025, https://pap.au.int/en/news/press-releases/2025-07-11/africas-lawmakers-commit-strengthening-ai-digital-health-and-smart
The Role of Telemedicine in Enhancing Surgical Care Delivery in Africa: A Literature Review - ResearchGate, accessed August 4, 2025, https://www.researchgate.net/publication/387165894_The_Role_of_Telemedicine_in_Enhancing_Surgical_Care_Delivery_in_Africa_A_Literature_Review
Digital Health Innovations in Africa: Harnessing AI, Telemedicine, and Personalized Medicine for Improved Healthcare - Frontiers, accessed August 4, 2025, https://www.frontiersin.org/research-topics/62391/digital-health-innovations-in-africa-harnessing-ai-telemedicine-and-personalized-medicine-for-improved-healthcare
A New Digital Health Platform for Africa - Africa CDC, accessed August 4, 2025, https://africacdc.org/news-item/a-new-digital-health-platform-for-africa/
Advancing One Health: African Union's Digital Platform Initiative Takes Shape - | AU-IBAR, accessed August 4, 2025, https://www.au-ibar.org/news/latest-news/advancing-one-health-african-unions-digital-platform-initiative-takes-shape
African Union and World Health Organization renew strategic partnership to drive impact and strengthen health systems in Africa, accessed August 4, 2025, https://www.who.int/news/item/24-05-2025-world-health-organization-and-african-union-renew-strategic-partnership-to-drive-impact-and-strengthen-health-systems-in-africa

The Digital Transformation Strategy for Africa (2020-2030), accessed August 4, 2025, https://www.iicba.unesco.org/en/africa-education-knowledge-platform/digital-transformation-strategy-africa-2020-2030

Licensure and Interstate Compacts, accessed August 4, 2025, https://www.ncsl.org/health/the-telehealth-explainer-series/licensure-and-interstate-compacts

New Challenges for Telehealth Reimbursement - Scribe-X, accessed August 4, 2025, https://scribe-x.com/resources/new-challenges-for-telehealth-reimbursement/

Telemedicine in Urology, accessed August 4, 2025, https://www.auanet.org/guidelines-and-quality/quality-and-measurement/quality-improvement/clinical-consensus-statement-and-quality-improvement-issue-brief-(ccs-and-qiib)/telemedicine-in-urology

Methods of Reimbursement for Telemedicine Services: A Scoping Review - PMC, accessed August 4, 2025, https://pmc.ncbi.nlm.nih.gov/articles/PMC9448495/

Economics - Telesurgery - Webnode, accessed August 4, 2025, https://stas325telesurgery.webnode.page/controversies/economics/

Opportunities and Barriers to Rural Telerobotic Surgical Health Care in 2021: Report and Research Agenda from a Stakeholder Workshop, accessed August 4, 2025, https://pmc.ncbi.nlm.nih.gov/articles/PMC9293678/

Market study on telemedicine - Public Health - European Commission, accessed August 4, 2025, https://health.ec.europa.eu/system/files/2019-08/2018_provision_marketstudy_telemedicine_en_0.pdf

Scaling up telemedicine in the WHO European Region - IRIS, accessed August 4, 2025, https://iris.who.int/bitstream/handle/10665/381574/WHO-EURO-2025-12185-51957-79682-eng.pdf?sequence=1

Beijing Introduces New Policy to Accelerate Surgical Robot Adoption | MedChina, accessed August 4, 2025, https://www.medchina.tech/news-article/beijing-introduces-groundbreaking-policy-to-accelerate-surgical-robot-adoption

Intuitive Surgical - Wikipedia, accessed August 4, 2025, https://en.wikipedia.org/wiki/Intuitive_Surgical

Asian Surgical Robotics Market Doubles by 2025, accessed August 4, 2025, https://asianroboticsreview.com/home316-html

SS Innovations International, Inc. Achieves Milestone with Over 100 SSi Mantra Surgical Robotic System Installations Worldwide | Nasdaq, accessed August 4, 2025, https://www.nasdaq.com/articles/ss-innovations-international-inc-achieves-milestone-over-100-ssi-mantra-surgical-robotic

The New Deal in New York City, 1933—1943 - Roosevelt House Public Policy Institute at Hunter College, accessed August 4, 2025, https://www.roosevelthouse.hunter.cuny.edu/exhibits/new-deal-new-york-city/

President Franklin Delano Roosevelt and the New Deal | Great Depression and World War II, 1929-1945 | U.S. History Primary Source Timeline | Classroom Materials at the Library of Congress, accessed August 4, 2025, https://www.loc.gov/classroom-materials/united-states-history-primary-source-timeline/great-depression-and-world-war-ii-1929-1945/franklin-delano-roosevelt-and-the-new-deal/

Agency History, accessed August 4, 2025, https://www.fsa.usda.gov/about-fsa/history-mission/agency-history

Presidents on health care | Miller Center, accessed August 4, 2025, https://millercenter.org/health-care-policy/presidents-health-care

will 5G-based robot-assisted telesurgery redefine modern surgery? - PMC - PubMed Central, accessed August 4, 2025, https://pmc.ncbi.nlm.nih.gov/articles/PMC12170204/

Grants & Programs - HRSA, accessed August 4, 2025, https://www.hrsa.gov/telehealth/grants

Telesurgery: current status and strategies for latency reduction - PubMed, accessed August 4, 2025, https://pubmed.ncbi.nlm.nih.gov/40220039/

Distance Learning & Telemedicine Grants - USDA Rural Development, accessed August 4, 2025, https://www.rd.usda.gov/programs-services/telecommunications-programs/distance-learning-telemedicine-grants

COVID-19 Telehealth Program (Invoices & Reimbursements), accessed August 4, 2025, https://www.fcc.gov/covid-19-telehealth-program-invoices-reimbursements

Assistance Listings Telehealth Programs - SAM.gov, accessed August 4, 2025, https://sam.gov/fal/96f0f8e6596748ac9962010b3dd61333/view

Exploring the ethical implications in the telesurgery ERA - ResearchGate, accessed August 4, 2025, https://www.researchgate.net/publication/379781749_Exploring_the_ethical_implications_in_the_telesurgery_ERA

ABBREVIATIONS & ARCHETYPES

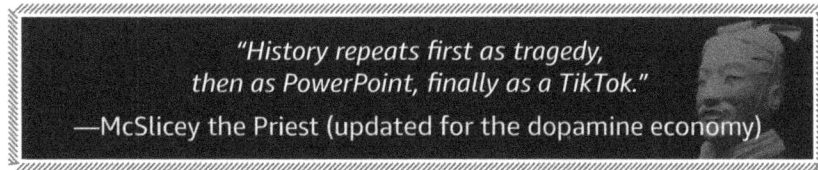

> *"History repeats first as tragedy,*
> *then as PowerPoint, finally as a TikTok."*
> —McSlicey the Priest (updated for the dopamine economy)

I. STRATEGIC ABBREVIATIONS

(Because policy debates now require more acronyms than actual policies.)

Power Players

★ **USA/US** — United States of America. The former marathon champion is now wheezing through the home stretch.
★ **PRC** — People's Republic of China. The patient, a Go master, is rearranging the global board.
★ **CCP** — Chinese Communist Party. China Inc.'s board of directors, now with AI-enhanced planning.

Economic Arsenal

★ **AI** — Artificial Intelligence. Silicon Valley's deity and Beijing's oracle, worshipped differently but with equal fervor.
★ **BRI** — Belt and Road Initiative. Infrastructure diplomacy on installment plans—paved with yuan and 99-year leases.
★ **AIIB** — Asian Infrastructure Investment Bank. The BRI's golden shovel fund.
★ **CBDC/e-CNY** — Digital Yuan. Programmable cash that geo-fences your latte and expires if hoarded.
★ **CIPS** — Cross-Border Interbank Payment System. China's SWIFT escape hatch—banking with Mandarin subtitles.
★ **GDP** — Gross Domestic Product. National bragging rights are measured in trillions and hubris.
★ **IMF** — International Monetary Fund. The macro-plumber you call when pipes burst—bills hurt more than floods.
★ **IP** — Intellectual Property. What gets "transferred" when you offshore everything.
★ **R&D** — Research and Development. Cash burned today, so tomorrow isn't worse.
★ **SWIFT** — Society for Worldwide Interbank Financial Telecommunication. Dollar hegemony's circulatory system.
★ **WTO** — World Trade Organization. Global referee whose whistle jammed circa 2001.

Military-Strategic Complex

★ **A2/AD** — Anti-Access/Area Denial. Beijing's geopolitical bouncer: "Carriers not on the list don't get in."
★ **ARPA-X** — Advanced Research Projects Agency-Experimental. DARPA's theoretical offspring, teaching America to build again.
★ **DoD** — Department of Defense. Where PowerPoint achieves sentience and budgets transcend physics.
★ **MIC** — Military-Industrial Complex. Pentagon-to-Capitol conveyor belt for gold-plated gizmos.
★ **NATO** — North Atlantic Treaty Organization. Democracy's oldest group chat, robust "mute" function included.
★ **PLA** — People's Liberation Army. World's largest uniformed comment section—now with hypersonics.
★ **QUAD** — Quadrilateral Security Dialogue. Indo-Pacific jazz quartet improvising freedom-of-navigation riffs.

Digital Infrastructure

★ **5G** — Fifth-generation wireless. The highway China built while others debated paint colors.
★ **DSR** — Digital Silk Road. Fiber-optic tentacles of the new empire.
★ **IoT** — Internet of Things. When your fridge joins the surveillance state.
★ **HPC** — High-Performance Computing. Where climate models arm-wrestle missile trajectories for cycles.

II. DRAMATIS PERSONAE

(Your allegorical guides through the theater of strategic absurdity.)

Economic Evangelists

Milton the Trickster Economist
Embodies: Market fundamentalism
Signature: Bow-tied necromancer who can offshore your soul and list it as "efficiency." Channels Friedman's ghost through Excel.
Catchphrase: "The invisible hand works perfectly—even when it's slapping democracy."

McSlicey the Priest
Embodies: Management consultancy
Signature: PowerPoint exorcist who slices supply chains thinner than prosciutto. Bills by the buzzword.
Achievement: Turned "synergy" into a sacrament and "resilience" into an afterthought.

Digital Deities

Algorithm Annie
Embodies: Engagement maximization
Signature: Turns outrage into quarterly earnings—democracy's dopamine dealer.
Motto: "If it enrages, it engages!"

Captain Panopticon
Embodies: Surveillance capitalism
Signature: Sells "smart cities" with firmware that phones home to Beijing.
Pitch: "Security through total visibility—privacy sold separately!"

Military Mythmakers

General Quagmire
Embodies: Forever-war mindset
Signature: Plans yesterday's war with tomorrow's budget, eternally shocked by today.
Philosophy: "Why win when you can persist?"

Admiral Procurement
Embodies: Acquisition dysfunction
Signature: Pentagon QVC host hawking hardware nobody can afford to lose.
Legacy: Made $1,200 toilet seats seem reasonable.

Strategic Seers

Cassandra the Cyber-Oracle
Embodies: Ignored foresight
Signature: Correctly predicts every breach, writes warnings that become post-mortems.
Tragedy: Being right while everyone checks Twitter.

Madame Créancière
Embodies: Debt diplomacy
Signature: Arrives with infrastructure loans, leaves with sovereignty receipts.
Method: Invoices written in concrete, payable in ports.

National Avatars

Uncle Sam
Embodies: American exceptionalism
Status: Former sprinter running marathons, occasionally trips on own slogans.
Condition: Chronic ideological whiplash, acute iPhone addiction.

Uncle Xi
Embodies: Chinese strategic patience
Method: Plays Go while others play Candy Crush—five-year plans with five-century implications.
Demeanor: Smiles like he knows your WiFi password (he does).

The Roosevelt Trinity
Cast: Teddy (Trust-Buster), Franklin (New Dealer), Eleanor (Conscience)
Role: Spectral board of directors for American renewal
Haunting: "We built the Hoover Dam. You can't fix a website."

Señor Cripto
Embodies: Post-dollar finance
Mission: Blockchain mariachi serenading central banks away from SWIFT.
Dream: Every currency gets sovereignty—except yours.

III. CONCEPTUAL APPENDIX

Strategic Catchphrases

- ★ **"Full-Spectrum Mammon"** — Market worship achieving strategic blindness
- ★ **"PowerPoint Paralysis"** — When slide decks replace strategy
- ★ **"Quarter-to-Quarter Quicksand"** — Short-termism as national suicide
- ★ **"Guanxi Goes Digital"** — Chinese networks, now with metadata
- ★ **"From Arsenal to Amazon Cart"** — America's industrial devolution

Philosophical Foundations

- ★ **The Art of War** — Sun Tzu's playbook, now with algorithmic annotations
- ★ **The Wealth of Nations** — Adam Smith's invisible hand giving an invisible finger
- ★ **Manufacturing Consent** — Chomsky's nightmare, Annie's business model
- ★ **Citizens United** — SCOTUS guide to democracy-as-auction
- ★ **Made in China 2025** — Beijing's shopping list for the future

> *"The best way to predict the future is to prevent your competitors from inventing it."*
> —The consolidated wisdom of strategic decline

BIBLIOGRAPHY AND KEY SOURCES

Geopolitics and US-China Relations

- ★ Allison, Graham. *Destined for War: Can America and China Escape Thucydides's Trap?* Boston: Houghton Mifflin Harcourt, 2017.
- ★ Brands, Hal. *American Grand Strategy in the Age of Trump.* Washington, D.C.: Brookings Institution Press, 2018.
- ★ Doshi, Rush. *The Long Game: China's Grand Strategy to Displace American Order.* New York: Oxford University Press, 2021.
- ★ Economy, Elizabeth C. *The World According to China.* Polity, 2022.
- ★ Kissinger, Henry. *On China.* New York: Penguin Books, 2012.
- ★ Mearsheimer, John J. *The Tragedy of Great Power Politics.* New York: W. W. Norton & Company, 2014.
- ★ Nye, Joseph S. *The Future of Power.* PublicAffairs, 2011.
- ★ Rudd, Kevin. *The Avoidable War: The Dangers of a Catastrophic Conflict between the U.S. and Xi Jinping's China.* PublicAffairs, 2022.
- ★ Shambaugh, David. *China's Military Modernization: Implications for Regional Security.* Carnegie Endowment for International Peace, 2023.

Satirical and Cultural Analysis

- ★ Carlin, George. *Brain Droppings.* New York: Hyperion, 1998.
- ★ Iannucci, Armando. *The Thick of It: The Scripts.* London: Faber & Faber, 2007.
- ★ Oliver, John, et al. *Last Week Tonight with John Oliver: Selected Episodes and Scripts.* HBO, 2014-2025.
- ★ Stewart, Jon. *America (The Book): A Citizen's Guide to Democracy Inaction.* New York: Grand Central Publishing, 2004.
- ★ Iannucci, Armando. *The Death of Stalin.* Film, 2017.
- ★ Carlin, George. *Jammin' in New York.* HBO special, 1992.

Economic and Financial Critique

- ★ Appelbaum, Eileen, and Rosemary Batt. *Private Equity at Work: When Wall Street Manages Main Street.* Russell Sage, 2014.
- ★ de Soto, Hernando. *The Mystery of Capital: Why Capitalism Triumphs in the West and Fails Everywhere Else.* New York: Basic Books, 2003.
- ★ Friedman, Milton. *Capitalism and Freedom.* Chicago: University of Chicago Press, 1962.
- ★ Mazzucato, Mariana. *The Value of Everything: Making and Taking in the Global Economy.* Penguin, 2018.
- ★ Piketty, Thomas. *Capital in the Twenty-First Century.* Cambridge, MA: Harvard University Press, 2014.
- ★ Stiglitz, Joseph E. *Globalization and Its Discontents Revisited: Anti-Globalization in the Era of Trump.* New York: W. W. Norton & Company, 2017.
- ★ Tooze, Adam. *Crashed: How a Decade of Financial Crises Changed the World.* Viking, 2018.
- ★ Zucman, Gabriel. *The Hidden Wealth of Nations: The Scourge of Tax Havens.* University of Chicago Press, 2015.

Historical Context and Rooseveltian Policies

- ★ Brands, H.W. *Traitor to His Class: The Privileged Life and Radical Presidency of Franklin Delano Roosevelt.* New York: Anchor Books, 2009.
- ★ Goodwin, Doris Kearns. *No Ordinary Time: Franklin & Eleanor Roosevelt: The Home Front in World War II.* New York: Simon & Schuster, 1994.
- ★ Morris, Edmund. *Theodore Rex.* New York: Random House, 2001.

Technological and AI Challenges

- ★ Kania, Elsa, and Lorand Laskai. *Myths and Realities of China's Military–Civil Fusion Strategy.* CNAS, 2021.
- ★ O'Neil, Cathy. *Weapons of Math Destruction: How Big Data Increases Inequality and Threatens Democracy.* New York: Crown Publishing Group, 2016.
- ★ Russell, Stuart. *Human Compatible: Artificial Intelligence and the Problem of Control.* New York: Viking, 2019.
- ★ Tegmark, Max. *Life 3.0: Being Human in the Age of Artificial Intelligence.* New York: Knopf, 2017.

- ★ Segal, Adam. *The Hacked World Order: How Nations Fight, Trade, Maneuver, and Manipulate in the Digital Age.* Vintage, 2020.

Infrastructure, Policy, and Institutional Analysis

- ★ Fukuyama, Francis. *The End of History and the Last Man.* New York: Free Press, 1992.
- ★ Mazzucato, Mariana. *The Entrepreneurial State: Debunking Public vs. Private Sector Myths.* London: Anthem Press, 2013.
- ★ Zakaria, Fareed. *The Post-American World: Release 2.0.* New York: W. W. Norton & Company, 2012.

Digital Surveillance and Security

- ★ Schneier, Bruce. *Data and Goliath: The Hidden Battles to Collect Your Data and Control Your World.* New York: W. W. Norton & Company, 2015.
- ★ Zuboff, Shoshana. *The Age of Surveillance Capitalism: The Fight for a Human Future at the New Frontier of Power.* New York: PublicAffairs, 2019.
- ★ Zeng, Jinghan. *China and Cyber Governance: China's Digital Silk Road and Cyber Sovereignty.* Routledge, 2024.

Additional Reports and Articles

- ★ Bureau of International Settlements & People's Bank of China. *e-CNY Research White Paper,* 2021.
- ★ Congressional Research Service. "China's Civil-Military Fusion Strategy," CRS Report R46475, July 2024.
- ★ McSlicey Global Institute Reports on globalization, offshoring, and digital transformation (2000-2025).
- ★ Council on Foreign Relations: Annual Reports on China's Belt and Road Initiative.
- ★ Permanent Court of Arbitration. *South China Sea Arbitration (Philippines v. China) Award,* 2016.
- ★ U.S. Department of Defense. *Military and Security Developments Involving the People's Republic of China,* 2024.
- ★ World Bank. *World Development Indicators,* 2025.

HUMBLE REQUEST TO REVIEW MY BOOK

I trust that you enjoyed reading this book. I'd appreciate hearing from you and would humbly request that you take a few minutes to post a review on Amazon. Your feedback and support will significantly improve my writing craft for future books and make this book even more commendable. This is a living manuscript that will continuously evolve based on your constructive feedback (direct contact details available at www.Epm-Mavericks.com). Thank you in advance!

This is a living manuscript and will continuously evolve based on your constructive feedback (contact @ www.EPM-Mavericks.com or www.Tiger-Rider.com)

Proceeds from this book will be donated to the Mother Teresa Mission (Missionaries of Charity) or similar missions.

www.ingramcontent.com/pod-product-compliance
Lightning Source LLC
Chambersburg PA
CBHW080415030426
42335CB00020B/2457
* 9 7 8 1 9 6 4 2 1 3 2 7 9 *